At two o'clock, under a brilliant moonlight, and with
a single guide, we started for the Pacific. The road was level
and wooded. We passed a trapiche or sugar-mill, worked
by oxen, and before daylight reached the village of Masagua,
four leagues distant, built in a clearing cut out of the woods,
at the entrance of which we stopped under a grove of orange-trees,
and by the light of the moon filled our pockets and alforgas
with the shining fruit. Daylight broke upon us in a forest
of gigantic trees, from seventy-five to a hundred feet high,
and from twenty to twenty-five feet in circumference, with creepers
winding around their trunks and hanging from the branches.
The road was merely a path through the forest, formed
by cutting away shrubs and branches. The freshness
of the morning was delightful.

—from Chapter XIII

Incidents of Travel in Central America, Chiapas, and Yucatan

Vols. I & II

JOHN LLOYD STEPHENS

COSIMOCLASSICS

NEW YORK

Incidents
of Travel
in Central
America,
Chiapas, and
Yucatan
Vol. I

Contents

CHAPTER IX

CHAPTER X

CHAPTER XI

CHAPTER XII

CHAPTER XIII

CHAPTER XVIII

CHAPTER XIX

List of Illustrations

Chapter I

HAVING been intrusted by the President with a Special Confidential Mission to Central America, on Wednesday, the third of October, 1839, I embarked on the British brig *Mary Ann* (Hampton, master) for the Gulf of Honduras. The brig was lying in the North River with her anchor apeak and sails loose, and in a few minutes, in company with a large whaling ship bound for the Pacific, we were under way. It was before seven o'clock in the morning. The streets and wharves were still and, although the Battery was desolate, at the moment of leaving on a voyage of uncertain duration it seemed to me more beautiful than I had ever known it.

Opposite the Quarantine Ground, a few friends who had accompanied me on board left; in an hour the pilot followed; at dusk the dark outline of the highlands of Navesink was barely visible; and the next morning we were fairly at sea.

My only fellow passenger was Mr. Catherwood, an experienced traveler and personal friend, who had passed more than ten years of his life in diligently studying the antiquities of the Old World. Immediately on receiving my appointment I had engaged him, as one familiar with the remains of ancient architectural greatness, to accompany me in exploring the ruins of Central America.

Hurried on by a strong northeaster, on the ninth we were within the region of the trade winds, on the tenth within the tropics, and on the eleventh, with the thermometer at 80° but with a refreshing breeze, we were moving gently between Cuba and Santo Domingo with both in full sight. As for the rest of the voyage, after eighteen days of boisterous weather, drenched with tropical rains, on the twenty-ninth we were driven inside the lighthouse reef; avoiding altogether the regular pilot ground, at midnight we reached St. George's Bay, about twenty miles from Belize. A large brig loaded with mahogany was lying at anchor with a pilot on board waiting for favorable weather to put to sea. The pilot had with him his son, a lad about sixteen, cradled on the water, whom Captain Hampton knew and determined to take on board.

It was full moonlight when the boy mounted the deck and gave us the pilot's welcome. I could not distinguish his features, but I could see that he was not white; his voice was as soft as a woman's. He took his place at the wheel and, loading the brig with canvass, told us of the severe gales on the coast, of the fears entertained for our safety, of disasters and shipwrecks, and of a pilot who, on a night which we well remembered, had driven his vessel over a sunken reef.

At seven o'clock the next morning we saw Belize,[1] appearing—if there be no sin in comparing it with cities consecrated by time and venerable associations, like Venice and Alexandria—to rise out of the water. A range of white houses extended a mile along the shore, terminated at one end by the Government House and at the other by the barracks, and intersected by the river Belize, the bridge across which formed a picturesque object. The fort on a little island at the mouth of the river, the spire of a Gothic church behind the Government House, and groves of cocoanut trees, which at that distance reminded us of the palm trees of

---

1. Belize is the capital of what we now know as British Honduras. Central Americans call the whole territory *Belice*.

Egypt, gave to it all an appearance of actual beauty. Four ships, three brigs, sundry schooners, bungos, canoes, and a steamboat, were riding at anchor in the harbor. Alongside the vessels were rafts of mahogany, and far out a negro was paddling a log of the same costly timber. The government dory which boarded us when we came to anchor was also made of the trunk of a mahogany tree.

We landed in front of the warehouse of Mr. Coffin, the consignee of the vessel. There was no hotel in the place, but Mr. Coffin undertook to conduct us to a lady who, he thought, could accommodate us with lodgings. The heavy rain from which we had suffered at sea had reached Belize. The streets were flooded, and in places there were large puddles which were difficult to cross. At the extreme end of the principal street we met the "lady," Miss——, a mulatto woman, who could give us only board, but Mr. Coffin kindly offered us the use of an unoccupied house on the other side of the river to sleep in.

Retracing our steps, for the second time I passed the whole length of the principal street, and the town seemed to me to be in the entire possession of blacks. The bridge, the market place, the streets and stores were thronged with them, and I might have fancied myself in the capital of a negro republic. They were a fine-looking race, tall, straight, and athletic, with skins black, smooth, and glossy as velvet. And they were well dressed, the men in white cotton shirts and trousers, with straw hats, and the women in white frocks with short sleeves and broad red borders, and adorned with large red earrings and necklaces. I could not help remarking that the frock was their only article of dress, and that it was the fashion of these sable ladies to drop this considerably from off the right shoulder, and to raise the skirt, which was held in the left hand, to any height necessary for crossing puddles.

I stopped at the house of a merchant, whom I found at what is called a second breakfast. The gentleman sat on one side of the table and his lady on the other. At the head was a British officer, and opposite him a mulatto; on his left was another officer, and opposite him also a mulatto. By chance

a place was made for me between the two colored gentlemen; some of my countrymen, perhaps, would have hesitated about taking it, but I did not. Both were well dressed,
well educated, and polite. They talked of their mahogany
works, of England, hunting, horses, ladies, and wine. Before I had been an hour in Belize I learned that the great
work of practical racial amalgamation, the subject of so
much angry controversy at home, had been going on quietly
here for generations; that color was considered a mere matter of taste; and that some of the most respectable inhabitants had black wives and mongrel children, whom they
educated with as much care, and made money for with as
much zeal, as if their skins were perfectly white. I hardly
knew whether to be shocked or amused at this condition of
society.

Rejoining Mr. Catherwood we went to visit the house
offered by Mr. Coffin, which was situated on the opposite
side of the river. The road to it was ankle deep in mud; at
the gate was a large puddle, which we cleared by a jump.
The house was built on piles about two feet high, and underneath was water nearly a foot deep. We ascended on a
plank to the sill of the door and entered a large room occupying the whole of the first floor and perfectly empty.
The upper story was tenanted by a family of negroes; in the
yard was a house swarming with negroes; and all over, in
the yard and in front, were picturesque groups of little negroes of both sexes, naked as they were born. We directed
the room to be swept and our luggage brought there. As we
left the house, we remembered Captain Hampton's description and felt the point of his concluding remark that "Belize
was the last place made."

While longing for the comfort of a good hotel, we received through Mr. Goff, the consul of the United States,
an invitation from His Excellency, Colonel MacDonald, to
the Government House, and information that he would
send the government dory to the brig for our luggage. As
this was the first appointment I had ever held from government and I was not sure of ever holding another, I deter-

mined to make the most of it and accepted at once His Excellency's invitation.

There was a steamboat for Izabal, the port of Guatemala, lying at Belize, and on my way to the Government House I called upon Señor Comyano, the agent, who told me that she was to sail the next day, but added with great courtesy that, if I wished it, he would detain her a few days for my convenience. Used to submitting to the despotic regulations of steamboat agents at home, this seemed a higher honor than the invitation of His Excellency, but not wishing to push my fortune too far I asked a delay of one day only.

The Government House stands in a handsome situation at the extreme end of the town, with a lawn extending to the water and ornamented with cocoanut trees. Colonel Mac-Donald, a veteran six feet tall, and one of the most military-looking men I have ever seen, received me at the gate. In an hour the dory arrived with our luggage, and at five o'clock we sat down to dinner. We had at table Mr. Newport, chaplain and for fifteen years parish clergyman at Belize; Mr. Walker, secretary of the government, who held, in addition, such a list of offices as would make the greatest pluralist among us feel insignificant; and several other gentlemen of Belize, officeholders, civil and military, in whose agreeable society we sat till eleven o'clock.

The next day we had to make preparations for our journey into the interior and to make use of our opportunity to see a little of Belize. The Honduras Almanac, which assumes to be the chronicler of this settlement, throws a romance around its early history by ascribing its origin to a Scotch buccaneer named Wallace. The fame of the wealth of the New World and the return of the Spanish galleons laden with riches of Mexico and Peru brought upon the coast of America hordes of adventurers—to call them by no harsher name—from England and France. Wallace,[2] one of the most noted and daring of these men, found refuge and

---

2. Local tradition has it that "Belize" is a corruption of the name of this seventeenth-century Scotch buccaneer. Another view derives "Belize" from the French *balise*, meaning "harbor beacon."

security behind the keys and reefs which protect the harbor of Belize. The place where he built his log huts and fortalice is still pointed out, but the site is now occupied by warehouses. Strengthened by a close alliance with the Indians of the Mosquito shore, and by the adhesion of numerous British adventurers, who descended upon the coast of Honduras for the purpose of cutting mahogany, he set the Spaniards at defiance. Ever since, the territory of Belize has been the subject of negotiation and contest, and to this day the people of Central America[3] claim it as their own. It grew by the exportation of mahogany but, since the supply of trees in the neighborhood is rapidly being exhausted and Central America so impoverished by wars that it offers but a poor market for British goods, the place is languishing, and will probably continue to dwindle away until the enterprise of her merchants discovers other channels of trade.[4]

At this day it contains a population of six thousand, of which four thousand are blacks who are employed by the merchants in gangs as mahogany cutters. Their condition had always been better than that of plantation slaves; even before the act for the general abolition of slavery throughout the British dominions, they were actually free, and on the thirty-first of August, 1839, a year before the time appointed by the act, by a general meeting and agreement of proprietors, even the nominal yoke of bondage was removed.

The event was celebrated, says the Honduras Almanac, by religious ceremonies, processions, bands of music, and banners with such devices as: "The sons of Ham respect the memory of Wilberforce";[5] "The Queen, God bless her"; "M'Donald forever"; "Civil and religious liberty all over the world." Nelson Schaw, "a snowdrop of the first water,"

---

3. At the time of Stephens' visit, Central America was a confederation of five states which were in the throes of civil war. These states have since become independent countries. Guatemala still maintains the claim to Belize.

4. Stephens' prediction concerning Belize has not been borne out. Today it has a population of more than seventeen thousand.

5. William Wilberforce (1759–1833) was an English philanthropist famous for his efforts to abolish the slave trade.

continues the Almanac, "advanced to his excellency, Colonel M'Donald, and spoke as follows: 'On the part of my emancipated brothers and sisters, I venture to approach your excellency, to entreat you to thank our most gracious Queen for all that she has done for us. We will pray for her; we will fight for her; and, if it is necessary, we will die for her. We thank you excellency for all you have done for us. God bless your excellency! God bless her excellency, Mrs. M'Donald, and all the royal family! Come, my countymen, hurrah! Dance, ye black rascals; the flag of England flies over your heads, and every rustle of its folds knocks the fetters off the limbs of the poor slave. Hubbabboo Cochalorum Gee!'"

The negro schools stood in the rear of the Government House, and the boys' department consisted of about two hundred boys from three to fifteen years of age and of every degree of tinge from nearly white down to the black of two little native Africans bearing on their cheeks the scars of cuts made by their parents at home. These two boys were taken from a slave ship captured and brought into Belize by an English cruiser. As provided for by the laws, on a drawing by lot, they fell to the share of a citizen who, upon entering into certain covenants for good treatment, was entitled to their services until they were twenty-one years old. Unfortunately, the master of the school was not present and I had no opportunity of learning the result of his experience in teaching; but in this school, I was told, the brightest boys and those who had improved most were those who had in them the most white blood.

The mistress of the female department had had great experience in teaching and she told us that, though she had had many clever black girls under her charge, her white scholars were always the most quick and capable.

From the negro school we went to the Grand Court. It had been open about half an hour when I entered. On the back wall, in a massive mahogany tablet, were the arms of England; on a high platform beneath was a large circular table around which were heavy mahogany chairs with high backs and cushions. The court consisted of seven judges, five of whom were in their places. One of them, Mr. Walker, invited me to one of the vacant seats. I objected on the ground that my costume was not becoming so dignified a position, but he insisted, and I, in a roundabout jacket, took my seat in a chair exceedingly comfortable for the administration of justice.

Of the five judges who were in their places, one was a mulatto. The jury was empaneled and two of the jurors were mulattoes; one of them, as the judge who sat next to me said, was a Sambo, or of the descending line, being the son of a mulatto woman and a black man. I was at a loss to determine the caste of a third juror and inquired of the judge, who answered that he was his, the judge's, brother, and that his mother was a mulatto woman. The judge was aware of the feeling which existed in the United States with regard to color, and said that in Belize there was, in political life, no distinction whatever, except on the ground of qualifications and character, and hardly any in social life, even in contracting marriages.

I had noticed the judges and jurors, but I missed an important part of an English court. Where were the gentlemen of the bar? Some of my readers will perhaps concur with Captain Hampton's observation that Belize was the last place made, when I tell them that there was not a single lawyer in the place and never had been. Lest some of my enterprising professional brethren should forthwith be tempted to pack their trunks for a descent upon the exempt city, I consider it my duty to add that I do not believe there is the least chance for one.

As there is no bar to prepare men for the bench, the judges, of course, are not lawyers. Of the five then sitting, two were merchants, one a mahogany cutter, and the mulatto, second to none of the others in character or qualifications, a doctor. This court is the highest tribunal for the trial of civil causes, and has jurisdiction of all amounts above £15. Belize is a place of large commercial transactions; contracts are daily made and broken, or misunderstood, which require the intervention of some proper tribunal to interpret and compel their fulfillment. There was no absence of litigation, the calendar was large, and the courtroom crowded. The first cause called was upon an account; when the defendant did not appear a verdict was taken by default. In the next, the plaintiff stated his case and swore to it; the defendant answered and called witnesses, and the cause was submitted to the jury. There was no case of particular interest. In one the parties became excited, and the defendant interrupted the plaintiff repeatedly, on which the latter, putting his hand upon the shoulder of his antagonist, said in a coaxing way, "Now don't, George; wait a little, you shall have your turn. Don't interrupt me, and I won't you." All was done in a familiar and colloquial way; the parties were more or less known to each other, and judges and jurors were greatly influenced by knowledge of general character. I remarked that regularly the merits of the case were so clearly brought out that when it was committed to the jury there was no question about the verdict. So satisfactory has this system proved that, though an appeal lies to the Queen in Council, as Mr. Evans, the foreman, told me, but one cause has been carried up in twenty-two years. Still it stands as an anomaly in the history of English jurisprudence for, I believe, in every other place where the principles of the common law govern, the learning of the bench and the ingenuity of the bar are considered necessary to elicit the truth.

At daylight the next morning I was roused by Mr. Walker for a ride to the barracks. There are no wheel carriages in Belize because there are no roads except the one we followed to the barracks. Immediately beyond the suburbs we entered upon an uncultivated country, low and flat, but very rich. We passed a racecourse, now disused and grown over. Between Belize and the inhabited part of Central America there is only wilderness unbroken even by an Indian path. The Golfo Dulce and the Belize River offer the only means of communication with the interior; from the want of roads, residence in Belize is more confining than living on an island.

In half an hour we reached the barracks, situated on the opposite side of a small bay. The soldiers were all black and were part of an old Jamaica regiment, most of them having been enlisted at English recruiting stations in Africa. Tall and athletic, with red coats, standing in a line bristling with steel, their ebony faces gave them a peculiarly warlike appearance. They carried themselves proudly, called themselves the "Queen's Gentlemen," and looked down with contempt upon the "niggers."

We returned to breakfast and immediately after made an excursion in the government pitpan. This was the same fashion of boat in which the Indians navigated the rivers of America before the Spaniards discovered it. European ingenuity had not contrived a better, though it had perhaps beautified the Indian model. Ours was about forty feet long and six feet wide in the center, running to a point at both ends, and made of the trunk of a mahogany tree. Ten feet from the stern, and running forward, was a light wooden top supported by fanciful stanchions, with curtains for protection against sun and rain. With its large cushioned seats it was fitted up almost as neatly as the gondolas of Venice. It was manned by eight negro soldiers; six sat two on a seat with paddles six feet long, and two stood up behind with paddles as steersmen. A few touches of the paddles gave brisk way to the pitpan, and we passed rapidly the whole length of the town. It was an unusual thing for His Excellency's pitpan to be upon the water; citizens stopped to gaze at us and all the idle negroes hurried to the bridge to cheer us. This excited our African boatmen, who, with a wild chant that reminded us of the songs of the Nubian boatmen on the Nile, swept under the bridge and hurried us into the still expanse of a majestic river. Before the cheering of the negroes died away we were in as perfect a solitude as if removed thousands of miles from human habitation. The Belize River, coming from sources but little known to civilized man, was then in its fullness. On each side was a dense, unbroken forest. The banks were overflowed and the trees seemed to grow out of the water. Their branches, spreading across so as almost to shut out the light of the sun were reflected in the water as in a mirror. The sources of the river were occupied by the aboriginal owners, wild and free as Cortes found them. We had an eager desire to follow the stream to the famous Lake of Petén,[6] where the skeleton of the conquering Spaniard's horse [7] had been erected into a god by the astonished Indians, but the toil of our boatmen reminded us that they were paddling against a rapid current. We turned the pitpan and, with the full power of the stream and with a pull stronger and a chant louder than before, amid the increased cheering of the negroes we swept under the bridge and in a few minutes landed at the Government House.

In order that we might embark for Izabal at the hour appointed, Colonel MacDonald had ordered dinner for two o'clock and, as on the two preceding days, had invited a small party to meet us. Perhaps I am wrong, but I should do violence to my feelings did I fail to express here my sense of the Colonel's kindness. My invitation to the Government House was the fruit of my official character, but I cannot help flattering myself that some portion of the kindness shown me was the result of personal acquaintance. Colonel MacDonald was a soldier of the Napoleonic Wars, the brother of Sir John MacDonald, adjutant-general of England, and the cousin of Marshal MacDonald of France. All his connections and associations were military. At eighteen he entered Spain as an ensign, one of an army of ten thousand men, of whom, in less than six months, but four thousand were left. After being actively engaged in all the trying service of the Peninsular War, at Waterloo he commanded a regiment, and on the field of battle received the order of Companion of the Military Order of the Bath from the King of England, and that of Knight of the Order of St. Anne from the Emperor of Russia. Rich in recollections of a long military life, personally acquainted with the public and private characters of the most distinguished military men of the age, his conversation was like reading a page of history. He is one of a race that is fast passing away and with whom an American seldom meets.

But to return to dinner. The large window of the dining-room opened upon the harbor; the steamboat lay in front

6. In the lowland jungles of northern Guatemala.
7. A sick horse left by Cortes on his march to Honduras.

of the Government House, and the black smoke, rising in columns from her pipe, gave notice that it was time to embark. Before rising, Colonel MacDonald, like a loyal subject, proposed the health of the Queen, after which he ordered the glasses to be filled to the brim and standing up gave, "The health of Mr. Van Buren, President of the United States," accompanying it with a warm and generous sentiment and the earnest hope of strong and perpetual friendship between England and America. I felt at the moment "cursed by the hand that attempts to break it," and albeit unused to taking the President and the people of my country upon my shoulders, I answered as well as I could. Another toast followed to the health and successful journey of Mr. Catherwood and myself, and we rose from the table.

Colonel MacDonald put his arm through mine and as we walked toward the government dory which lay at the foot of the lawn, he told me that I was going into a distracted country; that Mr. Savage, the American consul in Guatemala, had on a previous occasion protected the property and lives of British subjects; and that, if danger threatened me, I must assemble the Europeans, hang out my flag, and send word to him. I knew that these were not mere words of courtesy and, in the state of the country to which I was going, felt the value of such a friend at hand. With the warmest feelings of gratitude I bade him farewell and stepped into the dory. At the moment flags were run up at the government staff, the fort, the courthouse, and the government schooner, and a gun was fired from the fort. As I crossed the bay, a salute of thirteen guns was fired. Passing the fort, the soldiers presented arms, the government schooner lowered and raised her ensign, and when I mounted the deck of the steamboat, the captain, with hat in hand, told me that he had instructions to place her under my orders and to stop wherever I pleased.

The reader will perhaps ask how I bore all these honors. I had visited many cities, but it was the first time that flags and cannon announced to the world that I was going away. I was a novice, but I endeavored to behave as if I had been brought up to it; to tell the truth, my heart beat and I felt proud, for these were honors paid to my country, and not to me.

To crown the glory of the parting scene, my good friend Captain Hampton had charged his two four-pounders and, when the steamboat got under way, he fired one, but the other would not go off. The captain of the steamboat had on board one puny gun, with which he would have returned all their civilities, but, as he told me, to his great mortification he had no powder.

The steamboat in which we embarked was the last remnant of the stock in trade of a great Central American agricultural association formed for building cities, raising the price of land, accommodating emigrants, and improvement generally. On the rich plains of the province of Verapaz [8] they had established the site of New Liverpool, which only wanted houses and a population to become a city. On the wheel of the boat was a brass circular plate on which in strange juxtaposition were the words "Vera Paz," "London." The captain was a small, weather-beaten, dried-up old Spaniard, with courtesy enough for a don of old. The engineer was an Englishman, and the crew were Spaniards, mestizos, and mulattoes, not particularly at home in the management of a steamboat.

Our only fellow passenger was a Roman Catholic priest, a young Irishman, who had been eight months at Belize. He was now on his way to Guatemala by invitation of the provisor, who, by the exile of the archbishop, was the head of the church in Central America. The cabin was very comfortable, but the evening was so mild that we took our tea on deck. At ten o'clock the captain came to me for orders. I have had my aspirations, but I never expected to be able to dictate to the captain of a steamboat. Nevertheless, again as coolly as if I had been brought up to it, I designated the places I wished to visit and retired. Verily, thought I, if these are the fruits of official appointments, it is not strange that men are found willing to accept them.

---

8. Below the Petén in northern Guatemala there are now two departments called Alta Verapaz and Baja Verapaz.

Chapter II

〰〰〰〰〰〰〰〰〰〰〰〰〰〰〰〰〰〰〰〰〰〰〰〰

Everyone for himself. Travelers' tricks. Punta Gorda.
A visit to the Carib Indians. A Carib crone. A baptism.
Río Dulce. Beautiful scenery. Izabal. Reception of the
padre. A barber in office. A band of "Invincibles." Parties
in Central America. A compatriot. A grave in a foreign
land. Preparations for the passage of "the Mountain." A
road not macadamized. Perils by the way. A
well-spiced lunch. The mountain passed.

WE had engaged a young servant, a French Spaniard, Santo Domingo born and Omoa bred, bearing the name of Augustin, who we at first thought was not very sharp. Early in the morning he asked us what we would have for breakfast, naming eggs, chickens, etc. We gave him directions, and in due time sat down to breakfast. During the meal something occurred to put us on inquiry, and we learned that everything on the table, excepting the tea and coffee, belonged to the padre. Without asking any questions or thinking of the subject at all, we had taken for granted that the steamboat made all necessary provisions for passengers, but, to our surprise, we discovered that the boat furnished nothing, that passengers were expected to take care of themselves. The padre had been as ignorant and as improvident as we; but some good Catholic friends, whom he had married or whose children he had baptized, had sent on board contributions of various kinds, among other things —odd luggage for a traveler—a coop full of chickens. We congratulated the padre upon his good fortune in having us with him, and ourselves upon such a treasure as Augustin.

I may mention, by the way, that in the midst of Colonel MacDonald's hospitalities Mr. Catherwood and I exhibited rather too much of the old traveler. During our last dinner with the Colonel, Mr. Catherwood was called from the table to superintend the removal of some luggage. Shortly after, I, too, was called out and—fortunately for Colonel Mac-Donald and the reputation of my country—I found Mr. Catherwood quietly rolling up to send back to New York a large blue cloak belonging to the Colonel, supposing it to be mine. I returned to the table and mentioned to our host his narrow escape, adding that I was beginning to have some doubt about a large canvass sack for bedding which I had found in my room. Presuming it to be one that had been promised me by Captain Hampton, I had had it put on board the steamboat. This too, it turned out, belonged to Colonel MacDonald and for many years it had carried his camp bed. The Colonel insisted, however, that we use it, and I am afraid it was pretty well worn out before he received it back again. The reader will infer from all this that Mr. Catherwood and I, with the help of Augustin, were fit persons to travel in any country.

As we left Belize, our course lay nearly south, directly along the coast of Honduras. In his last voyage Columbus discovered this part of the Continent of America, but its verdant beauties could not win him to the shore. Without landing he continued on to the Isthmus of Darien in search of that passage to India which was the aim of all his hopes, but which it was destined he should never see.

Steamboats have destroyed some of the most pleasing illusions of my life. I had been hurried up the Hellespont, past Sestos and Abydos and the Plain of Troy, under the clatter of a steam engine; and now to follow the track of Columbus accompanied by the clamor of the same panting monster, struck at the root of all the romance connected with his adventures. Nevertheless, the day was beautiful with a hot sun and a refreshing breeze, and we found it very pleasant to sit on the deck under the shelter of an awning. The coast assumed an appearance of grandeur and beauty that realized my ideas of tropical regions. There was a dense forest to the water's edge. Beyond were lofty mountains covered to their tops with perpetual green, some isolated, others running off in ranges higher and higher till they were lost in the clouds.

At eleven o'clock we came in sight of Punta Gorda, a settlement of Carib Indians about a hundred and fifty miles down the coast, and the first place at which I had directed the captain to stop. As we approached we saw an opening on the water's edge with a range of low houses, reminding me of a clearing in our forests at home. It was but a speck on the great line of coast. On both sides were primeval trees and behind towered an extraordinary mountain, apparently broken into two like the back of a two-humped camel. As the steamboat turned in where steamboat had never been before, the whole village was in commotion: women and children were running on the bank, and four men descended into the water and came off in a canoe to meet us.

Our fellow passenger, the padre, during his residence at Belize had become acquainted with many of the Caribs and, upon one occasion, by invitation from its chief, had visited a settlement for the purpose of marrying and baptizing the inhabitants. He asked whether we had any objections to his taking advantage of the opportunity to do the same here. As we had none, at the moment of disembarking he appeared on deck with a large washhand basin in one hand, and in the other, a well-filled pocket handkerchief containing his priestly vestments.

We anchored a short distance from the beach and went ashore in the small boat. We landed at the foot of a bank about twenty feet high and, ascending to the top, came at once under a burning sun into all the richness of tropical vegetation. Besides cotton and rice, the cajun, banana, cocoanut, pineapple, orange, lemon, plantain, and many other fruits which we did not know even by name were growing with such luxuriance that at first their very fragrance was oppressive. Under the shade of these trees most of the inhabitants were gathered, and the padre immediately gave notice, in a wholesome way, that he had come to marry and baptize them. After a short consultation a house was selected for the performance of the ceremonies, and Mr. Catherwood and I, under the guidance of a Carib who had picked up a little English in his canoe expeditions to Belize, walked through the settlement. It consisted of about five hundred inhabitants. Their native place was on the seacoast below Truxillo within the government of Central America. Having taken an active part against Morazán,[1] when his party became dominant they had fled to their present location within the limits of the British authority. Though living apart as a tribe of Caribs, not mingling their blood with that of their conquerors, they were nevertheless completely civilized. They did retain, however, the Indian passion for beads and ornaments. The houses or huts were built of poles about an inch thick, set upright in the ground, tied together with bark strings, and thatched with cahoon leaves; some had partitions and bedsteads made of the same material. In every house were a grass hammock and a figure of the Virgin or of some tutelary saint. We were exceedingly struck with the great progress in civilization made by these descendants of cannibals, the fiercest of all the Indian tribes encountered by the Spaniards.

The houses extended along the bank at some distance apart; before reaching the last of them we found the heat so oppressive that we decided to turn back, but our guide urged us to go on and see "one old woman," his grandmother. We followed him and saw her. She was very old; no one knew her age, but it was considerably over a hundred. What gave her more interest in our eyes than the circumstance of her being the grandmother of our guide was that she came from the island of St. Vincent, the residence of the most indomitable portion of her race, and that she had never been baptized. She received us with an idiotic laugh. Her figure was shrunken, her face shriveled, weazened, and wicked; she looked indeed as though in her youth she might have gloried in dancing at a feast of human flesh.

We returned to the padre and found our friend dressed in the contents of his pocket handkerchief, quite a respectable-looking priest. By his side was our steamboat washbowl

---

1. Morazán was president of the Confederation of Central American States at the time of Stephens' visit (see pp. 156–157).

filled with holy water, and in his hand was a prayer book. Nearby stood Augustin holding the stump of a tallow candle.

The Caribs, like most of the other Indians of Central America, have received the doctrines of Christianity as presented to them by the priests and monks of Spain, and are in all things strict observers of the forms prescribed. In this settlement the visit of a padre was a rare but welcome occurrence. At first they seemed to have a suspicion that our friend was not orthodox because he did not speak Spanish, but when they saw him in his gown and surplice with the burning incense, all distrust vanished.

There was little to be done in the way of marrying, because of scarcity of men for that purpose; most of them were away fishing or at work. But a long file of women presented themselves, each with a child in her arms, for baptism. They were arranged around the wall in a circle, and the padre began. He asked the first mother a question which I believe is not to be found in the book, and which, in some places, it would be considered impertinent to put to one offering her child for initiation into the Church, that is, whether she was married. She hesitated, smiled, laughed, and answered No. The padre told her that this was very wrong and unbecoming a good Christian woman, and advised her to take advantage of the present opportunity to marry the child's father. She answered that she would like to do so, but that he was away cutting mahogany. As his questions and her answers had to pass through an interpreter, the affair began to get complicated; indeed, so many of the women interposed, all speaking at once, that the padre became aware that he had touched upon delicate ground and decided to quickly pass on to the next case.

In fact, the baptism service itself gave our friend more than enough to do. He understood but little Spanish and his book was in Latin. Not being able to translate as readily as the occasion required, he had employed the interval of our absence in copying on a slip of paper from a Spanish Protestant prayer book the formal part of the service. In the confusion this had been lost, and the padre was thrown back upon his Latin, to be translated into Spanish as required.

After laboring awhile, he turned to Augustin and gave him in English the questions to put to the women. Augustin was a good Catholic and listened to him with as much respect as if he had been the Pope, but did not understand a word he said. I explained to Augustin in French, who explained to one of the men in Spanish, who explained to the women. This, of course, led to confusion; but all were so devout and respectful that in spite of these tribulations the ceremony was solemn. When he came to the Latin parts, our friend rattled it off as fast as if fresh from the Propaganda[2] at Rome, and the Caribs were not much behindhand.

The padre had told us of the passion of the Caribs for a multiplicity of names. One of the women, after giving her child three or four, pointed to me and told the padre to add mine. I am not very strict, but I did not care to assume wantonly the obligations of a godfather. Stopping the ceremony, I begged the padre to get me released with the best grace he could and he promised to do so. But it was an excessively hot day, the room was crowded, the doors choked up, and by this time the padre, with his Latin, and English, and French, and Spanish, was in a profuse perspiration and somewhat confused. I thought myself clear until a few moments later a child was passed along for me to take in my arms. I was relieved on one point: I thought that it was the lady who had become a mother without being a wife who wished her child to bear my name, but fortunately its mother was an honest woman and the father stood by at the time. Still I most ungallantly avoided receiving the baby. On going away, however, the woman intercepted me and, thrusting forward the infant, called me *compadre,* so that without knowing it I became godfather to a Carib child. In all probability I shall never have much to do with its training; I can only hope that in due season it will multiply the name and make it respectable among the Caribs.

We returned to the steamboat and in a few minutes were again under way, steering for the Río Dulce. An amphitheater of lofty mountains stretched for many miles along

---

2. The College of Propaganda in Rome where priests are educated for missionary work.

the coast and back, until finally they were lost to the sight. In one small place this lofty range opens for the passage of a gentle river. On the right bank of the coast was one of the places I intended to visit. It was called by the familiar name of Livingston, in honor of the distinguished citizen of Louisiana whose criminal code had been introduced into Guatemala. It had been supposed, so advantageous was its position, that it would become the port of entry of Central America, but these expectations were not realized.[3]

It was four o'clock in the afternoon as we steered toward the bank, and the captain told me that if we cast anchor it would be necessary to lie there till morning. I was loath to lose the only opportunity I should probably ever have of stopping a steamboat; but I had an eager, almost a burning curiosity to see the Golfo Dulce, and we all agreed that it would be wanton to lose such an opportunity of seeing it to advantage. I therefore directed the captain just to move close to the bank and then pass on.

The bank was elevated about thirty feet above the water, and was as rich and luxuriant as at Punta Gorda. The site of the intended city was occupied by another tribe of Caribs, who, like the Caribs at Punta Gorda, having been driven from their home by war, had followed up the coast and, with that eye for the picturesque and beautiful in natural scenery which distinguished the Indians everywhere, had fixed themselves upon this spot. Their leaf-thatched huts were ranged along the bank, shaded by groves of plantain and cocoanut trees. Canoes with sails set were lying on the water, and men and women were sitting under the trees gazing at us. It was a soft and sunny scene, speaking peace and freedom from the tumults of a busy world.

But, beautiful as it was, we soon forgot it, for a narrow opening in a rampart of mountains wooed us on, and in a few moments we entered the Río Dulce. On each side, rising perpendicularly from three to four hundred feet, was a wall

---

3. Although Livingston has shown some growth since Stephens' time, expectations that it would become the port of entry to Central America are still not realized.

of living green. Trees grew from the water's edge with dense, unbroken foliage to the top; not a spot of barrenness was to be seen. On both sides, from the tops of the highest trees, long tendrils descended to the water, as if to drink and carry life to the trunks that bore them. It was, as its name imports, a Río Dulce, a fairy scene of Titan land, combining exquisite beauty with colossal grandeur. As we advanced the passage turned, and in a few minutes we lost sight of the sea and were enclosed on all sides by a forest wall; but the river, although showing us no passage, still invited us onward. Could this be the portal to a land of volcanoes and earthquakes, to one torn and distracted by civil war? For some time we looked in vain for a single barren spot. At length we saw a naked wall of perpendicular rock, but out of the crevices, and apparently out of the rock itself, grew shrubs and trees. Sometimes we were so enclosed that it seemed as if the boat must drive in among the trees. Occasionally, in an angle of the turns, the wall sank and the sun struck in with scorching force, but in a moment we would be again in the deepest shade. From the fanciful accounts we had heard we expected to see monkeys gamboling among the trees and parrots flying over our heads, but all was as quiet as if man had never been here before. The pelican, the stillest of birds, was the only living thing we saw, and the only sound was the unnatural bluster of our steam engine. The wild defile that leads to the excavated city of Petra is not more noiseless or more extraordinary, but its sterile desolation is in strange contrast to the luxuriant, romantic, and beautiful which is everywhere here.

For nine miles the passage continued thus, one scene of unvarying beauty, then suddenly the narrow river expanded into a large lake, encompassed by mountains and studded with islands, which the setting sun illuminated with gorgeous splendor. We remained on deck till a late hour, and awoke the next morning in the harbor of Izabal. A single schooner of about forty tons showed the low state of her commerce. We landed before seven o'clock in the morning, and even then it was hot. There were no idlers on the bank, and there was only the customhouse officer to receive us.

The town stands on a gentle elevation on the banks of the Golfo Dulce, with mountains piled upon mountains behind. We walked up the street to the square on one side of which was the house of Messrs. Ampudia and Pulleiro, the largest and, except for one they were engaged in building, the only frame house in the place, the rest being huts built of poles and reeds and thatched with leaves of the cajun plant. Opposite their door was a large shed, under which were bales of merchandise, and mules, muleteers, and Indians for transporting goods across Mico Mountain.

The arrival of the padre created a great sensation. It was announced by a joyful ringing of the church bells, and within an hour he was dressed in his surplice and saying mass. The church stood at the head of the square and, like the houses, was built of poles and thatched with leaves. In front, at a distance of ten or fifteen feet, was a large wooden cross. The floor was of bare earth, but swept clean and strewed with pine leaves; the sides were trimmed with branches and festoons of flowers; and the altar was ornamented with figures of the Virgin and saints and wreaths of flowers. It had been a long time since the people had had the privilege of hearing mass, and the whole population— Spaniards, mestizos, and Indians—answered the unexpected but welcome call of the matin bell. The floor was covered with kneeling women with white shawls over their heads, and behind, leaning against the rude pillars, were the men. Their earnestness and humility, the earthen floor and the thatched roof, were more imposing than the pomp of worship in the rich cathedrals of Europe or under the dome of St. Peter's.

After breakfast we inquired for a barber and were referred to the collector of the port, who, we were told, was the best haircutter in the place. His house was no bigger than his neighbors', but inside hung a military saddle with holsters and pistols, and a huge sword, the accouterments of the collector when he sallied out at the head of his one-man deputy to strike terror into the heart of a smuggler. Unfortunately, the honest democrat was not at home, but the deputy offered his own services. Mr. Catherwood and I submitted; but the padre, who wanted his crown shaved accord-

ing to the rules of his order, determined to await the return
of the collector.

I next called upon the commandant with my passport.
His house was on the opposite side of the square. A soldier
about fourteen years old, with a bell-crowned straw hat falling over his eyes like an extinguisher upon a candle, was
standing at the door as sentinel. The troops, consisting of
about thirty men and boys, were drawn up in front, and a
sergeant was smoking a cigar and drilling them. The uniform purported to be a white straw hat, cotton trousers with
shirt worn outside, and a musket and cartridge box. In one
particular, uniformity was strictly observed: all were barefooted. The customary first process of calling off rank and
file was omitted; as it happened, a long-legged fellow, six
feet tall, stood next to a boy twelve or thirteen years old.
The customhouse officer was with the sergeant, advising
him. After a maneuver and a consultation, the sergeant
walked up to the line and with the palm of his hand struck
a soldier on that part of the body which, in my younger days,
was considered by the schoolmaster the channel of knowledge into a boy's brain.

The commandant of this hopeful band was Don Juan
Peñol, a gentleman by birth and education, who with others
of his family had been banished by General Morazán, and
sought refuge in the United States. His predecessor, who
was an officer of Morazán, had been just driven out by the
Carrera party, and Don Juan had been but twenty days in
his place.

Three great parties at that time distracted Central America: that of Morazán, the former president of the Republic,
in El Salvador; of Ferrera [4] in Honduras; and of Carrera
in Guatemala. Ferrera, a mulatto, and Carrera, an Indian,
though not fighting for any common purpose, were in sym-
pathetic opposition to Morazán. When Mr. Montgomery [5]
visited Guatemala, it had been just thrown into a ferment by

4. Francisco Ferrera (1794–1851), general and president. For
Stephens' detailed discussion of Morazán and Carrera, see Chap. XI.
    5. G. W. Montgomery, author of *Narrative of a Journey to Guate-
mala in Central America in 1838* (New York: Wiley and Putnam,
1839).

the rising of Carrera, who was then regarded as the head of a troop of banditti, a robber and assassin. His followers were called *Cachurecos* and Mr. Montgomery told me that against him an official passport would be no protection whatever. Now he was the head of the party that ruled Guatemala. Señor Peñol gave us a melancholy picture of the state of the country. A battle had just been fought near San Salvador between General Morazán and Ferrera. Morazán had been wounded but Ferrera had been routed and his troops cut to pieces. Señor Peñol feared Morazán was about to march upon Guatemala. He could only give us a passport to Guatemala, which he said would not be respected by General Morazán. We felt interested in the position of Señor Peñol, a young man whose face bore the marks of care and anxiety, a consciousness of the miserable condition of the present, and fearful forebodings for the future. To our great regret, the intelligence we received induced our friend the padre to abandon for the present his intention of going to Guatemala City. He had heard all the terrible stories of Morazán's persecution and proscription of the priests and thought it dangerous to fall into his hands; I have reason to believe it was the apprehension of this which ultimately drove him from the country.

Toward evening I strolled through the town. The population consists of about fifteen hundred Indians, negroes, mulattoes, mestizos, and mixed blood of every degree, with a few Spaniards. Very soon I was accosted by a man who called himself my countryman, a mulatto from Baltimore whose name was Philip. He had been eight years in Guatemala and said that he had once thought of returning home as a servant by way of New Orleans, but that he had left home in such a hurry he had forgotten to bring with him his "Christian papers," from which I inferred that he was what would be called in Maryland a runaway slave. He was a man of considerable standing, being fireman on board the steamboat at $23 a month; he also did odd jobs at carpentering, and was in fact the principal architect in Izabal, having then on his hands a contract for $3500 for building the new house of Messrs. Ampudia and Pulleiro. In other things, I am sorry to say, Philip was not quite so respectable; I can only hope that it was not his American education that led him into some of the irregularities in which he seemed to think there was no harm. He asked me to go to his house and see his wife, but on the way I learned from him that he was not married; he said—and I hope it is a slander upon the good people of Izabal—that he only did as all the rest did. He owned the house in which he lived, and for which, with the ground, he had paid twelve dollars. Being myself a householder and an American, I tried to induce him to take advantage of the opportunity of the padre's visit and set a good example by getting married, but he was obstinate, and said that he did not like to be trammeled, and that he might go elsewhere and see another girl whom he liked better.

While I was standing at his door, Mr. Catherwood passed on his way to visit Mr. Rush, the engineer of the steamboat, who had been ill on board. We found him in one of the huts of the town, in a hammock with all his clothes on. He was a man of Herculean frame, six feet three or four inches tall and stout in proportion, but he lay helpless as a child. A single candle stuck upon the dirt floor gave a miserable light, and a group of men of different races and color, from the white-faced Saxon to the dark-skinned Indian and African, stood round him—rude nurses for one used to the comforts of an English home. I recollected that Izabal was noted as a sickly place; Mr. Montgomery, after his interesting visit to Guatemala in 1838, had told me that even to pass through it was like running the gauntlet for life, and I trembled for the poor stricken Englishman. I remembered, too, and it is strange that I had not done so earlier, that Mr. Shannon, our chargé to Central America, had died here. Philip was with me and knew where Mr. Shannon was buried, but in the dark he could not point out the spot. I intended to set out early in the morning and afraid that, in the hurry of departure, I might neglect altogether the sacred duty of visiting in this distant place the grave of an American, I returned to the house and requested Señor Ampudia to accompany me. We crossed the square, passed through the suburbs, and in a few minutes were outside the town. It was so dark that I could scarcely see my way. Crossing a deep gulley on a plank, we reached a rising ground, open on the right, stretching away to the Golfo Dulce, and in front bounded by a gloomy forest. On the top beside a rude fence of rough upright poles which enclosed the grave of some relative of Señor Ampudia, was the grave of Mr. Shannon. There was no stone or fence or hardly any elevation to distinguish it from the soil around. It was a gloomy burial place for one of my country-men, and I felt an involuntary depression of spirit. In fact, a certain sense of fatality hovered over our diplomatic ap-pointment to Central America: Mr. Williams, Mr. Shannon, Mr. De Witt, Mr. Leggett, all who had ever come here in such a capacity, were dead. I thought, too, of what a near relative of Mr. Dewitt had written me: "May you be more fortunate than either of your predecessors has been." It was melancholy that one who had died abroad in the service of his country was thus left on a wild mountain without any stone to mark his grave. I returned to the house, directed a fence to be built around the grave of Mr. Shannon, and my friend the padre promised to plant at its head a cocoanut tree.

At daylight the muleteers commenced loading for the passage of "the Mountain." At seven o'clock the whole cara-van, consisting of nearly a hundred mules and twenty or thirty muleteers, was fairly under way. Our immediate party consisted of five mules, two for Mr. Catherwood and my-self, one for Augustin, and two for luggage; in addition we had four Indian carriers. If we had been consulted, perhaps at that time we should have scrupled to use men as beasts of burden, but Señor Ampudia had made all the arrange-ments for us. The Indians were naked except for a small piece of cotton cloth wrapped around the loins and crossed in front between the legs. The loads were arranged so as to have on one side a flat surface. The Indians sat down on the ground with their backs to the loads; each passed a support-ing strap across his forehead and adjusted it on his shoul-ders; then, with the aid of staffs or the hands of bystanders, they rose to their feet as a unit. It seemed cruel, but before much sympathy could be expended upon them they were out of sight.

At eight o'clock Mr. Catherwood and I mounted, each armed with a brace of pistols and a large hunting knife, which we carried in a belt around the body. Afraid to trust it in other hands, I also had a mountain barometer slung over my shoulder. Augustin carried pistols and a sword. Our principal muleteer, who was mounted, carried a machete and, on his naked heels, a pair of murderous spurs with rowels two inches long; two other muleteers accompanied us on foot, each carrying a gun.

A group of friendly bystanders gave us their adieus and good wishes. After passing the few straggling houses which constituted the suburbs, we entered upon a marshy plain sprinkled with shrubs and small trees and in a few minutes were in an unbroken forest. At every step the mules sank to their fetlocks in mud, and very soon we came to great puddles and mudholes, which reminded me of the breaking-up of winter and the solitary horse-path in one of our primeval forests at home. As we advanced, the shade of the trees became thicker, the holes larger and deeper, and roots, rising two or three feet above the ground, crossed the path in every direction. I gave the barometer to the muleteer, for I had all I could do to keep myself in the saddle. All conversation was at an end, and we kept as close as we could to the track of the muleteer; when he descended into a mudhole and crawled out, the entire legs of his mule blue with mud, we followed and came out as blue as he.

The caravan of mules, which had started before us, was but a short distance ahead, and in a little while we heard ringing through the woods the loud shout of the muleteers and the sharp crack of the whip. We overtook them at the bank of a stream which broke rapidly over a stony bed, its waters darkened by the shade of the overhanging trees. The whole caravan was moving up the bed of the stream. The muleteers, without shirts and with their large trousers rolled up to the thighs and down from the waistband, were scattered among the mules. One was chasing a stray beast; a second darted toward one whose load was slipping off; a third was lifting up one that had fallen; another, with his foot braced against a mule's side, was straining at the girth— all were shouting, cursing, and lashing, the whole a mass of inextricable confusion.

We drew up to let them pass us. Before joining them, we wished to avoid a bend in the stream by crossing to a road on the opposite bank, which, though level, we found to be fetlock deep in mud. After a short distance on this road, we joined the caravan in the bed of the stream, following it until another road, no better than the first, brought us to the foot of the mountain. The ascent began precipitously and by an extraordinary passage, a narrow gulley worn by the tracks of mules and the washing of mountain torrents. It was so deep that the sides were higher than our heads, and so narrow that we could barely pass through without touching them. Our whole caravan moved singly through this muddy defile. The muleteers scattered among them and on the bank above, extricating the mules as they stuck fast, raising them as they fell, arranging their cargoes, cursing, shouting, and lashing them on; if one stopped, all behind were blocked up, unable to turn. Any sudden start pressed us against the sides of the gulley, and there was no small danger of getting a leg crushed. Emerging from this defile, we came again to deep mudholes and projecting roots of trees, which added to the difficulty of a steep ascent. The trees were large, their roots high and far-extending; above all, the mahogany tree threw out its giant roots, high at the trunk and tapering, not round like the roots of other trees, but straight with sharp edges, traversing rocks and the roots of other trees. It was the last of the rainy season. The heavy rains from which we had suffered at sea had deluged the mountain, and it was in the worst state it could be and still be passable; sometimes it was not passable at all. For the last few days there had been no rain, but we had hardly congratulated ourselves upon our good fortune in having a clear day when the forest became darker and the rain poured. The woods were of impenetrable thickness and we could see nothing beyond the detestable path before us. For five long hours we were dragged through mudholes, squeezed in gulleys, knocked against trees, and tumbled over roots. Every step required care and great physical exertion and, withal, I felt that our inglorious epitaph might well read: "tossed over the head of a mule, brained by the trunk of a mahogany tree, and buried in the mud of Mico Mountain." We attempted to walk, but the rocks and roots were so slippery, the mudholes so deep, and the ascents and descents so steep, that it was impossible to continue.

The mules were only half loaded, but, even so, several broke down and the lash could not move them; scarcely one passed over the mountain without a fall. Of our immediate party, mine fell first. Finding that I could not save her with the rein, by an exertion that strained every nerve I lifted myself from off her back and flung myself clear of roots and trees (but not of mud) to discover I had escaped an even worse danger: my dagger had fallen from its sheath and was standing upright with the handle in the mud, a foot of naked blade. Then Mr. Catherwood, too, was thrown from his mule with such violence that for a few moments, feeling the helplessness of our condition, I was horror-struck. Long before this he had broken silence to utter an exclamation which seemed to come from the bottom of his heart: "If I had known of this mountain, you might have come to Central America alone!" If I had had any tendency to be a little uplifted by the honors I received at Belize, I was quickly brought down by this highway to my capital. Shortly after, Augustin's mule fell backward; he kicked his feet out of the stirrups and attempted to slide off behind, but the mule rolled and caught him with his left leg under. But for his kicking, I should have thought that every bone in his body was broken, and the mule kicked worse than he. But they rose together and without any damage, except that the mud, which before lay upon them in spots, was now formed into a regular plaster.

We were toiling on toward the top of the mountain, when, at a sudden turn, we met a solitary traveler. He was a tall, dark-complexioned man, with a broad-brimmed Panama hat rolled up at the sides, a striped woolen Guatemala jacket with fringe at the bottom, plaid pantaloons, leather spatterdashes, spurs, and sword. He was mounted on a noble mule with a high-peaked saddle, and the butts of a pair of horseman's pistols peeped out of the holsters. His face was covered with sweat and mud, his breast and legs were spattered, and his right side was a complete incrustation; altogether, his appearance was fearful. It seemed strange to meet anyone on such a road and, to our surprise, he accosted us in English. He had set out with muleteers and Indians but, having lost them in some of the windings of the woods, he was now seeking his way alone. He had crossed the mountain twice before, but had never known it to be so bad; he had been thrown twice, once his mule had rolled over him and nearly crushed him, and now she was so frightened that he could hardly urge her along. He dismounted, and the trembling beast and his own exhausted state confirmed all that he had said. He asked us for brandy, wine, or water, anything to revive him, but unfortunately our stores were up ahead and for him to go back even one step was out of the question.

Imagine our surprise when, with his feet buried in the mud, he told us that for two years he had been in Guatemala City "negotiating" for a bank charter. Fresh as I was from the land of banks, I almost thought he intended a fling at me, but he did not look like one in a humor for jesting and, for the benefit of those who will regard it as an evidence of incipient improvement, I am able to state that he already had the charter secured when he rolled over in the mud and was then on his way to England to sell the stock. He told us, too, what seemed in better keeping with the scene, that Carrera had marched toward San Salvador and that a battle was daily expected between him and Morazán.

But neither of us had time to lose, and parting, though with some reluctance, almost as abruptly as we had met, we continued our ascent. At one o'clock, to our inexpressible satisfaction, we reached the top of the mountain. Here we found a clearing about two hundred feet in diameter, made for the benefit of benighted muleteers; in various places were heaps of ashes and burned stumps of wood, the remains of their fires. It was the only place on the mountain which the sun could reach, and here the ground was dry. The view, however, was bounded by the clearing.

We dismounted, and would have lunched if we had had any water to drink; after a few minutes' rest we resumed our journey. The descent was as bad as the ascent; instead of stopping to let the mules breathe as they had done in ascending, the muleteers seemed anxious to determine in how short a time they could tumble them down the mountain. In one of the muddiest defiles, shut up by the falling of a mule in front of us and the crowding upon us of all behind, we stopped at the first convenient place to let the whole caravan pass. The carefulness of the mules was extraordinary. For an hour I watched the movements of the one ahead of me. At times he put one of his forefeet on a root or stone and tried it as a man would; sometimes he drew his forelegs out of a bed of mud from the shoulders, and sometimes it was one continued alternation of sinking and pulling out.

This was the great highroad to the city of Guatemala, which has always been a place of distinction in Spanish America; almost all the travel and merchandise from Europe passes over it. Our guide said that the reason it was in such bad condition was because it was traversed by so many mules. In some countries this would be a good reason for improving it, but it was pleasant to find that the people here to whom I was accredited were relieved from one of the sources of contention at home, since they did not trouble themselves with the complicated questions attendant upon internal improvements.[6]

In two hours we reached a wild river or mountain torrent, foaming and breaking over its rocky bed, and shaded by large trees. It was called *El Arroyo del Muerto*, or Stream of the Dead. The muleteers were already distributed on the

---

6. Stephens noted that for the improvement of the road the Constituent Assembly of Guatemala had imposed a tax of one dollar upon every bale of merchandise that passed over the mountain. A railroad now carries much of the freight from the Atlantic Coast to Guatemala City.

rocks or under the shade of the trees, eating their frugal meal of corncakes; the mules were in the river or scattered along the bank. We selected a spot under a large tree, which spread its branches over us like a roof, and which was so near the stream that we could dip our drinking cups into the water.

All the anxiety which during the day I had been able to spare from myself I bestowed upon my barometer. The guide who carried it on his back also carried on the belt of his machete a small white pitcher with a red rim, of which he was very proud and very careful. Several times, after a stumble and a narrow escape, he turned round and held up the pitcher with a smile, which gave me hopes for the barometer. In fact, he had carried the barometer through without its being broken, although, unfortunately, all the quicksilver, which was not well secured, had escaped. It was impossible to repair it in Guatemala, and its loss was a source of regret during our whole journey, for we ascended many mountains, the heights of which had never been ascertained.

But we had another misadventure, which, at the moment, touched us more nearly. We sat on the ground Turkish fashion with a vacant space between us, and Augustin placed before us a well-filled napkin. As we dipped water from the clear stream by our side, a spirit of other days came over us, and we spoke in contempt of railroads, cities, and hotels. But O Publicans, you were avenged! We unrolled the napkin, and the scene that presented itself was too shocking even for the strongest nerves. We had provided bread for three days, eggs boiled hard, and two roasted fowls for as long as they might last. Augustin had forgotten salt, but he had placed in the napkin a large paper of gunpowder as an adventure of his own. The paper was broken, and the bread, fowls, and eggs were thoroughly seasoned with this new condiment. All the beauty of the scene, all our equanimity, everything except our tremendous appetites, left us in a moment. As the vision of country taverns rose before us, we who had been so amiable abused Augustin and wished him the whole murderous seasoning in his own body. We picked and made excavations for our immediate use, but most of our stores were lost and there was not enough to satisfy hunger. Perhaps it was the most innocent way of tasting gunpowder, but even so it was a bitter pill.

This over, we mounted and, fording the stream, continued our descent. Passing off by a spur of the mountain, we came out upon an open ridge which commanded a view of an extensive savannah. Very soon we reached a fine table of land where a large party of muleteers on their way to Izabal were encamped for the night, their fires for cooking supper already burning. Bales of indigo, which formed their cargoes, were piled up like a wall; nearby the mules were pasturing quietly. It was a great satisfaction to be once more in the open country, and to see the mountain, with its dense forest, lighted up by the setting sun, grand and gloomy, and ourselves fairly out of it. With ten hours of the hardest riding I ever went through, we had made only twelve miles.

Descending from this table, we entered a thickly wooded plain and in a few minutes reached a grove of wild palm trees of singular beauty. From the top of a tall naked stem grew branches twenty or thirty feet long, spreading from the trunk and falling outward with a graceful bend, like enormous plumes of feathers. The trees stood so close that the bending branches met to form arches, in some places as regular as if constructed by an artist. As we rode among them there was a solemn stillness, an air of desolation, that reminded us of the columns of an Egyptian temple.

Toward dark we reached the rancho of Mico. It was a small house, built of poles and plastered with mud. Near it and connected by a shed thatched with branches was a larger house, built of the same material and expressly for the use of travelers. This was already occupied by two parties from Guatemala City, one of which consisted of the Canónigo Castillo, his clerical companion or secretary, and two young Pavons. The other was a French merchant on his way to Paris. Mr. Catherwood and I were picturesque-looking objects, not spattered but plastered with mud from head to foot, but we soon became known, and received from the whole company a cordial welcome to Central America.

Their appearance was such as to give me a highly favorable opinion of the kind of people I could expect to meet at Guatemala City. The canónigo was one of the first men in the country in position and character, and was then on his way to Havana on a delicate political mission, having been sent by the Constituent Assembly to invite back the archbishop banished by General Morazán ten years before. He undertook to do the honors, and set before us chocolate and what he called the "national dish," *frijoles*, or fried black beans, which, fortunately for our subsequent travels, we "cottoned to" at once. We were very tired, but agreeable company was better than sleep. The canónigo had been educated at Rome and had passed the early part of his life in Europe; the Frenchman was from Paris; the young Pavons had been educated in New York. We sat till a late hour, our clothes stiff with mud, talking of France, Italy, and home. At length we hung up our hammocks. We had been so much occupied that we had paid no attention to our luggage, and now, wanting a change of raiment, we could not find our men and were obliged to turn in as we were. However, with the satisfactory feeling that we had passed "the mountain," we soon fell asleep.

Chapter III

〰〰〰〰〰〰〰〰〰〰〰〰〰〰〰〰〰〰〰〰〰〰〰〰〰〰〰〰

*A canónigo. How to roast a fowl. Extempore shoemaking.
Motagua River. Beautiful scene. Crossing the river. The
luxury of water. Primitive costumes. How to make tortillas. Costly timber. Gualán. Oppressive heat. Shock of an
earthquake. A stroll through the town. A troublesome
muleteer. A lawsuit. Important negotiations. A modern
Bona Dea. How to gain a husband. A kingdom of
flora. Zacapa. Making free with a host.*

BEFORE daylight I was out of doors. Twenty or thirty
men, muleteers and servants, were asleep on the
ground, each lying on his back with his black *chamarra*
wound round him and covering his head and feet. As the day
broke they arose. Very soon the Frenchman, too, got up,
took chocolate, and after an hour's preparation started his
journey. The canónigo set off next. He had crossed the
mountain twenty years before on his first arrival in the country and still retained a full recollection of its horrors. He set
off on the back of an Indian, in a *silla*, a chair with a high
back and top to protect him from the sun. Three other Indians followed as relay carriers, and a noble mule for his relief if he should become tired of the chair. The Indian was
bent almost double, but the canónigo was in high spirits,
smoking his cigar and waving his hand till he was out of
sight. The Pavons started last, and we were left alone.

Still none of our men came. At about eight o'clock two
made their appearance; they had slept at a rancho near by,
and the others had gone on with the luggage. We were excessively provoked but, enduring as best we could the discomfort of our clothes stiff with mud, we saddled and set off.

We saw no more of our caravan of mules, and our mule-teer of the barometer had disappeared without notice, leaving us in the hands of two understrappers.

Our road lay over a mountainous country, but one generally clear of wood. In about two hours we reached a collection of ranchos, called El Pozo. One of our men rode up to a hut and dismounted as if he were at home. When the woman of the house chided him for not having come the night before, he gruffly ascribed the cause to us, and it was evident that we stood a chance of losing him too. But in the desire for breakfast we had a subject of more immediate interest. Our tea and coffee, all that we had left after the destruction of our stores by gunpowder, had gone forward, and it would be some time before we would be able to get them. And here, in the beginning of our journey, we found a scarcity of provender greater than we had ever met with before in any inhabited country. The people lived exclusively upon tortillas—flat cakes made of crushed Indian corn and baked on a clay griddle—and black beans. Augustin bought some of the latter, but they required several hours' soaking before they could be eaten. At length he succeeded in buying a fowl and, running a stick through it, smoked it over a fire without dressing of any kind. With tortillas, it made a good meal for a penitentiary system of diet. As we had expected, our principal muleteer found it impossible to tear himself away; but, like a dutiful husband, he sent, by the only one of our men now left us, a loving message to his wife at Gualán.

At the moment of starting our remaining attendant said he could not go until he had made a pair of shoes, and we were obliged to wait; but it did not take long. Standing on an untanned cowhide, he marked the size of his feet with a piece of coal, cut the shapes out with his machete, made proper holes, and, passing a leather string under the instep, around the heel, and between the great *doigt du pied* and the one next to it, was shod.

Again our road lay on the ridge of a high mountain, with a valley on each side. At a distance were beautiful green hillsides, ornamented with pine trees and grazing cattle, that reminded us of park scenery in England. Often points of land presented themselves which at home would have been selected as sites for dwellings and embellished by art and taste. It was a land of perpetual summer—the blasts of winter never reach it—but, with all its softness and beauty, it was dreary and desolate.

At two o'clock it began to rain, but in an hour it cleared off. From the high mountain ridge we saw the Motagua River, one of the noblest in Central America, rolling majestically through the valley on our left. Descending by a wild, precipitous path, at four o'clock we reached the bank directly opposite Encuentros.[1] It was one of the most beautiful scenes I ever beheld: all around were giant mountains, and the river, broad and deep, rolled through them with the force of a mighty torrent.

On the opposite bank were a few houses, and two or three canoes lay in the water, but not a person was in sight. By loud shouting we brought a man to the bank who entered one of the canoes and set it adrift. He was immediately carried far down the stream, but, taking advantage of an eddy, he brought her across to the place where we stood. Our luggage, the saddles, bridles, and other trappings of the mules were put on board, and we embarked. Augustin sat in the stern holding the halter of one of the mules and leading her like a decoy duck, but the rest had no disposition to follow. The muleteer drove them in up to their necks, but they ran back to the shore. Several times, by pelting them with sticks and stones, he drove them in as before. At length he stripped himself and, wading to the depth of his breast with a stick ten or twelve feet long, succeeded in getting them all afloat, and on a line within the reach of his stick. In the event that one of them turned toward the shore, he received a blow on his nose. At last they all set their faces for the opposite bank, their little heads being all that we could see, aimed directly across but carried down by the current. When one who had been carried below the rest saw her companions landing, she raised a frightened cry and almost drowned herself in her struggle to reach them.

During all this time we sat in the canoe with the hot sun beating upon our heads. For the last two hours we had suf-

---

1. At present no such village exists on the lower Motagua.

fered excessively from heat. Our clothes were saturated with
perspiration and stiff with mud, and we looked forward almost with rapture to a bath in the Motagua and a change of
linen. We landed and walked up to the house in which we
were to pass the night. It was plastered and whitewashed,
and adorned with streaks of red in the shape of festoons; in
front was a fence made of long reeds, six inches in diameter,
split into two. Altogether the appearance was favorable. To
our great vexation, our luggage had gone on to a rancho
three leagues beyond and our muleteers refused to go any
farther. We were unpleasantly situated, but we did not care
to leave the Motagua River so soon. Our host told us that
his house and all that he had were at our disposal. But he
could give us nothing to eat and, telling Augustin to ransack
the village, we returned to the river. Everywhere the current was too rapid for a quiet bath. Calling our canoe man,
we returned to the opposite side, and in a few minutes were
enjoying an ablution, the luxury of which can only be appreciated by those who, like us, had crossed Mico Mountain
without throwing away their clothes.

There was an enjoyment in this bath greater even than
that of cooling our heated bodies, for it was the moment of
a golden sunset. At the margin of a channel along which the
stream was rushing with arrow-like speed, we stood up to
our necks in water clear as crystal and as calm as that of some
diminutive lake. On each side were mountains several thousand feet high, whose tops were illuminated by the setting
sun. On a point above us was a palm-leafed hut, and before
it a naked Indian sat looking at us, as flocks of parrots, with
brilliant plumage, almost in thousands, flew over our heads,
catching up our words, and filling the air with noisy mock-
ings. It was one of those beautiful scenes that so rarely occur in human life, almost realizing dreams. Old as we were,
we might have become poetic had not Augustin come down
to the opposite bank and, with a cry that rose above the chattering of parrots and the loud murmur of the river, called
us to supper.

We had one moment of agony when we returned to our
clothes. They lay extended upon the bank, emblems of men

who had seen better days. The setting sun, which shed over all a soft and mellow luster, laid bare the seams of mud and dirt, and made them hideous. We had but one alternative, and that was to go on without them. But, as this seemed to be trenching upon the proprieties of life, we picked them up and put them on reluctantly. I am not sure, however, but that we made an unnecessary sacrifice of personal comfort. The proprieties of life are after all only matters of conventional usage. When we presented our letter, our host, a don, received us with great dignity in a single garment, loose, white, and very laconic, not quite reaching his knees. The dress of his wife was no less easy, being somewhat in the style of the old-fashioned shortgown and petticoat, except that the shortgown and whatever else is usually worn under it were wanting and their place supplied by a string of beads with a large cross at the end. A dozen men and half-grown boys, naked except for the small covering formed by rolling the trousers up and down in the manner I have mentioned, were lounging about the house, as were women and girls in such extremes of undress that a string of beads seemed quite a modest covering.

Mr. Catherwood and I were in a rather awkward predicament for the night. The general reception room contained three beds made of strips of cowhide interlaced. The don occupied one; he had not much undressing to do, but what little he had, he did by pulling off his shirt. Another bed was at the foot of my hammock. I had been dozing, when I opened my eyes and saw a girl about seventeen sitting sideways upon it, smoking a cigar. She had a piece of striped cotton cloth tied around her waist and falling below her knees. The rest of her dress was that which Nature bestows alike upon the belle of fashionable life and the poorest girl; in other words, it was the same as that of the don's wife, with the exception of the string of beads. At first I thought it was something I had conjured up in a dream. As I waked up perhaps I raised my head, for she gave a few puffs of her cigar, drew a cotton sheet over her head and shoulders, and lay down to sleep. I endeavored to do the same, recalling the proverb that "traveling makes strange bedfellows." I had slept pell-mell with Greeks, Turks, and Arabs. Now I was beginning a journey in a new country and I felt it my duty to conform to the customs of the people, to be prepared for the worst, and to submit with resignation to whatever might befall me.

As guests, it was pleasant to feel that the family made no strangers of us. Several times during the night we were wakened by the clicking of flint and steel, and saw one of our neighbors lighting a cigar. At daylight the wife of the don, who had retired with no more ceremony than the others, was enjoying her morning slumber. While I was dressing she bade me good morning, removed the cotton covering from her shoulders, and arose dressed for the day.

We departed early, and for some distance our road lay along the banks of the Motagua, almost as beautiful by morning as by evening light. In an hour we began to ascend the spur of a mountain. Reaching the top, we followed a high and narrow ridge which commanded on both sides an almost boundless view, and seemed selected for picturesque effect. The scenery was grand, but the land was wild and uncultivated, without fences, enclosures, or habitation. A few cattle were wandering wild over the great expanse but without imparting that domestic aspect which in other countries attends the presence of cattle. We met a few Indians who with their machetes were going to their morning's work, and a man who was riding a mule, with a woman before him, his arm encircling her waist.

I was riding ahead of my companions, and on the summit of the ridge, a little aside from the road, I saw a little white girl, perfectly naked, playing before a rancho. As most of the people we had met were Indians or Ladinos, I was attracted by her appearance and rode up to the rancho. The proprietor, in the easy costume of our host of Encuentros, was swinging in a hammock under the portico smoking a cigar. At a little distance was a shed thatched with stalks and leaves of Indian corn called the *cocina*, or kitchen. As usual, while the don was lolling in his hammock, the women were at work.

I rode on to the *cocina* and dismounted. The party consisted of the mother and a pretty daughter-in-law of about nineteen, and two daughters of about fifteen and seventeen. In honor of my visit, the mother snatched up the little girl who had attracted me to the rancho, carried her inside, and slipped over her head a garment which, I believe, is generally worn by little girls; but in a few minutes my young friend disencumbered herself of her finery and was toddling about with it under her arm.

The whole family was engaged in making tortillas. This is the bread of Central and of all Spanish America and the only kind to be found except in the principal towns. At one end of the *cocina* was an elevation on which stood a *comal*, or griddle, resting on three stones wih a fire blazing under it. The daughter-in-law had before her an earthen vessel containing Indian corn which had been soaked in limewater to remove the husk. Placing a handful on an oblong stone curving inward, she mashed it with a stone roller into a thick paste. The girls took it as it was mashed, patted it with their hands into flat cakes, and laid them on the griddle to bake. This is repeated for every meal, and a great part of the work of the women consists in making tortillas.

By the time Mr. Catherwood arrived the tortillas were smoking, and we stopped to breakfast. They gave us the only luxury they had, coffee made of parched corn, which, in compliment to their kindness, we drank. Like me, Mr. Catherwood was struck with the personal beauty of this family group. With the advantages of dress and education they might well have become ornaments in cultivated society; but it has been decreed otherwise, and these young girls will go through life making tortillas.

For another hour we continued on the ridge of the mountain and then entered a more woody country. Half an hour later we came to a large gate, which stood directly across the road like a toll bar, the first token we had seen of individual or territorial boundary. In other countries it would have formed a fitting entrance to a princely estate, for the massive frame, with all its posts and supporters, was of solid mahogany. The heat was now intense. We entered a thick wood and forded a wild stream, across which pigs were swimming. Soon after we came to a cochineal plantation and passed through a long lane thickly bordered and overshaded with shrubs and trees, close to suffocation. We emerged into an open plain on which the sun beat with almost intolerable power; crossing the plain, at about three o'clock we entered Gualán. There was not a breath of air; the houses and the earth seemed to throw out heat. I was confused, my head swam, and I felt in danger of sunstroke. At that moment there was a slight shock of earthquake. I was unconscious of it, but was almost overpowered by the excessive heat and closeness of atmosphere which accompanied it.

We rode up to the house of Doña Bartola to whom we had a letter of recommendation, and I cannot describe the satisfaction with which I threw myself into a hammock. Shade and quiet restored me. For the first time since we left Izabal we changed our clothes; for the first time, too, we dined.

Toward evening we strolled through the town. It stood on a table of breccia rock at the junction of two noble rivers, and was encircled by a belt of mountains. Its population of about ten thousand was chiefly mestizos. One principal street, the houses of one story with piazzas in front, terminated in a plaza or public square. At the head of the square stood a large church with a Gothic door, before which, at a distance of ten or twelve yards, was a cross about twenty feet high. Leaving the plaza, we walked down to the Motagua. On the bank a boat about fifty feet long and ten wide was in the process of construction and it was being made entirely of mahogany. Near it a party of men and women were fording the stream, carrying their clothes above their heads; around a point three women were bathing. There were no ancient associations connected with this place, but the wildness of the scene, the clouds, the tints of the sky, and the setting sun reflected upon the mountains, were beautiful. At dark we returned to the house. Except for the companionship of some thousands of ants, which blackened the candles and covered everything perishable, we had a room to ourselves.

Early in the morning we were served with chocolate and a small roll of sweet bread. While at breakfast our muleteer came, reiterating a demand for settlement, and claiming that

an additional three dollars were due him. We refused to pay
him, and he went away furious. Within half an hour an
alguacil [2] came to me with a summons to the alcalde. [3] Mr.
Catherwood, who was at the moment cleaning his pistols,
cheered me by threatening to bombard the town if they put
me in prison. The cabildo, or town hall, was at one side of
the plaza. We entered a large room, one end of which was
partitioned off by a wooden railing. Inside sat the alcalde
and his clerk, and outside was the muleteer with a group of
half-naked fellows as his backers. He had reduced his claim
to one dollar, doubtless supposing that I would pay that
rather than have any trouble. It was not very respectable to
be sued for a dollar, but when I looked into his face on entering, I resolved not to pay a cent. I did not, however,
claim my privilege under the law of nations, but defended
the action on its merits. The alcalde decided in my favor
and then when I showed him my passport, he asked me inside the bar and offered me a cigar.

This over, I had more important business to attend to. I
had to hire mules, which I found could not be procured until
two days later. Next I negotiated for having some clothes
washed, which was a complicated business, for it was necessary to specify which articles were to be washed, which
ironed, and which starched, and to pay separately for washing, ironing, soap, and starch. Lastly, I negotiated with a
tailor for a pair of pantaloons, purchasing separately stuff,
lining, buttons, and thread, the tailor finding needles and
thimble himself.

Toward evening we again walked to the river, and on our
return taught Doña Bartola how to make tea. By this time
the whole town was in a commotion in anticipation of the
great ceremony of praying to Santa Lucía. Early in the
morning, the firing of muskets, petards, and rockets had
announced the arrival of this unexpected but welcome visitor, one of the holiest saints of the calendar, and, next to
San Antonio, the most celebrated for the power of working

2. Policeman.
3. Mayor.

miracles. Morazán's rise to power had been signalized by a persecution of the clergy: his friends said that it was the purification of a corrupt body; his enemies, that it was a war against morality and religion. The country was at that time overrun with priests, friars, and monks of various orders. Everywhere the largest buildings, the best-cultivated lands, and a great portion of the wealth of the country were in their hands. Many, no doubt, were good men, but some used their sacred robes as a cloak for rascality and vice, and most were drones, reaping where they did not sow and living luxuriously by the sweat of other men's brows. At all events, and whatever the cause, the early part of Morazán's administration was signalized by hostility to the clergy as a class. From the Archbishop of Gautemala down to the poorest friar, they were in danger; some fled, others were banished, and many were torn by rude soldiers from their convents and churches, hurried to the seaports, and shipped to Cuba and old Spain under sentence of death if they returned. The country was left comparatively destitute. Many of the churches fell to ruins; others stood, but their doors were seldom opened and the practice and memory of their religious rites were fading away. Carrera and his Indians, with the mystic rites of Catholicism ingrafted upon the superstitions of their fathers, had acquired a strong hold upon the feelings of the people by endeavoring to bring back the exiled clergy and to restore the influence of the church. The tour of Santa Lucía was regarded as an indication of a change of feeling and government, and as a prelude to the restoration of the influence of the church and the revival of ceremonies dear to the heart of the Indian. As such, it had been hailed by all the villages through which she had passed, and that night she would receive the prayers of the Christians of Gualán.

Santa Lucía enjoyed a peculiar popularity because of her miraculous power over the affections of the young. Any young man who prayed to her for a wife, or any young woman who prayed for a husband, was sure to receive the object of such prayer; and if the person praying indicated to the saint the individual wished for, the prayer would be granted, provided such individual was not already married.

It was not surprising that a saint with such extraordinary powers, touching so directly the tenderest sensibilities, should create such a sensation in a place where the feelings, or, rather, the passions, are particularly turned to love.

Doña Bartola invited us to go with her to call upon a friend of hers; during the whole visit, a servant girl sat with her lap full of tobacco, making straw cigars for immediate use. It was the first time we had smoked with ladies and, at first, it was rather awkward to ask one for a light; but we were so thoroughly broken in that night that we never felt any delicacy about it afterward. The conversation turned upon the saint and her miraculous powers. When we avowed ourselves somewhat skeptical, the servant girl, with that familiarity—though not want of respect—which exists throughout Central America, said that it was wicked to doubt, that she had prayed to the saint herself and two months afterward had been married to the very man she prayed for, though at the time he had had no idea of her, in fact, had wanted another girl.

With this encouragement, we locked the house and, accompanied by children and servants, set out to pay our homage to the saint. The sound of a violin and the firing of rockets indicated the direction of her temporary domicile. She had taken up her residence in the hut of a poor Indian in the suburbs. For some time before reaching the hut, we encountered crowds of both sexes, of all ages and colors, and in every degree of dress and undress, smoking and talking, and sitting or lying on the ground in every variety of attitude. Room was made for our party, and we entered the hut.

It was about twenty feet square, thatched on the top and sides with leaves of Indian corn, and filled with a dense mass of kneeling men and women. On one side was an altar, about four feet high, covered with a clean white cotton cloth. On the top of the altar was a frame, with three elevations, like a flower stand, and on the top of that a case containing a large wax doll, dressed in blue silk and ornamented with gold leaf, spangles, and artificial flowers. This was Santa Lucía. Over her head was a canopy of red cotton cloth on which was emblazoned a cross in gold. On the right was a sedan chair, the traveling equipage of the saint, trimmed with red cotton and gold leaf, with festoons of oranges hung from the roof, and rough posts enwrapped with leaves of sugar cane; near it were the Indians in half sacerdotal dress on whose shoulders she traveled. At the foot of the altar was a mat, on which girls and boys were playing; and a little fellow about six years old, habited in the picturesque costume of a straw hat—and that only—was coolly surveying the crowd.

The ceremony of praying had already begun, and the music of a drum, a violin, and a flageolet, under the direction of the Indian master of ceremonies, drowned the noise of voices. Doña Bartola, who was a widow, and the other ladies of our party fell on their knees. Recommending myself to their prayers, I looked on without doing anything for myself, but I studied attentively the faces of those around me. There were some of both sexes who could not strictly be called young, but they did not, on that account, pray less earnestly. In some places the imputation of being desirous to procure husband or wife would be repellent to the people, but not so in Gualán: they prayed publicly for what they considered a blessing. Some of the men were so much in earnest that perspiration stood in large drops upon their faces; and none thought that praying for a husband need tinge the cheek of a modest maiden. I watched the countenance of a young Indian girl, beaming with enthusiasm and hope; while her eyes rested upon the image of the saint and her lips moved in prayer, I could not but imagine that her heart was full of some truant, and perhaps unworthy, lover.

Outside the hut the scene was entirely different. Near by were rows of kneeling men and women, but beyond were wild groups of half-naked men and boys, setting off rockets and fireworks. As I moved through the throng, a flash rose from under my feet, and a petard exploded so near that the powder singed me; turning round, I saw hurrying away my rascally muleteer. Beyond were parties of young men and women dancing by the light of blazing pine sticks. In a hut at some little distance were two haggard old women, who were stirring up large caldrons over blazing fires and serving

out the contents with long wooden ladles, like witches deal-
ing out poison instead of love potions.

At ten o'clock the prayers to the saint died away, the
crowd separated into groups and couples, and many fell into
what in English would be called flirtations. A mat was
spread for our party against the side of a hut, and we all
lighted cigars and sat down upon it. Cups made of small
gourds and filled from the caldrons with a preparation of
boiled Indian corn sweetened with various *dulces* were
passed from mouth to mouth, each one taking a sip and passing it on to the next; this continued, without any interruption, for more than an hour. Although we remained on the
ground till after midnight, we were, nevertheless, among
the first to leave. On the whole, we concluded that praying
to Santa Lucía must lead to matrimony. I could not but remark, however, that in the matter of getting husbands and
wives, most seemed disposed to do something for themselves and not leave all to the grace of the saint.

The next day it was excessively hot, and we remained
within doors. In the evening we visited the padre, who had
just returned from a neighboring village. He was a short,
fat man, dressed in a white nightcap, a blue striped jacket,
and white pantaloons, and we found him swinging in a hammock and smoking a cigar. He had a large household of
women and children, but as to the relation in which each
stood to him, people differed. He gave us more information
about the country than we had yet been able to obtain, and
particularly about Copán, a ruined city which we wished to
visit. He was familiar with the history of the Indians, and
understood thoroughly the character of the present race. In
answer to our question if they were all Christians, he said
that they were devout and religious, and had a great respect
for the priests and saints. With this he hitched up his bursting pantaloons, and lighted another cigar. We might have
smiled at the idea of his confounding his comfortable figure
with the saints, but he had so much good sense and good
feeling that we were not disposed to be captious.

The next morning our muleteer came, but through some
misunderstanding he did not bring enough mules to carry
all our luggage. Rather than wait any longer we started with-

out him, leaving part of the baggage for him to bring on to Zacapa the next day.

To the right of us as we left Gualán, was the Motagua River, now become to us a friend. Beyond the river was the great range of the mountains of Verapaz, six or eight thousand feet high, which an hour later we began to ascend. Soon we were in a wilderness of flowers. Shrubs and bushes were clothed in purple and red and, on the sides of the mountain and in the ravines leading down to the river, in the wildest positions, were large trees so covered with red that they seemed a single flower. In three hours we descended from our mountain height, and came once more to the river side, where it was rolling swiftly, and in some places breaking into rapids. After following the river for about an hour, we again ascended several thousand feet. At two o'clock we reached the village of San Pablo, situated on a lofty table of land, looking down upon the river and having its view bounded by the mountains of Verapaz. The church stood at the entrance of the village and after turning our mules loose to graze we ate our meal on its porch. It was a beautiful location, and two waterfalls, shining like streaks of silver on the distant mountain side, reminded us of cascades in Switzerland.

We procured a guide from the alcalde to conduct us to Zacapa and, for two hours after resuming our journey, we had the same great range upon our right. The sun was obscured, but occasionally it broke through and lighted up the sides of the mountains, although the tops were covered with clouds. At four o'clock we had a distant view of the great plain of Zacapa, bounded on the opposite side by a triangular belt of mountains at the foot of which stood the town. We descended and crossed the plain, which was green and well cultivated; fording a stream, we ascended a rugged bank and entered the town.

It was by far the finest we had seen. The streets were regular, and the houses plastered and whitewashed, with large balconied windows and piazzas. The church was two hundred and fifty feet long, with walls ten feet thick and a façade rich with Moorish devices. It was built in the form of a Latin cross. In one end of the cross was a tailor's shop; the other end was roofless. At one corner was a belfry, consisting of four rough trunks of trees supporting a peaked roof covered with tiles. Two bells were suspended from a rude beam; as we passed, a half-naked Indian was standing on a platform underneath, ringing for vespers.

We rode up to the house of Don Mariano Durante, one of the largest and best in the place, having about a hundred-foot front and a corridor, extending the whole length, paved with square stones. The door was opened by a respectable-looking Santo Domingo negro who told us, in French, that Señor Durante was not at home, but that the house was at our service. Going around to a porte-cochère alongside, he admitted us into a large courtyard ornamented with trees and flowers, at one side of which was a *caballeriza*, or stable. We left our mules in the hands of the servants and entered a *sala*, or reception room, covering nearly the whole front, with large windows reaching down to the floor and iron balconies, and furnished with tables, a European bureau, and chairs. In the center of the room and in the windows hung cages, handsomely made and gilded, containing beautiful singing birds of the country, and two fine canary birds from Havana. This was the residence of two bachelor brothers, who, feeling for the wants of travelers in a country entirely destitute of hotels, kept a door always open for their accommodation. We had candles lighted and made ourselves at home. I was sitting at a table writing when we heard the tramp of mules outside, and a gentleman entered, took off his sword and spurs, and laid his pistols upon the table. Supposing him to be a traveler like ourselves, we asked him to take a seat, and when supper was served, invited him to join us. It was not till bedtime that we discovered that we were doing the honors of the house to one of its masters. He must have thought us cool, but I flatter myself he had no reason to complain of any want of attention.

Chapter IV

~~~~~~

Purchasing a bridle. A school and its regulations. Conversation with an Indian. Spanish translation of The Spy. *Chiquimula. A church in ruins. A veteran of* The French Empire. *San Esteban. A land of mountains. An affair with a muleteer. A deserted village. A rude assault. Arrest. Imprisonment. Release.*

THE next day we were obliged to wait for our muleteer. Our guide of the night before had stolen one of our bridles and, in trying to replace it, we began to experience an annoyance which was to attend us throughout Central America, that is, the difficulty of buying anything ready-made. We found a blacksmith who had a bit partly made, but he did not have charcoal enough to finish it. Fortunately, during the day an Indian arrived with a backload of the fuel and the bridle was completed. The headstall we bought of a saddler, and the reins, which were of platted leather like the lash of a whip, we were lucky enough to obtain ready-made. The arrival of the charcoal also enabled the blacksmith to fit us out with one pair of spurs.

At Zacapa, for the first time, we saw a schoolhouse, a respectable-looking building with columns in front. Against the wall hung a large card which was headed:

1st Decurion [1]   2nd Decurion
MONITOR, *etc.*

"Interior regulation for the good government of the school of first letters of this town, which ought to be observed strictly by all the boys composing it . . ."

---

1. "A student who has the care of ten other students."

with a long list of complicated Articles enumerating rewards and punishments. The school, for the government of which these regulations were intended, consisted of five boys, the two decurions, the monitor, and two others. It was nearly noon, and the master, who was also the clerk of the alcalde, had not yet made his appearance. The only books I saw were a Catholic prayer book and a translation of Montesquieu's *Spirit of the Laws*. The boys were fine little fellows, half white. With one of them I had a trial of sums in addition, and then of exercises in handwriting, in which he showed himself very proficient, writing "Give me sixpence" in Spanish in a hand which I could not mistake.

We were rather at a loss as to what to do with ourselves, but in the afternoon our host called in an Indian for the purpose of enabling us to make a vocabulary of Indian words. I asked him first to tell me the Indian expression for "name of God," to which he answered, *Santísima Trinidad*. Through our host I explained to him that it was the Indian not the Spanish name that I wanted, but he answered as before, *Santísima Trinidad*, or *Dios*. Although I shaped my question in a variety of ways, I could get no other answer. He was of a tribe called Chinaute,[2] and it might be inferred either that they had never known any Great Spirit who governed and directed the universe, or that they had undergone such an entire change in matters of religion that they had lost their own appellation for the Deity.

In the evening the town was thrown into excitement by the entry of a detachment of Carrera's soldiers on their way to Izabal to receive and escort a purchase of muskets. The house of our friend was a gathering place for residents of the town and, as usual, the conversation turned to the revolutionary state of the country. Some of them, as soon as they knew my official character, were anxious for me to go directly to San Salvador, the headquarters of the Morazán or Federal Party, and assured me that the road to Guatemala City was occupied by the troops of Carrera, and dangerous to

2. Probably a misspelling of Chinautla, which is now the name of a village in the State of Guatemala.

travel over. I was too well aware of the effect of party spirit to put implicit faith in what partisans told me, and endeavored to change the subject. Our host asked me whether we had any wars in my country, and said he knew that we had had one revolution, for he had read *La Historia de la Revolución de los Estados Unidos del Norte*, in four volumes, in which General Washington appeared under the name of Harper, and Jack Lawton and Dr. Sitgreaves were two of the principal characters; I am sure that my readers will be as surprised as I to learn that in the Spanish translation the tale of *The Spy* is called a history of the American Revolution.

Our muleteer did not make his appearance till late the next day. In the meantime, I had had an opportunity to acquire considerable information about the roads and the state of the country. I became satisfied that as far as the purpose of my mission was concerned, it was not necessary to proceed immediately to Guatemala City, that, in fact, it would be better to delay a little while and see the result of the convulsions that then distracted the country. We decided, therefore, to visit Copán, a city completely out of the usual line of travel. Though only a few days' journey distant, it was in a region of country but little known even at Zacapa. However, our muleteer said that he knew the road. We made a contract with him to conduct us thither in three days, arranging the various stages beforehand, and from Copán to take us directly to Guatemala.

At seven o'clock the next morning we started. Although both my companion and myself were old travelers, our luggage was not packed well for traveling with mules over a mountainous country; our packages were difficult to load and fell off easily. Another traveling difficulty lay in the fact that we had but one pair of spurs between us. Within an hour we forded the Motagua, at this point still a broad stream, deep, and with a rapid current; the wet feet and legs with which we emerged from the stream diminished somewhat the regret with which we bade farewell for a while to the beautiful river. For an hour longer we continued on the plain of Zacapa, cultivated for corn and cochineal, and divided by fences of brush and cactus. Beyond this the country became broken, arid, and barren, and very soon we began the ascent of a steep mountain.

Two hours later we reached the top, three or four thousand feet high, from which looking back, we had a fine view of the plain and town of Zacapa. Crossing the ridge, we reached a bold precipitous spur, and very soon saw before us another extensive plain, and, afar off, the town of Chiquimula with its giant church. On each side of the ridge were immense ravines with the opposite heights covered with pale and rose-colored mimosa. We descended by a long and zigzag path to the plain, on which were growing corn, cochineal, and plantain. Once more fording a stream, we ascended a bank, and at two o'clock entered Chiquimula, the capital of the department of that name.

In the center of the plaza was a fine fountain shaded by palm trees, at which women were filling their water jars, and on the sides were the church and cabildo. On one corner was a house to which we were attracted by the appearance of a woman at the door—I may call her a lady, for she wore a frock not open behind, and shoes and stockings. She had a face of uncommon interest, dark, with finely penciled eyebrows. Her gracious welcome to her house heightened the effect of her appearance, and in a few minutes the shed was lumbered with our multifarious luggage.

After a slight lunch we took our guns and, walking down to the edge of the table of land, saw that the gigantic church which had attracted our attention from the top of the mountain was in ruins. With a frontage of seventy-five feet it was two hundred and fifty feet deep, with walls ten feet thick. The façade was adorned with ornaments and figures of the saints, larger than life. The roof had fallen, and inside were huge masses of stone and mortar and a thick growth of trees. Built by the Spaniards on the site of an old Indian village, after twice being shattered by earthquakes both the church and the village were abandoned and the new town built where it now stands. The site of the ruined village was now a campo santo, or burial place; inside the church were the graves of the principal inhabitants and in the niches of the wall were the bones of priests and monks, identified by names. Outside were the graves of the common people, untended and uncared for; on the top of each grave, only slightly covered with earth, lay the barrow of laced sticks which had carried the body to the grave. The bodies had decayed, the dirt fallen in, and the graves were yawning. Around this scene of desolation and death nature was rioting in beauty. The ground was covered with flowers, and on every bush and tree and flying in flocks over our heads, wanton in gaiety of color, were parrots, whose senseless chattering disturbed the stillness of the grave.

Returning to the town, we found about twelve hundred soldiers drawn up in the plaza for evening parade, their aspect ferocious and banditti-like. Convicts peeped through the gratings of the prison and walked in chains on the plaza, and the whole scene inspired the refreshing realization that sometimes crimes were punished. With all their ferocity of appearance, the officers, mounted on prancing mules or very small horses, almost hidden in saddlecloth and armor, had an air bordering upon the mock heroic. While we were looking at them, General Cascara, the commandant of the department, rode up to the line attended by a servant. He was an Italian, about sixty years old, who had served under Napoleon in Italy; on the downfall of the emperor he had fled to Central America. Banished by Morazán, after eight years in exile he had just recently returned to this country, and six months before had been appointed to this command. He was ghastly pale, and evidently in feeble health. I could not but think that, if recollections of the pomp of war under the Emperor ever crossed his mind, he must needs blush to contemplate the barefooted detachment he now commanded.

When he returned to his house, we followed him and presented our passport. Like the commandant at Izabal, he seemed ill at ease and spoke much of the distracted state of the country. He was dissatisfied, too, with the route I proposed to take; although I told him my purpose was merely to visit the ruins of Copán, he was evidently apprehensive that I intended going to San Salvador to present my credentials to the Federal government. He gave me a visa, however, as I required; but after we left, he called Augustin back and questioned him very closely as to our purposes. This made me indignant, but I smothered my feelings when I considered the distracted state of the country and the game of life and death that was then being played throughout the land.

We did not at first know whether the interesting lady who had welcomed us was a señora or a señorita, but unhappily we found out that the man whom we supposed to be her father was, in fact, her husband. When we asked her about a fine ten-year-old boy whom we supposed to be her brother, she answered, "*es mío* (he is mine)." As if it were fated that the charm of her appearance be broken, when, according to the rules of courtesy, I offered for her choice a cigar and a *puro*,[3] she took the *puro*. But it had been a long time since I had seen a woman who was at all attractive, and her face was so interesting, her manners so good, her voice so sweet, the Spanish words rolled so beautifully from her lips, and her frock was tied so close behind, that, in spite of the ten-year-old boy and *puro*, I clung to my first impression.

The next morning we rose early but our interesting hostess and her fatherly husband were already up and eager to assist us. It would have been an offence to the laws of hospitality to have offered them money, but Mr. Catherwood gave the boy a penknife, and I put on the finger of the señora a gold ring with the motto, *Souvenir d'amitié.* Her husband could not understand French nor, unfortunately, could she.

At seven o'clock we started. Passing the ruined church and the old village, we rode over a rich valley so well cultivated with Indian corn that we began to understand why the boy had asked us whether we had come to Chiquimula to buy maize. At a league's distance we came to the village of San Esteban, where, amid a miserable collection of thatched huts, stood a gigantic church which, like that at Chiquimula, was roofless and falling to ruins. We were now in a region which

---

3. The *puro* would be a cigar and the "cigar" what we now call a cigarette.

had been scourged by civil war; only a year before the village had been laid waste by the troops of Morazán.

Passing the village, we came to the bank of a stream, in some places diverted into watercourses for the irrigation of the land; on the other side of the stream was a range of high mountains. As we continued along the bank of the river we met an Indian who advised our muleteer that the *camino real* for Copán was on the opposite side across the range of mountains. Turning back and fording the river, we found a great part of the bed dry, but after riding along it for some distance, could find no path that led up the mountain. When at length we struck one, it proved to be only a cattle path, and we wandered for more than an hour before we found the *camino real*, and this royal road was barely a track by which a single mule could climb. It became evident that our muleteer did not know the road, and the region we were entering was so wild that we had some doubts about following him. At eleven o'clock we reached the top of the mountain and looking back saw at a great distance and far below us, the town of Chiquimula; on the right, up the valley, the village of Santa Elena; and, rising above a few thatched huts, another gigantic and roofless church. On each side of us rose mountains still higher than ours. Some were grand and gloomy, with their summits buried in the clouds; others in the form of cones and pyramids were so wild and fantastic that they seemed to be sporting with the heavens, and I almost wished for wings that I might fly and alight upon their summits. Here, on heights apparently inaccessible, we saw the wild hut of an Indian, with his *milpa*, or patch of Indian corn. Clouds gathered around the mountains, and for an hour we rode in the rain. When the sun broke through we saw the mountaintops still towering above us, and on our right, far below us, a deep valley. We descended, and found it narrower and more beautiful than any we had yet seen. Bounded by ranges of mountains several thousand feet high, on its left was a range of extraordinary beauty covered with gigantic pines without any brush or underwood and with a red soil of sandstone. In front, rising above the miserable huts of the village and seeming to bestride the valley,

was the gigantic church of San Juan Ermita, reminding me
of the Church of St. John in the wilderness of Judea, although the immediate scene was even more beautiful. At
two o'clock we crossed the stream and entered the village.
When we were opposite the church, the muleteer told us that
the day's work was over; with all our toils, we had made
only fifteen miles and were unwilling to stop so soon. The
exceeding beauty of the place might have tempted us, but
the only good plastered hut was occupied by a band of ruffianly soldiers, and we rode on. The muleteer followed with
curses, and vented his spite by lashing the mules. Again we
crossed the stream, and continued up the valley along the
dry bed, which bore marks of the flood that washed it in the
rainy season; in one hour we crossed the river half a dozen
times. Heavy clouds rested on the mountains, and again we
had rain. At four o'clock we saw on a high table on the left
the village of Jocotán, with another gigantic church. According to the route agreed upon with the muleteer, this
should have been the end of our first day's journey. We had
been advised that the cura would be able to give us much
information about the ruins of Copán, so we told the muleteer to cross over and stop there. But he refused to stop and,
hurrying on the mules, added that since we had refused to
stop when he wished, he would not now stop for us. I could
not spur my mule beyond her own gait to overtake him, so
I jumped off and ran after him on foot. Accidentally I put
my hand on my pistols to steady them in my belt, at which
he fell back and drew his machete. We came to a parley.
He claimed that if we stopped now we could not reach Copán
the next day. Willing to make a retreat, and since I did not
wish to leave him any excuse for a future failing, I agreed
to continue on our way.

At six o'clock we reached a beautiful table of land, on
which stood another gigantic church, the seventh of its kind
we had seen that day. Coming upon these churches in a
region of desolation, and by mountain paths which human
hands had never attempted to improve, their colossal grandeur and costliness were startling, and their abandoned state
gave evidence of a retrograding and expiring people. This

particular edifice stood in a more desolate place than any we had yet seen. The grass was green, the sod unbroken even by a mule path; not a human being was in sight, not a single pair of eyes peered through the gratings of the prison. It was, in fact, a picture of a deserted village. We rode up to the cabildo, the door of which was fastened and the shed barricaded, probably to prevent the entrance of straggling cattle. We tore away the fastenings, broke open the door, and, unloading the mules, sent Augustin on a foraging expedition. In half an hour he returned from the nearby village of Camotán with *one* egg, being all that he was able to procure; but he had waked up the village, and the alcalde, an Indian with a silver-headed cane, and several alguaciles with long thin rods or wands of office, came down to examine us. We showed them our passport, and told them where we were going, at which, with their characteristic indifference of manner, they expressed no surprise. They could not read the passport, but they examined the seal and returned it. We asked them for eggs, fowls, milk, etc., to which they answered, *"no hay* (there is none)," a reply which was to become all too familiar; in a few minutes they retired and left us to ourselves.

The cabildo was about forty feet long and twenty feet broad, with plastered walls; its furniture consisted of a large table and two benches with high backs. The alcalde sent us a jar of water, and abusing the muleteer for stopping at a place where we could get nothing to eat, we made our dinner and supper of bread and chocolate, taking care not to give him any. There were pins in the walls for swinging hammocks, and in the evening we prepared for sleep. Mr. Catherwood was in his hammock and I was half undressed when the door was suddenly burst open and twenty-five or thirty men rushed in, the alcalde, alguaciles, soldiers, Indians, and mestizos, ragged and ferocious-looking fellows armed with staves of office, swords, clubs, muskets, and machetes, and carrying blazing pine sticks. The leader was a young officer of about twenty-eight or thirty with a glazed hat and sword and a knowing and wicked expression; we were informed later that he was a captain of one of Carrera's companies. The alcalde who was evidently intoxicated said that he wished to see my passport again. I delivered it to him, and he handed it over to the young officer who examined it and said that it was not valid. In the meantime, Mr. Catherwood and I dressed. I was not very familiar with the Spanish language but, using Augustin as interpreter, I attempted to explain my official character, directing him to emphasize particularly the endorsements of Commandant Peñol and General Cascara. The alcalde paid no attention to my explanations; he said that he had seen a passport once before and that it had been printed on a small piece of paper not bigger than his hand, unlike mine, which had been issued by the government on a quarto sheet. Besides, they objected, the seal of General Cascara was only that of the department of Chiquimula, and it ought to be that of the State of Guatemala. I did all in my power to show the insufficiency of these objections but to no avail. After a warm altercation, the young officer told us that we could not proceed on our journey but must remain at Camotán until information could be sent to Chiquimula and orders received from that place. We had no disposition to remain in such hands but, unable to move them by threats of the consequences of their action, I told them that, rather than be detained here and lose time, I would abandon my journey to Copán altogether, and would, instead, return by the road on which I had come. But even to this solution they would not agree; both the officer and the alcalde peremptorily commanded us not to leave Camotán.

The young man then ordered me to give up my passport. I answered that the passport had been given me by my own government, that it was the evidence of my official character and necessary for my personal security, and that I would not give it up. Mr. Catherwood made a learned exposition of the law of nations, the right of an ambassador, and the danger of bringing down upon them the vengeance of the government *del Norte*, which I sustained with some warmth—but it was of no use. At length I told him again that I would not give up the passport, but that I would go with it myself, under a guard of soldiers, to Chiquimula, or whatever place they chose to send it. He answered insultingly that we would not go to Chiquimula or anywhere else—neither forward nor backward—that we must stay where we were, and must give up the passport. Finding arguments and remonstrances of no use, I placed the paper inside my vest, buttoned my coat tight across my breast, and told him he must get it by force, to which the officer, with a gleam of satisfaction crossing his villainous face, responded that he would. I added, however, that whatever the immediate result, ultimately such action would be fatal to them, but he answered, with a sneer, that they would run the risk. During all this time, the band of cowardly ruffians stood with their hands on their swords and machetes, and two assassin-looking scoundrels sat on a bench with muskets against their shoulders, the muzzles pointed within three feet of my breast. If we had been longer in the country we should have been more alarmed, but as yet we did not know the sanguinary character of the people, and the whole proceeding was so outrageous and insulting that it roused our indignation more than our fears. Augustin, having previously suffered a cut on the head from a machete, was always bellicose, and he begged me in French to give the order to fire, claiming that one round would scatter them all; we had eleven charges, all sure, and we were excited. If the young man himself had laid his hands upon me, I think I should have knocked him down at least, but, most fortunately, before he had time to give his order a man wearing a glazed hat and roundabout jacket entered and asked to see the passport. I was determined not to trust it out of my hands, and held it up before a blazing pine stick while, at Mr. Catherwood's request, he read it aloud.

I have since doubted whether at first the officer had read it, or if he had, whether he had communicated its contents to the others, for when it was now read aloud it produced an effect upon the alcalde and his alguaciles who, after some moments of anxious suspense to us, decided not to execute their threat, although they insisted we remain in custody. I then demanded a courier to take a letter immediately to General Cascara, which at first they refused; but when I offered to pay the expense of the courier, the alcalde promised to send it. Knowing General Cascara to be an Italian and afraid to trust my Spanish, I wrote a note in English, which Mr. Catherwood translated into Italian, informing the General of our arrest and imprisonment. The note explained the refusal of the alcalde and the soldiers who arrested us to accept my special passport from my own government, with its endorsements by Commandant Peñol and himself certifying my official character. I demanded that we be set at liberty immediately and allowed to proceed on our journey without further molestation, adding that we should, of course, report to my own government and that at Guatemala City the manner in which we had been treated. Not to mince matters, Mr. Catherwood signed the note as Secretary, and, having no official seal with me, we sealed it unobserved by anybody with a new American half dollar and gave it to the alcalde. The eagle spread his wings and the stars glittered in the torchlight. All gathered round to examine it, and then after locking us up in the cabildo and stationing twelve men at the door with swords, muskets, and machetes, they retired. At parting, the officer warned the alcalde that if we escaped during the night his head should answer for it.

The excitement over, Mr. Catherwood and I were exhausted. What a beautiful beginning to our travels—only a month from home and here we were in the hands of men who would have been turned out of any decent state prison lest they contaminate the other boarders. A peep at our beautiful keepers did nothing to reassure us. They were sitting under the shed directly before the door, and smoking cigars around a fire, their arms in reach. Their whole stock of wearing apparel was not worth a pair of old boots, and with their rags, their arms, and their dark faces reddened by the firelight, their appearance was ferocious; if we had attempted to escape, they would have been glad, doubtless, of the excuse for murder. We opened a basket of wine with which Colonel MacDonald had provided us, and drank his health. Relieved from immediate apprehensions, our prospects were, nevertheless, not pleasant, but, fastening the door as well as we could inside, we again betook ourselves to our hammocks.

Suddenly during the night the door was again burst open, and the whole ruffianly band entered, as before, with swords, muskets, machetes, and blazing pine sticks. In an instant we were on our feet. In my first hurried impression, I thought that they had come to take the passport, but instead, to our surprise, the alcalde handed me back the letter with the big seal, saying there was no need to send it, that we were at liberty to proceed on our journey when we chose.

We were too well pleased to ask any questions, and to this day do not know why we were arrested or set free. My belief is, however, that if we had quailed at all, if we had not kept up a high, threatening tone to the last, we should not have been set free; and I have no doubt that the big seal did much in our behalf. Our indignation, however, was no less strong now that we considered ourselves safe in pouring it out, and we insisted that the matter should not end here and that the letter should go to General Cascara. The alcalde objected, but we told him that, if it were not sent, it would be the worse for him; after some delay, he thrust it into the hands of an Indian and beat him out of doors with his staff. In a few minutes the guard was withdrawn, and they all left us.

It was now nearly daylight, and we did not know what to do; to continue to Copán was to risk exposing ourselves to a repetition of the same treatment, and perhaps, as we advanced farther into the interior, with a worse result. Still undecided, for the third time we turned into our hammocks. At broad daylight we were again roused by the alcalde and his alguaciles, but this time they came to pay us a visit of ceremony. The soldiers who had made all the disturbance during the night had just happened to pass through the village, and by now had left. After some further deliberation we made up our minds to continue. Charging the alcalde again about the letter to General Cascara, we turned our backs upon him and his alguaciles; in a few minutes they all withdrew. We took a cup of chocolate, loaded our mules, and left the place now as desolate as when we entered it. Not a person had been there to welcome us, no one was there to bid us farewell.

Chapter V

~~~~~~

An Indian funeral. Copán River. Woman's kindness.
Hacienda of San Antonio. Strange customs. A mountain
of aloes. The State of Honduras. Village of Copán. An
ungracious host. Wall of Copán. History of Copán. First
view of the ruins. Vain speculations. Applications for
medicine. Search for an abode. A sick woman. Plagues of
a muleteer. An unpleasant situation. A thunder-
storm. Thoughts of buying Copán.

SOON after we resumed our journey to Copán we began
to ascend another mountain. We had not proceeded
very far when we met some Indians, naked except for loin
cloths, who bore on their shoulders a rude bier of sticks on
which was a corpse which shook awfully under the movements of its carriers. Soon after we met another group, three
or four men and a young woman, who were also carrying
one of their dead to the graveyard of the village church; in
this case the corpse was wrapped in matting. As we reached
the top of a mountain we saw behind us a beautiful valley
extending toward Jocotán; but all was wasteland, and we
could not help but regret that so beautiful a country should
be in such miserable hands.

At half past twelve we descended to the banks of the
Copán River. It was broad and rapid, and in the middle
was a large sand bar. We had difficulty in fording it, and
some of the baggage, particularly the beds and bedding, got
wet during the crossing. From the opposite side we again
ascended another ridge, and from the top we saw the river
winding through the valley. As we crossed the summit, by
a sudden turn the river flowed along its base, and we could

look directly down upon it. Descending this mountain, we came to a beautiful stream where a gray-haired Indian woman and a pretty little girl, pictures of youth and old age, were washing clothes. We dismounted and sat down on the bank to wait for the muleteer.

I have forgotten to mention that the muleteer had with him a boy about thirteen or fourteen years old, a fine little fellow upon whom he imposed the worst part of the burden, that of chasing the mules, and who really seemed, like Baron Munchausen's dog, in constant danger of running his legs off. Our breach with the muleteer had not been healed, and at first we ascribed to him some part in our troubles at Camotán; at all events, if it had not been for him, we should not have stopped there. All day he had been particularly furious with the mules and they had been particularly perverse; now they had gone astray, and it was an hour before we heard his spiteful voice cursing as he loaded them.

Mounting again, we continued on our way, and at four o'clock saw in the distance a hacienda; it was on the opposite side of a valley and stood alone, promising a quiet resting place for the night. We turned off from the *camino real* into a wild path, stony and overgrown with bushes, and so steep that in order to make the descent we were obliged to dismount, let the mules go ahead, and help ourselves down by holding onto the bushes. At the foot of the hill we mounted and crossed a stream where a little boy playing in the water saluted first me and then Mr. Catherwood by crossing his arms upon his breast. This was a favorable omen; as we climbed a steep hill, I felt that here, in this lonely spot, away from the gathering places of men, we must meet kindness. On the top of the hill a woman with a naked child in her arms and a smile on her face stood watching our toilsome ascent. When we asked her if we could make posada there, she answered, in the kindest phrase of the country, with a face that spoke even a warmer welcome than her words, "*cómo no?* (why not?)" and when she saw that our servant had pineapples in his alforjas, she asked why he brought them, and if he did not know that she had plenty.

The situation of this hacienda of San Antonio was wildly beautiful. It had a clearing for a cowyard, a plantation of corn, tobacco, and plantains, and a view of the high mountains by which it was surrounded. The house was built of poles plastered with mud, and against the wall in front of the door, on a white cotton cloth hung round with votive offerings, was a figure of the Saviour on the cross. The naked child which the mother carried in her arms was called María de los Angeles. While supper was in preparation, the master of the house arrived, a swarthy, grim-looking fellow, with a broad-brimmed sombrero and huge whiskers, and mounted on a powerful young horse, which he was just breaking to the mountain roads. When he knew that we were strangers asking hospitality, his harsh features relaxed, and he repeated the welcome the woman had given us.

Unfortunately, the boy of the muleteer became very ill. His master paid no attention to him; while the poor little fellow was groaning under a violent fever, the muleteer continued to eat with perfect indifference. We made the boy a comfortable bed on the piazza, and Mr. Catherwood gave him a dose of medicine. But our evening passed very differently from the last. Our host and hostess were a kind-hearted and simple couple. It was the first time they had ever met men from another country, and they asked many questions and examined our little traveling apparatus, particularly our plated cups, knives, forks, and spoons. We showed them our watches, compass, sextant, chronometer, thermometer, telescope, etc., and the woman, with great discernment, said that we must be very rich, and had *muchas ideas* (many ideas). They asked us about our wives, and we learned that our simple-minded host had two, one of whom lived at Jocotán, and that he passed a week alternately with each. We told him that in England he would be transported and in the North imprisoned for life for such indulgences, to which he responded that they were barbarous countries, and the woman, although she thought a man ought to be content with one, said that it was no *pecado*, or crime, to have two; but I heard them say, sotto voce, that we were *más cristianos*, or better Christians than they. He assisted us in swinging our hammocks, and about nine o'clock we drove out the dogs and pigs, lighted cigars, and went to bed. Including servants, women, and children, we numbered eleven in the room. All around were little balls of fire, shining and disappearing with the puffs of the cigars. One by one these went out, and we fell asleep.

In the morning we all rose together. The boy was much better, but we did not think him in a condition to travel. His brutal master, however, insisted upon his going. For all that our kind friends had done for us, they would have charged us nothing; but, besides compensating them in money, we distributed among them various trifles. When bidding them farewell, I noticed with regret that a ring which I had given to the woman was then sparkling on her husband's finger! After we had mounted, the little boy who had saluted us at the stream came toward us, staggering under a load of six freshly cut pineapples; even after we had started, the woman ran after me with a piece of fresh sugar cane. All parted at the hacienda of San Antonio with kind feelings except our surly muleteer, who was indignant, as he said, that we made presents to everybody except him. The poor boy was most grateful, and, unfortunately for him, we had given him a knife, which made the muleteer jealous.

Almost immediately from the hacienda we entered a thick wood, dense as that of Mico Mountain, and almost as muddy. The ascent was toilsome, but the top was open and so covered with that beautiful plant that we called it the Mountain of Aloes. Some of these plants were just peeping out of the ground, others were twenty or thirty feet high, and some gigantic stalks were dead; these flowers, which would have kindled rapture in the breast of beauty, had bloomed and died on this desolate mountain, unseen except by a passing Indian.

In descending we lost the path and wandered for some time before recovering it. Almost immediately we began to ascend another mountain, from whose summit, looking completely over yet another mountain, we could see at a great distance a large hacienda. Our road lay directly along the edge of a precipice from which we looked down upon the tops of gigantic pines at a great distance beneath us. Very soon the path became so broken and ran so near the edge of a precipice, that I called to Mr. Catherwood to dismount. The precipice was on the left side, and I had advanced so far that, on the back of a perverse mule, I did not venture to make any irregular movement, and rode for some moments in great anxiety. Somewhere on this road, but unmarked by any visible sign, we crossed the boundary line of the State of Guatemala and entered Honduras.

At two o'clock we reached the village of Copán, which consisted of half a dozen miserable huts thatched with corn. Our appearance created a great sensation. All the men and women gathered around to gaze at us. We inquired immediately for the ruins, but none of the villagers could direct us to them, and all advised us to go to the hacienda of Don Gregorio. We had no wish to stop at the village and told the muleteer to go on, but he refused, saying that his engagement was to conduct us to Copán. After a long wrangle we prevailed, and, riding through a piece of woods, once more forded the Copán River and came out upon a clearing. On one side was a hacienda, with a tile roof and a *cocina* and other outbuildings, evidently the residence of a rich proprietor. We were greeted by a pack of barking dogs, and all the doorways were filled with women and children, who seemed in no small degree surprised at our appearance; there was not a man in sight. The women received us kindly, and told us that Don Gregorio would return soon and would conduct us to the ruins. Immediately the fire was rekindled in the *cocina*, the sound of the patting of hands gave notice of the making of tortillas, and in half an hour dinner was ready. It was served up on a massive silver plate, with water in a silver tankard, but without knife, fork, or spoon; soup, or *caldo*, was served in cups to be drunk. Nevertheless, we congratulated ourselves upon having fallen into such good quarters.

In a short time a young man gaily dressed with an embroidered shirt arrived on horseback accompanied by several men driving a herd of cattle. An ox was selected and, by a rope thrown around its horns, the animal was drawn up to the side of the house, and by another rope around its legs, thrown down. Its feet were tied together, its head drawn back by a rope tied from its horns to its tail, and with one thrust of the machete the artery of life was severed. The pack of hungry dogs stood ready, and, with a horrible clicking, lapped up the blood with their tongues. All the women were looking on, and a young girl took a puppy dog and rubbed its nose in the crimson stream to give it an early taste for blood. The ox was skinned, the meat separated from the bones, and, to the entire destruction of steaks, sirloins, and roasting pieces, in an hour the whole animal was hanging in long strings on a line before the door.

During this operation Don Gregorio arrived. He was about fifty, had large black whiskers, and a beard of several days' growth; from the behavior of all around, it was easy to see that he was a domestic tyrant. The glance which he threw at us before dismounting seemed to say, Who are *you*? but, without a word, he entered the house. In my intercourse with the world I have more than once found my overtures to an acquaintance received coldly, but I have never experienced anything quite so cool as the don's reception of me. I told him that we had come into that neighborhood to visit the ruins of Copán, and his manner said, What's that to me?, but he answered that they were on the other side of the river. I asked him whether we could procure a guide, and again he said that the only man who knew anything about them lived on the other side of the river. As yet we had not made sufficient allowance for the distracted state of the country, nor the circumstance that a man might incur danger to himself by giving shelter to suspected persons. Having relied on the reputation of the country for hospitality, the proof of which we had already enjoyed, I was rather slow in coming to the disagreeable conclusion that we were not welcome. This conclusion, however, could not be avoided; the don was certainly not pleased with our looks. I ordered the muleteer to saddle the mules, but that rascal, enjoying our confusion, positively refused to saddle his beasts again that day. We appealed to Don Gregorio himself, offering him payment, and, as Augustin said, in the hope of getting rid of us he lent us two mules on which we rode back to the village. Unfortunately, when we reached the village we found that the guide we sought was away; a brisk cockfight was then pending, and we received no en-

couragement, either from the appearance of the people or
from invitation, to bring back our luggage to the village.
And we learned, which was very provoking, that Don
Gregorio was the great man of Copán, the richest man, the
petty tyrant, and that it would be most unfortunate to have
a rupture with him or even to let it be known at the village
that we were not well received at his house. Reluctantly, but
in the hope of making a more favorable impression, we returned to the hacienda. Mr. Catherwood dismounted on the
steps, and took a seat on the piazza. I happened to dismount
outside and, before moving, took a survey of the party. The
don sat on a chair, with our detestable muleteer by his side
and a half-concealed smile of derision on his face, talking of
idols, and looking at me. By this time eight or ten men—
sons, servants, and laborers—had come in from their day's
work, but not one offered to take my mule, or made any of
those demonstrations of civility which are always shown a
welcome guest. The women turned away their heads, as if
they had been reproved for receiving us; and all the men,
taking their cue from the don, looked so insulting that I
told Mr. Catherwood we would tumble our luggage into
the road and curse the don for an inhospitable churl. But
Mr. Catherwood warned me against it, urging that, if we
had an open quarrel with him, after all our trouble we might
be prevented from seeing the ruins. The don probably
suspected something of what was in my mind and, fearing
to push things too far and thus bring a stain upon his name,
he pointed to a chair and asked me to take a seat. With a
great effort, I resolved to smother my indignation until I
could pour it out with safety. Augustin, too, was very indignant at the treatment we were receiving. On the road he
had sometimes swelled his own importance by telling of the
flags hoisted and cannon fired when we left Belize; and
here he had hoisted more flags and fired more guns than
usual, beginning with forty guns and going on to a cannonade. But it would not do; the don did not like us, and
probably was willing to hoist flags and fire cannons too when
we should go away.

Toward evening the skin of an ox was spread upon the
piazza, ears of corn were thrown upon it, and all the men,

with the don at their head, sat down to shell them. The cobs were carried to the kitchen for fuel, the corn taken up in baskets, and three pet hogs, which had been grunting outside in expectation of the feast, were let in to pick up the scattered grains. During the evening no notice was taken of us, except that the wife of the don sent a message by Augustin that supper was being prepared; an additional message, that they had an oven and flour and would bake us some bread if we wished to buy it, somewhat relieved our wounded pride and discontent.

After supper all prepared for sleep. The don's house had two sides, an inside and an outside. The don and his family occupied the former, and we the latter. But we did not have even this to ourselves. All along the wall were frames made of sticks about an inch thick and tied together with bark strings; the workmen spread an untanned oxhide over the frames and prepared for bed. There were three hammocks besides ours, and I had so little room for mine that my body described an inverted parabola, with my heels as high as my head. It was vexatious and ridiculous or, in the words of the English tourist in *Fra Diávolo*,[1] "shocking! positively shocking!"

In the morning we found Don Gregorio's humor unchanged. We took no notice of him, but made our toilet under the shed with as much respect as possible to the presence of the female members of the family, who were constantly passing and repassing. We had made up our minds to hold on and see the ruins; fortunately, early in the morning, one of the crusty don's sons, a civil young man, brought from the village the guide of whom we stood in need.

By reason of many vexatious delays growing out of difficulties between the guide José and the muleteer, we did not get away until nine o'clock. Very soon we left the path, or road, and entered a large field partially cultivated with corn, which belonged to Don Gregorio. After riding for some distance through the field, on the edge of the woods

---

1. A comic opera by Scribe and Auber, based on the life of the famous Neapolitan bandit Michele Pezza (1760–1806).

we reached a hut thatched with corn leaves where some
workmen were preparing their breakfast. Dismounting and
tying our mules to trees near by, we entered the woods,
José clearing a path before us with a machete. Soon we came
to the bank of a river and saw directly opposite a stone wall,

FIG. 1 *Wall of Copán*

with furze growing out of the top. Perhaps a hundred feet
high, it ran north and south along the river, in some places
fallen but in others entire; it had more the character of a
structure than any we had ever seen ascribed to the aborigines of America. This was part of the wall of Copán (figure 1), an ancient city on whose history, books throw but
little light.

Volumes without number have been written to account
for the first peopling of the Americas. By some, the inhabitants of these continents have been regarded as a separate race and not one descended from the common father
as the rest of mankind. Others have considered them the
most ancient race of people upon the earth, ascribing their
origin to some remnant of the antediluvian inhabitants of
the earth who survived the deluge which swept away the
greatest part of the human species in the days of Noah.
Under the broad range allowed by a descent from the sons
of Noah, many peoples have had ascribed to them the honor

of peopling the Americas: the Jews, the Canaanites, the Phoenicians, the Carthaginians, the Greeks, and the Scythians in ancient times; the Chinese, the Swedes, the Norwegians, the Welsh, and the Spaniards in modern times. North and South America have been joined together and rent asunder by the shock of an earthquake; the fabled island of Atlantis has been lifted out of the ocean; and, not to be left behind, an enterprising American has turned the tables on the Old World and planted the ark itself within the state of New York.

The monuments and architectural remains of the aborigines have heretofore formed only a small part of the groundwork for these speculations. Dr. Robertson[2] in his *History of America*, claims as "a certain principle, that America was not peopled by any nation of the ancient continent which had made considerable progress in civilization." "The inhabitants of the New World," he says, "were in a state of society so extremely rude as to be unacquainted with those arts which are the first essays of human ingenuity in its advance toward improvement." Discrediting the glowing accounts of Cortes and his companions, and those of soldiers, priests, and civilians, all of which concur in their representations of the splendor exhibited in the buildings of Mexico, Dr. Robertson goes on to say that the "houses of the people were mere huts, built with turf, or mud, or the branches of trees, like those of the rudest Indians." The temple of Cholula, this historian tells us, was nothing more than "a mound of earth, without any steps or any facing of stone, covered with grass and shrubs"; and, on the authority of persons long resident in New Spain who professed to have visited every part of it, he reports that "there is not, in all the extent of that vast empire, a single monument or vestige of any building more ancient than the conquest." In Dr. Robertson's time distrust was perhaps the safest side for the historian; but since that time a new flood of light has poured

---

2. William Robertson (1721–1793), well-known Scottish historian and author of a *History of America*, 2 vols., 1777.

upon the world, and the field of American antiquities has been opened.

The ignorance, carelessness, and indifference with which the inhabitants of Spanish America view this subject is a matter of wonder. In our own country, wild and wandering ideas in regard to its first peopling have been inspired by the opening of forests, the discovery of tumuli, or mounds, and fortifications extending in ranges from the lakes through the valleys of the Ohio and Mississippi, the finding of mummies in a cave in Kentucky, the discovery on the rock at Dighton of an inscription supposed to be in Phoenician characters, and the unearthing of ruins of walls and a great city in Arkansas and Wisconsin Territory. From such evidence there arose a strong belief that powerful and populous nations had once occupied the country and had passed away, leaving little knowledge of their histories.

In Mexico the evidence assumes a still more definite form. The first new light was thrown upon this subject in respect to Mexico by the great Humboldt, who visited that country at a time when, by the jealous policy of the government, it was almost as much closed against strangers as China is now. No man could have better deserved such fortune. Although at that time the monuments of the country were not a leading object of research, Humboldt collected from various sources information and drawings, particularly of Mitla, or the Vale of the Dead; of Xochicalco, the Hill of Flowers, a mountain hewed down and terraced; and of the great pyramid or Temple of Cholula which he, himself, visited. His own eloquent account of all this is within reach of the reader.[3] Unfortunately, of the great cities beyond the Vale of Mexico—cities buried in forests, ruined, desolate, and without a name—Humboldt never heard; or, if he did, he never visited them. It was only lately that accounts of their existence reached Europe and our own country, accounts which, however vague and unsatisfactory, had roused both

---

3. Alexander van Humboldt. *Vues des Cordillères, et Monuments des Peuples Indigènes de l'Amérique*, Paris, 1816.

our curiosity and our skepticism—Mr. Catherwood and I arrived at Copán with the hope rather than the expectation of finding wonders.

Since the discovery of these ruined cities, the prevailing theory has been that they belonged to a race long anterior to that which inhabited the country at the time of the Spanish conquest. Early Spanish historians mention, for instance, a place called Copán which offered formidable resistance to Spanish arms. They describe its location as the same region of country in which we now find these ruins of a once inhabited city. There are, however, indications in their reports that the city of which they wrote was of inferior strength and solidity of construction, and of more modern origin.

Their city stood in the old province of Chiquimula de la Sierra, which was conquered by the officers of Pedro de Alvarado. Although no Spanish historian has given any particulars of this conquest,[4] we know that in 1530 the Indians of the province revolted and attempted to throw off the yoke of Spain. Hernando de Chávez was sent to subdue them, and after many sanguinary battles he encamped before Esquipulas, a place of arms belonging to a powerful cacique. On the fourth day, to use the words of the cacique himself, "more out of respect for the public tranquillity than from fear of the Spanish arms," the cacique "determined to surrender." The whole province thus was submitted again to Spanish dominion.

The cacique of Copán, whose name was Copán Calel, had been active in exciting the revolt and assisting the insurgents, so Hernando de Chávez, determined to punish him, marched against Copán, then one of the largest, most opulent, and most populous places of the kingdom. The camp of the cacique, with his auxiliaries, consisted of thirty thousand men, well-disciplined veterans in war armed with wooden

---

4. Stephens obtained his information from *A History of the Kingdom of Guatemala* (ch. XXIV) by Domingo Juarros, translated by John Baily and published in 1823 in London by John Hearne. The original Spanish edition was published in Guatemala in 1808. An earlier account of the same events can be found in Fuentes y Guzmán, *Recordación florida*, Guatemala, 1933 (modern edition).

swords having stone edges, and with arrows and slings. One side of the camp, says the historian, was defended by the ranges of mountains of Chiquimula and Gracias a Dios, and the opposite side by a deep fosse and an intrenchment formed of strong beams of timber, the interstices filled with earth, which had embrasures and loopholes for the discharge of arrows. Chávez, accompanied by some horsemen, rode well armed to the fosse from where he signaled his desire to hold conference. The cacique answered with an arrow, and then a shower of arrows, stones, and darts compelled the Spaniards to retreat. The next day Chávez made an attack upon the intrenchment. His infantry wore loose coats stuffed with cotton and were armed with swords and shields; the horsemen wore breastplates and helmets, and their horses were covered. The Copanes carried shields covered with the skin of the danta and guarded their heads with bunches of feathers. The attack lasted the whole day. The Indians, with their arrows, javelins, and pikes, the heads of which were hardened by fire, maintained their ground, and at the end of the day the Spaniards were obliged to retreat. Chávez, who had fought in the thickest of the battle, was alarmed at the difficulties of the enterprise and the danger to the credit of the Spanish arms. Receiving information that in one place the depth of the ditch which defended Copán was but trifling, the next day he proceeded to attack the spot. The Copanes, who had watched his movements, manned the intrenchment with their bravest soldiers. When Chávez's infantry were unable to make a lodgment, the cavalry came to their assistance. The Indians brought up their whole force, but the Spaniards stood like rocks, impassable to pikes, arrows, and stones. Several times they attempted to scale the intrenchments and were driven back into the fosse. Many were killed on both sides, but the battle continued without advantage to either until a brave horseman leaped the ditch. His horse was thrown so violently against the barrier that the earth and palisadoes gave way, and the frightened animal plunged among the Indians. Other horsemen quickly followed, spreading such terror among the Copanes that their lines broke and they fled. Copán Calel rallied his forces at a place where he had posted a body of reserve, but unable to resist long, he was forced to retreat, leaving Copán to its fate. As we gazed on the wall of the city on the opposite side of the river, this account of the city's conquest which the Spanish historians have given us, seemed to us most meager and unsatisfactory. It did not appear to us that the massive stone structures before us could have belonged to a city the intrenchment of which could be broken down by the charge of a single horseman. Since at this place the river was not fordable, we returned to our mules, mounted, and rode to another part of the bank, a short distance above. Here the stream was wide, and in some places deep, rapid, and with a broken and stony bottom. Fording it, we rode along the bank by a footpath encumbered with undergrowth, which José opened by cutting away the branches. At the foot of the wall which we had seen from the opposite bank we again dismounted and tied our mules.

The wall was of cut stone, well laid, and in a good state of preservation. We ascended by large stone steps, only some of which were well preserved, and reached a terrace, the form of which it was impossible to make out because of the density of the forest in which it was enveloped. Following a path which our guide cleared for us with his machete, we passed a large fragment of stone elaborately sculptured and half buried in the earth, and came to the angle of a structure with steps on the sides, which in so far as the trees allowed us to make them out, resembled the sides of a pyramid in form and appearance. Diverging from the base of the structure, and working our way through the thick woods, we came upon a square stone column, about fourteen feet high and three feet on each side, sculptured on all four of the sides, from the base to the top, in very bold relief. On the front side was carved the figure of a man (evidently a portrait) curiously and richly dressed, whose face was solemn, stern, and well fitted to excite terror. The design on the opposite side was unlike anything we had ever seen before; the remaining two sides were covered with hieroglyphics. About three feet in front of the column was a large block of stone, also sculptured with figures and emblematical

devices. From our guide we learned that the square column
was an "idol" [5] and the block of stone an "altar." The sight
of this unexpected monument put at rest once and forever
all uncertainty in our minds as to the character of American
antiquities, and gave us the assurance that the objects we
were in search of were not only interesting as the remains
of an unknown people, but were works of art as well, prov-
ing, like newly discovered historical records, that the people
who once occupied the American continents were not savages.
With an interest perhaps stronger than we had ever felt in
wandering among the ruins of Egypt, we followed our
guide, who, sometimes missing his way, with a constant and
vigorous use of his machete conducted us through the thick
forest, among half-buried fragments, to fourteen more
monuments of the same character and appearance, some
with more elegant designs, and some in workmanship equal
to the finest monuments of the Egyptians. One, we found,
had been displaced from its pedestal by enormous roots; another, locked in the close embrace of branches of trees, was
almost lifted out of the earth; and still another had been
hurled to the ground and bound down by huge vines and
creepers. One with its altar before it stood in a grove of
trees which grew around it, seemingly to shade and shroud
it as a sacred thing; in the solemn stillness of the woods,
it seemed a divinity mourning over a fallen people. The
only sounds that disturbed the quiet of this buried city were
the noise of monkeys moving among the tops of the trees
and the cracking of dry branches broken by their weight.
They moved over our heads in long and swift processions,
forty or fifty at a time. Some with little ones wound in their
long arms walked out to the end of boughs and, holding
on with their hind feet or a curl of the tail, sprang to a
branch of the next tree; with a noise like a current of wind,
they passed on into the depths of the forest. It was the first
time we had seen these mockeries of humanity and, amid
these strange monuments, they seemed like wandering

5. Modern archeologists use the term *stela* rather than *idol*. Stephens
enclosed the word *idol* in quotation marks because of his doubts as to
the accuracy of the term. In the subsequent pages of the present edition, this use of quotation marks has been eliminated.

spirits of the departed race guarding the ruins of their former habitations. We returned to the base of the pyramidal structure and ascended by regular stone steps, which in some places had been forced apart by bushes and saplings and in others thrown down by the growth of large trees. In parts they were ornamented with sculptured figures and rows of death's heads. Climbing over the ruined top, we reached a terrace overgrown with trees and, crossing it, descended by stone steps into an area so covered with trees that at first we could not make out its form. When the machete had cleared the way, we saw that it was a square with steps on all the sides almost as perfect as those of the Roman amphitheatre. The steps were ornamented with sculpture, and on the south side, about halfway up, forced out of its place by roots, was a colossal head, again evidently a portrait. We ascended these steps and reached a broad terrace a hundred feet high overlooking the river and supported by the wall which we had seen from the opposite bank. The whole terrace was covered with trees, and even at this height were two gigantic ceibas (kapok trees), over twenty feet in circumference; their half-naked roots extended fifty or a hundred feet around, binding down the ruins and shading them with their wide-spreading branches.

We sat down on the very edge of the wall and strove in vain to penetrate the mystery by which we were surrounded. Who were the people that built this city? In the ruined cities of Egypt, even in the long-lost Petra, the stranger knows the story of the people whose vestiges he finds around him. America, say historians, was peopled by savages; but savages never reared these structures, savages never carved these stones. When we asked the Indians who had made them, their dull answer was "Quién sabe? (Who knows?)" There were no associations connected with this place, none of those stirring recollections which hallow Rome, Athens, and "The world's great mistress on the Egyptian plain." But architecture, sculpture, and painting, all the arts which embellish life, had flourished in this overgrown forest; orators, warriors, and statesmen, beauty, ambition, and glory had lived and passed away, and none knew that such things had been, or could tell of their past existence. Books, the records of knowledge, are silent on this theme.

The city was desolate. No remnant of this race hangs round the ruins, with traditions handed down from father to son and from generation to generation. It lay before us like a shattered bark in the midst of the ocean, her masts gone, her name effaced, her crew perished, and none to tell whence she came, to whom she belonged, how long on her voyage, or what caused her destruction—her lost people to be traced only by some fancied resemblance in the construction of the vessel, and, perhaps, never to be known at all. The place where we were sitting, was it a citadel from which an unknown people had sounded the trumpet of war? or a temple for the worship of the God of peace? or did the inhabitants worship idols made with their own hands and offer sacrifices on the stones before them? All was mystery, dark, impenetrable mystery, and every circumstance increased it. In Egypt the colossal skeletons of gigantic temples stand in unwatered sands in all the nakedness of desolation; but here an immense forest shrouds the ruins, hiding them from sight, heightening the impression and moral effect, and giving an intensity and almost wildness to the interest.

Late in the afternoon we worked our way back to the mules, bathed in the clear river at the foot of the wall, and returned to the hacienda. Our grateful muleteer-boy had told of his dreadful illness and of the extraordinary cure effected by Mr. Catherwood; as a result, we found at the hacienda a ghastly looking man, worn down by fever and ague, who begged us for *remedios*. There awaited us, also, an old lady who had delayed the termination of her visit to the family in the hope that we would cure her of a malady from which she had suffered for twenty years. The sight of the medicine chest which we brought out converted the wife of the don into a patient also. Mr. Catherwood's reputation rose with the medicines he distributed and in the course of the evening he had under his care four or five women and as many men. We would have liked very much to practice on the don, but he was cautious. The percussion caps of our pistols attracted the attention of the men, so we showed them the compass and the other possessions which had made our friend at San Antonio suppose us to be "very rich" and to have "many ideas." By degrees we became on social terms with all the house except the master. Having taken his ground, the don was too dignified and obstinate to unbend, but he did find a congenial spirit in the muleteer. When we were ready to retire our new friends made more room for our hammocks, and we had a better swing for the night.

In the morning we continued to astonish the people by our strange ways, particularly by brushing our teeth, an operation which, probably, they saw then for the first time. While thus engaged, the door of the house opened and Don Gregorio appeared, turning his head away to avoid giving us a *buenos días*. We resolved not to sleep another night under his shed, but to take our hammocks to the ruins, where if there was no building to shelter us, we would hang them up under a tree. My contract with the muleteer allowed us to stop three days at Copán but did not provide for any use of the mules during that time. Undoubtedly he hoped that the vexations we met with would make us go on immediately, for when he found us bent on remaining, he swore he would not carry the hammocks and would not remain one day longer, but at length he consented to hire out the mules for the day.

Before we started for the ruins, a newcomer who had been conversing for some time with Don Gregorio stepped forward and said that he was the owner of the idols and that no one could go on the land without his permission; as proof of his claim he handed me his title papers. This was a new difficulty. I was not disposed to dispute his title, but I read his papers as attentively as if I meditated an action in eject-ment. He seemed relieved when I told him that his title was good and that if my plans were not disturbed I would make him a compliment at parting. Fortunately, he had a favor to ask. Our fame as physicians had reached the village, and he wished *remedios* for a sick wife. It was important for us to make him our friend, so, after some conversation, it was arranged that Mr. Catherwood, with several workmen whom we had hired, should go on to the ruins and make a lodgment there as we had intended; I promised in the meantime to go to the village and visit his sick wife.

This new acquaintance, Don José María Acevedo, was about fifty, tall, and well dressed (that is to say, his cotton shirt and pantaloons were clean). One of the most respectable inhabitants of Copán, he was inoffensive though ignorant. He lived in one of the best huts of the village; it was made of poles thatched with corn leaves and furnished with a wooden frame on one side for a bed and a few pieces of pottery for cooking. A heavy rain had fallen during the night and the ground inside the hut was wet. His wife seemed as old as he and, fortunately, was suffering from a rheumatism of several years' standing. I say fortunately, but I speak only in reference to ourselves as medical men and to the honor of the profession accidentally confided to our hands. I told her that a recent affliction would be more within the reach of art but, as this was an illness of long standing, it would require time, skill, and the watching of symptoms and the effect of medicine from day to day. For the present, I advised her to take her feet out of a puddle of water in which she was standing, and promised to consult Mr. Catherwood, an even better medico than I, and to send her a liniment with which to bathe her neck.

Don José María then accompanied me to the ruins where I found Mr. Catherwood with the Indian workmen. Again we wandered over the whole ground in search of some ruined building in which we could take up our abode, but there was none. To hang up our hammocks under the trees was madness; the branches were still wet, the ground muddy, and again there was a prospect of early rain. But we were determined not to go back to Don Gregorio's and when Don José María said that there was a hut near by, I asked him to conduct me to it. As we approached, we heard the screams of a woman inside and, entering, saw her rolling and tossing on a bull's-hide bed, wild with fever and pain. Starting to her knees at the sight of me, with her hands pressed against her temples and tears bursting from her eyes, she begged me, for the love of God, to give her some *remedios*. Her skin was hot, her pulse very high; she had a violent intermittent fever. While I was inquiring into her symptoms, her husband, Don Miguel, entered the hut. He was a white man, about forty, dressed in a pair of dirty cotton drawers with a nether garment hanging outside. He had a handkerchief tied around his head and his feet were bare. I told him that we wished to pass a few days among the ruins, and asked permission to stop at his hut. The woman, most happy at having a skilful physician near her, answered for him, and I returned to relieve Mr. Catherwood, having added another to his list of patients. The whole party escorted us to the hut, bringing along only the mule that carried the hammocks. With the addition of Mr. Catherwood to the medical corps and his mysterious display of drawing materials and measuring rods, the poor woman's fever seemed frightened away.

The hut (figure 8) stood on the edge of a clearing, on the ground once covered by the city; almost at the very door was a stone fragment, which had been hollowed out and used as a drinking-vessel for cattle. The clearing was planted with corn and tobacco, and was bounded on each side by the forest. The hut was about sixteen feet square; its peaked roof, thatched with husks of Indian corn, was made by setting in the ground two upright poles with crotches, in which another pole was laid to support the peak of the roof; similar supports were on each side, but only about four feet high. The gable end was at the front; one half of it was thatched with corn leaves, whereas the other half remained open. The back part of the hut was also thatched, and piled up against it was Indian corn three ears wide. One side of the pile was unbroken, but the other side had been reduced to within three or four feet of the ground. In the front corner inside the hut was the bed of Don Miguel and his wife, protected by a bull's hide fastened at the head and side. The furniture consisted of a stone roller for mashing corn, and a *comal*, or earthen griddle, for baking tortillas. On a rude shelf over the bed were two boxes, which contained the wardrobe and all the property of Don Miguel and his wife except Bartolo, their son and heir. Bartolo was an overgrown

lad of twenty, whose naked body seemed to have burst up
out of a pair of boy's trousers, disdaining a shirt. His stomach was swollen by a distressing liver complaint, and both
his stomach and his livid face were clouded with dirt. There
was only room enough for one hammock; in fact, the cross-
sticks were not strong enough to support more than one man.
The used side of the pile of corn, however, was just high
and broad enough for a bed; by common consent, I took
this for my sleeping place, and Mr. Catherwood hung up
his hammock. We were so glad to be relieved from the
churlish hospitality of Don Gregorio, and to be so near the
ruins, that all seemed snug and comfortable.

After a noonday meal I mounted the luggage mule, with
only a halter to hold her, and, accompanied by Augustin on
foot, set out for Don Gregorio's to get the luggage. The
heavy rains had swollen the river and Augustin was obliged
to strip himself in order to ford it. Don Gregorio was not
at home, and the muleteer, glad as usual of a difficulty, said
that it would be impossible to cross the river with a cargo
that day. Regularly, instead of helping us in our little difficulties, he did all that he could to increase them. He knew
that if we discharged him, the only way left us to get mules
at Copán would be to send someone to a place at least a two-
day journey distant; he was also aware we had no one to
send on whom we could rely. Uncertain at what moment
it might be advisable for us to leave and not wishing to be
left destitute, I was compelled to hire him to remain at a
price so exorbitant that it gave me a reputation for having
mucha plata, which, though it might be useful at home, I
did not covet at Copán. Afraid to trust me, the rascal stipu-
lated daily payments. At that time I was not acquainted with
the cash system of business prevailing in the country. The
barbarians are not satisfied with your custom unless you pay
them besides, and the whole, or a large portion of it, must
be in advance. I was accidentally in arrears to the muleteer;
and while I was congratulating myself on this only security
for his good behavior, he was torturing himself with the
apprehension that I did not mean to pay at all.

In the meantime it had begun to rain. I settled my accounts with the señora, thanked her for her kindness, and

gave her an order to have some bread baked for the next day. Then taking with me an umbrella and a blue bag, contents unknown, belonging to Mr. Catherwood which he had particularly requested me to bring, I set out on my return to the ruins. Augustin followed with a tin teapot and some other articles for immediate use. As we entered the woods, my umbrella struck against the branches of the trees, frightening the mule. While I was endeavoring to close it, she fairly ran away with me. Having only a halter, I could not hold her back. Knocking me against the branches, she ran through the woods and splashed into the river, and, missing the fording-place, never stopped till she was breast-deep in the water. The river was swollen and angry, the rain was pouring down, and rapids were foaming a short distance below. In the effort to restrain her, I lost Mr. Catherwood's blue bag, but would have saved it if the beast had stood still. I tried to retrieve it with the handle of my umbrella, but as it floated under her nose she snorted and started back. I broke the umbrella in driving her across, and, just as I touched the shore, I saw the bag floating toward the rapids; Augustin, with his clothes in one hand and the teapot in the other, holding both above his head, was steering down the river after it. Supposing it to contain some indispensable drawing materials, I dashed among the thickets on the bank in the hope of intercepting it, but I became entangled among branches and vines. I dismounted and tied my mule, and was two or three minutes working my way to the river. I saw Augustin's clothes and the teapot, but nothing of him, and, with the rapids roaring below, I had horrible apprehensions. It was impossible for me to continue along the bank, so, with a violent effort, I jumped across a rapid channel to a ragged island of sand covered with scrub bushes and, running to the end of it, saw the whole face of the river and the rapids, but nothing of Augustin. I shouted with all my strength and, to my inexpressible relief, I heard an answer, very faint above the noise of the rapids. Presently Augustin appeared in the water and, working himself around a point of land, pulled himself up on the bushes. Relieved about him, I now found myself in a quandary. The jump back to

the bank was to higher ground and the stream was a torrent; with the excitement over, I was afraid to attempt it.
It would have been exceedingly inconvenient for me at
this moment if Augustin had been drowned, for now I
needed rescue. Making his way through the bushes and
down to the opposite bank with his dripping body, he
stretched a pole across the stream. By springing upon the
pole I touched the edge of the bank, slipped, and then, with
the help of Augustin and the bushes, hauled myself up on
the bank. All this time it had been raining very hard and
now I found that I had forgotten where I had tied my mule.
We were several minutes looking for her and, wishing
everything but good luck to the old bag, I again mounted.
Augustin, principally because he could carry them more conveniently on his back, put on his clothes.

Reaching the village, I took shelter in the hut of Don
José María, while Augustin, being in that happy state that
cannot be made worse, continued through the rain. There
was no one in the hut but a little girl, and the moment the
rain abated I followed Augustin. I had another stream to
cross and it, too, was much swollen; the road which lay
through a thick forest was also flooded. Very soon the clouds
became blacker than ever; on the left was a range of naked
mountains and the old stone quarries of Copán, along which
the thunder rolled fearfully while the lightning wrote
angry inscriptions on its sides. An English tourist in the
United States once admitted the superiority of our thunder
and lightning. Although I am pertinacious on all points of
national honor, I concede this claim in favor of the tropics.
The rain fell as if floodgates had been opened from above
and, while my mule was slipping and sliding through the
mud, I lost my road. Returning for some distance and again
retracing my steps, I met a woman, barefooted and holding
her dress above her knees. She proved to be my rheumatic
patient, the wife of Don José María. While inquiring about
the road, I told her that she was setting at naught the skill
of the physician, and added, what I believed to be very true,
that she need not expect to get well under our treatment.
I rode on some distance and then again lost my way. I had

come out of the woods by a footpath which I had not noticed particularly and it was necessary to find it now to re-enter the woods. With cattle paths in every direction, for a mile I kept going in and out of them without hitting the right one. Several times I saw the prints of Augustin's feet, but soon, losing them in puddles of water, they only confused me more. It was nearly dark and not knowing which way to turn, like Mr. Henry Pelham when in danger of drowning in one of the gutters of Paris, I stood still and hallooed. To my great joy, I was answered by a roar from Augustin, who had been lost longer than I and was in even greater tribulation. He had the teapot in his hand, the stump of an unlighted cigar in his mouth, and was plastered with mud from his head to his heels—altogether a most distressful object. After comparing notes we selected a path to try. Shouting as we went, our united voices were soon answered by barking dogs and Mr. Catherwood, who, alarmed at our absence and apprehending what had happened, was coming out with Don Miguel to look for us. Back at the hut, having no change of clothes, I stripped and rolled myself up in a blanket in the style of a North American Indian. All evening peals of thunder clashed over our heads, lightning illuminated the dark forest and flashed through the open hut, and the rain fell in torrents. Don Miguel said that there was a chance that we would be cut off for several days from all communication with the opposite side of the river and from our luggage. Nevertheless, we passed the evening with great satisfaction, smoking cigars of Copán tobacco, the most famed in Central America, of Don Miguel's own growing and his wife's own making.

Don Miguel, like myself that evening, had but little wearing apparel, but he was an intelligent and educated man. He could read and write, bleed, and draw teeth or a law paper. Literary in his tastes, he asked Augustin if we had any books, adding that if they were in English, it would make no difference for "books were good things." It was delightful to hear him express his contempt for the understanding of Don Gregorio. A sub-tenant on the estate, Don Miguel was generally behind in his rent of four dollars a year. He said he had not much to offer us, but we felt what was better than a canopied bed, that we were welcome guests. In fact, everyone was pleased: his wife expected us to drive away her fever and ague; Bartolo made sure that we would reduce the protuberance of his stomach; and Don Miguel liked our society. In these happy circumstances, the raging of the elements without did not disturb us.

All day I had been brooding over the title deeds of Don José María and, drawing my blanket around me, suggested to Mr. Catherwood "an operation" (hide your heads, ye speculators in uptown lots!) to buy Copán and remove the monuments of a bygone people from the desolate region in which they were buried, set them up in the "great commercial emporium," and found an institution to be the nucleus of a great national museum of American antiquities! But query, Could the idols be removed? They were on the banks of a river that emptied into the same ocean by which the docks of New York are washed, but there were rapids below, which, in answer to my inquiry, Don Miguel said were impassable. Nevertheless, I should have been unworthy of having passed through the times "that tried men's souls" if I had not had an alternative. I could exhibit by sample: I could cut up one idol and remove it in pieces, and then make casts of the others. The casts of the Parthenon are regarded as precious memorials in the British Museum; would not the casts of Copán be similarly regarded in New York? Other ruins might be discovered that would be even more interesting and more accessible. Very soon their existence would become known and their value appreciated, and it would be the friends of science and the arts in Europe who would get possession of them. They belonged by right to us and, though we did not know how soon we might be kicked out ourselves, I resolved that ours they should remain. With visions of glory and indistinct fancies of receiving the thanks of the corporation flitting before my eyes, I drew my blanket around me and fell asleep.

Chapter VI

~~~~~~

How to begin. Commencement of explorations. Interest created by these ruins. Visit from the alcalde. Vexatious suspicions. A welcome visitor. Letter from General Cascara. Buying a city. Visit from Don Gregorio's family. Distribution of medicines.

AT daylight the clouds still hung over the forest, but as the sun rose they cleared away; our workmen made their appearance, and at nine o'clock we left the hut. The branches of the trees were dripping wet and the ground very muddy. Trudging once more over the district which contained the principal monuments, we were startled by the immensity of the work before us, and very soon we concluded that to explore the whole extent of the ruins would be impossible. Our guides knew only of this district; but having seen columns beyond the village, a league distant, we had reason to believe that others were strewed in different directions, completely buried in the woods and entirely unknown. The woods were so dense that it was almost hopeless to think of penetrating them. The only way to make a thorough exploration would be to cut down the whole forest and burn the trees. This was incompatible with our immediate purposes and might be considered as taking liberties; besides it could only be done in the dry season. After deliberation, we resolved first to obtain drawings of the sculptured columns. Even in this there was great difficulty. The designs were very complicated, and so different from anything Mr. Catherwood had ever seen before as to be perfectly unintelligible. The cutting was in very high relief and required a strong body of light to bring up the figures; the foliage was so thick and the shade so deep that drawing was impossible.

After much consultation, we selected one of the idols and determined to cut down the trees around it and thus lay it open to the rays of the sun. Here again was difficulty: there was no axe. The only instrument which the Indians possessed was the machete, or chopping-knife, which varies in form in different sections of the country. Wielded with one hand, it was useful in clearing away shrubs and branches but almost harmless upon large trees. The Indians, as in the days when the Spaniards discovered them, applied to work without ardor, carried it on with little activity, and, like children, were easily diverted from it. One hacked into a tree and when tired, which happened very soon, sat down to rest, and another relieved him. While one worked there were always several looking on. I remembered the ring of the woodman's axe in the forests at home, and wished for a few long-sided Green Mountain boys. But we had been buffeted into patience, and as we watched the Indians while they hacked with their machetes, we even wondered that they succeeded so well. At length the trees were felled and dragged aside; a space was cleared around the base, in which Mr. Catherwood's frame was set up, and he began to work. I took two mestizos, Bruno and Francisco, and, offering them a reward for every new discovery, with a compass in my hand set out on a tour of exploration. Neither of them had seen the idols until the morning of our first visit, when they followed in our train to laugh at *los ingleses,* but very soon they had exhibited such an interest that I hired them. Bruno attracted my attention by his admiration, as I supposed, of my person; but I found it was of my coat, which was a long shooting frock with many pockets. He said that he could make one just like it except for the skirts. He was a tailor by profession and, in the intervals of a great job upon a roundabout jacket, worked with his machete. But he had an inborn taste for the arts. As we passed through the woods nothing escaped his eye, and he was professionally curious, touching the costumes of the sculptured figures. I was struck with the first development of antiquarian taste in these two mestizos. Francisco found the feet and legs of a statue and Bruno a part of the body to match, and the effect was electric upon both. They searched and raked up the ground with their machetes till they found the shoulders, and then they set up the entire statue except for the head. They were both eager for the possession of instruments with which to dig and find this remaining fragment.

It is impossible to describe the interest with which I explored these ruins. The ground was entirely new; there were no guidebooks or guides; the whole was a virgin soil. We could not see ten yards before us, and never knew what we should stumble upon next. At one time we stopped to cut away branches and vines, which concealed the face of a monument, and dig around and bring to light a fragment, a sculptured corner of which protruded from the earth. I leaned over with breathless anxiety while the Indians worked, and an eye, an ear, a foot, or a hand was disentombed; and when the machete rang against the chiseled stone, I pushed the Indians away and cleared out the loose earth with my hands. The beauty of the sculpture, the solemn stillness of the woods disturbed only by the scrambling of monkeys and the chattering of parrots, the desolation of the city, and the mystery that hung over it, all created an interest higher, if possible, than I had ever felt among the ruins of the Old World. After several hours' absence I returned to Mr. Catherwood and reported upward of fifty objects to be copied.

I found him not so well pleased as I had expected with my report. Standing with his feet in the mud, he was drawing with his gloves on to protect his hands from the mosquitoes. As we feared, the designs were so intricate and complicated, the subjects so entirely new and unintelligible that he was having great difficulty in drawing. He had made several attempts both with the camera lucida and without, but failed to satisfy himself or even me, who was less severe in criticism. The idol seemed to defy his art; two monkeys on a tree on one side appeared to be laughing at him, and I felt discouraged and despondent. In fact, I made up my mind with a pang of regret that we must abandon the idea of carrying away any materials for antiquarian speculation, and must be content with having seen them ourselves. Of that satisfaction nothing could deprive us. We returned to the hut with our interest undiminished, but sadly out of heart as to the result of our labors.

Our luggage had not been able to cross the river, but the blue bag which had caused me so many troubles was recovered. I had offered a dollar reward, and Bartolo, the heir apparent of the lesseeship of our hut, had passed the day in the river and found it entangled in a bush upon the bank. His naked body seemed glad of its accidental washing, and when the bag, which we supposed to contain some of Mr. Catherwood's drawing materials, was shaken, it gave out a pair of old boots. Being waterproof, the boots cheered Mr. Catherwood's drooping spirits, for he was ill with a prospective attack of fever and ague or rheumatism, from standing all day in the mud. Our men went home, and before coming to work in the morning, Francisco had orders to go to Don Gregorio's and buy bread, milk, candles, lard, and a few yards of beef. The door of the hut looked toward the west, and the sun set over the dark forest in front with a gorgeousness I have never seen surpassed. Again, during the night, we had rain with thunder and lightning, but not so violent as the night before, and in the morning it was again clear.

That day Mr. Catherwood was much more successful in his drawings; indeed, at the beginning the light fell exactly as he wished, and he mastered the difficulty. His preparations, too, were much more comfortable, as he had his waterproofs and stood on a piece of oiled canvas used for covering luggage on the road. I passed the morning in selecting another monument, clearing away the trees, and preparing it for him to copy. At one o'clock Augustin came to call us to dinner. Don Miguel had a patch of beans from which Augustin gathered as many as he pleased, and, with the fruits of a standing order for all the eggs in the village (being three or four a day), strings of beef, and bread and milk from the hacienda, we did very well. In the afternoon we were again called off by Augustin with a message that the alcalde had come to pay us a visit. As it was growing late, we broke up for the day and went back to the hut. We shook hands with the alcalde, gave him and his attendants cigars, and were disposed to be sociable, but the dignitary was so tipsy he could hardly speak. His attendants sat crouching on the ground, swinging themselves on their knee joints; though their positions were different, they reminded us of the Arabs. In a few minutes the alcalde started up suddenly, made a staggering bow, and left us, and they all followed, Don Miguel with them. While we were at supper he returned, and it was easy to see that he, his wife, and Bartolo were in trouble. As we feared, the matter concerned us.

While we had been busy with our own affairs, we had but little idea what a sensation we were creating in the village. Not satisfied with getting us out of his house, Don Gregorio wanted to get us out of the neighborhood. Unluckily, besides his instinctive dislike, we had offended him in drawing off some of his workmen by the high prices which as strangers we were obliged to pay. He had begun to look upon us as rivals, saying everywhere that we were suspicious characters, that we had been the cause of disturbing the peace of Copán and of introducing soldiers and war into the neighborhood. In confirmation of this, two Indians who passed through the village reported that we had escaped from imprisonment, had been chased to the borders of Honduras by a detachment of twenty-five soldiers under Landaveri, the officer who arrested us, and that, if we had been taken, we would have been shot. The alcalde, who had been drunk ever since our arrival, resolved to visit us, to solve the doubts of the village, and to take whatever measures the presence of such dangerous persons and the safety of the country might require. But this doughty purpose was frustrated by a ludicrous circumstance. We had made it a rule to carry our arms with us to the ruins, and when we returned to the hut to receive his visit, each of us had, as usual, a brace of pistols in his belt and a gun in hand. Our appearance was so formidable that the alcalde was frightened at his own audacity in having thought of catechizing us, and he fairly sneaked off. As soon as he reached the woods, his attendants reproached him for not executing his purpose, but he said, doggedly, that he was not going to have anything to say to men armed as we were. Roused at the idea of our terrible appearance, we told Don Miguel to advise the alcalde and the people of the village that they had better keep out of our way and let us alone. Don Miguel gave a ghastly smile; but all was not finished. He said that he had no doubt himself of our being good men, but we were suspected, the country was in a state of excitement, and he had been warned that he ought not to harbor us, and would get into difficulty by doing so. Don Miguel's wife could not conceal her distress; her head was full of assassinations and murders. Though alarmed for their safety, she was not unmindful of ours; she said that if any soldiers came into the village we would be murdered, and begged us to go away.

We were exceedingly vexed and disturbed by these communications, but we had too much at stake to consent to be driven away by apprehensions. We assured Don Miguel that no harm could happen to him, that it was all false and a mistake, and that we were above suspicion. At the same time, in order to convince him, I opened my trunk and showed him a large bundle of papers, sealed credentials to the government and private letters of introduction in Spanish to prominent men in Guatemala, describing me as *Encargado de los Negocios de los Estados Unidos del Norte*. One very special letter was from Don Antonio Aycinena, formerly colonel in the Central army, who was banished by Morazán and who is at this time living in New York. He had written to his brother the Marquis Aycinena, the leader of the Central Party, which was dominant in that district in the civil war then raging, recommending me very highly and stating my purpose in traveling through the country. This last letter was more important than anything else; if it had been directed to one of the opposite party in politics, it would have been against us, as confirming the suspicion of our being *enemigos*. Never was greatness so much under a shade. Though vexatious, it was almost amusing to be obliged to clear up our character to such a miserable party as Don Miguel, his wife, and Bartolo. But it was indispensable to relieve them from doubts and anxieties, enabling us to remain quietly in their wretched hut; the relief they experienced, and the joy of the woman in learning that we were tolerably respectable people, not enemies and not in danger of being put up and shot at, were most grateful to us. Nevertheless, Don Miguel advised us to go to Guatemala or to General Cascara to procure an order to visit the ruins, and then return. We had made a false step in one particular: we should have gone directly to Guatemala and returned with a passport and letters from the government; but, as we had had no time to spare and did not know what there was at Copán, probably if we had not taken it on the way we should have missed it altogether. And we did not know that the country was so completely secluded; the people are less accustomed to the sight of strangers than the Arabs about Mount Sinai, and they are much more suspicious. Colonel Galindo [1] was the only stranger who had been there before us, and he could hardly be called a stranger, for he was a colonel in the Central American service and had visited the ruins under a commission from the government. Our visit did have perhaps some influence upon the feelings of the people; it had, at all events, taught Don Gregorio that strangers are not easily got rid of. But I advise anyone who wishes to visit these ruins in peace, to go to Guatemala first and apply to the government for all the protection it can give. As to us, it was too late to think of this, and all we could do was maintain our ground as quietly as we could. We had no apprehension of soldiers coming from any other place merely to molest us. Don Miguel told us, what we had before observed, that there was not a musket in the village; the quality and excellence of our arms were well known; the muleteer had reported that we were outrageous fellows and had threatened to shoot him; and the alcalde was an excessive coward. We formed an alliance, offensive and defensive, with Don Miguel, his wife, and Bartolo, and went

---

1. Col. Juan Galindo, author of "The Ruins of Copán in Central America," in *Proceedings* of the American Antiquarian Society, Vol. II, 543–50, 1836.

to sleep. Don Miguel and his wife, by the way, were curious people; they slept with their heads at different ends of the bed, so that, in the unavoidable accompaniment of smoking, they could clear each other.

In the morning we were relieved from our difficulty and put in a position to hurl defiance at the traducers of our character. While the workmen were gathering outside the hut, an Indian courier came trotting through the cornfield up to the door. He inquired for *el Señor Ministro* and, pulling off his hat, took out of the crown a letter, which he said he was ordered by General Cascara to deliver into the right hands. It was directed to *Señor Catherwood, a Camotán o donde se halle,* and conveyed the expression of General Cascara's regret for the arrest at Camotán, ascribing it to the ignorance or mistake of the alcalde and soldiers, and enclosed besides a separate passport for Mr. Catherwood. I have great satisfaction in acknowledging the receipt of this letter; and the promptness with which General Cascara despatched it to "Camotán, or wherever he may be found," was no less than I expected from his character and station. I requested Don Miguel to read it aloud, told the Indian to deliver our compliments to General Cascara, and sent him to the village to breakfast with a donation which I knew would make him publish the story with right emphasis and discretion. Don Miguel smiled, his wife laughed, and a few spots of white flashed along Bartolo's dirty skin. Stocks rose, and I resolved to ride to the village, strengthen the cords of friendship with Don José María, visit our patients, defy Don Gregorio, and get up a party in Copán.

Mr. Catherwood went to the ruins to continue his drawings, and I to the village, taking Augustin with me to fire the Belize guns and to buy up eatables for a little more than they were worth. My first visit was to Don José María. After clearing up our character, I broached the subject of a purchase of the ruins. I told him that, on account of my public business, I could not remain as long as I desired, but that I wished to return with spades, pickaxes, ladders, crowbars, and men, build a hut to live in, and make a thorough exploration, but that I could not incur the expense at the risk of being refused permission to do so. In short, in plain English, I asked him, What will you take for the ruins? I think he was not more surprised than if I had asked to buy his poor old wife, our rheumatic patient, to practice medicine upon. He seemed to doubt which of us was out of his senses. The property was so utterly worthless that my wanting to buy it seemed very suspicious. On examining the paper, I found that he did not own the fee, but held it under a lease from Don Bernardo de Aguila, of which three years were unexpired; the tract consisted of about six thousand acres, for which he paid eighty dollars a year. He was at a loss as to what to do, but told me that he would reflect upon it, consult his wife, and give me an answer at the hut the next day. I then visited the alcalde, but he was too tipsy to be susceptible of any impression. I prescribed for several patients and, instead of going to Don Gregorio's, sent him a polite request by Don José María to mind his own business and let us alone, after which I returned to pass the rest of the day among the ruins. It rained during the night, but again cleared off in the morning, and we were on the ground early. My business was to go around with workmen to clear away trees and bushes, dig, and excavate, and prepare monuments for Mr. Catherwood to copy. While so engaged, I was called off by a visit from Don José María, who was still undecided as to what to do. Not wishing to appear too anxious, I told him to take more time and to come again the next morning.

The next morning he came, and his condition was truly pitiable. He was anxious to convert unproductive property into money but afraid, saying that I was a stranger and it might bring him into difficulty with the government. I again went into proof of character, and engaged to save him harmless with the government or release him. Don Miguel read aloud my letters of recommendation, and re-read the letter of General Cascara. Don José was convinced, but these papers did not give him a right to sell me his land; the shade of suspicion still lingered. For a finale, I opened my trunk and put on a diplomatic coat with a profusion of large eagle buttons. I had on a Panama hat, soaked with rain and spotted with mud, a checked shirt, white pantaloons, yellow up to the knees with mud, and was about as *outré* as the negro king who received a company of British officers on the coast of Africa in a cocked hat and military coat, without any inexpressibles. But Don José María could not withstand the buttons on my coat; the cloth was the finest he had ever seen and Don Miguel, his wife, and Bartolo realized fully that they had in their hut an illustrious incognito. The only question was who should find paper on which to draw the contract. I did not stand upon trifles and gave some paper to Don Miguel, who took our mutual instructions and appointed the next day for the execution of the deed.

The reader is perhaps curious to know how old cities sell in Central America. Like other articles of trade, they are regulated by the quantity in the market and the demand; but, not being staple articles like cotton and indigo, they were held at fancy prices, and at that time were dull of sale. I paid fifty dollars for Copán. There was never any difficulty about price. I offered that sum, for which Don José María thought me only a fool; if I had offered more, he would probably have considered me something worse.

We had regular communications with the hacienda by means of Francisco, who brought thence every morning a large *guacal* of milk, carrying it a distance of three miles, and fording the river twice. The ladies of the hacienda had sent us word that they intended to pay us a visit, and this morning Don Gregorio's wife appeared, leading a procession of all the women of the house, servants, and children with two of her sons. We received them among the ruins, seated them as well as we could, and, as the first act of civility, gave them cigars all around. It can hardly be believed, but not one of them, not even Don Gregorio's sons, had ever seen the idols before, and now they were much more curious to see Mr. Catherwood's drawings. In fact, I believe it was the fame of these drawings that procured us the honor of their visit. In his heart Mr. Catherwood was not much happier to see them than the old don was to see us, as his work was stopped and every day was precious. As I considered myself in a manner the proprietor of the city, I was bound to do the honors; having cleared paths, I led them around, showing off all the lions as the cicerone does in the Vatican or the Pitti Palace. But I could not keep them away and to the distress of Mr. Catherwood brought them all back upon him.

Obliged to give up work, we invited them down to the hut to see our accommodations. Some of them were our patients, and reminded us that we had not sent the medicines we promised. The fact is, we avoided giving medicines when we could, among other reasons, from an apprehension that if anyone happened to die on our hands we should be held responsible; but our reputation was established, honors were buckled on our backs and we were obliged to wear them. These ladies, in spite of Don Gregorio's crustiness, had always treated us kindly, and we would fain have shown our sense of it in some other mode than by giving them physic. But to gratify them in their own way, we distributed among them powders and pills, with written directions for use; and when they went away we escorted them some distance, and had the satisfaction of hearing that they avenged us on Don Gregorio by praises of our gallantry and attentions.

Chapter VII

~~~~~~

*Survey of the ruins. Account of them by Juarros and by
Colonel Galindo. Their situation. Their extent. Plan of
survey. Pyramidal structures. Rows of death's heads. Remarkable portrait. Idols. Character of the engravings.
Ranges of terraces. A portrait. Courtyards. Curious altar.
Tablets of hieroglyphics. Gigantic head. Stone quarries.
More applicants for medicine. Idols and altars. Buried
image. Material of the statues. Idols originally
painted. Circular altar. Antiquity of Copán.*

THAT night there was no rain, and the next day, as the
ground was somewhat dry, we commenced a regular
survey of the ruins. It was my first essay in engineering. Our
surveying apparatus was not very extensive; we had a good
surveying compass, and the rest consisted of a reel of tape
which Mr. Catherwood had used in a survey of the ruins of
Thebes and Jerusalem. My part of the business was very
scientific. I had to direct the Indians in cutting straight lines
through the woods, make Bruno and Francisco stick their
hats on poles to mark the stations, and measure up to them.
The second day we were thoroughly in the spirit of it.

That day Don José María refused to execute the contract.
Don Gregorio was the cause. He had ceased to interfere with
us, but at the idea of our actually taking root in the neighborhood he could not contain himself and persuaded Don
José María that he would get into difficulty by having anything to do with us; he even told him that General Cascara's
passport was worthless, and that General Cascara himself
had gone over to Morazán. He carried his point for the

moment, but in the end we beat him, and the contract was executed. After three days of very hard but very interesting labor, we finished the survey, the results of which I intend to inflict upon the reader; but before doing so I will mention the little that was previously known of these ruins.

Juarros, the historian of Guatemala, says, "Francisco de Fuentes, who wrote the Chronicles of the Kingdom of Guatemala, assures us that in his time, that is, in the year 1700, the great circus of Copán still remained entire. This was a circular space surrounded by stone pyramids about six yards high, and very well constructed. At the bases of these pyramids were figures, both male and female, of very excellent sculpture, which then retained the colours they had been enameled with, and, what was not less remarkable, the whole of them were habited *in the Castilian costume.*[1] In the middle of this area, elevated above a flight of steps, was the place of sacrifice. Fuentes also affirms that a short distance from the circus there was a portal constructed of stone, on the columns of which were the figures of men, likewise represented in *Spanish habits,* with hose, and ruff around the neck, sword, cap, and short cloak. On entering the gateway there are two fine stone pyramids, moderately large and lofty, from which is suspended a hammock that contains two human figures, one of each sex, clothed in the Indian style. Astonishment is forcibly excited on viewing this structure, because, large as it is, there is no appearance of the component parts being joined together; and though entirely of one stone, and of an enormous weight, it may be put in motion by the slightest impulse of the hand." [2]

From this time, that is, from the year 1700, there is no account of these ruins until the visit of Colonel Galindo in 1836, before referred to, who examined them under a commission from the Central American government, and whose communications on the subject were published in the pro-

---

1. This is, of course, not true, but rather a flight of fancy on the part of Fuentes y Guzmán.
2. Domingo Juarros. *A History of the Kingdom of Guatemala,* translated by John Baily, London: John Hearne, 1923, pp. 56 and 57.

ceedings of the Royal Geographical Society of Paris, and in
the Literary Gazette of London. He is the only man in
Central America who has given any attention at all to the
subject of antiquities, or who has ever presented Copán to
the consideration of Europe and our own country. Not being
an artist, his account is necessarily unsatisfactory and imperfect, but it is not exaggerated. Indeed, it falls short of the
marvelous account given by Fuentes one hundred and thirty-
five years before, and makes no mention of the movable
stone hammock with the sitting figures, which were our
great inducement to visit the ruins. No plans or drawings
have ever been published, nor anything that can give even
an idea of that valley of romance and wonder where, as has
been remarked, the genii who attended on King Solomon
seem to have been the artists.

It lies in the district of country now known as the State of
Honduras, one of the most fertile valleys in Central America and to this day famed for the superiority of its tobacco.
Mr. Catherwood made several attempts to determine the
longitude, but the artificial horizon which we took with us
expressly for such purposes had become bent and, like the
barometer, was useless. The ruins are on the left bank of the
Copán River, which empties into the Motagua and so passes
into the Bay of Honduras near Omoa, distant perhaps three
hundred miles from the sea. The Copán River is not navigable, even for canoes, except for a short time in the rainy
season. Falls interrupt its course before it empties into the
Motagua. Cortes, in his terrible journey from Mexico to
Honduras,[3] of the hardships of which even now, when the
country is comparatively open and free from masses of enemies, it is difficult to form a conception, must have passed
within two days' march of this city.

The extent along the river, as ascertained by monuments
still found, is more than two miles. On the opposite side of
the river, at the distance of a mile, there is one monument on

---

3. The incredible overland journey from Mexico to Honduras un-
dertaken by Cortes to punish Cristóbal de Olid, a rebellious lieutenant.
A good account of it can be found in Chap. 3, Book VII, of Prescott's
Conquest of Mexico.

the top of a mountain two thousand feet high. Whether the city ever crossed the river and extended to that monument, it is impossible to say. I believe not. To the rear of the city is an unexplored forest in which there may be ruins. There are no remains of palaces or private buildings, and the principal part is that which stands on the bank of the river, which may perhaps with propriety be called the temple.

This temple is an oblong enclosure. The front or river wall extends on a right line north and south six hundred and twenty-four feet, and it is from sixty to ninety feet in height. It is made of cut stones, from three to six feet in length, and a foot and a half in breadth. In many places the stones have been thrown down by bushes growing out of the crevices, and in one place there is a small opening, from which the ruins are sometimes called by the Indians *Las Ventanas,* or the windows. The other three sides consist of ranges of steps and pyramidal structures, rising from thirty to one hundred and forty feet in height on the slope. The whole line of survey is two thousand, eight hundred and sixty-six feet; that the reader's imagination may not mislead him, I consider it necessary to say that, though gigantic and extraordinary for a ruined structure of the aborigines, the base of the structure is not so large as that of the great Pyramid of Ghizeh. The engraving (figure 9) gives the plan according to our survey; reference to it will assist the reader to understand the description.

To begin on the right: Near the southwest corner of the river wall and the south wall is a recess which was probably once occupied by a colossal monument fronting the water, no part of which is now visible; probably it fell and broke, the fragments being buried or washed away by the floods of the rainy season. Beyond are the remains of two small pyramidal structures, to the largest of which is attached a wall running along the west bank of the river; this appears to have been one of the principal walls of the city. Between the two pyramids there seems to have been a gateway or principal entrance from the water.

The south wall runs at right angles to the river, beginning with a range of steps about thirty feet high, each step

being about eighteen inches square. At the southeast corner
is a massive pyramidal structure one hundred and twenty-
feet high on the slope. On the right are other remains of
terraces and pyramidal buildings, and probably a gateway,
a passage about twenty feet wide into a quadrangular area
two hundred and fifty feet square, two sides of which are

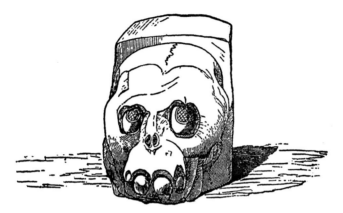

FIG. 2 *Death's Head at Copán*

massive pyramids one hundred and twenty feet high on the
slope.

At the foot of these structures, and in different parts of
the quadrangular area, are numerous remains of sculpture.
At the point marked *E* is a colossal monument richly sculptured, now fallen and ruined. Behind it fragments of sculpture, thrown from their places by trees, are strewed and
lying loose on the side of the pyramid from the base to the
top. Among them our attention was forcibly arrested by rows
of death's heads of gigantic proportions, still standing in
their places about halfway up the side of the pyramid; the
effect was extraordinary. The engraving (figure 2) represents one of them.

At the time of our visit we had no doubt that these were
death's heads, but it has been suggested to me since that the
drawing is more like the skull of a monkey than that of a
man. And, in connection with this remark, I add that our

attention was attracted at the time, though not so forcibly, to the remains of a colossal ape or baboon among the fragments on this side. It strongly resembled in outline and appearance the four monstrous animals which once stood in front of, and attached to the base of, the obelisk of Luxor, now in Paris,[4] animals which, under the name of Cynocephali, were worshiped at Thebes. This fragment was about six feet high; the head was wanting and the trunk lay on the side of the pyramid. We rolled the trunk down several steps when it fell among a mass of stones from which we could not disengage it. We had no such idea at the time, but it is not absurd to suppose the sculptured skulls to be intended for the heads of monkeys, and that these animals were worshiped as deities by the people who built Copán.

Among the fragments lying on the ground near this place, is a remarkable portrait, of which the engraving (figure 3) is a representation. It is probably the portrait of some king, chieftain, or sage. The mouth is injured, and also part of the ornament over the wreath that crowns the head. The expression is noble and severe, and the whole character shows a close imitation of nature.

At the point marked D stands one of the columns or idols which give the peculiar character to the ruins of Copán; the front view of the idol is reproduced in figure 10, to which I particularly request the attention of the reader. It stands with its face to the east, about six feet from the base of the pyramidal wall. It is thirteen feet in height, four feet in front, and three deep, and sculptured on all four of its sides from the base to the top; it is one of the richest and most elaborate specimens in the whole extent of the ruins. Originally it was painted, the marks of red color being still distinctly visible. Before it, at a distance of about eight feet, is a large block of sculptured stone, which the Indians call an altar. The subject of the front is a full-length figure, the face wanting beard and of a feminine cast, though the dress seems that of a man. On the two sides are rows of

4. Stephens notes that "as it stands in Paris, these figures are wanting to make it complete as it stood at Thebes, the obelisk alone having been removed."

hieroglyphics, which probably recite the history of this mysterious personage.

As the monuments speak for themselves, I shall abstain from any verbal description; I have so many to present to

FIG. 3 *Portrait at Copán*

the reader, all differing very greatly in detail, that it will be impossible, within reasonable limits, to present our own speculations as to their character. I will only remark that, from the beginning, our great object and effort was to procure true copies of the originals, adding nothing for effect as pictures. Mr. Catherwood made the outline of all the drawings with the camera lucida, and divided his paper into sections, so as to preserve the utmost accuracy of proportion. The engravings were made, with the same regard to truth, from drawings reduced by Mr. Catherwood himself, the originals being also in the hands of the engraver. I consider it proper to mention that a portion of them (one of which is reproduced in this volume as figure 10) were sent to London, and executed on wood by engravers whose names stand among the very first in England; yet, though done with exquisite skill, and most effective as pictures, they failed to give the true character and expression of the originals; at some considerable loss both of time and money, they were all thrown aside, and re-engraved on steel. Proofs of every plate were given to Mr. Catherwood, who made such corrections as were necessary; in my opinion, they are as true copies as can be presented and, except for the stones themselves, the reader could not have better materials for speculation and study.

Following the wall, at the place marked C is another monument or idol (figure 11) of the same size and in many respects similar. The character of this image as it stands at the foot of the pyramidal wall with masses of fallen stone resting against its base, is grand, and it would be difficult to exceed the richness of the ornament and sharpness of the sculpture. This, too, was painted, and the red is still distinctly visible.

The whole quadrangle is overgrown with trees and interspersed with fragments of fine sculpture, particularly on the east side, and at the northeast corner is a narrow passage, which was probably a third gateway.

On the right, running off into the forest, is a confused range of terraces ornamented with death's heads, some of which are still in position, while others lie about as they have fallen or been thrown down. Turning northward, the range on the left hand continues a high, massive, pyramidal structure, with trees growing out of it to the very top. At a short distance is a detached pyramid (marked Z on the plan) about fifty feet square and thirty feet high, which is tolerably perfect. Along this range, which continues for a distance of about four hundred feet, decreasing somewhat in height, are but few remains of sculpture.

The range of structures turns at right angles to the left and runs to the river, joining the other extremity of the wall at which we began our survey. The bank was elevated about thirty feet above the river and had been protected by a wall

of stone, most of which had fallen down. Among the fragments lying on the ground on this side is the portrait shown
in figure 4.

The plan was complicated and, the whole ground being
overgrown with trees, difficult to make out. There was no
entire pyramid, but, at most, two or three pyramidal sides
joined onto terraces or other structures of the same kind.
Beyond the wall of enclosure were walls, terraces, and pyramidal elevations running off into the forest, which sometimes confused us. Probably the whole was not erected at

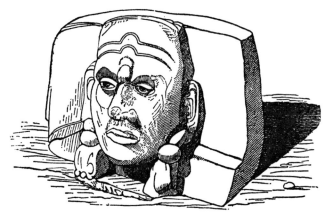

FIG. 4 *Portrait at Copán*

the same time; probably additions were made and statues
erected by different kings or, perhaps, in commemoration
of important events in the history of the city. Along the
whole line were ranges of steps with pyramidal elevations
probably crowned on the top with buildings or altars now
ruined. All these steps and the pyramidal sides were painted,
and the reader may imagine the effect when the whole country was clear of forest, and priest and people were ascending
from the outside to the terraces and thence to the holy places
within to pay their adoration in the temple.

Within this enclosure are two rectangular courtyards having ranges of steps ascending to terraces. The area of each is
about forty feet above the river. Of the larger and most dis-

tant from the river, the steps have all fallen and now constitute mere mounds. On one side, at the foot of the pyramidal wall, is the monument or idol marked *B*, of which figure 12 represents the front. It is about the same height as the others, but differs in shape, being larger at the top than below. Its appearance and character are tasteful and pleasing, but the sculpture is in much lower relief; the expression of the hands is good though somewhat formal. The figure of a man shows the relative height. The back and sides are covered with hieroglyphics.

Near this, at the point marked *A*, is a remarkable altar which perhaps presents as curious a subject of speculation as any monument in Copán. The altars, like the idols, are all of a single block of stone. In general they are not so richly ornamented, and they are more faded and worn, or covered with moss; some were completely buried, and of others it was difficult to make out more than the form. All differed in fashion, and doubtless had some distinct and peculiar reference to the idols before which they had been placed. This one stands on four globes cut out of the same stone; the sculpture is in bas-relief, and it is the only specimen of that kind of sculpture found at Copán, all the rest being in bold alto-relievo. It is six feet square and four feet high, and the top is divided into thirty-six tablets of hieroglyphics which beyond doubt record some event in the history of the mysterious people who once inhabited the city. The lines are still distinctly visible, and a faithful copy appears in figure 5.

Figures 13 and 14 exhibit the four sides of this altar. Each side represents four individuals. On the west side are the two principal personages, chiefs or warriors, with their faces opposite each other, apparently engaged in argument or negotiation. The other fourteen are divided into two equal parties and seem to be following their leaders. Each of the two principal figures is seated cross-legged, in the Oriental fashion, on a hieroglyphic which probably designates his name and office, or character, and on three of which the serpent forms a part. Between the two principal personages is a remarkable cartouche containing two hieroglyphics well preserved, which reminded us strongly of the Egyptian method

of giving the names of the kings or heroes in whose honor
monuments were erected. The headdresses are remarkable
for their curious and complicated form; the figures all have
breastplates, and one of the two principal characters holds in

FIG. 5 *Tablet of Hieroglyphics at Copán*

his hand an instrument, which may, perhaps, be considered
a sceptre. Each of the others holds an object which can be
only a subject for speculation and conjecture; it may be a
weapon of war, and, if so, it is the only thing of the kind
found represented at Copán. In other countries, battle scenes,
warriors, and weapons of war are among the most prominent
subjects of sculpture, but from the entire absence of them

here, there is reason to believe that the people were not war-like, but peaceable and easily subdued.

The other courtyard is near the river. By cutting down the trees, we discovered the entrance to be on the north side, by a passage thirty feet wide and about three hundred feet long. On the right is a high range of steps rising to the terrace of the river wall. At the foot of this are six circular stones, from eighteen inches to three feet in diameter, perhaps once the pedestals of columns or monuments now fallen and buried. On the left side of the passage is a high pyramidal structure, with steps six feet high and nine feet broad, like the side of one of the pyramids at Saccara,[5] and one hundred and twenty-two feet high on the slope. The top is fallen and has two immense ceiba trees growing out of it, the roots of which have thrown down the stones and now bind the top of the pyramid. At the end of the passage is the area or courtyard, probably the great circus of Fuentes,[6] but which instead of being circular is rectangular, one hundred and forty feet long and ninety broad, with steps on all the sides. This was probably the most holy place in the temple. Beyond doubt it had been the theatre of great events and of imposing religious ceremonies; but what those ceremonies were, or who were the actors in them, or what had brought them to such a fearful close, were mysteries which it was impossible to fathom. There was no idol or altar, nor were there any vestiges of them.

On the left, standing alone, two-thirds of the way up the steps, is the gigantic head pictured in figure 18. It is moved a little from its place, and a portion of the ornament on one side has been thrown down some distance by the expansion of the trunk of a large tree, as shown in the drawing. The head is about six feet high, and the style good. Like many of the others, with the great expansion of the eyes it seems intended to inspire awe. On either side of it, distant about thirty or forty feet, and rather lower down, are other frag-

---

5. The name of these Egyptian pyramids is sometimes spelled Saqqara.

6. Fuentes y Guzmán, the seventeenth-century Guatamalan historian (see note 4, p. 76.)

ments of sculpture of colossal dimensions and good design; and at the foot are two colossal heads turned over and partly buried, which are well worthy the attention of future travelers and artists. The whole area is overgrown with trees and encumbered with decayed vegetable matter, with fragments of curious sculpture protruding above the surface, which, probably with many others completely buried, would be brought to light by digging.

On the opposite side, parallel with the river, is a range of fifteen steps to a terrace twelve feet wide, and then fifteen steps more to another terrace twenty feet wide, extending to the river wall. On each side of the center of the steps is a mound of ruins, apparently of a circular tower. About halfway up the steps on this side is a pit five feet square and seventeen feet deep, cased with stone. At the bottom is an opening two feet four inches high, with a wall one foot nine inches thick, which leads into a chamber ten feet long, five feet eight inches wide, and four feet high. At each end is a niche one foot nine inches high, one foot eight inches deep, and two feet five inches long. Colonel Galindo, who first broke into this sepulchral vault, found the niches and the ground full of red earthenware dishes and pots, more than fifty of which, he says, were full of human bones packed in lime. He also found several sharp-edged and pointed knives of *chaya* (obsidian) and a small death's head carved in a fine green stone, with its eyes nearly closed, the lower features distorted, and the back symmetrically perforated by holes, the whole of exquisite workmanship. Immediately above the pit which leads to this vault is a passage leading through the terrace to the river wall, from which, as before mentioned, the ruins are sometimes called *Las Ventanas,* or the windows. It is one foot eleven inches at the bottom, and one foot at the top, barely large enough for a man to crawl through on his face.

There were no remains of buildings. In regard to the stone hammock mentioned by Fuentes, which was in fact our great inducement to visit these ruins, we made special inquiry and search, but we saw nothing of it. Colonel Galindo does not mention it. Still it may have existed, and may be there still, broken and buried. The padre of Gualán told us that he had seen it, and in our inquiries among the Indians we met with one who told us that he had heard his father say that *his* father, two generations back, had spoken of such a monument.

I have omitted the particulars of our survey: the difficulty and labor of opening lines through the trees, climbing up the sides of the ruined pyramids, measuring steps, and the aggravation of all these from our want of materials and help and our imperfect knowledge of the language. The people of Copán could not comprehend what we were about, and thought we were practising some black art to discover hidden treasure. Bruno and Francisco, our principal coadjutors, were completely mystified. And even the monkeys seemed embarrassed and confused; these counterfeit presentments of ourselves aided not a little in keeping alive the strange interest that hung over the place. They had no "monkey tricks," but were grave and solemn as if officiating as the guardians of consecrated ground. In the morning they were quiet, but in the afternoon they came out for a promenade on the tops of the trees; and sometimes, as they looked steadfastly at us, they seemed on the point of asking us why we disturbed the repose of the ruins. I have omitted, too, what aggravated our hardships and disturbed our sentiment: apprehensions from scorpions, and bites of mosquitoes and *garrapatas*, or ticks, the latter of which, in spite of precautions (pantaloons tied tight over our boots and coats buttoned close in the throat), got under our clothes, and buried themselves in the flesh. At night, moreover, the hut of Don Miguel was alive with fleas, to protect ourselves against which, on the third night of our arrival we sewed up the sides and one end of our sheets, and thrust ourselves into them as we would into a sack. And while in the way of mentioning our troubles, I may add that, during this time, the flour of the hacienda gave out, so we were cut off from bread and brought down to tortillas.

The day after our survey was finished, as a relief we set out for a walk to the old stone quarries of Copán. Very soon we abandoned the path along the river and turned off to the left. The ground was broken, the forest thick, and all the way we had an Indian before us with his machete, cutting down branches and saplings. The range lies about two miles north from the river and runs east and west. At the foot of it we crossed a wild stream. The side of the mountain was overgrown with bushes and trees. The top was bare and commanded a magnificent view of a dense forest, broken only by the winding of the Copán River and the clearings for the haciendas of Don Gregorio and Don Miguel. The city was buried in forest and entirely hidden from sight. Imagination peopled the quarry with workmen and laid bare the city to their view. Here, as the sculptor worked, he turned to the theatre of his glory, as the Greek did to the Acropolis of Athens, and dreamed of immortal fame. Little did he imagine that the time would come when his works would perish, his race be extinct, his city a desolation and the abode of reptiles for strangers to gaze at and wonder by what race it had once been inhabited.

The stone is of a soft grit. The range extended a long distance, seemingly unconscious that enough stone had been taken from its sides to build a city. How the huge masses were transported over the irregular and broken surface we had crossed, and particularly how one of them was set up on the top of a mountain two thousand feet high, it was impossible to conjecture. In many places were blocks which had been quarried out and rejected for some defect; and at one spot, midway in a ravine leading toward the river, was a gigantic block, much larger than any we saw in the city, which had probably been on its way thither to be carved and set up as an ornament when the labors of the workmen were arrested. Like the unfinished blocks in the quarries at Aswan and on Pentelikon Mountain, it remains as a memorial of baffled human plans.

We remained all day on the top of the range. The close forest in which we had been laboring made us feel more sensibly the beauty of the extended view. On the top of the range was a quarried block. With the *chaya* stone found among the ruins and supposed to be the instrument of sculpture, we wrote our names upon it. They stand alone, and few will ever see them. Late in the afternoon we returned from our walk and struck the river about a mile above the ruins, near a stone wall with a circular building and a pit, apparently for a reservoir.

As we approached our hut, we saw tied outside two horses with sidesaddles, and heard the cry of a child within. A party had arrived, consisting of an old woman and her daughter, her son, and his wife and child, and their visit was to "the medicos." We had had so many applications for *remedios,* our list of patients had increased so rapidly, and we had been so much annoyed every evening with weighing and measuring medicines, that, influenced also by the apprehensions before referred to, we had given out our intention to discontinue practice. But our fame had extended so far that these people had actually come from beyond San Antonio, more than thirty miles distant, to be cured, and it was hard to send them away without doing something for them. As Mr. Catherwood was the medico in whom the public had most confidence, I scarcely paid any attention to them, unless to observe that they were much more respectable in dress and appearance than any patients we had had except the members of Don Gregorio's family. But during the evening I was attracted by the tone in which the mother spoke of the daughter, and for the first time noticed in the latter an extreme delicacy of figure and a pretty foot with a neat shoe and clean stocking. She had a shawl drawn over her head which, when I spoke to her, she removed, turning up a pair of the most soft and dovelike eyes that mine had ever met. She was the first of our patients in whom I took any interest, and I could not deny myself the physician's privilege of taking her hand in mine. While she thought we were consulting in regard to her malady, we were speaking of her interesting face. But the interest which we took in her was melancholy and painful, for we felt that she was a delicate flower, born to bloom but for a season and, even at the moment of unfolding its beauties, doomed to die.

The reader is aware that our hut had no partition walls. Don Miguel and his wife gave up their bed to two of the women; she herself slept on a mat on the ground with the other. Mr. Catherwood slept in his hammock, I on my bed of Indian corn, and Don Miguel and the young men under a shed out of doors.

I passed two or three days more in making the clearings and preparations, and then Mr. Catherwood had occupation for at least a month. When we turned off to visit these ruins, we did not expect to find employment for more than two or three days, and I did not consider myself at liberty to remain longer. I apprehended a desperate chase after a government and, fearing that among these ruins I might wreck my own political fortunes and bring reproach upon my political friends, I thought it safer to set out in pursuit. A council was called at the base of an idol at which Mr. Catherwood and I were both present. It was resumed in Don Miguel's hut. The subject was discussed in all its bearings. All the excitement in the village had died away; we were alone and undisturbed; and Mr. Catherwood had under his dominion Bruno and Francisco, Don Miguel, his wife, and Bartolo. We were very reluctant to separate, but it was agreed, *nem. con.*, for me to go on to Guatemala, and for Mr. Catherwood to remain and finish his drawings. Mr. Catherwood did remain until, after many privations and difficulties, he was compelled to leave on account of illness. But he returned a second time and completed the drawings, and I give the result of the whole.

At a short distance from the temple, within terraced walls probably once connected with the main building, are the idols which give the distinctive character to the ruins of Copán (if the reader will look at the plan of Copán, figure 9, and follow the line marked "pathway to Don Miguel's house," he will see toward the end on the right the place where they stand). Near as they are, the forest was so dense that one could not be seen from the other. In order to ascertain their juxtaposition, we cut vistas through the trees and took the bearings and distances, and I introduce them in the order in which they stand.

The first is on the left of the pathway, at the point marked *K*. This statue is fallen and the face destroyed. It is twelve feet high, three feet three inches on one side, and four feet on the other. The altar is sunk in the earth, and we made no drawing of either the idol or the altar.

At a distance of two hundred feet stands the idol marked *S*. It is eleven feet eight inches high and three feet four inches on each side; it stands with its front to the east on a pedestal six feet square, the whole resting on a circular stone foundation sixteen feet in diameter. Before it, at a distance of eight feet ten inches, is an altar partly buried; measuring three feet three inches above the ground and seven feet square, it stands diagonally to the idol. It is in high relief, boldly sculptured, and in a good state of preservation.

The engravings reproduced in figures 15 and 16 represent the front and back view of the idol. From the absence of a beard and from the dress, we supposed the figure on the front to be that of a woman; the countenance presents traits of individuality which lead to the supposition that it is also a portrait.

The back is a different subject. The head is in the center, with complicated ornaments over it, the face broken, and the border gracefully disposed; at the foot are tablets of hieroglyphics. The altar is introduced on one side, and consists of four large heads strangely grouped together, so as not to be easily made out. It could not be introduced in its proper place without hiding the lower part of the idol. In drawing the front, Mr. Catherwood always stood between the altar and the idol.

A little behind this is the monument marked *T* (figure 17). It is one of the most beautiful in Copán and in workmanship is equal to the finest Egyptian sculpture. Indeed, it would be impossible, with the best instruments of modern times, to cut stone more perfectly. It stands at the foot of a wall of steps, with only the head and part of the breast rising above the earth. The rest is buried but it is probably as perfect as the portion which is now visible. When we first discovered it, it was buried up to the eyes. Arrested by the beauty of the sculpture and by its solemn and mournful position, we commenced excavating. As the ground was level up to that mark, the excavation was made by loosening the earth with the machete and scooping it out with the hands. As we proceeded, the earth formed a wall around and increased the labor. The Indians struck so carelessly with their machetes that, afraid to let them work near the stone, we cleared it with our own hands. It was impossible, however, to continue; the earth was matted together by roots which entwined and bound the monument. It required a complete throwing out of the earth for ten or twelve feet around, and, without any proper instruments and afraid of injuring the sculpture, we preferred to let it remain to be excavated by ourselves at some future time or by some future traveler. Whoever he may be, I almost envy him the satisfaction of doing it. The outline of the trees growing around it is given in the engraving.

Toward the south, at a distance of fifty feet, is a mass of fallen sculpture, with an altar, marked R on the map; and at ninety feet distance is the statue marked Q, standing with its front to the east, twelve feet high and three feet square, on an oblong pedestal seven feet in front and six feet two inches on the sides. Before it, at a distance of eight feet three inches, is an altar five feet eight inches long, three feet eight inches broad, and four feet high.

The face of this idol (figure 19) is decidedly that of a man. The beard is of a curious fashion and joined to the mustache and hair. The ears are large, though not resembling nature; the expression is grand with the mouth partly open and the eyeballs seeming to start from the sockets. The intention of the sculptor seems to have been to excite terror. The feet are ornamented with sandals, probably of the skins of some wild animals, in the fashion of that day.

The back of this monument (figure 20) contrasts remarkably with the horrible portrait in front. It had nothing grotesque or pertaining to rude conceits of Indians, but it was noticeable for its extreme grace and beauty. In our daily walks we often stopped to gaze at it, and the more we gazed the more it grew upon us. Others seemed intended to inspire terror and, with their altars before them, sometimes suggested the idea of a blind, bigoted, and superstitious people, and of sacrifices of human victims. This always left a pleasing impression, but there was an even higher interest, for we considered that in its medallion tablets the people who reared it had published a record of themselves through which we might one day hold conference with a perished race and unveil the mystery that hung over the city.

At a distance of one hundred and forty-two feet in a southeasterly direction is the idol marked *P*. It stands at the foot of a wall rising in steps to the height of thirty or forty feet; the wall was originally much higher, but the rest had fallen and was now in ruins. Its face is to the north; its height is eleven feet nine inches, the breadth of its sides, three feet, and the pedestal, seven feet square. Before it, at a distance of twelve feet, is a colossal altar. It is of good workmanship, and had been painted red, though scarcely any vestige of the paint remains, and the surface is timeworn. The two engravings (figures 21 and 22) represent the front and back view. The former appears to represent the portrait of a king or hero, perhaps erected into a deity. It is judged to be a portrait, from certain marks of individuality in the features which are also observable in most of the others; its sex is ascertained by the beard, as in the Egyptian monuments, though it also has a mustache, which is not found in Egyptian portraits.

Again, the back of this idol presents an entirely different subject; consisting of tablets, each contains two figures oddly grouped together, ill-formed, and in some cases with hideous heads, while in others the natural countenance is preserved. The ornaments, diadems, and dresses are interesting, but what these personages are doing or suffering it is impossible to make out. This statue had suffered so much from the action of time and weather that it was not always easy to make out the characters; the light, coming through irregular openings among the branches of trees, is in all cases very bad.

The stone of which all these altars and statues are made is a soft grit stone from the quarries before referred to. At the quarries we observed many blocks with hard flint stones distributed through them which had been rejected by the workmen after they were quarried out. The back of this monument originally contained two such blocks, but between the second and third tablets the flint had been picked out, and the sculpture is blurred; the other, in the last row but one from the bottom, remains untouched. An inference from this is that the sculptor had no instruments with which he could cut so hard a stone, and, consequently, that iron was unknown. We had, of course, directed our searches and inquiries particularly to this point, but did not find any pieces of iron or other metal, nor could we hear of any having ever been found there. Don Miguel had a collection of *chaya*, or flint stones, cut in the shape of arrowheads which he thought —and Don Miguel was no fool—were the instruments employed. They were sufficiently hard to scratch into the stone. Perhaps by men accustomed to the use of them, the whole of these deep relief ornaments might have been scratched, but the *chaya* stones themselves looked as if they had been cut by metal.

The engraving (figure 23) represents the altar as it stands before the last monument. It is seven feet square and four feet high, richly sculptured on all its sides. The front represents a death's head. The top is sculptured, and contains grooves, perhaps for the passage of the blood of victims, animal or human, offered in sacrifice. The trees in the engraving give an idea of the forest in which these monuments are buried.

At the distance of one hundred and twenty feet north is the monument marked *O*, which, unhappily, is fallen and broken (figure 24). In sculpture it is the same as the beautiful half-buried monument before given, and, I repeat, in workmanship equal to the best remains of Egyptian art. The fallen part was completely bound to the earth by vines and creepers, and before it could be drawn, it was necessary to unlace them and tear the fibers out of the crevices. The paint is very perfect and has preserved the stone, which makes it more to be regretted that it is broken. The altar is buried, with the top barely visible, which by excavating we made out to represent the back of a tortoise.

The next engravings (figures 25, 26, and 27) exhibit the front, back, and one of the sides of monument *N*, distant twenty feet from the last. It is twelve feet high, four feet on one side, three feet four inches on the other, and stands on a pedestal seven feet square, with its front to the west. There is no altar visible; probably it is broken and buried. The front view seems to be a portrait, probably of some deified king or hero. The two ornaments at the top appear like the trunk of an elephant, an animal unknown in that country. The crocodile's head is seven feet from it, but it appears to have no connection with it. It is four feet out of

FIG. 6 *Fallen Idol at Copán*

the ground, and has been chosen for illustration here as one of the many fragments found among the ruins.

The back presents an entirely different subject from the front. At the top is a figure sitting cross-legged, almost buried under an enormous headdress, and three of the compartments contain tablets of hieroglyphics.

Not to multiply engravings, I have omitted side views, as they are, in general, less interesting. But in this case, the side view is particularly beautiful; the tablets of hieroglyphics are very distinct.

At the distance of twenty-eight feet in the same direction is the statue marked *M*, which is fallen, and lies on its back, with a tree across it nearly lengthwise, leaving visible only the outline, feet, and sandals, both of which are well sculptured (figure 6). Opposite is a circular altar with two grooves on the top. It is three feet high and five feet six inches in diameter (figure 7).

The next three engravings (figures 28, 29, and 30) are the front, back, and side view of the monument marked *L*, distant seventy-two feet north from the last, with its front toward the west; it is twelve feet high, three feet in front, two feet eight inches on the side, with a pedestal six feet square. Before it, at a distance of eleven feet, is an altar very much defaced and buried in the earth.

FIG. 7 *Circular Altar at Copán*

The front view is a portrait. The back is entirely made up of hieroglyphics, and each tablet has two hieroglyphics joined together, an arrangement which afterward we observed occasionally at Palenque. The side presents a single row of hieroglyphics, joined in the same manner. The tablets probably contain the history of the king or hero delineated, and the particular circumstances or actions which constituted his greatness.

I have now given engravings of all the most interesting monuments of Copán, and I repeat, they are accurate and faithful representations. I have purposely abstained from all comment. If the reader can derive from them but a small portion of the interest that we did, he will be repaid for whatever he may find unprofitable in these pages.

Of the moral effect of the monuments themselves, standing as they do in the depths of a tropical forest, silent and solemn, strange in design, excellent in sculpture, rich in ornament, different from the works of any other people, their uses and purposes and whole history so entirely unknown, with hieroglyphics explaining all but being perfectly unintelligible, I shall not pretend to convey any idea. Often the imagination was pained in gazing at them. The tone which pervades the ruins is that of deep solemnity. An imaginative mind might be infected with superstitious feelings. From constantly calling them by that name in our intercourse with the Indians, we regarded these solemn memorials as idols—deified kings and heroes—objects of adoration and ceremonial worship. We did not find on either the monuments or sculptured fragments any delineations of human, or, in fact, any other kind of sacrifice, but we had no doubt that the large sculptured stone invariably found before each idol had been employed as a sacrificial altar. The form of sculpture most frequently met with was a death's head, sometimes the principal ornament and sometimes only accessory. There were whole rows of them on the outer wall, adding gloom to the mystery of the place, keeping death and the grave before the eyes of the living, presenting the idea of a holy city—the Mecca or Jerusalem of an unknown people.

In regard to the age of this desolate city I shall not at present offer any conjecture. Some idea might perhaps be formed from the accumulations of earth and the gigantic trees growing on the top of the ruined structures, but it would be uncertain and unsatisfactory. Nor shall I at this moment offer any conjecture in regard to the people who built it; or to the time when or the means by which it was depopulated to become a desolation and ruin; or as to whether it fell by the sword, or famine, or pestilence. The trees which shroud it may have sprung from the blood of its slaughtered inhabitants; they may have perished howling with hunger; or pestilence, like the cholera, may have piled its streets with the dead and driven forever the feeble remnants from their homes. Of such dire calamities to other cities we have authentic accounts, in eras both prior and subsequent to the discovery of the country by the Spaniards.

FIG. 8 *The Hut at Copán*

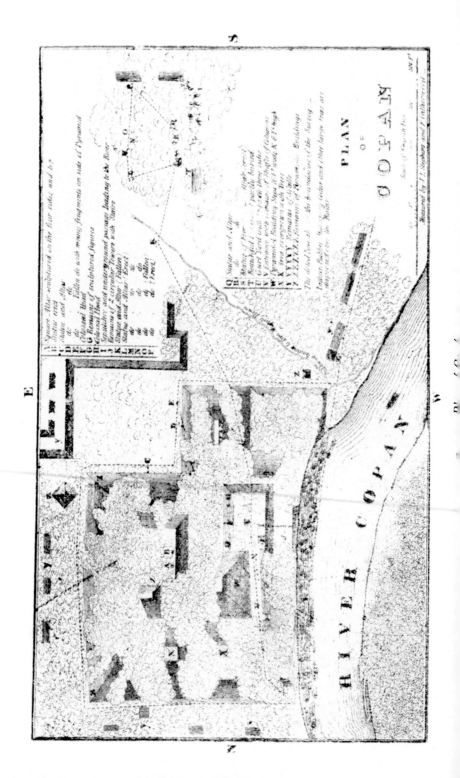

PLAN
OF
COPAN.
Scale of 1000 feet to 1 Inch.

RIVER COPAN

Drawn by F. Catherwood.

FIG. 10 *Stone Idol D at Copán* — front view

FIG. 11 *Stone Idol C at Copán* — front view

FIG. 12 *Stone Idol B at Copán* — front view

FIG. 13 *Stone Altar at Copán* — west and north sides

FIG. 14 *Stone Altar at Copán* — south and east sides

FIG. 15 *Stone Idol S at Copán*—front view

FIG. 16 *Stone Idol S at Copán* — back view

FIG. 17 *Half Buried Stone Idol at Copán*

FIG. 18 *Gigantic Head at Copán*

FIG. 19 *Stone Idol Q at Copán*—front view

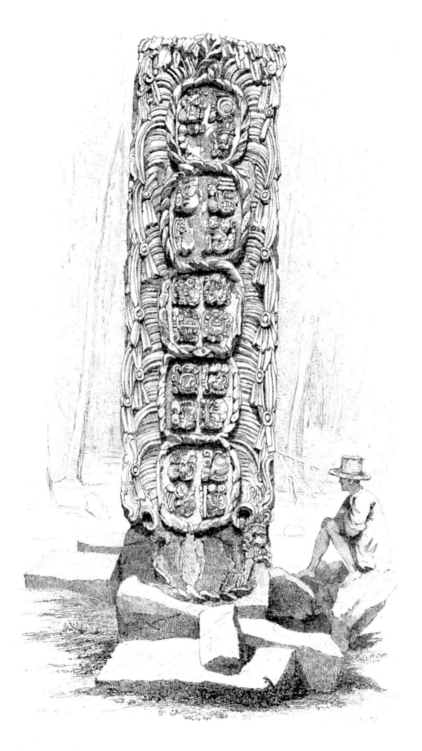

FIG. 20 *Stone Idol Q at Copán*—back view

FIG. 21 *Stone Idol P at Copán* — front view

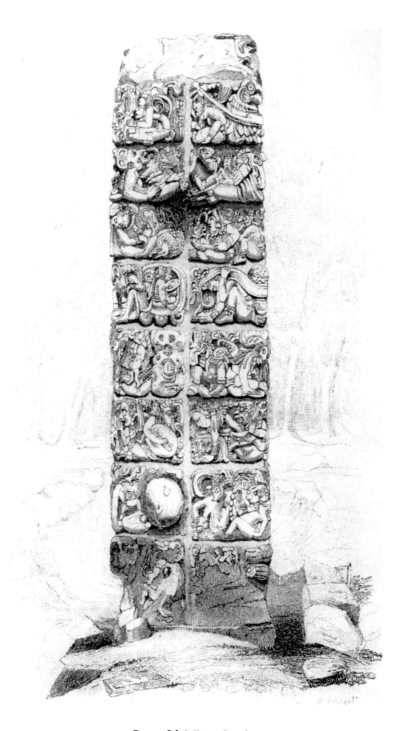

FIG. 22 *Stone Idol P at Copán* — back view

FIG. 23 *Stone Idol and Altar at Copán*

FIG. 24 *Fallen Stone Idol O at Copán*

FIG. 25 *Stone Idol N at Copán* — front view

FIG. 26 *Stone Idol N at Copán*—back view

FIG. 27 *Stone Idol N at Copán*—side view

FIG. 28 *Stone Idol I. at Copán* — front view

FIG. 29 *Stone Idol I. at Copán* — back view

FIG. 30 *Stone Idol L at Copán* — side view

FIG. 31 *Great Square of Antigua Guatemala*

One thing I believe: its history is graven on its monuments. No Champollion [7] has yet brought to them the energies of his inquiring mind. Who shall read them?

Chaos of ruins! who shall trace the void,
O'er the dim fragments cast a lunar light,
And say 'here was or is,' where all is doubly night?

In conclusion, I will barely remark, that if this is the place referred to by the Spanish historian as that conquered by Hernando de Chávez (which I almost doubt), at that time its broken monuments, terraces, pyramidal structures, portals, walls, and sculptured figures were entire, and all were painted. The Spanish soldiers must have gazed at them with astonishment and wonder, and it seems strange that a European army could have entered the city without spreading its fame through the official reports of generals and exaggerated stories of soldiers; at least, no European army could enter such a city now without this result following. But the silence of the Spaniards may be accounted for by the fact that these conquerors of America were illiterate and ignorant adventurers, eager in pursuit of gold, and blind to everything else. Or, if reports were made, the Spanish government, with a jealous policy observed down to the last moment of her dominion, could have suppressed everything that might attract the attention of rival nations to her American possessions.

---

7. The French archeologist who deciphered the Egyptian hieroglyphics (1788–1867).

Chapter VIII

~~~~~~

Separation. An adventure. Copán River. Don Clementino.
A wedding. A supper. A wedding ball. Buying a mule.
The Sierra. View from the top. Esquipulas. The cura.
Hospitable reception. Church of Esquipulas. Responsi-
bility of the cura. Mountain of Quezaltepeque. A narrow
escape. San Jacinto. Reception by the padre. A village
fête. An ambuscade. Motagua River. Village
of Santa Rosalía. A death scene.

HAVING decided that under the circumstances it was
best to separate, we lost no time in acting upon the
conclusion. I had difficulty in coming to a right understanding with my muleteer, but at length a treaty was established.
The mules were loaded and at two o'clock I mounted. Mr.
Catherwood accompanied me to the edge of the woods where
I bade him farewell and left him to difficulties worse than
we had apprehended. I passed through the village, crossed
the river, and, leaving the muleteer on the bank, rode to the
hacienda of Don Gregorio; but I was deprived of the satisfaction which I had promised myself at parting of pouring
upon him my indignation and contempt, by the consideration that Mr. Catherwood was still within the reach of his
influence. And even now my hand is stayed by the reflection
that when Mr. Catherwood, in great distress, robbed by his
servant and broken down by fever, took refuge in his house,
the don received him as kindly as his bearish nature would
permit. My only comfort was in making the lordly churl
foot up the account of sixpences and shillings for eggs, milk,
meat, etc., to the amount of two dollars, which I put into
his hands. I afterward learned that I had elevated myself

very much in his estimation, and in that of the neighborhood generally, by my handsome conduct in not going off without paying.[1]

My good understanding with the muleteer was of short duration. At parting, Mr. Catherwood and I had divided our stock of plates, knives and forks, spoons, etc., and Augustin had put my share in the basket which had carried the whole. Being loose, they made such a clattering that it frightened the mule. The beast ran away, setting us all off after her with a crashing noise, till she threw herself among the bushes. We had a scene of terrible confusion, and I escaped as fast as I could from the hoarse and croaking curses of the muleteer.

For some distance the road lay along the river. The Copán has no storied associations, but the Guadalquivir[2] cannot be more beautiful. On each side were mountains, and at every turn a new view. We crossed a high range, and at four o'clock again came down upon the river, which was here the boundary line of the State of Honduras. It was broad and rapid, deep, and broken by banks of sand and gravel. Fording it, I again entered the State of Guatemala. There was no village, not even a house in sight, and no difficulty about passport. Late in the afternoon, ascending a little eminence, I saw a large field, with stone fences, bars, and a cattleyard, that looked like a Westchester farm. We entered a gate and rode up through a fine park to a long, low, substantial-looking hacienda. It was the house of Don Clementino, whom I knew to be the kinsman of Don Gregorio; it was the one of all others I would have avoided, but it was also the very one at which the muleteer had determined to contrive a halt. The family consisted of a widow with a large family of children, the principal of whom were

---

1. According to Mr. Stephens "On Mr. Catherwood's second visit, finding the rancho of Don Miguel deserted, he rode to Don Gregorio's. The don had in the meantime been to Esquipulas, and learned our character from the cura; and it is due to him to say, that he received Mr. Catherwood kindly, and made many inquiries after me. The rest of the family were as cordial as before."

2. A famous river in southern Spain.

Don Clementino, a young man of twenty-one, and his sister of about sixteen or seventeen, a beautiful fair-haired girl. Under the shed was a party of young people in holiday dresses; five or six mules with fanciful saddles were tied to the posts of the piazza. Don Clementino was jauntily dressed in white jacket and trousers, braided and embroidered. He wore a white cotton cap and over it a steeple-crowned glazed hat with red and yellow stripes under the brim. It had a silver cord twisted round as a band and a silver ball with a sharp piece of steel as a cockade. He had the consequential air and feelings of a boy who had suddenly become the head of an establishment. He asked me, rather superciliously, if I had finished my visit to the idols, and then, without waiting for an answer, he asked if I could mend an accordion; then, if I could play on the guitar; then, if I would sell him a pair of pocket pistols which had been the admiration of Don Gregorio's household; and, finally, if I had anything to sell. With this young gentleman, I should have been more welcome as a pedler than as an ambassador from any court in Europe, though it must be admitted that I was not traveling in a very imposing way. Finding I had nothing to make a bargain for, he picked up a guitar, danced off to his own music, and sat down on the earthen floor of the piazza to play cards.

Within, preparations were going on for a wedding at the house of a neighbor two leagues distant, and a little before dark the young men and girls appeared dressed for the journey. All were mounted; for the first time, I admired exceedingly the fashion of the country in riding. My admiration was called forth by the sister of Don Clementino and the happy young gallant who escorted her. Both rode the same mule and on the same saddle. She sat sidewise before him, his right arm encircling her waist. At starting, the mule was restive, and to support her in her seat, he was obliged, from necessity, to draw her close to himself; her ear invited a whisper, and when she turned her face toward him her lips almost touched his. I would have given all the honors of diplomacy for his place.

Don Clementino was too much of a coxcomb to set off in this way. He had a fine mule gaily caparisoned; he swung a large basket-hilted sword through a strap in the saddle, buckled on a pair of enormous spurs, and, mounting, wound his poncho around his waist so that the hilt of the sword appeared about six inches above it. Giving the animal a sharp thrust with his spurs, he drove her up the steps, through the piazza, and down the other side, and asked me if I wanted to buy her. I declined and, to my great satisfaction, he started to overtake the others, leaving me alone with his mother, a respectable-looking, gray-haired old lady, who called together all the servants and Indian children for vesper prayers. I am sorry to say it, but for the first time I was reminded that it was Sunday. I stood in the doorway, and it was interesting to see them all kneeling before the figure of the Virgin. An old gray-nosed mule walked up the piazza and, stopping by my side, put his head in the doorway; more forward than I, he walked in, gazed a moment at the figure of the Virgin, and, without disturbing anybody, walked out again.

Soon after I was called in to supper, which consisted of fried beans, fried eggs, and tortillas. The beans and eggs were served on heavy silver dishes, and the tortillas were laid in a pile by my side. There was no plate, knife, fork, or spoon. Fingers were made before forks, but bad habits make the latter, to a certain degree, necessary. Poultry, mutton, beef, and the like, do not come amiss to fingers, but beans and fried eggs were puzzling. How I managed I will not publish, but from appearances afterward, the old lady could not have supposed that I had been at all at a loss. I slept in an outbuilding constructed of small poles and thatched, and for the whole I paid eighteen and three-quarters cents. I gave a pair of earrings to a woman whom I supposed to be a servant, but who, I found, was only a visitor, and who went away at the same time that I did.

At a distance of two leagues from the hacienda we passed the house of the wedding party. The dancing was not yet over, and I had a strong fancy to see again the fair-haired sister of Don Clementino. Having no better excuse, I determined to call the latter out and "talk mule." As I rode up, the doorway and the space thence to the middle of the room were filled with girls, all dressed in white, with the roses in their hair faded and the brightness of their eyes somewhat dimmed by a night's dissipation. The sister of Don Clementino was modest and retiring and, as if she suspected my object, shrank back from observation, while he made all open a way for him and his guitar. I had no idea of buying his mule, but made him an offer which, to my surprise and regret at the time, he accepted; but virtue is its own reward, and the mule proved a most faithful animal.

Mounted on my new purchase, we commenced ascending the great Sierra, which divides the streams of the Atlantic from those that empty into the Pacific Ocean. The ascent was rugged and toilsome, but in two hours we reached the top. That the scenery was wild and grand, I have no doubt, but the fact is, it rained very hard all the time; while I was floundering among mudholes I would have given the chance of the sublime for a good macadamized road. Mr. Catherwood, who crossed on a clear day, says that the view from the top, in both directions, was the most magnificent he saw in the country. Descending, the clouds were lifted, and I looked down upon an almost boundless plain running from the foot of the Sierra, and afar off saw, standing alone in the wilderness, the great church of Esquipulas, like the Church of the Holy Sepulcher in Jerusalem, and the Caaba in Mecca, the holiest of temples. My muleteer was very anxious to stop at a collection of huts on this side of the town, and he told me first that the town was occupied by Carrera's soldiers, and then that he was ill. I had a long and magnificent descent to the foot of the Sierra. The plain reminded me of the great waste places of Turkey and Asia Minor, but was more beautiful, being bounded by immense mountains. For three hours the church was our guide. As we approached, it stood out more clearly defined against mountains whose tops were buried in the clouds.

Late in the afternoon we entered the town and rode up to the convent. I was a little nervous, but presented my passport as a letter of introduction. But could I have doubted the hospitality of a padre? Don Gregorio's reception made me feel more deeply the welcome of the cura of

Esquipulas. None can know the value of hospitality but those who have felt the want of it, and they can never forget the welcome of strangers in a strange land.

The whole household of the cura turned out to assist, and in a few minutes the mules were munching corn in the yard, while I was installed in the seat of honor in the convent. It was by far the largest and best building in the place. The walls were three or four feet thick. A large portico extended in front; the entrance was by a wide hall, which was used as a sleeping place for servants and which communicated with a courtyard in the rear. On the left was a large *sala*, or reception room, with lofty windows and deep recesses; on one side of the wall was a long wooden settee, with a high back and arms at each end, before which was a massive unpolished mahogany table above which hung a painting of our Saviour. Against the wall were large antiquated chairs, the backs and seats covered with leather and studded with nails having large brass heads.

The cura was a young man under thirty, of delicate frame; his face beamed with intelligence and refinement of thought and feeling. He was dressed in a long black bombazet gown, drawn tight around the body, with a blue border around the neck, and from his cross was suspended his rosary. His name was *Jesús* María Gutiérrez. It was the first time I had ever heard that name applied to a human being, and even in respect to him it seemed a profanation.

On a visit to him and breaking the monotony of his secluded life, was an old schoolfellow and friend, Colonel San Martín of Honduras, who, having been wounded in the last battle against Morazán, was staying at the convent to recover his health and strength. His case showed the distracted state of the country; his father was of the same politics as himself, but his brother had been fighting on the other side in the battle in which the Colonel had been wounded.

They gave me disagreeable information in regard to my road to Guatemala. Carrera's troops had fallen back from the frontiers of El Salvador and now occupied the whole line of villages to the capital. They were mostly Indians, ignorant, intemperate, and fanatic, who could not comprehend my official character, could not read my passport, and, in the excited state of the country, would suspect me as a stranger. They had already committed great atrocities; there was not a curate on the whole road, and to attempt traversing it would be to expose myself to robbery and murder. I was very loth to protract my journey, but it would have been madness to proceed; in fact, no muleteer would undertake to go on with me, and I was obliged to turn my eyes to Chiquimula and the road I had left. The cura said I must be guided by him. I put myself in his hands, and at a late hour lay down to rest with the strange consciousness of being a welcome guest.

I was awakened by the sound of the matin bell, and accompanied the cura to mass. The church for everyday use was directly opposite the convent, spacious and gloomy, and the floor was paved with large square bricks or tiles. Rows of Indian women were kneeling around the altar, cleanly dressed, with white mantillas over their heads but without shoes or stockings. A few men stood up behind or leaned against the walls.

We returned to breakfast and afterward set out to visit the only object of interest, the great church of the pilgrimage, the Holy Place of Central America. Every year, on the fifteenth of January, pilgrims visit it, even from Peru and Mexico, the latter being a journey not exceeded in hardship by the pilgrimage to Mecca. As in the East "it is not forbidden to trade during the pilgrimage" and, when there are no wars to make the roads unsafe, eighty thousand people have assembled among the mountains to barter and pay homage to "our Lord of Esquipulas."

The town contains a population of about fifteen hundred Indians. There was one street nearly a mile long with mud houses on each side; but most of the houses were shut, being occupied only during the time of the fair. At the head of this street, on elevated ground, stood the great church. About halfway to it we crossed a bridge over a small stream, one of the sources of the great Lempa. It was the first stream

I had seen that emptied into the Pacific Ocean, and I saluted it with reverence. Ascending by a flight of massive stone steps in front of the church, we reached a noble platform a hundred and fifty feet broad and paved with bricks a foot square. The view from this platform of the great plain and the high mountains around was magnificent; and the church, rising in solitary grandeur in a region of wildness and desolation, seemed almost the work of enchantment. The façade was rich with stucco ornaments and figures of saints larger than life. At each angle was a high tower, and over the dome a spire, rearing aloft in the air the crown of that once proud power which wrested the greatest part of America from its rightful owners, ruled it for three centuries with a rod of iron, and now has not within it a foot of land or a subject to boast of.

We entered the church by a lofty portal, rich in sculptured ornaments. Inside was a nave, with two aisles separated by rows of pilasters nine feet square, and a lofty dome guarded by angels with expanded wings. On the walls were pictures, some drawn by artists of Guatemala, and others that had been brought from Spain; the recesses were filled with statues, some of which were admirably well executed. The pulpit was covered with gold leaf, and the altar was protected by an iron railing with a silver balustrade ornamented with six silver pillars about two feet high and two angels standing as guardians on the steps. In front of the altar, in a rich shrine, was an image of the Saviour on the cross, "our Lord of Esquipulas," to whom the church is consecrated, an image famed for its power of working miracles. Every year thousands of devotees ascend the steps of his temple on their knees or laden with a heavy cross; they are not permitted to touch the sacred image, but go away contented in having obtained a piece of riband stamped with the words "*Dulce nombre de Jesús.*"

We returned to the convent; while I was sitting with Colonel San Martín the curate entered and, closing the door, asked me if my servant was faithful. Augustin's face was an unfortunate letter of recommendation. Colonel MacDonald, Don Francisco, and, as I afterward heard, General

Cascara, distrusted him. I told the cura all I knew of him, and mentioned his conduct at Camotán; but he still cautioned me to beware of him. Soon after, Augustin, who seemed to suspect that he had not made a very favorable impression, asked me for a dollar to pay for a confession. My intelligent friend was not free from the prejudices of education; though he could not at once change his opinion so warmly expressed, he said that Augustin had been well brought up.

In the course of the day I had an opportunity of seeing what I afterward observed throughout all Central America: the life of labor and responsibility passed in an Indian village by the cura, who devotes himself faithfully to the people under his charge. Besides officiating in all the services of the church, visiting the sick, and burying the dead, my worthy host was looked up to by every Indian in the village as a counsellor, friend, and father. The door of the convent was always open, and Indians were constantly resorting to him: a man who had quarreled with his neighbor; a wife who had been badly treated by her husband; a father whose son had been carried off as a soldier; a young girl deserted by her lover—all who were in trouble or affliction came to him for advice and consolation, and none went away without it. And, besides this, he was principal director of all the public business of the town, the right hand of the alcalde; it was he who had been consulted as to whether or not I ought to be considered a dangerous person. But the performance of these multifarious duties, and the excitement and danger of the times, were wearing away his frame. Four years before, he gave up Guatemala City and took upon himself this curacy, and since that time he had been living a life of labor, anxiety, and peril, cut off from all the delights of social intercourse that make labor welcome. He was beloved by the Indians, but was without anyone to sympathize with him in his thoughts and feelings. Once when the troops of Morazán invaded the town he lay for six months concealed in a cave of the mountains, supported by Indians. Lately the difficulties of the country had increased, and the cloud of civil war was darker than ever. He mourned, but, as he said, he had not long to mourn; and the whole tone of his thoughts and conversation was so good and pure that it seemed like a green spot in a sandy desert. We sat in the embrasure of a large window; within, the room was already dark. He took a pistol from the window sill and, looking at it, said with a faint smile that the cross was his protection; and then he put his thin hand in mine and told me to feel his pulse. It was slow and feeble and seemed as if every beat would be the last; but he said it was always so and, rising suddenly, added that this was the hour of his private devotions, and then retired to his room. I felt as if a good spirit had flitted away.

My anxiety to reach Guatemala would not permit me long to enjoy the cura's hospitality. I intended to discharge my muleteer but, unable to replace him immediately and unwilling to lose another day, I was obliged to retain him. The usual course was to leave Esquipulas in the afternoon and ride four leagues, but, having seven mules and only four cargoes, I determined to make these four leagues and the next day's journey also that same day. Early in the morning I started. When I bade farewell, the priest and the soldier stood side by side, pictures of Christian humility and man's pride; both recommended me to God at parting.

As we crossed the plain the mountains of Esquipulas seemed to have gained in grandeur. In half an hour we commenced to ascend the Mountain of Quezaltepeque, which was thickly wooded and, like Mico Mountain, muddy and full of gullies and deep holes. Heavy clouds were hanging over it, and as we ascended, it rained hard; but before we reached the top the clouds were lifted, the sun shone, and the plain of Esquipulas, with the great Sierra behind it covered with lofty pines and clouds chasing each other over its sides, all blended together, made one of the grandest spectacles I ever beheld; and the great church still presented itself for the farewell view of the pilgrim. But the gleam of sunshine did not last long, and again the rain poured. For a while I had great satisfaction in seeing the muleteer drenched and in hearing him grumble, but an unaccountable fit of good humor came over me, and I lent him my bear's skin greatcoat. At intervals the sun shone, and we saw at a great distance below us the village of Quezalte-peque. The descent was very precipitous, and the mudholes and gullies were very deep; the clouds which hung over the mountain were typical of my fortune. Mr. Catherwood, who followed on this road about three weeks afterward, heard from the padre of Quezaltepeque that a plan had been formed to murder and rob me on the supposition that I had a large amount of money about my person, which laud-able project was defeated by my crossing in the morning instead of in the afternoon as is usually done.

We passed through Quezaltepeque without dismounting. It is usual, in dividing the stages to Guatemala City, to make an afternoon's journey to this place and sleep. It was now but eleven o'clock, clear and bright as a September day at home. Leaving the village, we crossed a beautiful stream, at which some women were washing. Very soon we ascended again, and on the top of the mountain came to an abrupt precipice, forming the side of a deep ravine. We de-scended by a narrow path on the very edge of the precipice, part of the way on a narrow protruding ledge, and in other places by a path built against the rock to the bottom of the ravine. On the other side rose another precipitous wall. The ravine was deep and narrow and wild to sublimity. The stream ran through it over a rocky bed, and for some dis-tance the road lay in this bed. We ascended by a steep and difficult path to the top of the other side of the ravine and rode for some distance along its edge. The opposite side was a perpendicular mass of limestone rock, black with ex-posure; in some places were patches of grass on a brown ground, lighted up occasionally by brief gleams of sunshine. We descended again to the very bottom of the ravine and, crossing the stream, ascended almost immediately a narrow path built along the side of the precipice to the top and on the same side of the river from which we started. It is im-possible to give any idea of the wildness of this double cross-ing of the ravine. It terminated abruptly, and on a point at the extreme end was a small hacienda, on one side looking directly up this awful opening and on the other upon a soft valley.

At three o'clock we struck the *riachuelo* of San Jacinto. On the opposite side was a fine table of land, with mountains rising beyond, which was covered to the top with noble pines. There was no cultivation, and the whole country was in primeval wildness. At five o'clock we crossed the stream and entered the village of San Jacinto. It consisted of a collection of huts, some made of poles and some plastered with mud. The church was of the same simple construction. On each side was an arbor thatched with leaves of Indian corn, and at the corners were belfries with three bells each. In front were two gigantic ceiba trees; the roots ran along even with the ground more than a hundred feet and the branches spread to an equal extent.

The village was under the care of the cura of Quezaltepeque, who was then at San Jacinto. I rode up to his house and presented the letter of the cura of Esquipulas. My muleteer, without unloading the mules, threw himself down on the piazza and, with my greatcoat on his unthankful body, began abusing me for killing him with long marches. I retorted, and before the padre had time to recover from his surprise at our visit, he was confounded by our clamor.

But he was a man who could bear a great deal, being about six feet, broad-shouldered, and with a protuberance in front that required support to keep it from falling. His dress consisted of a shirt and a pair of pantaloons with buttonholes begging for employment. But he had a heart as big as his body and as open as his wearing apparel; and when I told him I had ridden from Esquipulas that day, he said I must remain a week to recruit. As to going on the next day, he would not hear of it; in fact, very soon I found that it would be impossible without other aid, for my abominable muleteer filled up the measure of his iniquities by falling ill with a violent fever.

At my earnest solicitation, the padre endeavored to procure me mules for the next day, and during the evening we had a levee of villagers. The man upon whom he principally relied said that it was dangerous traveling, that two *ingleses* had been arrested in Honduras and although they had escaped, their muleteers and servants had been murdered. I could perhaps have thrown some light upon this story, but did not think it worth while to know anything about such suspicious characters. The padre was distressed that he could not serve me, but at length he said that a man of my rank and character (I had shown him my passport, and Augustin had fired the Belize guns) ought to have every facility, and he would provide for me himself. He ordered a man to go early in the morning to his hacienda for mules; then, fatigued with such unusual efforts, he threw his gigantic body into a hammock, and swung himself to sleep.

The household of the padre consisted of two young men, one deaf and dumb, and the other a fool. The former possessed extraordinary vivacity and muscular powers and entertained the padre by his gesticulations, stories, and sleight-of-hand tricks, and particularly with a steel puzzle. There was something intensely interesting in the kindness with which the padre played with him and the earnestness with which he hung around his gigantic master. At times the young man became so excited that it seemed as if he would burst in the effort to give utterance to his thoughts, but all ended in a feeble sound, which grated upon my nerves yet seemed to knit him more closely to the goodhearted padre. The latter was continually changing the puzzle, but the ingenuity of the lad could not be defeated. The poor simpleton meanwhile looked on with admiration. The padre offered him half a dollar if he could open it, and both he and the deaf and dumb lad laughed at the awkward attempts of the simpleton. The padre finished with a warm panegyric upon the worth of both, which the deaf and dumb boy seemed to understand and thank him for, but which he that had ears seemed not to hear.

The padre insisted on my taking his own *catre*, which was unusually neat and had a mosquito netting. It was my best bed since I left Colonel MacDonald's at Belize. Before I was up he stood over me with a flask of *aguardiente;* soon after came chocolate with a roll of sweet bread. Finding that

it was impossible to get away that day, I became a willing
victim to his hospitality. At nine o'clock we had breakfast;
at twelve, fruit; at two, dinner; at five, chocolate and sweet
bread; and at eight, supper, with constant intermediate invitations to *aguardiente*, which the padre, with his hand on
that prominent part of his own body, said was good for the
stomach. In everything except good feeling he was the complete antipodes of the cura of Esquipulas. I had had some
suspicion that my muleteer was not as unwell as he pretended, but his neglect of the padre's good fare convinced
me that he was really in a bad way. I gave him some medicine, but I believe he suspected me and was afraid to take it.

At twelve o'clock the mules sent for by the padre arrived
with a strapping young ladino, or mestizo, as muleteer; but
they were not in a condition to set off that day. In the afternoon I took a long walk on the bank of the river. On returning, I stopped under the ceiba trees, where a traveling
merchant was displaying his wares, consisting of two trunks
of striped cottons, beads, horn combs, scissors, etc. His mule
was tied by a long rope, and a pair of pistols lay on one
of the boxes.

Passing on, I met a party of women dressed in white with
red shawls over the tops of their heads. I have seen enough
of fancy colors in women to remove some prejudices, but I
retain an old-fashioned predilection for white faces, and
here I remarked that the whitest women were the prettiest,
though the padre did not agree with me entirely. Under the
shed of a deserted house near by was an old Indian with ten
or twelve Indian girls; he was teaching them the catechism.
They were dressed in red plaid cotton, drawn round the
waist and tied in a knot on the left side, with a white handkerchief over the shoulders. Other parties were out in different places organizing for a village fête in honor of some
saint. Toward evening, while sitting with the padre, now
dressed in his long black gown, a procession advanced,
headed by the oldest man in the village with white hair and
beard, and a lame man and two or three associates playing
on violins. Before reaching the house they set off five or six
rockets, and then all went up and saluted the padre, kissing

the back of his hand. The women went inside, carrying bundles wrapped in clean white napkins; and when I went in to take my chocolate, I found the table piled up with cakes and confectionery. Afterward all went to the church for vesper prayers. I could but think what afterward impressed itself upon me more and more in every step of my journey in that country, that blessed is the village that has a padre.

During the day, the deaf and dumb boy had contrived several times to make me understand that he wished to accompany me, and in the evening the padre concluded to make him happy by giving him a journey to Guatemala City. Early in the morning the convent was in commotion. The good padre was unused to fitting out an expedition for Guatemala City. Many things were wanting besides the mules, and the village was laid under contribution. During the bustle, a single soldier entered the village and created an alarm that he was the pioneer of others come to quarter upon them. The padre told him who I was, and that the guard must not molest me. At length all was ready; a large concourse of people, roused by the requisitions of the padre, were at the door, and among them were two men with violins. The padre directed his own gigantic energies particularly to the eatables; he had put up chocolate, bread, sausages, and fowl, and a box of cakes and confectionery. As the finale, the deaf and dumb lad came out of the house, holding at arm's length above his head the whole side of an ox with merely the skin taken off and the ribs cracked. It was spread as a wrapper over one of the cargoes and secured by a netting. A large pot, with the bottom upward, was secured on the top of another cargo. The padre took a kind leave of me, and a most affectionate one of the deaf and dumb lad; at nine o'clock, with violins playing and a turnout that would have astonished my city friends, I made another start for the capital. A low groan from the piazza reminded me of my muleteer. I dismounted and, at the moment of parting, exchanged a few words of kindness with him. His brawny figure was prostrated by fever; at times he had vexed me almost beyond endurance, but, with all my malice against him, I could not have wished him in a worse condition. The boy sat by his side, apparently softened by the illness of his master and indifferent as to my going.

For the first time in a long while we had a level road. The land was rich and productive: brown sugar sold for three cents a pound and white lump sugar, even under their slow process of making it, for eight cents; indigo could be raised for two shillings a pound. I was riding quietly when four soldiers sprang into the road almost at my mule's head. They were perfectly concealed until I approached, and their sudden appearance was rather footpad-like. They could not read my passport and said that they must conduct me to Chiquimula. My road lay a little off from that town but, fortunately, while under escort, the soldier whom I had seen in San Jacinto overtook us, satisfied them, and released me. A short distance beyond I recognized the path by which we had turned off to go to Copán; three weeks had not elapsed, yet it seemed an age. We passed by the old church of Chiquimula and, winding up the same zigzag path by which we had descended, we crossed the mountain and descended to the plain of Zacapa and the Motagua River, which I hailed as an old acquaintance. It was growing late, and we saw no signs of habitation. A little before dark, on the top of a small eminence on the right, we saw a little boy, who conducted us to the village of Santa Rosalía, beautifully situated on a point formed by the bend of the river. The village consisted of a miserable collection of huts; before the door of the best was a crowd of people, but they did not ask us to stop, and we rode up to one of the poorest. All we wanted was *zacate* [3] for the mules. The stores of the padre were abundant for me, and the deaf and dumb lad cut a few ribs from the side of the ox and prepared supper for himself and the muleteer.

While supping we heard a voice of lamentation from the house before which the crowd was assembled. After dark I walked over and found that they were mourning over the

---

3. Stephens explains that "*Zacate* means any kind of grass or leaves for mules. The best is *zacate de maíz*, or the stalks and leaves of Indian corn."

dead. Inside were several women; one was wringing her hands, and the first words I distinguished were, "Oh, our Lord of Esquipulas, why have you taken him away?" She was interrupted by the tramp of horses' hoofs. A man rode up, whose figure in the dark I could not see, but who, without dismounting, in a hoarse voice said that the priest asked six dollars to bury the corpse. One of the crowd cried out "Shame! shame!" and others said they would bury it in *el campo*, the field. The horseman, in the same hoarse voice, said that it would be the same if it were buried in the road, the mountain, or the river—the priest must have his fee. There was a great outcry; but the widow, in a weeping tone, declared that the money must be paid, and then she renewed her exclamations: "My only help, my consolation, my head, my heart, you who were so strong, who could lift a seroon of indigo, you said you would go and buy cattle; I said, 'yes; bring me fine linen and jewelry.'" The words and the piercing tone of distress reminded me of a similar scene I had once beheld on the banks of the Nile. By invitation of one of the friends I entered the house. The corpse lay on the ground in a white cotton dress extending from the neck to the feet. It was that of a young man, not more than twenty-two, with the mustache just budding on his upper lip, tall, and but a month before so strong that he could "lift a seroon of indigo." He had left home to buy cattle and had returned with a fever; in a week he was dead. A bandage was tied under his chin to hold up his jaw, his thin wrists were secured across his breast, and his taper fingers held a small crucifix made of corn husks stitched together. On each side of his head was a lighted candle, and ants, which burden the ground, were swarming over his face. The widow did not notice me, but the mother and two young sisters asked me if I had no *remedios*, if I could not cure him, if I could have cured him if I had seen him before.

I left the bereaved family and withdrew. The man who had asked me to enter met me at the door and gave me a seat among the friends. He inquired about my country—where it was, and whether the customs were like theirs—and very soon, but for the lamentations of the widow, many would have forgotten that a few yards from them lay a dead friend.

I remained with them an hour and then returned to my hut. The piazza was full of hogs; the interior was a perfect piggery, full of fleas and children; and the woman, with a cigar in her mouth, and the harshest voice I ever heard, still brought in child after child and piled them up on the floor. My men were already asleep outside and, borrowing an undressed ox hide, I spread it on the floor at the end of the house; upon this I laid my *pellón*,[4] and upon that I laid myself. The night before I had slept under a mosquito netting! Oh, padre of San Jacinto, that a man of my "rank and character" should come to this! The woman was sleepless; a dozen times she came out to smoke a cigar or to drive away the hogs; and her harsh voice, and the screams from the house of mourning, made me rejoice when the cocks crew for morning.

4. Fur robe.

Chapter IX

~~~~~~

Chimalapa. The cabildo. A scene of revelry. Guastatoya.
A hunt for robbers. Approach to Guatemala. Beautiful
scenery. Volcanoes of Agua and Fuego. First view of the
city. Entry into the city. First impressions. The diplomatic
residence. Parties in Central America. Murder of Vice-
President Flores. Political state of Guatemala. An em-
barrassing situation. The Constituent
Assembly. Military police.

AT peep of day I bathed in the Motagua. In the meantime the deaf and dumb boy prepared chocolate, and
the corpse of the young man was borne to its final resting
place. I went over to the desolate house, bade farewell to
the mourners, and resumed my journey. Again we had on
our right the Motagua River and the mountains of Verapaz.
The road was level, but it was excessively hot and we suffered from thirst. At noon we stopped for two hours at the
village of Fisioli.[1] Late in the afternoon we came upon a
table of land covered with trees bearing a flower, which
looked like apple trees in blossom; there was cactus or *tuna*,
too, with branches from three to fifteen feet long. I was in
advance; having been in the saddle all day and wishing to
relieve my mule, I dismounted and walked. A man overtook
me on horseback, who touched me by telling me that my
mule was tired. The mule, unused to being led, pulled back,
and my new acquaintance followed, whipping her. Remembering the fable and that I could not please everybody,
I mounted again, and we rode into Chimalapa[2] together.

1. At the present time, no such village exists.
2. This village is now called Cabañas.

It was a long, straggling village with a large church, but there was no cura, so I rode to the cabildo. This, besides being the town house, is a sort of caravansary, or stopping place for travelers, a remnant of Oriental usages which still existed in Spain, and which she had introduced into her former American possessions. It was a large building, situated on the plaza, plastered and whitewashed. At one end the alcalde was holding a sort of court, and at the other were the gratings of a prison. Between them was a room about thirty feet by twenty with naked walls and destitute of chair, bench, or table. The luggage was brought in, the hammock hung up, and the alcalde sent me my supper. Hearing the sound of a drum and violin, I walked to the house whence it issued, and found it crowded with men and women smoking, lounging in hammocks, dancing, and drinking *aguardiente,* in celebration of a marriage. Only the night before I had been present at a death scene. Before me now was an exhibition of disgusting revelry; when a prominent vagabond seemed disposed to pick a quarrel with me, I quietly walked back to the cabildo, shut the door, and betook myself to my hammock.

The next morning we started early. As we left the town, for some distance on each side were fences made of rails upon crotches four feet high and filled with long pieces of *tunas.* The road was the same as we had found it on the preceding day, level and abounding with cactus. Again it was desperately hot, and in the afternoon we saw at the foot of a high mountain a cluster of cocoanut trees, glittering in the sunbeams like plates of silver, which concealed the town of Guastatoya. At four o'clock we entered the town, which was beautifully situated, overlooking a valley in the rear of the square waving with Indian corn; we rode up to the house of the brother of Doña Bartola, our hostess of Gualán, who had recommended him to us.

I had a good supper of eggs, *frijoles,* chocolate, and tortillas, and was lying in a hammock with my boots off when the alcalde entered with a sword under his arm, followed by my host and several other persons. He told me that a party of robbers was out after me, that he had men on their traces, and wished to borrow my arms and servants. The latter I was willing enough to lend, for I knew they would find their way back, but the former, I thought, were more secure under my own eye. Being on the main road, I had considered it so safe that I had that day taken off the caps of my pistols and gun; but, drawing on my boots, recapping and distributing my surplus arms, I sallied forth. The muleteer would not go, but the deaf and dumb lad, with face of fire, drew his machete and followed.

It was pitchy dark and, on first going out from the light, I could not see at all, but stumbled along after my companions, who moved swiftly and without noise through the plaza and along the whole length of the town. In the suburbs we approached a hut which stood alone; the side toward us was closed, but the light of a fire issued from both ends. Here it was supposed the robbers were, unconscious of pursuit or suspicion. After a brief consultation, it was agreed that the party should separate, and one half enter at each end; the alcalde's charge was to shoot the villains rather than let them escape. Stealing toward the hut, we rushed in at the same time from the opposite sides and captured an old woman, who sat on the ground replenishing the fire. She was not surprised at our visit, and, with a bitter laugh, said that the birds had flown. At that moment we heard the report of a musket, which was recognized as the signal of the men who had been stationed to watch them. All rushed out; another report hurried us on faster, and very soon we reached the foot of a mountain. As we ascended, the alcalde said that he saw a man crawling on his hands and feet up the side of the mountain and, snatching my double-barreled gun, he fired at him as coolly as he would have done at a woodcock; they all scattered in pursuit and I was left with Augustin and the deaf and dumb boy.

Moving on, but not very fast, and looking back occasionally to the distant lights in the village, with an unknown mountain before me and a dark night, I began to think that it was about enough for me to defend myself if attacked; although the affair had been got up on my account, it was straining a point for me to pass the night in helping to rid the town of its robbers. Next I reflected that, if the gentlemen we were in pursuit of should take it into their heads to double back, my cap and white dress would make me conspicuous, and it might be awkward to meet them at this place. In order to gain time for consideration of what it was best to do, I walked back toward the town, and had not fully made up my mind when I reached the plaza.

Here I stopped, and in a few minutes a man passed, who said that he had met two of the robbers on the main road and that they had told him they would catch me in the morning. They had got it into their heads that I was an aide-de-camp of Carrera, and was returning from Belize with a large amount of money to pay the troops. In about an hour the alcalde and his *posse comitatus* returned. I had no notion of being robbed by mistake and, knowing the facility with which the robbers might go ahead and take a long shot at me, I asked the alcalde to furnish me with two men to go in advance and keep a lookout; but I was heartily sick of the country and the excitement of its petty alarms.

Daylight dispelled the gloom which night had cast over my spirits. Leaving Guastatoya, for some distance I rode through a cultivated country where the fields were divided by fences. Very soon I forgot all apprehensions of robbers and, tired of the slow pace of the cargo mules, I rode on leaving them far behind. At eleven o'clock I entered a ravine so wild that I thought it could not be the main road to Guatemala. There were no mule tracks visible and, returning, I took another road, with the result that I lost my way and rode the whole day alone. I could gain no certain intelligence of Augustin and the muleteer, but continued on in the belief that they were ahead of me. Pushing on rapidly, at dark I rode up to a hacienda on one side of the road, where I was very kindly received by the proprietor, who was a mulatto. To my great surprise, I learned from him that I had advanced to within one long day's journey of Guatemala.[3] He made me anxious, however, about the safety of

3. Since locally Guatemala City is often referred to simply as Guatemala, no attempt has been made to differentiate between the city and country of that name in instances where the intent is obvious.

my luggage; but for that night I could do nothing. I lay down opposite a large household altar, over which was a figure of the Virgin. At about ten o'clock I was roused by the arrival of Augustin and the muleteer. Besides their apprehensions about me, they had had their own difficulties: two of the mules had broken down, obliging them to stop and rest and feed them.

Early the next morning, leaving the luggage with the muleteer (which, by the way, was at that time a very imprudent proceeding), and taking merely a change of apparel, I set out with Augustin. Almost immediately we commenced ascending a very steep and rugged mountain, which commanded at every step a wild and magnificent view. From the top we saw, at a great distance below us in the hollow of an amphitheatre of mountains, the village of El Puente,[4] the ground around which was white and trodden hard by caravans of mules. We descended to the village and crossed the bridge, which was laid on a stone arch thrown across a ravine with a cataract foaming through it; at this point we were completely encircled by mountains, wild to sublimity, and reminding me of some of the finest parts of Switzerland. On the other side of the bridge we commenced ascending another mountain. The road was winding, and when we reached the top, the view of the village and bridge at the immense distance below was surpassingly fine. Descending a short distance, we passed a village of huts, situated on the ridge of the mountain, commanding on both sides a view of an extensive valley four or five thousand feet below us. Continuing on this magnificent ridge, we descended upon a table of rich land and saw a gate opening into grounds which reminded me of park scenery in England, undulating, and ornamented with trees. In the midst of this stood the hacienda of San José, a long, low stone building with a corridor in front. It was one of those situations which, when least expected, touch a tender chord, call up cherished associa-

---

4. If there ever was a Guatemalan village called El Puente (The Bridge), it seems to have disappeared.

tions, and make a traveler feel as though he could linger around it forever; it was particularly welcome to us, as we had not breakfasted.

It was a *hacienda de ganados*, or cattle hacienda, with hundreds of cattle roaming over it; but all that it could give us to eat were eggs, tortillas, and beans softened in hot water, the last being about equal to a basket of fresh chips. This over, we made a last push for Guatemala. The road lay over a table of land, green and rich as a European lawn, ornamented with trees, and with features of scenery peculiarly English. Muleteers, who had left the city at midnight and had already finished their day's work, were lying under the shade of the trees, with their saddles and cargoes piled up like walls and their mules pasturing near. Along the table was a line of huts, and if adorned instead of being deformed by the hand of man, this would be a region of poetic beauty. Indians, men and women, with loads on their backs, every party with a bundle of rockets, were returning from the "Capitol," [5] as they proudly called it, to their villages among the mountains. All told us that two days before Carrera had re-entered the city with his soldiers.

When we were yet two leagues from the city, Augustin's horse gave out, but being anxious to have a view of the city before dark, I rode on. Late in the afternoon, as I was ascending a small eminence, two immense volcanoes stood up before me, seeming to scorn the earth and towering to the heavens. They were the great volcanoes of Agua and Fuego, forty miles distant, and nearly fifteen thousand feet high, wonderfully grand and beautiful. In a few moments the great plain of Guatemala appeared in view, surrounded by mountains; in its center was the city, a mere speck on the vast expanse, with churches and convents, and numerous turrets, cupolas, and steeples, still as if the spirit of peace rested upon it. It had no storied associations, but by its own

5. An attempt has been made throughout the text to correct Stephens' frequent misspellings of Spanish words. In this instance, however, Stephens may have been intentionally recording an Indian pronunciation.

beauty it created an impression on the mind of a traveler which could never be effaced. I dismounted and tied my mule. As yet the sun lighted up the roofs and domes of the city, giving a reflection so dazzling that I could only look at them by stealth. By degrees its disk touched the top of the Volcán de Agua; slowly the whole orb sank behind it, illuminating the background with an atmosphere fiery red. A rich golden cloud rolled up its side and rested on the top and, while I gazed, the golden hues disappeared and the glory of the scene was gone.

Augustin came along with his poor horse hobbling after him and a pistol in his hand. He had been told on the way that Carrera's soldiers were riotous and that there were many ladrones about the suburbs of the city; he was in the humor to fire upon anyone who asked a question. I made him put up his pistols, and we both mounted. An immense ravine was still between us and the city. It was very dark when we reached the bottom of this ravine, and we were almost trodden down by a caravan of loaded mules coming out. Rising on the other side to the top, we entered the outer gate to the city, still a mile and a half from Guatemala. Inside were miserable huts, with large fires before them, surrounded by groups of drunken Indians and vagabond soldiers firing their muskets at random in the air. Augustin told me to spur, but his poor horse could not keep up, and we were obliged to move on at a walk. As yet I did not know where to stop; there was no hotel in Guatemala. What's the use of a hotel in Guatemala? Who ever goes to Guatemala? were the answers of a gentleman of that place to my inquiries on this subject. I had several letters of introduction, and one was to Mr. Hall, the English vice-consul; fortunately, I resolved to throw myself upon his hospitality.

We picked up a ragged Indian, who undertook to conduct us to the vice-consul's house, and under his guidance we entered the city at the foot of a long straight street. My country-bred mule seemed astonished at the sight of so many houses; he would not cross the gutters, which were wide and in the middle of the street. In spurring her over one, she gave a leap that, after her hard journey, made me proud of her, but she broke her bridle and I was obliged to dismount and lead her. Augustin's poor beast was really past carrying him, and he followed on foot, whipping mine, the guide lending a hand before and behind. In this way we traversed the streets of Guatemala. Perhaps no diplomatist ever made a more unpretending entry into a capital. Our stupid Indian did not know where Mr. Hall lived and there were hardly any people in the streets to inquire of; I was an hour hauling my mule over the gutters and grumbling at the guide before I found the house. I knocked some time without receiving any answer. At length a young man opened the shutter of a balconied window, and told me that Mr. Hall was not at home. This would not serve my turn. I gave my name, and he retired; in a few minutes the large door was unlocked and Mr. Hall, himself, received me. He gave me a reason for not opening the door sooner, saying that the soldiers had mutinied that day for want of pay, and had threatened to sack the city. Carrera had exerted himself in trying to pacify them, and had borrowed fifty dollars from his (Mr. Hall's) neighbor, a French merchant. But the inhabitants were greatly alarmed and, when I knocked at his door, he had been afraid that the soldiers were beginning to put their threat into execution. Mr. Hall had taken down his staff, because on their last entry when he had had his flag flying, the soldiers had fired upon it, calling it a *bandera de guerra*. They were mostly Indians from the villages, ignorant and insolent. A few days before he had his hat knocked off by a sentinel because he did not raise it in passing, for which his complaint was then before the government.[6] The whole city was kept in a state of awe. No one ventured out at night, and Mr. Hall wondered how I had been able to wander through the streets without being molested. All this was not very agreeable, but it could not destroy my satisfaction in reaching Guatemala. For the first time since I entered the country, I had a good bed and a pair of clean sheets. It was two months that day since I

---

6. Stephens comments that "It is due to Carrera to say that by his orders the soldier received two hundred lashes."

embarked from New York and only one since I entered the country, but it seemed at least a year.

The luxury of my rest that night still lingers in my recollections, and the morning air was the most pure and invigorating I ever breathed. Situated in the *tierras templadas*, or temperate regions, on a tableland five thousand feet above the sea, the climate of Guatemala is that of perpetual spring. The general aspect reminded me of the best class of Italian cities. It is laid out in regular blocks of from three to four hundred feet square, the streets crossing each other at right angles. The houses, made to resist the action of earthquakes, are of only one story, but very spacious, with large doors and windows protected by iron balconies. In the center of the city stands the plaza, a square of one hundred and fifty yards on each side, paved with stone, with a colonnade on three sides. On one side stands the old viceregal palace and hall of the Audiencia; on another are the cabildo and other city buildings; on the third the customhouse and palace of the ci-devant Marquisate of Aycinena; and situated between the archiepiscopal palace and the Colegio de Infantes is the Cathedral, a beautiful edifice in the best style of modern architecture. In the center is a large stone fountain of imposing workmanship which is supplied with pipes from the mountains about two leagues distant; the area is used as a market place. The churches and convents correspond with the beauty of the plaza, and their costliness and grandeur would attract the attention of tourists in Italy or old Spain.

The foundation of the city was laid in 1776, a year memorable in our own annals, and a time when our ancestors thought but little of the troubles of their neighbors. At that time the old capital, twenty-five miles distant, shattered and destroyed by earthquakes, was abandoned by its inhabitants and the present city built in the rich valley of Las Vacas, in a style commensurate with the dignity of a captaincy-general of Spain. I have seldom been more favorably impressed with the first appearance of any city, and the only thing that pained me in a two hours' stroll through the streets was the sight of Carrera's ragged and insolent-looking soldiers; my first thought was that in any city in Europe or the United States the citizens, instead of submitting to be lorded over by such barbarians, would rise en masse and pitch them out of the gates. In the course of the morning I took possession of the house that had been occupied by Mr. DeWitt, our late chargé d'affaires. If I had been favorably impressed with the external appearance of the houses, I was charmed with the interior. The entrance was by a large double door through a passage paved with small black and white stones into a handsome patio or courtyard paved in like manner. On the sides were broad corridors paved with square red bricks, and along the foot of the corridors were borders of flowers. In front, on the street, and adjoining the entrance, was an anteroom with one large balconied window, and next to it was a *sala*, or parlor, with two windows. At the farther end a door opened from the side into the *comedor*, or dining room. At the end of the dining room was a door leading to a sleeping room, which, in turn, had a door which led into another room of the same size, all also had doors and windows opening upon the corridor. The building and corridor were continued across the foot of the lot; in the center were rooms for servants, and in the corners were a kitchen and stable, completely hidden from sight and each furnished with a separate fountain. This is the plan of all the houses in Guatemala; others are much larger—as, for instance, that of the Aycinena family which covered a square of two hundred feet—but mine combined more beauty and comfort than any habitation I ever saw.

At two o'clock my luggage arrived, and I was most comfortably installed in my new domicile. The *sala*, or reception room, was furnished with a large bookcase, containing rows of books with yellow bindings, which gave me twinging recollections of a law office at home; the archives of the legation had quite an imposing aspect. Over Mr. DeWitt's writing table hung another memorial of home: a facsimile of the Declaration of Independence.

My first business was to make arrangements to send a trusty escort for Mr. Catherwood; with this accomplished, it was incumbent upon me to look around for the government to which I was accredited.

From the time of the conquest, the Kingdom of Guatemala had remained in a state of profound tranquillity as a colony of Spain. The Indians submitted quietly to the authority of the whites, and all bowed to the divine right of the Romish Church. In the beginning of the present century a few scattering rays of light penetrated to the heart of the American Continent, and in 1823 the Kingdom of Guatemala, as it was then called, declared its independence of Spain; after a short union with Mexico, it constituted itself a republic under the name of the United States of Central America. By the articles of agreement the confederacy was composed of five states: Guatemala, El Salvador, Honduras, Nicaragua, and Costa Rica. Chiapas had the privilege of entering the union if it should think proper, but it never did. Quezaltenago, a district of Guatemala, was afterward erected into a separate state and added to the confederacy.

The monster party-spirit was rocked in the very cradle of their independence, and a line of demarcation was at once drawn between the aristocratic and democratic parties. The local names of these at first confused me, the former being called the Central, or Servile, and the latter the Federal, or Liberal or Democratic Party. Substantially they were the same as our own Federal and Democratic Parties. The reader will perhaps find it difficult to understand that in any country, in a political sense, Federal and Democratic can mean the same thing, or that when I speak of a Federalist I mean a Democrat; to prevent confusion in referring to them hereafter, I shall call the aristocratic, the Central, and the democratic, the Liberal Party. The former, like our own Federal Party, was for consolidating and centralizing the powers of the general government, and the latter contended for the sovereignty of the states. The Central Party consisted of a few leading families, who had, by reason of certain privileges of monopoly for importations under the old Spanish government, assumed the tone of nobles, sustained by the priests and friars, and the religious feeling of the country. The Liberal Party was composed of men of intellect and energy; they had thrown off the yoke of the Romish Church and, in the first enthusiasm of emancipated minds, tore away at once the black mantle of superstition which had been thrown like a funeral pall over the genius of the people. The Centralists wished to preserve the usages of the colonial system, and they resisted every innovation and every attack, direct or indirect, upon the privileges of the Church and their own prejudices or interests. The Liberals, ardent and cherishing brilliant schemes of reform, aimed at an instantaneous change in popular feelings and customs, and they considered every moment lost that did not establish some new theory or sweep away some old abuse. The Centralists forgot that civilization is a jealous divinity which does not admit of partition and cannot remain stationary. The Liberals forgot that civilization requires a harmony of intelligence, of customs, and of laws. The example of the United States and of their free institutions was held up by the Liberals; but the Centralists contended that, with their ignorant and heterogeneous population, scattered over a vast territory without facilities of communication, it was a hallucination to take our country as a model. At the third session of Congress the parties came to an open rupture, and the deputies of El Salvador, always the most liberal state in the confederacy, withdrew.

Flores, the vice-chief of the State of Guatemala, a Liberal, had made himself odious to the priests and friars by laying a contribution upon the convent at Quezaltenango. While he was on a visit to that place, the friars of the convent had excited the populace against him as an enemy to religion. A mob had gathered before his house with cries of "Death to the heretic!" Flores fled to the church, but as he was entering the door a mob of women seized him, wrested a stick from his hands, beat him with it, tore off his cap, and dragged him by the hair. He escaped from these furies and ran up into the pulpit. The alarm bell was sounded, and all the rabble of the town poured into the plaza. A few soldiers endeavored to cover the entrance to the church, but were assailed with stones and clubs; and the mob, bearing down all opposition, forced its way into the church, making the roof ring with cries of "Death to the heretic!" Rushing toward the pulpit, some tried to unhinge it, others to scale it. Others struck at the unhappy vice-chief with knives tied to the ends of long poles, while a young fiend, with one foot on the mouldings of the pulpit and the other elevated in the air, leaned over and seized him by the hair. The curate, who was in the pulpit with him, frightened at the tempest he had assisted to raise, held up the Holy of Holies, and begged the mob to spare Flores, promising that he should leave the city immediately. The unhappy Flores, on his knees, confirmed these promises, but the friars urged on the mob, who became so excited with religious frenzy that, after kneeling before the figure of the Saviour exclaiming, "We adore thee, Oh Lord, we venerate thee," rose up with the ferocious cry, "but for thy honor and glory this blasphemer, this heretic, must die!" They dragged him from the pulpit across the floor of the church, and in the cloisters threw him into the hands of the fanatic and furious horde, where the women, like unchained furies, with their fists, sticks, and stones, beat him to death. His murderers stripped his body, leaving it disfigured and an object of horror, exposed to the insults of the populace, and then they dispersed throughout the city, demanding the heads of Liberals, and crying *"Viva la Religión, y mueran los herejes del Congreso."* About the same time religious fanaticism swept the state, and the Liberal Party was crushed in Guatemala.

But the state of El Salvador, from the beginning the leader in liberal principles, was prompt in its efforts of vengeance, and on the sixteenth of March, 1827, its army appeared within the outer gates of Guatemala, threatening the destruction of the capital. But religious fanaticism was too strong; the priests ran through the streets exhorting the people to take up arms, the friars headed mobs of women who with drawn knives swore destruction to all who attempted to overturn their religion; and the Salvadorans were defeated and driven back. For two years the parties were at open war. In 1829 the troops of El Salvador, under General Morazán, who had now become the head of the Liberal Party, again marched upon Guatemala and, after three days' fighting, entered the city in triumph. All the leaders of the Central Party, the Aycinenas, the Pavons, and Peñoles, were banished or fled; the convents were broken up, the institution of friars was abolished, and the friars themselves put on board vessels and shipped out of the country; the archbishop, anticipating banishment, or perhaps fearing a worse fate, sought safety in flight.

In 1831 General Morazán was elected president of the republic; at the expiration of his term he was re-elected, and for eight years the Liberal Party had the complete ascendancy. During the latter part of his term, however, there was great discontent, particularly on account of forced loans and exactions for the support of government, or, as the Centralists said, to gratify the rapacity of unscrupulous and profligate officeholders. The Church party was always on the alert. The exiles in the United States and Mexico, and on the frontier, with their eyes always fixed upon home, kept up constant communications and fostered the growing discontents. Some of them, in a state of penury abroad, ventured to return, and when these were not molested, others soon followed. At this time came the rise of Carrera, which was at first more dreaded by the Centralists than by the Liberals, but suddenly, and to the Centralists' utter astonishment, his rise to power placed them nominally at the head of government.

In the May preceding my arrival, the term of the president, senators, and deputies expired, and no elections had been held to supply their places. The vice-president, who had been elected during an unexpired term, was the only existing officer of the Federal government. The states of Guatemala, Honduras, Nicaragua, and Costa Rica had declared themselves independent of the Federal government. The states of El Salvador and Quezaltenango sustained the Federal government, and Morazán, as commander-in-chief of the Federal forces, had defeated Ferrera and established troops in Honduras, which gave the Liberal Party the actual control of three states.

Virtually, then, the states stood "three and three." Where was my government? The last Central American Congress, before its dissolution, had recommended that panacea for political ills, a convention to amend the Constitution. The governments of England and France were represented in Central America by consuls-general. Neither had any treaty with Central America. England could not procure one except by the surrender of all claim to the Island of Roatán in the Gulf of Honduras, and to Belize. One had been drawn up with France, but, though pressed with great earnestness by the consul-general of that country, the senate refused to ratify it. The government of the United States was the only government that had any treaty with Central America, and up to the time of Mr. DeWitt's departure from the country, we were represented by a chargé d'affaires. The British consul-general had published a circular denying the existence of the general government, and the French consul was not on good terms with either party. My arrival, and the course I might take, were a subject of some interest to politicians.

There was but one side to politics in Guatemala. Both parties had a beautiful way of producing unanimity of opinion by driving out of the country all who did not agree with them. If there were any Liberals, I did not meet them, or they did not dare to open their lips. The Central Party, only six months in power, and still surprised at being there, was fluttering between arrogance and fear. The old families, whose principal members had been banished or politically ostracized, and the clergy were elated at the expulsion of the Liberal Party, and their return to what they considered their natural right to rule the state. They talked of recalling the banished archbishop and friars, restoring the privileges of the Church, repairing the convents, reviving monastic institutions, and making Guatemala what it had once been, the jewel of Spanish America.

One of my first visits of ceremony was to Señor Rivera Paz, the chief of state. I was presented by Mr. Henry Savage, who had formerly acted as United States consul at Guatemala. He was the only American resident there and to him I am under many obligations for his constant attentions. The State of Guatemala, having declared its independence of the Federal government, was at that time governed by a temporary body called a Constituent Assembly. On the last entry of Carrera into the city, in the March preceding my arrival, Salazar, the chief of state, fled; Carrera, on horseback, knocked at the door of Señor Rivera

Paz before daylight and, by his individual pleasure, installed him as chief. It was a fortunate choice for the people of Guatemala. He was about thirty-eight and gentlemanly in his appearance and manners; in all the trying positions in which he was afterward placed, he exhibited more than ordinary prudence and judgment.

I had been advised that it would be agreeable to the government of Guatemala for me to present my credentials to the chief of that state, and afterward to the chiefs of the other states, and that the states separately would treat of the matters for which I was accredited to the general government. The object of this was to preclude a recognition on my part of the power which was, or claimed to be, the general government. The suggestion was of course preposterous, but it showed the dominion of party spirit with men who knew better. Señor Rivera Paz expressed his regret at my happening to visit the country at such an unfortunate period; he assured me of the friendly disposition of that state, and that it would do all in its power to serve me. During my visit I was introduced to several of the leading members of the administration, and I left with a favorable opinion of Rivera Paz, which was never shaken in regard to him personally.

In the evening, in company with Mr. Hall, I attended the last meeting of the Constituent Assembly, which was held in the old Hall of Congress. The room was large, hung with portraits of old Spaniards distinguished in the history of the country, and dimly lighted. The deputies sat on a platform at one end, elevated about six feet, the president on an elevation in a large chair, and two secretaries at a table beneath. On the wall were the arms of the republic, the groundwork of which was three volcanoes, emblematic, I suppose, of the combustible state of the country. The deputies sat on each side, about thirty being present, nearly half of whom were priests with black gowns and caps. By the dull light, the scene carried me back to the dark ages and seemed a meeting of inquisitors.

The subject under discussion was a motion to revive the old law of tithes, which had been abolished by the Liberal

Party. The law was passed unanimously; but there was a discussion upon a motion to appropriate a small part of the proceeds for the support of hospitals for the poor. The priests took part in the discussion, and with liberal sentiments; but a lay member, with big black whiskers, opposed it, saying that the Church stood like a light in darkness, and the Marquis of Aycinena, a priest and the leading member of the party, said that "what was raised for God should be given to God alone." There was another discussion as to whether the law should operate upon cattle then in being, or also upon those to be born thereafter, and finally, as to the means of enforcing it. One gentleman contended that coercive measures should not be used and, with a fine burst of eloquence, said that reliance might be placed upon the religious feelings of the people, that the poorest Indian would come forward and contribute his mite. But the Assembly decided that the law should be enforced by *Las leyes antiguas de los Españoles*, the old laws of the Spaniards, the severities of which had been one of the great causes of revolution in all Spanish countries. There was something horrible in this retrograde legislation. I could hardly realize that, in the nineteenth century, men of sense, in a country through the length and breadth of which free principles were struggling for the ascendancy, would dare fasten on the people a yoke which, even in the dark ages, was too galling to be borne. The tone of debate was respectable, but it was calm and unimpassioned, from the entire absence of any opposition party. Yet the Assembly purported to be a popular body, representing the voice of the people. It was a time of great excitement, and the last night of the session; Mr. Hall and I, in addition to four men and three boys were the only listeners.

As it was not safe to be in the streets after eight o'clock, the Assembly was adjourned. After a short session the next morning, it assembled at a state breakfast. The place of meeting was in the old library, a venerable room containing a valuable collection of rare old Spanish books and manuscripts, among which had lately been discovered the two missing volumes of Fuentes, and where I promised myself much satisfaction. The only guests were Mr. Hall, the French consul-general, Colonel Monte Rosa, an aide of Carrera, and myself. Carrera had been invited but had not come. The table was profusely ornamented with flowers and fruits. There was very little wine drunk, no toasts, and no gaiety. There was not a gray-haired man at table; all were young, and so connected that it seemed a large family party. More than half of them had been in exile, and if Morazán returned to power they would all be scattered again.

I had been but three days in Guatemala, and already the place was dull. The clouds which hung over the political horizon weighed upon the spirits of the inhabitants, and in the evening I was obliged to shut myself up in my house alone. In the uncertainty which hung over my movements, and to avoid the trouble of housekeeping for perhaps a few weeks, I dined and supped at the house of the señora, an interesting young widow, who owned my house (her husband had been shot in a private revolution of his own getting up) and lived nearly opposite. The first evening I remained there till nine o'clock; but as I was crossing on my return home a fierce *"Quién vive?* (Who goes?)" *"Qué gente?* (What people?)" *"Qué Regimiento?* (What regiment?)" and then fire. One fellow had already obeyed his orders literally and, hurrying through the three questions without waiting for answers, fired and shot a woman. The answers were, *"Patria Libre* (Country free)"; *"Paisano* (Country-man)"; and *"Paz* (Peace)."

This challenge was a subject of annoyance all the time I was in Guatemala. The streets were not lighted and, hearing it, sometimes at the distance of a square, in a ferocious voice, without being able to see the sentinel, I always imagined him with his musket at his shoulder, peering through the darkness to take aim. I felt less safe by reason of my foreign pronunciation; but I never met anyone, native or stranger, who was not nervous when within reach of the sentinel's challenge, or who would not go two squares out of the way to avoid it.

Chapter X

~~~~~~

Hacienda of Naranjo. Lassoing. Diplomatic correspond-
ence. Formulas. Fête of La Concepción. Taking the black
veil. A countrywoman. Renouncing the world. Fireworks.
Procession in honor of the Virgin. Another exhibition of
fireworks. A fiery bull. Insolent soldiery.

THE next day, in company with Mr. Savage, I rode to
Naranjo, a small hacienda of the Aycinena family,
about seven miles from the city; beyond the walls all was
beautiful. In the palmy days of Guatemala, the Aycinenas
rolled to the Naranjo in an enormous carriage, full of
carving and gilding, in the style of the grandees of Spain;
the carriage now stands in the courtyard of the family house
as a memorial of better days. We entered by a large gate
into a road upon their land, undulating and ornamented
with trees. We rode around the borders of a large artificial
lake, made by damming up several streams, and entered a
large cattle yard, in the center of which, on the side of a declivity, stood the house, a strong stone structure with a broad
piazza in front which commanded a beautiful view of the
volcanoes of Antigua.

The hacienda was only valuable because of its vicinity to
Guatemala, being what would be called at home a country-
seat; it contained only seven thousand acres of land, about
seventy mules, and seven hundred head of cattle. It was
the season for marking and numbering the cattle, and two
of the Señores Aycinena were at the hacienda to superintend
the operations. The cattle had already been caught and
brought in, but as I had never seen the process of lassoing,
after dinner a hundred head which had been kept for two

days without food were let loose into a field two or three miles in circumference. Eight men were mounted, with iron spurs an inch long on their naked heels. Each held a lasso in hand, which consisted of an entire cow's hide cut into a single cord about twenty yards long; one end was fastened to the horse's tail, which was first wrapped in leaves to prevent its being lacerated, and the rest, wound into a coil, was held by the rider in his right hand, which rested on the pommel of the saddle. The cattle had all dispersed; we placed ourselves on an elevation commanding a partial view of the field, and the riders scattered in search of them. In a little while thirty or forty cattle rushed past, followed by the riders at full speed, and very soon they were out of sight. We had either to lose the sport or follow; and in one of the doublings, taking particularly good care to avoid the throng of furious cattle and headlong riders, I drew up to the side of two men who were chasing a single ox, and followed over hill, through bush, brush, and underwood. Finally one rider threw his lasso beautifully over the horns of the ox and then turned his horse; the ox bounded to the length of the lasso and, without shaking horse or rider, pitched headlong to the ground.

At this moment a herd swept by with the whole company in full pursuit. A large yellow ox separated from the rest and all followed him. For a mile he kept ahead, doubling and dodging, but the horsemen crowded him down toward the lake and, after an ineffectual attempt to bolt, he rushed into the water. Two horsemen followed and drove him out and gave him a start, but in a few moments the lasso whizzed over his head and, while horse and rider stood like marble, the ox again came with a plunge to the ground. The riders scattered, and one horse and rider rolled over in such a way that I thought every bone in the rider's body must be broken. The sport was so exciting that I, who at the beginning had been particularly careful to keep out of harm's way, felt very much disposed to have my own horse's tail tied up and to take a lasso in my hand. The effect of the sport was heightened by the beauty of the scene, with the great volcanoes of Agua and Fuego towering above us and, toward evening, throwing a deep shade over the plain. It was nearly dark when we returned to the house. With that refinement of politeness (which I believe is exclusively Spanish) the gentlemen escorted us some distance on our road back to the city. At dark we reached Guatemala and, to our great satisfaction, learned at the gate that the soldiers were confined to the barracks.

The news of my arrest and imprisonment, with great exaggeration of circumstance, had reached Guatemala before me, and I was advised that the state government intended to make me a communication on the subject. I waited several days and, not receiving any, made a formal complaint, setting forth the facts and concluding that I would not attempt to suggest what ought to be done, but felt satisfied that the government would do what was consistent with its own honor and the rights of a friendly nation. In a few days I received an answer from the Secretary of State, conveying the regrets of the President for the occurrence, and stating that, before receiving my note, the government had taken the measures which it deemed proper in the premises. This was very indefinite. I bore considerable anger against the parties concerned and, moreover, I had heard out of doors something about these "measures." For the future protection of Americans who were or might be in that country, I considered it necessary to see to it that so notorious an outrage not be treated lightly With this in mind, I addressed a further note to the Secretary, asking specifically whether the officer and alcalde referred to had been punished, and if so, in what way. To this I received for answer that, in the circumstances in which the country was placed by means of an extraordinary popular revolution, and because of the distrust prevailing in the frontier villages, local authorities were more suspicious than usual in the matter of passports; and that the outrage, *el atropellamiento*, which I had suffered, had had its origin in the orders of a military officer, *un oficial militar*, who suspected that I and my companion were "enemies"; and that General Cascara, as soon as he was informed of the circumstances, had removed the officer from his command. The reply went on to say that the government, much to its regret, because of the difficult circumstances in which the country was placed, did not have the power to give that security to travelers which it desired to give, but that it would issue preventive orders to the local authorities to secure me in my further travels.

I had understood that General Cascara had removed the officer, but the intelligence was hardly received in Guatemala before Carrera ordered him to be restored; and I afterward saw in a San Salvador paper that the officer had threatened to shoot General Cascara if his degradation was not revoked. In further communications with the secretary and the chief of the state, they confessed their inability to do anything, and being satisfied that they desired to do something even more than myself, I did not consider it worth while to press the subject; indeed, in strictness, I had no right to call upon the state government. The general government had not the least particle of power in the state, and I mention this circumstance to show the utter feebleness of the administration and the wretched condition of the country generally. It troubled me on one account, as it showed the difficulty and danger of prosecuting the travels I had contemplated.

From the moment of my arrival I was struck with the devout character of the city of Guatemala. At matins and vespers the churches were all open, and the people, particularly the women, went regularly to prayers. Every house had its figure of the Virgin, the Saviour, or some tutelary saint, and on the door were billets of paper with prayers:

La verdadera sangre de Cristo, nuestro redentor que sólo representado en Egipto libró a los Israelitas de un brazo fuerte y poderoso, líbrenos de la peste, guerra, y muerte repentina. Amén. (The true blood of Christ our Redeemer, which merely exhibited in Egypt, freed the Israelites from a strong and powerful arm, deliver us from pestilence, war, and sudden death. Amen.)

O María, concebida sin pecado, rogad por nosotros, que recurrimos a vos. (O Virgin, conceived without sin, pray for us, who have recourse to thee.)

Ave María, gracia plena, y la santísima Trinidad nos favorezca. (Hail Mary, full of grace, and may the Holy Trinity favour us.)

El dulce nombre de Jesús
Sea con nosotros. Amén.

On the first Sunday after my arrival was celebrated the
fête of La Concepción, a fête always honored in the observances of the Catholic Church and more important this day
from the circumstance that a probationer in the convent of
La Concepción intended to take the black veil. At break of
day the church bells rang throughout the city, cannon were
fired in the plaza and rockets and fireworks set off at the
corners of the streets. At nine o'clock crowds of people were
hurrying to the Church of La Concepción. Before the door,
and extending across the streets, were arches decorated with
evergreens and flowers. The broad steps of the church were
strewed with pine leaves, and on the platform were men
firing rockets. The church was one of the handsomest in
Guatemala, rich with gold and silver ornaments, pictures,
and figures of saints, and adorned with arches and flowers.
The Padre Aycinena, the vice-president of the state and the
leading member of the Constituent Assembly, was the
preacher of the day, and his high reputation attracted a
large concourse of people. The pulpit was at one end of the
church, and the great mass of people who faced it were anxious to hear the sermon. The other end was comparatively
vacant, and I placed myself on a step of the nearest altar,
directly in front of the grating of the convent. At the close
of the sermon there was a discharge of rockets and crackers
from the steps of the church, the smoke of which clouded
the interior; the smell of powder was stronger than that of
the burning incense. The floor was strewed with pine leaves
and covered with kneeling women, each with a black man-
tilla drawn close over the top of the head and held together
under the chin. I never saw a more beautiful spectacle than
these rows of kneeling women, their faces pure and lofty in
expression, lighted up by the enthusiasm of religion. Among
them, fairer than most and lovely as any, was one from my
own land; not more than twenty-two, she was married to a
gentleman belonging to one of the first families of Guatemala, a gentleman who was once an exile in the United
States. In a new land and among a new people, she had embraced a new faith; with the enthusiasm of a youthful convert, no lady in Guatemala was more devout, more regular

at mass, or more strict in all the discipline of the Catholic Church than the Sister Susannah.

After the fireworks there was a long ceremony at the altar, and then a general rush toward the other extremity of the church. The convent was directly adjoining, and in the partition wall, about six feet from the floor, was a high iron grating; about four feet beyond it was another grating at which the nuns attended the services of the church. Above the iron grating was a wooden one, and from this in a few minutes issued a low strain of wild Indian music. Presently a figure in white, with a long white veil and a candle in her right hand and both arms extended, walked slowly to within a few feet of the grating, and then as slowly retired. Presently the same low note issued from the grating below, and we saw advancing a procession of white nuns, with long white veils, each holding in her hand a long lighted candle. The music ceased and a chant arose, so low that it required intent listening to catch the sound. Advancing two and two with this low chant to within a few feet of the grating, the sisters turned off different ways. At the end of the procession were two black nuns, leading between them the probationer dressed in white, with a white veil and a wreath of roses round her head. The white nuns arranged themselves on each side, their chant ceased and the voice of the probationer was heard alone, but so faint that it seemed the breathing of a spirit of air. The white nuns strewed flowers before her, and she advanced between the two black ones. Three times she stopped and kneeled, continuing the same low chant, and the last time the white nuns gathered around her, strewing flowers upon her head and in her path. Slowly they led her to the back part of the chapel, and all kneeled before the altar.

At this time a strain of music was heard at the other end of the church. A way was cleared through the crowd and a procession advanced, consisting of the principal priests clothed in their richest robes, and headed by the venerable provisor, an octogenarian with white hair and tottering on the verge of the grave, who was as remarkable for the piety of his life as for his venerable appearance. A layman bore on a rich frame a gold crown and scepter studded with jewels. The procession advanced to a small door on the right of the grating, and the two black nuns and the probationer appeared in the doorway. Some words passed between her and the provisor, which I understood to be an examination by him of whether her proposed abandonment of the world was voluntary or not. This over, the provisor removed the wreath of roses and the white veil, and put on her head the crown and in her hand the scepter. The music sounded loud notes of triumph and in a few moments she reappeared at the grating with the crown and scepter and a dress sparkling with jewels. The sisters embraced her and again threw roses upon her. It seemed horrible to heap upon her the pomp and pleasures of the world at the moment when she was about to bid farewell to them forever. Again she kneeled before the altar; and when she rose the jewels and precious stones, the rich ornaments with which she was decorated, were taken from her, and she returned to the bishop, who took away the crown and scepter, and put on her head the black veil. Once again she appeared before the grating for the last, the fatal step was not yet taken: the black veil was not drawn. Again the nuns pressed round, and this time they almost devoured her with kisses.

I knew nothing of her story. I had not heard that the ceremony was to take place till late in the evening before, and I had made up my mind that she would be old and ugly; but she was not, nor was she faded and worn with sorrow, the picture of a broken heart, nor yet a young and beautiful enthusiast. She was not more than twenty-three and had one of those good faces which, without setting men wild by their beauty, bear the impress of a nature well qualified for the performance of all duties belonging to daughter and wife and mother, speaking the kindliness and warmth of a woman's heart. It was a pale face, and she seemed conscious of the important step and the solemn vows she was taking, and to have no pangs—yet, who can read what is passing in the human breast?

She returned to the provisor who drew over her face a black veil; and music rose in bursts of rejoicing that one who was given to the world to take a share in its burdens had withdrawn herself from it. Immediately commenced the hum of restrained voices and, working my way through the crowd, I joined a party of ladies, one of whom was my fair countrywoman. She was from a small country town in Pennsylvania, and the romance of her feelings toward convents and nuns had not yet worn off. On Carrera's first invasion she had taken refuge in the convent of La Concepción, and she spoke with enthusiasm of the purity and piety of the nuns, describing some as surpassing in all the attributes of woman. She knew particularly the one who had just taken the veil, and told me that in a few days the nun would appear at the grating of the convent to embrace her friends and bid them farewell, and she promised to take me there and procure for me a share in the distribution.

During this time rockets were fired from the steps, and in the street, immediately in front, was a frame of fireworks thirty feet high, which the whole crowd waited on the steps and in the street to see set off. Everybody spoke of the absurdity of such an exhibition by daylight, but they said it was the custom. The piece was complicated in its structure, and in the center was a large box. There was a whizzing of wheels, a great smoke, and occasionally a red flash; and for the finale, as the extremities burned out, with a smart cracking the box flew open and, when the smoke cleared away, disclosed the figure of a little black nun, at which all laughed and went away.

In the afternoon there was a procession in honor of the Virgin. Although Guatemala was dull and, by the convulsions of the times, debarred all kinds of gaiety, religious processions went on as usual; it would have been an evidence of an expiring state to neglect them. All the streets through which the procession was to pass were strewed with pine leaves, and crossing them were arches decorated with evergreens and flowers. The long balconied windows were ornamented with curtains of crimson silk and flags with fanciful devices. At the corners of the streets were altars, under arbors of evergreens as high as the tops of the houses, which were adorned with pictures and silver ornaments from the churches, the whole being covered with flowers. Rich as the whole of Central America is in natural productions, the valley of Guatemala is distinguished for the beauty and variety of its flowers. For one day the fields had been stripped of their clothing to beautify the city. I have seen great fêtes in Europe, got up with lavish expenditure of money, but never anything so simply beautiful. My stroll through the streets before the procession was the most interesting part of the day. All the inhabitants, in their best dresses, were there: the men standing at the corners, and the women, in black mantillas, seated in long rows on each side. The flags and curtains in the balconied windows, the green of the streets, the profusion of flowers, the vistas through the arches, and the simplicity of manners which permitted ladies of the first class to mingle freely in the crowd and sit along the street, formed a picture of beauty that even now relieves the stamp of dullness with which Guatemala is impressed upon my mind.

The procession for which all these beautiful preparations had been made opened with a single Indian, old, wrinkled, dirty, ragged, bareheaded, and staggering under the load of an enormous bass drum, which he carried on his back; the drum seemed as old as the conquest, with every cord and the head on one side broken. Another Indian in the same ragged costume followed him with one ponderous drumstick, with which from time to time he struck the old drum. Then came an Indian with a large whistle, corresponding in venerableness of aspect to the drum. From time to time, he gave a fierce blast on the whistle and looked around with a comical air of satisfaction for applause. Next followed a little boy about ten years old, wearing a cocked hat, boots above his knees, a drawn sword, and the mask of a hideous African. He was marshaling twenty or thirty persons not inaptly called "the Devils," all wearing grotesque and hideous masks and ragged, fantastic dresses; some had reed whistles, some were knocking sticks together. The principal actors were two pseudo-women, with broad-brimmed European hats, frocks which were high in the neck with the waist across the breast, large boots, and each with an old guitar,

waltzing and dancing an occasional fandango. How it happened that these devils, who of course excited laughter in
the crowd, came to form part of a religious procession, I
could not learn. The boys followed them just as they do the
military with us on a Fourth of July; in fact, with the Guatemala boys, there is no good procession without good devils.

Next, and in striking contrast, came four beautiful boys,
six or eight years old, dressed in white frocks and pantalettes,
with white gauze veils over wreaths of roses, perfect emblems of purity. Then came four young priests, bearing
golden candlesticks, with wax candles lighted. Following the
priests were four Indians, carrying on their shoulders the
figure of an angel larger than life, with expanded wings
made of gauze, and puffed out like a cloud. It was intended
to appear to float in air but it was dressed more after the
fashion of this world, with the frock rather short, and the
suspenders of the stockings of pink ribbons. Then, borne as
before on the shoulders of Indians, and again larger than
life, came the figure of Judith, with a drawn sword in one
hand and the gory head of Holofernes in the other. After
one more angel with a cloud of silk over her head was the
great object of veneration, *La Virgen de la Concepción*, on
a low handbarrow, richly decorated with gold and silver
and a profusion of flowers, and protected by a rich silken
canopy upborne on the ends of four gilded poles. Priests followed in their costly dresses—one under a silken canopy
holding up the Host—before the imaginary splendor of
which all fell on their knees. The whole concluded with a
worse set of devils than those which led the procession: five
hundred of Carrera's soldiers, dirty and ragged, and carrying their muskets without any order, with fanaticism added
to their usual expression of ferocity. The officers were
dressed in any costume they could command. A few, with
black hat and silver or gold band, like footmen, carried their
heads very high; many were lame from gunshot wounds
badly cured. A gentleman who was with me pointed out
several who were known to have committed assassinations
and murders, for which, in a country that had any government, they would have been hung. The city was at their

mercy, and Carrera was the only man living who had any control over them.

At the head of the street the procession filed off into the cross streets, and the figure of the Virgin was taken from its place and set up on the altar. The priests kneeled before it and prayed, and the whole crowd fell on their knees. I was at the corner near the altar which commanded a view of four streets, and rising a little on one knee, saw in all the streets a dense mass of kneeling figures, rich men and beggars, lovely women and stupid-looking Indians, fluttering banners and curtains in balconied windows, and the figures of angels in their light gauze drapery seeming to float in air. The loud chant of the crowd, swollen by the deep chorus of the soldiers' voices, produced a scene of mingled beauty and deformity at once captivating and repulsive. This over, all rose, the Virgin was replaced on her throne, and the procession again moved. At the next altar I turned aside and went to the square in front of the Church of San Francisco, the place fixed for the grand finale of the honors to the Virgin, the exhibition of fireworks!

At dark the procession entered the foot of a street leading to the square. It approached with a loud chant, and at a distance nothing was visible but a long train of burning candles, making the street light as day. The devils were still at its head, and its arrival in the square was announced by a discharge of rockets. In a few minutes the first piece of fireworks was set off from the balustrade of the church; the figures on the roof were lighted by the glare, and, though not built expressly for that purpose, the church answered exceedingly well for the exhibition.

The next piece, on the ground of the square, was a national one called the *Toro*, or Bull, and as much a favorite in an exhibition of fireworks as the devils in a religious procession. It consisted of a frame covered with pasteboard in the form of a bull, on the outside of which were the fireworks. Into this figure of the bull, a man thrust his head and shoulders and then, with nothing but his legs visible, he rushed into the thickest of the crowd, scattering on all sides streams of fire. I was standing with a party of ladies and with several members of the Constituent Assembly who were speaking of an invasion of troops from Quezaltenango, and of the sally of Carrera to repel them. As the *Toro* came at us, we retreated till we could go no farther; the ladies screamed, and we bravely turned our backs and, holding down our heads, sheltered them from the shower of fire. All said it was dangerous, but it was the custom. There was more cheerfulness and gaiety than I had yet seen in Guatemala, and I felt sorry when the exhibition was over.

All day I had felt particularly the influence of the beautiful climate; the mere breathing of the air was a luxury. And the evening was worthy of such a day; the moonbeams were lighting up the façade of the venerable church, showing in sadness a rent made by an earthquake from top to bottom. As we walked home, the streets were lighted with a brilliancy almost unearthly; and the ladies, proud of their moonlight, almost persuaded me that it was a land to love.

Continuing on our way, we passed a guardhouse, where a group of soldiers were lying at full length, so as to make everybody pass off the walk and go round them. Perhaps three or four thousand people, a large portion of them ladies, were turned off. All felt the insolence of these fellows, and I have no doubt some felt a strong disposition to kick them out of the way; but, though young men enough passed to drive the whole troop out of the city, no complaint was made, and no notice whatever taken of it. In one of the corridors of the plaza another soldier lay on his back crosswise with his musket by his side, muttering to everybody that passed, "Tread on me if you dare, and you'll see!" and we all took good care not to tread on him. I returned to my house to pass the evening in solitude, and it was melancholy to reflect that, with the elements of so much happiness, Guatemala was made so miserable.

Chapter XI

THE next three or four days I passed in receiving and
paying visits, and in making myself acquainted with
the condition of the country. Among the most interesting
visitors was the venerable provisor, who, since the banishment of the archbishop, had been acting as head of the
church; by a late bull of the Pope, he had been appointed
bishop, but he had not yet been ordained owing to the
troubled times. A friend in Baltimore had procured for me
a letter from the archbishop in that city, to whom I here
acknowledge my obligations, recommending me to all his
brother ecclesiastics in Central America. The venerable provisor received this letter as from a brother in the Church,
and upon the strength of it, when I set out later for Palenque, gave me a letter of recommendation to all the curas
under his charge.

During the day my time passed agreeably enough; but the
evenings, in which I was obliged to keep within doors, were
long and lonely. My house was so near the plaza that I
could hear the sentinel's challenge and from time to time the
report of a musket. These reports, in the stillness of night,
were always startling. For some time I did not know the
cause; but at length I learned that cows and mules straggled

about the city, and when they were heard moving at a distance and not answering the challenge, they were fired upon without ceremony.

There was but one newspaper in Guatemala, and that a weekly, a mere chronicler of decrees and political movements. City news passed by word of mouth. Every morning everybody asked his neighbor what was the news. One day it was that an old deaf woman, who could not hear the sentinel's challenge, had been shot; another day it was that Asturias, a rich old citizen, had been stabbed; and one morning the report circulated that thirty-three nuns in the convent of Santa Teresa had been poisoned. This latter news was the subject of excitement for several days, until the nuns all recovered and it was ascertained that they had suffered from the unsentimental circumstance of eating food that did not agree with them.

On Friday, in company with my fair countrywoman, I visited the convent of La Concepción for the purpose of embracing a nun, or rather the nun who had taken the black veil. The room adjoining the locutory of the convent was crowded, and she was standing in the doorway with the crown on her head and a doll in her hand. It was the last time her friends could see her face; but this puerile exhibition of the doll detracted from the sentiment. It was an occasion that addressed itself particularly to ladies; some wondered that one so young should abandon a world to them beaming with bright and beautiful prospects; others, for whom the dreams of life had passed, looked upon her retirement as the part of wisdom. They embraced her and retired to make room for others. By her side was a black nun, with a veil so thick that not a lineament of her face could be seen, whom my countrywoman had known during her own seclusion in the convent; she described her as young, of exceeding beauty and loveliness, and around her she threw a charm which almost awakened a spirit of romance. I would have made some sacrifice for one glimpse of her face.

Before our turn came there was an irruption of those objects of my detestation, the eternal soldiers, who, leaving their muskets at the door, forced their way through the crowd, and presenting themselves—though respectfully—for an embrace, retired. At length our turn came; my fair companion embraced her and, after many farewell words, recommended me as her countryman. I had never had much practice in embracing nuns; in fact, it was the first time I ever attempted such a thing, but it came as natural as if I had been brought up to it. My right arm encircled her neck, her right arm mine; I rested my head upon her shoulder, and she hers upon mine; but a friend's grandmother never received a more respectful embrace. "Stolen joys are always dearest"; there were too many looking on. The grating closed, and the face of the nun will never be seen again.

That afternoon Carrera returned to the city. I was extremely desirous to know him, and I made an arrangement with Mr. Pavón to call upon him the next day. At ten o'clock the next morning Mr. Pavón called for me. I was advised that this formidable chief would be taken by external show, so I put on the diplomatic coat with a great profusion of buttons which had produced such an effect at Copán, and which, by the way, owing to the abominable state of the country, I never had an opportunity of wearing afterward; the cost of the coat was a dead loss.

Carrera was living in a small house in a retired street. Sentinels were at the door, and eight or ten soldiers were basking in the sun outside; they were part of a bodyguard, who had been fitted out with red bombazet jackets and tartan plaid caps, and they made a much better appearance than any of his soldiers I had before seen. Along the corridor was a row of muskets, bright and in good order. We entered a small room adjoining the *sala*, and saw Carrera sitting at a table counting money.

Ever since my arrival in the country this name of terror had been ringing in my ears. Mr. Montgomery, to whom I have before referred, and who arrived in Central America about a year before me, says, "An insurrection, I was told, had taken place among the Indians, who, under the directions of a man called Carrera, were ravaging the country and committing all kinds of excesses. Along the coast, and in some of the departments, tranquillity had not been disturbed; but in the interior there was no safety for the traveller, and every avenue to the capital was beset by parties of brigands, who showed no mercy to their victims, especially if they were foreigners." In referring to the posture of affairs at his departure he adds, "It is probable, however, that while this is being written, the active measures of General Morazán for putting down the insurrection have been successful, and that the career of this rebel hero has been brought to a close." But the career of the "rebel hero" was not brought to a close; the "man called Carrera" was now absolute master of Guatemala; and, if I am not deceived, he is destined to become more conspicuous than any other leader who has yet risen in the convulsions of Spanish America.[1]

He is a native of one of the wards of Guatemala City. His friends, in compliment, call him a mulatto; I, for the same reason, call him an Indian, considering that the better blood of the two. In 1829 he had been a drummer boy in Colonel Aycinena's regiment. When the Liberal or Democratic Party prevailed and General Morazán entered the city, Carrera broke his drum and retired to the village of Mataquescuintla. Here he entered into business as a pig driver, and for several years he continued in this respectable occupation, probably as free as one of his own pigs from any dreams of future greatness. The excesses of political parties, severe exactions for the support of government, encroachments upon the property of the Church, and innovations, particularly the introduction of the Livingston Code, which established trial by jury and made marriage a civil contract, created discontent throughout the country. The last gave great offence to the clergy, who exercised an unbounded influence over the minds of the Indians.

In 1837 the cholera, which, in its destructive march over the habitable world had hitherto spared this portion of the American continent, made its terrible appearance, and, besides strewing the land with dead, proved to be the imme-

---

1. From 1840 until his death in 1865 Carrera was the strong man of Guatemala. Elected president in 1847 and re-elected in 1851, he was in 1854 named president for life.

diate cause of political convulsions. The priests persuaded the Indians that the foreigners had poisoned the waters. Gálvez, who was at that time the chief of the state, sent into all the villages medicines which, being ignorantly administered, sometimes produced fatal consequences; and the priests, always opposed to the Liberal Party, persuaded the Indians that the government was endeavoring to poison and destroy their race. The Indians became excited all over the country and, in Mataquescuintla, they rose in mass, with Carrera at their head, crying *Viva la Religión, y muerte a los extranjeros!* The first blow was struck by murdering the judges appointed under the Livingston Code. Gálvez sent a commission with detachments of cavalry and a white flag to hear their complaints, but while conferring with the insurgents, they were surrounded and almost all of them cut to pieces. The number of the disaffected increased to more than a thousand, and Gálvez sent against them six hundred troops, who routed them, plundered and burned their villages, and, among other excesses, perpetrated the last outrage upon Carrera's wife. Roused to fury by this personal wrong, he joined with several chiefs of villages, vowing never to lay down his arms while an officer of Morazán remained in the state. With a few infuriated followers he went from village to village, killing the judges and government officers. When pursued, he escaped to the mountains, begging tortillas at the haciendas for his men, and sparing and protecting all who assisted him.

At this time he could neither read nor write; but, urged on and assisted by some priests, particularly one Padre Lobo, a notorious profligate, he issued a proclamation, with his name stamped at the foot of it, against strangers and the government, for attempting to poison the Indians. He demanded the destruction of all foreigners except the Spaniards, the abolition of the Livingston Code, a recall of the archbishop and friars, the expulsion of heretics, and a restoration of the privileges of the Church and old usages and customs. His fame spread as a highwayman and murderer. The roads about Guatemala were unsafe and all traveling was broken up; the merchants were thrown into consternation by intelligence that the whole of the goods sent to the fair at Esquipulas had fallen into his hands (which, however, proved untrue). Very soon he became so strong that he attacked villages and even towns.

The reader will bear in mind that this was in the State of Guatemala. The Liberal Party was dominant, but at this critical moment a fatal division took place among its members; Barundia, a leading member, disappointed of a high office for a profligate relative, deserted the administration and appeared in the Assembly at the head of the opposition. Party distraction and the rising of Carrera stirred up all who were dissatisfied with the government; the citizens of Antigua, about twenty-five miles distant, sent a petition to the Assembly for a decree of amnesty for political offences, which would allow exiles to return and redress other grievances. A deputation of the Assembly was sent to confer with them. It returned unsuccessful, and the Antiguans threatened to march against Guatemala.

On Sunday, the twentieth of February 1838, proclamations of the Antiguans were found strewed in the streets, and there was a general alarm that they were on their march to attack the city. The troops of the general government (less than five hundred in number) and the militia were mustered; cannon were placed at the corners of the square and sentinels in the streets; and General Prem published a bando, calling upon all citizens to take up arms. Gálvez, the chief of the state, mounted his horse, and rode through the streets, endeavoring to rouse the citizens, and giving out that Morazán was on his march and had defeated three hundred of Carrera's gang.

On Monday all business was suspended. Gálvez, in great perplexity, reinstated some officers who had been dismissed; he appointed Mexía, a Spaniard, lieutenant-colonel, which gave such disgust that Prem and all the officers sent in their resignations. Gálvez begged and implored them to continue, reconciling himself to each individually; and at length, on his revoking the commission of Mexía, they consented. At two o'clock it was rumored that Carrera had joined the Antiguans. Prem published a decree that all males from fourteen to sixty, except priests and persons laboring under physical imbecility, should take up arms. At nine o'clock at night there was an alarm that a party of Carrera's gang was at the Aycetuna.[2] The square was again garrisoned, and sentinels and cannons placed at the corners of the streets. To add to the excitement, during the night the provisor died, and news was received that the Livingston Code had been publicly burned at Chiquimula and that the town had declared itself against Gálvez. On Wednesday morning fosses were commenced at the corners of the public square; but on Thursday the Marquis of Aycinena, the leader of the Central Party, by a conference with the divided Liberals, succeeded in inducing a majority of deputies to sign a convention of amnesty, which gave general satisfaction.

On Friday morning the city was perfectly quiet. But by midday this calm proved to be only the forerunner of a dreadful storm. The troops of the Federal government, the only reliable force, revolted; with bayonets fixed, colors flying, and cannon in front, they left the barracks and marched into the plaza. They refused to ratify the convention by which, it was represented to them, Gálvez was to be deposed and Valenzuela, the vice-chief and a tool of Barundia, appointed in his stead. They refused to serve under any of the opposition and said they could give protection and had no occasion to ask it. Deputies were cited to attend a meeting of the Assembly, but they were afraid to convene. The officers had a conference with the soldiers and Merino, a sergeant, drew up a document requiring that President Morazán be sent for, Gálvez to remain chief until his arrival. This was assented to. Deputies were sent requesting Morazán to come to Guatemala, and also to Antigua, to explain the circumstances of violating the convention, but the deputies were unsuccessful.

The same night the alarm bell announced the approach of eight hundred men to attack the city. The militia were called to arms, but only about forty appeared. At half past five

---

2. In spite of extensive searching, the editor finds it impossible to identify "Aycetuna."

Gálvez formed the government troops and, accompanied by Prem, marched from the plaza to meet the rebels. But before he reached the gate a conspiracy broke out among the troops, and with the cry *Viva el General Merino, y muera el Jefe del Estado, que nos ha vendido—fuego, muchachos!* (Long live General Merino, and die the chief of the state, who has sold us—fire, boys!) the infantry fired upon the *état-major*. A ball passed through Prem's hat; Gálvez was thrown from his horse, but he escaped and took refuge behind the altar of the Church of La Concepción. Yáñez, a cavalry officer, succeeded in dispersing the troops with his cavalry; he returned to the square, leaving fifteen dead in the street. Merino, with about a hundred and twenty men, took possession of the small fieldpiece of the battalion, and stationed himself in the square of Guadalupe. Parties of the dispersed troops remained out all night, firing their muskets and keeping the city in a state of alarm; but Yáñez saved it from plunder by patrolling with his cavalry. In the morning Merino asked permission to march into the plaza. His numbers had increased by the return of straggling parties; but, on forming in the plaza, he and three or four ringleaders were ordered to leave the ranks, and were sent to prison in the convent of Santo Domingo, where, on Monday afternoon, he was tied to a stake in his cell and shot. His grave at the foot of the stake and his blood spattered on the wall were among the curiosities shown to me in Guatemala.

On Sunday morning the bells again sounded the alarm; the rebel Antiguans were at the old gate, and commissioners were sent out to treat with them. They demanded an evacuation of the plaza by the soldiers, but the soldiers answered, indignantly, that the rebels might come and take the square. Prem softened this into an answer that they could not surrender to rebels, and at about half past twelve at night the attack commenced. The rebels scattered in the suburbs, wasting powder and bullets, and in the morning Yáñez, with seventy cavalry, made a sally and, routing three hundred of them, returned into the plaza with lances reeking with blood. Probably, if he had been seconded by the citizens, he would have driven them all posthaste back to Antigua.

On Wednesday Carrera joined the rebels. He had sent his emissaries to the villages to rouse the Indians, promising them the plunder of Guatemala; and on Thursday, with a tumultuous mass of half-naked savages, men, women, and children, estimated at ten or twelve thousand, he presented himself at the gate of the city. The Antiguans themselves were struck with consternation, and the citizens of Guatemala were thrown into a state bordering on distraction. Commissioners were again sent out to treat with Carrera, who demanded the deposition of Gálvez, the evacuation of the plaza by the Federal troops, and a free passage into the city. Probably, even at this time, if the Federal troops had been supported by the citizens, they could have resisted the entry; but the consternation and the fear of exasperating the rebellious hordes were so great that nothing was thought of but submission. The Assembly met in terror and distraction, and the result was an assent to all that was demanded.

At five o'clock the small band of government troops evacuated the plaza. The infantry, amounting to three hundred, marched out by the Calle Real, or Royal Street. The cavalry, seventy in number exclusive of officers, on their march through another street, met an aide-de-camp of Carrera, who ordered them to lay down their arms. Yáñez answered that he must first see his general; but the dragoons, suspecting some treachery on the part of Valenzuela, became panic-stricken and fled. Yáñez, with thirty-five men, galloped through the city and escaped by the road to Mixco. The rest rushed back into the plaza, threw down their lances in disgust, dismounted, and disappeared; not a single man was left under arms.

In the meantime Carrera's hordes were advancing. The commandant of the Antiguans asked him if he had his masses divided into squares or companies to which Carrera answered, *No entiendo nada de eso. Todo es uno.* (I don't understand anything of that. It is all the same.) Among his leaders were Monreal and other known outlaws, criminals, robbers, and murderers. He himself was on horseback, with a green bush in his hat, which was hung round with pieces of dirty cotton cloth covered with pictures of saints. A gentleman who saw them from the roof of his house, and who was familiar with all the scenes of terror which had taken place in that unhappy city, told me that he never felt such consternation and horror as when he saw the entry of this immense mass of barbarians. Choking up the streets, all with green bushes in their hats, they seemed to him at a distance like a moving forest. They were armed with rusty muskets, old pistols, fowling pieces, some with locks and some without; they carried sticks formed into the shape of muskets, with tin-plate locks, and clubs, machetes, and knives tied to the ends of long poles. And swelling the multitude were two or three thousand women, with sacks and alforjas for carrying away the plunder. Many, who had never left their villages before, looked wild at the sight of the houses and churches, and the magnificence of the city. They entered the plaza, vociferating *Viva la religión, y muerte a los extranjeros!* Carrera himself, amazed at the immense ball he had set in motion, was so embarrassed that he could not guide his horse. He afterward said that he was frightened at the difficulty of controlling this huge and disorderly mass. The traitor Barundia, the leader of the opposition, the Catiline of this rebellion, rode by his side on his entry into the plaza.

At sundown the whole multitude set up the *Salve,* or Hymn to the Virgin. The swell of human voices filled the air and made the hearts of the inhabitants quake with fear. Carrera entered the cathedral; the Indians, in mute astonishment at its magnificence, thronged in after him and set up around the beautiful altar the uncouth images of their village saints. Monreal broke into the house of General Prem and seized a uniform coat richly embroidered with gold, into which Carrera slipped his arms, still wearing his straw hat with its green bush. A watch was brought him, but he did not know the use of it. Probably, since the invasion of Rome by Alaric and the Goths, no civilized city was ever visited by such an inundation of barbarians.

And Carrera alone had power to control the wild elements around him. As soon as possible some of the authorities sought him out and in the most abject terms begged him to state on what conditions he would evacuate the city. He demanded the deposition of Gálvez, the chief of the state, all the money, and all the arms the government could command. The priests were the only people who had any influence with him, and words cannot convey any idea of the awful state of suspense which the city suffered, dreading every moment to hear the signal given for general pillage and massacre. The inhabitants shut themselves up in their houses, which, being built of stone, with iron balconies to the windows and doors several inches thick, resisted the assaults of straggling parties; but atrocities more than enough were committed, preliminary, as it seemed, to a general sacking. The vice-president of the republic was murdered. The house of Flores, a deputy, was sacked and his mother knocked down by a villain with the butt of a musket, and one of his daughters shot in the arm with two balls.

The house of Messrs. Klee, Skinner, & Co., the principal foreign merchants in Guatemala, which was reported to contain ammunition and arms, was several times attacked with great ferocity; having strong balconied windows, and the door being secured by bales of merchandise piled up within, it resisted the assaults of an undisciplined mob armed only with clubs, muskets, knives, and machetes. The priests ran through the streets bearing the crucifix, in the name of the Virgin and saints restraining the lawless Indians, stilling the wildness of passion, and saving the terrified inhabitants. And I cannot help mentioning one whose name was in everybody's mouth, Mr. Charles Savage, at that time United States consul, who, in the midst of the most furious assault upon Mr. Klee's house, rushed down the street under a shower of bullets and, knocking up bayonets and machetes, drove the mob back from the door. Branding them as robbers and murderers, with his white hair streaming in the wind, he poured out such a torrent of indignation and contempt that the Indians, amazed at his audacity, desisted. After this, with an almost wanton exposure of life, he was seen in the midst of every mob; to the astonishment of everybody, he was not killed. The foreign residents presented him with a unanimous letter of thanks for his fearless and successful exertions in the protection of life and property.

Pending the negotiation, Carrera, dressed in Prem's uniform, endeavored to restrain his tumultuous followers; but several times he said that he could not himself resist the temptation to sack Klee's house, and those of the other *ingleses*. There was a strange dash of fanaticism in the character of this lawless chieftain. The battle cry of his hordes was *Viva la religión!* The palace of the archbishop had been suffered to be used as a theatre by the Liberals; Carrera demanded the keys and, putting them in his pocket, declared that, to prevent any future pollution, it should not be opened again until the banished archbishop returned to occupy it.

At length the terms upon which he consented to withdraw were agreed upon: eleven thousand dollars in silver, ten thousand to be distributed among his followers, and one thousand for his own share; a thousand muskets; and a commission as lieutenant-colonel for himself. The amount of money was small as the price of relief from such imminent danger, but it was an immense sum in the eyes of Carrera and his followers, few of whom were worth more than the rags on their backs and the stolen arms in their hands. But even this sum was not easily raised; the treasury was bankrupt, and the money was not very cheerfully contributed by the citizens. The madness of consenting to put in the hands of Carrera a thousand muskets was only equaled by the absurdity of making him a lieutenant-colonel.

On the afternoon of the third day the money was paid, the muskets delivered, and Carrera was invested with the command of the province of Mita, a district near Guatemala City. The joy of the inhabitants at the prospect of his immediate departure was without bounds. But at the last moment an awful rumor spread that the wild bands had evinced an uncontrollable eagerness to sack the city before leaving. A random discharge of muskets in the plaza confirmed this rumor, and the effect was dreadful. An hour of terrible suspense followed, but at five o'clock Carrera and his men filed off in straggling crowds from the plaza. At the Plaza de Toros they halted and, firing their muskets in the air, created another panic. Again a rumor was revived that Carrera had demanded four thousand dollars more, and that, unless he received it, he would return and take it by force. Carrera himself did actually return and demand a fieldpiece, which was given him. But, at length, leaving behind him a document requiring the redress of certain grievances, to the unspeakable joy of all the inhabitants, he left the city.

The delight of the citizens at being relieved from the pressure of immediate danger was indeed great, but there was no return of confidence, and, unhappily, no healing of political animosities. Valenzuela was appointed chief of the state; the Assembly renewed its distracted sessions; Barundia, as the head of the now ministerial party, proposed to abolish all the unconstitutional decrees of Gálvez; money was wanted, and recourse to the old system of forced loans had to be taken. This exasperated the moneyed men; and in the midst of discord and confusion news was received that Quezaltenango, one of the departments of Guatemala, had seceded and declared itself a separate state. At this time, too, the government received a letter from Carrera, stating that he had been informed since his arrival at Mataquescuintla that people spoke ill of him in the capital, and if they continued to do so he had four thousand men, and would return and put things right. From time to time he sent a message to the same effect by some straggling Indian who happened to pass through his village. Afterward it was reported that his followers had renounced his authority and commenced operations on their own account, threatening the city with another invasion, determined, according to their proclamations, to exterminate the whites and establish a government of *pardos libres* (free tigers) [3] and enjoy in their own right the lands which had devolved upon them by their emancipation from the dominion of the whites. To the honor of

---

3. Stephens has probably mistranslated *pardo*. In various parts of Latin America it means "mestizo" or "mulatto."

Guatemala, a single spark of spirit broke forth, and men of all classes took up arms; but it was a single flash and soon died away.

Again intelligence arrived that Carrera himself had sent out his emissaries to summon his hordes for another march upon the city. Several families received private information and advice to seek safety in flight. Hundreds of people did so, and the roads were crowded with processions of mules, horses, and Indians loaded with luggage. On Sunday everybody was going, and early on Monday morning guards were placed at the barriers. Hundreds of passports were applied for and refused. Again a decree was published that all should take up arms, and the militia were again mustered. At ten o'clock on Tuesday night it was said that Carrera was at Palencia, at eleven that he had gone to suppress an insurrection of his own bandits, and on Wednesday night that he was at a place called Canales. On Sunday, the fourth of March, a review took place of about seven hundred men. Antigua sent three hundred and fifty muskets and ammunition, which they did not consider it prudent to keep, as there had been cries of *muera Guatemala, y viva Carrera!* and placards, bearing the same ominous words, posted on the walls. At this time a letter was received from Carrera by the government, advising them to disband their troops, and assuring them that he was collecting forces only to destroy a party of four hundred rebels, headed by one Gálvez (the former chief of the state, whom he had deposed), and requesting two cannon and more ammunition. At another time, probably supposing that the government must be interested in his fortunes, he sent word that he had narrowly escaped being assassinated. Monreal had taken advantage of an opportunity, seduced his men, tied him to a tree, and was in the very act of having him shot, when his brother Laureano Carrera rushed in and ran Monreal through with his bayonet. The government now conceived the project of inducing his followers, by the influence of the priests, to surrender their arms on paying them five dollars apiece; but very soon he was heard of stronger than ever, occupying all the roads and sending in imperious proclamations to the government. At length the news came that he was actually marching upon the city.

At this time, to the unspeakable joy of the inhabitants, General Morazán, the President of the Republic, arrived from San Salvador with fifteen hundred men. But party spirit was even yet dominant. General Morazán encamped a few leagues from the city, hesitating to enter it or to employ the forces of the general government in putting down a revolution in the state except with the consent of the state government. The state government was jealous of the Federal government, tenacious of prerogatives it had not the courage to defend. It demanded from the President a plan of his campaign; it also passed a decree offering Carrera and his followers fifteen days to lay down their arms. But General Morazán would not permit the decree to be published at his headquarters, and two days later, it was annulled and the President of the Republic authorized to act as circumstances might require.

During this time one of Morazán's pickets had been cut off and the officers murdered, which created a great excitement among his soldiers. Anxious to avoid shedding more blood, he sent into the city for the Canónigo Castillo and Barundia, deputing them as commissioners to persuade the bandits to surrender their arms, even offering to pay fifteen dollars a head rather than come to extremities. The commissioners found Carrera at one of his old haunts among the mountains of Mataquescuintla surrounded by hordes of Indians living upon tortillas. The traitor Barundia had been received by Morazán's soldiers with groans, and his poor jaded horse had been tied up at Morazán's camp a day and a half without a blade of grass. As a further reward of his treason, Carrera refused to meet him under a roof, because, as he said, he did not wish to plunge his new lance, a present from a priest, into Barundia's breast.

The meeting took place in the open air and on the top of a mountain. Carrera refused to lay down his arms unless all his former demands were complied with and unless also the Indian capitation tax was reduced to one-third of its amount;

but he softened his asperity against foreigners to the demand
that only those not married should be expelled from the
country, and that thereafter they should be permitted to
traffic only, and not to settle in it. The atrocious priest Padre
Lobo, his constant friend and adviser, was with him. The
arguments of the Canónigo Castillo, particularly in regard to
the folly of charging the government with an attempt to
poison the Indians, were listened to with much attention by
them, but Carrera broke up the conference by asserting ve-
hemently that the government had offered him twenty dollars a head for every Indian he poisoned.

All hope of compromise was now at an end, and General
Morazán marched directly to Mataquescuintla; but before
he reached it Carrera's bands had disappeared among the
mountains. He heard of them in another place, devastating
the country, desolating villages and towns, and again before
his troops could reach them, the muskets were concealed and
the Indians either in the mountains or quietly working in
the fields. Mr. Hall, the British vice-consul, received a letter
from eleven British subjects of Salamá, a distance of three
days' journey, stating that they had been seized at night by
a party of Carrera's troops, stripped of everything, confined
two nights and a day without food, and sentenced to be shot,
but that they had finally been ordered to leave the country,
which they were then doing, destitute of everything and
begging their way to the port. A few nights after, at ten
o'clock, the cannon of alarm was sounded in the city, and it
was reported that Carrera was again at the gates.

All this time party strife was as violent as ever: the Centralists trembling with apprehension but in their hearts
rejoicing at the distraction of the country under the administration of the Liberals, and rejoicing that one had risen up
capable of inspiring the Liberals with terror, and the divided
Liberals hating each other with a more intense hate even
than the Centralists bore them. Finally, the excitement became so great that all the parties drew up separate petitions
to General Morazán, representing the deplorable state of
insecurity, and begging him to enter the city and provide
for its safety. Separate sets of deputies hurried to anticipate

each other at General Morazán's headquarters and to pay court to him by being the first to ask for his protection. General Morazán had become acquainted with the distracted condition of the city, and was in the act of mounting his horse when the deputies arrived. On Sunday he entered with an escort of two hundred soldiers, amid the ringing of bells, firing of cannon, and other demonstrations of joy.

The same day the merchants, with the Marquis of Aycinena and others of the Central Party, presented a petition representing the dreadful state of public feeling, and requesting Morazán to depose the state authorities, to assume the reins of government, and to convoke a Constituent Assembly, as the only means of saving Guatemala from utter ruin. In the evening, deputies from the different branches of the Liberal Party had long conferences with the President. Morazán answered all that he wished to act legally, and that he would communicate with the Assembly the next day and be governed by their decision. The proceedings in the Assembly are too afflicting and disgraceful to dwell upon. So far as I can understand the party strife of that time (after wading through papers and pamphlets emanating from both sides), General Morazán conducted himself with probity and honor. The Centralists made a desperate effort to attach him to them, but he would not accept the offered embrace, nor the sycophantic service of men who had always opposed him; nor would he sustain what he believed to be wrong in his own partisans.

In the meantime Carrera was gaining ground; he had routed several detachments of the Federal troops, massacred men, and increased his stock of ammunition and arms. At length all agreed that something must be done; and at a final meeting of the Assembly, with a feeling of desperation, it was decreed without debate: (1) that the state government should retire to Antigua; and (2) that the President, in person or by delegate, should govern the district according to Article 176 of the Constitution.

Amid these scenes within the city, and rumors of worse from without, on Sunday night a ball was given to Morazán; the Centralists, displeased at his not acceding to their overtures, did not attend. Gálvez, the chief deposed by Carrera, made his first appearance since his deposition and danced the whole time.

Though Morazán was irresolute in the cabinet, he was all energy in the field; and being now invested with full power, he sustained his high reputation as a skillful soldier. The bulletin of the army for May and June exhibits the track of Carrera as he devastated villages and towns, and the close pursuit of the government troops who beat him wherever they found him but who were never able to secure his person. In the meantime party jealousies continued and the state government was in a state of anarchy. The Assembly could not meet, because, since the state party was not attending, it was incumbent on the vice-chief to retire and his place to be taken by the oldest counsellor, and there was no such official, for the term of the council had expired and no new elections had been held. While Morazán was dispersing the wild bands of Carrera, and relieving the Guatemalans from the danger which had brought them to their knees before him, the old jealousies revived; incendiary publications were issued, charging him with exhausting the country to support idle soldiers, and of keeping the city in subjection by bayonets.

About the first of July General Morazán considered Guatemala relieved from all external danger and returned to El Salvador, leaving troops in various towns under the command of Carvallo, and appointing Carlos Salazar commandant in the city. Carrera was supposed to be completely put down; and to bring things to a close, Carvallo published the following:

NOTICE

The person or persons who may deliver the criminal Rafael Carrera, dead or alive (if he does not present himself voluntarily under the last pardon), shall receive a reward of fifteen hundred dollars and two *caballerías* of land, and pardon for any crime he has committed.

The general-in-chief,

Guatemala, July 20, 1838   *J. N. CARVALLO*

But the "criminal" Carrera, the proscribed outlaw, was not yet put down; one by one, he surprised detachments of Federal troops. And while the city exhibited the fierceness of party spirit, complained of forced loans and the expense of maintaining idle soldiers, he made plans to abolish the state government and form a provisional junta, and to organize a Constituent Assembly with M. Rivera Paz at its head. With still increasing numbers, he attacked Amatitlán, took Antigua, and, barely waiting to sack a few houses, stripped it of cannon, muskets, and ammunition, and again marched against Guatemala, proclaiming his intention to raze every house to the ground and to murder every white inhabitant.

The consternation in the city cannot be conceived. General Morazán was again solicited to come. A line in pencil was received from him by a man who carried it sewed up in the sleeve of his coat, urging the city to defend itself and to try to hold out for a few days. But the danger was too imminent. Salazar, at the head of the Federal troops (the idle soldiers complained of), marched out at two o'clock in the morning and, aided by a thick fog, came upon Carrera suddenly at Villa Nueva, killed four hundred and fifty of his men, and completely routed him, Carrera himself being badly wounded in the thigh. The city was thus saved from destruction. The next day Morazán entered the city with a thousand men. The shock of the immense danger which they had escaped was not yet over; on the morrow it might return. Party jealousies were scared away, and all looked to General Morazán as the only man who could effectually save them from Carrera, and they begged him to accept the office of dictator.

About the same time Guzmán, the general of Quezaltenango, arrived with seven hundred men, and General Morazán made formidable arrangements to enclose and crush the *Cachurecos*.[4] The result was the same as before: Carrera was constantly beaten but as constantly escaped.

---

4. The Liberals applied this name to the Conservatives. Here *Cachurecos* refers to Carrrera and his forces, by means of which the Conservatives came to power.

His followers were scattered, his best men taken and shot, and he himself was penned up and almost starved on the top of a mountain, with a cordon of soldiers around its base, and only escaped by the remissness of the guard. In three months, chased from place to place, his old haunts broken up, and hemmed in on every side, he entered into a treaty with Guzmán by which he agreed to deliver up one thousand muskets and to disband his remaining followers. In executing the treaty, however, he delivered only four hundred muskets, and those old and worthless; Guzmán merely winked at this breach of the convention, little dreaming of the terrible fate reserved for himself at Carrera's hands.

This over, Morazán deposed Rivera Paz, restored Salazar, and again returned to El Salvador, first laying heavy contributions on the city to support the expense of the war, and taking with him all the soldiers of the Federal government, belying one of the party cries against him that he was attempting to retain an influence in the city by bayonets. Guzmán returned to Quezaltenango, and the garrison consisted only of seventy men.

The contributions, and the withdrawal of the troops from the city, created great dissatisfaction with Morazán, and the political horizon became cloudy throughout the Republic. The Marquis of Aycinena, who, banished by Morazán, had resided several years in the United States studying our institutions, hurried on the crisis by a series of articles which were widely circulated and which purported to illustrate our constitution and laws. Honduras and Costa Rica declared their independence of the general government, and in Guatemala all this added fuel to the already flaming fire of dissension.

On the twenty-fourth of March, 1839, Carrera issued a bulletin from his old quarters in Mataquescuintla, in which, referring to the declaration of independence by the States, he said: "When those laws came to my hands, I read them and returned to them very often; as a loving mother clasps in her arms an only son whom she believed lost and presses him against her heart, so did I with the pamphlet that contained the declaration; for in it I found the principles that

I sustain and the reforms I desire." This was rather figurative, as Carrera could not at that time read; but it must have been quite new to him and a satisfaction to find out what principles he sustained. Again he threatened to enter the city.

All was anarchy and distraction in the councils, when on the twelfth of April his hordes appeared before the gates. All were aghast, but there was no rising to repel him. Morazán was beyond the reach of their voices, and they who had been loudest in denouncing him for attempting to control the city by bayonets, now denounced him for leaving them to the mercy of Carrera. All who could, hid away their treasures and fled; the rest shut themselves up in their houses, barring their doors and windows. At two o'clock in the morning, routing the guard, Carrera entered with fifteen hundred men. Salazar, the commandant, fled, and Carrera, riding up to the house of Rivera Paz, knocked at the door and reinstalled him as chief of the state. His soldiers took up their quarters in the barracks, and Carrera established himself as the guardian of the city; it is due to him to say that he acknowledged his own incompetency to govern and placed men at the disposition of the municipality to preserve the peace. The Central Party was thus restored to power.

Carrera's fanaticism bound him to the Church party; he was flattered by his association and connection with the aristocracy, who made him a brigadier general and presented him with a handsome uniform. Besides these empty honors, he had the city barracks and pay for his men, which was better than Indian huts and foraging expeditions. The league had continued since the April preceding my arrival. The great bond of union was hatred of Morazán and the Liberals. The Centralists had their Constituent Assembly; they abolished the laws made by the Liberals, and revived old Spanish laws and old names for the courts of justice and officers of government, and they passed any laws they pleased so long as they did not interfere with him. Their great difficulty was to keep him quiet. Unable to remain inactive in the city, he marched toward El Salvador for the

ostensible purpose of attacking General Morazán. This put
the Centralists in a state of great anxiety; Carrera's success
or his defeat was alike dangerous to them. If he was defeated, Morazán might march directly upon the city and
take signal vengeance upon them; if successful, he might
return with his barbarians so intoxicated by victory as to be
utterly uncontrollable.

A little circumstance shows the position of things. Carrera's mother, an old woman well known as a huckster on
the plaza, died. Formerly it was the custom with the higher
classes to bury their dead in vaults constructed within the
churches; but from the time of the cholera, all burials, without distinction, were forbidden in the churches and even
within the city, and a *campo santo* was established outside
the town, in which all the principal families had vaults.
Carrera signified his pleasure that his mother should be
buried in the Cathedral! The government charged itself
with the funeral and issued cards of invitation; all the
principal inhabitants followed in the procession. No efforts
were spared to conciliate and keep Carrera in good temper;
but he was subject to violent bursts of passion, and, it was
said, that he had cautioned the members of the government
at such moments not to attempt to argue with him, but to
let him have his own way. Such was Carrera at the time of
my visit—more absolute master of Guatemala than any king
in Europe of his dominions, and by the fanatic Indians called
el Hijo de Dios, the Son of God, and *nuestro Señor*, our
Lord.

When I entered the room he was sitting at a table counting sixpenny and shilling pieces. Colonel Monte Rosa, a
dark mestizo in a dashing uniform, was sitting by his side,
and several other persons were in the room. Carrera was
about five feet six inches in height, with straight black hair
and an Indian complexion and expression; he wore a black
bombazet roundabout jacket and pantaloons. He was without beard, and did not seem to be more than twenty-one
years old. As we entered, he rose and pushed the money to
one side of the table and, probably out of respect to my coat,
received me with courtesy and gave me a chair at his side.

My first remark was an expression of surprise at his extreme youth; he answered that he was but twenty-three years old —certainly he was not more than twenty-five. Then, as a man conscious that he was something extraordinary and that I knew it, without waiting for any leading questions he continued that he had begun (he did not say what) with thirteen men armed with old muskets, which they were obliged to fire with cigars. He pointed to eight places in which he had been wounded, and said that he had three balls then in his body.

It was hard to recognize in him the man who, less than two years before, had entered Guatemala with a horde of wild Indians, proclaiming death to strangers. Indeed, in no particular had he changed more than in his opinion of foreigners, a happy illustration of the effect of personal intercourse in the breaking down of prejudices against individuals or classes. He had become personally acquainted with several, and one, an English doctor, had extracted a ball from his side. His intercourse with all had been so satisfactory that his feelings had undergone an entire revulsion; he said that they were the only people who never deceived him. He had done, too, what I consider extraordinary: in the intervals of his hurried life he had learned to write his name and had thrown aside his stamp.

I never had the fortune to be presented to any legitimate king, nor to any usurper of the prerogatives of royalty except Mohammed Ali, to whom, old as he was, I gave some good advice; it grieves me that the old lion is now shorn of his mane. Considering Carrera a promising young man, I told him that he had a long career before him and might do much good to his country. Laying his hand upon his heart, with a burst of feeling that I did not expect, he said that he was determined to sacrifice his life for his country. With all his faults and his crimes, none ever accused him of duplicity or of saying what he did not mean; perhaps, as many self-deceiving men have done before him, he believes himself a patriot.

I considered that he was destined to exercise an important, if not a controlling influence on the affairs of Central America, and trusting that hopes of honorable and extended fame might have some effect upon his character, I told him that his name had already reached my country and that I had seen in our newspapers an account of his last entry into Guatemala, with praises of his moderation and his exertions to prevent atrocities. He expressed himself pleased that his name was known and that such mention was made of him among strangers, and said he was not a robber and murderer, as he was called by his enemies. He seemed intelligent and capable of improvement, and I told him that he ought to travel into other countries, and particularly, from its contiguity, into mine. He had a very indefinite notion as to where my country was; he knew it only as *El Norte*, or the North, and inquired about the distance and facility for getting there, adding that, when the wars were over, he would endeavor to make *El Norte* a visit.

But he could not fix his thoughts upon anything except the wars and Morazán; in fact, he knew of nothing else. He was boyish in his manners and manner of speaking, but very grave; he never smiled, and, conscious of power, was unostentatious in the exhibition of it, though he always spoke in the first person of what he had done and what he intended to do. One of the hangers-on, evidently to pay court to him, looked for a paper bearing his signature to show me as a specimen of his handwriting, but did not find one. My interview with him was much more interesting than I had expected. So young, so humble in his origin, so destitute of early advantages, with honest impulses, perhaps, but ignorant, fanatic, sanguinary, and the slave of violent passions, he wielded absolutely the physical force of the country, and that force entertained a natural hatred of the whites. At parting he accompanied me to the door, and in the presence of his villainous soldiers made me a free offer of his services. I understood that I had had the good fortune to make a favorable impression; later, but unluckily during my absence, he called upon me in full dress and in state, which for him was an unusual thing.

At that time, as Don Manuel Pavón told me, Carrera professed to consider himself a brigadier general, subject to the orders of the government. He had no regular allowance for the maintenance of himself and troops. He did not like keeping accounts and called for money when he wanted it; but, with this understanding, in eight months he had not required more than Morazán did in two. He really did not want money for himself, and as a matter of policy he paid the Indians but little. This operated powerfully with the aristocracy, upon whom the whole burden of raising money devolved. It may be a satisfaction to some of my friends, however, to know that this lawless chief was under a dominion to which meeker men are loth to submit: his wife accompanied him on horseback in all his expeditions, influenced by a feeling which is said to proceed sometimes from excess of affection (I have heard that it is no unimportant part of the business of the chief of the state to settle family jars).

As we were returning to my house, we met a gentleman who told Mr. Pavón that a party of soldiers was searching for a member of the Assembly who was lying under the displeasure of Carrera, but who was a personal friend of theirs. As we passed on, we saw a file of soldiers drawn up before his door, while others were inside searching the house. This was being done by Carrera's personal orders, without any knowledge on the part of the government.

Chapter XII

~~~~~~

*Party to Mixco. A scene of pleasure. Procession in honor
of the patron saint of Mixco. Fireworks. A bombardment.
Smoking cigars. A night brawl. Suffering and sorrow. A
cockfight. A walk in the suburbs. Sunday
amusements. Return to the city.*

IN consequence of the convulsions and danger of the
times, the city was dull, and there was no gaiety in private circles. But an effort had been made by some enterprising ladies to break the monotony, and a party, to which I was invited, was formed for that afternoon to go to Mixco, an Indian village about three leagues distant, where on the following day the festival of its patron saint was to be celebrated with Indian rites.

At four o'clock in the afternoon I left my door on horseback to call on Don Manuel Pavón. His house was next to that of the proscribed deputy, and a line of soldiers had been drawn around the whole block to prevent an escape while every house was being searched. I always gave these gentlemen a wide berth when I could, but it was necessary to ride along the whole line. As I passed the house of the deputy, with the door closed and sentinels before it, I could not but think of his distressed family in agony lest his hiding place should be discovered.

Don Manuel was waiting for me, and we rode to the house of one of the ladies of the party, a young widow whom I had not seen before and who, in her riding dress, made a fine appearance. Her horse was ready, and when she had kissed the old people good-by we carried her off. The women servants, with familiarity and affection, followed her to the door and continued farewell greetings and cautions to take good care of herself, which the lady answered as long as we were within hearing. We called at two or three other houses, and then all assembled at the place of rendezvous. The courtyard was full of horses with every variety of fanciful mountings. Although we were going only nine miles, and to a large Indian village, it was necessary to carry beds, bedding, and provisions. A train of servants large enough to carry stores for a small military expedition was sent ahead, and we all started. Outside the gate all the anxieties and perils which slumbered in the city were forgotten. Our road lay over an extensive plain, which, as the sun went down behind the volcanoes of Agua and Fuego, seemed a beautiful bowling green in which our party, preceded by a long file of Indians with loads on their backs, formed a picture. I was surprised to find that the ladies were not good horsewomen. They never rode for pleasure and, on account of the want of accommodation on the road, seldom traveled.

It was after dark when we reached the borders of a deep ravine separating the plain from Mixco, into which we descended. Rising on the other side, we emerged from the darkness of the ravine into an illuminated street, and, at two or three horses' lengths, into a plaza blazing with lights and crowded with people, nearly all of whom were Indians in holiday costume. In the center of the plaza was a fine fountain, and at the head of it a gigantic church. We rode up to the house that had been provided for the ladies, and, leaving them there, the gentlemen scattered to find lodgings for themselves. The door of every house was open, and the only question asked was whether there was room. Some of the young men did not give themselves the trouble of finding lodgings, as they were disposed to make a night of it, but Mr. Pavón and I secured a place and returned to the house occupied by the ladies. In one corner of the house was a *tienda*, or store, about ten feet square, partitioned off and shelved, which served as a place for their hats and shawls;

the rest of the house was one large room containing merely
a long table and benches.

In a few moments the ladies were ready, and we all sallied out for a walk. All the streets and passages were bril-
liantly illuminated, and across some were arches decorated
with evergreens and lighted, and at the corners under arbors
of branches were altars adorned with flowers. The spirit
of frolic seemed to take possession of our file leaders, who,
as the humor prompted them, entered any house, and after
a lively chat left it, contriving to come out just as the last
of the party were going in. In one house they found a
poncho rolled up very carefully, with the end of a guitar
sticking out. The proprietor of the house only knew that it
belonged to a young man from Guatemala, who had left it
as an indication of his intention to pass the night there. One
of the young men unrolled the poncho, and some loaves of
bread fell out, which he distributed; with half a loaf in his
mouth he struck up a waltz, which was followed by a
quadrille. The good people of the house seemed pleased at
this free use of their roof; shaking hands all around, with
many expressions of good will on both sides, we left as unceremoniously as we had entered. We made the tour of all
the principal streets, and as we returned to the plaza the
procession was coming out of the church.

The village procession in honor of its patron saint is the
great pride of the Indian and the touchstone of his religious
character. Every Indian contributes his labor and money
toward getting it up, and he is most honored who is allowed
the most important part in it. This was a rich village, at
which all the muleteers of Guatemala lived, and nowhere
had I seen an Indian procession so imposing. The church
stood on an elevation at the head of the plaza, its whole
façade rich in ornaments illuminated by the light of torches,
the large platform and the steps being thronged with women
in white. A space was cleared in the middle before the great
door, and with a loud chant the procession passed out of the
doorway. First came the alcalde and his alquaciles, all Indians, with rods of office in one hand and lighted wax candles
six or eight feet long in the other. They were followed by

a set of devils, which, while not as playful as the devils of Guatemala, were more hideous and probably better likenesses according to the notions of the Indians. Then there came, borne aloft by Indians, a large silver cross, richly chased and ornamented, which was followed by the curate, with a silken canopy held over his head on the ends of long poles borne by Indians. As the cross advanced all fell on their knees, and a stranger would have been thought guilty of an insult to their holy religion who omitted conforming to this ceremony. Next came figures of saints larger than life, borne on the shoulders of Indians, and then a figure of the Virgin, gorgeously dressed, her gown glittering with spangles. There followed, carrying lighted candles, a long procession of Indian women dressed in costume, with a thick red cord twisted in the hair to look like a turban. The procession passed through the illuminated streets, under the arches, and, stopping from time to time before the altars, made a tour of the village. In about an hour, with a loud chant, they ascended the steps of the church. The re-entry of the procession to the church was announced by a discharge of rockets, after which all gathered in the plaza for the exhibition of fireworks.

It was some time before these were ready, for those who had figured in the procession, particularly the devils, were also the principal managers of the fireworks. Our party was well known in Mixco and, though the steps of the church were crowded, one of the best places was immediately vacated for us. From their nearness to Guatemala, the people of Mixco knew all the principal families of the former place and were glad to see so distinguished a party at their fiesta. The familiar but respectful way in which we were everywhere treated, manifested a simplicity of manners and a kindliness of feeling between the rich and the poor which to me was one of the most interesting parts of the whole fête.

The exhibition began with the *Toro*. The man who played the part of the bull gave universal satisfaction; scattering and putting to flight the crowd in the plaza, he rushed up the steps of the church and, amid laughing and screaming, went out. Other pieces, including flying pigeons, followed, and the whole was concluded with the grand national piece of the Castle of San Felipe, which was a representation of the repulse of an English fleet. A tall structure represented the castle, and a little brig perched on the end of a stick like a weathercock, the fleet. The brig fired a broadside and then, by a sudden jerk, turned on a pivot and fired another; long after, until she had riddled herself to pieces, the castle continued pouring out on all sides a magnanimous stream of fire.

When all was over we returned to the posada, or lodging house. A cloth was spread over the long table, and in a few minutes, under the direction of the ladies, it was covered with the picnic materials brought from Guatemala. The benches were drawn up to the table and as many as could find seats sat down. Before supper was over there was an irruption of young men from Guatemala, who with their glazed hats, ponchos, and swords presented a rather disorderly appearance; but they were mostly juveniles, brothers and cousins of the ladies. With their hats on, they seated themselves at the vacated tables. As soon as they had finished eating, they hurried off the plates and piled the tables away in a corner, one on the top of the other, with the candles on the top of all; the violins struck up, and gentlemen and ladies, lighting cigars and *cigarillos*, commenced dancing.

I am sorry to say that generally the ladies of Central America, not excepting Guatemala, smoke; married ladies smoke *puros*, or all tobacco, and unmarried ladies cigars, or tobacco wrapped in paper or straw. Every gentleman carries in his pocket a silver case, with a long string of cotton, steel, and flint, which takes up nearly as much space as a handkerchief. One of the offices of gallantry is to strike a light; by doing it well, he may help to kindle a flame in a lady's heart, but at all events, to do it bunglingly would be ill-bred. I will not express my sentiments on smoking as a custom for the sex. I have recollections of beauteous lips profaned; nevertheless, I have seen a lady show her prettiness and refinement, barely touching the straw to her lips, as if kissing it gently. When a gentleman asks a lady for a light, she always removes the cigar from her lips. Happily, the dangerous proximity which sometimes occurs in a similar circumstance between gentlemen in the street is not in vogue.

The dancing continued till two o'clock, and the breaking up was like the separation of a gay family party. The young men dispersed to sleep or to finish the night with merriment elsewhere, and Don Manuel and I retired to the house he had secured for us.

We were in our hammocks, talking over the affairs of the night, when we heard a noise in the street, a loud tramping past the door, and a clash of swords. Presently Mr. Pavón's servant knocked for admission and told us that a few doors off a man had been killed by a sword cut across the head. Instead of going out to gratify an idle curiosity, like prudent men we secured the door. The tramping passed up the street, and presently we heard reports of firearms. The whole place seemed to be in an uproar. We had hardly lain down again before there was another knock at the door. Our host, a respectable old man, and his wife slept in a back room, and, afraid of rioters, they went into consultation about opening the door. The man was unwilling to do so, but his wife, with a mother's apprehensions, said that she was afraid some accident might have hapepned to Chico. As the knocking continued, we heard Rafael, a known companion of their son, cry out that Chico was wounded. The old man rose for a light, and, apprehending the worst, the mother and a young sister burst into tears. But the old man sternly checked them; he said that he had always cautioned Chico against going out at night and that he deserved to be punished. The sister ran and opened the door, and two young men entered. We could see the glitter of their swords, and that one was supporting the other, and just as the old man procured a light, the wounded man fell on the ground. His face was ghastly pale and spotted with blood, his hat cut through the crown and rim as smoothly as if done with a razor, and his right hand and arm were wound in a pocket handkerchief, which was stained with blood. The old man looked at him with the sternness of a Roman, and told him that he knew this would be the consequence of his running out at night. The mother and sister cried, and the young man, with a feeble voice, begged his father to spare him. His companion carried him into the back room, but before they could lay him on the bed he fell again and fainted. The father was alarmed and, when the boy recovered, asked him whether he wished to confess. Chico, with a faint voice, answered, "As you please." The old man told his daughter to go for the padre, but the uproar was so great in the street that she was afraid to venture out.

In the meantime we examined Chico's head, which, notwithstanding the cut through his hat, was barely touched; he himself said that he had received the blow on his hand and that it was cut off. There was no physician nearer than Guatemala, and not a person who was able to do anything for him. I had had some practice in medicine, but none in surgery; I knew, however, that it was at all events proper to wash and cleanse the wound, and with the assistance of Don Manuel's servant, a young Englishman whom Don Manuel had brought from the United States, I laid him on a bed. This servant had had some experience in the brawls of the country, having killed a young man in a quarrel growing out of a love affair, and having been confined to the house for seven months by wounds received in the same encounter. With his assistance I proceeded to unwind the bloody handkerchief, but I found that my courage began to fail me, and when, with the last coil, a dead hand fell in mine, a shudder and a deep groan ran through the spectators and I almost let the hand drop. It was cut off through the back above the knuckles, and the four fingers hung merely by the fleshy part of the thumb. The skin was drawn back, and showed on each side four bones protruding like the teeth of a skeleton. I joined them together, and as he drew up his arm they jarred like the grating of teeth. I saw that the case was beyond my art. Possibly the hand could have been restored by sewing the skin together, but I believed that the only thing to be done was to cut it off entirely, and this I was not willing to do. Unable to give any further assistance, I wound it up again in the handkerchief. The young man had a mild and pleasing countenance, and was as thankful for my ineffectual attempt as if I had really served him; he told me not to give myself any more trouble, but to return to bed. His mother and sister, with stifled sobs, hung over his head; his father retained the sternness of his manner, but it was easy to see that his heart was bleeding. To me, a stranger, it was horrible to see a fine young man mutilated for life in a street brawl.

As Chico, himself, told the story, he had been walking with some of his friends when he met one of the Espinozas from Guatemala, who was also with a party of friends. Espinoza, who was known as a bully, approached them with an expression in Spanish about equivalent to the English one, "I'll give it to you." Chico answered, "No you won't," and immediately they drew their swords. Chico, in attempting to ward off a stroke, received it on the edge of his raised right hand. In passing through all the bones, its force was so much broken that it only cut the crown and rim of his hat. The loss of his hand had no doubt saved his life, for, if the whole force of the stroke had fallen on his head, it must have killed him. But the unfortunate young man, instead of being thankful for his escape, swore vengeance against Espinoza; and Espinoza, as I afterward learned, swore that the next time Chico should not escape with the loss of his hand. In all probability, when they do meet again one of them will be killed.

All this time the uproar continued, shifting its location, with occasional reports of firearms; an aunt was wringing her hands because her son was out, and we had reason to fear a tragical night. We went to bed, but for a long time the noise in the street, the groans of poor Chico, and the sobbing of his mother and sister kept us from sleeping.

We did not wake till nearly ten o'clock. It was Sunday and the morning was bright and beautiful. The arches and flowers still adorned the streets, and the Indians, in their clean clothes, were going to Sunday mass. None except the immediate parties knew or cared about the events of the night. Crossing the plaza, we met a tall, dashing fellow on horse-

back, with a long sword by his side, who bowed to Mr.
Pavón and rode on past the house of Chico. This was Espinoza. No one attempted to molest him, and no notice whatever was taken of the circumstance by the authorities.

The door of the church was so crowded that we could not
enter and, passing through the curate's house, we stood in a
doorway on one side of the altar. The curate, in his richest
vestments, with young Indian assistants in sacerdotal dresses,
their long black hair and sluggish features contrasting
strangely with their garb and occupations, was officiating at
the altar. On the front steps, with their black *mantones*
drawn over their heads and their eyes bent on the ground,
were the dancers of our party the preceding night. Kneeling
along the whole floor of the immense church was a dense
mass of Indian women, with red headdresses, and, leaning
against the pillars and standing up in the background, were
Indians wrapped in black *chamarras*, or ponchos.

We waited till mass was over and then accompanied the
ladies to the house and breakfasted. Sunday though it was,
the occupations for the day were a cockfight in the morning
and a bullfight in the afternoon. Our party was increased by
the arrival of a distinguished family from Guatemala, and
we all set out for the cockfight. It was held in the yard of
an unoccupied house, which was already crowded. I noticed,
to the honor of the Indians and the shame of the better
classes, that they were all mestizos, or white men, and, always excepting Carrera's soldiers, I never saw a worse looking or more assassin-like set of men. All along the walls of
the yard were cocks tied by one leg, and men were running
about with other cocks under their arms, putting them on
the ground to compare size and weight, regulating bets, and
trying to cheat each other. At length a match was made;
the ladies of our party had seats in the corridor of the house,
and a space was cleared before them. The gaffs were murderous instruments, more than two inches long; they were
thick and sharp as needles. The birds were hardly on the
ground before the feathers of the neck were ruffled and they
flew at each other. In less time than had been taken to gaff
them, one was lying on the ground dead, with its tongue

hanging out and the blood running from its mouth. The eagerness and vehemence, noise and uproar, wrangling, betting, swearing, and scuffling of the crowd, exhibited a dark picture of human nature and a sanguinary people. I owe it to the ladies to say that in the city they never are present at such scenes. Here they went for no other reason that I could see than because they were away from home, and it was part of the fête. We must make allowances for an education and a state of society every way different from our own. They were not wanting in sensibility or refinement; though they did not turn away with disgust, they seemed to take no interest in the fight and when it was over they were not disposed to tarry for a second.

Leaving the disgusting scene, we walked around the suburbs, where at one point we beheld a noble view of the plain and city of Guatemala, with the surrounding mountains, and we could not help but wonder how, amid objects so grand and glorious, men can grow up with tastes so groveling. Crossing the plaza, we heard music in a large house belonging to a rich muleteer; and entering, we found a young harpist, and two mendicant friars with shaved crowns, dressed in white, with long white mantles and hoods, of an order newly revived in Guatemala. They were all drinking *aguardiente*. Mantas and hats were thrown off and tables and seats placed against the wall; in a few moments my friends were waltzing. Two or three cotillons followed before we returned to the posada, where, after fruit of various kinds had been served, we all took seats on the back piazza. A horse happened to be loose in the yard, and a young man, putting his hands on its hind quarters, jumped on its back; the rest of the young men followed suit. Then one of them lifted the horse up by its forelegs and, when he dropped them, another took them up, to be followed, in turn, by all the others, very much to the astonishment of the poor animal. Then there followed a game in which the young men stood on the piazza and jumped over each other's heads; then one man leaned down with his hands resting on the piazza while another man mounted on his back, the first man trying to shake the second man off without letting go his hands. Other feats followed, all impromptu, and each more absurd than the one before it. The last game was a bull-fight, in which two young men mounted on the backs of two others as matadors, and a third man, with his head between his shoulders, ran at them like a bull. Though these amusements were not very elegant, all were so intimate with each other, and there was such perfect abandonment, that the whole went off with shouts of laughter.

The young men now brought out the ladies' mantas and again we sallied forth for a walk. But, when we reached the plaza, the young men changed their minds and, seating the ladies to whom I attached myself in the shade, they commenced to play prisoner's base. All who passed stopped, and the villagers seemed delighted with the gaiety of our party. The players tumbled each other in the dust, to the great amusement of the lookers-on, until we saw trays coming across the plaza, which was a sign of dinner. After dinner, thinking that I had seen enough for one Sunday, I determined to forego the bullfight. In company with Don Manuel and another prominent member of the Assembly and his family, I set out on my return to the city. Their mode of traveling was primitive. All were on horseback: the Assemblyman with a little son behind him, his daughter alone, his wife on a pillion with a servant to support her, a servant-maid with a child in her arms, and a servant on the top of the luggage. It was a beautiful afternoon, and the plain of Guatemala, with its green grass and dark mountains, was a lovely scene. As we entered the city we encountered another religious procession, with priests and monks all bearing lighted candles and preceded by men throwing rockets. We avoided the plaza on account of the soldiers and, in a few minutes, I was in my house, alone.

Chapter XIII

~~~~~~

ON Tuesday, the seventeenth of December, I set out on
an excursion to La Antigua Guatemala and the Pacific
Ocean. I was accompanied by a young man who lived opposite me and who wished to ascend the Volcán de Agua. I
had discharged Augustin and with great difficulty procured
a man who knew the route. Rumaldo had but one fault: he
was married! Like some other married men, he had a fancy
for roving, but his wife set her face against this propensity.
She said that I was going to *el mar*, the sea, and might carry
him off and she would never see him again; [1] the affectionate
woman wept at the bare idea, but upon my paying the
money into her hands before going, she consented. My only
luggage was a hammock and pair of sheets, which Rumaldo
carried on his mule, and each of us had a pair of alforjas. At
the gate we met Don José Vidaurre, whom I had first seen
in the president's chair of the Constituent Assembly, who
was setting out to visit his hacienda at Antigua. Though it
was only five or six hours' distant, Señor Vidaurre, being a

---

1. Rumaldo, Stephens tells us, was killed at the battle of Comitán,
May 15th, 1841.

very heavy man, had two led horses, one of which he insisted on my mounting. When I expressed my admiration
of the animal, he told me, in the usual phrase of Spanish
courtesy, that the horse was mine. It was done in the same
spirit in which a Frenchman, who, entertained hospitably in
a country house in England, would offer himself to seven
of the daughters of his host, merely as a compliment. My
worthy friend would have been very much astonished if I
had accepted his offer.

The road to Mixco I have already described. In the village I stopped to see Chico. His hand had been cut off and
he was doing well. Leaving the village, we ascended a steep
mountain, from the top of which we had a fine view of the
village at its foot, the plain and city of Guatemala, and the
Lake of Amatitlán, enclosed by a belt of mountains. Descending by a wild and rugged road, we reached a plain and
saw on the left the village of San Lucas, and on the right,
at some distance, San Mateo. We then entered a piece of
woodland and crossed another mountain, descending its
precipitous side, with a magnificent ravine on our right, to
a beautiful stream. At this place mountains rose all around
us; but the banks of the stream were covered with delicate
flowers, and parrots with gay plumage were perched on the
trees and flying over our heads, making, in the midst of
gigantic scenery, a fairy spot. The stream passed between
two ranges of mountains so close together that there was
barely room for a single horsepath by its side. As we continued, the mountains turned to the left, and on the other
side of the stream were a few openings cultivated with
cochineal into the very hollow of the mountainside. Again the
road turned and then ran straight, making a vista of more
than a mile between the mountains. At the end of the road
in a delightful valley stood Antigua, shut in by mountains
and hills that always retain their verdure, watered by two
rivers that supply numerous fountains, with a climate in
which heat or cold never predominates. Yet this city, surrounded by more natural beauty than any location I ever
saw, has perhaps undergone more calamities than any city
that was ever built. We passed the gate and rode through

the suburbs in the opening of the valley, on one side of which was a new house, that reminded me of an Italian villa, with a large cochineal plantation extending to the base of the mountain. We crossed a stream bearing the poetical name of El Río Pensativo; on the other side was a fine fountain, and at the corner of the street was the ruined church of Santo Domingo, a monument of the dreadful earthquakes which had prostrated the old capital and driven the inhabitants from their home.

On each side were the ruins of churches, convents, and private residences, large and costly; some were lying in masses, some with fronts were still standing. Richly ornamented with stucco, they were cracked and yawning and roofless, without doors or windows, and with trees growing inside above the walls. Many of the houses have been repaired, and the city, now repeopled, presents a strange appearance of both ruin and recovery. The inhabitants, like the dwellers over the buried Herculaneum, seemed to entertain no fears of renewed disaster. I rode up to the house of Don Miguel Manrique, which had been occupied by his family at the time of the destruction of the city, and, after receiving a kind welcome, in company with Señor Vidaurre, I walked to the plaza.

The print (figure 31) will give an idea, which I cannot, of the beauty of this scene. The great volcanoes of Agua and Fuego look down upon the plaza in the center of which is a noble stone fountain. Facing the square is the palace of the captain-general, which displays on its front the armorial bearings granted by Emperor Charles the Fifth to the loyal and noble city, and is surmounted by the Apostle St. James on horseback, armed and brandishing a sword. And there, also, is the majestic but roofless and ruined cathedral, three hundred feet long, one hundred and twenty broad, and nearly seventy high, lighted by fifty windows. These and other buildings show at this day that Antigua was once one of the finest cities of the New World, that she deserved the proud name which Alvarado gave it, The City of St. James of Gentlemen.[2]

---

2. The complete name is "The Very Noble and Very Loyal City of St. James of the Knights of Guatemala."

This was the second capital of Guatemala, founded in 1543 after the destruction of the first by a water volcano. Its history is one of uninterrupted disasters. "In 1558 an epidemic disorder, attended with a violent bleeding at the nose, swept away great numbers of people; nor could the faculty devise any method to arrest the progress of the distemper. Many severe shocks of earthquake were felt at different periods; the one in 1565 seriously damaged many of the principal buildings; those of 1575, 76, and 77 were not less ruinous. On the 27th of December, 1581, the population was again alarmed by the volcano, which began to emit fire; and so great was the quantity of ashes thrown out and spread in the air, that the sun was entirely obscured, and artificial light was necessary in the city at midday.

"The years 1585 and 6 were dreadful in the extreme. On January 16th of the former, earthquakes were felt, and they continued through that and the following year so frequently that not an interval of eight days elapsed during the whole period without a shock more or less violent. Fire issued incessantly, for months together, from the mountain, and greatly increased the general consternation. The greatest damage of this series took place on the 23d of December, 1586, when the major part of the city again became a heap of ruins, burying under them many of the unfortunate inhabitants; the earth shook with such violence that the tops of the high ridges were torn off and deep chasms formed in various parts of the level ground.

"In 1601 a pestilential distemper carried off great numbers. It raged with so much malignity that three days generally terminated the existence of such as were affected by it.

"On the 18th of February, 1651, about one o'clock in the afternoon, a most extraordinary subterranean noise was heard, and was immediately followed by three violent shocks, at very short intervals from each other, which threw down many buildings and damaged others; the tiles from the roofs of the houses were dispersed in all directions, like light straws by a gust of wind; the bells of the churches were rung by the vibrations; masses of rock were detached from the mountains; and even the wild beasts were so terrified that, losing their natural instinct, they quitted their retreats and sought shelter among the habitations of men.

"The year 1686 brought with it another dreadful epidemic, which in three months swept away a tenth part of the inhabitants . . . . From the capital the pestilence spread to the neighbouring villages and thence to the more remote ones, causing dreadful havoc, particularly among the most robust of the inhabitants.

"The year 1717 was memorable; on the night of August 27th the mountain began to emit flames, attended by a continued subterranean rumbling noise. On the night of the 28th the eruption increased to great violence and very much alarmed the inhabitants. The images of saints were carried in procession, public prayers were put up day after day; but the terrifying eruption still continued and was followed by frequent shocks, at intervals, for more than four months. At last, on the night of September 29th, the fate of Guatemala appeared to be decided, and inevitable destruction seemed to be at hand. Great was the ruin among the public edifices; many of the houses were thrown down, and nearly all that remained were dreadfully injured; but the greatest devastation was seen in the churches.

"The year 1773 was the most melancholy epoch in the annals of this metropolis; it was then destroyed, and, as the capital, rose no more from its ruins. . . . About four o'clock, on the afternoon of July 29, a tremendous vibration was felt, and shortly after began the dreadful convulsion that decided the fate of the unfortunate city. . . . On the 7th of September there was another, which threw down most of the buildings that were damaged on the 29th of July; and on the 13th of December, one still more violent terminated the work of destruction. . . .

"The people had not well recovered from the consternation inflicted by the events of the fatal 29th of July, when a meeting was convoked for the purpose of collecting the sense of the inhabitants on the subject of the removal. . . . In this meeting it was determined all the public authorities should remove provisionally to the village of La Hermita until the valleys of Jalapa and Las Vacas could be surveyed and until the king's pleasure could be ascertained on the subject. . . .

"On the 6th of September the governor and all the tribunals withdrew to La Hermita; the surveys of the last-mentioned places being completed, the inhabitants were again convoked to decide upon the transfer. This congress was held in the temporary capital, and it lasted from the 12th to the 16th of January, 1774: the report of the commissioners was read, and, by a plurality of votes, it was resolved to make a formal translation of the city of Guatemala to the Valley of Las Vacas. The king gave his assent to this resolution on the 21st of July, 1775; and, by a decree of the 21st of September following, he approved most of the plans that were proposed for carrying the determination into effect, granting very liberally the whole revenue arising from the customs, for the space of ten years, toward the charges of building, &c. By virtue of this decree, the ayuntamiento was in due form established in the new situation on the 1st of January, 1776; and on the 29th of July, 1777, a proclamation was issued in Old Guatemala, commanding the population to remove to the new city within one year and totally abandon the remains of the old one."

Such is the account given by the historian [3] of Guatemala concerning the destruction of this city. I, myself, saw on the spot Padre Antonio Croquer, an octogenarian (who died on August 6, 1841) and the oldest canónigo in Guatemala, who was living in the city during the earthquake which completed its destruction. He was still vigorous in frame and intellect, writing his name with a free hand in my memorandum book, and he had vivid recollections of the splendor of the city in his boyhood, when, as he said, carriages rolled through it as in the streets of Madrid. On the fatal day he was in the Church of San Francisco with two padres, one of whom, at the moment of the shock, took him by the hand and hurried him into the patio; the other was buried under the ruins of the church. He remembered that the tiles

---

3. Quoted from pages 148–157 of the English translation of Juarros history of Guatemala (see note 4, p. 76).

flew from the roofs of the houses in every direction; the clouds of dust were suffocating, and the people ran to the fountains to quench their thirst. The fountains were broken, and one man snatched off his hat to dip for water. The archbishop slept that night in his carriage in the plaza. Father Antonio described to me the ruins of individual buildings, the dead who were dug from under them, and the confusion and terror of the inhabitants; though his recollections were only those of a boy, he had material enough for hours of conversation.

In company with the cura we visited the interior of the cathedral. The gigantic walls were standing but roofless. The interior was occupied as a burying ground, and the graves were shaded by a forest of dahlias and trees, seventy or eighty feet high, which rose above the walls. The grand altar stood under a cupola supported by sixteen columns faced with tortoise shell and adorned with bronze medallions of exquisite workmanship. On the cornice there had once been placed statues of the Virgin and the twelve apostles in ivory, but all these were now gone. Even more interesting than the recollections of its ancient splendor or its mournful ruins, was the empty vault where once reposed the ashes of Alvarado the Conqueror.

Toward evening my young companion Rumaldo rejoined me, and we set out for Santa María, an Indian village at two leagues' distance situated on the side of the Volcán de Agua, which we intended to ascend the next day to the summit. As we entered the valley, the scene was so beautiful I did not wonder that even earthquakes could not make it desolate. At the distance of a league we reached the village of San Juan del Obispo. The church and convent had been conspicuous from below and their site commanded a magnificent view of the valley and city of Antigua.

At dark we reached the village of Santa María, perched at a height of two thousand feet above Antigua and seven thousand feet above the level of the Pacific. The church stands in a noble court with several gates, and before it is a gigantic white cross. We rode up to the convent, which is under the care of the cura of San Juan del Obispo, but it was unoccupied, and there was no one to receive us except a talkative little old man, who had only arrived that morning. Very soon there was an irruption of Indians, who, with the alcalde and his alguaciles, came to offer their services as guides up the mountain. They were the first Indians I had met who did not speak Spanish, and their eagerness and clamor reminded me of my old friends the Arabs. They represented the ascent as very steep, with dangerous precipices; they said the path was extremely difficult to find, and that it would be necessary for each of us to have sixteen men with ropes to haul us up and to pay twelve dollars for each man. They seemed a little astonished when I told them that we wanted only two men each and would give them half a dollar apiece, but they fell immediately to eight men for each at a dollar apiece. After a noisy wrangling, we picked out six from forty, and they all retired.

In a few minutes we heard a violin out of doors, which we thought was in honor of us; but it was for the little old man, who was a *titiritero*, or puppet-player, who intended to give an exhibition that night. The music entered the room, and a man stationed himself at the door to admit visitors. The price of admission was three cents, and there were frequent wranglings to have one cent taken off or two admitted for three cents. The high price preventing the entrance of common people, the company was very select, and all sat on the floor. The receipts, as I learned from the doorkeeper, were upward of five shillings. Rumaldo, who was a skillful amateur, led the orchestra—that is, the other fiddler. The puppet-player was in an adjoining room, and when the door opened, a black *chamarra* was disclosed hanging as a curtain, the rising of which discovered the puppet-player sitting at a table with his little figures before him. The sports of the puppets were carried on with ventriloquial conversations, in the midst of which I fell asleep.

We did not get off till seven o'clock the next morning. The day was very unpromising, and the whole mountain was covered with clouds. At this point the side of the volcano was still cultivated. In half an hour the road became so steep and slippery that we dismounted and continued the ascent on foot; each of us was equipped with a strong staff. The Indians went on before, carrying water and provisions. At a quarter before eight we entered the middle region, which is covered with a broad belt of thick forest; the path was steep and muddy, and every three or four minutes we were obliged to stop and rest. At a quarter before nine we reached a clearing in which stood a large wooden cross. This was the first resting place, and we sat down at the foot of the cross and lunched. A drizzling rain had commenced, but, in the hope of a change, at half past nine we resumed our ascent. The path became steeper and muddier, the trees were so thickly crowded together, their branches and trunks covered with green excrescences, that the sun never found its way through them. The path was made and kept open by Indians, who go up in the wintertime to procure snow and ice for Guatemala. The labor of toiling up this muddy acclivity was excessive, and very soon my young companion became so fatigued that he was unable to continue without help. One of the ropes, with which the Indians were provided, was tied around his waist, and two Indians went ahead of him with the other end of the rope over their shoulders.

At half past ten we were above the region of forest and came out upon the open side of the volcano. There was still a scattering of trees, long grass, and a great variety of curious plants and flowers, furnishing rich materials for the botanist. Among them was a plant with a red flower, called the *mano del mico*, or hand-plant,[4] but more like a monkey's paw, growing to a height of thirty or forty feet, the inside a light vermilion color, and the outside vermilion with stripes of yellow. My companion, tired with the toil of ascending even with the aid of the rope, at length mounted an Indian's shoulders. I was obliged to stop every two or three minutes, and my rests were about equal to the actual time of walking. The great difficulty was on account of the wet and mud, which, in ascending, made us lose part of every step. It was so slippery that, even with the staff and the assistance of

4. The Spanish phrase means literally "monkey's hand."

branches of trees and bushes, it was difficult to keep from
falling. About half an hour before reaching the top, and
perhaps one thousand or fifteen hundred feet from it, the
trees became scarce and seemed blazed by lightning or
withered by cold. The clouds gathered thicker than before,
and I lost all hope of a clear day.

At half an hour before twelve we reached the top and
descended into the crater. A whirlwind of cloud and vapor
was sweeping around it. We were in a perspiration, our
clothes were saturated with rain and mud, and in a few moments the cold penetrated our very bones. We attempted to
build a fire, but the sticks and leaves were wet and would
not burn. For a few moments we raised a feeble flame and
all crouched around it, but a sprinkling of rain came down,
just enough to put it out. We could see nothing, and the
shivering Indians begged me to return. On rocks near us
were inscriptions, one of which bore the date of 1548, and
on a cut stone were the words:

> ALEXANDRO LDVERT
> DE SAN PETERSBURGO;
> EDVARDO LEGH PAGE,
> DE INGLATERRA;
> *JOSE CROSKEY,*
> *DE FYLADELFYE,*
> BIBYMOS AQUI UNAS BOTEAS
> DE CHAMPANA, EL DIA 26
> DE AGOSTO DE 1834.

It seemed strange that three men from such distant and
different parts of the world—St. Petersburg, England, and
Philadelphia—had met to drink champagne on the top of
this volcano. While I was blowing my fingers and copying
the inscription, the vapor cleared away a little and gave me
a view of the interior of the crater. It was a large oval basin,
the area level and covered with grass. The sides were sloping and about one hundred or one hundred and fifty feet
high; all around were masses of rock piled up in magnificent
confusion and rising to inaccessible peaks. There is no tradition of this mountain having ever emitted fire, and there is

no calcined matter or other mark of volcanic eruption anywhere in its vicinity. The historical account is that in 1541
an immense torrent, not of fire but of water and stones, was
vomited from the crater, by which the old city was destroyed.
Father Remesal [5] relates that on this occasion the crown of
the mountain fell down. The height of this detached part
was one league, and the distance from the remaining summit
to the plain was three leagues, which he affirms he measured
in 1615. The area, by my measurement, is eighty-three paces
long and sixty wide. According to Torquemada [6] (and such
is the tradition according to Padre Alcántara of Ciudad
Vieja), this immense basin, probably the crater of an extinct volcano with sides much higher than they are now,
became filled with water by accumulations of snow and rain.
There never was any eruption of water, but one of the sides
gave way, and the immense body of fluid rushed out with
horrific force, carrying with it rocks and trees, inundating
and destroying all that opposed its progress. The immense
barranca, or ravine, by which it descended was still fearfully
visible on the side of the mountain. The height of this mountain has been ascertained by barometrical observation to be
fourteen thousand four hundred and fifty feet above the
level of the sea. The edge of the crater commands a beautiful view of the old city of Guatemala, thirty-two surrounding villages, and the Pacific Ocean—at least so I am told,
but I saw nothing of it. Nevertheless, I did not regret my
labor and, though drenched with rain and plastered with
mud, I promised myself that in the month of February,
when the weather is fine, I would ascend again, prepared
for the purpose, and would pass two or three days in the
crater.

At one o'clock we began our descent. It was rapid and
sometimes dangerous from the excessive steepness and slip-
periness, and the chance of pitching head foremost against

5. Fray Antonio de Remesal, author of *Historia General de las
Indias Occidentales y particular de la Gobernación de Chiapa y Guatemala.* (Modern Edition, Guatemala, 1932.)
6. Juan Torquemada, author of *Monarquía indiana,* Madrid, 1613.

the trunk of a tree. At two o'clock we reached the cross. I mention as a hint for others, that, because of the pressure of heavy waterproof boots upon the *doigts du pied,* I was obliged to stop frequently; and, after changing the pressure by descending sidewise and backward, catching at the branches of trees, I was obliged to pull off my boots and go down barefooted, ankle deep in mud. My feet were severely bruised by the stones, and I could hardly walk at all, when I met one of the Indians pulling my horse up the mountain to meet me. At four o'clock we reached Santa María; at five, Antigua; and at a quarter past, I was in bed.

The next morning I was still asleep when Señor Vidaurre rode into the courtyard to escort me on my journey, but, leaving Rumaldo to follow, I was soon mounted. Emerging from the city, we entered the open plain, shut in by mountains cultivated to their base with cochineal. At about a mile's distance we turned in to the hacienda of Señor Vidaurre. In the yard were four oxen grinding sugar cane, and behind was his nopal, or cochineal plantation, one of the largest in Antigua. The plant is a species of cactus, set out in rows like Indian corn, which, at that time, was about four feet high. On every leaf was pinned with a thorn a piece of cane, in the hollow of which were thirty or forty insects. These insects cannot move, but they do breed; the young crawl out and fasten upon the leaf and, when they have once fixed, they never move; a light film gathers over them and, as they feed, the leaves become mildewed and white. At the end of the dry season some of the leaves are cut off and hung up in a storehouse for seed; the insects are brushed off from the rest and dried, and are then sent abroad to minister to the luxuries and elegances of civilized life, and to enliven with their bright colors the salons of London, Paris, and St. Louis in Missouri. The crop is valuable but uncertain, as an early rain may destroy it, and sometimes all the workmen of a hacienda are taken away for soldiers at the moment when they are most needed for its culture. The situation was ravishingly beautiful at the base and under the shade of the Volcán de Agua, and the view was bounded on all sides by mountains of perpetual green; the morning air was soft and balmy, but pure and refreshing. With good government and laws, and one's friends around, I never saw a more beautiful spot on which man could desire to pass his allotted time on earth.

Resuming our ride, we came out upon a rich plain between the bases of the two great volcanoes; it was covered with grass and on it cattle and horses were pasturing. On the left, at a distance, on the side of the Volcán de Agua, we saw the Church of Ciudad Vieja, the first capital of Guatemala, which was founded by Alvarado the Conqueror. I was now on classic ground. The fame of Cortes and his exploits in Mexico had spread among the Indian tribes to the south, and the Kakchiquel kings sent an embassy offering to acknowledge themselves vassals of Spain. Cortes received the ambassadors with distinction, and sent Pedro de Alvarado, an officer distinguished in the conquest of New Spain, to receive the submission of the native kings and take possession of Guatemala. On the thirteenth of November, 1523, Alvarado left the city of Mexico with three hundred Spaniards, and a large body of Tlascaltecas, Cholultecas, Chimapas, and other auxiliary Mexican Indians. He fought his way through the populous provinces of Soconusco and Tonalá and, on the fourteenth of May, by a decisive victory over the Quiché Indians, he arrived at the capital of the Kakchiquel kingdom, now known as the village of Tecpán Guatemala. After remaining a few days to recover from their fatigues, the conquering army continued their route by the villages on the coast, overcoming all that disputed their progress. On the 24th of July, 1524, they arrived at a place called by the Indians Almolonga, meaning, in their language, a spring of water (or the mountain from which water flows), situated at the base of the Volcán de Agua. The situation, says Remesal, pleased them so much by its fine climate, by the beauty of the meadows delightfully watered by running streams, and particularly by its position lying as it did between two lofty mountains, from one of which descended runs of water in every direction, and from the summit of the other issued volumes of smoke and fire, that they determined to build a city which should be the capital of Guatemala.

On the twenty-fifth of July (the festival of St. James, the patron of Spain), the soldiers, with martial music, and with splendid armor, waving plumes, and horses superbly caparisoned in trappings glittering with jewels and plates of gold, proceeded to the humble church which had been constructed for that purpose, where Juan Godínez, the chaplain to the army, said mass. The whole body invoked the protection of the apostle, and called by his name the city they had founded. On the same day Alvarado appointed alcaldes, regidores, and the chief alguacil. The appearance of the country harmonized with the romantic scenes of which it had been the theatre; as I rode over the plain I could almost imagine the sides of the mountains covered with Indians, and Alvarado and his small band of daring Spaniards, soldiers and priests, with martial pride and religious humility, unfurling the banners of Spain and setting up the standard of the cross.

As we approached the town its situation appeared more beautiful. But very early in its history dreadful calamities befell it. "In 1532 the vicinity of the city was ravaged, and the inhabitants thrown into consternation by a lion of uncommon magnitude and ferocity, that descended from the forests on the mountain called the Volcán de Agua, and committed great devastation among the herds of cattle. A reward of twenty-five gold dollars, or one hundred bushels of wheat, was offered by the town council to any person that could kill it; but the animal escaped, even from a general hunting party of the whole city with Alvarado at the head of it. After five or six months' continual depredations, he was killed on the thirtieth of July by a herdsman, who received the promised reward. The next great disaster was a fire that happened in February, 1536, and caused great injury; as the houses were at the time nearly all thatched with straw, a large portion of them was destroyed before it could be extinguished. The accident originated in a blacksmith's shop; to prevent similar misfortunes in the future, the council prohibited the employment of forges within the city.

"The most dreadful calamity that had as yet afflicted this unfortunate place occurred on the morning of September 11, 1541. It had rained incessantly, and with great violence, on the three preceding days, particularly on the night of the tenth, when the water descended more like the torrent of a cataract than rain; the fury of the wind, the incessant appalling lightning, and the dreadful thunder, were indescribable. . . . At two o'clock on the morning of the eleventh, the vibrations of the earth were so violent that the people were unable to stand. The shocks were accompanied by a terrible subterranean noise, which spread universal dismay; and, shortly afterward, an immense torrent of water rushed down from the summit of the mountain, forcing away with it enormous fragments of rocks and large trees, which, descending upon the ill-fated town, overwhelmed and destroyed almost all the houses, and buried a great number of the inhabitants under the ruins; among the many, Doña Beatriz de la Cueva, the widow of Pedro de Alvarado, lost her life." [7]

All the way down the side of the volcano we saw the seams and gullies made by the torrents of water which had inundated the city. Again we crossed the beautiful stream of El Río Pensativo, and rode up to the convent. It stands adjoining the gigantic and venerable church of the Virgin. In front was a high stone wall. A large gate opened into a courtyard, at the extremity and along the side of which were the spacious corridors of the convent, and on the left the gigantic wall of the church, with a door of entry from one end of the corridor. The patio was sunk about four feet below the level of the corridor, and divided into parterres, with beds of flowers; in the center was a large white circular fountain, with goldfish swimming in it, and rising out of it, above a *jet d'eau*, an angel with a trumpet and flag.

Señor Vidaurre had advised Padre Alcántara of my intended visit and he was waiting to receive us. He was about thirty-three, intelligent, educated, and energetic, with a passion for flowers, as was shown by the beautiful arrangements

---

7. Quoted from pages 146–148 of the English translation of Juarros history of Guatemala (see note 4, p. 76).

of the courtyard. He had been banished by Morazán and had only returned to his curacy about a year before. On a visit to him was his friend and neighbor Don Pepe Asteguieta, proprietor of a cochineal hacienda and a man of the same stamp and character. They were among the few whom I met who took any interest in the romantic events connected with the early history of the country.

After a brief rest in the convent, with a feeling more highly wrought than any that had been awakened in me except by the ruins of Copán, we visited a tree standing before the church and extending wide its branches, under whose shade, tradition says, Alvarado and his soldiers first encamped. We visited also the fountain of Almolonga, or, in the Indian language, the mountain from which water flows, which first induced Alvarado to select this spot as the site for the capital. The fountain is a large natural basin of clear and beautiful water, shaded by trees, under which thirty or forty Indian women were washing. The ruined cathedral, on the spot where Juan Godínez first said mass, next claimed our attention. The walls of the cathedral were standing, and in one corner was a chamber filled with the sculls and bones of those destroyed by the inundation from the volcano. After breakfast we visited the church, which was very large and more than two hundred years old; its altar was rich in ornaments of gold and silver, among which was a magnificent crown of gold studded with diamonds and emeralds, which had been presented by one of the Philips to the Virgin, to whom the church was consecrated.

Returning to the house, I found that Padre Alcántara had prepared for me a visit from a deputation of Indians, which consisted of the principal chiefs and women, descendants of caciques of the Mexican auxiliaries of Alvarado, who called themselves, like the Spaniards, *conquistadores*, or conquerors. They entered wearing the same costumes which their ancestors had worn in the time of Cortes and bearing on a salver covered with velvet a precious book bound in red velvet, with silver corners and clasp, which contained the written evidence of their rank and rights. Dated 1639, it was written on parchment and contained the order of Philip the Fourth, acknowledging them as conquerors, and exempting them, as such, from the tribute paid by the native Indians. This exemption continued until the revolution of 1825, and even yet they call themselves descendants of the conquerors and the head of the Indian aristocracy. The interest which I felt in these memorials of the conquerors was increased in no small degree by the beauty and comfort of the convent and by Padre Alcántara's kindness. In the afternoon we walked down to the bridge across the Río Pensativo. The plain on which the Spanish soldiers had glittered in armor was shaded by the high volcanoes, and the spirit of romance rested upon it.

The day which I passed at the "old city" is one of those upon which I look back with pleasure. Señor Vidaurre and Don Pepe remained with us all day. Afterward, when Padre Alcántara had again been obliged to flee from the convent at the approach of an invading army, and after we had all passed through the crash of the revolution, on leaving Guatemala to return home, I diverged from my road to pay them a visit; they were the last friends to whom I said farewell.

In the morning, with great regret, I left Ciudad Vieja. Padre Alcántara and Don Pepe accompanied me, and, to help me on my journey, the latter lent me a noble mule, and the padre an excellent servant. The exit from this mountain-girt valley was between the two great volcanoes of Agua and Fuego, rising on each side nearly fifteen thousand feet; and from between the two, so unexpectedly to me as almost to induce a burst of enthusiasm, we overlooked an immense plain, and saw the Pacific Ocean. At a league's distance we reached the village of Alotenango, where, among Indian huts, stood another gigantic church, roofless and ruined by an earthquake, and where, with the hope, in which I was not disappointed, of seeing them again, I took leave of the cura and Don Pepe. The road between the two great volcanoes was singularly interesting; one with its base cultivated, girt by a belt of thick forests, and verdant to the very summit; the other with three bare and rugged peaks, covered with dried lava and ashes, shaken by the strife of the elements within and the working of internal fires, and emitting constantly a pale blue smoke. The road bears marks of the violent convulsions to which it has been subject. In one place the horse path lies through an immense chasm rent asunder by a natural convulsion, over which huge stones, hurled in every direction, lay in the wildest confusion; in another it crosses a deep bed of ashes, cinders, and scorified lava; and a little farther on, strata of decomposed vegetable matter covers the volcanic substances, and high shrubs and bushes have grown up, forming a thick shady arbor, fragrant as the fields of Araby the Blessed. At every step there was a strange contrast of the horrible and the beautiful. The last eruption of the Volcán de Fuego took place about twelve years ago, when flames issued from the crater and ascended to a great height; immense quantities of stones and ashes were cast out, and the race of monkeys inhabiting the neighboring woods was almost extirpated. But it can never burst forth again; its crater is no longer *la Boca del Infierno*, or the Mouth of the Infernal Regions, for, as a very respectable individual told me, it has been blessed by a priest.

After a beautiful ride under a hot sun, but shaded nearly all the way, at three o'clock we reached Escuintla, where there was another magnificent church, roofless, and again with its rich façade cracked by an earthquake. Before it were two venerable ceiba trees, and the platform commanded a splendid panoramic view of the volcanoes and mountains of Antigua.

In the streets were soldiers and drunken Indians. I rode to the house of the corregidor, Don Juan Dios de Guerra, and, with Rumaldo for a guide, I walked down to the banks of a beautiful stream which makes Escuintla in the summer months of January and February the great watering place of Guatemala. The bank was high and beautifully shaded. Descending to the river through a narrow passage between perpendicular rocks, in a romantic spot where many a Guatemalan lover has been hurried by the charming influences around into a premature outpouring of his hopes and fears, I sat down on a stone and washed my feet.

Returning, I stopped at the church. The front was cracked from top to bottom by an earthquake; the divided portions stood apart but the towers were entire. I ascended to the top and looked down into the roofless area. On the east the dark line of forest was broken by the curling smoke of a few scattered huts and backed by verdant mountains, by the cones of volcanoes with their tops buried in the clouds, and by the Rock of Mirandilla, an immense block of bare granite held up among the mountain tops, riven and blasted by lightning. On the west the setting sun illuminated a forest of sixty miles, and beyond it shed its dying glories over the whole Pacific Ocean.

At two o'clock in the morning, under a brilliant moon-light, and with a single guide, we started for the Pacific. The road was level and wooded. We passed a *trapiche*, or sugar-mill, worked by oxen, and before daylight we reached the village of Masagua, four leagues distant, which was built in a clearing cut out of the woods. At the entrance to the village we stopped under a grove of orange trees and by the light of the moon filled our pockets and alforjas with the shining fruit. Daylight broke upon us in a forest of gigantic trees, from seventy-five to a hundred feet high and from twenty to twenty-five feet in circumference, with creepers winding around their trunks and hanging from the branches. The road was merely a path through the forest, formed by cutting away shrubs and branches.

The freshness of the morning was delightful. We had descended from the table of land called the *tierras templadas* and were now in the *tierras calientes*, but at nine o'clock the glare and heat of the sun did not penetrate the thick shade of the woods. In some places the branches of the trees, trimmed by the machete of a passing muleteer and hung with a drapery of vines and creepers bearing red and purple flowers, formed for a long distance natural arches more beautiful than any ever fashioned by man. And there were parrots and other birds of beautiful plumage flying among the trees; among them were the *guacamayas*, or great ma-caws, large birds clothed in red, yellow, and green, which when on the wing displayed a splendid plumage. But there were also vultures and scorpions, and, running across the road and up the trees, innumerable iguanas, or lizards, from an inch to three feet long. The road was a mere track among the trees and perfectly desolate, though twice we met mule-teers bringing up goods from the port.

At the distance of twelve miles we reached the hacienda of Naranjo, occupied by a major-domo, who looked after the cattle of the proprietor, which roamed wild in the woods. The house which stood alone in the midst of a clearing was built of poles, with a cattle yard in front where I spied a cow with a calf, which was a sign of milk. But you must catch a cow before you can milk her! The major-domo went out with a lasso and, playing upon the chord of nature, caught the calf first and then the cow, which he hauled up by the horns to a post. The hut had but one *guacal*, or drinking shell, made of a gourd, and it was so small that we sat down by the cow so as not to lose much time. We had bread, chocolate, and sausages, and after a ride of twenty-four miles, they made a glorious breakfast; but we exhausted the poor cow, and I was ashamed to look the calf in the face.

Resuming our journey, at a distance of nine miles we reached the solitary hacienda of Overo. The whole of this great plain was densely wooded and entirely uncultivated, but the soil was rich and capable of maintaining with very little labor thousands of people. Beyond Overo the country was open in places, and the sun beat down with scorching force. At one o'clock we crossed a rustic bridge, and through the opening in the trees saw the river Michatoya. We fol-lowed along its bank, and very soon we heard breaking on the shore the waves of the great southern ocean. The sound was grand and solemn, giving a strong impression of the immensity of those waters which had been rolling from the creation for more than five thousand years, unknown to civilized man. I was loth to disturb the impression, and rode slowly through the woods, listening in profound silence to the grandest music that ever fell upon my ear. The road terminated on the bank of the river, and I had crossed the Continent of America.

On the opposite side was a long sand bar, with a flagstaff, two huts built of poles and thatched with leaves, and three sheds of the same rude construction; over the bar were seen the masts of a ship, riding on the Pacific. This was the port of Iztapa. We shouted above the roar of the waves, and a man came down to the bank, and loosing a canoe, came over for us. In the meantime, the interest of the scene was somewhat broken by a severe assault of mosquitoes and sand flies. The mules suffered as much as we; but I could not take them across with us, and was obliged to tie them under the trees. Neither Rumaldo nor my guide could be prevailed upon to remain and watch them; they said it would be death to sleep there.

The river is the outlet of the Lake of Amatitlán, and is said to be navigable from the Falls of San Pedro Mártir, seventy miles from its mouth; but there are no boats upon it, and its banks are in the wildness of primeval nature. The crossing place was at the old mouth of the river. The sand bar extends about a mile farther, and has been formed since the conquest. Landing, I walked across the sand to the house, or hut, of the captain of the port, and a few steps beyond saw the object of my journey, the boundless waters of the Pacific. When Núñez de Balboa, after crossing swamps and rivers, mountains and woods which had never been passed but by straggling Indians, came down upon the shores of this newly discovered sea, he rushed up to his middle in the waves with his buckler and sword, and took possession of it in the name of the king, his master, vowing to defend it in arms against all his enemies. But Núñez had the assurance that beyond that sea "he would find immense stores of gold, out of which people did eat and drink"; I had only to go back again. I had ridden nearly sixty miles and the sun was intensely hot, the sand burning; very soon I entered the hut and threw myself into a hammock. The hut, built of poles set up in the sand and thatched with the branches of trees, was furnished with a wooden table, a bench, and some boxes of merchandise, and was swarming with mosquitoes. The captain of the port, as he brushed them away, complained of the desolation and dreariness of the place, its isolation and separation from the world, its unhealthiness, and the misery of a man doomed to live there; and yet he feared the result

of the war, a change of administration, and being turned
out of office!

Toward evening, rested and refreshed, I walked out upon
the shore. The port is an open roadstead, without bay, headland, rock or reef, or anything whatever to distinguish it
from the line of the coast. There is no light at night, and
vessels at sea take their bearings from the great volcanoes
of Antigua, more than sixty miles inland. A buoy was anchored outside of the breakers with a cable attached, and
under the sheds were three large launches for embarking
and disembarking cargoes. The ship whose masts we had
seen as we approached lay off more than a mile from the
shore. She had come from Bordeaux and since her boat had
landed the supercargo and passengers, she had had no communication with the land, seeming, in fact, to be proudly
independent of so desolate a place. Behind the sand bar were
a few Indian huts, and Indians nearly naked were sitting by
me on the shore. Yet this desolate place was once the focus
of ambitious hopes, high aspirations, lust of power and gold,
and romantic adventure. Here Alvarado fitted out his arma-
ment and embarked with his followers to dispute with
Pizarro the riches of Peru. The sun was sinking, and the red
globe touched the ocean; clouds were visible on its face, and
when it disappeared, ocean and land were illuminated with
a ruddy haze. I returned to the hut and threw myself into
my hammock. Could it be that I was again so far from home,
and that these were the waves of the great southern ocean
breaking on my ears?

Chapter XIV

〰〰〰〰〰〰〰〰〰〰〰〰〰〰〰〰〰〰〰〰〰〰〰〰〰〰〰〰

The return. Hunt for a mule. Overo. Masagua. Escu-
intla. Falls of San Pedro Mártir. Michatoya River. Village
of San Pedro. A major-domo. San Cristóbal. Amatitlán.
A roving American. Entry into Guatemala. Letter from
Mr. Catherwood. Christmas Eve. Arrival of Mr. Cather-
wood. Plaza de Toros. A bullfight. The theatre. Official
business. The aristocracy of Guatemala. State of the
country. New Year's Day. Ferocity of party.

AT three o'clock in the morning Rumaldo woke me to
set out on my return to Guatemala City. The moonbeams were glancing over the water and the canoe was
ready. I bade farewell to my host as he lay in his hammock,
and crossed the river to find an unexpected difficulty: my
spare mule had broken her halter and was nowhere to be
seen. We beat about among the woods till daylight, when,
concluding that she must have taken the only path open and
set out for home on her own account, we saddled and rode
on back to the hacienda of Overo, a distance of twenty miles.
But no stray mule had passed Overo, so I stopped there
and sent Rumaldo back to the port.

Very soon I became tired of waiting at the miserable
hacienda and, saddling my mule, I started alone. The road
was so shaded that I did not stop for the noonday heat. For
twenty-one miles the road was perfectly desolate, the only
sound being the occasional crash of a falling tree. At the
village of Masagua I rode up to a house, at which I saw a
woman under the shed. Unsaddling my mule, I got her to
send a man out to cut *zacate*, and to make me some chocolate. I was so pleased with my independence that I almost

resolved to travel altogether by myself, without servant or change of apparel. In half an hour I resumed my journey. Toward sundown I met drunken Indians coming out from Escuintla, and, as I looked back over the great plain, I saw the sun fast sinking into the Pacific. It was some time after dark when I rode up to the house of the corregidor, having performed in two days a hundred and ten miles. Unfortunately, there was no *zacate* for my mule. This article is brought into the towns daily by the Indians, and every person buys just enough for the night and no more. There was not a spare lock of grass in the place. With a servant of the corregidor's I made an exploring expedition through the town, and by an affecting appeal to an old woman (enforced by treble price), I bought from under their very noses the ration of two mules and left them supperless.

I waited till two o'clock the next day for Rumaldo and the mule, and, after a vain endeavor to procure a guide to the falls of San Pedro Mártir, I set out alone direct for Guatemala City. At the distance of two leagues, in ascending a steep hill I passed a *trapiche*, or sugar mill, in a magnificent situation commanding a full view of the plain I had crossed and the ocean beyond. Two oxen were grinding sugar cane, and under a shed was a large boiling caldron for making *panela*, a brown sugar, in lumps of about two pounds each, an enormous quantity of which is consumed in the country. Here the humor seized me to make some inquiries about the falls of San Pedro Mártir. A man, out at the elbows and every other mentionable and unmentionable part of his body, who was glad to get rid of regular work, offered to conduct me. I had passed a league back the place where I ought to have turned off, so now, with my guide, I proceeded onward to the village of San Pedro, where we turned off to the right and, going back almost in the same direction, descended by a narrow path through thick woods choked with bushes into a ravine where we reached the Michatoya River, which I had crossed at Iztapa. The river was narrow and rapid, breaking wildly over a stony bed, with a high mountain on the opposite side. Following it, we reached the cataract which was partly concealed by bushes. Consisting of four streams separated by granite rock, and precipated from a height of about two hundred feet, it formed with the wild scenery around a striking and romantic view. A little below the cataract were a sugar mill worked by water and an uncommonly fine hacienda, which commanded a view of the falls and at which I was very much disposed to pass the night. The major-domo, a black man, was somewhat surprised at my visit, but when he learned that I did not come to see the mill, but only the falls, he seemed to suspect that I was no better than I should be; and when I asked him if I could reach San Cristóbal before dark, he answered that I could if I started immediately. This was not exactly an invitation to stay, and I left him. It shows the want of curiosity and indolence of the people, that, though these falls are but a pleasant afternoon's ride from Escuintla, which for two months is thronged with visitors from Guatemala, nobody ever visits them.

Hurrying back by the same wild path, we reached the main road, and, as it was late, I hired my guide to go on with me to San Cristóbal. We passed through the village of San Pedro, a collection of miserable huts with an *estanco*, or place for the sale of *aguardiente*, which was thronged with half-intoxicated Indians. As we advanced, clouds began to gather around the mountains, and there was every appearance of heavy rain. I had no cloak or greatcoat and, being particularly apprehensive of fevers and rheumatisms, after riding about a mile I returned to San Pedro. The most respectable citizens of the place were reeling round the *estanco*. They urged me to stop, but my guide said that they were a bad set and advised me to return and pass the night at the sugar mill. Presuming that he knew the people of whom he spoke better than I did, I was in no way inclined to disregard his caution. It was after dark when we reached the *trapiche*. Some of the workmen were sitting around a fire smoking; others were lying asleep under a shed; and I had but to

"*Look around and choose my ground,
And take my rest.*"

I inquired for the major-domo and was escorted to a mud house. In the dark I heard a harsh voice and, presently by the light of a pine stick, I saw an old and forbidding face, and by its side that of a young woman so soft and sweet that it seemed to appear expressly for the sake of contrast; and these two were one. I was disposed to pity the young wife; but the old major-domo was a noble fellow in heart, and she managed him so beautifully that he never suspected it. He was about to go to bed, but on my arrival he sent men out to cut *zacate;* both he and his wife were pleased that accident had brought me to their hut. The workmen sympathized in their humor, and we sat for two hours around a large table under the shed, with two candles sticking up in their own tallow. They could not comprehend that I had been to the top of the Volcán de Agua, and then had ridden down to the coast merely to see the Pacific. One of the men, a fine, open-faced young man, had a great desire to travel, but he did not like to go away from home. I offered to take him with me and give him good wages. The subject was discussed aloud: It was an awful thing for him to go away from home, and among strangers, where no one would care for him. His house was the outside of the major-domo's hut, but his home was in the hearts of his friends, and perhaps some of them would be dead before he returned. The wife of the major-domo seemed a good spirit in tempering the hearts and conduct of these wild and half-naked men. I promised to give him money to pay his expenses home when he should wish to return, and before we retired he agreed to go with me. At three o'clock the old major-domo was shouting in my ears. I was not familiar with my own name with the *don* prefixed, and thought he had "waked up the wrong passenger." The courage of the young man who wished to travel failed him, and he did not make his appearance; in the expectation of his going, my guide also did not come, so I set out alone.

Before daylight I passed for the third time through the village of San Pedro, and a little beyond overtook a bundle on horseback which proved to be a boy and a woman with one poncho over both. The River Michatoya was foaming and breaking in a long succession of rapids on our right, as we rode on together to San Cristóbal. I rode up to the convent, pounced upon the cura at the witching hour of breakfast, and, mounting again, rode around the base of the Volcán de Agua, with its cultivated fields and belt of forest and verdure to the top. Opposite was another volcano, its sides covered with immense forests. Between the two I passed a single *trapiche* belonging to a convent of Dominican friars; in a large and beautiful valley, I passed hot springs, smoking for more than a mile along the road, and then entered among the nopals, or cochineal plantations, of Amatitlán. On both sides were high clay fences, and the nopals within the enclosures were more extensive than those of Antigua, and more valuable, for though Amatitlán is only twenty-five miles from Antigua, the climate here is so different they can produce two crops in each season.

Approaching the town, I remembered that Mr. Handy, who had traveled from the United States through Texas and Mexico with a caravan of wild animals, had told me in New York of an American in his employ who had been left at this place to take charge of a cochineal plantation, and I was curious to see how this man looked and flourished in such employment. I had forgotten his name, but when I inquired on the road for an American *del Norte*, I was directed to the nopal of which he had charge. It was one of the largest in the place and contained four hundred thousand plants. I rode up to a small building in the middle of the plantation, which looked like a summerhouse, and was surrounded by workmen, one of whom announced me as a "Spaniard," as the Indians generally called foreigners. Dismounting and giving my mule to an Indian, I entered and found Don Enrique sitting at a table with an account book before him, settling accounts with the workmen. He was dressed in the *cotón*, or jacket of the country, and had a very long beard, but I should have recognized him anywhere as an American. I addressed him in English, and he stared at me, as if startled by a familiar sound, and answered in Spanish. By degrees he comprehended the matter. He was under thirty, from Rhinebeck Landing on the Hudson River where his father kept a store, and his name was Henry Pawling. He had been a clerk in New York and then in Mexico. Induced by a large offer and a strong disposition to ramble and see the country, he had accepted the proposal from Mr. Handy. His business had been to go on before the caravan, hire a place, give notice, and make preparation for the exhibition of the animals. In this capacity he had traveled all over Mexico and from thence to Guatemala; it had been seven years since he left home. Since parting with Mr. Handy he had not spoken a word of his own language and, as he spoke it now, it was more than half Spanish. I need not say that he was glad to see me. He conducted me over the plantation and explained the details of the curious process of making cochineal. He was somewhat disappointed in his expectations and spoke with great feeling of home; but when I offered to forward letters, he said he had resolved never to write to his parents again, nor to inform them of his existence, until he retrieved his fortunes and saw a prospect of returning rich. He accompanied me into the town of Amatitlán. As it was late, and as I expected to return there, I did not stop to visit the lake but continued direct for Guatemala.

The road lay across a plain, with a high, precipitous, and verdant wall on the left. At a distance of a league we ascended a steep hill to the tableland of Guatemala. I regret that I cannot communicate to the reader the highest pleasure of my journey in Central America, that derived from the extraordinary beauty of scenery constantly changing. At the time I thought this the most delightful ride I had had in the country.

On the way I overtook a man and his wife on horseback, he with a gamecock under his arm, and she with a guitar. A little boy was hidden away among bedding on a luggage mule and four lads were with them on foot, each with a gamecock wrapped in matting with only the head and tail visible. They were going to Guatemala to pass the Christmas holidays, and with this respectable party I entered the gate of the city on the eighth day after my departure. I found a letter from Mr. Catherwood, dated at Esquipulas, advising me that after he had been robbed by his servant and taken ill, he had left the ruins and gone to Don Gregorio's, and that he was then on his journey to Guatemala. He also informed me that my messenger had passed through Copán and gone on he did not know where. I was in great distress, and resolved, after a day's rest, to set off in search of him.

I dressed myself and went to a party at the home of Señor Zebadúa, formerly minister to England, where I surprised the *guatemaltecos* by the tour I had made, and particularly by having come alone from Iztapa. Here I met Mr. Chatfield, her Britannic majesty's consul-general, and Mr. Skinner, who had arrived during my absence. It was Christmas Eve, the night of *El Nacimiento*, or birth of Christ. At one end of the *sala* was a raised platform with a green floor and decorated with branches of pine and cypress, on which birds were sitting; pieces of looking glass and sandpaper, and figures of men and animals represented a rural scene in which there was an arbor and a wax doll in a cradle—in short, the grotto of Bethlehem and the infant Saviour. Always, at this season of the year, every house in Guatemala has its *Nacimiento*, according to the wealth and taste of the proprietor. In time of peace the figure of the Saviour is adorned with family jewels, pearls, and precious stones, and at night every house is open, and the citizens, without acquaintance or invitation or distinction of rank or persons, go from house to house visiting; the week of *El Nacimiento* is the gayest of the year. Unfortunately, at this time it was observed only in form; the state of the city was too uncertain to permit the general opening of houses and running in the streets at night. Carrera's soldiers might enter.

The party was small, but consisted of the élite of Guatemala. It commenced with supper, after which followed dancing, and, I am obliged to add, smoking. The room was badly lighted, and the company, from the precarious state of the country, not gay; but the dancing was kept up till twelve o'clock, when the ladies put on their mantillas and we all went to the cathedral where were to be performed the imposing ceremonies of the Christmas Eve. The floor of the church was crowded with citizens and a large concourse from the villages around. Mr. Savage accompanied me home, and we did not get to bed till three o'clock in the morning.

The bells had done ringing and Christmas mass had been said in all the churches before I awoke. In the afternoon was the first bullfight of the season. My friend Vidaurre had called for me, and I was in the act of going to the Plaza de Toros, when there was a loud knock at the *puerta cochera*, and in rode Mr. Catherwood. He was armed to the teeth, pale and thin, and most happy at having reached Guatemala, but he was not half so happy as I was to see him. He was in advance of his luggage, but I dressed him up and carried him immediately to the Plaza de Toros.

The Plaza de Toros stands near the church of El Calvario, at the end of the Calle Real, in shape and form like the Roman amphitheatre. It was about three hundred and fifty feet long and two hundred and fifty broad, and was capable of containing, as we supposed, about eight thousand people, at least one-fourth of the population of Guatemala. When we arrived, it was crowded with spectators of both sexes and all classes, the best and the vilest in the city, but all were conducting themselves with perfect propriety. We recognized several parties; in fact, the greater part of our Guatemalan acquaintances were present.

The seats commenced about ten feet above the area, with a corridor and open wooden fence in front to protect the spectators. Astride sat Carrera's disorderly soldiers to keep order. At one end, underneath the corridor, was a large door through which the bull was to be let in. At the other end, separated by a partition from the part occupied by the rest of the spectators, was a large unoccupied box, formerly intended for the captain-general and other principal officers of government, and now reserved for Carrera. Underneath was a military band composed mostly of Indians. Notwithstanding the collection of people and the expectation of an animating sport, there was no clapping or stamping, or other expression of impatience and anxiety for the performance to begin.

At length Carrera entered the captain-general's box, dressed in a badly fitting blue military frock coat embroidered with gold; he was attended by Monte Rosa and other richly dressed officers, the alcalde, and members of the municipality. All eyes were turned toward him, as when a king or emperor enters his box at the theatre in Europe. A year before he had been hunted among the mountains with a reward for his body "dead or alive," and nine-tenths of those who now looked upon him would then have shut the city against him as a robber, murderer, and outcast.

Soon after, the picadores entered. They were eight in number and mounted, each carrying a lance and a red poncho. After galloping round the area, they stopped with their lances opposite the door at which the bull was to enter. The door was pulled open by a padre, a great cattle proprietor, who owned the bulls of the day. The animal rushed out into the area, kicking up his heels as if in play, but at the sight of the line of horsemen and lances he turned about and ran back quicker than he had entered. The padre's bull was an ox and, like a sensible beast, he would rather run than fight; but the door was closed upon him, and perforce he ran around the area, looking up to the spectators for mercy, and below for an outlet of escape. The horsemen followed, "prodding" him with their lances; and all round the area, men and boys on the fence threw barbed darts with ignited fireworks attached, which, sticking in his flesh and exploding on every part of his body, irritated him, and sometimes made him turn on his pursuers. The picadores led him on by flaring ponchos before him; as he pressed them, the skill of the picador consisted in throwing the poncho over his horns so as to blind him, and then fixing in his neck, just behind his jaw, a sort of balloon of fireworks. When this was done successfully it created shouts of applause.

The government, in an excess of humanity, had forbidden the killing of bulls, restricting the fight to worrying and torturing. Consequently, it was entirely different from the bullfight in Spain, and wanted even the exciting interest of a fierce struggle for life, and the chance of the *picador* being gored to death or tossed over among the spectators. But, watching the earnest gaze of thousands, it was easy to imagine the intense excitement of a martial age, when gladiators fought in the arena before the nobility and beauty of Rome.

Our poor ox, after being tired out, was allowed to withdraw. Others followed and went through the same round. All the padre's bulls were oxen. Sometimes a picador on foot was chased to the fence under a general laugh of the spectators. After the last ox had run his rounds, the picadores withdrew, and men and boys jumped over into the arena in such numbers that they fairly hustled the ox. The noise and confusion, and the flaring of colored ponchos, the running and tumbling, attacking and retreating, and the clouds of dust made this the most stirring scene of any. But altogether it was a puerile exhibition, and the better classes, among whom was my fair countrywoman, regarded it merely as an occasion for meeting acquaintances.

In the evening we went to the theatre, which opened for the first time. A large building had been commenced in the city, but in one of the revolutions it had been demolished and the work abandoned. The performance was in the courtyard of a house. The stage was erected across one of the corners; the patio was the pit, and the corridor was divided by temporary partitions into boxes. The audience sent beforehand, or servants brought with them, their own seats. We had invitations to the box of Señor Vidaurre. Carrera was there, sitting on a bench a little elevated against the wall of the house and at the right hand of Rivera Paz, the chief of the state. Some of his officers were with him in their showy uniforms, but he had laid his aside; he had on his black bombazet jacket and pantaloons and was very unpretending in his deportment. I considered him the greatest man in Guatemala, and made it a point to shake hands with him in passing.

The first piece was *Saide*,[1] a tragedy. The company consisted entirely of *guatemaltecos*, and their performance was

---

1. The editor has been unable to identify a play by this name. Possibly the play was *Zaïre*, the tragedy by Voltaire. *Saide* may represent what Stephens thought he heard when his Guatemalan friends tried to pronounce the foreign word *Zaïre*.

very good. There was no change of scenery, and, when the curtain fell, all lighted cigars, ladies included; fortunately, there was an open courtyard for the escape of smoke. When the performance was over, the boxes waited till the pit was emptied. Special care had been taken in placing sentinels, and all went home quietly.

During the week there was an attempt at gaiety, but it was all more or less blended with religious solemnities. One was that of the Novena, or term of nine days' praying to the Virgin. One lady, who was distinguished for the observance of this term, had an altar built across the whole end of the *sala*, with three steps decorated with flowers and a platform adorned with looking glasses, pictures, and figures, in the center of which was an image of the Virgin richly dressed. The whole was ornamented in a way impossible for me to describe, but which can be imagined in a place where natural flowers are in the greatest profusion and artificial ones made more perfect than in Europe, and where the ladies have extraordinary taste in the disposition of them. When I entered, the gentlemen were in an anteroom, with hats, canes, and small swords; and in the *sala* the ladies, with female servants cleanly dressed, were on their knees praying. In front of the fairy altar was one who seemed a fairy herself; while her lips moved, her bright eye was roving, and she looked more worthy of being kneeled to than the pretty image before her, and as if she thought so too.

In regard to my official business I was perfectly at a loss what to do. In Guatemala all were on one side; all said that there was no Federal government. And Mr. Chatfield, the British consul-general, whose opinion I respected more, concurred; he had even published a circular denying its existence. But the Federal government claimed to be in existence, and the bare suggestion of General Morazán's marching against Guatemala excited consternation. Several times there were rumors to that effect, one being that he had actually determined to do so, and that not a single priest would be spared, and that the streets would run with blood. The boldest partisans trembled for their lives. Morazán had never been beaten; Carrera had always run before him, and they had no faith in his being able to defend them, and they could not defend themselves. At all events, I had as yet heard only one side and did not consider myself justified in assuming that there was no government. I was bound to make "diligent search," and then I might return, in legal phrase, *cepi corpus*,[2] or *non est inventus*,[3] according to circumstances.

For this purpose I determined to go to San Salvador, which was formerly, and still claimed to be, the capital of the Confederation and the seat of the Federal government, or, rather, to Cojutepeque, to which place the government had been lately transferred on account of earthquakes at San Salvador. This project was not without its difficulties. One Rascón, with an insurgent and predatory band, occupied an intervening district of country, acknowledging neither party and fighting under his own flag. Mr. Chatfield and Mr. Skinner had come by sea, a circuitous route, to avoid him; and Captain Le Nonvel, master of a French ship lying at the port of San Salvador, who arrived in Guatemala almost on a run, having ridden sixty miles the last day over a mountainous country, reported horrible atrocities. He said that three men had been murdered near San Vicente, on their way to the fair at Esquipulas, and their faces so disfigured that they could not be recognized. Immediately on his arrival he sent a courier to order his ship up to Iztapa merely to take him back and save him from returning by land. I had signified my intention of going to San Salvador to the state government; they were dissatisfied with my going at all, but offered me an escort of soldiers, warning me, however, that if we met any of Morazán's soldiers there would certainly be a fight. This was not at all pleasant. I was loth to travel a third time the road to Iztapa, but, under the circumstances, I accepted Captain Le Nonvel's invitation to take a passage in his ship.

Meanwhile I passed my time in social visiting. In our own city the aristocracy is called by the diplomatic corps at

2. "I have found the body."
3. "It has not been found."

Washington "the aristocracy of streets." In Guatemala it is the aristocracy of houses, as certain families live in the houses built by their fathers at the time of the foundation of the city, and they are really aristocratic old mansions. These families, by reason of certain monopolies of importation, acquired under the Spanish dominion immense wealth and rank as "merchant princes." Still they were excluded from all offices and all part in the government. At the time of the revolution one of these families was noble with the rank of marquisate, but its head tore off the insignia of his rank and joined the revolutionary party. Next in position to the officers of the crown, these families thought that, emancipated from the yoke of Spain, they would have the government in their own hands; and so they had, but it was only for a short time. The principles of equal rights began to be understood, and they were put aside. For ten years they had been in obscurity, but accidentally they were again in power, and at the time of my visit ruled in social as well as political life. I do not wish to speak harshly of them, for they were the only people who constituted society. My intercourse was almost exclusively with them; my fair countrywoman was one of them; I am indebted to them for much kindness; and, besides, they are personally amiable. But I speak of them as public men; I did not sympathize with them in politics.

To me the position of the country seemed most critical, and from a cause which in all Spanish America had never operated before. At the time of the first invasion a few hundred Spaniards, by superior bravery and skill, and with more formidable arms, had conquered the whole Indian population. Naturally peaceable, and kept without arms, the conquered people had remained quiet and submissive during the three centuries of Spanish dominion. In the civil wars following the independence they had borne but a subordinate part, and down to the time of Carrera's rising they were entirely ignorant of their own physical strength. But this fearful discovery had now been made. The Indians constituted three-fourths of the inhabitants of Guatemala. They were the hereditary owners of the soil, and, for the first time since they fell under the dominion of the whites, they were organized and armed under a chief of their own, who chose for the moment to sustain the Central Party. I did not sympathize with that party, for I believed that in their hatred of the Liberals they were courting a third power that might destroy them both, that they were consorting with a wild animal which might at any moment turn and rend them in pieces. I believed that they were playing upon the ignorance and prejudices of the Indians. Through the priests, they played upon their religious fanaticism, amusing them with fêtes and church ceremonies, and persuading them that the Liberals aimed at a demolition of churches and the destruction of the priests. They were hurrying back the country into darkness and, in the general heaving of the elements, there was not a man of nerve enough among them, with the influence of name and station, to rally round him the strong and honest men of the country, reorganize the shattered republic, and save it from the disgrace and danger of truckling to an ignorant, uneducated Indian boy.

Such were my sentiments. Of course I avoided expressing them but, because I did not denounce their opponents, some looked coldly upon me. With them political differences severed all ties. Our worst party abuse is moderate and mild compared with the terms in which they speak of each other. We seldom do more than call men ignorant, incompetent, dishonest, dishonorable, false, corrupt, subverters of the Constitution, and bought with British gold; but here a political opponent is a robber, an assassin, and it is praise to admit that he is not a bloodthirsty cutthroat. We complain that our ears are constantly offended and our passions roused by angry political discussions; yet here it would have been delightful to hear a good, honest, hot, and angry political dispute. I traveled in every state, and never heard such a dispute, for I never met two men together who differed in political opinions. Defeated partisans are shot or banished, they run away or get a moral lockjaw, but they never dare express their opinions before one of the dominant party. We have just passed through a violent political struggle; [4] twenty millions of people have been divided almost man to

---

4. Stephens was writing this book in 1840 when "Tippecanoe and Tyler too" won the presidential election.

man, friend against friend, neighbor against neighbor, brother against brother, and son against father. Honest differences of opinion, ambition, want, and lust of power and office, have roused passions sometimes to fierceness. Two millions of men highly excited have spoken out their thoughts and sentiments fearlessly and openly. They have all been counted, and the first rule in arithmetic has decided between them. But the defeated party are still permitted to live in the country; their wives and children are spared; nay, more, they may grumble in the streets and hang out their banners of defiance, of continued and determined opposition; and, more than all, the pillars of the republic are not shaken! Among a million of disappointed men, never, with all the infirmities of human passion, has one breathed resistance to the Constitution and laws. The world has never presented such a spectacle, such a proof of the capacity of the people for self-government. Long may it continue! May the tongue wither that dares preach resistance to the ballot boxes; and may the moral influence of our example reach our distracted sister republics, staying the sword of persecution in the hands of victors and crushing the spirit of revolution in a defeated party.

January 1, 1840. This day, so full of home associations —snow and red noses and blue lips out of doors, and blazing fires and beauteous faces within—opened in Guatemala like a morning in spring. The sun seemed to rejoice in the beauty of the land it shone upon. The flowers were blooming in the courtyards, and the mountains, visible above the tops of the houses, were smiling in verdure. The bells of thirty-eight churches and convents proclaimed the coming of another year. The shops were shut as on a Sunday; there was no market in the plaza. Gentlemen well dressed, and ladies in black mantas were crossing the plaza to attend grand mass in the cathedral. Mozart's music swelled through the aisles. A priest in a strange tongue proclaimed morality, religion, and love of country. The floor of the church was thronged with whites, mestizos, and Indians.

On a high bench opposite the pulpit sat the chief of the state, and by his side Carrera, again dressed in his rich uniform. I leaned against a pillar opposite and watched Car-

rera's face; if I read him right, he had forgotten war and
the stains of blood upon his hands, and his very soul was
filled with fanatic enthusiasm, exactly as the priests would
have him. I did verily believe that he was honest in his impulses and would do right if he knew how. They who undertake to guide him have a fearful responsibility. The service
ended, and a way was cleared through the crowd. Carrera, accompanied by the priests and the chief of the state, awkward
in his movements, with his eyes fixed on the ground, or with
furtive glances, as if ill at ease in being an object of so much
attention, walked down the aisle. A thousand ferocious-
looking soldiers were drawn up before the door. A wild burst
of music greeted him, and the faces of the men glowed with
devotion to their chief. A broad banner was unfurled, with
stripes of black and red; there was a device of a death's head
and legs in the center, and on one side the words *Viva la
religion!* and on the other *Paz o muerte a los Liberales!*
Carrera placed himself at their head, and with Rivera Paz
by his side, and the fearful banner floating in the air, and
wild and thrilling music, and the stillness of death around,
they escorted the chief of the state to his house. How different from New Year's Day at home!

Fanatic as I knew the people to be in religion, and violent
as they were in political animosities, I did not believe that
they would countenance such an outrage as flaunting in the
plaza of the capital a banner linking together the support
of religion and the death or submission of the Liberal Party.
Afterward, in a conversation with the chief of the state, I
referred to this banner. He had not noticed it, but thought
that the last clause was *Paz o muerte a los que no la quieren,*
"to those who do not wish it." This does not alter its atrocious
character, and only adds to fanaticism what it takes from
party spirit. I think, however, that I am right, for on the
return of the soldiers to the plaza, Mr. Catherwood and I
followed the banner till, as we thought, the standard-bearer
contracted its folds expressly to hide it and some of the
officers looked at us so suspiciously that we withdrew.

For the sake of home associations, I called on my fair
countrywoman, and dined at Mr. Hall's. In the afternoon
I went to the cockpit, a large circular building handsomely

proportioned, with a high seat for the judges. When the judges rang a bell as a signal for the fight, there commenced a clamor: "I offer five dollars!" "I offer twenty," etc. I am happy to say that in this crowded den I saw but one man whom I had ever seen before. From the cockpit I went to the bullfight, and then to the theatre. The reader will admit that I made a brilliant beginning to the year 1840.

Chapter XV

O N Sunday, the fifth of January, I rose to set out in search of a government. Don Manuel Pavón, with his usual kindness, brought me a packet of letters of introduction to his friends in San Salvador. But Mr. Catherwood, who intended to accompany me to the Pacific, and I had not yet packed up, the muleteer had not made his appearance, and my passport had not been sent to me. Captain Le Nonvel waited till nine o'clock and then went on in advance. In the midst of my confusion I received a visit from a distinguished canónigo. The reverend prelate was surprised at my setting out on that day but, as I was about to plead my necessities as an excuse for traveling on the Sabbath, he relieved me by adding that there was to be a dinner party, a bullfight, and a play, and he wondered that I could resist such temptations.

At eleven o'clock the muleteer came with his mules, his wife, and a ragged little son. Mr. Savage, who was always my help through the little vexations attendant upon doing anything in that country, as well as in more important matters, returned from the Government House with word that my passport had been sent to my house. I knew that the government was displeased with my purpose of going to the capital. The night before it had been currently reported that I intended to present my credentials at San Salvador and to recognize the existence of the Federal government. And newspapers, received the same night by the courier from Mexico, were burdened with accounts of an invasion of that country by the Texans. I had before received a piece of information that was new to me, and of which it was considered diplomatic that I should profess ignorance, that is, that, though not so avowed, the Texans were supported and urged on by the government of the United States. We were considered here as bent upon the conquest of Mexico, and, of course, Guatemala would come next. The odium of our ambitious pretensions increased the feeling of coldness and distrust toward me arising from my not having attached myself to the dominant party. In general I was considered as the successor of Mr. DeWitt. It was known among politicians that proceedings were pending for the renewal of a treaty and that our government had a claim for the destruction of property of our citizens in one of the revolutions of the country, but some imagined that the special object of my mission was very deep and in favor of the party of San Salvador.

When Mr. Savage returned without my passport, I suspected an intention to embarrass me and make me lose the opportunity of going by sea, so I went immediately to the Government House, but I received the same answer that had been given to Mr. Savage. I thereupon requested another passport, but the secretary of state objected on the ground that none could be made out on that day. There were several clerks in the office, and I urged my pressing necessity, the actual departure of Captain Le Nonvel, my seasonable application, and the promise made me that it would be sent to my house. After an unpleasant parley, a passport was given me, but it was one which did not assign to me any official character. When I pointed out the omission, the secretary said that I had not presented my credentials. I answered that my credentials were to the general government and not to the State of Guatemala, which alone he represented, but he persisted that it was not the custom of his government to recognize an official character unless he presented his credentials. His government had been in existence about six months, and during that time no person claiming to be official had been near the country. I put into his hands my passport from my own government and, reminding him that I had been arrested and imprisoned once, I assured him that I should at all events set out for San Salvador and wished to know definitively whether he would give me such a passport as I had a right to ask for. After much hesitation, and with a very bad grace, he interlined before the official title the words *con el carácter*.

I make great allowance for party feeling in a country where political divisions are matters of life and death, and, more particularly, I made allowance for Don Joaquín Durand, whose brother, a priest, had been shot a short time before by the Morazán party. But this attempt to embarrass my movements by depriving me of the benefit of official character excited a feeling of indignation which I did not attempt to conceal. To refuse to accept the passport altogether or to wait a day for remonstrance would cause me to lose my passage by sea and make it necessary for me to either undertake a dangerous journey by land or abandon going to the capital. This, I believe, was precisely what was wished, and I was resolved not to be prevented by any indirect means. I only needed a passport to the port; the best they could give I did not value very highly and in San Salvador it would be utterly worthless. Therefore, with the uncourteous paper thus ungraciously bestowed, I returned to the house, and at two o'clock we started. It was the hottest hour of the day and when we passed the gate the sun was scorching. Late as it was, our muleteer had not finished his leave-taking. His wife and little son accompanied him, and at some distance outside we were obliged to stop in the hot sun and wait till they came up. We were extremely glad when they exchanged their last embraces and the wife and son turned off for their home in Mixco.

Notwithstanding the lateness of the hour, we diverged from the regular road for the purpose of passing by the Lake of Amatitlán, but it was dark when we reached the top of the high range of mountains which bounds that beautiful water. Looking down, it seemed like a gathering of fog in the bottom of a deep valley. The descent was by a rough zigzag path on the side of the mountain, very steep, and, in the extreme darkness, difficult and dangerous. We felt happy when we reached the bank of the lake, though still a little above it. The mountains rose around it like a wall and cast over it a gloom deeper than the shade of night. We rode for some distance with the lake on our left and a high and perpendicular mountainside on our right. A cold wind had succeeded the intense heat of the day, and when we reached Amatitlán, I was perfectly chilled. We found Captain Le Nonvel in the house he had indicated. It was nine o'clock, and, not having touched anything to eat since seven in the morning, we were prepared to do justice to the supper he had provided for us.

To avoid the steep descent to the lake with the cargo mules, our muleteer had picked up a guide for us on the road and had gone on himself direct, but to our surprise he had not yet arrived. While at supper we heard an uproar in the street, and a man ran in to tell us that a mob was murdering our muleteer. The Captain, a frequent visitor to the country, said it was probably a general machete fight, and he cautioned us against going out. While we were in the corridor, hesitating, the uproar was hurrying toward us. The gate burst open, and a crowd rushed in dragging with them our muleteer—that respectable husband and father—with his machete drawn and so tipsy that he could hardly stand, but wanting to fight all the world. With difficulty we got him entangled among some saddle gear; he dropped down, and, after vain efforts to rise, he fell asleep.

I woke the next morning with a violent headache and pain in all my bones. Nevertheless, we started at daylight and rode till five o'clock in the evening. The sun and heat increased the pain in my head, and for three hours before reaching Escuintla I was in great suffering. I avoided going to the corregidor's, for I knew that his sleeping apartment was open to all who came, and I wanted quiet. But I made a great mistake in stopping at the house of the captain's friend, the proprietor of an *estanco*, or distillery for making *aguardiente.* He gave us a large room directly back of a store and separated from it by a low board partition open over the top; the store was constantly filled with noisy and wrangling drinking men and women. My bed was next to the partition, and we had eight or ten men in our room. All night I had a violent fever, and in the morning I was unable to move. Captain Le Nonvel regretted it, but he could not wait, as his ship was ready to lie off and on without coming to anchor. Mr. Catherwood had me removed to a storeroom filled with casks and demijohns, where, except for occasional entries to draw off liquor, I was quiet; but the odor was sickening.

In the afternoon the fever left me, and we rode to Masagua, a level and shady road of four leagues. To our surprise and great satisfaction, we found Captain Le Nonvel at the house at which I had stopped on my return from Iztapa. He had advanced two leagues beyond this place when he heard a band of robbers at some distance farther on, and returned to wait for company, sending, in the meantime, to Escuintla for a guard of soldiers. We afterward learned that the "robbers" were a body of exiles, who, having been expelled from Guatemala, were crossing from Quezalte-nango to San Salvador; but, being in desperate circum-stances, they were nevertheless dangerous persons to meet on the road.

The hut at which we stopped was hardly large enough for the family that occupied it, and our luggage, with two ham-mocks and a *catre*, drove them into a very small space. Cry-ing children are said to be healthy, and, if so, the good woman of this house was blessed; besides this, a hen was hatching a brood of chickens under my head. During the night a party of soldiers entered the village in pursuance of the Captain's requisition and passed on to clear the road. We started before daylight but, as the sun rose, my fever re-turned, and at eleven o'clock when we reached Overo I could go no farther.

I have before remarked that this hacienda is a great stop-ping-place for people from Iztapa and the salt works; un-fortunately for me, several parties of muleteers in appre-hension of the robbers had joined together and, starting at

midnight, had already finished their day's labor. In the afternoon a wild boar was hunted, which our muleteer, with my
gun, killed; there was a great feast in cooking and eating it.
The noise racked my brain, and night brought no relief;
quiet was all I wanted, but that it seemed impossible to
have. In addition, the rancho was more than usually abundant in fleas. All night I had violent fever. Mr. Catherwood, who, from not killing anyone at Copán had conceived
a great opinion of his medical skill, gave me a powerful dose
of medicine, and toward morning I fell asleep.

We started at daylight and arrived at Iztapa at nine
o'clock. Captain Le Nonvel had not yet gone on board. Two
French ships were then lying off the port: the *Belle Poule*
and the *Mélanie,* both from Bordeaux, the latter being the
vessel of Captain Le Nonvel. He had accounts to arrange
with the captain of the *Belle Poule,* and we started first for
that vessel.

I have before remarked that Iztapa is an open roadstead,
without bay, headland, rock, reef, or any protection whatever from the open sea. Generally the sea is, as its name
imports, pacific, and the waves roll calmly to the shore; but
even in the smoothest times there is a breaker, and to pass
this, as a part of the fixtures of the port, an anchor is dropped
outside with a buoy attached from which a long cable is
secured on shore. The longboat of the *Mélanie* lay hard
ashore, stern first, with a cable run through a groove in her
bows and passing through the sculling-hole in the stern.
She was filled with goods, among which we took our seats.
The mate sat in the stern, and, taking advantage of a wave
that raised the bows, gave the order to haul. The wet rope
whizzed past, and the boat moved till, with the receding
wave, it struck heavily on the sand. Another wave and another haul, and she swung clear of the bottom. Meeting the
coming wave and hauling fast on the receding, in a few
minutes we passed the breakers; the rope was thrown out
of the groove and the sailors took to their oars.

It was one of the most beautiful of those beautiful days on
the Pacific. The great ocean was as calm as a lake; the fresh-

ness of the morning still rested upon the water, and already I felt revived. In a few minutes we reached the *Belle Poule*, one of the most beautiful ships that ever floated, and considered a model in the French commercial marine. The whole deck was covered with an awning, having a border trimmed with scarlet and fluttering in the wind. The quarter-deck was raised and protected by a fanciful awning; it was furnished with settees, couches, and chairs, and on a brass railing in front sat two beautiful Peruvian parrots. The door of the cabin was high enough to admit a tall man without stooping. On each side were four staterooms, and the stern was divided into two chambers for the captain and super-cargo, each with a window in it and furnished with a bed (not a berth), a sofa, books, drawers, writing-desk, and everything necessary for luxurious living on shipboard—just the comforts with which one would like to circumnavigate the world. She was on a trading voyage from Bordeaux with an assorted cargo of French goods. She had touched at the ports of Peru, Chile, Panama, and Central America, and had left at each place merchandise to be sold, the proceeds to be invested in the products of the country. She was now bound for Mazatlán, on the coast of Mexico, whence she would return and pick up her cargo, and in two years return to Bordeaux. We had a *déjeuner à la fourchette*, abounding in Paris luxuries, with wines and *café*, as in Paris, to which, fortunately for the ship's stores, I did not bring my accustomed vigor. There was style in everything, even to the name of the steward, who was called the maître d'hôtel.

At two o'clock we went on board the *Mélanie*. She was about the same size as the *Belle Poule*, and if we had not seen the latter ship first, we should have been delighted with her. The comfort and luxury of these "homes on the sea" were in striking contrast with the poverty and misery of the desolate shore. The captain of the *Belle Poule* came on board to dine. It was a pleasure to us to see the delight with which these two Bordeaux men and their crews met on this distant shore. Cape Horn, Peru, and Chile were the subjects of conversation, and we found on board a file of papers which gave us the latest news from our friends in the Sandwich Islands. Mr. Catherwood and the captain of the *Belle Poule* remained on board the *Mélanie* till we got under way. We bade them good-by over the railing and, as the evening breeze filled our sails, for a few moments we saw them, a dark spot on the water; then the wave sank and we lost sight of them entirely.

I remained on deck but a short time. I was the only passenger, and the maître d'hôtel made me a bed with settees directly under the stern windows, but I could not sleep. Even with windows and doors wide open the cabin was excessively warm; the air was heated, and it was full of mosquitoes. The captain and mates slept on deck. I had been advised not to do so, but at twelve o'clock I went out. It was bright starlight; the sails were flapping against the mast, the ocean was like a sheet of glass, and the coast dark, irregular, gloomy, and portentous with volcanoes. The Great Bear was almost upon me, and the North Star, lower than I had ever seen it before, like myself, seemed waning. A young sailor of the watch on deck spoke to me of the deceitfulness of the sea, of shipwrecks, of the wreck of an American vessel which he had fallen in with on his first cruise in the Pacific, and of his beautiful and beloved France. The freshness of the air was grateful and, while he was entertaining me, I stretched myself on a settee and fell asleep.

The next day I had a recurrence of fever, which continued upon me all day, and the captain put me under ship's discipline. In the morning the maître d'hôtel stood by me with cup and spoon, *"Monsieur, un vomitif,"* and in the afternoon, *"Monsieur, une purge."* When we arrived at Acajutla I was unable to go ashore. As soon as we cast anchor, the captain landed and, before leaving for Sonsonate, engaged mules and men for me. The port of Acajutla is not quite so open as that of Iztapa, having on the south a slight projecting headland of rock. In the offing were a *goélette* brig for a port in Peru, a Danish schooner for Guayaquil, and an English brig from London. All the afternoon I sat on the upper deck. Some of the sailors were asleep and others playing cards. In sight were six volcanoes; one was constantly emitting smoke, and another flames. At night the volcano of Izalco seemed a steady ball of fire.

The next morning the mate took me ashore in the launch. The process was the same as at Iztapa, and we were detained some time by a boat of the English vessel occupying the cable. As soon as we struck the shore, a crowd of Indians, naked except for a band of cotton cloth which was wound around the loins and passed between the legs, backed up against the side of the boat. I mounted the shoulders of one of them; as the wave receded he carried me several paces onward, then stopped and braced himself against the coming wave. I clung to his neck, but was fast sliding down his slippery sides when he deposited me on the shore of El Salvador, called by the Indians "Cuscatlán," or "the land of riches." Alvarado, on his voyage to Peru, had been the first Spaniard to set foot upon this shore; as I took special care to keep my feet from getting wet, I could but think of the hardy frames as well as iron nerves of the conquerors of America.

The mate and sailors took leave of me and returned to the ship. I walked along the shore and up a steep hill. It was only eight o'clock, but already it was excessively hot. On the bank fronting the sea were the ruins of large warehouses, which had been occupied as receptacles for merchandise under the Spanish dominion, when all the ports of America were closed against foreign vessels. In one corner of the ruined building was a sort of guardroom where a few soldiers were eating tortillas and one was cleaning his musket. Another apartment was occupied by the captain of the port, who told me that the mules engaged for me had got loose, and that the muleteers were looking for them. Here I had the pleasure to meet Dr. Drivon, a gentleman from the Island of St. Lucia, who had a large sugar hacienda a few leagues distant; he was at the port to superintend the disembarkation of machinery for a mill from the English brig. While waiting for the mules, he conducted me to a hut where he had two Guayaquil hammocks hung, and feeling already the effect of my exertions, I took possession of one of them.

The woman of the rancho was a sort of ship's husband; there being three vessels in port, the rancho was encumbered with vegetables, fruit, eggs, fowls, and ship's stores. It was close and hot, but very soon I required all the covering I could get. I had a violent ague, followed by a fever, in comparison with which all I had suffered before was nothing. I called for water till the old woman was tired of giving it to me, and went out and left me alone. I became light-headed, wild with pain, and wandered among the miserable huts with only the consciousness that my brain was scorching. I have an indistinct recollection of speaking English to some Indian women, of begging them to get me a horse to ride to Sonsonate; of some laughing, others looking at me with pity, and others leading me out of the sun and making me lie down under the shade of a tree. At three o'clock in the afternoon the mate came ashore again. I had changed my position, and he found me lying on my face asleep and almost withered by the sun. He wanted to take me back on board the ship, but I begged him to procure mules and take me to Sonsonate, within the reach of medical assistance. It is hard to feel worse than I did when I mounted. I passed three hours of agony scorched by the intense heat, and a little before dark I arrived at Sonsonate, fortunate, as Dr. Drivon afterward told me, in not having suffered a stroke of the sun. Before entering the town and crossing the bridge over the Río Grande, I met a gentleman, well mounted with a scarlet Peruvian *pellón* over his saddle, with whose appearance I was struck, and we exchanged low bows. This gentleman, as I afterward learned, was the government I was looking for.

I rode to the house of Captain Le Nonvel's brother, one of the largest in the place, where I had that comfort seldom known in Central America, a room to myself and everything else necessary. For several days I remained within doors. The first afternoon I went out I called upon Don Manuel de Aguilar, formerly chief of the State of Costa

Rica, who had about a year before been driven out by a revolution and banished for life. At his house I met Don Diego Vigil, the vice-president of the Republic, the same gentleman whom I had met on the bridge and the only existing officer of the Federal government. From observation and experience in my own country, I had learned never to take the character of a public man from his political enemy; and I will not soil this page with the foul aspersions which men of veracity, blinded by party prejudice, threw upon the character of Señor Vigil. He was about forty-five, six feet high, thin, and suffering from a paralytic affection which almost deprived him of the use of both legs; in dress, conversation, and manners, he was eminently a gentleman. He had traveled more extensively in his own country than most of his countrymen, and knew all the objects of interest. With a politeness which I appreciated, he made no reference to my position or my official character.

His business at Sonsonate showed the wretched state of the country. He had come expressly to treat with Rascón, the head of the band which had prevented my coming from Guatemala by land. Chico Rascón, as he was familiarly called in Sonsonate, was of an old and respectable family; he had spent a large fortune in dissipation in Paris and, returning here in desperate circumstances, had turned patriot. About six months before, he had made a descent upon Sonsonate, killed the garrison to a man, robbed the customhouse, and retreated to his hacienda. He was then on a visit in the town, publicly, by appointment with Señor Vigil; he demanded, as the price of disbanding his troops, a colonel's commission for himself, other commissions for some of his followers, and four thousand dollars in money. Vigil assented to all except the four thousand dollars in money, offering instead the credit of the State of El Salvador, which Rascón agreed to accept. Papers were drawn up and that afternoon appointed for their execution; but, while Vigil was waiting for him, Rascón and his friends, without a word of notice, mounted their horses and rode out of town. The place was thrown into great excitement, and in the evening I saw the garrison busily engaged in barricading the plaza in apprehension of another attack.

The next day I made a formal call upon Señor Vigil. I was in a rather awkward position. When I left Guatemala in search of a government, I did not expect to meet it on the road. In that state I had heard but one side; I was just beginning to hear the other. If there was any government, I had treed it. Was it the real thing or was it not? In Guatemala they said it was not; here they said it was. It was a knotty question. I was in no great favor in Guatemala, and in endeavoring to play a safe game I ran the risk of being hustled by all parties. In Guatemala they had no right to ask for my credentials, and took offence because I did not present them; here, if I refused, they had a right to consider it an insult. In this predicament I opened my business with the Vice-President and told him that I was on my way to the capital with credentials from the United States, but that, in the state of anarchy in which I found the country, I was at a loss what to do. I was desirous to avoid making a false step and anxious to know whether the Federal government really existed, or whether the Republic was dissolved.

Our interview was long and interesting, and the purport of his answer was that the government did exist *de facto* and *de jure;* that he himself had been legally elected vice-president; that the act of the four states in declaring themselves independent was unconstitutional and rebellious; that the union could not be dissolved except by a convention of deputies from all the states; that the government had the actual control in three states: one had been reduced to subjection by arms, and very soon the Federal Party would have the ascendancy in the others. He was familiar with the case of South Carolina, and he said that our Congress had sustained the right of the general government to coërce states into subjection, and that they were in the same position here. I referred to the shattered condition of the government, to its absolute impotence in other states, and to the non-existence of senate and other co-ordinate branches, or even of a secretary of state, the officer to whom my credentials were addressed. He answered that he had in his suite an acting secretary of state, confirming what had been told me before, and that the "government" would, at a moment's notice, make any officer I wanted. But I owe it to Señor Vigil to say that, after going over fully the whole ground of the unhappy contest, and although at that critical juncture the recognition of the Federal government by that of the United States would have been of moment to his party, and not to recognize it would have been disrespectful and would have favored the cause of the rebellious or independent states, he did not ask me to present my credentials. The Convention, which was expected to compose the difficulties of the Republic, was then about to assemble in Honduras. The deputies from El Salvador had gone to take their seats, and it was understood that I should await the decisions of this body. The result of my interview with the Vice-President was much more agreeable than I expected. I am sure that I left him without the least feeling of ill will on his part, but my great perplexity as to whether I had any government was not yet brought to a close.

In the meantime, while the political repairs were going on, I remained in Sonsonate recruiting. The town is situated on the banks of the Río Grande, which is formed by almost innumerable springs; in the Indian language its name means four hundred springs of water. It stands in one of the richest districts of the rich State of El Salvador, and has its plaza with streets at right angles and white houses of one story, some of them very large; but it has borne its share of the calamities which have visited the unfortunate Republic: The best houses are deserted, and their owners in exile. There are seven costly churches and but one cura.

I was unable to undertake any journey by land, and, feeling the enervating effect of the climate, swung all day in a hammock. Fortunately, the proprietors of the brig which I had seen at Acajutla bound for Peru, changed her destination and determined to send her to Costa Rica, the southernmost state of the Confederacy. At the same time, a man offered himself as a servant who was very highly recommended, and whose appearance I liked. I resolved to have the benefit of the sea voyage and, in returning by land, to explore the canal route between the Atlantic and Pacific by the Lake of Nicaragua, a thing which I had desired much but which I had despaired of being able to accomplish.

Before leaving I roused myself for an excursion. The window of my room opened upon the volcano of Izalco. All day I heard at short intervals the eruptions of the burning mountain, and at night I saw the column of flame bursting from the crater and streams of fire rolling down its side. Fortunately, Mr. Blackwood, an Irish merchant for many years resident in Peru, arrived and agreed to accompany me.

The next morning before five o'clock we were in the saddle. At the distance of a mile we forded the Río Grande, here a wild river, and riding through a rich country, in half an hour we reached the Indian village of Naguisal, a lovely spot and literally a forest of fruits and flowers. Large trees were perfectly covered with red, and at every step we could pluck fruit. Interspersed among these beautiful trees were the miserable huts of Indians, and lying on the ground, or at some lazy work, were the miserable Indians themselves. Continuing another league through the same rich country, we rose upon a table of land, from which, looking back, we saw an immense plain, wooded and extending to the shore, and beyond it, the boundless waters of the Pacific. Before us, at the extreme end of a long street, was the church of Izalco, standing out in strong relief against the base of the volcano, which at that moment, with a loud report like the rolling of thunder, threw in the air a column of black smoke and ashes lighted by a single flash of flame.

With difficulty we obtained a guide, but he was so tipsy that he could scarcely guide himself along a straight street. He would not leave till the next day, as he said it was so late that we would be caught on the mountain at night and that it was full of tigers. In the meantime the daughter of our host found another guide, and, stowing four green cocoanuts in his alforjas, we set out. Soon we came out upon an open plain. Without a bush to obstruct the view, we saw on our left the whole volcano from its base to its top. It rose from near the foot of a mountain to a height perhaps of six thousand feet; its sides were brown and barren, and all around for miles the earth was covered with lava. Being in a state of eruption, it was impossible to ascend it; behind it was a higher mountain, which commanded a view of the burning crater. The whole volcano was in full sight, spouting into the air a column of black smoke and an immense body of stones, while the earth shook under our feet. Crossing the plain, we commenced ascending the mountain.

At eleven o'clock we sat down by the bank of a beautiful stream to breakfast. My companion had made abundant provision and for the first time since I left Guatemala I felt the keenness of returning appetite. In half an hour we mounted, and soon after twelve o'clock entered the woods; we had a very steep ascent by a faint path which we soon lost altogether. Our guide changed his direction several times and at length, becoming lost, he tied his horse, and left us to wait while he searched the way. We knew that we were near the volcano, for the explosions sounded like the deep mutterings of dreadful thunder. Shut up as we were in the woods, these reports were awful. Our horses snorted with terror, and the mountain quaked beneath our feet. Our guide returned, and in a few minutes we came out suddenly upon an open point, higher than the top of the volcano, which commanded a view of the interior of the crater, and which was so near it that we saw the huge stones as they separated in the air and fell pattering around the sides of the volcano. In a few minutes our clothes were white with ashes, which fell around us with a noise like the sprinkling of rain.

The crater had three orifices: one was inactive; another emitted constantly a rich blue smoke; and, after a report, deep in the huge throat of the third there appeared a light blue vapor and then a mass of thick black smoke, whirling and struggling out in enormous wreaths and rising in a dark majestic column, lighted for a moment by a sheet of flame. When the smoke dispersed, the atmosphere was darkened by a shower of stones and ashes. This over, a moment of stillness followed, and then another report and eruption; these continued regularly, at intervals, as our guide said, of exactly five minutes, and really he was not much out of the way. The sight was fearfully grand. We refreshed ourselves

with a draught of cocoanut milk, thought how this grandeur
would be heightened when the stillness and darkness of
night were interrupted by the noise and flame, and forthwith resolved to sleep upon the mountain.

The cura of Sonsonate, still in the vigor of life, told me
that he remembered when the ground on which this volcano
stands had nothing to distinguish it from any other spot
around. In 1798 a small orifice was discovered puffing out
small quantities of dust and pebbles. He was then living at
Izalco and, as a boy, was in the habit of going to look at it;
he had watched it and marked its increase from year to year
until it had grown into what it is now. Captain Le Nonvel
told me he could observe from the sea that it had grown
greatly within the last two years. Two years before, its light
could not be seen at night on the other side of the mountain
on which I stood. Night and day it forces up stones from the
bowels of the earth, spouts them into the air, and receives
them upon its sides. Every day it is increasing, and probably
it will continue to do so until the inward fires die, or by some
violent convulsion the whole is rent to atoms.

Old travelers are not precluded occasional bursts of enthusiasm, but they cannot keep it up long. In about an
hour we began to be critical and even captious. Some eruptions were better than others, and some were comparatively
small affairs. In this frame of mind we summed up our
want of comforts for passing the night on the mountain and
determined to return to the town. Mr. Blackwood and I
thought that we could avoid the circuit of the mountain by
descending directly to the base of the volcano, and by crossing it, reach the *camino real;* but our guide said it was a
tempting of Providence and refused to accompany us. We
had a very steep descent on foot, and in some places our
horses slid down on their haunches. An immense bed of lava,
stopped in its rolling course by the side of the mountain,
filled up the wide space between us and the base of the
volcano. We stepped directly upon this black and frightful
bed, but we had great difficulty in making our horses follow.
The lava lay in rolls as irregular as the waves of the sea,
sharp, rough, and with huge chasms, difficult for us and

dangerous for the horses. With great labor we dragged them to the base and around the side of the volcano. Massive stones, hurled into the air, fell and rolled down the sides, so near that we dared not venture farther. Afraid of breaking our horses' legs in the holes into which they were constantly falling, we turned back. On the lofty point from which we had looked down into the crater of the volcano sat our guide, gazing, and, as we could imagine, laughing at us. We toiled back across the bed of lava and up the side of the mountain; when we reached the top both my horse and I were almost exhausted. Fortunately, the road home was down hill. It was long after dark when we passed the foot of the mountain and came out upon the plain. Every burst of the volcano sent forth a pillar of fire; in four places were steady fires and, in one, a stream of fire was rolling down its side. At eleven o'clock we reached Sonsonate. Besides toiling around the base of the volcano, we had ridden upward of fifty miles; but such had been the interest of the day's work, that, though my first effort, I never suffered from it.

The arrangements for my voyage down the Pacific were soon made. The servant to whom I referred was a native of Costa Rica, then on his way home after a long absence, with a cargo of merchandise belonging to himself. He was a tall, good-looking fellow, dressed in a Guatemala jacket, or *cotón,* a pair of Mexican leather trousers with buttons down the sides, and a steeple-crowned, broad-brimmed, drab wool hat; he was altogether far superior to any servant I saw in the country, and I think if it had not been for him I should not have undertaken the journey. The reader will perhaps be shocked to hear that his name was Jesús, pronounced in Spanish "Hezoos," by which latter appellation, to avoid what might be considered profanity, I shall hereafter call him.

Chapter XVI

ON Monday, the twenty-second of January, two hours before daylight, we started for the port. Hezoos led the way, carrying before him all my luggage, rolled up in a *vaqueta,* which was simply a cowhide, after the fashion of the country. At daylight we heard behind us the clattering of horses' hoofs, and Don Manuel de Aguilar with his two sons overtook us. Before the freshness of the morning was past we reached the port and rode up to the old hut which I had hoped never to see again. The hammock was swinging in the same place. The miserable rancho seemed destined to be the abode of sickness. In one corner lay Señor de Iriarte, my captain, who, exhausted by a night of fever, was unable to sail that day.

Dr. Drivon was again at the port. He had not yet disembarked his machinery; in fact, the work was suspended by a mutiny on board the English brig, the ringleader of which, as the doctor complained to me, was an American. I passed the day on the seashore. In one place, a little above high-water mark and almost washed by the waves, were rude wooden crosses, marking the graves of unhappy sailors who had died far from their homes.

Returning to the hut, I found Captain Jay of the English brig, who also complained to me of the American sailor.

The captain was a young man, making his first voyage as master; his wife, whom he had married a week before sailing, accompanied him. He had had a disastrous voyage of eight months from London; in doubling Cape Horn his crew had been all frost-bitten and his spars carried away. With only one man on deck he had worked up to Guayaquil, where, after incurring great loss of time and money in making repairs, he shipped an entirely new crew. At Acajutla he found that his boats were not sufficient to land the doctor's machinery, and he was obliged to wait until a raft could be constructed. In the meantime his crew mutinied, and part of them refused to work. His wife was then at the doctor's hacienda and I noticed that, while writing her a note with pencil, his sunburned face was pale and large drops of perspiration stood on his forehead. Soon after he threw himself into the hammock and, as I thought, fell asleep; but in a few minutes I saw the hammock shake and, remembering my own shaking there, thought it was at its old tricks of giving people the fever and ague; but very soon I saw that the poor captain was in convulsions. Excepting Captain de Iriarte, who was lying against the wall perfectly helpless, I was the only man in the hut. As there was danger of Mr. Jay throwing himself out of the hammock, I endeavored to hold him in, but with one convulsive effort, he threw me to the other side of the hut and hung over the side of the hammock with one hand entangled in the cords and his head almost touching the ground. The old woman said that the devil had taken possession of him, and she ran out of doors screaming.

Fortunately, this brought in a man whom I had not seen before, a Mr. Warburton, an engineer who had come out to set up the machinery, and who was himself a machine of many horsepower, having a pair of shoulders that seemed constructed expressly for holding men in convulsions. At first he was so shocked that he did not know what to do. I told him that the captain was to be held, whereupon he opened his powerful arms and closed them around the captain's with the force of a hydraulic press, turning the legs over to me. These legs were a pair of the sturdiest that ever

supported a human body, and I verily believe that if the feet
had once touched my ribs, they would have sent me through
the wall of the hut. Watching my opportunity, I wound
the hammock around his legs, and my arms around the hammock. In the meantime he broke loose from Mr. Warburton's hug. The latter, taking the hint from me, doubled
his part in with the folds of the hammock and gave his clinch
from the outside. The captain struggled and, worming like a
gigantic snake, slipped his head out of the top of the hammock and twisted the cords around his neck, so that we were
afraid of his strangling himself. We were in utter despair
when in rushed two of his sailors, who, being at home with
ropes, extricated his head, shoved him back into the hammock, and wrapped it around him as before. At this point I
withdrew completely exhausted.

The two recruits were Tom, a regular tar of about forty,
and the cook, a black man and a particular friend of Tom,
who called him Darkey. Tom undertook the whole direction of securing the captain. Although Dr. Drivon and several Indians came in, Tom's voice was the only one which
was heard, and it was addressed only to "Darkey." "Stand
by his legs, Darkey!" "Hold fast, Darkey!" "Steady,
Darkey!"—but all together could not hold him. Turning
on his face and doubling himself inside, he braced his back
and drove both legs through the hammock, striking his feet
violently against the ground; his whole body passed through.
His struggles were dreadful. Suddenly the mass of bodies
on the floor rolled against Captain de Iriarte's bed, which
broke down with a crash and, with a fever upon him, he was
obliged to scramble out of the way. In the interval of one
of the most violent struggles, we heard a strange idiotic
noise, which seemed like an attempt to crow. When the
Indians who crowded the hut laughed, Dr. Drivon was so
indignant at their heartlessness that he seized a club and
drove them all out of doors. An old naked African, who had
been a slave at Belize and had lost his language without ac-
quiring much of any other, returned with a bunch of
feathers which he wished to stick in the captain's nose and

set fire to, saying it was the remedy of his country; but the doctor showed him his stick, and he retreated.

The convulsions continued for three hours, during which time the doctor considered the captain's situation to be very critical. The old woman persisted that the devil was in him and would not give him up, and that he must die; I could not but think of his young wife, who was sleeping a few miles off, unconscious of the calamity that threatened her. The fit was brought on, as the doctor said, by anxiety and distress of mind occasioned by his unfortunate voyage and particularly by the mutiny of his crew.

At eleven o'clock he fell asleep, and now we learned the cause of the strange noise which had affected us so unpleasantly. Tom had just been preparing to go on board the vessel when the African ran down to the shore and told him that the captain was at the hut drunk. Tom, being himself in that state, felt that it was his duty to look after the captain. He had just bought a parrot for which he had paid a dollar, and, afraid to trust him in other hands, he had hauled his baggy shirt a foot more out of his trousers and thrust the parrot into his bosom, almost smothering it with his neckcloth. The parrot, indignant at this confinement, was driving his beak constantly into Tom's breast, which was scarified and covered with blood; and once, when Tom thought it was going too far, he had put his hand inside and pinched it, thus producing the extraordinary sounds we had heard.

In a little while Tom and Darkey got the Indians to relieve them and went out to drink the captain's health. On their return they took their places on the ground, one on each side of their commander. I threw myself into the broken hammock and Dr. Drivon, charging them if the captain awoke not to say anything that could agitate him, went off to another hut.

It was not long before the captain, raising his head, called out, "What the devil are you doing with my legs?" which was answered by Tom's steady cry, "Hold on, Darkey!" Darkey and an Indian were holding the captain's legs, two Indians, his arms, and Tom was spread over his body. The captain looked perfectly sensible and utterly amazed at being pinned to the ground. "Where am I?" said he. Tom and Darkey had agreed not to tell him what had happened; but, Tom, after the most extraordinary lying, while the captain was looking at him and us in utter amazement, became so entangled that, swearing the doctor might stay and tell his own stories, he began to tell how he and Darkey had come in and found the captain kicking in the hammock. The captain was given to understand that if it had not been for him and Darkey he would have kicked his own brains out. I relieved Tom's story from some obscurity, and a general and noisy conversation followed, which was cut short by poor Captain de Iriarte; he had not had a wink of sleep all night and begged us to give him a chance.

In the morning, while I was taking chocolate with Doctor Drivon, the mate came to the hut with the mutinous American sailor in the custody of four soldiers, to make a complaint to me. The sailor was a young man of twenty-eight, short, well made, and very good-looking, whose name was Jemmy. He, too, complained to me. He wanted to leave the brig, and said that he would stop on a barren rock in the midst of the ocean rather than remain on board. I told him I was sorry to find an American sailor a ringleader in mutiny, and I represented to him the distress and danger in which it had placed the captain. Doctor Drivon had had some sharp passages with him on board the brig and, after a few words, started up and struck him. Jemmy fell back in time to avoid the full blow; as if by no means unused to such things, he continued to fall back and ward off, but when pressed too hard, he broke loose from the soldiers and tore off his jacket for a regular fight.

I had no idea of favoring a mutinous sailor, but still less of suffering an American to be maltreated by odds, and I hauled off the soldiers. In a moment the doctor's passion was over and he discontinued his attack, whereupon Jemmy surrendered himself to the soldiers, who carried him, as I supposed, to the guardhouse. I waited a little while and, going down, saw Jemmy sitting on the ground in front of the *cuartel,* or barracks, with both legs in the stocks above his knees. He was keenly alive to the disgrace of his situation, and my blood boiled. I hurried to the captain of the port and complained warmly of his conduct as high-handed and insufferable; I insisted that Jemmy must be released or I would ride to San Salvador on the instant and make a complaint against him. Doctor Drivon joined me and Jemmy was released from the stocks, but he was put under guard in the cuartel.

This will probably never reach the eyes of any of his friends, but I will not mention his name. He was from the little town of Esopus on the Hudson. In 1834 he had sailed from New York in the sloop-of-war *Peacock* for the Pacific station. Transferred to the *North Carolina* he had been regularly discharged at Valparaiso. He entered the Chilean naval service and, after plenty of fighting and no prize money, he had shipped on board this brig. I represented that he was liable to be tried for mutiny and had only escaped the stocks by my happening to be at the port, that I could do nothing more for him, and that he might be kept on shore till the vessel sailed and be carried on board in irons. It was a critical moment in the young man's life. I regarded him as one destitute of early opportunities and probably doomed by necessity to a wayward life. Still, as he was a countryman, I was anxious to save him from the effects of headstrong passion. The captain said he was the best sailor on board. As the captain was short of hands, I procured from him a promise that, if Jemmy would return to his duty, he would take no notice of what had passed and would give him his discharge at the first port where he could procure a substitute.

Fortunately, in the afternoon Captain de Iriarte was sufficiently recovered to sail, and before going on board my vessel I took Jemmy to his. She was the dirtiest vessel I ever saw, and her crew a fair sample of the villainous sailors picked up in ports of the Pacific. Among them and as bad as any in appearance, was another countryman, Jemmy's American accomplice. I did not wonder that Jemmy was discontented; I left him on board in a bad condition, but, unfortunately, I afterward heard of him in a worse.

A few strokes of the oar brought me on board our vessel, and, as before, with the evening breeze we got under way. The vessel in which I embarked was called *La Cosmopolita*. She was a *goélette* brig and the only vessel that bore on the Pacific the Central American flag. She was built in England for a cutter and called the *Britannia*. By some accident she reached the Pacific Ocean and was bought by the State of El Salvador when at war with Guatemala and called by that state's Indian name of *Cuscatlán*. Afterward she was sold to an Englishman, who called her *Eugenia*, and from him she came to Captain de Iriarte, who called her *La Cosmopolita*.

My first night on board was not particularly agreeable. I was the only cabin passenger. Besides the bugs that always infest an old vessel, I had in my berth mosquitoes, spiders, ants, and cockroaches. Yet there is no part of my tour upon which I look back with so much quiet satisfaction as this voyage on the Pacific. I had on board *Gil Blas* and *Don Quixote* in the original, and all day I sat under an awning, my attention divided between them and the great range of gigantic volcanoes which stud the coast. Before this became tedious we reached the Gulf of Papagayo, the only outlet by which the winds of the Atlantic pass over to the Pacific. The dolphin, the most beautiful fish that swims, played under our bows and stern and accompanied us slowly alongside. But the sailors had no respect for his golden back. The mate, a murderous young Frenchman, stood for hours with a harpoon in his hand, driving it into several of these fish, and at length he brought one on board. The king of the sea seemed conscious of his fallen state; his beautiful colors faded, and he became spotted and at last heavy and lustreless like any other dead fish.

We passed in regular succession the volcanoes of San Salvador, San Vicente, San Miguel, Telica, Momotombo, Managua,[1] Nindiri, Masaya, and Nicaragua,[1] each one a noble spectacle. All together they formed a chain with which

1. The editor has been unable to identify volcanoes with these two names.

no other in the world can be compared; indeed, this coast has well been described as "bristling with volcanic cones." For two days we lay with sails flapping in sight of Cape Blanco, the upper headland of the Gulf of Nicoya,[2] and on the afternoon of the thirty-first we entered the gulf. On a line with the point of the cape was an island of rock with high, bare, and precipitous sides, the top of which was covered with verdure. It was about sunset; for nearly an hour the sky and sea seemed blazing with the reflection of the departing luminary, and the island of rocks seemed like a fortress with turrets. It was a glorious farewell view. I had passed my last night on the Pacific, and the highlands of the Gulf of Nicoya closed around us.

Early in the morning we had the tide in our favor, and very soon, leaving the main body of the gulf, we turned off to the right and entered a beautiful little cove forming the harbor of Caldera. In front was the range of mountains of Aguacate, on the left the old port of Puntarenas, and on the right the volcano of San Pablo. On the shore was a long low house; it was set upon piles and had a tile roof. Near it were three or four thatched huts and two canoes. We anchored in front of the houses, apparently without exciting the attention of a soul on shore.

All the ports of Central America on the Pacific are unhealthy, but this one was considered deadly. I had entered without apprehension cities where the plague was raging, but here, as I looked ashore, there was a death-like stillness that was startling. To spare me the necessity of sleeping at the port, the captain sent the boat ashore with my servant to procure mules with which I could proceed immediately to a hacienda two leagues beyond.

Our boat had hardly started before we saw three men coming down to the shore, who presently put off in a canoe, met our boat, turned her back, and boarded us themselves. They were two paddles and a soldier. The soldier informed our captain that, by a late decree, no passenger would be permitted to land without the special permission of the gov-

2. The Gulf of Nicoya is in Costa Rica, the southernmost republic of Central America.

ernment, for which it was necessary to send an application to the capital and to wait on board for an answer. He added that the last vessel was full of passengers who were obliged to remain twelve days before the permission was received. I was used to vexations in traveling, but I could not bear this quietly. The captain made a bold attempt in my favor by saying that he had no passengers, but that he did have on board the Minister of the United States, who was making the tour of Central America, and who had been treated with courtesy in Guatemala and El Salvador, adding that it would be an indignity for the government of Costa Rica not to permit his landing.

He wrote to the same effect to the captain of the port, who, on the return of the soldier, came off himself. I was almost sick with vexation, and the captain of the port finished two glasses of wine before I had the courage to introduce the subject. He answered with great courtesy, regretting that the law was imperative and that he had no discretionary powers. I replied that the law was intended to prevent the entrance of seditious persons, emigrés, and *expulsados* from other states who might disturb the peace of Costa Rica, but that it could not contemplate a case like mine. In my discourse I laid great stress upon my official character. Fortunately for me, he had a high sense of the respect due to that character and, though holding a petty office, he had a feeling of pride that his state should not be considered wanting in courtesy to an accredited stranger. For a long time he was at a loss as to what to do; but finally, after much deliberation, he requested me to wait till morning, when he would dispatch a courier to advise the government of the circumstances and take upon himself the responsibility of permitting me to land. Fearful of some accident or some change of purpose and anxious to get my feet on shore, I suggested that in order to avoid traveling in the heat of the day it would be better to sleep on shore, so as to be ready for an early start. To this he assented.

In the afternoon the captain took me ashore. At the first house we saw two candles lighted to burn at the body of a dead man. All whom we saw were ill, and all complained that the place was fatal to human life: in fact, it was almost deserted. Notwithstanding its advantages as a port, the government, a few days afterward, issued an order for breaking it up and moving back to the old port of Puntarenas. The captain was still suffering from fever and ague, and he would not on any account remain on shore after dark. I was so rejoiced to find myself on shore that if I had met a death's head at every step it would hardly have turned me back.

The last stranger who had been at the port was a distinguished American whose name was Handy. I had first heard of him at the Cape of Good Hope, hunting giraffes, and afterward I had met him in New York; I regretted exceedingly to miss him here. He had traveled from the United States through Texas, Mexico, and Central America with an elephant and two dromedaries as his file leaders! The elephant was the first ever seen in Central America, and I often heard of him in the *pueblos* under the name of *El Demonio*. Six days before, Mr. Handy, with his interesting family, had embarked for Peru, and perhaps he was at this moment crossing the pampas to Brazil.

Determined not to lose sight of my friend, the captain of the port, with my luggage at my heels I walked down the beach to the customhouse. It was a frame building about forty feet long, standing at a little distance above high-water mark on piles about six feet above ground. It was the gathering place of different persons in the employ of the government (civil and military) and of two or three women employed by them. The military force consisted of the captain of the port and the soldier who boarded us, so that I had not much fear of being sent back at the point of the bayonet. During the evening a new difficulty arose about my servant; but, considering myself tolerably secure, I insisted that he was my suite and obtained permission for him to accompany me. My host gave me a bedstead with a bull's hide for a bed. It was a warm night, and I placed it opposite an open door and looked out upon the water of the gulf. The waves were breaking gently upon the shore, and it was beautiful to see the *Cosmopolita* riding quietly at her anchor without even Hezoos or the luggage in her.

At two o'clock in the morning we rose, and before three we started. The tide was low, and for some distance we rode along the shore by moonlight. At daylight we overtook the courier sent to give advice of my coming. An hour later we crossed the river of Jesús María, and at seven o'clock stopped to breakfast at the hacienda of the same name.

It was a miserable shell with an arbor of branches around it, but it had an appearance of cleanliness and comfort. Hezoos told me that the proprietor had two thousand head of cattle and owned all the land over which we had ridden from the sea. Hezoos was quite at home; as he afterward told me, he had once wanted to marry one of the daughters, but that the father and mother had objected because he was not good enough. He added that they were surprised at seeing him return in such prosperous circumstances and that the daughter told him she had always refused to marry any one else on account of her affection for him.

While I was breakfasting, the mother told me of a sick daughter, asked me for *remedios*, and finally requested me to go in and see her. The door opened from the shed, and all the apertures in the room were carefully closed so as to exclude even a breath of air. The invalid lay in a bed in one corner, which had a cotton covering over it like a mosquito-netting but lower and pinned close all around. When the mother raised the covering, I encountered a body of hot and unwholesome air that almost overcame me. The poor girl lay on her back with a cotton sheet wound tightly around her body, and already she seemed like one laid out for burial. She was not more than eighteen; the fever had just left her and her eye still sparkled, but her face was pale and covered with spots, seams, and creases of dirt. She was suffering from intermitting fever, that scourge which breaks down the constitution and carries to the grave thousands of the inhabitants of Central America.

According to the obstinate prejudice of the country, her face had not been washed for more than two months! I had often been disgusted with the long beards and unwashed faces of fever and ague subjects, and with the ignorance and prejudice of the people on medical subjects. An illustration of this ignorance was a case of practice by an old quack woman which Dr. Drivon told me about. She had directed her patient, a rich cattle proprietor, to be extended on the ground naked every morning, and over him a bullock was to be slaughtered, so that the blood could run warm upon his body. The man submitted to the operation more than a hundred times and was bathed with the blood of more than a hundred bullocks; afterward he underwent a much more disgusting process, and, strange to say, he lived.

But to return to the case of the young girl. In general, my medical practice had been confined to men, and with them I considered myself a powerful practitioner. I did not like prescribing for women. In this case, I struck at all the prejudices of the country and cheapened my medical skill by directing first that the poor girl's face be washed, but I saved myself somewhat by making a strong point that it should be washed with warm water. Whether they thanked me or not I do not know, but I had my reward, for I saw a lovely face; long afterward I remembered the touching expression of her eyes as she turned toward me and listened to the advice I gave her mother.

At ten we resumed our journey. The land was level and rich but uncultivated. We passed several miserable cattle haciendas, the proprietors of which lived in the towns and kept men on the estate, from time to time, to gather and number the cattle, which roamed wild in the woods. At eleven we passed the hacienda of San Felipe, which belonged to a Welshman engaged in mining. It was in a large clearing and a fine situation, and its cleanliness, neatness, and good fences showed that the Welshman had not forgotten what he had learned at home.

Crossing the river Surubris and the Río Grande, or Machuca, we reached the hacienda of San Mateo, situated at the foot of the mountain of Aguacate, and from this place we began to ascend. The road had been much improved lately, but the ascent was steep, wild, and rugged. As we toiled up the ravine, we heard before us a loud noise that sounded like distant thunder, but regular and continued, and becoming louder as we advanced. At length, coming out on a small clearing, we saw on the side of the mountain a neat frame building of two stories with a light and graceful balcony in front, alongside of which was the thundering machine which had startled us by its noise. Strangers from the other side of the Atlantic were piercing the sides of the mountain and pounding its stones into dust in a search for gold. The whole range, the very ground which our horses spurned with their hoofs, contained that treasure for which man forsakes kindred and country.

I rode up to the house and introduced myself to Don Juan Bardh, the superintendent, a German from Freiburg. It was about two o'clock and excessively hot. The house was furnished with chairs, sofa, and books, and it had in my eyes a delightful appearance; but the view without was even more delightful. The stream which turned the immense pounding machine had made the spot, from time immemorial, a *descansadero*, or resting place for muleteers. All around were mountains, and directly in front one rose to a great height, receding and covered to the top with trees.

Don Juan Bardh had been superintendent of the Quebrada del Ingenio for about three years. The company which he represented was called the Anglo Costa Rican Economical Mining Company. It had been in operation these three years without losing anything, which was considered doing so well that it had increased its capital and was about to continue on a larger scale. The machine, which had just been set up, was a new German patent, called a *Machine for Extracting Gold by the Zillenthal Patent Self-acting Cold Amalgamation Process* (I believe that I have omitted nothing). Its great value was that it required no preliminary process, but by one continued and simple operation it could extract the gold from the stone. It was an immense wheel of cast iron, by which the stone, as it came from the mountain, was pounded into powder. This powder passed into troughs filled with water and then into a reservoir containing vases, where the gold detached itself from the other particles and combined with the quicksilver with which the vases were provided.

There were several mines under Don Juan's charge, and after dinner he accompanied me to that of Corralillo, which was the largest and, fortunately, lay on my road. After a hot ride of half an hour, ascending through thick woods, we reached the spot.

According to the opinion of the few geologists who have visited that part of the country, immense wealth lies buried in the mountain of Aguacate; and so far from being hidden, the proprietors say, its places are so well marked that all who search may find. The lodes or mineral veins run regularly north and south in ranges of greenstone porphyry with strata of basaltic porphyry, and they average about three feet in width. In some places side-cuts or lateral excavations are made from east to west, and in others shafts are sunk until they strike the vein.

The first opening we visited was a side-cut four feet wide, which pentrated two hundred and forty feet before it struck the lode, but it was so full of water that we did not enter. Above it was another cut, and higher still a shaft was sunk. We descended the shaft by a ladder made of the trunk of a tree, with notches cut in it, until we reached the vein, which we followed with a candle as far as it was worked. It was about a yard wide, and the sides glittered—but not with gold; it was quartz and feldspar, impregnated with sulphuret of iron and gold in such small particles as to be invisible to the naked eye. The most prominent objects in these repositories of wealth were naked workmen with pickaxes, bending and sweating under heavy sacks of stones.

It was late in the afternoon when I came out of the shaft. Don Juan conducted me by a steep path up the side of the mountain to a small table of land, on which was a large building occupied by miners. The view was magnificent: below was an immense ravine; above, perched on a point like an eagle's nest, the house of another superintendent; and on the opposite side the great range of the mountains of Candelaria. I waited till my mules came up and then, with many thanks for his kindness, I bade Don Juan farewell.

As we continued ascending, every moment the view became more grand and beautiful; suddenly, from a height of six thousand feet, I looked down upon the Pacific, the Gulf of Nicoya, and, sitting like a bird upon the water, our brig,

La Cosmopolita. And here, on the very highest points, in the wildest and most beautiful spots that ever men chose for their abodes, were the huts of the miners. The sun touched the sea, lighting up the surface of the water and softening the rugged mountains. It was the most beautiful scene I ever saw, and this liveliest view was the last that day, for suddenly it became dark, and very soon the darkest night I ever knew came on.

As we descended, the woods were so thick that even in the daytime they shut out the light, and in some places the road was cut through steep hills higher than our heads and roofed over by the dense foliage. Hezoos was before me, with a white hat and jacket and with a white dog running by his side, but I could not see the outline of his figure. The road was steep but good, and I did not pretend to direct the mule. In one of the darkest passages Hezoos stopped and, with a voice that made the woods ring, cried out "a lion! a lion!" I was startled, but he dismounted and lighted a cigar. This was cool, I thought, but he relieved me by telling me that here a lion was a different animal from the roarer of the African desert, that it was small, frightened by a shout, and only ate children.

Long as it seemed, our whole descent did not occupy three hours, and at ten o'clock we reached the house at the foot of the mountain. It was shut, and all were asleep; but when we knocked hard, a man opened the door and, before we could ask any questions, disappeared. Once inside, however, we made noise enough to wake everybody and got corn for the mules and a light. There was a large room open to all comers, with three bedsteads, all occupied; in addition two men were sleeping on the floor. The occupant of one of the beds, after eying me a few moments, vacated it, and I took his place. The reader must not suppose that I am perfectly unscrupulous; he took all his bedclothes, that is, his *cha-marra*, with him. The bed and all its furniture consisted of an untanned bull's hide.

Chapter XVII

〰〰〰〰〰〰〰〰〰〰〰〰〰〰〰〰〰〰〰〰〰〰〰〰〰〰〰〰〰

La Garita. Alajuela. A friendly people. Heredia. Río Segundo. Coffee plantations of San José. The sacrament for the dying. A happy meeting. Traveling embarrassments. Quarters in a convent. Señor Carrillo, Chief of State. Vicissitudes of fortune. Visit to Cartago. Tres Ríos. An unexpected meeting. Ascent of the volcano of Cartago. The crater. View of the two seas. Descent. Stroll through Cartago. A burial. Another attack of fever and ague. A vagabond. Cultivation of coffee.

THE next morning we entered an open, rolling, and undulating country which reminded me of scenes at home. At nine o'clock we came to the brink of a magnificent ravine, and, as we wound down by a steep descent of more than fifteen hundred feet, the mountains closed around us forming an amphitheatre. At the bottom of the ravine was a rough wooden bridge crossing a narrow stream running between perpendicular rocks a hundred and fifty feet high; it was very picturesque and reminded me of Trenton Falls.

We ascended by a steep road to the top of the ravine, where a long house stood across the road, which prevented all passing except directly through it. It was called La Garita [1] and commanded the road from the port to the capital. Officers were stationed here to take an account of merchandise and to examine passports. The officer then in command had lost an arm in the service of his country, that is, in a battle between his own town and another fifteen miles off; his place here had been given to him as a reward for his patriotic services.

---

1. La Garita, or "sentry box," is now the name of a village at this point on the main road to San José.

As we advanced the country improved, and for a league before entering Alajuela it was lined on both sides with houses three or four hundred yards apart, built of sun-dried bricks and whitewashed. The fronts of some of the houses were ornamented with paintings, and several had chalked in red on each side of the door the figure of a soldier with his musket shouldered and bayonet fixed, large as life and stiff as a martinet. But all imperfections were hidden by rows of trees on both sides of the road, many of them bearing beautiful flowers, which in some places completely imbowered the houses. The fields were cultivated with sugar cane, and every house had its little *trapiche*, or sugar mill. There were marks of carriage wheels and very soon we heard a vehicle approaching. The creaking of its wheels made almost as much noise as the Zillenthal Patent Cold Amalgamating Machine in the mountain of Aguacate. They were made of a cut, about ten or twelve inches thick, from the trunk of a guanacaste tree, with a hole in the center which played upon the axle almost *ad libitum*, making the most mournful noise that can be conceived. The body was constructed of sugar cane; it was about four feet high, and drawn by oxen fastened by the horns instead of by the neck.

At the entry of Alajuela I stopped to inquire for one who bore a name immortal in the history of the Spanish conquest. It was the name of Alvarado. Whether this man was a descendant or not I do not know, nor did he; and strange to say, though I met several bearing that name, not one attempted to trace his lineage to the conqueror. Don Ramón Alvarado, however, was recommended to me for qualities which allied him in character with his great namesake. He was the courier of the English Mining Company for Sarapiquí and the River San Juan,[2] one of the wildest roads in all Central America.

Next to the advantage of the sea voyage, my principal object in leaving Sonsonate had been to acquire some information in regard to the canal route between the Atlantic and

---

2. The San Juan river marks the frontier between Costa Rica and Nicaragua.

Pacific by means of the Lake of Nicaragua and the River
San Juan, and my business with Alvarado was to secure him
as a guide to the port of San Juan.[3] In half an hour all these
arrangements were made, and the day fixed and half the
contract money paid. In the meantime Hezoos was busily
engaged in drawing a black glazed covering over my hat and
fixing in it an American eagle which I had taken off on shipboard.

There are four cities in Costa Rica, all of which lie within
the space of fifteen leagues; yet each has a different climate
and different productions. Including the suburbs, Alajuela
contains a population of about ten thousand. The plaza was
beautifully situated, and the church, the cabildo, and the
houses fronting it were handsome. The latter were long and
low, with broad piazzas and large windows, and balconies
made of wooden bars. It was Sunday, and the inhabitants,
cleanly dressed, were sitting on the piazzas, or, with doors
wide open, reclining in hammocks or on high-backed wooden
settees inside. The women were dressed like ladies, and
some were handsome, and all were white. A respectable-
looking old man, standing in the door of one of the best
houses, called out *amigo* (friend), and asked us who we
were, whence we came, and whither we were going, recommending us to God at parting. All along the street we were
accosted in the same friendly spirit.

At a distance of three leagues we passed through Heredia
without dismounting. I had ridden all day with a feeling of
extraordinary satisfaction; and if such were my feelings,
what must have been those of Hezoos? He was returning to
his country, with his love for it increased by absence and
hardship away from home. All the way he met old acquaintances and friends. He was a good-looking fellow, dashingly
dressed, and wore a basket-hilted Peruvian sword more than
six feet long. Behind him was strapped a valise of scarlet
cloth with black borders, part of the uniform of a Peruvian
soldier. It would have been curious to remember how many

---

3. There are two ports in Nicaragua by this name. It is safe to
assume that Stephens is referring here to San Juan del Sur on the
Pacific coast.

times he told his story: of military service and two battles in Peru, of impressment for the navy and desertion, of a voyage to Mexico and his return to Guatemala by land. He always concluded by inquiring about his wife, from whom he had not heard since he left home, *la pobre* being regularly his last words. As we approached his home his tenderness for *la pobre* increased. He could not procure any direct intelligence of her, but one good-natured friend suggested that she had probably married someone else, and that he would only disturb the peace of the family by his return.

A league beyond Heredia we came to another great ravine. We descended and crossed a bridge over the Río Segundo. A few months before, this river had risen suddenly and, without any apparent cause, swept away a house and family near the bridge, carrying with it consternation and death. Little is known of the geography of the interior of the country, but it is supposed that a lake had burst its bounds. As we were coming out of the ravine, Hezoos pointed out the scene of the battle in which the officer of La Garita had lost his arm, and in which he himself had taken part. Being a San José man, he spoke of the people of the other town as an Englishman in Lord Nelson's time would have spoken of a Frenchman.

On the top of the ravine we came upon a large table of land covered with the rich coffee plantations of San José. It was laid out into squares of two hundred feet and enclosed by living fences of trees bearing flowers; its roads were sixty feet wide and, except the small horsepath, had a sod of unbroken green. The deep green of the coffee plantations, the sward of the roads, and the vistas through the trees at all the crossroads were lovely. At a distance on each side were mountains, and in front, rising above all, was the great volcano of Cartago. It was about the same hour as when, the day before, from the top of the mountain of Aguacate, I had looked down into great ravines and over the tops of high mountains and seen the Pacific Ocean. This scene was as soft as that had been wild; and it addressed itself to other senses than the sight, for it was not, like the rest of Central America, retrograding and going to ruin, it was smiling as the reward of industry. Seven years before the whole plain had been an open waste.

At the end of this table of land we saw San José on a plain below us. On the top of the hill we passed a house with an arch of flowers before the door, which indicated that within there lay one who was waiting to receive the last sacrament before going to his final account in another world. Descending, we saw at a distance a long procession headed by a cross with the figure of the Saviour crucified. It approached with the music of violins and a loud chorus of voices, escorting the priest, who was carried in a sedan chair, to the house of the dying man. As it approached, horsemen pulled off their hats and pedestrians fell on their knees. We met it near a narrow bridge at the foot of the hill and waited till the priest passed. Then, taking advantage of a break in the procession, we crossed the bridge and passed a long file of men and a longer one of women. The sun was low, but its last rays were scorching to the naked head and, being some distance ahead, I put on my hat. A fanatic fellow, with a scowl on his face, cried out, "*quítese su sombrero* (take off your hat)." I answered by spurring my horse, and at the same moment the whole procession was thrown into confusion. A woman darted from the line, and Hezoos sprang from his horse and caught her in his arms and hugged and kissed her as much as decency in the public streets would allow. To my great surprise, the woman was only his cousin, but she told him that his wife, who was the principal milliner in the place, was up ahead in the procession. Hezoos was beside himself; he ran back, returned, caught his horse, and dragged the beast after him; then mounting and spurring, he begged me to hurry on and let him go back to his wife.

Entering the town, we passed a respectable-looking house, where four or five well-dressed women were sitting on the piazza. They screamed and Hezoos drove his mule up the steps and, throwing himself off, embraced them all around. After a few hurried words, he embraced them all over again. Some male friends attempted to haul him off, but he returned to the women. In fact, the poor fellow seemed beside himself, though I could not but observe that there was method in his madness, for after two rounds with the very respectable old ladies he abandoned them, and dragging forward a very pretty young girl, with his arms around her waist and kissing her every moment, he told me she was the apprentice of his wife. Though at every kiss he asked her questions about his wife, he did not wait for answers, and the kisses were repeated faster than the questions.

During all this time I sat on my horse looking on. Doubtless it was all very pleasant for him, but I began to be impatient. Seeing this, he tore himself away, mounted, and accompanied by half a dozen of his friends, he again led the way. As we advanced, his friends increased. It was rather vexatious, but I could not disturb him in the sweetest pleasures in life, the welcome of friends after a long absence. As we were crossing the plaza, two or three soldiers of his old company, leaning on the railing of the cuartel, cried out *compañero*, and, with the sergeant at their head, they passed over and joined us. We crossed the plaza with fifteen or twenty in our suite—or rather in his suite—some of whom, particularly the sergeant, in compliment to him, were civil to me.

While he had so many friends to welcome him, I had none. In fact, I did not know where I should sleep that night. In the large towns of Central America I was always at a loss where to stop. Throughout the country the traveler finds no public accommodation save the cabildo and a jar of water. Everything else he must carry with him or purchase on the spot—if he can. But in the large towns he has not even this resource, for it is not considered respectable to stop at the cabildo. I had letters of recommendation, but it was excessively disagreeable to present one from the back of a mule with my luggage at my heels, as it was, in fact, a draft at sight for board and lodging.

Hezoos had told me that there was an old *chapetón*, that is, a person from Spain, in whose house I could have a room to myself and pay for it; but, unfortunately, time had made its changes, and the old Spaniard had been gone so long that the occupants of his house did not know what had become of him. I had counted upon him with so much certainty that I had not taken out my letters of recommendation and did not even know the names of the persons to whom they were addressed. The cura was at his hacienda, and his house shut up; and a padre who had been in the United States was sick and could not receive anyone. My servant's friends all recommended different persons, as if I had the whole town at my disposal; and principally they urged me to honor with my company the chief of the state. In the midst of this street consultation, I longed for a hotel at a hundred dollars a day, with the government as paymaster.

Hezoos, who was all the time in a terrible hurry, after an animated interlude with some of his friends, spurred his mule and hurried me back. He crossed a corner of the plaza and turned down a street to the right, stopping opposite a small house where he dismounted and begged me to do the same. In a moment the saddles were whipped off and carried inside. I was ushered into the house and seated on a low chair in a small room where a dozen women, friends of Hezoos and his wife, were waiting to welcome him to his home. He told me that he had not known where his house was, or that it had an extra room, till he learned it from his friends. Carrying my luggage into a little dark apartment, he said that I could have that to myself, and that he and his wife and all his friends would wait upon me, and that I could be more comfortable there than in any house in San José.

I was excessively tired, having made three days' journey in two, and I was worn out with the worry of searching for a resting place. If I had been younger and had no character to lose, I should not have given myself any further trouble; but, unfortunately, the dignity of office might have been touched by my remaining in the house of my servant. Besides, I could not move without running against a woman and, more than all, Hezoos threw his arms around any one of them he chose and kissed her as much as he pleased. In the midst of my irresolution *la pobre* herself arrived, and half the women in the procession, amateurs of tender scenes, followed. I shall not attempt to describe the meeting. Hezoos, as in duty bound, forsook all the rest and, notwithstanding all that he had done, wrapped her little figure in his arms as tightly as if he had not looked at a woman for a month; and *la pobre* lay in his arms as happy as if there were no pretty cousins or apprentices in the world.

All this was too much for me. I worked my way out of doors and, after a consultation with the sergeant, I ordered my horse to be saddled. Riding a third time across the plaza, I stopped before the convent of Don Antonio Castro. The woman who opened the door said that the padre was not at home; I answered that I would walk in and wait, and ordered my luggage to be set down on the portico. She invited me inside, and I ordered the luggage in after me. The room occupied nearly the whole front of the convent, and, besides some pictures of saints, its only furniture was a large wooden table and a long, high-backed, wooden-bottomed settee. I laid my pistols and spurs upon the table and, stretching myself upon the settee, waited to welcome the padre to his house.

It was some time after dark when he returned. He was surprised and evidently did not know what to do with me, but he seemed to recognize the principle that possession is nine points of the law. I saw, however, that his embarrassment was not from want of hospitality, but from a belief that he could not make me comfortable. In Costa Rica the padres are poor, and I afterward learned that there it is unusual for a stranger to plant himself upon one. I have since thought that Padre Castro must have considered me particularly cool; but, at all events, when his nephew came in soon after, they forthwith procured me chocolate. At each end of the long room was a small one, one occupied by the padre and the other by his nephew. The latter vacated his and, with a few pieces from the padre's room, they fitted me up so well that when I lay down I congratulated myself upon my forcible entry; probably before they had recovered from their surprise, I was asleep.

My arrival was soon known, and the next morning I received several invitations to the house of residents—one was from the lady of Don Manuel de Aguilar; but I was so well pleased with the convent that I was not disposed to leave it.

As a matter of course, I soon became known to all the foreign residents, who, however, were but four: Messrs. Steipel
and Squire, a German and an Englishman associated in business; Mr. Wallenstein, German; and a countryman, Mr.
Lawrence, from Middletown, Connecticut. All four lived
with Mr. Steipel, and I had immediately a general invitation to make his house my home.

San José is, I believe, the only city that has grown up or
even improved since the independence of Central America.
Under the Spanish dominion Cartago was the royal capital;
but, on the breaking out of the revolution, the fervor of
patriotism was so hot that it was resolved to abolish this
memorial of colonial servitude and to establish the capital at
San José. Their local advantages are perhaps equal. Cartago
is nearer the Atlantic, and San José the Pacific, but they are
only six leagues apart. The buildings in San José are all
republican: not one is of any grandeur or architectural
beauty, and the churches are inferior to many erected by
the Spaniards in the smallest villages. Nevertheless, it exhibited a development of resources and an appearance of
business unusual in this lethargic country. There was one
house in the plaza which showed that the owner had been
abroad and had returned with his mind so liberalized as to
adopt the improvements of other countries and build differently from the custom of his fathers and the taste of his
neighbors.

My first visit of ceremony was to Señor Carrillo, the
Jefe del Estado. The State of Costa Rica enjoyed at that
time a degree of prosperity unequalled by any in the dis-
jointed confederacy. At a safe distance, without wealth
enough to excite cupidity, and with a large tract of wilderness to protect it against the march of an invading army, it
had escaped the tumults and wars which desolated and devastated the other states. And yet, but two years before, it
had had its own revolution: a tumultuous soldiery had entered the plaza shouting *abajo Aguilar, viva Carrillo*. My
friend Don Manuel had been driven out by bayonets and
banished from the state; Carrillo was installed in his place,
and he appointed his father-in-law, a quiet, respectable old

man, vice-chief. He called the soldiery, officers, civil and
military, into the plaza, and all went through the solemn
farce of swearing fealty to the Constitution. The time fixed
by the Constitution for holding new elections came, but they
were not permitted to be held. Having tried this once and
having failed, Carrillo did not mean to run the risk of holding another; probably he will hold on till he is turned out
by the same force that put him in. In the meantime, he uses
prudent precautions: he does not permit emigrés, nor revolutionists, nor suspected persons from other states to enter his
dominions; he has sealed up the press; and he imprisons, or
banishes under pain of death if they return, all who speak
aloud against the government.

He was about fifty, short, stout, and plain but careful in
his dress, with an appearance of dogged resolution in his
face. His house was republican enough, and had nothing to
distinguish it from that of any other citizen; in one part his
wife had a little store, and in the other was his office for
government business. His office was not larger than the
counting room of a third-rate merchant; he had three clerks
who, at the moment of my entering, were engaged in writing, while he, with his coat off, was looking over papers. He
had heard of my coming and welcomed me to Costa Rica.
Though the law under which I had come near being detained at the port was uppermost in my mind, and I am sure
was not forgotten by him, neither of us referred to it. He
inquired particularly about Guatemala; though sympathizing in the policy of that state, he had no good opinion of
Carrera. He was uncompromising in his hostility to General
Morazán and the Federal government. In fact, it seemed
to me that he was against any general government and
strongly impressed with the idea that Costa Rica could stand
alone; doubtless he believed that the state, or he, himself,
which is the same thing, could disburse revenues better than
any other authority. Indeed, this is the rock on which all the
politicians of Central America split; there is no such thing as
national feeling. Every state would be an empire; the officers of state cannot brook superiors; a chief of state cannot
brook a president. He had not sent deputies to the Conven-

tion and did not intend to do so, but he said that Costa Rica would remain neutral until the other states had settled their difficulties.

He spoke with much interest of the improvement of the roads, particularly to the ports on the Atlantic and Pacific, and expressed great satisfaction at the project of the British government, which I mentioned to him, of sending steamboats to connect the West India Islands with the American coast, which, by touching at the port of San Juan, could bring his secluded capital to within eighteen or twenty days of New York. In fact, usurper and despot as he is, Carrillo works hard for the good of the state, and for twelve hundred dollars a year, with perquisites and leave to be his own paymaster. In the meantime, all who do not interfere with him are protected. A few who cannot submit to despotism talk of leaving the country, but the great mass are contented, and the state prospers. As for myself, I admire him. In that country the alternative is a strong government or none at all. Throughout his state I felt a sense of personal security which I did not enjoy in any other. For the benefit of travelers, may he live a thousand years!

In the afternoon I dined with the foreign residents at the house of Mr. Steipel. This gentleman is an instance of the vicissitudes of fortune. A native of Hanover, at fifteen he left college and entered the Prussian army. He fought at Dresden and Leipsig, and at the battle of Waterloo he received a ball in his brain, which, unfortunately, only within the month preceding, caused him to lose the use of one eye. Disabled for three years by his wound, on his recovery, with three companions he had sailed for South America, where he had entered the Peruvian army, married an *Hija del Sol* (Daughter of the Sun) and turned merchant. Later he came to San José, where he was then living in a style of European hospitality. I shall lose all reputation as a sentimental traveler, but I cannot help mentioning honorably every man who gave me a good dinner; and with this determination, I shall offend the reader but once more.

Early the next morning, accompanied by my countryman, Mr. Lawrence, and mounted on a noble mule lent me by

Mr. Steipel, I set off for Cartago. We left the city by a long, well-paved street, and a little beyond the suburbs passed a neat coffee plantation, which reminded me of a Continental villa. It was the property of a Frenchman, who had died just as he completed it; but his widow had provided another master for his house and father for his children. On both sides were mountains, and in front was the great volcano of Cartago. The fields were cultivated with corn, plantains, and potatoes. The latter, though indigenous, and now scattered all over Europe, is no longer the food of the natives and is but rarely found in Spanish America. The Cartago potatoes are of good flavor, but not larger than a hickory nut, doubtless from the want of care in cultivating them. We passed a campo santo, a square enclosure of mud walls whitewashed, and came to an Indian village, the first I had seen in Costa Rica. It was much better than any in the other states, the houses of *tejas,* or tiles, were more substantial, and the inhabitants had clothes on.

Halfway between San José and Cartago we reached the village of Tres Ríos. From this place the road was more broken, without fences, and the land but little cultivated.

Entries have been found in the records of Cartago dated in 1598,[4] which show it to be the oldest city in Central America. Coming as we did from San José, its appearance was that of an ancient city. The churches were large and imposing, the houses had yard walls as high as themselves, and the quiet was extraordinary. We rode up a very long street without seeing a single person; the cross streets, extending to a great distance in both directions, were desolate. A single horseman crossing at some distance was an object to fix our attention.

The day before we had met at San José Dr. Bridley, the only foreign resident in Cartago, who had promised to procure a guide and make arrangements for us to ascend the volcano of Cartago;[5] we found that, besides doing all that he had promised, he was himself prepared to go with us. While

4. Cartago was founded in 1522.
5. Now known as the "Volcán Irazú."

dinner was being prepared, Mr. Lawrence and I visited another countryman, Mr. Lovel, a gentleman whom I had known in New York. He had brought with him from New York a newly married wife, a young lady who, to my surprise and great pleasure, I recognized as an acquaintance—a very slight acquaintance, it is true, but the merest personal knowledge, so far from home, was almost enough to constitute an intimacy. She had encountered many hardships, and her home was indeed in a strange land; but she bore all with the spirit of a woman who had given up all for one and was content with the exchange. Their house, situated on one side of the plaza, commanded a view of the volcano almost from its base to its top; though one of the best houses in the place, the rent was only six dollars per month.

Immediately after dinner we set out to ascend the volcano. It was necessary to sleep en route, and Mr. Lovel furnished me with a poncho from Mexico for a covering and a bear's skin from the Rocky Mountains for a bed. Passing down the principal street, we crossed in front of the cathedral and immediately began to ascend. Very soon we reached a height which commanded a view of a river, a village, and an extensive valley not visible from the plain below. The sides of the volcano are particularly favorable for cattle and, although the plains below were unappropriated, all the way up were *potreros*, or pasture grounds, and huts occupied by persons who had charge of the cattle.

Our only anxiety was lest we should lose our way. A few months before my companions had attempted to ascend with Mr. Handy, but, by the ignorance of their guide, they had become lost; after wandering the whole night on the sides of the volcano, they had returned without reaching the top. As we ascended, the temperature became colder, and I put on my poncho, but before we reached our stopping place my teeth were chattering, and before dismounting I had an ague. The situation was most wild and romantic, hanging on the side of an immense ravine, but I would have exchanged all its beauties for a blazing coal fire. The hut, built of mud, was the highest on the mountain; there was no opening but the door and there were cracks in the wall. Opposite the door was a figure of the Virgin, and on each side was a frame for a bed; my friends spread the bear's skin on one of the frames, and tumbling me upon it, wrapped me up in the poncho. I had promised myself a social evening, but who can be sure of an hour of pleasure? I was entirely unfit for use, but the place was perfectly quiet and my friends made me some hot tea; upon the whole, I had as comfortable a chill and fever as I had ever experienced.

Before daylight we resumed our journey. The road was rough and precipitous; in one place where a tornado had swept the mountain and the trees lay across the road so thickly as to make it almost impassable, we were obliged to dismount and climb over some and creep under others. Beyond this we came into an open region, where nothing but cedar and thorns grew; and here I saw whortleberries for the first time in Central America. In that wild region there was a charm in seeing anything that was familiar to me at home, and I should perhaps have become sentimental, but they were hard and tasteless. As we rose we entered a region of clouds which very soon became so thick that we could see nothing; the figures of our own party were barely distinguishable, and we lost all hope of any view from the top of the volcano. Grass still grew here, and we ascended till we reached a belt of barren sand and lava where to our great joy we emerged from the region of clouds and saw the top of the volcano, without a vapor upon it, seeming to mingle with the clear blue sky; at that early hour the sun was not high enough to play upon its top.

Mr. Lawrence, who had exerted himself in walking, lay down to rest, and the doctor and I walked on. The crater was about two miles in circumference, rent and broken by time or some great convulsion; the fragments stood high, bare, and grand as mountains, and within were three or four smaller craters. We ascended on the south side by a ridge running east and west till we reached a high point, at which there was an immense gap in the crater impossible to cross. The lofty point on which we stood was perfectly clear, the atmosphere was of transparent purity, and, looking beyond the region of desolation, below us at a distance of perhaps

two thousand feet the whole country was covered with clouds
and the city at the foot of the volcano invisible.

By degrees the more distant clouds were lifted, and over
the immense bed we saw at the same moment the Atlantic
and Pacific Oceans. This was the grand spectacle we had
hoped, but scarcely expected, to behold. My companions had
ascended the volcano several times, but on account of the
clouds had only seen the two seas once before. The points at
which they were visible were at the Gulf of Nicoya and the
harbor of San Juan, which were not directly opposite but
nearly at right angles to each other, so that we could see
both oceans without turning the body. In a right line over
the tops of the mountains neither ocean was more than
twenty miles distant, and from the great height at which
we stood they seemed almost at our feet. This is the only
point in the world which commands a view of the two seas;
and I ranked the sight with those most interesting occasions
when, from the top of Mount Sinai, I looked out upon the
Desert of Arabia, and when, from Mount Hor, I saw the
Dead Sea.[6]

There is no history or tradition of the eruption of this
volcano; probably it took place long before the country was
discovered by Europeans. This was one of the occasions in
which I regretted the loss of my barometer, as the height
of the mountain had never been measured; it is believed to
be about eleven thousand feet.

We returned to our horses and found Mr. Lawrence and
the guide asleep. We woke them, kindled a fire, made chocolate, and descended. In an hour we reached the hut at which
we had slept, and at two o'clock, Cartago.

Toward evening I set out with Mr. Lovel for a stroll.
The streets were all alike, long and straight, and there was
nobody in them. We fell into one which seemed to have no
end, and at some distance were intercepted by a procession
coming down a cross street. It was headed by boys playing
on violins. A small barrow tastefully decorated and strewed

6. Stephens notes that "several persons who have crossed the
Isthmus from Chagres to Panama" report "that there is no point on
the road from which the two seas are visible."

with flowers followed; it was a bier carrying the body of a child to the cemetery. We followed the procession and, passing it at the gate, entered the cemetery through a chapel, at the door of which sat three or four men selling lottery tickets, one of whom asked us if we wished to see the grave of our countryman. When we assented, he conducted us to the grave of a young American whom I had known by sight, and several members of whose family I knew personally. He had died about a year before my visit, and his funeral was attended with mournful circumstances. The vicar had refused him burial in consecrated ground, but Dr. Bridley, the only European resident in Cartago, at whose house he died, had ridden over to San José and, making a strong point of the treaty existing between the United States and Central America, had obtained an order from the government for his burial in the cemetery. Still the fanatic vicar, acting, as he said, under a higher power, refused. A messenger had then been sent to San José, and two companies of soldiers were ordered to the doctor's house to escort the body to the grave. That night men had been stationed by the grave to watch that the body was not dug up and thrown out. The next day the vicar, with the cross and images of saints and all the emblems of the church, and a large concourse of citizens, moved in solemn procession to the cemetery and formally reconsecrated the ground which had been polluted by the burial of a heretic.

In an honored place among the principal dead of Cartago, lay the body of another stranger, an Englishman named Baillie. The day before his death the alcalde had been called in to draw his will. When, according to the customary form, the alcalde asked him if he was a Christian, Mr. Baillie answered yes, and the alcalde recorded him as *Católico Romano Apostólico Cristiano*. Mr. Baillie, having known of the difficulty in the case of my countryman about six months before and wishing to spare his friends a disagreeable and, perhaps, unsuccessful controversy, had already indicated a particular tree under which he wished to be buried. He did not see what the alcalde recorded, and before the will was read to him, he died. His recorded answer to the alcalde had been considered evidence of his orthodoxy and, his friends not wishing to interfere, he had been buried under the special direction of the priests, with all the holiest ceremonies of the Church. It had been the greatest day ever known in Cartago. The funeral had been attended by all the citizens. The procession had started from the door of the church, headed by violins and drums; priests followed with all the crosses, figures of saints, and banners that had been accumulating from the foundation of the city. At the corners of the plaza and of all the principal streets, the procession stopped to sing hallelujahs to represent the joy in heaven over a sinner that repents.

From where we were standing we saw the man who had accompanied the bier in this day's procession pass by with the child in his arms. He was its father, and with a smile on his face he was carrying it to its grave. He was followed by two boys playing on violins, while others were laughing around. As the child, dressed in white with a wreath of roses around its head, lay in its father's arms, it did not seem dead, but sleeping. The grave not being quite ready, the boys sat on the heap of dirt thrown out and played the violin till it was finished. The father then laid the child carefully in its final resting place with its head to the rising sun. He folded its little hands across its breast, and closed its fingers around a small wooden crucifix; and it seemed, as they thought it was, happy at escaping the troubles of an uncertain world. There were no tears shed; on the contrary, all were cheerful. And though it appeared heartless, it was not because the father did not love his child, but because he and all his friends had been taught to believe, and were firm in the conviction, that, taken away so young, it was transferred immediately to a better world. The father sprinkled a handful of dirt over its face; the grave digger took his shovel and in a few moments the little grave was filled up; then, preceded by the boy playing on his violin, we all went away together. The next morning with great regret I took leave of my kind friends and returned to San José.

It is my misfortune to be the sport of other men's wives. I lost the best servant I had in Guatemala because his wife was afraid to trust him with me. On my return I found Hezoos at the convent waiting for me, and, while he was putting my things in order, without looking me in the face he began to tell me of the hardships of his wife, of how much *la pobre* had suffered during his absence, and of how difficult it was for a married woman to get along without her husband. I saw to what he was tending, and feeling, particularly since the recurrence of my fever and ague, the importance of having a good servant in the long journey I had before me, with the selfishness of a traveler I encouraged his vagabond propensities by telling him that in a few weeks he would be tired of home and would not have so good an opportunity of getting away. This seemed so sensible to him that he discontinued his hints and went off contented.

At three o'clock I felt uncertain in regard to my chill, but, determined not to give way, I dressed myself and went to dine with Mr. Steipel. Before sitting down, the blueness of my lips and a tendency to use superfluous syllables betrayed me; and my old enemy shook me all the way back to the convent and into bed. Fever followed, and I lay in bed all next day, receiving many visits at the door and a few inside. One of the latter was from Hezoos, who returned stronger than before. Coming to the point, he said that although he, himself, was anxious to go with me, his wife would not consent. I felt that if she had fairly taken the field against me it was all over, but I told him that he had made a contract and was already overpaid, and I sent her a pair of gold ear rings to keep her quiet.

On each of four days in succession I had a recurrence of chill and fever. Every kindness was shown me in the convent; friends visited me and Dr. Bridley came over from Cartago to attend me, but withal I was desponding. When the day fixed for setting out with Alvarado arrived, it was impossible for me to go; Dr. Bridley had advised me that it would be unwise, while any tendency to the disease remained, to undertake a journey. There would be six days of desert traveling to the port of San Juan, without a house on the road, and with mountains to cross and rivers to ford. The whole party was to go on foot except myself; four extra men would be needed to pass my mule over some difficult

places, and there would always be more or less rain. San
Juan was a collection of miserable shanties, and from that
place it would be necessary to embark in a bungo for ten or
fifteen days on an unhealthy river. Besides all this, I had
either to return by the *Cosmopolita* to Sonsonate, or to go to
Guatemala by land, a journey of twelve hundred miles
through a country destitute of accommodations for travelers
and dangerous from the convulsions of civil war. At night,
as I lay alone in the convent and by the light of a small
candle saw the bats flying along the roof, I felt gloomy and
would have been glad to have been at home.

Still I could not bear the idea of losing all I came for.
The land route which lay along the coast of the Pacific, was
for three days the same as to the port. I determined to go
by land, but, by the advice of Dr. Bridley, to start in time
to reach the vessel. In the hope that I would not have another chill, I bought two of the best mules in San José, one
being that on which I had ascended the volcano of Cartago,
and the other a *macho,* or he-mule, which, though not more
than half broken, was the finest animal I ever mounted.

But to return to Hezoos. The morning after I gave him
the earrings he did not come, but he sent word that he had
the fever and ague. The next day he had it much worse and,
satisfied that I must lose him, I sent him word that if he
would procure me a good substitute I would release him.
This raised him from bed, and in the afternoon he came
with his substitute, who had very much the air of being the
first man he had picked up in the street. His dress was a pair
of cotton trousers, with a shirt outside, and a high, bell-
crowned, narrow-brimmed black straw hat; all that he had
in the world was on his back. His hair was cut very close
except in front, where it hung in long locks over his face;
in short, he was the *beau ideal* of a Central American loafer.
I did not like his looks, but I was at the time under the influence of fever, and told him I could give him no answer.
He came again the next day at a moment when I wanted
some service; and by degrees, though I never hired him,
he quietly engaged me as his master.

The morning before I left, Don Agustín Gutiérrez called
upon me and, seeing this man at the door, expressed his sur-

prise, telling me that he was the town blackguard, a drunkard, gambler, robber, and assassin; that the first night on the road he would rob and perhaps murder me. Shortly after Mr. Lawrence entered and told me that he had just heard the same thing. I discharged this loafer at once, and apparently not much to his surprise, though he still continued round the convent, as he said, in my employ. It was very important for me to set out in time for the vessel, and I had but that day to look out for another guide. Hezoos was astonished at the changes time had made in the character of his friend. He said that he had known him when a boy, and had not seen him in many years till the day he brought him to me, when he had stumbled upon him in the street. Not feeling perfectly released, after a great deal of running about he brought me another man whose name was Nicolás. In any other country I should have called him a mulatto, but in Central America there are so many different shades that I am at a loss how to designate him. By trade a mason, Hezoos had encountered him at his work and talked him into a desire to see Guatemala and Mexico and come back as rich as himself. He presented himself just as he left his work, with his shirt sleeves rolled up above his elbows and his trousers above his knees: a rough diamond for a valet. But he was honest, could take care of mules, and make chocolate; I did not ask more. He was married, too, and as his wife did not interfere with me, I liked him the better for it.

In the afternoon, being the last before I started, in company with Mr. Lawrence I visited the coffee plantations of Don Mariano Montealegre. It was a lovely situation, and with great good taste Don Mariano lived there a great part of the year. He was at his factory, and his son mounted his horse and accompanied us. It was a beautiful walk, but in that country gentlemen never walk.

The cultivation of coffee on the plains of San José had increased rapidly within a few years. Seven years before, the whole crop had not been more than five hundred quintals, but this year it was supposed that it would amount to more than ninety thousand. Don Mariano was one of the largest planters, and had three *cafetales* in that neighborhood; we visited one which contained twenty-seven thousand trees, to which he was preparing to make great additions the next year. He had expended a large sum of money in buildings and machinery; and though his countrymen said he would ruin himself, every year he planted more trees. His wife, la señora, was busily engaged in superintending the details of husking and drying the grains. In San José, by the way, all the ladies were what might be called good businessmen—they kept stores, bought and sold goods, looked out for bargains, and were particularly knowing in the article of coffee.

Chapter XVIII

~~~~~~

Departure for Guatemala. Esparta. Town of Costa Rica.
The barranca. History of a countryman. Wild scenery.
Hacienda of Aranjuez. River Lagartos. Cerro of Collito.
Herds of deer. Santa Rosa. Don Juan José Bonilla. An
earthquake. A cattle farm. Bagaces. Guanacaste. An agree-
able welcome. Belle of Guanacaste. Pleasant lodgings.
Cordilleras. Volcanoes of Rincón and Orosi. Hacienda
of Santa Teresa. Sunset view.
The Pacific again.

ON the thirteenth day of February I mounted for my
journey to Guatemala. My equipage was reduced to
articles of the last necessity: a hammock of striped cotton
cloth laid over my *pellón*, a pair of alforjas, and a poncho
strapped on behind. Behind him Nicolás had strung across
his *albarda*, or packsaddle, a pair of leather *cojines*, in shape
like buckets with the inner side flat, which contained biscuit,
chocolate, sausages, and *dulces*; and in front, he carried on
the pommel my wearing apparel rolled up in an oxhide after
the fashion of the country. During my whole stay at the
convent the attentions of the padre were unremitted. Besides
the services he actually rendered me, I have no doubt he
considers that he saved my life for, during my sickness,
he entered my room while I was preparing to shave and
made me desist from so dangerous an operation. I washed
my face by stealth, but his kindness added another to the
list of obligations I was already under to the padres of Central America.

I felt great satisfaction at being able once more to resume
my journey, pleased with the lightness of my equipage and

the spirit of my mules. I looked my journey of twelve hundred miles boldly in the face. Then, all at once I heard a clattering from behind, and Nicolás swept by me on a full run. My macho was what was called *espantadizo*, or scary, and he was startled; I had very little strength, and was fairly run away with. If I had bought my beasts for racing I should have had no reason to complain; but, unluckily, my saddle turned, and I came to the ground. Fortunately I cleared the stirrups. The beast ran, scattering on the road pistols, holsters, saddlecloths, and saddle, and he continued on bare-backed toward the town. To my great relief, some muleteers intercepted him and saved my credit as a horseman in San José. We were more than an hour in recovering scattered articles and repairing broken trappings.

For three days my road was the same that I had traveled in entering Costa Rica. The fourth morning I rose without any recurrence of fever. Mr. Lawrence had kindly borne me company from San José, and was still with me; he had relieved me from all trouble and had made my journey so easy and comfortable that, instead of being wearied, I was recruited, and I abandoned all idea of returning by sea.

At seven o'clock we started and in half an hour reached Esparta. From this place to Nicaragua, a distance of three hundred miles, the road lay through a wilderness; except the frontier town of Costa Rica,[1] there were only a few straggling haciendas, twenty, thirty, and forty miles apart. I replenished my stock of provisions, my last purchase being a yard and a half of American cotton from a Massachusetts factory, a material called by the imposing name of *Manta del Norte*.

In half an hour we crossed the Barranca, a broad, rapid, and beautiful river; but it lost in my eyes all its beauty, for here Mr. Lawrence left me. Since the day of my arrival at San José he had been almost constantly with me; he had accompanied me on every excursion, and during my sickness had attended me constantly. He was a native of Middletown in Connecticut, about fifty years old, and by trade a silver-

1. Stephens is probably referring to the town of Liberia.

smith; with the exception of a single return visit, he had been nineteen years away from home. In 1822 he had gone to Peru, where, besides carrying on his legitimate business upon a large scale, his science and knowledge of the precious metals brought him into prominent public positions. In 1830 he sold a mint to the government of Costa Rica, and was offered the place of its director. Business connected with the mint brought him to Costa Rica, and during his absence he left his affairs in the hands of a partner, who mismanaged them and died. Mr. Lawrence returned to Peru, but without engaging in active business; in the meantime the mint which the government had purchased from him had become worn out, and another, imported from Europe, was so complicated that no one in Costa Rica could work it. Offers were made to Mr. Lawrence of such a nature that, connected with mining purposes of his own, they induced him to return. Don Manuel de Aguilar was then *Jefe del Estado*, but when Mr. Lawrence arrived at the port he met Don Manuel banished and flying from the state. The whole policy of the government was changed. Mr. Lawrence remained quietly in San José, and when I left he intended to establish himself at Puntarenas to traffic with the pearl fishermen. Such is, in brief, the history of one of our many countrymen scattered in different parts of the world; it would be a proud thing for the country if all sustained as honorable a reputation as his. We exchanged adieus from the backs of our mules, and, not to be sentimental, lighted our cigars. Whether we shall ever meet again or not is uncertain.

I was again setting out alone. I had traveled so long with companions or in ships that, when the moment for plunging into the wilderness came, my courage almost failed me. And it was a moment that required some energy, for we struck off immediately into one of the wildest paths that I met on the whole of that desolate journey. The trees were so close as to darken it, and the branches so low that it was necessary to keep the head constantly bent to avoid hitting them. The noise of the locusts, which had accompanied us since we reached the mountain of Aguacate, here became startling.

Very soon families of monkeys, walking heavily on the tops of the trees, disturbed these noisy tenants of the woods and sent them flying around us in such swarms that we were obliged to beat them off with our hats. My macho snorted and pulled violently on the bit, dragging me against the trees; and I could not help thinking, if this is the outset, what will be the end?

Parting with Mr. Lawrence advanced the position of Nicolás. Man is a talking animal; Nicolás was particularly so, and very soon I knew the history of his life. His father was a muleteer, and he seemed constructed for the same rough business; but after a few journeys to Nicaragua he retired in disgust, married, and had two children. The trying moment of his life was when he was compelled to serve as a soldier. His great regret was that he could not read or write; and his great astonishment, that he worked hard and yet could not get on. He wanted to go with me to Mexico, to go to my country, to be away two years, and to return with a sum of money in hand, as Hezoos had done. He knew that General Morazán was a great man, for when he visited Costa Rica there was a great firing of cannons and a ball. He was a poor man himself, and did not know what the wars were about. He supposed that Don Manuel de Aguilar had been expelled because Carrillo wanted to be chief.

We continued in the woods till about two o'clock, when, turning off by a path to the right, we reached a clearing, on one side of which was the hacienda of Aranjuez. The entrance to the house was by a ladder from the outside, and underneath was a sort of storehouse. It was occupied by a major-domo, a mestizo, and his wife. Near it was the *cocina*, where the wife and another woman were at work. The major-domo was sitting on the ground doing nothing, and two able-bodied men were helping him.

The major-domo told us that he had a good *potrero* for the mules, and the house promised a good resting place for me. Outside and extending all around was a rough board piazza, one side of which commanded a view of the ocean. I seated myself on this side, and very soon Nicolás brought me my dinner which consisted of tortillas, rice cooked with lard, which he brought in a shell, and salt which he brought in his hands. As I finished with a cup of chocolate, I could not but think of the blessings wasted by this major-domo. In the same situation, one of our backwoodsmen, with his axe, his wife, and two pairs of twins, would in a few years surround himself with all the luxuries that good land can give.

After dinner I led the mules to a stream, on the banks of which were tufts of young grass. While I was sitting there, two wild turkeys flew over my head and lighted on a tree near by. Sending Nicolás for my gun, I soon had a bird large enough for a household dinner and I sent it immediately to the house to be converted into provender. At sundown I returned to the house to discover a deficiency in my preparations which I was to feel during the whole journey, that is, of candles. A light was manufactured by filling a broken clay vessel with grease and coiling in it some twisted cotton, leaving one end sticking out about an inch. The workmen on the hacienda took advantage of the light and brought out a pack of cards. The wife of the major-domo joined them and, seeing no chance of a speedy termination of the game, I undressed myself and went to bed. When they finished the game, the woman got into a bed directly opposite mine and, before lying down, lighted another cigar. The men did the same on the floor, and till the cigars went out they continued discussing the game. The major-domo was already asleep in the hammock. All night the wife of the major-domo smoked, and the men snuffled and snored.

At two o'clock I rose and went out of doors. The moon was shining, and the freshness of the morning air was grateful. I woke Nicolás, and paying the major-domo as he lay in his hammock, at three o'clock we resumed our journey. I had been charmed with this place when we reached it, but disgusted when we left it. The people were kind and of as good disposition as the expectation of pay could make them, but their habits were intolerable. But the freshness of the morning air restored my equanimity. The moon shed a glorious light over the clearing, lifting the darkness of the forest; we heard only the surge of monkeys, as, disturbed by our noise, they moved on the tops of the trees.

At eight o'clock we reached the River Lagartos, breaking rapidly over a bed of white sand and gravel; it was clear as crystal and shaded by trees, the branches of which met at the fording place to form a complete arbor. We dismounted, took off the saddles from our mules and tied the mules to a tree; we then kindled a fire on the bank and breakfasted. Wild scenes had long lost the charm of novelty, but this I would not have exchanged for a *déjeuner à la fourchette* at the best restaurant of Paris. The wild turkey was not more than enough for my household, which consisted of Nicolás.

Resuming our journey, in two hours we emerged from the woods and came into an open country in sight of the Cerro of Collito, a fine bare conical peak, which stood alone and was covered with grass to the top. At twelve o'clock we reached the rancho of an Indian. On one side was a group of orange trees loaded with fruit, and in front a shed thatched with leaves of Indian corn. An old Indian woman was sitting in the door, and a sick Indian was lying asleep under the shed. It was excessively hot and, riding under the shed, I dismounted, threw myself into a ragged hammock, and while quenching my thirst with an orange fell asleep. The last thing I remembered was seeing Nicolás drive into the hut a miserable half-starved chicken. At two o'clock he woke me and set before me the unfortunate little bird, nearly burned up; the expense of the chicken, with oranges *ad libitum*, was six and a quarter cents, which the old woman wished to commute for a charge of gunpowder. I was very poor in this and would rather have given her a dollar, but I could not help adding the charge of gunpowder to the coin.

At two o'clock we set off again. We had already made a day's journey, but I had a good resting place for the night in view. It was excessively hot, but very soon we reached the woods again. We had not gone far before a deer crossed our path. It was the first I had seen in the country, which was almost destitute of all kinds of game. Indeed, during my whole journey, except at the wild turkey, I had fired but twice, and then merely to procure curious birds; and most unfortunately, in pursuance of my plan of encumbering myself as little as possible, I had with me but a few charges of duck shot and half a dozen pistol balls. Very soon I saw two deer together and within reach of a ball. Both barrels of my gun were loaded with duck shot, and I dismounted and followed them into the woods, endeavoring to get within reach. In the course of an hour I saw perhaps a dozen deer, and in that hour I fired away my last duck shot. I was resolved not to use my pistol balls, and as both barrels were empty, I kept quiet. As the evening approached the deer increased, and I am safe in saying I saw fifty or sixty, and many within rifle shot. Occasionally cattle peeped at us through the trees as wild as the deer. The sun was getting low when we came out into a large clearing, on one side of which stood the hacienda of Santa Rosa. The house stood on the right, and directly in front, against the side of a hill, was a large cattle yard, enclosed by a hard clay wall; it was divided into three parts and filled with cows and calves. On the left was an almost boundless plain interspersed with groves of trees; as we rode up, a gentleman in the yard sent a servant to open the gate. Don Juan José Bonilla met me at the porch and, before I had time to present my letter, welcomed me to Santa Rosa.

Don Juan was a native of Cartago, a gentleman by birth and education, and of one of the oldest families in Costa Rica. He had traveled over his own country and, what was very unusual in that region, had visited the United States; and though laboring under the disadvantage of not knowing the language, he spoke with great interest of our institutions. He had been an active member of the Liberal Party; he had labored to carry out its principles in the administration of the government and to save his country from the disgrace of falling back into despotism. He had been persecuted and heavy contributions had been laid upon his property; and four years before he had withdrawn from Cartago and retired to this hacienda.

But political animosity never dies. A detachment of soldiers was sent to arrest him, and, that no suspicion might be excited, they were sent by sea and landed at a port on the

Pacific within the bounds of his own estate. Don Juan received an intimation of their approach, and sent a servant to reconnoiter. When the servant returned with the intelligence that they were within half a day's march, he mounted his horse to escape, but near his own gate he was thrown and his leg badly broken. He was carried back to his house insensible; when the soldiers arrived and found him in bed, they made him rise. They put him on horseback and hurried him to the boundary line of the state of Costa Rica which is a river in the midst of a wilderness. After communicating to him his sentence of banishment, and death if he returned, they left him at the frontier. He had been obliged to travel on horseback to Nicaragua, a journey of four days. He never recovered the use of his leg, which remained two or three inches shorter than the other. After two years in exile, on the election of Don Manuel de Aguilar as chief of the state, he returned. On the expulsion of Don Manuel he retired again to his hacienda, and at the time of our arrival he was busily engaged in making repairs for the reception of his family; but he did not know at what moment another order might come to expel him from his home.

While sitting at the supper table we heard a noise over our heads, which seemed to me like the opening of the roof. Don Juan threw his eyes to the ceiling and suddenly started from his chair, threw his arms around the neck of a servant, and with the fearful word *"temblor!* (an earthquake! an earthquake!)" all rushed for the doors. I sprang from my chair, made one bound across the room, and cleared the piazza. The earth rolled like the pitching of a ship in a heavy sea. My step was high, my feet barely touched the ground, and my arms were thrown up involuntarily to save myself from falling. I was the last to start, but, once under way, I was the last to stop. Halfway across the yard I stumbled over a man on his knees, and fell. I never felt myself so feeble a thing before. At this moment I heard Don Juan calling to me. He was leaning on the shoulder of his servant, with his face to the door, crying to me to come out of the house. It was pitchy dark; within was the table at which we had sat with a single candle, the light of which extended far enough to show a few of the kneeling figures with their faces

to the door. We looked anxiously in and waited for the
shock which should prostrate the strong walls and lay the
roof on the ground. There was something awful in our position, with our faces to the door, shunning the place which
at all other times offers shelter to man. The shocks were
continued for perhaps two minutes, during which time it required an effort to stand firm. The return of the earth to
steadiness was almost as violent as the shock. We waited a
few minutes after the last vibration, and then Don Juan said
it was over and, assisted by his servant, he entered the house.
I had been the last to leave it, but I was the last to return;
and my chair lying with its back on the floor gave an intimation of the haste with which I had decamped. The houses
in Costa Rica are the best in the country for resisting these
shocks. They are long and low, and built of adobes, or un-
dried bricks, two feet long and one broad, which are made
of clay mixed with straw to give adhesion. The bricks are
laid when soft with upright posts between, so that they are
dried by the sun into one mass, which moves with the surface
of the earth.

Before the evening was over I forgot the earthquake in a
minor trouble. The uncultivated grounds of Central America teem with noxious insects. Riding all day in the woods,
striking my head against the branches of trees had brought
ticks down upon me in such numbers that I could brush
them off with my hand. I had suffered so much during the
day that twice I was obliged to strip at a stream and tear
them out of my flesh, which gave me only temporary relief
for lumps of irritation were left. In the midst of serious
disquisitions with Don Juan, impolite as it was, I was obliged
to use my nails violently and constantly. I was fain to entreat him to go out and give me the room to myself. A
moment after he retired all my clothes were out of doors,
and I tore the vipers out by the teeth; but Don Juan to my
relief sent a deaf and dumb boy, who, by touching them
with a ball of black wax, drew them from their burrowing
places without any pain; yet they left behind wounds from
which I did not recover in a long time.

Early in the morning two horses were at the door and two
servants in attendance for a ride. Don Juan mounted the

same horse which he had ridden in his exile, and was attended by the same servants. Heretofore I had always heard constant complaints of servants, and to do them justice, I think they are the worst I ever knew; but Don Juan's were the best in the world, and it was evident that they thought he was the best master.

The estate of Don Juan covered as much ground as a German principality, containing two hundred thousand acres, and bounded on one side for a long distance by the Pacific Ocean. A small portion of it was cultivated, but not more than enough to raise maize for the workmen; the rest was a roaming ground for cattle. More than ten thousand animals were wandering over it, almost as wild as the deer; they were never seen except as they crossed a path in the woods, or at the season when they were lassoed for the purpose of taking an account of the increase.

We had not gone far before we saw three deer all close together and not far from us; in the course of an hour we saw more than twenty. It was exceedingly vexatious, the first time I was in a country where there was anything to shoot at, to be so wholly unprovided with ammunition, and I had no chance of supplying myself till I was out of that region. Don Juan was incapacitated for sporting by his lameness; in fact, deer shooting was not considered sporting, and venison not fit to eat.

I had set out on this long journey without any cargo mule because of the difficulty of procuring one that could keep pace with the riding beasts and because we had felt the inconvenience of being encumbered with luggage. Besides Don Juan's kindness to me at his house, he also furnished me with a mule which he had broken expressly for his own use in rapid journeys between Cartago and the hacienda, and which he warranted me, with a light load, would trot and keep up with mine.

Late in the afternoon I left his hospitable dwelling. Don Juan, with his deaf and dumb boy, accompanied me a league on the way, when we dismounted and took leave of each other. My new mule, like myself, was very reluctant to leave Don Juan; she seemed to have a sentiment that she should never see her old master again. Indeed, it was so difficult to

get her along that Nicolás tied her by the halter to his mule's
tail, after a manner common in the country, and led her
along with me following at her heels. The deer were more
numerous than I had yet seen them, and I now looked at
them only as animating a beautiful landscape.

At dark we began to have apprehensions about the road.
There was a difficult mountain pass before us, and Nicolás
wanted to stop and wait till the moon rose; but as that would
derange the journey for the next day, I pushed on for more
than an hour through the woods. The mules stumbled along
in the dark, and very soon we lost all traces of a path. While
trying to find it, we heard the crash of a falling tree, which
in the darkness sounded appalling and made us hesitate to
enter the woods. Determined to wait for the moon, I dismounted. Peering into the darkness, I saw a glimmering
light on the left. We shouted with all our strength, and were
answered by a pack of barking dogs; moving in the direction of the light, we reached a hut where three or four workmen were lying on the ground. They were at first disposed
to be merry and impertinent when we asked for a guide to
the next hacienda, but then one of them recognized my
cargo mule. He said that he had known it since he was a
child (rather doubtful praise of my new purchase), and he
was at length induced to make us an offer of his services. A
horse was brought around; he was large, wild, and furious,
as if never bitted. He snorted, reared, and almost made the
ground shake at every tread; and, before the rider was fairly
on his back, he was tearing in the dark across the plain. Making a wide sweep, he returned, and the guide, releasing the
cargo mule from that of Nicolás, tied her to the tail of his
horse and started to lead the way. Even with the drag of
the cargo mule it was impossible to moderate his pace, and
we were obliged to follow at a most unhappy rate. It was
the first piece of bad road we had met with; it was broken
and stony, with many sharp turns, and ascents and descents.
Fortunately, while we were in the woods, the moon rose,
touching with a silvery light the tops of the trees; when we
reached the bank of the river it was almost as light as day.
Here my guide left me, and I lost all confidence in the

moon, for by her deceitful light I had slipped into his hand a gold piece instead of a silver one, without either of us knowing it.

As we ascended the bank after crossing the stream, the hacienda was in full sight. The occupants were in bed, but Don Manuel, to whom I had been recommended by Don Juan, rose to receive me. On the bank of the river, near the house, was a large sawmill, the first I had seen in the country; it had been built, Don Manuel told me, by an American, who afterward straggled to Guatemala and was killed in some popular insurrection.

At daylight the next morning, as the workmen on the hacienda were about to go to work, we set off again. In an hour we heard the sound of a horn, giving notice of the approach of a drove of cattle. We drew up into the woods to let them pass; they came with a cloud of dust, the faces of the drivers covered, and would have trampled to death anything that impeded their progress.

At eleven o'clock we entered the village of Bagaces. We had made tremendous journeys, and it was the first time in four days that we had seen anything but single haciendas, but we rode through without stopping, except to ask for a cup of water.

Late in the afternoon we came into a broad avenue and saw marks of wheels. At dusk we reached the river which runs by the suburbs of Guanacaste,[2] the frontier town of Costa Rica. The pass was occupied by an ox-cart, drawn by four stubborn oxen, which would not go ahead and could not go back. We were detained half an hour, and it was dark when we entered the town. We passed through the plaza, before the door of the church, which was lighted up for vespers, and rode to a house at which I had been directed to stop. Nicolás went in to make preliminary inquiries; returning, he told me to dismount and unloaded the luggage mule. I went in, took off my spurs, and stretched myself on a bench. Soon it struck me that my host was not particularly

2. There is no town in this location with this name. Stephens is probably again referring to Liberia, the capital of the province of Guanacaste.

glad to see me. Several children came in and stared, and then ran back into another room. In a few minutes I received the compliments of the lady of the house, and her regret that she would not be able to accommodate me. I was indignant at Nicolás, who had merely asked whether such a person lived there, and without more ado had sent me in. I left the house, and with the halter of my macho in one hand and spurs in the other, and Nicolás following with the mules, I sought the house of the commandant. I found him standing on the piazza with the key in his hand and all his household stuff packed up outside; he was only waiting for the moon to rise before setting out for another post. I believe he regretted that he could not accommodate me, nor could he refer me to any other house; but he sent his servant to look for one, and I waited nearly an hour for a bidder.

In the meantime I made inquiries about my road. I did not wish to continue on the direct route to Nicaragua, but to go first to the port of San Juan on the Pacific, the proposed termination of the canal to connect the Atlantic and Pacific Oceans. The commandant regretted that I had not come one day sooner. He mentioned a fact of which I was aware before, that Mr. Baily, an English gentleman, who had been employed by the government to survey the canal route, had resided for some time at the port, and added that since his departure the place had been perfectly desolate; no one ever visited it, not a person in the place knew the road to it, and, unluckily, a man who had been in Mr. Baily's employ there had left that morning for Nicaragua. Most fortunately, on inquiry, the man was found to be still in the place, but he, too, intended to set out as soon as the moon rose. I had no inducement to remain; nobody seemed very anxious for the honor of my company, and I would have gone on immediately if the mules had been able to continue. I made an arrangement with him and his son to wait till three in the morning, then to conduct me to the port, and thence to Nicaragua.

At length the commandant's servant returned and conducted me to a house with a little shop in front, where I was received by an old lady with a *buenas noches* that almost

surprised me into an idea that I was welcome. I entered
through the shop and passed into a parlor which contained a
hammock, an interlaced bedstead, and a very neat *catre* with
a gauze mosquito netting and pink bows at the corners. I
was agreeably disappointed with my *posada*, and while I was
conversing with the old lady and dozing over a cup of chocolate, I heard a lively voice at the door. A young lady entered,
with two or three young men in attendance, who came up
to the table in front of me, and throwing back a black man-
tilla, bade me *buenas noches*. Putting out her hand, she said
that she had heard in church that I was at her house; she
said that she was so glad of it, that no strangers ever came
there, that the place was completely out of the world, that
it was very dull, etc., etc. I was so surprised that I must
have looked very stupid. She was not regularly handsome,
but her mouth and eyes were beautiful; and her manner was
so different from the cold, awkward, and bashful air of her
countrywomen, and so much like the frank and fascinating
welcome which a young lady at home might extend to a
friend after a long absence, that if the table had not been
between us I could have taken her in my arms and kissed
her. As it was I pulled up my coat collar and forgot all my
troubles and perplexities.

Though living in that little remote town, like young ladies
in large cities, she had a fancy for strangers, which at the
time I regarded as a delightful trait of character in a woman.
Her everyday beaux had no chance. At first they were very
civil to me, but then they became short and crusty, and, very
much to my satisfaction, took themselves off. It had been
so long since I had felt the least interest in a woman that
I gave myself a benefit. The simplest stories of other countries and other people were to her romance, and her eye
kindled as she listened. Soon the transition came from facts
to feelings, and then that highest earthly pleasure of being
lifted above everyday thoughts by the enthusiasm of a high-
minded girl.

We sat up till twelve o'clock. The mother, who at first
wearied me, I found exceedingly agreeable. Indeed, I had
seldom known a more interesting old lady, for she pressed

me to remain two or three days and rest. She said the place was dull, but that her daughter would try to make it agreeable; her daughter said nothing, but looked unutterable things.

All pleasure is fleeting. Twelve o'clock was an unprecedented hour for that country. My ordinary prudence in looking out for a sleeping place had not deserted me. Two little boys had taken possession of the leather bed and the old lady had retired; the beautiful little *catre* remained unoccupied, and the young lady withdrew, telling me that this was to be my bed. I do not know why, but I felt uneasy. I opened the mosquito net. In that country beds are not used, and an oxhide or mat, often not so clean as it might be, is the substitute. This was a mat, very fine, and clean as if perfectly new. At the head was a lovely pillow with a pink muslin covering, and over it was a thin white pillowcase with a bewitching ruffle. Whose cheek had rested on that pillow? I pulled off my coat, walked up and down the room, and waked up one of the boys. It was as I supposed. I lay down, but could not sleep and determined not to continue my journey the next day.

At three o'clock the guide knocked at the door. The mules were already saddled, and Nicolás was putting on the luggage. I had often clung to my pillow, but never as I did to that pink one with its ruffled border. I told Nicolás that the guide must go home and wait another day. The guide refused. It was the young man; his father had already gone and had ordered him to follow. Very soon I heard a light footstep, and a soft voice expostulating with the guide. Indignant at his obstinacy, I ordered him away; but very soon I reflected that I could not procure another and might lose the great object I had in view in making this long journey. I called him back and attempted to bribe him, but his only answer was that his father had started at the rising of the moon and had ordered him to follow. At length it was arranged that he should go and overtake his father and bring him back, but perhaps his father would not come. I was pertinacious until I carried the point, and then I was more indifferent. After all, why should I wait? Nicolás said we could get our clothes washed in Nicaragua. I walked out of doors and resolved that it was folly to lose the chance of examining a canal route for the belle of Guanacaste. I hurried through my preparations and bade her, I may say, an affectionate farewell. There is not the least chance that I shall ever see her again. Living in a secluded town unknown beyond the borders of its own unknown state between the Andes and the Pacific Ocean, probably she is already the happy wife of some worthy townsman and has forgotten the stranger who owes to her some of the happiest moments he passed in Central America.

It was now broad daylight. It was very rare that I had left a place with so much regret, but I turned my sorrow into anger, and wreaked it upon Nicolás and the guide. The wind was very high, and, sweeping over the great plain, it raised such clouds of dust that riding was both disagreeable and difficult. This ought to have had some effect in restoring my equanimity, but it did not. All day we had on our right the grand range of Cordilleras, and crowning it at this point the great volcanoes of Rincón and Orosi. From thence a vast plain, over which the wind swept furiously, extended to the sea.

At one o'clock we came in sight of the hacienda of Santa Teresa, standing on a great elevation and still a long way before us. The hacienda was the property of Don Agustín Gutiérrez of San José and, with two others, was under the charge of his son, Don Manuel. A letter from his father had advised him of my coming, and he received me as an old acquaintance. The situation of the house was finer than that of any I had seen. It was high and commanded a view of an immense plain studded with trees in groups and in forest. The ocean was not visible, but we could see the opposite coast of the Gulf of Nicoya, and the point of the port of Culebra, the finest on the Pacific, only three and a half leagues distant. The hacienda contained a thousand mares and four hundred horses, more than a hundred of which were in sight from the door. It was grand enough to give the owner ideas of empire.

Toward evening I counted from the door of the house seventeen deer, and Don Manuel told me that he had a con-

tract for furnishing two thousand skins. In the season a good
hunter gets twenty-five a day. Even the workmen will not
eat them, and they are only shot for the hide and horns. He
had forty workmen, and an ox was killed every day. Near
the house was an artificial lake, more than a mile in circumference, which had been built as a drinking place for cattle.
And yet the proprietors of these haciendas are not rich. The
ground is worth absolutely nothing; the whole value is in
the stock. Allowing ten dollars a head for the horses and
mares would probably give the full value of this apparently
magnificent estate.

Here, too, I could have passed a week with great satisfaction, but the next morning I resumed my journey.
Though early in the dry season, the ground was parched
and the streams were dried up. We carried a large calabash
with water, and stopping under the shade of a tree, we
turned our mules out on the plain and breakfasted. As we resumed our journey, I was riding in advance with my poncho
flying in the wind, when I saw a drove of cattle stop and look
wildly at me, and then rush furiously toward me. I attempted to run, but, remembering the bullfights at Guatemala, I tore off my poncho and had just time to get behind a
high rock as the whole herd darted by at their full speed. We
continued our route, from time to time catching glimpses of
the Pacific, till we reached a clear, open place, completely
protected from the wind which was called the Boca of the
Mountain of Nicaragua. A large caravan had already encamped, and among the muleteers Nicolás found acquaintances from San José. Their cargoes consisted of potatoes,
sweet bread, and *dulces* for Nicaragua.

Toward evening I climbed to the top of one of the hills,
and had a magnificent sunset view. On the top the wind blew
so fiercely that I was obliged to shelter myself under the
lee. Behind me was the great range of Cordilleras, along
which we had ridden all day, with their volcanoes. On the
left were the headlands of the bays of Tortugas and Salinas,
and in front, the great body of the Pacific Ocean; and, what
was quite as agreeable a spectacle to a traveler, my mules
were up to their knees in grass. I returned to the encamp-

ment and found that my guide had made me a *casita*, or small house, to sleep in. It was formed by cutting two forked sticks about four feet high and as thick as a man's arm, and driving them into the ground. Another stick was laid in the crotches, and against this other sticks were laid slanting, with leaves and branches wound in between them to protect me from the dew and tolerably well from the wind.

I never had a servant in Central America who was not a brute with mules. I was obliged to look out myself for their food, and also to examine their backs to see if they were hurt by the saddles. My macho I always saddled myself. Nicolás had saddled the cargo mule so badly the day before that when he took off the *aparejo* (a huge saddle covering half the beast) her shoulder was raw, and in the morning even pointing at it made her shrink as if touched with a hot iron. I was unwilling to put the *aparejo* upon her back, and tried to hire a mule from one of the muleteers. Since I could not, I put the cargo upon the other mule, made Nicolás walk, and let the cargo mule go loose. I left the *aparejo* at the base of the mountain: a great piece of profligacy, as Nicolás and the guide considered it.

We wound for a short distance among the hills that enclosed us, ascended a slight range, and came down directly upon the shore of the sea. I always had a high feeling when I touched the shore of the Pacific, and never more so than at this desolate place. The waves rolled grandly and broke with a solemn roar. The mules were startled, and my macho shrank from the heaving water. I spurred him into it, and at a moment when I was putting in my pocket some shells which Nicolás had picked up, he ran away. He had attempted it several times before in the woods; and now, having a fair chance, I gave him the full sweep of the coast. We continued nearly an hour on the shore, and then, crossing a high, rough headland, we again came down upon the sea. Four times we mounted headlands and again descended to the shore, and the heat became almost intolerable. The fifth ascent was steep, but we came upon a table covered with a thick forest, through which we proceeded until we came to a small clearing with two huts. We stopped at the first, which was occupied by a black man and his wife. He had plenty of corn; there was a fine pasture ground near, so hemmed in by the woods that there was no danger of the mules escaping. I hired the man and woman to sleep out of doors and give me the hovel to myself.

Chapter XIX

~~~~~~

The Flores. The San Juan. Nature's Solitude. Primitive cookery. Harbor of San Juan. Route of the great canal to connect the Atlantic and Pacific Oceans. Nicaragua. Survey for the canal. Lake of Nicaragua. Plan of the canal. Lockage. Estimate of cost. Former efforts to construct the canal. Its advantages. Central American hospitality. Tierra Caliente. Horrors of civil war.

I ROSE about an hour before daylight and was in my saddle by break of day. We watered our mules at the River Flores, the boundary line of the states of Costa Rica and Nicaragua.[1] In an hour we reached Skamaika, the name given to a single hut occupied by a negro, sick and alone. He was lying on a bedstead made of sticks, the very picture of wretchedness and desolation, worn to a skeleton by fever and ague. Soon after, we came to another hut, where two women were sick with fever. Nothing could be more wretched than these huts along the Pacific. They asked me for *remedios,* and I gave them some quinine, but with little hope of their ever benefiting by it. Probably both the negro and they are now in their graves.

At twelve o'clock we reached the River San Juan, the mouth of which was the proposed terminating point of the great canal. The road to Nicaragua crossed the stream, and ours followed it to the sea, the port being situated at its mouth. Our whole road had been desolate enough, but this far surpassed anything I had seen; as I looked at the little path that led to Nicaragua, I felt as if we were leaving a

---

1. The San Juan River forms most of the boundary. The Flores is a small river on the Pacific side.

great highway. The valley of the river is about a hundred yards broad, and in the season of rain the whole is covered with water; but at this time the stream was small, and a great part of its bed dry. The stones were bleached by the sun, and there was no track or impression which gave the slightest indication of a path. Very soon this stony bed became contracted and lost; the stream ran through a different soil, and high grass, shrubs, and bushes grew luxuriantly up to its bank. We searched for the track on both sides of the river, and it was evident that since the last wet season no person had passed.

Leaving the river, we found the bushes higher than our heads, and so thick that at every two or three paces I became entangled and held fast; at length I dismounted, and my guide cleared a way for me on foot with his machete. Soon we reached the stream again and, crossing it, we entered the same dense mass on the opposite side. In this way we continued for nearly two hours, with the river for our line. We crossed it more than twenty times, and when it was shallow we rode in its bed. Farther down, the valley was open, stony, and barren, and the sun beat upon it with prodigious force; flocks of *zopilotes*, or turkey buzzards, hardly disturbed by our approach, moved away on a slow walk, or, with a lazy flap of the wings, rose to a low branch of the nearest tree. In one place a swarm of the ugly birds were feasting on the carcass of an alligator. Wild turkeys were more numerous than we had seen them before, and so tame that I shot one with my pistol. Deer looked at us without alarm, and on each side of the valley large black apes walked on the tops of the trees or sat quietly in the branches looking at us. Having, for the last time, crossed the river, which became broader and deeper until it emptied into the Pacific,[2] we entered the woods on the right, and reached the first station of Mr. Baily, which we found covered with young trees and bushes; the woods were thicker than before and the path

2. On two or three occasions Stephens speaks of the San Juan River as emptying into the Pacific. Actually the San Juan connects the Atlantic and the Lake of Nicaragua, but it does not flow into the Pacific.

entirely undistinguishable. I had read reports, papers, and pamphlets on the subject of the great canal, and had expected at least to find a road to the port; but the desert of Arabia is not more desolate, and the track of the Children of Israel to the Red Sea a turnpike compared with it.

My beautiful gray, degraded into a cargo mule, chafed under her burden, and she began to obstruct and jerk first one way and then the other. The girths of the saddle became loose, the load turned on her side, and she rushed blindly forward, kicking, and threw herself among the bushes. Her back was badly hurt, and she was desperately frightened, but we were obliged to reload her. Fortunately, we were near the end of our day's journey.

On the border of the woods we reached the last stream at which fresh water was procurable; after filling our calabash, we entered a plain covered with high grass. In front was another piece of woodland, and on the left the River San Juan, now a large stream, emptying into the Pacific. In a few minutes we reached a small clearing so near the shore that the waves seemed breaking at our feet. We tied our mules under the shade of a large tree on the edge of the clearing. The site of Mr. Baily's rancho was on a nearby eminence, but hardly a vestige remained; though it commanded a fine view of the port and the sea, the afternoon sun was so hot that I fixed our encampment under the large tree. We hung our saddles, saddlecloths, and arms upon its branches and, while Nicolás and José gathered wood and made a fire, I found, what was always the most important and satisfactory part of the day's journey, excellent pasture for the mules.

The next thing was to take care of ourselves. We had no trouble in deciding what to have for dinner. We had made provision, as we supposed, for three days; but, as always, however abundant our supplies, they did not last more than one day. At this time all was eaten up by ourselves or by vermin; but for the wild turkey, we should have been obliged to dine upon chocolate. How the turkey should be cooked was a matter of deeply interesting consideration. Boiling it was the best way, but we had nothing to boil it in except a small coffeepot. We attempted to make a gridiron of our stirrups and broil it, but those of Nicolás were wooden, and mine alone were not large enough. Roasting was a long and tedious process; but our guide had often been in such straits and, fixing in the ground two sticks with crotches, he laid another across, split open the turkey, and, securing it by sticks crosswise, hung it like a spread eagle before a blazing fire. When one side was burned, he turned the other. In an hour it was cooked, and in less than ten minutes eaten up. A cup of chocolate, heavy enough to keep the turkey from rising if it had been eaten with its wings on, followed, and I had dined.

Rested and refreshed, I walked down to the shore. Our encampment was in about the center of the harbor,[3] which was the finest I saw on the Pacific. It was not large, but it was beautifully protected, being almost in the form of the letter U. The arms are high and parallel, running nearly north and south and terminating in high perpendicular bluffs. As I afterward learned from Mr. Baily, the water is deep, and under either bluff, according to the wind, vessels of the largest class can ride with perfect safety. Supposing this to be correct, there is but one objection to this harbor, which I derived from Captain de Iriarte with whom I made the voyage from Sonsonate to Caldera. He had been nine years navigating the coast of the Pacific from Peru to the Gulf of California, and had made valuable notes, which he intends to publish in France. He told me that during the summer months, from November to May, the strong north winds which sweep over the Lake of Nicaragua pass with such violence through the Gulf of Papagayo that it is almost impossible for a vessel to enter the port of San Juan. Whether this is true to the extent that Captain de Iriarte supposes, and if it is true, how far steam tugs would be adequate to bring vessels in against such a wind, is for others to determine. But at the moment there seemed more palpable difficulties.

I walked along the shore down to the estuary of the river, which was here broad and deep This was the proposed

3. The harbor of San Juan del Sur.

termination of the great canal to connect the Atlantic and Pacific Oceans. I had read and examined all that had been published on this subject in England or this country; I had conferred with individuals; I had been sanguine, almost enthusiastic, in regard to this gigantic enterprise; but on the spot the scales fell from my eyes. The harbor was perfectly desolate and for years not a vessel had entered it; primeval trees grew around it and for miles there was not a habitation. I walked the shore alone. Since Mr. Baily left, not a person had visited it; probably the only thing that keeps it alive even in memory is the theorizing of scientific men, or the occasional visit of some Nicaragua fisherman, who, too lazy to work, seeks his food in the sea. It seemed preposterous to consider it the focus of a great commercial enterprise and to imagine that a city was to rise up out of the forest, that its desolate harbor was to be filled with ships, and that it was to become a great portal for the thoroughfare of nations. But the scene was magnificent. The sun was setting, and the high western headland threw a deep shade over the water. It was perhaps the last time in my life that I should see the Pacific; and in spite of fever and ague tendencies, I bathed once more in the great ocean.

It was after dark when I returned to my encampment. My attendants had not been idle; blazing logs of wood, piled three or four feet high, lighted up the darkness of the forest. We heard the barking of wolves, the scream of the mountain cat, and other wild beasts of the forest. I wrapped myself in my poncho and lay down to sleep. Nicolás threw more wood upon the burning piles and, as he stretched himself on the ground, hoped we would not be obliged to pass another night in this desolate place.

In the morning I had more trouble. My gray mule, running loose and drinking at every stream with her girths tight, had raised a swelling eight or ten inches. I attempted to put the cargo on my macho, with the intention of walking myself; but it was utterly impossible to manage him, and I was obliged to transfer it to the raw back of the cargo mule.

At seven o'clock we started; we recrossed the stream at which we had procured water and returned to the first station of Mr. Baily on the River San Juan, a mile and a half from the sea. The river here had sufficient depth of water for large vessels, and it was from this point that Mr. Baily had commenced his survey to the Lake of Nicaragua. I sent Nicolás with the mules by the direct road, and set out with my guide to follow, as far as practicable, his line of survey. I did not know, until I found myself in this wilderness, how fortunate I had been in securing this guide. He had been Mr. Baily's pioneer in the whole of his exploration. He was a dark mestizo, and he gained his living by hunting bee-trees and cutting them down for the wild honey, which made him familiar with all the watercourses and secret depths of almost impenetrable forests. He had been selected by Mr. Baily out of all Nicaragua; for the benefit of any traveler who may feel an interest in this subject, his name is José Dionisio de Lerda and he lives at Nicaragua.[4]

It had been two years since Mr. Baily had taken his observations, and already in that rank soil the clearings were overgrown with trees twelve or fifteen feet high. My guide cleared a path for me with his machete and, working our way across the plain, we entered a valley, which ran in a great ravine called Quebrada Grande, between the mountain ranges of Zebadea and El Platina.[5] By a vigorous use of the machete I was enabled to follow Mr. Baily's line up the ravine to the station of Panama, so called from a large Panama tree near which Mr. Baily had built his rancho.

Up to this place manifestly there could be no difficulty in cutting a canal; beyond, the line of survey follows the small stream of El Cacao for another league and then crosses the mountain; but there was such a rank growth of young trees that it was impossible to continue without sending men forward to clear the way. We therefore left the line of the canal and, crossing the valley to the right, we reached the foot of the mountain over which the road to Nicaragua passes. A path had been opened for carrying Mr. Baily's supplies to

---

4. On this page and again on pp. 327–328, Stephens refers to a Nicaraguan town now usually called Rivas. He was already in the country of Nicaragua.

5. The editor has been unable to identify ranges with these names, the correct spellings of which are probably *Cebadea* and *El Platino*.

that station, but it was difficult to find it. We took a long draught at a beautiful stream called Loco de Agua, and my guide pulled off his shirt and commenced with his machete. It was astonishing how he found anything to guide him, but he knew a tree as the face of a man. The side of the mountain was very steep, and besides large trees, was full of brambles, thorn bushes, and ticks. I was obliged to dismount and lead my macho; the dark skin of my guide glistened with perspiration, and it was almost a climb till we reached the top.

Coming out into the road, we found the change beautiful. The road was about ten feet wide, straight, and shaded by the noblest trees in the Nicaragua forests. In an hour we reached the foot of the mountain, where Nicolás was waiting with the mules under the shade of a large tree, which threw its branches fifty feet from its trunk, and seemed reared by a beneficent hand for the shelter of a weary traveler. Soon we reached another of Mr. Baily's stations. Looking back, I saw the two great mountain ranges standing like giant portals, and could but think what a magnificent spectacle it would be to see a ship, with all its spars and rigging, cross the plain, pass through the great door, and move on to the Pacific. Beyond, the whole plain was on fire; the long grass, scorched by the summer's sun, crackled, flashed, and burned like powder. The road was a sheet of flame, and when the fire had passed, the earth was black and hot. We rode some distance on the smoking ground along the line of flame, and finding a favorable place, spurred the mules through; but part of the luggage took fire, my face and hands were scorched, and my whole body heated.

Off from the road, on the edge of the woods, and near the River Las Lajas, was another of Mr. Baily's stations. From that place the line runs direct over a plain till it strikes the same river near the Lake of Nicaragua. I attempted to follow the lines again, but was prevented by the growth of underwood.

It was late in the afternoon, and I hurried on to reach the *camino real*. Beautiful as the whole country had been, I found nothing equal to this two hours before we entered Nicaragua. The fields were covered with high grass, studded with noble trees, and bordered at a distance by a dark forest, while in front, high and towering, of a conical form, rose the beautiful volcano of the island. Herds of cattle gave it a homelike appearance.

Toward dark we again entered the woods, and for an hour saw nothing, but at length we heard the distant sound of the vesper bell, and very soon were greeted by the barking of dogs in the suburbs of Nicaragua. Fires were burning in the streets, which served as kitchens for the miserable inhabitants, and at which they were cooking their suppers. We passed round a miserable plaza and stopped at the house of the *licenciado* Pineda. A large door was wide open; the *licenciado* was swinging in one hammock, his wife and a mulatto woman in another. I dismounted and entered his house, and told him that I had a letter to him from Don Manuel de Aguilar. He asked me what I wished, and when I told him a night's lodging, said that he could accommodate me, but had no room for the mules. I told him that I would go to the cura, and he said that the cura could do no better than he. In a word, his reception of me was very cool. I was indignant and went to the door, but without it was dark as Erebus. I had made a long and tiresome journey through a desolate country, and that day had been one of extreme labor.

The first words of kindness came from the lady of the *licenciado*. I was so tired that I was almost ready to fall; I had left San José with the fever and ague, had been twelve days in the saddle, and the last two nights I had slept in the open fields. I owe it to both of them, however, to say that, once the ice was broken, they did all they could for my comfort; and, in fact, treated me with distinguished attention. A traveler never forgets kindness shown him in a strange land, and I never felt so sensible of it as in Central America; in other countries, with money, a man can command comforts, but here, whatever his means may be, he is entirely dependent upon individual hospitality.

The whole of the next morning I devoted to making inquiries on the subject of the canal route. More is known of it in the United States than at Nicaragua. I did not find one man who had been to the port of San Juan, or who even knew Mr. Baily's terminating point on the Lake of Nicaragua. I was obliged to send for my old guide, and after a noonday dinner started for the lake. The town consisted of a large collection of straggling houses, without a single object of interest. Though Nicaragua is the richest state in the confederacy in natural gifts, its population is the most miserable.

Passing through the suburbs, very soon we entered the woods and rode under a beautiful shade. We met no one. Before reaching the lake we heard the waves breaking upon the shore like the waves of the sea, and when we emerged from the woods the view before us was grand. On one side no land was visible; a strong north wind was sweeping over the lake, and its surface was violently agitated; the waves rolled and broke upon the shore with solemn majesty, and opposite, in the center of the lake, were the islands of Isola and Madera with giant volcanoes rising as if to scale the heavens. The great volcano of Ometepe reminded me of Mount Etna, rising, like the pride of Sicily, from the water's edge, a smooth unbroken cone, to the height of nearly six thousand feet.

We rode for an hour along the shore, and so near the water that we were wetted by the spray. The bank was all wooded; and in one place, on a little clearing by the side of a stream, was a hut occupied by a mulatto, the view from which princes might envy. Farther on we passed some women washing, and at a distance of a league and a half we reached the River Las Lajas, which, according to Mr. Baily's survey, was the terminating point on the lake. A flock of wild fowl were sitting on the water, and long-legged birds, with wings outstretched, were walking on the shore.

I had now examined, as well as circumstances would permit, the canal route from the Pacific to the Lake of Nicaragua. A direction had been given to my investigations by getting on the track of Mr. Baily's survey, but I should be able to communicate nothing if it were not for Mr. Baily himself, whom I afterward met at Granada. This gentleman is a half-pay officer in the British navy. Two years before he was employed by the government of Central America to make a survey of this canal route, and he had completed all except the survey of an unimportant part of the River San Juan when the revolution broke out. The states declared their independence of the general government, and disclaimed all liability for its debts. Mr. Baily had given his time and labor, and when I saw him he had sent his son to make a last appeal to the shadow of the Federal government; but before he reached the capital this government was utterly annihilated, and Mr. Baily remains with no reward for his arduous services beyond the satisfaction of having been a pioneer in a noble work. On my arrival at Granada he laid before me all his maps and drawings with liberty to make what use of them I pleased. I passed an entire day in taking notes and memoranda, and in receiving explanations. The measurements which I have recorded [6] began on the side of the Pacific Ocean, and were carried over to the Lake of Nicaragua; the levels were taken from Mr. Baily's survey. To sum up these measurements: The length from the Pacific Ocean to the Lake of Nicaragua is 28,365⅔ yards, or 15⅔ miles. The sum of the ascents is 1047 feet 5.45 inches; the sum of the descents is 919 feet 2.4 inches; and the difference, 128 feet 3.05 inches, is the height of the lake above the Pacific Ocean at low water.

We now come to the communication with the Atlantic by means of the Lake of Nicaragua and the River San Juan. The lake is ninety-five miles long and, in its broadest part, about thirty; it averages, according to Mr. Baily's soundings, fifteen fathoms of water. The length of the river, by measurement with all its windings from the mouth of the lake to the sea, is seventy-nine miles. There are no cataracts or falls; all the obstructions are from rapids, and it is at all times navigable both up and down for piraguas drawing from three to four feet of water.

From the lake to the river of El Sábalo, a distance of about eighteen miles, the depth is from two to four fathoms.

6. Stephens detailed record of these measurements is given on pp. 343–346.

At El Sábalo commence the rapids of Toros, which extend for one mile with water from one and a half to two fathoms deep. The river is then clear for four miles, with an average depth of from two to four fathoms. Then come the rapids of the Old Castle, but little more than half a mile in extent, with water from two to four fathoms. The river is clear again for about two miles, with water from two and a half to five fathoms, where begin the rapids of Mico and Las Balas, connected and running into each other, and both together not more than a mile, with water from one to three fathoms. The river then runs clear for one mile and a half to the rapids of Machuca; these rapids, which extend for a mile, are the worst of all, the water being more broken from running over a broken rocky bottom.

From this point the river is clear and without any obstruction for ten miles to the River San Carlos, with water from two to seven fathoms, and then for eleven miles, with some islands interspersed to the River Sarapiquí, with water from one to six fathoms, the measurements of one fathom being about the points or bends, where there is an accumulation of sand and mud. It then continues seven miles clear, with water from two to five fathoms, to the Río Colorado. The River Colorado runs *out* of the San Juan in another direction into the Atlantic. The loss to the latter, according to measurement taken in the month of May, 1839, was twenty-eight thousand one hundred and seventy-eight cubic yards of water per minute; in the month of July of the same year, during the rising of the waters, it was eighty-five thousand eight hundred and forty yards per minute. This immense body of water might be saved to the San Juan by damming up the mouth of the River Colorado.

From this point there are thirteen miles, with soundings of from three to eight fathoms. The bottom is of sand and mud, and there are many small islands and aggregations of sand without trees, very easily cleared away. The last thirteen miles might be reduced to ten by restoring the river to its old channel, which has been filled up by collections, at points, of drifted matter. An old master of a piragua told Mr. Baily that within his memory trees grew half a mile back. The soundings were all taken with the plotting scale when the river was low, and the port of San Juan, though small, Mr. Baily considers unexceptionable.

The detailed memoranda were placed in the hands of my friend, Mr. Horatio Allen, the engineer on our Croton Aqueduct, who kindly prepared from them the plan shown in figure 32.

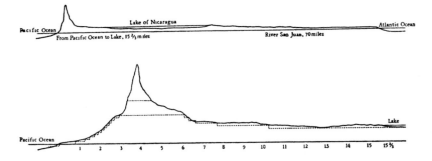

FIG. 32 *Profile of Nicaragua Canal*

I ought perhaps to remark, for the benefit of those who are not familiar with such plans, that in order to bring the profile of the country within a small compass, the vertical lines, which represent elevations and depressions, are on a scale many times greater than the base lines or horizontal distances. Of the former, the scale is one thousand feet, and of the latter it is twenty miles to the inch. This, of course, gives a distorted view of the country; but, to preserve the relative proportions, it would be necessary for the base line in the plan to be one thousand times longer.

The whole length of the canal from the Lake of Nicaragua to the Pacific is fifteen and two-thirds miles. According to the plan, in the first eight miles from the lake but one lock is necessary. In the next mile sixty-four feet of lockage are required. In the next three miles there are about two of deep cutting and one of tunnel, and then a descent of two hundred feet in three miles by lockage to the Pacific.

So much for the canal across the isthmus. The Lake of Nicaragua is navigable for ships of the largest class down to the mouth of the River San Juan. This river has an average fall of one and six-sevenths feet per mile to the Atlantic. If the bed of the river cannot be cleared out, a communication can be made either by lock and dam, or by a canal along the bank of the river. The latter would be more expensive, but, on account of the heavy floods of the rainy season, it is preferable.

I am authorized to state that the physical obstructions of the country present no impediment to the accomplishment of this work. A canal large enough for the passage of boats of the usual size could be made at a trifling expense. A tunnel of the length required is not considered a great work in the United States. According to the plan of the Chesapeake and Ohio Canal, a tunnel is contemplated upward of four miles in length. The sole difficulty is the same which would exist in any route in any other region of country, that is, the great dimensions of the excavation required for a ship canal.

The data here given are, of course, insufficient for great accuracy; but I present a rough estimate of the cost of this work, furnished me with the plan. It is predicated upon the usual contract prices in the United States, and I think I am safe in saying that the cheapness of labor in Nicaragua will equalize any advantages and facilities that exist here. The total of the estimate which follows is about the same as the sum contemplated as the cost of our enlarged Erie Canal.

From the lake to the east end of the tunnel, from...	$ 8,000,000 to $10,000,000
Descent to the Pacific.....	$ 2,000,000 to $ 3,000,000
From the lake to the Atlantic, by canal along the bank of the river........	$10,000,000 to $12,000,000
	$20,000,000 to $25,000,000

The idea of a communication between the Atlantic and Pacific is not new. Columbus wore out the last days of his checkered life in searching for a natural passage, and the vastness and sublimity of the enterprise suited the daring imagination of the early Spaniards.

From the formation of the continent and the falling off in height of the range of the Andes, it has ever since engaged the attention of reflecting men. Even during the deathlike sleep of Spanish dominion a survey was made under the direction of the captain-general; but the documents remained buried in the archives of Guatemala until the emancipation of the colonies, when they were procured and published by Mr. Thompson,[7] who visited that country under a commission from the British government.

In 1825 an envoy-extraordinary from the new Republic of Central America called the special attention of our government to the canal project, requesting our co-operation in preference to that of any other nation; he proposed, by means of a treaty, "effectually to secure its advantages to the two nations." As a result a chargé d'affaires was appointed by our government who was specially instructed to assure the government of Central America of the deep interest of the United States in the execution of an undertaking "so highly calculated to diffuse an extensive influence on the affairs of mankind," and to investigate with the greatest care the facilities offered by the route, and to remit the information to the United States.

Unfortunately, being far removed from the capital, none of our diplomatic agents ever visited the spot. But, in 1826, as appears by documents accompanying the report of a committee of the House of Representatives on a memorial "praying the aid of the government of the United States in procuring the construction of a ship channel or navigable canal across the isthmus between North and South America," a contract was made by the government of Central America with the agent of a New York company, under the name, style, and designation of the "Central American and United States' Atlantic and Pacific Canal Company." Although the names of Dewitt Clinton and other most distinguished men

7. G. A. Thompson, *Narrative of an Official Visit to Guatemala from Mexico*, London, 1829. Stephens calls attention to the fact that Baily knew of the prior survey made by the captain-general; that he had even helped Thompson gain access to it; and that the work appeared much more easy by the captain-general's survey than by Baily's, but that the former survey purports to have been taken by the water level.

of that day appear as associates, the scheme fell through.

In 1830 the government of Central America made another contract with a society of the Netherlands, under the special patronage of the King of Holland, who embarked in it a large amount of his private fortune; but, owing to the difficulties between Holland and Belgium, and the separation of the two countries, this also fell through.

On the third of March, 1835, a resolution passed the Senate of the United States, "that the president be requested to consider the expediency of opening negotiations with the governments of other nations, and particularly with the governments of Central America and Granada,[8] for the purpose of effectually protecting, by suitable treaty stipulations with them, such individuals or companies as may undertake to open a communication between the Atlantic and Pacific Oceans, by the construction of a ship canal across the isthmus which connects North and South America, and of securing forever, by such stipulations, the free and equal right of navigating such canal to all nations, on the payment of such reasonable tolls as may be established, to compensate the capitalists who may engage in such undertaking and complete the work."

Under this resolution a special agent appointed by General Jackson was instructed to proceed without delay by the most direct route to Port San Juan, ascend the River San Juan to the Lake of Nicaragua, and thence by the contemplated route of communication, by canal or railroad, to the Pacific Ocean. After having completed an examination of the route of the canal, he was directed to repair to Guatemala, the capital of that Republic, and, with the aid of Mr. DeWitt, the chargé d'affaires of the United States, procure all such public documents connected with the subject as might be had, and especially copies of all such laws as may have been passed to incorporate companies to carry into effect the undertaking of any convention or conventions that may have been entered into with a foreign power upon the sub-

8. In Stephens' day, Colombia was known as the Republic of New Granada.

ject, and of any plans, surveys, or estimates in relation to it. From Guatemala he was directed to proceed to Panama, and make observations and inquiries relative to the proposed connection of the two oceans at that point.

Unfortunately, from the difficulty of procuring a conveyance to the River San Juan, the agent went to Panama first; from adverse circumstances he never did reach Nicaragua, and on his return to this country died before reaching Washington. From his imperfect report, it appears to be the result of his observations that a ship canal was not practicable across the Isthmus of Panama. It was therefore valuable in that it turned attention, which was before divided between the two routes, exclusively to that by the Lake of Nicaragua. In regard to this route much has been written, many speculations and even estimates of the cost of constructing the canal have been made, but the actual knowledge on the subject has been very limited. In fact, the notes from Mr. Baily's survey in this volume are the most reliable data that have ever been published. I can but hope that the same liberal spirit which prompted the sending out of an agent may induce our government to procure from Mr. Baily and to give to the world the whole of his maps and drawings.[9]

As yet the subject of this communication has not taken any strong hold upon the public mind. It will be discussed, frowned upon, sneered at, and condemned as visionary and impracticable. Many in established business will oppose it as deranging the course of their trade. Capitalists will not risk their money in an unsettled and revolutionary country. The pioneers will be denounced and ridiculed, as Clinton was when he staked his political fortunes upon the "big ditch" that was to connect the Hudson with Lake Erie; but, if the peace of Europe be not disturbed, I am persuaded that the time is not far distant when the attention of the whole civilized and mercantile world will be directed toward it, and steamboats will give the first impulse. In less than a year,

9. T. Saunders of London published a general history of Central America by John Baily in 1850. In the same year Saunders also published a map of Central America showing the proposed routes between the Atlantic and Pacific oceans engraved from the original drawings of John Baily.

English mailboats will be steaming to Cuba, Jamaica, and the principal ports of Spanish America, touching once a month at San Juan and Panama. To men of leisure and fortune, jaded with rambling over the ruins of the Old World, a new country will be opened. After a journey on the Nile, a day in Petra, and a bath in the Euphrates, English and American travelers will be bitten by mosquitoes on the Lake of Nicaragua, and will drink champagne and Burton ale on the desolate shores of San Juan on the Pacific. The random remarks of the traveler for amusement, and the observations of careful and scientific men, will be brought together, a mass of knowledge will be accumulated and made public, and in my opinion the two oceans will be united.

In regard to the advantages of this work I shall not go into any details; I will remark, however, that on one point there exists a great and very general error. In the documents submitted to Congress before referred to, it is stated that "the trade of the United States and of Europe with China, Japan, and the Indian Archipelago would be facilitated and increased by reason of shortening the distance above four thousand miles;" and in that usually correct work, the *Modern Traveler*, it is stated that from Europe "the distance to India and China would be shortened more than 10,000 miles!" but by measurement on the globe the distance from Europe to India and China will not be shortened at all. This is so contrary to the general impression that I have some hesitation in making the assertion, but it is a point on which the reader may satisfy himself by referring to the globe. The trade of Europe with India and Canton, then, will not necessarily pass through this channel from any saving of distance; but, from conversations with masters of vessels and other practical men, I am induced to believe that, by reason of more favorable latitudes for winds and currents, it will be considered preferable to the passage by the Cape of Good Hope. At all events, all the trade of Europe with the western coast of the Pacific and the Polynesian Islands, and all her whale fishing, and *all* the trade of the United States with the Pacific without the exception of a single vessel, would pass through it. The amount of saving in time, interest of money, navigating expenses and insurance, by avoiding the stormy passage around Cape Horn, I have no data for calculating.

On broad grounds, this work has been well characterized as "the mightiest event in favour of the peaceful intercourse of nations which the physical circumstances of the globe present to the enterprise of man." It will compose the distracted country of Central America; turn the sword, which is now drenching it with blood, into a pruning hook; remove the prejudices of the inhabitants by bringing them into close connection with people of every nation; furnish them with a motive and a reward for industry; and inspire them with a taste for making money, which, after all, opprobrious as it is sometimes considered, does more to civilize and keep the world at peace than any other influence whatever. A great city will grow up in the heart of the country, with streams issuing from it, fertilizing as they roll into the interior; her magnificent mountains and valleys, now weeping in desolation and waste, will smile and be glad. The commerce of the world will be changed, the barren region of Tierra del Fuego be forgotten, Patagonia become a land of fable, and Cape Horn live only in the recollection of sailors and insurers. Steamboats will go smoking along the rich coasts of Chile, Peru, Equador, Granada, Guatemala, California, our own Oregon Territory, and the Russian possessions on the borders of Behring's Straits. New markets will be opened for products of agriculture and manufactures, and the intercourse and communion of numerous and immense bodies of the human race will assimilate and improve the character of nations.

The whole world is interested in this work. I would not speak of it with sectional or even national feeling; but if Europe is indifferent, it would be glory surpassing the conquest of kingdoms to make this greatest enterprise ever attempted by human force entirely our own work; nay, more, to make it, as it was once attempted, entirely the work of our city; for it is to furnish a new field for the action of that tremendous power which, first brought into being under our own eyes, is now changing the face of the whole moral, social, and political world. Is it too much to hope that, in honor of services poorly paid but never to be forgotten, a steamboat bearing the glorious name of Fulton may start from the spot where he made his first experiment, and open the great "highway of nations" to the Pacific Ocean?

THURSDAY, FEBRUARY 27. At three o'clock in the morning we left the yard of the *licenciado*. The inhabitants of the town were still sleeping. At daylight we passed a village, where, before the door of one of the houses, a traveler was making preparation to set out on a journey. We accosted him, and he said that he would overtake us on the road. At eight o'clock we reached a house, where we stopped to break-fast. The hospitality of Central America is in the country and in the villages; here I never knew it to fail. The traveler may stop where he pleases, and have house, fire, and water free, paying only for the articles which he consumes. We had milk in abundance, and the charge was six cents.

Before we resumed our journey the traveler whom we had passed at the last village arrived, and, after he had taken chocolate, we all started together. He was a merchant, on his way to León, accoutered in the style of the country, with pistols, sword, spatterdashes, and spurs. As he was then suffering from fever and ague, he wore a heavy woollen poncho, a striped cotton pocket handkerchief around his head, and over it two straw hats, one inside of the other. A young man, mounted and armed with a gun, was driving a cargo mule, and three *mozos* with machetes followed on foot.

The whole of this region along the coast of the Pacific is called the *Tierra Caliente*. At half past two, after a des-perately hot and dusty ride without any water, we reached a hacienda, the name of which I have lost. It was built of poles and plastered with mud. The major-domo was a white man, in bad health but very obliging, who lived by selling occa-sionally a fowl or a few eggs to a traveler, and corn and water for mules. There were no more of those beautiful streams which had given such a charm to my journey in Costa Rica; the earth was parched, and water a luxury sold

for money. There was a well on the hacienda, and I paid two
cents apiece for our mules to drink. There was a bedstead in
the hut, and at four o'clock I lay down for a few moments'
rest, but I did not waken till five the next morning. On a
line with the head of my bed was a long log, squared and
hollowed out, with a broad lid on the top secured by a lock
and key, which contained the corn and household valuables;
on the top of this crude bed were sleeping a woman, rather
yellow, and a little girl. I took chocolate, and in a few minutes was in the saddle. Very soon we came in sight of the
highlands of Mombacho, a high, dark range of mountains
behind which stood Granada,[10] which in half an hour we
entered. Built by those hardy adventurers who conquered
America, even yet this city is a monument worthy of their
fame. The houses are of stone, large and spacious, with balconies to the windows of turned wood, and projecting roofs
with pendent ornaments of wood curiously carved.

I rode to the house of Don Federico Derbyshire, to whom
I had a letter from friends in New York. Don Federico had
gone to the United States, but his clerk, a young Englishman, offered me the house, gave me a room, and in a few
moments my traveling clothes were off and I was in the
street. My first visit was to Mr. Baily, who lived nearly
opposite with an English lady whose husband had died two
years before, and who, besides carrying on his business, received into her house the few Englishmen or foreigners
whom chance brought to that place. My appearance at
Granada created surprise, and I was congratulated upon
my liberation or escape from prison. News had reached
there that I had been arrested (I do not know for what)
and was in prison in San Salvador; as all news had a
party bias, it was told as another of the outrages of General
Morazán.

The house of this lady was a comfort to a battered traveler. I could have remained there a month, but unfortunately, I heard news which did not allow me much time for

---

10. Stephens refers here to the Nicaraguan city of Granada, not to
the Republic of New Granada (cf. note 8 of this chapter).

rest. The black clouds which hung over the political horizon had burst, and civil war had broken out anew. The troops of Nicaragua, fourteen hundred strong, had marched into Honduras and, uniting with those of the latter state, had routed with great slaughter the troops of Morazán stationed at Tegucigalpa. The latter consisted of but four hundred and fifty men, under the command of General Cabañas, and the records of civil wars among Christian people nowhere present a bloodier page. No quarter was given or asked. After the battle, fourteen officers were shot in cold blood, and not a single prisoner lived as a monument of mercy. Cabañas, fighting desperately, escaped. Colonel Galindo, to whom I have before referred as having visited the ruins of Copán, known both in this country and in Europe for his investigation of the antiquities of that country, and to whom I had a letter of introduction from Mr. Forsyth, was murdered. After the battle, in attempting to escape with two dragoons and a servant boy, he had passed through an Indian village, where they were recognized and all murdered with machetes. A disgraceful quarrel ensued between Quijano and Ferrera, the leaders of the Nicaragua and Honduras troops, for the paltry spoils; the former got Ferrera into his power, and for twenty-four hours had him under sentence to be shot. Afterward the matter was accommodated, and the Nicaraguans returned to León in triumph with three hundred and fifty muskets, several stands of colors, and as a proof of the way in which they had done their work, without a single prisoner.

At San Salvador there had been an ominous movement. General Morazán had resigned his office of chief of the state, retaining command of the army, and had sent his wife and family to Chile. The crisis was at hand, the notes of war sounded fearfully, and it was all important for the prosecution of my ultimate designs and for my personal safety to reach Guatemala while yet the road was open.

I would have gone on immediately, but I felt that I might exert myself too far and break down at an awkward place. In the afternoon, in company with Mr. Baily and Mr. Wood, I walked down to the lake. At the foot of the street by which we entered, built out into the lake, was an old fort, dismantled, and overgrown with bushes and trees, a relic of the daring Spaniards who first drove the Indians from the lake; it was probably the very fortress that Córdoba [11] built, and it was, in its ruins, beautifully picturesque. Under the walls, and within the shade of the fort and trees growing near it, the Indian women of Granada were washing; garments of every color were hanging on the bushes to dry and waving in the wind; women were wading out with their water-jars, passing beyond the breakers to obtain it clear of sand; men were swimming, and servants were bringing horses and mules to drink—all together they presented a beautifully animated picture. There were no boats on the water, but about half a dozen piraguas, the largest of which was forty feet long and drew three feet of water, lay on the shore.

11. Francisco Hernández de Córdoba, principal conqueror of Nicaragua and founder of the city of Granada in 1524.

NICARAGUAN CANAL MEASUREMENTS
RECORDED BY STEPHENS
(A chain equals 25 varas and a vara, 32½ inches)

At a distance of: Chains		*Elevation in Feet*
17.50	. . . .	8.93
34.37	. . . .	12.04
52.38	. . . .	7.99
67.50	. . . .	16.82
80.95	. . . .	26.90
103.06	. . . .	38.12
120.07	. . . .	52.62
134.94	La Desperansedera de la Quebrada la Palma. Boring 3½ feet, loose sand; 66 feet, clay, not very firm	66.12
149.61	. . . .	76.12
164.71	. . . .	94.66
185.34	. . . .	132.95
201.50	Panama, water on the surface. Boring 11 feet, gravel; 24 feet 5 inches, slate-stone . . .	201.50
221.87	. . . .	223.00
226.14	. . . .	214.235
235.48	. . . .	241.35
253.63	First limestone *rock*	284.20
264.28	. . . .	356.770
273.18	. . . .	389.700
280.26	. . . .	425.95
287.01	. . . .	461.525
288.97	. . . .	519.391
292.99	Top of the Palma, and summit level. Boring 5 feet, yellow clay; 59 feet, stone, soft and loose. No water	615.673
299.05	. . . .	570.157
300.53	Second limestone rock	506.300
314.11	. . . .	460.891
317.05	. . . .	442.858
319.27	. . . .	443.899
332.25	. . . .	410.524
336.92	To this point national lands	393.216
340.28	Third limestone rock. Boring 31½ feet, water; 49 feet, limestone, soft and loose . . .	350.776
358.50	. . . .	311.152
361.40	. . . .	318.235
370.55	. . . .	291.419

Chains		Elevation in Feet
373.85	. . . .	295.160
382.86	. . . .	283.352
401.04	. . . .	269.236
409.30	. . . .	258.378
413.51	. . . .	261.486
423.75	Water on the surface. Boring 3 feet, sand; 12 feet, earth	247.780
437.55	. . . .	237.570
448.90	. . . .	250.370
464.78	. . . .	228.237
477.76	. . . .	214.695
489.29	. . . .	200.530
	Between this and next, boring 5 feet, earth; 10 feet, white clay; 11 feet, water; 38 feet, soft stone.	
506.22	. . . .	184.511
510.53	. . . .	186.869
519.47	. . . .	180.244
533.04	. . . .	170.161
543.25	. . . .	159.311
545.98	. . . .	160.411
553.85	. . . .	158.736
	In the next six stations the elevations do not differ one foot.	
604.82	. . . .	153.461
612.62	. . . .	160.077
622.54	Water on the surface. Boring 12 feet, sand and hard stone. This station is in a hole of the Quebrada, very deep.	149.553
627.27	. . . .	150.052
630.32	. . . .	149.336
634.20	. . . .	157.102
638.86	. . . .	147.044
643.31	. . . .	154.785
685.55	. . . .	143.343
661.35	. . . .	155.076
664.47	. . . .	140.243
671.22	. . . .	151.185
675.86	. . . .	139.352
685.93	. . . .	150.927
692.55	. . . .	146.977
696.91	. . . .	148.569
712.85	. . . .	144.436

Chains		Elevation in Feet
716.17	. . . .	149.152
723.29	. . . .	142.994
728.29	. . . .	148.552
739.95	. . . .	139.702
749.10	. . . .	164.360
756.40	. . . .	142.560
760.80	. . . .	144.830
766.80	. . . .	141.177
770.61	Water at 8 feet. Boring 12 feet, black earth; 22 feet, white clay; 4 feet, stone . . .	142.718
774.73	. . . .	140.560
779.49	. . . .	142.743
805.50	. . . .	138.485
808.31	Water on the surface. Boring 5 feet, sand; 15 feet, stone	124.312
812.01	. . . .	139.150
828.77	. . . .	133.802
832.24	. . . .	134.377
837.43	. . . .	130.994
841.76	. . . .	129.486
846.45	. . . .	129.994
	In six stations there is a difference of but from one to two feet.	
880.12	Water on the surface. Boring 9 feet, loose sand; 18 feet, soft stone.	126.569
887.23	. . . .	107.553
891.96	. . . .	123.903
901.22	. . . .	118.112
910.80	. . . .	120.628
	In four stations there is a difference of but one foot.	
933.74	Boring 8 feet, black earth; 10 feet, white mud; 18 feet, soft stone	
957.62	. . . .	117.178
971.48	. . . .	108.802
976.30	. . . .	135.168
986.06	. . . .	107.643
992.93	. . . .	119.176
1001.03	. . . .	108.576
1006.65	. . . .	118.592
1014.28	. . . .	108.692
1033.51	. . . .	124.808
1036.44	. . . .	126.663

Chains										Elevation in Feet
1043.06	.	.	.	.	.	.	.	.	.	141.416
1047.39	.	.	.	.	.	.	.	.	.	157.583
1062.87	.	.	.	.	.	.	.	.	.	118.042
1068.43	.	.	.	.	.	.	.	.	.	131.942
1077.69	.	.	.	.	.	.	.	.	.	120.584
1083.96	.	.	.	.	.	.	.	.	.	125.784
1100.19	.	.	.	.	.	.	.	.	.	135.709
1113.35	.	.	.	.	.	.	.	.	.	152.176
1128.97	.	.	.	.	.	.	.	.	.	127.201
1133.79	.	.	.	.	.	.	.	.	.	163.276
1140.94	.	.	.	.	.	.	.	.	.	129.776
1145.18	.	.	.	.	.	.	.	.	.	151.401
1156.44	.	.	.	.	.	.	.	.	.	129.335
1176.61	.	.	.	.	.	.	.	.	.	140.835
1190.87	.	.	.	.	.	.	.	.	.	129.396
1193.77	.	.	.	.	.	.	.	.	.	132.801
1203.21	.	.	.	.	.	.	.	.	.	128.093
1210.14	.	.	.	.	.	.	.	.	.	140.985
1123.50	.	.	.	.	.	.	.	.	.	128.243

Incidents
of Travel
in Central
America,
Chiapas, and
Yucatan
Vol. II

Contents

CHAPTER IV

CHAPTER V

CHAPTER VI

CHAPTER VII

CHAPTER VIII

CHAPTER XXIII

CHAPTER XXIV

CHAPTER XXV

CHAPTER XXVI

List of Illustrations

Chapter I

MARCH 1. Anxious as I was to hurry on, I resolved nevertheless to give one day to the volcano of Masaya. For this purpose I sent a courier ahead to procure me a guide for the ascent, and did not get off till eleven o'clock. At a short distance from the city of Masaya we met a little negro on horseback; he was dressed in the black suit that nature made him and had two large plantain leaves for a saddle. At the distance of two leagues we came in sight of the volcano, and at four o'clock, after a hot ride, entered the town, one of the oldest and largest in Nicaragua; though completely inland, it contained, with its suburbs, a population of twenty thousand. We rode to the house of Don Sabino Satroon, who lay snoring in a hammock with his mouth open; but his wife, a pretty young half-blood, received me cordially, and with a proper regard for the infirmities of an old husband and for me, she did not wake him up. But all at once he shut his mouth and opened his eyes, and gave me a cordial welcome. Don Sabino was a Colombian who had been banished for ten years, as he said, for services rendered his country. Having found his way to

Masaya, he had married the pretty young half-breed and set up as a doctor. Inside the door, behind the little stock of sugar, rice, sausages, and chocolate, was a formidable array of jars and bottles, which exhibited as many colors and as puzzling labels as an apothecary's shop at home.

I had time to take a short walk around the town. Turning down the road, at the distance of half a mile I came to the brink of a precipice more than a hundred feet high, at the foot of which, and a short distance beyond, was the Lake of Masaya. One descended almost perpendicularly, in one place by a rough ladder, and then by steps cut in the rock. I was obliged to stop while fifteen or twenty women, most of them young girls, passed. Their water jars were made of the shell of a large gourd, round, with fanciful figures scratched on them, and painted or glazed; a gourd was supported on the back of the girl by a strap across the forehead and secured by fine network. Below they were chattering gaily; but by the time they reached the place where I stood, they were silent, their movements very slow, their breathing hard, and their faces covered with profuse perspiration. This was a great part of the daily labor of the women of the place, and in this way they procured enough water for domestic use; but every horse, mule, or cow was obliged to go for water by a circuitous road of more than a league. Why a large town had grown up and been continued so far from this element of life, I do not know. The Spaniards originally found it a large Indian village, and as they immediately made the owners of the soil their drawers of water, they did not feel this burden, nor do their descendants now.

In the meantime my guide arrived, who, to my great satisfaction, was no less a personage than the alcalde himself. The arrangements were soon made, and I was to join him the next morning at his house in Nindiri. I gave my mules and Nicolás a day's rest and the next morning started on Don Sabino's horse, with a boy to act as guide and to carry a pair of alforjas with provisions. In half an hour I reached Nindiri, having met more people than on my whole road from San José to Nicaragua. The alcalde was ready, and in

company with an assistant, who carried a pair of alforjas
with provisions and a calabash of water, we set out.

At the distance of half a league we left the main road and
turned off on a small path in the woods on the left. We
emerged from this into an open field covered with lava,
which extended to the base of the volcano in front and on
each side as far as I could see; the lava was black, several
feet deep—in some places lying in high ridges—and showed
a faint track beaten by cattle. In front were two volcanoes,
from both of which streams of lava had run down the sides
into the plain. The one directly in front of us my guide said
was the volcano of Masaya. In the volcano on the right and
farthest from us, the crater was broken and the great chasm
inside visible. He said that this was called Ventero,[1] a name
I never heard before, and that it was inaccessible. Riding
toward the volcano in front of us, we crossed the field of
lava and reached the foot of Masaya. Here the grass was
high, but the ground was rough and uneven, being covered
with decomposed lava. We ascended on horseback until it
became too steep for the horses to carry us; we then dismounted, tied them to a bush, and continued on foot. I was
already uneasy as to my guides' knowledge of localities,
and soon I also found that they were unwilling or unable
to endure much fatigue. Before we were halfway up they
disencumbered themselves of the water jar and provisions,
and yet they lagged behind. The alcalde, a man about forty,
rode his own horse; since he was a man of consequence in the
town, I could not order him to go faster. His associate, some
ten years older, was physically incapable. When, in addition,
I saw that they did not know any particular path, I left them
and went on alone.

At eleven o'clock, or three hours from the village of
Nindiri, I reached the high point at which we had been aiming. From this point I had expected to look down into the
crater of the volcano, but there was no crater; the whole

1. Ventero is not the official name of any volcano in Nicaragua, but
since it would be an appropriate nickname for a volcano still active,
perhaps it is used locally.

surface was covered with gigantic masses of lava and overgrown with bushes and scrub trees. When my guides came
up they told me that this *was* the volcano of Masaya, and
that this was all there was to see. The alcalde insisted that
two years before he had ascended with the cura, since deceased, and a party of villagers, and that they all stopped
at this place. I was disappointed and dissatisfied. Directly opposite rose a high peak, which I thought from its position
must command a view of the crater of the other volcano.
I attempted to reach it by passing round the circumference
of the mountain, but was obstructed by an immense chasm.
Returning I struck directly across. I had no idea what I was
attempting. The whole was covered with lava lying in ridges
and irregular masses, the surface varying at every step and
overgrown with trees and bushes. After an hour of the hardest work I ever had in my life, I reached the point at which
I aimed, and, to my astonishment, instead of seeing the
crater of the distant volcano, I was on the brink of another.

Among the recorded wonders of the discoveries in America, this mountain was one; and the Spaniards, who in those
days never stopped halfway in any matter that touched the
imagination, had called it *El Infierno de Masaya,* or The
Hell of Masaya. The historian,[2] in speaking of Nicaragua,
says, "There are burning mountains in this province, the
chief of which is Masaya, where the natives at certain times
offered up maids, throwing them into it, thinking by their
lives to appease the fire, that it might not destroy the country, and they went to it very cheerful." And in another place
he says, "Three leagues from the city of Masaya is a small
hill, flat and round, called Masaya, being a burning mountain, the mouth of it being half a league in compass, and the
depth within it two hundred and fifty fathoms. There are
no trees nor grass, but birds build without any disturbance
from the fire. There is another mouth like that of a well
about a bowshot over, the distance from which to the fire
is about a hundred and fifty fathoms. It is always boiling up,

---

2. The historian to which Stephens refers here does not appear to
be Juarros; the editor was unable to further identify the reference.

and that mass of fire often rises and gives a great light, so that it can be seen at a considerable distance. It moves from one side to the other, and sometimes roars so loud that it is dreadful, yet never casts up anything but smoke and flame. The liquor never ceasing at the bottom, nor its boiling, imagining the same to be gold, *F. Blase de Yniesta,* of the Order of St. Dominic, and two other Spaniards, were let down into the first mouth in two baskets, with a bucket made of one piece of iron, and a long chain to draw up some of the fiery matter, and know whether it was metal. The chain ran a hundred and fifty fathoms, and as soon as it came to the fire, the bucket melted, with some links of the chain, in a very short time, and therefore they could not know what was below. They lay there that night without any want of fire or candles, and came out again in their baskets sufficiently frighted."

Either the monk, disappointed in his search for gold, had fibbed, or nature had made one of its most extraordinary changes. The crater was about a mile and a half in circumference, five or six hundred feet deep, with sides slightly sloping, and so regular in its proportions that it seemed an artificial excavation. The bottom was level, both sides and bottom were covered with grass, and it seemed an immense conical green basin. There were none of the fearful marks of a volcanic eruption, nothing to terrify or suggest an idea of *el infierno;* on the contrary, it was a scene of singular and quiet beauty. I descended to the side of the crater and walked along the edge, looking down into the area. Toward the other end was a growth of *arbolitos,* or little trees, and in one place no grass grew and the ground was black and loamy, like mud drying up. This was perhaps the mouth of the mysterious well that had sent up the flame, which gave its light a "considerable distance," into which the Indian maidens were thrown, and which melted the monk's iron bucket.

Like the monk, I felt curious to "know what was below." Both sides of the crater were perpendicular; entirely alone, and with an hour's very hard work between me and my guides, I hesitated about making any attempt to descend. But I disliked to return without trying. In one place, and near the black earth, the side was broken, and there were some bushes and scrub trees. I planted my gun against a stone, tied my handkerchief around it as a signal of my whereabouts, and very soon was below the level of the ground. Letting myself down by the aid of roots, bushes, and projecting stones, I descended to a scrub tree which grew out of the side about halfway from the bottom; below this the side of the crater was a naked and perpendicular wall. It was impossible to go any farther; I was even obliged to keep on the upper side of the tree. At this point I was more anxious than ever to reach the bottom, but it was of no use. Hanging midway, impressed with the solitude and the extraordinary features of a scene upon which so few human eyes had ever rested, and with the power of the great Architect who has scattered his wonderful works over the whole face of the earth, I could not but reflect what a waste this was of the bounties of Providence in this favored but miserable land! At home this volcano would be a fortune; there would be a good hotel on top, with a railing round to keep children from falling in, a zigzag staircase down the sides, and a glass of iced lemonade at the bottom. Cataracts are good property with people who know how to turn them to account. Niagara and Trenton Falls pay well, and the owners of volcanoes in Central America might make money out of them by furnishing facilities to travelers. This one could probably be bought for ten dollars, and I would have given twice that sum for a rope and a man to hold it. Meanwhile, though anxious to be at the bottom, I was casting my eyes wistfully to the top. The turning of an ankle, the breaking of a branch, the rolling of a stone, or a failure of strength might put me where I should have been as hard to find as the government of Central America. I commenced climbing up slowly and with care, and in due time I hauled myself out in safety.

On my right was a full view of the broken crater of the volcano of Nindiri. The side toward me was hurled down, showing the whole interior of the crater. This the alcalde had declared inaccessible; and partly from sheer spite against him, with extreme labor and difficulty I worked my way to it. At length, after five hours of most severe toil among the rugged heaps of lava, I descended to the place where we had left our provisions. Here I seized the calabash of water and stood for several minutes with my face turned up to the skies, and then I began upon the alcalde and the eatables. Both he and his companion expressed their utter astonishment at what I described, and persisted in saying that they did not know of the existence of such a place.

I dwell upon this matter for the benefit of any future traveler who may go out competent and prepared to explore the interesting volcanic regions of Central America. Throughout my journey, my labors were much increased by the ignorance and indifference of the people concerning the objects of interest in their immediate neighborhood. A few intelligent and educated men know of their existence as part of the history of the country, but I never met one who had visited the volcano of Masaya; and in the village at its foot the traveler will not obtain even the scanty information afforded in these pages. The alcalde was born near this volcano; from boyhood he had hunted stray cattle on its side. He told me that he knew every foot of the ground, yet he stopped me short of the only object of interest, ignorant, as he said, of its existence. Now either the alcalde lied and was too lazy to encounter the toil which I had undergone, or he was imposing upon me. In either case he deserves a flogging, and I beg the next traveler, as a particular favor to me, to give him one.

I was too indignant with the alcalde to have anything further to do with him; but, bent upon making another attempt, on my return to the village I rode to the house of the cura to obtain his assistance in procuring men and making other needful preparations. On the steps of the back piazza I saw a young negro man, in a black gown and cap, sitting by the side of a good-looking, well-dressed white woman, and, if I mistake not, discoursing to her of other things than those connected with his priestly duties. His black reverence was by no means happy to see me. I asked him if I could make an inn of his house, which, though it sounds somewhat free, is the set phrase for a traveler to use; without rising from his seat, he said his house was small and incommodious, and that the alcalde had a good one. He was the first black priest I had seen, and the only one in the country who failed in hospitality. I must confess that I felt a strong impulse to lay the butt of a pistol over his head, but, spurring my horse so that he sprang almost upon him, I wheeled short and galloped out of the yard. With the alcalde and the cura both against me, I had no chance in the village. It was nearly dark, so I returned to Masaya. My vexation was lost in a sense of overpowering fatigue. It would be impossible to repeat the severe labor of the day without an interval of rest, and there was so much difficulty in making arrangements that I determined to mount my macho and push on.

The next morning I resumed my journey. My mules had not been watered. To send them to the lake and back would give them a journey of two leagues; to save them I bought water, which was measured out in a gourd holding about a quart. At about a league's distance we came in sight of the Lake of Managua, and before us the whole country was a bed of lava from the base of the volcano to the lake. I met a traveling party, the principal of which I recognized as a stranger. We had already passed them when I turned round and accosted him in English; after looking at me for a minute, to my great surprise he called me by name. He was an American named Higgins, whom I had seen last at my own office in New York. He was coming from Realejo and was on his way to San Juan, with the intention of embarking for the United States. We sent our luggage on and dismounted; and besides the pleasure of the meeting, I am under great obligation to him. I was riding at the time on an *albarda*, or common saddle of the country, very painful for one not used to it, and painful also to my macho. As Mr. Higgins' journey was nearly at an end, he gave me his in exchange; I used it till I left it on the shores of Yucatán. He gave me, too, a line in pencil to a lady in León, and I charged him with messages to my friends at home. When he rode off, I almost envied him; he was leaving behind him tumults and convulsions, and was going to a quiet home, but I had still a long and difficult journey before me.

In about three hours, after a desperately hot ride, we reached Managua, beautifully situated on the banks of the lake. Entering through a collection of thatched huts, we passed a large aristocratic house, with a courtyard occupying a whole square. It was the mansion of an expatriated family, decaying and going to ruin.

Late in the afternoon I walked down to the Lake of Managua. It was not so grand as the Lake of Nicaragua, but it was a noble sheet of water, and in full sight was the volcano of Momotombo. The shore presented the same animated spectacle of women filling their water jars, men bathing, horses and mules drinking; in one place was a range of fishermen's huts, and on the edge of the water where stakes had been set up in a triangular form, women with small hand nets were catching fish, which they threw into hollow places dug, or rather, scraped, in the sand. The fish were called *sardinitos,* which, at the door of the huts, the men were building fires to cook. The beauty of this scene was enhanced by the reflection that it underwent no change. Here was perpetual summer; no winter ever came to drive the inhabitants shivering to their fires. Still it may be questioned whether, with the same scenery and climate, with wants few and easily supplied, luxuriating in the open air by the side of this lovely lake, even the descendants of the Anglo-Saxon race would not lose their energy and industry.

This lake empties into the Lake of Nicaragua by means of the River Tipitapa, and another communication between the two seas has been spoken of, that is, by means of a canal from the Lake of Managua to the Pacific at the port of Realejo.[3] The ground is perfectly level, and the port is perhaps the best in Spanish America; but the distance is sixty miles, and there are other difficulties which it seems to me are insuperable. The River Tipitapa has been represented as navigable the whole length for the largest ships; but no survey was ever made until Mr. Baily's, according to which the river is thirty miles in length. Beginning at the Lake of Nicaragua, for twenty-four miles the water is from one to three fathoms in depth. Above this there are rapids, and at the distance of four and a half miles a fall of thirteen feet.

---

3. This port is now called Corinto.

The whole rise within the six miles is twenty-eight feet eight inches. The Lake of Managua, from observation and information without survey, is about fifteen leagues long and thirty-five in circumference, and averages ten fathoms of water. There is not a single stream on the contemplated line of canal from this lake to the Pacific, and it would be necessary for this lake to furnish the whole supply of water for communication with both oceans.

At three o'clock the next morning we started. In all the *tierras calientes* it is the custom to travel at night, or rather, very early in the morning. At eight o'clock we entered the village of Mateare, where we procured some eggs and breakfasted. From this village our road lay directly along the lake, but a few paces from the shore and shaded by noble trees. Unfortunately, we were obliged to turn off to avoid a large rock which had rolled down several months before and which probably blocks up the road still. This brought us round by the Cuesta del Reloj, so called from a venerable sundial which stands on one side of the road; it is of a dark gray stone with an inscription in Castilian, but the characters were so worn and indistinct that I could not make them out. It has no history except that it was erected by the conquerors, but it stands as an indication of the works with which the Spaniards began the settlement of the country.

At half past eleven we left the lake for the last time, and entered an open plain. We rode an hour longer and reached Nagarote, a miserable village, the houses of which were built partly of mud, with yards in front trodden bare by mules and baked white by the sun. I entered one of the houses for shelter, and found in it a young negro priest on his way to Cartagena with orders from the Church of León. The house was occupied by an old man alone. It had a bedstead with a mat over it, upon which I lay down, glad to rest a while and to escape the scorching heat. Opposite the bed was a rude frame about six feet high, on the top of which was a sort of baby house with the figure of the Virgin sitting on a chair dressed in cheap finery.

At three we started again. The sun had lost some of its force, the road was wooded, and I observed more than the

usual number of crosses. The people of Nicaragua are said
to be the worst in the Republic of Central America; the inhabitants of the other states always caution a stranger against
them. But their devotion is proportionate to their bad reputation. Everywhere, in the cities and country, on the tops of
mountains and by the side of rivers, these religious memorials stared me in the face. I noticed one in a cleared place
by the roadside; it was painted black and on a black board
suspended to it, was an inscription in faded white letters; it
had been erected to the memory of a padre who had been
murdered and buried at its foot. I stopped to copy the inscription, but, while so engaged, I saw a traveling party
approaching and, knowing the jealousy of the people, I shut
my notebook and rode on. The party consisted of two men
with their servants, and a woman. The younger man accosted me, and said that he had seen me at Granada and
regretted that he had not known of my proposed journey.
From the style of his dress and equipments I supposed him
to be a gentleman, and I was sure of it from the circumstance
of his carrying a gamecock under his arm. As we rode on the
conversation turned to these interesting birds, and I learned
that my new acquaintance was going to León to fight a
match, of which he offered to give me notice. The bird
which he carried had won three matches in Granada; its
fame had reached León and drawn forth a challenge from
that place. It was rolled up as carefully as a fractured leg,
with nothing but the head and tail visible; suspended by a
string, it was as easily carried as a basket. The young man
sighed over the miseries of the country and the distress and
ruin caused by the wars; he represented the pit at Granada
as being in a deplorable condition, but said that in León it
was very flourishing on account of León being the headquarters of the military. The building where the cockpit was
located also did honor to the city; it was only open on Sun-
days, but since he knew the proprietor, he could at any time
make an arrangement for a match. He made many inquiries
about the state of the science in my country; he told me that
he had imported two cocks from England, which were game
enough, but not sufficiently heavy for theirs. He gave me,

in addition, much valuable information on this subject, of which I neglected to make any memorandum.

Before dark we reached Pueblo Nuevo, and all went to the same *posada*. His companion was not so much of a sportsman, though he knew the qualities of a good bird and showed a familiarity in handling them. It was the first time I had fallen in with travelers for the night. I have avoided details in all places where I was partaking of private hospitality, but this was like a hotel at home, in the main point that is, that all were expected to pay. For supper we had poached eggs and beans, without plate, knife, fork, or spoon. My companions used their tortillas to take up an egg and also, by turning up the edges, to scoop out *frijoles* from the dish; but withal, they were courteous and gentlemanly. We had a species of chocolate, made of pounded cocoa and sweetened; it was served in hickories,[4] which, having bottoms like the butts of large eggs, could not stand on the table. My companions twisted their pocket handkerchiefs, and winding them on the table in circular folds, set the hickories inside the hollow; one of them did the same with my handkerchief for me. After supper the younger of the two dressed the birds in their *robes de nuit*, a cotton cloth wound tight around the body, compressing the wings; then, with a string fastened to the back of the cloth, so that the body was balanced, he hooked each of them to the hammock. While he was preparing them, the woman was showing horn combs, beads, earrings, and rosaries; and she entrapped the daughter of the host into the purchase of a comb. The house had an unusual influx of company. The young man, the female merchant, and I do not know how many of the family, slept in a back room. The elder traveler offered me the hammock, but I preferred the long chest made from the trunk of a tree, which in every house in Nicaragua served as a sort of cupboard.

---

4. Hickory may possibly be Stephens' terminology for the Spanish *jícara*, or chocolate cup.

Chapter II

~~~~~~

Beautiful plain. León. Stroll though the town. Baneful effects of party spirit. Scenes of horror. Unpleasant intelligence. Journey continued. A fastidious beggar. Chinandega. Gulf of Conchagua. Visit to Realejo. Cotton factory. Harbor of Realejo. El Viejo. Port of Naguiscolo. Importance of a passport. Embarking mules. A bungo. Volcano of Cosegüina. Eruption of 1835. La Unión.

AT two o'clock we were awakened by the crowing of the cocks, and at three the cargo mules were loaded and we set off. The road was level and wooded, but desperately dusty. For two hours after daylight we had shade, then we came upon an open plain, bounded on the Pacific side by a low ridge and, on the right, by a high range of mountains which formed part of the great chain of the Cordilleras. Before us, at a great distance, rising above the level of the plain, we saw the spires of the cathedral of León. This magnificent plain, in richness of soil not surpassed by any land in the world, lay as desolate as when the Spaniards first traversed it. The dry season was near its close; for four months there had been no rain, and the dust hung around us in thick clouds, hot and fine as the sands of Egypt. At nine o'clock we reached León and I parted from my companions, but not without a courteous invitation from the younger to take up my rest at the house of his brother.

The suburbs were more miserable than anything I had yet seen. Passing up a long street across which a sentinel was patrolling, I saw in front of the cuartel a group of vagabond soldiers, a match for Carrera's, who cried out insolently, *Quítese su sombrero* (Take off your hat). I had to traverse the whole extent of the city before I reached the house to which I had been recommended. I dismounted and entered it with confidence of a warm reception, but the lady, with considerable expedition, told me that her husband was not at home. I gave her a note with which I had been furnished, addressed to herself; but she said she could not read English, and handed it back. I translated it word for word, being a request that she would give me lodgings. Her brow actually knit with vexation; she said she had but one spare room, and that was reserved for the English vice-consul from Realejo. I answered that the vice-consul did not intend leaving Realejo for the present. She asked me how long I intended to stay; and when I replied only that night, she said that if such was the case I might remain. The reader will perhaps wonder at my want of spirit; but the fact is, I was loth to consider any incivility personal. My only alternative was to seek out the young man whose invitation I had declined and whose name I did not know, or to ask admission from door to door.

It is said that women are governed by appearances, and mine was not very seductive. My dress was the same with which I had left Granada, and, soiled by the ascent of the volcano of Masaya, was now covered with dust. Making the most of my moderate wardrobe, on my reappearance I was more favorably received; at least I had a capital breakfast. As it was very hot and I wanted to rest, I remained indoors and played with the children. At dinner I had the seat of honor at the head of the table; I had made such progress that, if I had desired it, I would have ventured to broach the subject of remaining another day. I owe it to the lady to say that, having assented to my remaining, she treated me with great civility and attention, and particularly, she used great exertions in procuring me a guide to enable me to set out the next day.

After dinner Nicolás came to my room, and with uplifted hands cried out against the people of León, *Gente indecente, sin vergüenza* (literally: Indecent people, without shame). He had been hooted in the streets and had heard such stories of the state of the country before us that he wanted to return home. I was extremely loth to make another change, and particularly for any of the assassin-looking scoundrels whom I had seen on my entry; but not liking the responsibility of taking him against his will, I told him that if he would procure me two honest men he might leave me. I had advanced him more than was due, but I had a security against his deserting me in his apprehension of being taken for a soldier.

This over, I walked out to take a view of the town. It had an appearance of old and aristocratic respectability, which no other city in Central America possessed. The houses were large, and many of the fronts were full of stucco ornaments; the plaza was spacious, and the squares of the churches and the churches themselves magnificent. It was the seat of a bishopric and distinguished for the costliness of its churches and convents, its seats of learning, and its men of science, down to the time of its revolution against Spain; but in walking through its streets I saw palaces, in which nobles had lived, dismantled and roofless, and occupied by half-starved wretches, pictures of misery and want; on one side was an immense field of ruins, covering half the city.

Almost immediately on the establishment of independence and the drawing of the great party lines between the Centralists and Federalists, the State of Nicaragua had become the theatre of a furious struggle. In an unfortunate hour the people elected a Central governor and Liberal vice-governor. A divided administration led to drawing of blood and the most sanguinary conflict known in civil wars. Inch by inch the ground was disputed, till the whole physical force and deadly animosity of the state were concentrated in the capital. The contending parties fought up to the very heart of the city; the streets were barricaded, and for three months not a person could pass the line without being shot at. Scenes of horror surpassing human belief were fresh in the memory of the inhabitants. The Liberals prevailed; the Central chief was killed, his forces massacred, and in the frenzy of the moment, the part of the city occupied by the Centralists was burned and razed to the ground; besides the blood of murdered citizens and the tears and curses of widows and orphans, the victors had the rich enjoyment of a desolated country and a ruined capital. The same ruthless spirit still characterized the inhabitants of León. The heroes of Tegucigalpa,[1] without a single prisoner as a monument of mercy, had been received with ringing of bells, firing of cannon, and other demonstrations of joy, and they were still in the city, flushed with their brutal victory and anxious to be led on to more such triumphs.

I must confess that I felt a degree of uneasiness in walking the streets of León that I never felt in any city in the Near East. My change of dress did not make my presence more acceptable, and the eagle on my hat attracted particular attention. At every corner was a group of scoundrels, who stared at me as if disposed to pick a quarrel. With some, my official character made me an object of suspicion, for in their disgraceful fights they thought that the eyes of the whole world were upon them, and that England, France, and the United States were secretly contending for the possession of their interesting country. I intended to pay a visit to the chief of the state but, afraid of being insulted or getting into some difficulty that might detain me, I returned to the house.

By means of the servants Nicolás had found two men who were willing to accompany me, but I did not like their looks, or even to let them know when I intended to set out. I had hardly disposed of them before my guide came to advise me not to set out the next day, as five hundred soldiers, who had been making preparations for several days, were to march the next morning against El Salvador. This was most unpleasant intelligence. I did not wish to travel with them, or to fall in with them on the road; calculating that their march would be slower than mine, I told the guide to ascertain their time for starting, and that we would set out two hours before them. Nicolás went out with him to take the mules to water, but the two returned in great haste with the intelligence that piquets were scouring the city for men and mules,

---

1. A brief account of the battle of Tegucigalpa is given in volume I, p. 341.

having entered the yard of a padre nearby and taken three of his animals. The lady of the house ordered all the doors to be locked and the keys brought to her; an hour before dark we were all shut in and my poor mules had to go without water.

At about eight o'clock we heard the tramp of cavalry in the streets, and gathering inside the doorway, we saw about six hundred men taking up their line of march. There was no music, no shouting, no waving of handkerchiefs to cheer them as defenders of their country or as adventurers on the road to glory; but in the dark, and barefooted, their tread seemed stealthy; people looked at them with fear; and it seemed rather the sally of a band of conspirators than a march by the soldiers of the Republic.

My muleteer did not return till daylight the next morning. Fortunately for us, he had learned that the troops were destined on another but even more inglorious expedition. Expenses had been incurred in sending troops into Honduras, of which Granada refused to pay its portion on the ground that, by the constitution, it was not liable except for expenses incurred in defending the borders of its own state. This was admitted; but the expense had been incurred; León had fought the battle and had the same materials with which she gained it to enforce the contribution. In order that Granada might be taken unawares, it was given out that the troops were destined for El Salvador, and they were actually marched out on the El Salvador road; but at midnight they made a circuit and took the route for Granada. War between different states was bad enough, but here the flame which had before laid the capital in ruins was lighted again within its own borders. What the result of this expedition was I never heard; but probably, taken unawares and without arms, Granada was compelled by bayonets to pay what, by the constitution, she was not bound to pay.

Outside of León, and once more on the back of my macho, I breathed more freely. Nicolás was induced to continue when he heard that there was a vessel at Realejo for Costa Rica, and I hoped to find one there for Sonsonate. The great plain of León was even more beautiful than before—too

beautiful for the thankless people to whom the bounty of
Providence had given it. On the left was the same low ridge
separating it from the Pacific Ocean, and on the right the
great range of Cordilleras, terminated by the volcano of El
Viejo.

I had passed through the village of Chichigalpa when I
heard a cry of *Caballero!* behind me, and turning, I saw
divers people waving their hands, and a woman running, almost out of breath, with a pocket handkerchief which I had
left at the house where I breakfasted. As I was going on, a
respectable-looking gentleman stopped me, who, with many
apologies for the liberty, asked for a *medio* (sixpence). I
gave him one, which he examined and handed back, saying,
"*No corre* (It does not pass)." It was always, in paying
money, a matter of course to have two or three pieces returned, and this I sometimes resisted; but as in this land
everything was *al revés,* it seemed regular for beggars to be
choosers, so I gave him another.

My stopping place was at the house of Mr. Bridges, an
Englishman from one of the West India Islands, who had
been resident in the country many years; he was married
to a lady of León, but, on account of the convulsions of the
country, they lived on his hacienda. The soil was rich for
cotton and sugar, and Mr. Bridges said that here fifty men
could manufacture sugar cheaper than two hundred in the
islands; but the difficulty was, no reliance could be placed
upon Indian labor. Here again, thanks to the kindness of
Mr. Bridges and his lady, and to the magnificent wildness
of hacienda life, I could have passed several days with much
satisfaction; but I stopped only for dinner, after which Mr.
Bridges accompanied me to Chinandega.

As usual, my first business was to make arrangements for
continuing my journey. My whole road was along the coast
of the Pacific, but beyond Chinandega the Gulf of Conchagua [2] made a large indentation in the land, which it was
customary to cross in a bungo, sending the mules around the

2. This is now called the Gulf of Fonseca. Between El Salvador and
Nicaragua, it represents Honduras' only outlet to the Pacific.

head of the Gulf. I was advised that it would be hazardous thus to send the mules, as the Honduras troops were marching upon El Salvador and would seize them. I might save them by going myself, but it was a journey of six days through a country so desolate that it was necessary to carry food for the mules, and as I had still a long road beyond, I felt it necessary to economize my strength. I was loth to run the risk of losing my mules, and sent a courier to El Viejo, where the owners of the bungoes lived, to hire the largest, determined to run the risk of taking the mules with me. The next morning the courier returned, having procured a bungo to be ready the next evening, and with a message from the owner that the embarkation must be at my risk.

Obliged to wait the day, after breakfast I started for Realejo. On the way I met Mr. Foster, the English vice-consul, coming to see me. He turned back and took me first to the *máquina*, or cotton factory, of which I had heard much on the road. It was the only one in the country and owed its existence to the enterprise of a countryman, having been erected by Mr. Higgins, who, disappointed in his expectations or disgusted with the country from other causes, had sold it to Don Francisco and Mr. Foster. They were sanguine in their expectations of profit, for they supposed that, by furnishing a market, the people would be induced to work and raise cotton enough for exportation to Europe. The resources of this distracted country are incalculable. Peace and industry would open fountains which would overflow with wealth; and I have no doubt the influence of this single factory will be felt in quieting and enriching the whole district within its reach.

I accompanied Mr. Foster to Realejo, which was only half an hour's ride. The harbor, Juarros says, is capable of containing a thousand ships; but, being two or three leagues distant, I was unable to visit it. The town, consisting of two or three streets with low straggling houses enclosed by a thick forest, was founded by a few of the companions of Alvarado, who stopped there on their expedition to Peru; but, being so near the sea and exposed to the incursions of the buccaneers, the inhabitants had moved inland and founded León.

At dark we returned to the factory, and Don Francisco and I reached Chinandega, where I was greeted with intelligence that the proprietor of the boat had sent word that he supposed I had a permission to embark from the chief of the state, as, by a late order, no person could embark without such an order. He was most provokingly out in his supposition. I had entered the state by a frontier of wilderness, and had not once been asked for a passport. The reader may remember how I was prevented from visiting the chief of the state; besides, when at León, I did not know whether I should continue by land or cross the Gulf, and I had supposed that at the port of embarkation I could procure all that was necessary. I was excessively disturbed; but Don Francisco sent for the commandant of the town, who said that the order had not yet been sent to the port, but that it was in his hands and he would retain it.

Early the next morning I sent on an ox wagon with the luggage and a stock of corn and grass for the mules during the voyage, and, after a pleasant ride of a league, I reached El Viejo, one of the most respectable-looking towns in Nicaragua. The house of the owner of the bungo was one of the largest in the place, and furnished with two mahogany sofas made by a Yankee cabinetmaker in Lima, two looking glasses with gilt frames, a French clock, gilt chairs with cane bottoms, and two Boston rocking chairs, which had made the passage round Cape Horn. Don Francisco went over to the commandant. He, unluckily, had received his orders direct from the government, and dared not let me pass. I went over myself with Mr. Foster. The order was positive, and I was in agony. Here I made a push with my official character, and after an hour's torment, by the warm help of Mr. Foster, and upon his undertaking to save the commandant harmless, and to send an express immediately to León for a passport from the chief of the state, it was agreed that in the meantime I might go on.

I did not wait long, but, taking leave of Mr. Foster and Don Francisco, I set out for the port. It was seven leagues through an unbroken forest. On the way I overtook my bungo men, who, nearly naked, were moving in single file with the pilot at their head, each carrying on his back an open network containing tortillas and provisions for the voyage. At half past two we reached the port of Naguiscolo.[3] There was a single hut, at which a woman was washing corn; near her on the ground was a naked child, its face, arms, and body one running sore, a picture of squalid poverty. In front of us was a large muddy plain, through the center of which ran a straight cut called a canal, with an embankment on one side dry, the mud baked hard and bleached by the sun. In this ditch lay several bungoes high and dry, adding to the ugliness of the picture. I had a feeling of great satisfaction that I was not obliged to remain there long; but the miserable woman, with a tone of voice that seemed to rejoice in the chance of making others as miserable as herself, desisted from washing her maize and screeched in my ears that a *guarda* had been sent direct from the capital with orders to let no one embark without a passport. The *guarda* had gone down the river in a canoe, in search of a bungo which had attempted to go away without a passport; and I walked down the bank of the canal in the hope of catching him alone when he returned. The sun was scorching hot, and as I passed the bungoes, the boatmen asked me if I had a passport. At the end of the canal, under the shade of a large tree, were two women; they had been in that place three days, waiting for one of their party who had gone to León to procure a passport.

It was more than an hour before the *guarda* appeared. He was taken by the' eagle on my hat, and as I told him my story, he said *Sí, señor*, to everything; but when I talked of embarking, he said, "*Señor*, you have no passport." I will not inflict upon the reader the details of all my vexations and anxiety that afternoon. I was most eager to hurry on. To send a courier to León would keep me in suspense in-

---

3. The editor was unable to identify a town with this name. It is evident, however, that Stephens embarked some miles northwest of Corinto, possibly at Playa Grande.

sufferable. Some difficulty might happen, and the only way
for peace of mind was to return myself. I had already made
a longer journey than is ever made in the country without
an interval of rest. The road before me led through the seat
of war, and four days' detention might throw me into the
midst of it. (In fact, the result proved that one day would
have done so.) I walked with the *guarda* to the hut, and in
greater anxiety than I had felt since my departure from
home, showed him my papers—a larger bundle, perhaps,
than he had ever seen before, and with bigger seals, particularly my original passport from my own government. I jum-
bled together his government and my government, I reminded him of the amicable relations existing between them,
and I tried to give him an overwhelming idea of my importance. But he knew no more what it meant than if I had
repeated to him in English the fifth problem in Euclid. The
poor man was almost in as great perplexity as I was. Several
times he assented and retracted; and at length, upon my
giving him a letter promising him the protection of Mr.
Foster and the commandant at El Viejo, he agreed to let
the bungo go.

It was about an hour before dark when we went down to
embark the mules. My bungo was at the extreme end of the
canal, and the tide had risen so that she was afloat. We began
with the gray, by casting a noose around her legs, drawing
them together, and throwing her down. The men then attempted to lift her up bodily over the side of the bungo;
failing in this, they took off the rudder and, leaning it
against the side, hauled the mule up it, then, tilting the rudder, they dropped her into the boat. In the meantime the
macho stood under a tree, looking on very suspiciously, and
with fearful forebodings. The noose was put round his legs,
with a rope before and behind to pull on, and struggling desperately, he was thrown down; but hardly had he touched
the ground when, with a desperate effort, he broke the ropes
and rose upon his feet. A second attempt was more successful; but the two mules abreast made a close fit and I was
obliged to leave behind the luggage mule. I paid the *guarda*

to take her to Mr. Foster, but whether she reached him or not I have never heard.

We were assisted by the boatmen of another bungo, and I ordered supper and *aguardiente* for everybody. This was furnished at the hut by the *guarda*, and when it was over, the men, all in good spirits, commenced taking the luggage on board. At this time as some who were detained were grumbling, a new man entered the hut, as he said direct from the *pueblo*. He croaked in my ears the odious order, and the guard again made objections. I was excessively vexed by this last interruption; and fairly bullying the newcomer out of the hut, I told the guard that the thing was settled and I would not be trifled with. I, thereupon, took up my gun and told the men to follow me. I saw beforehand that they were elevated by their good cheer, and that I could rely upon them. The guard, and all those compelled to wait, followed; but we got on board, and my crew were so tipsy that they defied all opposition. One push cleared the bungo from the canal; as she was passing out, a stranger unexpectedly stepped on board and, in the dark, slipped down under the awning with the mules. I was surprised and a little indignant that he had not asked leave, and it occurred to me that perhaps he was a partisan who might compromise me; but to return might lead to new difficulty, and anyway, he was probably some poor fellow escaping for his life, and it was better that I should know nothing about it. In the midst of my doubts a man on the bank cried out that fifty soldiers had arrived from León. It was pitchy dark; we could see nothing, and my men answered with a shout of defiance.

In the meantime we were descending rapidly, whirling around and hitting against the branches of trees; the mules were thrown down, the awning carried away, and in the midst of darkness and confusion we struck with a violent crash against another bungo, which knocked us all into a heap, and would, I thought, send us to the bottom. The men rose with roars of laughter. It was a bad beginning. Still I was overjoyed at being clear of the port, and there was a wild excitement in the scene itself. At length the men sat down to the oars and pulled for a few minutes as if they would tear the old bungo out of the water, shouting all the time like spirits of darkness let loose. The pilot sat quietly at the helm without speaking, and dark as it was, at times I saw a smile steal over his face at wild sallies of the boatmen. Again they began rowing furiously as before, and then suddenly one of the sweeps broke and the oarsman fell backward. The bungo was run up among the trees, and the men climbed ashore by the branches. The blows of machetes mingled with shouts and laughter rang through the woods; they were the noisiest party I met in Central America. In the dark they cut down a dozen saplings before they found what they wanted. In about an hour they returned, and the shattered awning was refitted. By this time they were more sobered and, taking their sweeps, they moved us silently down the dark river until one o'clock, when we came to anchor.

The bungo was about forty feet long, dug out of the trunk of a Guanacaste tree. It was about five feet wide and nearly as deep, with the bottom round; and a *toldo,* or awning, round like the top of a market wagon, made of matting and bulls' hides, covered ten feet of the stern. Beyond were six seats across the sides of the bungo for the oarsmen. The whole front was necessary for the men, and in reality I had only the part occupied by the awning, where, with the mules as tenants in common, there were too many of us. They stood abreast, with their halters tied to the first bench. The rounded bottom gave them an unsteady foothold and when the boat heaved they had a scramble to preserve their center of gravity. The space between their heels and the end of the log, or stern of the bungo, was my sleeping room. Nicolás was afraid to pass between the mules to get a place among the men, and he could not climb over the awning. I had their heads tethered close up to the bench, and putting Nicolás outside to catch the first kick, I drew up against the stern of the bungo and went to sleep.

At half past seven we weighed anchor, or hauled up a large stone, and started with oars. My boatmen were peculiar in their way of wearing pantaloons. First they pulled

them off, then folding them about a foot wide and two feet
long, they suspended them over the belts of their machetes
like little aprons. At nine o'clock we reached the mouth of
the river. Here we hoisted sail and, while the wind was fair,
did very well. The sun was scorching, and under the awning
the heat was insufferable. Following the coast, at eleven
o'clock we were opposite the volcano of Coseguina, a long,
dark mountain range, with another ridge running below it,
and then an extensive plain covered with lava to the sea. The
wind headed us, and in order to weather the point of headland from which we could lay our course, the boatmen got
into the water to tow the bungo. I followed them, and with
a broad-brimmed straw hat to protect me from the sun, I
found the water delightful. During this time one of the men
brought sand from the shore to break the roundness of the
bottom of the boat and thus give the mules a foothold. Unable to weather the point, at half past one we came to anchor,
and very soon every man on board was asleep.

I woke with the pilot's legs resting on my shoulder. It was
rather an undignified position, but no one saw it. Before me
was the volcano of Coseguina, with its field of lava and its
desolate shore; not a living being was in sight except my
sleeping boatmen. Five years before, on the shores of the
Mediterranean, and at the foot of Mount Etna, I read in a
newspaper an account of the eruption of this volcano; little
did I then ever expect to see it. It was the most awful in the
history of volcanic eruptions, the noise startling the people
of Guatemala four hundred miles off; at Kingston, Jamaica,
eight hundred miles distant, it was thought to be signal guns
of distress from some vessel at sea. The face of nature was
changed: the cone of the volcano was gone; a mountain and
field of lava ran down to the sea; a forest old as creation had
entirely disappeared; two islands were formed in the sea;
shoals were discovered, in one of which a large tree was
fixed upside down; one river was completely choked up,
and another formed running in an opposite direction; seven
men in the employ of my bungo proprietor ran down to the
water, pushed off in a bungo, and were never heard of again;
wild beasts, howling, left their caves in the mountains; and

ounces,[4] leopards, and snakes fled for shelter to the abodes of men.

This eruption took place on the twentieth of January, 1835. Mr. Savage was on that day at the side of the volcano of San Miguel, distant one hundred and twenty miles, looking for cattle. At eight o'clock he saw a dense cloud rising in the south in a pyramidal form, and heard a noise which sounded like the roaring of the sea. Very soon, the thick clouds were lighted up by vivid flashes, rose-colored and forked, shooting and disappearing, which he supposed to be some electrical phenomenon. These appearances increased so fast that his men became frightened and said it was a *ruina*, and that the end of the world was nigh. Very soon he himself was satisfied that it was the eruption of a volcano. As Coseguina was at that time a quiet mountain, not suspected to contain subterraneous fires, he supposed it to proceed from the volcano of Tigris.[5] He returned to the town of San Miguel, and in riding three blocks felt three severe shocks of earthquake. The inhabitants were distracted with terror. Birds flew wildly through the streets and, blinded by the dust, fell dead on the ground. At four o'clock it was so dark that, as Mr. Savage says, when he held up his hand before his eyes he could not see it. Nobody moved without a candle, which gave a dim and misty light, extending only a few feet. At this time the church was full and could not contain half who wished to enter. The figure of the Virgin was brought out into the plaza and borne through the streets, followed by the inhabitants with candles and torches in penitential procession, crying upon the Lord to pardon their sins. Bells tolled, and during the procession there was another earthquake, so violent and long that it threw to the ground many people walking in the procession. The darkness continued till eleven o'clock the next day, when the sun was partially visible, but dim and hazy and without any brightness. The dust on the ground was four inches thick; the branches of

---

4. A lynx-like cat.
5. Stephens must refer to the volcano on the island El Tigre in the Gulf of Fonseca.

trees broke with its weight, and people were so disfigured by it that they could not be recognized.

At this time Mr. Savage set out for his hacienda at Sonsonate. He slept at the first village, and at two or three o'clock in the morning was roused by a report like the breaking of most terrific thunder or the firing of thousands of cannon. This was the report which startled the people of Guatemala when the commandant sallied out supposing that the cuartel was attacked, and that which was heard at Kingston in Jamaica. It was accompanied by an earthquake so violent that it almost threw Mr. Savage out of his hammock. Although this may at first appear no great feat for an earthquake, no stronger proof can be cited of the violence with which the shock affects the region in which it occurs.

Toward evening my men all woke; the wind was fair, but they took things quietly and after supper hoisted sail. About twelve o'clock, by an amicable arrangement, I stretched myself on the pilot's bench under the tiller. When I woke, we had passed the volcano of Tigris,[6] and were in an archipelago of islands more beautiful than the islands of Greece. The wind died away, and the boatmen, after playing for a little while with the oars, again let fall the big stone and went to sleep. Outside the awning the heat of the sun was withering, under it the closeness was suffocating, and my poor mules had had no water since their embarkation. In the confusion of getting away I had forgotten it till the moment of departure, and then there had been no vessel in which to carry it. After giving the men a short nap I roused them and, with the promise of a reward, induced them to take to their oars. Fortunately, before they got tired, we had a breeze, and at about four o'clock in the afternoon the big stone was dropped in the harbor of La Unión,[7] in front of the town. One ship was lying at anchor, a whaler from Chile which had put in in distress and had been condemned.

The commandant was Don Manuel Romero, one of Morazán's veterans, who was anxious to retire altogether

---

6. See note 5, p. 28.
7. The port of La Unión in El Salvador.

from public life, but who had remained in office because, in his present straits, he could be useful to his benefactor and friend. He had heard of me, and his attentions reminded me of what I sometimes forgot but which others very rarely did —my official character; he invited me to his house while I remained in La Unión, but he gave me intelligence which made me more anxious than ever to hurry on. General Morazán had left the port but a few days before, having accompanied his family thither on their way to Chile. On his return to San Salvador, he intended to march directly against Guatemala. By forced marches I might overtake him and go up under the escort of his army, trusting to chance to avoid being on the spot in case of a battle, or to my acquaintance with Carrera to get passed across the lines. Fortunately, the captain of the condemned ship wished to go to San Salvador, and agreed to accompany me the next day.

There were two strangers in the place, Captain R. of Honduras, and Don Pedro, a mulatto, both of whom were particularly civil to me. In the evening my proposed traveling companion and I called upon them, and very soon a game of cards was proposed. The doors were closed, wine was placed on the table, and monte was begun with doubloons. Captain R. and Don Pedro tried hard to make me join them. When I rose to leave, Captain R., as if he thought there could be but one reason for my resisting, took me aside and said that if I wanted money he was my friend. Don Pedro declared that he was not rich, but that he had a big heart, that he was happy of my acquaintance, that he had had the honor to know a consul once before at Panama, and that I might count upon him for anything I wanted. Gambling is one of the great vices of the country, and that into which strangers are most apt to fall. The captain had fallen in with a set of gamblers at San Miguel, and these two had come down to the port expressly to fleece him. When during the night he detected them cheating, telling them that he had learned in Chile how to use a knife as well as they could, he laid his cane over the shoulders of him who had had the honor to know a consul once before, and broke up the party. There is an old-fashioned feeling of respect for a man who wears a sword, but that feeling wears off in Central America.

Chapter III

〰〰〰〰〰〰〰〰〰〰〰〰〰〰〰〰〰〰〰〰〰〰〰〰〰〰〰

*Journey to San Salvador. A new companion. San Alejo.
San Miguel. War alarms. Another countryman. State of
El Salvador. River Lempa. San Vicente. Volcano of
San Vicente. Thermal springs. Cojutepeque. Arrival at
San Salvador. Prejudice against foreigners. Contribu-
tions. Pressgangs. Vice-President Vigil. Taking of San
Miguel and San Vicente. Rumors of a march upon
San Salvador. Departure from San Salvador.*

AT five o'clock the next afternoon we set out for San
Salvador. Don Manuel Romero furnished me with
letters of introduction to all the *jefes políticos*, and the captain's name was inserted in my passport.

I must introduce the reader to my new friend, Captain
Antonio V. F., a little over thirty. When six months out on
a whaling voyage, with a leaky ship and a mutinous crew he
had steered across the Pacific for the Continent of America,
and had reached the port of La Unión with seven or eight
feet of water in the hold and half his crew in irons. He had
known nothing of Central America until necessity threw him
upon its shore. While Captain F. was awaiting the slow process of a regular condemnation and order for the sale of his
ship, General Morazán with an escort of officers came to the
port to embark his wife and family for Chile. Captain F.
had become acquainted with them, and through them with
their side of the politics of the country. In the evening,
while we were riding along the ridge of a high mountain, he
told me that he had been offered a lieutenant-colonel's commission, and was then on his way to join Morazán in his
march against Guatemala. His ship was advertised for sale,
and he had written an account of his misadventures to his

owners and his wife; he was tired of remaining at the port
and a campaign with Morazán was the only other thing
offered. He liked General Morazán, and he liked the country and thought his wife would; if Morazán succeeded, there
would be vacant offices and estates without owners, and some
of them were worth having. He went from whaling to campaigning as coolly as a Yankee would go from cutting down
trees to editing a newspaper. It was no affair of mine, but I
suggested that there was no honor to be gained; that he
would get his full share of hard knocks, bullets, and sword
cuts; that if Morazán succeeded, he would have a desperate
struggle for his share of the spoils; and if Morazán failed,
he would certainly be shot. All this was matter he had
thought on, and before committing himself he intended to
make observations at San Salvador.

At ten o'clock we reached the village of San Alejo and
stopped for the night at a very comfortable house where all
were in a state of excitement because of the report of an invasion from Honduras. Early the next morning we started
with a new guide, and a little beyond the village he pointed
out a place where his uncle had been murdered and robbed
about a year before. Four of the robbers had been caught and
sent by the alcalde, under a guard of the relations of the
murdered man, to San Miguel, with directions to the guard
to shoot them if they became refractory. The guard found
them refractory at the very place where the murder had
been committed, and shot them on the spot.

At eight o'clock we came in sight of the volcano of San
Miguel, and at two we entered the city. Riding up the street,
we passed a large church with its front fallen, and saw paintings on the walls, an altar forty feet high with columns, and
images sculptured and gilded, all exposed to the open air.
All along the road we had heard of war, and we found the
city in a state of great excitement. The troops of Honduras
were marching upon it and were then only twelve leagues
distant. There were no soldiers to defend it; all had been
drawn off for Morazán's expedition. Many of the citizens
had already fled; in fact, the town was half depopulated, and
the rest were preparing to save themselves by concealment
or flight. We stopped at the house of John, or Don Juan,

Denning, an American from Connecticut, who had sold an armed brig to the Federal government and commanded her himself during the blockade of Omoa.[1] He had married in the country, and several years ago he had retired and gone to live at his hacienda. His house was deserted and stripped, the furniture and valuables hidden, and his mother-in-law, an old lady, remained in the empty tenement. No one thought of resistance. The captain bought a silver-mounted sword from one of the most respectable citizens who was converting his useless trappings into money; this man, with a little trunk in his hand containing *la plata*, pointed to a fine horse in the courtyard and, without a blush on his face, said that that was his security.

The captain had great difficulty in procuring mules; he had two enormous trunks, containing, among other things, Peruvian chains and other gold trinkets to a large amount — in fact, all he was worth. In the evening we walked to the plaza; groups of men, wrapped in their ponchos, were discussing in low tones the movements of the enemy: how far they had marched that day, how long they would require for rest, and at what moment it would be necessary to flee. We returned to the house, placed two naked wooden-bottomed bedsteads in one, and, having ascertained by calculation that we were not likely to be disturbed during the night, we forgot the troubles of the flying inhabitants and slept soundly.

On account of the difficulty of procuring mules, we did not set out the next morning till ten o'clock. The climate is the hottest in Central America, and insalubrious under exposure to the sun; but we would not wait. Every moment there were new rumors of the approach of the Honduras army, and it was all important for us to keep in advance of them. I shall hasten over our hurried journey through the State of El Salvador, the richest in Central America, which extended a hundred and eighty miles along the shores of the Pacific, and which produced tobacco, the best indigo, and the richest balsam in the world. We had mountains and rivers, valleys and immense ravines, and the three great volcanoes of San Miguel, San Vicente, and San Salvador, one or

---

1. A port on the Atlantic coast of Honduras.

the other of which was almost constantly in sight. The whole surface is volcanic; for miles the road lay over beds of decomposed lava, inducing the belief that here the whole shore of the Pacific is an immense arch over subterraneous fires. From the time of the independence, this state stood foremost in the maintenance of liberal principles; it exhibits throughout an appearance of improvement, a freedom from bigotry and fanaticism, and a development of physical and moral energy not found in any other. The Salvadorans are the only men who speak of sustaining the integrity of the Republic as a point of national honor.

In the late afternoon of the second day we came in sight of the Lempa, now a gigantic river rolling on to the Pacific. Three months before I had seen it a little stream among the mountains of Esquipulas. Here we were overtaken by Don Carlos Rivas, a leading Liberal from Honduras, who was flying for life before partisan soldiers of his own state. We descended to the bank of the river and followed it through a wild forest which had been swept by a tornado, the trees still lying as they fell. At the crossing place the valley of the river was half a mile wide; but being the dry season, on this side there was a broad beach of sand and stones. We rode to the water's edge and shouted for the boatman on the opposite side. Other parties arrived, all fugitives, among them the wife and family of Don Carlos, and we formed a crowd upon the shore. At length the boat came and took on board sixteen mules, saddles, luggage, and as many men, women, and children as could stow themselves away, leaving a multitude behind. We crossed in the dark, and on the opposite side we found every hut and shed filled with fugitives; there were families in dark masses under the trees, and men and women crawled out to congratulate friends who had put the Lempa between them and the enemy. We slept upon our luggage on the bank of the river, and before daylight were again in the saddle.

That night we slept at San Vicente, and the next morning the captain, in company with an invalid officer of Morazán's, who had been prevented by sickness from accompanying the general on his march against Guatemala, rode on with the luggage, while I, with Colonel Hoyas, made a circuit to visit

El Infierno of the volcano of San Vicente. Crossing a beautiful plain running to the base of the volcano, we left our animals at a hut and walked some distance to a stream in a deep ravine, which we followed upward to its source at the very base of the volcano. The water was warm and had a taste of vitriol, and the banks were incrusted with white vitriol and flour of sulphur. At a distance of one or two hundred yards it formed a basin, where the water was hotter than the highest grade of my Reaumur's thermometer. In several places we heard subterranean noises, and toward the end of the ravine, on the slope of one side, was an orifice about thirty feet in diameter, from which, with a terrific noise, boiling water spouted into the air. This is called *El Infiernillo,* or the little infernal regions. The inhabitants say that the noise is increased by the slightest agitation of the air, even by the human voice. Approaching to within range of the falling water, we shouted several times, and as we listened and gazed into the fearful cavity, I imagined that the noise was louder and more angry, and that the boiling water spouted higher at our call. Colonel Hoyas conducted me to a path from which I saw my road, like a white line, over a high verdant mountain. He told me that many of the inhabitants of San Miguel had fled to San Vicente, and at that place the Honduras arms would be repelled; we parted, little expecting that we would see each other again soon and under unpleasant circumstances for him.

I overtook the captain at a village where he had breakfast prepared, and in the afternoon we arrived at Cojutepeque, which until two days before had been the temporary capital. It was beautifully situated at the foot of a small extinct volcano whose green and verdant sides were broken only by a winding path, and on the top of which stood a fortress, which Morazán had built as his last rallying place under the flag of the Republic.

The next day at one o'clock we reached San Salvador.[2] Entering by a fine gate and through suburbs teeming with fruit

---

2. San Salvador is the capital of El Salvador. Since Stephens uses the first name for both city and state, his intent is not always quite clear. In cases where there was no ambiguity, correction has been made.

and flower trees, we hardly noticed the meanness of the houses. Advancing, we saw heaps of rubbish and large houses with their fronts cracked and falling, marks of the earthquakes which had broken the city up as the seat of government and almost depopulated it. This series of earthquakes commenced on the third of the preceding October (the same day on which I sailed for that country), and for twenty days the earth was tremulous, sometimes suffering fifteen or twenty shocks in twenty-four hours; there was one so severe, Mr. Chatfield told me, that a bottle standing in his sleeping room had been thrown down. Most of the inhabitants abandoned the city, and those who remained slept under matting in the courtyards of their houses. Every house had been more or less injured, some having been rendered untenantable, and many thrown down. Two days before, the vice-president and officers of the Federal and State governments, impelled by the crisis of the times, had returned to their shattered capital.

It was intensely hot, and there was no shade; the streets were solitary, the doors and windows of the houses closed, the shops around the plaza shut, and the little matted tents of the market women deserted; the inhabitants, forgetting earthquakes and that a hostile army was marching upon them, were taking their noonday siesta. In a corner of the plaza was a *burricada*, constructed with trunks of trees, rude as an Indian fortress; fortified with cannon, it was intended as the scene of the last effort for the preservation of the city. A few soldiers were asleep under the corridor of the cuartel, and a sentinel was pacing before the door. Inquiring our way of him, we turned the corner of the plaza and stopped at the house of Don Pedro Negrete, who at that time was acting as vice-consul both of England and France; he was the only representative of a foreign power at the capital.

It was one of the features of this unhappy revolution, that the Liberal Party manifested a violent feeling against foreigners before their friends and supporters, and particularly against the English, ostensibly on account of their occupation of the miserable little Island of Roatán in the Gulf of Honduras. The press, that is, a little weekly published at San Salvador, teemed with inflammatory articles against *los ingleses*, their usurpation and ambition, and their unjust design of adding to their extended dominions the Republic of Central America. It was a desperate effort to sustain a party menaced with destruction by rousing the national prejudice against strangers. A development of this spirit was seen in the treaty of alliance between El Salvador and Quezaltenango,[3] the only two states that sustained the Federal government. By this treaty in the preceding August, it was agreed that their delegates to the national convention should be instructed to treat, in preference to all other things, upon measures to be taken for the recovery of the Island of Roatán; and that no production of English soil or industry, even though it came under the flag of another nation, and no effect of any other nation, even a friendly one, if it came in an English vessel, should be admitted into the territory until England restored to Central America the possession of that island. I do not mean to say that they were wrong in putting forth their claims to this island—the English flag was planted upon it in a very summary way—nor that they were wrong in recommending the only means in their power to redress what they considered an injury, for, as England had not declared war with China, it would have been rash for the states of El Salvador and Los Altos to involve themselves in hostilities with that overgrown power. But no formal complaint was ever made, and no negotiation proposed. On the publication of the treaty, Mr. Chatfield, the British consul-general, who considered it disrespectful and injurious to his government, addressed a note to the vice-president, requesting a categorical answer to the question "whether the Federal government did exist or not" (precisely what I was anxious to know). But he received no answer.

Later Mr. Chatfield visited Nicaragua, and the government of that state sent him a communication requesting his mediation in settling the difficulties between the states of El Salvador and Honduras, then at war, and through him the

---

3. Quezaltenango is the capital of Los Altos, the western highlands of Guatemala, which tried to secede during the regime of Carrera.

guarantee of the Queen of England to compel the fulfilment of any treaty made between them. Mr. Chatfield, in his answer, referred to his previous letter to the vice-president, and spoke of the government as the "so-called Federal government." The correspondence was published, and increased the exasperation against Mr. Chatfield and foreigners generally; they were denounced as instigators and supporters of the revolution, their rights and privileges as residents discussed, and finally the injustice of their enjoying the protection of the government (!) without contributing to the expense of supporting it. The result was, that on the levying of a new forced loan, foreigners were included in the liability, and a peremptory order was issued requiring them, in case of refusal to pay, to leave the country in eight days. The foreigners were violently exasperated. There were not more than a dozen in the state, and most of them, being engaged in business which it would be ruinous to leave, were compelled to pay. Two or three who had wanted to leave before walked off, called themselves martyrs, threatened the vengeance of their government, and talked of the arrival of a British ship-of-war. Mr. Kilgour, a British subject, refused to pay. The authorities had orders to give him his passport to leave the state. Don Pedro Negrete, as vice-consul of France, *Encargado de Inglaterra*, presented a remonstrance. The vice-president's answer (in part but too true), as it contains the grounds of the law and shows the state of feeling existing at the time, I give in his own words:

"Strangers in these barbarous countries, as they call them, ought not to expect to have the advantage of being protected in their property without aiding the government in it. We are poor, and if, in any of the convulsions which are so frequent in new countries that have hardly begun their political career, strangers suffer losses, they at once have recourse to their governments to oblige the nations in which they come to speculate, not without knowledge of the risks, to pay them double or treble of what they have lost. This is unjust from every point of view, when they do not care with a slight loan to aid the government in its most urgent necessities. What ought the government to do? Shall it tell them, 'Away with you, I cannot secure your property'; or, 'Lend me a certain sum in order to enable me to secure it'? On the other hand, if it happens that a strong party or faction, as it is called, prevails and falls upon your property the same as upon the property of the sons of the country and upon the public rents, and you complain to your nation, she comes and blockades our ports and makes the poor nation pay a thousand per cent."

Mr. Mercher, a French merchant, was absent at the time of enforcing the contributions. Don Pedro, who was his agent under a power of attorney and in charge of his goods, refused to pay. The government insisted; Don Pedro was determined. The government sent soldiers to his house. Don Pedro said he would hoist the French flag; the chief of the state said he would tear it down. Don Pedro was imprisoned in his own house, his family excluded from him, and his food handed in by a soldier, until, finally a friend paid the money. Don Pedro contended that the majesty of France was violated in his person; the government said that the proceedings were against him as the agent of Mercher, and not as French consul; but any way, consul or agent, Don Pedro's body bore the brunt, and as this took place but two days before our arrival, Don Pedro was still in bed from the indisposition brought upon him by vexation and anxiety. We received the above, with many details, from Don Pedro's son, as an apology for his father's absence, and an explanation of the ravings we heard in the adjoining room.

In the evening I called upon the vice-president. Great changes had taken place since I saw him at Sonsonate. The troops of the Federal government had been routed in Honduras; Carrera had conquered Quezaltenango, garrisoned it with his own soldiers, destroyed its existence as a separate state, and annexed it to Guatemala. El Salvador stood alone in support of the Federal government. But Señor Vigil had risen with the emergency. The chief of the state, a bold-looking mulatto, and other officers of the government were with him. They knew that the Honduras troops were marching upon the city, and they had reason to fear they would be joined by those of Nicaragua, but they were not dismayed; on the contrary, all showed a resolution and energy I had not seen before. General Morazán, they said, was on

---

his march against Guatemala. Tired as they were of war, the people of El Salvador, Señor Vigil said, had risen with new enthusiasm. Volunteers were flocking in from all quarters with a determination that was imposing; though called out by civil war they were resolved to sustain the Federation or die under the ruins of San Salvador.

This was the first time my feelings had been at all roused. In all the convulsions of the time I had seen no flash of heroism, no high love of country. Self-preservation and self-aggrandizement were the ruling passions. It was a bloody scramble for power and place; and sometimes, as I rode through the beautiful country and saw what Providence had done for them, and how unthankful they were, I thought it would be a good riddance if they would play out the game of the Kilkenny cats.[4] This was a higher tone than I was accustomed to: the chief men of a single state, with an invading army at their door and their own soldiers away, expressing the stern resolution to sustain the Federation or die under the ruins of the capital. But they did not despair of the Republic; the Honduras troops would be repulsed at San Vicente, and General Morazán would take Guatemala. The whole subject of the revolution was discussed, and the conversation was deeply interesting to me, for I regarded it as touching matters of life and death. I could not compromise them by anything I might say, for they are all in exile, under sentence of death if they return. They did not speak in the ferocious and sanguinary spirit I afterward heard imputed to them at Guatemala, but they spoke with great bitterness of gentlemen whom I considered personal friends, and who, they said, had been before spared by their lenity; and they added, in tones that could not be misunderstood, that they would not make such a mistake again.

In the midst of this confusion, where was my government? I had traveled all over the country, led on by a glimmering light shining and disappearing, and I could not conceal from myself that the crisis of my fortune was at

---

4. Two cats which fought until nothing was left of them but their tails.

hand. All depended upon the success of Morazán's expedition. If he failed, my occupation was gone; but in this darkest hour of the Republic I did not despair. In ten years of war Morazán had never been beaten. Carrera would not dare fight him. Guatemala would fall. The moral effect would be felt all over the country: Quezaltenango would shake off its chains; the strong minority in the other states would rise; the flag of the Republic would once more wave triumphantly; and out of chaos the government I was in search of would appear.

Nevertheless, I was not so sure of it as to wait quietly till it came to me at San Salvador. The result was very uncertain, and if it should be a protracted war, I might be cut off from Guatemala without any opportunity of serving my country by diplomatic arts, and I might be prevented from prosecuting other objectives more interesting than the uncertain pursuit in which I was then engaged. The design which the captain had had in coming up to San Salvador had failed—he could not join Morazán's expedition. But he had nothing to do at the port, he was anxious to see Guatemala, and he had a stock of jewelry and other things which he might dispose of there; he was so sure of Morazán's success that he determined to go on and pay him a visit, and have the benefits of balls and other rejoicings attendant upon his triumph.

In the excitement and alarm of the place, it was very difficult to procure mules. To procure them direct for Guatemala was impossible; no one would move on that road until the result of Morazán's expedition was known. Even to get them for Sonsonate it was necessary to wait a day. That day I intended to abstract myself from the tumult of the city and ascend the volcano of San Salvador, but the next morning a woman came to inform us that one of our men had been taken by a pressgang of soldiers and was in the *cárcel*. We followed her to the place and, being invited in by the officer to pick out our man, we found ourselves surrounded by a hundred of Vigil's volunteers of every grade in appearance and character from the frightened servant boy torn from his master's door to the worst of desperadoes, some asleep on the ground, some smoking stumps of cigars, some sullen, and others perfectly reckless. Two of the supreme worst did me the honor to say they liked my looks; they called me captain and asked me to take them into my company.

Our man was not ambitious, and could do better than be shot at for a shilling a day; but we could not take him out without an order from the chief of the state. We went immediately to the office of the government, where I was sorry to meet Señor Vigil, as the subject of my visit and the secrets of the prison were an unfortunate comment upon his boasts of the enthusiasm of the people in taking up arms. With his usual courtesy, however, he directed the proper order to be made out and the names of all in my service to be sent to the captains of the different pressgangs with orders not to touch them. All day men were caught and brought in, and petty officers were stationed along the street drilling them. In the afternoon intelligence was received that General Morazán's advanced guard had defeated a detachment of Carrera's troops, and that he was marching with an accession of forces upon Guatemala. A *feu de joie* was fired in the plaza, and all the church bells rang peals of victory.

In the evening I saw Señor Vigil again and alone. He was confident of the result. The Honduras troops would be repulsed at San Vicente; Morazán would take Guatemala. He urged me to wait; he had his preparations all made, his horses ready, and, on the first notice of Morazán's entry, he intended to go up to Guatemala and establish that city once more as the capital. But I was afraid of delay, and we parted to meet in Guatemala. But we never met again. A few days afterward he was flying for his life, and is now in exile under sentence of death if he returns. The party that rules Guatemala is heaping opprobrium upon his name; but in the recollection of my hurried tour I never forget him who had the unhappy distinction of being vice-president of the Republic.

I did not receive my passport till late in the evening, and though I had given directions to the contrary, the captain's name was inserted. We had already had a difference of opinion in regard to our movements. He was not so bent as I was upon pushing on to Guatemala, and besides, I did not consider it right, in an official passport, to have the name of a partisan. Accordingly, early in the morning I went to the Government House to have it altered. The separate passports were just handed to me when I heard a clatter in the streets, and fifteen or twenty horsemen galloped into the courtyard, covered with sweat and dust, among whom I recognized Colonel Hoyas, with his noble horse so broken that I did not know him. They had ridden all night. The Honduras troops had taken San Miguel and San Vicente, and were then marching upon San Salvador. If not repulsed at Cojutepeque, that day they would be upon the capital. For four days I had been running before these troops, and now, by a strange caprice, at the prospect of actual collision, I regretted that my arrangements were so far advanced and that I had no necessity for remaining. I had a strong curiosity to see a city taken by assault, but, unfortunately, I had not the least possible excuse. I had my passport in my hand and my mules were ready. Nevertheless, before I reached Don Pedro's house, I determined to remain. The captain had his sword and spurs on and was only waiting for me. I told him the news, and uttering an exclamation of thankfulness that we were all ready, he mounted immediately. I added that I intended to remain. He refused, said that he knew the sanguinary character of the people better than I did, and did not wish to see an affair without having a hand in it. I replied, and after a short controversy, the result was as usual between two obstinate men: I would not go and he would not stay. I sent my luggage mules and servants under his charge, and he rode off, to stop for me at a hacienda on the road, while I unsaddled my horse and gave him another mess of corn.

In the meantime the news had spread, and great excitement prevailed in the city. Here there was no thought of flight; the spirit of resistance was general. The impressed soldiers were brought out from the prisons and furnished with arms, and drums beat through the streets for volunteers. On my return from the Government House I noticed a tailor on his board at work; when I passed again his horse was at the door, his sobbing wife was putting pistols in his holsters, and he was fastening on his spurs. Afterward I saw him mounted before the cuartel; he received a lance with a red flag, and then galloped off to take his place in the line. In two hours, all that the impoverished city could do was done. Vigil, the chief of the state, clerks, and household servants were preparing for the last struggle. At twelve o'clock the city was as still as death. I lounged on the shady side of the plaza, and the quiet was fearful. At two o'clock intelligence was received that the troops of San Vicente had fallen back upon Cojutepeque, and that the Honduras troops had not yet come up. An order was immediately issued to make Cojutepeque the rallying place and to send thither the mustering of the city. About two hundred lancers set off from the plaza with a feeble shout under a burning sun, and I returned to the house. The commotion subsided; my excitement died away. Just as I was regretting that I had not set out with the captain, to my surprise he rode into the courtyard. On the road he had begun to think that he had left me in the lurch, and that, as a traveling companion, he ought to have remained with me. I had no such idea, but I was glad of his return, and I mounted and left my capital to its fate, even yet uncertain whether I had any government.

Chapter IV

~~~~~~

*Contributions. La Barranca de Guaramal. Volcano of
Izalco. Depredations of Rascón. Sonsonate. News from
Guatemala. Journey continued. Aguisalco. Apaneca.
Mountain of Ahuachapán. Subterranean fires. Ahua-
chapán. Defeat of Morazán.
Confusion and terror.*

THE captain had given me a hint in the led horse which
he kept for emergencies, and I had bought one of an
officer of General Morazán, who sold him because he would
not stand fire and recommended him for a way he had of
carrying his rider out of the reach of bullets. At the distance
of two leagues we reached a hacienda where our men were
waiting for us with the luggage. It was occupied by a miserable old man alone, with a large swelling under his throat
which is very common all through this country, the same
as it is among the mountains of Switzerland.

While the men were reloading, we heard the tramp of
horses, and fifteen or twenty lancers galloped up to the
fence. The leader, a dark, stern, but respectable-looking man
about forty, in a deep voice called to the old man to get ready
and mount; the time had come, he said, when every man
must fight for his country; if they had done so before, he
told them, their own ships would be floating on the Atlantic
and the Pacific, and they would not now be at the mercy of
strangers and enemies. Altogether the speech was a good
one, and would have done for a Fourth of July oration or a
ward meeting at home; but when made from the back of a
horse by a powerful man, well armed, and with twenty
lancers at his heels, it was not pleasant in the ears of the

"strangers" for whom it was intended. Really I respected the man's energy, but his expression and manner precluded all courtesies; though he looked at us for an answer, we said nothing. When the old man answered that he was too old to fight, the officer told him to help others then to do so, and to contribute his horses or mules. This touched us again and, taking our mules aside, we left exposed and alone an object more miserable as a beast than his owner was as a man. This animal, the old man said, was his all. The officer, looking as if he would like a pretext for seizing ours, told him to give her up; and the old man, slowly untying her, without a word led her to the fence and handed the halter across to one of the lancers. They laughed as they received the old man's all, and pricking the mule with their lances, galloped off in search of more "contributions."

Unluckily, they continued on our road, and we feared that parties were scouring the whole country to Sonsonate. This brought to mind a matter that gave us much uneasiness. As the mail routes were all broken up and there was no traveling, I was made letter carrier all the way from Nicaragua. I had suffered so much anxiety from not receiving any letters myself that I was glad to serve any one that asked me; but I had been treated with great frankness by the "party" at San Salvador, and was resolved not to be the means of communicating anything to their enemies. With this view, I always asked whether the letters contained any political information, never taking them until I had been assured that they did not. But many of them were to Mr. Chatfield and the other *ingleses* in Guatemala; there was a most bitter feeling against Mr. Chatfield, and the rudeness of this really respectable-looking leader of the lancers gave us some idea of the exasperation against foreigners generally. As the latter were identified in the revolution, the directions on the letters alone might expose us to danger with any band of infuriated partisans who might take it into their heads to search us on the road. If I had had a safe opportunity, I should have sent them back to San Salvador. I could not intrust them with the old man, and we deliberated whether it was not better to return and await the crisis at the capital; but remembering our objective to get near the coast and perhaps within reach of a vessel, we determined to continue.

In about an hour we passed the same party of lancers dismounted at some distance from the road before the door of a large hacienda; some of the men were inside, and they were all, fortunately, so far off that, though we heard them hallooing at us, we could not understand what they said. Soon after we descended a wild mountain pass and entered La Barranca de Guaramal, a narrow opening with high perpendicular sides covered with bushes, wild flowers, and moss, and roofed over by branches of large trees, which crossed each other from the opposite banks. A large stream forced its way through the ravine, broken by trunks of trees and huge stones. For half a league our road lay in the bed of the stream, knee deep for the mules. In one place, on the right-hand side, a beautiful cascade precipitated itself from the top of the bank almost across the ravine. A little before dark, in a grassy recess at the foot of the bank, we encountered a pig merchant who had encamped for the night. His pigs were harnessed with straps and tied to a tree, and his wife was cooking supper; when we told him of the foraging party at the other end of the ravine, he trembled for his pigs. Some time after dark we reached the hacienda of Guaramal. There was plenty of *zacate* in an adjoining field, but we could not get any one to cut it; the major-domo was an old man, and the workmen were afraid of snakes. Aside from this, however, we fared well, and had wooden bedsteads to sleep on; in one corner was a small space partitioned off for the major-domo and his wife.

Before daylight we were in the saddle, and we rode till eleven, when we stopped at a small village to feed our mules and avoid the heat of the day. At three we again started, and toward evening I heard once more the deep rumbling noise of the volcano of Izalco, sounding like distant thunder. We passed along its base, and stopped at the same house at which I had put up on my previous visit to the volcano. The place was in a state of perfect anarchy and misrule. Since my departure, Rascón, rendered more daring by the abject policy

of the government, had entered Sonsonate, robbed the customhouse again, and laid contributions upon some of the
citizens; he had then marched to Izalco and quartered his
whole band upon the town. Unexpectedly, he had been surprised at night by a party of Morazán's soldiers; he himself
escaped in his shirt, but nineteen of his men were killed and
his band was broken up. Lately the soldiers were called off
to join Morazán's expedition, and the dispersed band
emerged from their hiding places. Some were then living
publicly in the town, perfectly lawless; they had threatened
to kill the alcalde if he attempted to disturb them, and they
kept the town in a state of terror. I was told that among those
who had reappeared was a young American *del Norte;* from
the description I recognized him as Jemmy, whom I had
put on board his ship at Acajutla. He and the other American had deserted and attempted to cross over to the Atlantic
on foot. On the way they had fallen in with Rascón's band
and joined them. The other man had been killed at the time
of the rout, but Jemmy escaped. I was happy to hear that
Jemmy, by his manners and good conduct, had made a favorable impression upon the ladies of Izalco. He had remained only three days, and whither he had gone no one
knew.

While listening to this account we heard a noise in the
street. Looking out of the window, we saw a man on the
ground, and another striking at him with a white club,
which by the moonlight looked like the blade of a broad-
sword or machete. A crowd gathered, mostly of women, who
endeavored to keep him off; but he struck among them with
blows that would have killed the man if they had hit him.
He was one of the Rascón gang, a native of the town and
known from boyhood as a bad fellow. All called him by
name, and more by entreaties than by force, they made him
desist. As he walked off with several of his companions, he
said that the man was a spy of Morazán, and that the next
time he met him he would kill him. The poor fellow was
senseless; and as the women raised up his head, we saw with
horror hairs white as snow and the face of a man of seventy.

He was all in rags, and they told us that he was a beggar and crazy. He had given no provocation whatever, but the young scoundrel, happening to fix his eyes upon him in passing, had called him a spy of Morazán and knocked him down with his club. Very soon the crowd dispersed, and the women remained to take care of the old man. These were times which required the natural charity of woman to be aided by supernatural strength. Every woman dreaded that her husband, son, or brother should cross the street at night, in the fear of quarrels and worse weapons than clubs. We saw five women, one with a candle, without a single man or boy to help them, support the old man across the street and set him up with his back against the side of the house. Afterward a woman came to the door and called to the woman in our house that if the young man passed again he would kill the old man; and the two, going out again with a candle, carried him into the courtyard of a house and locked the door.

The reader will perhaps cry shame upon us, but we went out once and were urged to retire, and two men were standing at the window all the time. It was natural to wish to break the head of the young man, but it was natural also to avoid bringing upon ourselves a gang which, though broken, was strong enough to laugh at the authorities of the town and to waylay us in the wild road we had to pass. There was one ominous circumstance in the affair: that in a town in the state of El Salvador a man dared threaten publicly to kill another because he was a partisan of Morazán showed a disaffection in that state which surprised me more than anything I had yet encountered. Our men were afraid to take the mules to water, and it was indispensable for the beasts to drink. We were cautioned against going with them, but at length, upon our standing in the doorway ready to go to their assistance, they set off with loaded pistols. When I passed through Izalco before, it had been a tranquil place.

Starting early in the morning, we arrived at Sonsonate before breakfast and rode to the house of my friend Mr. Le Nonvel. It was exactly two months ago that I had left it, and, with the exception of my voyage on the Pacific and my sickness at Costa Rica, I had not had a day of repose.

I was now within four days of Guatemala, but the difficulty of going on was greater than ever. The captain could procure no mules, no intelligence had been received of Morazán's movements, and intercourse was entirely broken off and business at a stand. The people were anxiously waiting for news from Guatemala, and nobody would set out on that road. I was very much distressed. My engagement with Mr. Catherwood was for a specific time; the rainy season was coming on, and by the loss of a month I would be prevented visiting Palenque.[1] I considered it actually safer to pass through while all was in this state of suspense than after the floodgates of war were opened; Rascón's band had prevented my passing the road before, and other Rascóns might spring up. The captain had not the same inducement to push ahead that I had. I had no desire to incur any unnecessary risk, and on the road I would have had no hesitation at any time in putting spurs to my horse; but, on deliberate consideration, my mind was so fully made up that I determined to procure a guide at any price and set out alone.

In the midst of my perplexity, a tall, thin, gaunt-looking Spaniard, whose name was Don Saturnino Tinocha, came to see me. He was a merchant from Costa Rica, who had come this far on his way to Guatemala, and who, by advice of his friends rather than by his own judgment, had been already waiting a week at Sonsonate. He was exactly in the humor to suit me, in that he was very anxious to reach Guatemala; and his views and opinions were just the same as mine. The captain was indifferent and, at all events, could not go unless he could procure mules. I told Don Saturnino that I would go at all events, and he undertook to provide for the captain. In the evening he returned with intelligence that he had scoured the town and could not procure a single mule,

---

1. An ancient Mayan city in the state of Chiapas in southern Mexico.

but he offered to leave two of his own cargoes and take the captain's, or to sell him two of his mules. I offered to lend him my horse or macho, and the matter was thus arranged. In the midst of the war rumors, the next day, which was Sunday, was one of the most quiet I passed in Central America. I was at the hacienda of Dr. Drivon, about a league from Sonsonate. This was one of the finest haciendas in the country. The doctor had imported a large sugar mill, which was not yet set up, and he was preparing to manufacture sugar upon a larger scale than any other planter in the country. He was from the island of St. Lucia. Before settling down in this out-of-the-way place, he had traveled extensively in Europe and all the West India Islands; he knew America from Halifax to Cape Horn, but he surprised me by saying that he looked forward to a cottage in Morristown, New Jersey, as the consummation of his wishes. I learned from him that Jemmy, after his disappearance from Izalco, had straggled here to this hacienda in wretched condition and sick of campaigning, and that he was now at the port on board the *Cosmopolita*, bound for Peru.

On our return to Sonsonate we were again in the midst of tumult. Two of Captain de Iriarte's passengers for Guayaquil, whom he had given up, arrived that evening direct from Guatemala, and reported that Carrera, with two thousand men, had left the city at the same time to march upon El Salvador. Carrera knew nothing of Morazán's approach; his troops were a disorderly and tumultuous mass; and at three leagues from the city, where they halted, the horses were already tired. Here our informants slipped away, and three hours afterward met Morazán's army, in good order, marching single file, with Morazán himself at their head; Morazán and all his cavalry had dismounted and were leading their horses, which were fresh and ready for immediate action. Morazán stopped them and made them show their passports and letters, and they told him of the sally of Carrera's army and of its condition. We all formed the conclusion that Morazán had attacked them the same day, defeated them, and was then in possession of Guatemala. Upon the whole, we considered the news favorable to us, as his first business would be to make the roads secure.

At three o'clock the next morning we were again in the saddle. A stream of fire was rolling down the volcano of Izalco, bright, but paler by the moonlight. The road was good for two leagues, at which distance we reached the Indian village of Aguisalco.[2] Our mules were overloaded, and one of Don Saturnino's gave out entirely. We tried to procure others, or Indian carriers, but no one would move from home. Don Saturnino loaded his saddle mule and walked; and if it had not been for his indefatigable perseverance, we should have been compelled to stop.

At one o'clock we reached Apaneca, and rode up to one of the best houses, where an old man and his wife undertook to give us breakfast. Our mules presented a piteous spectacle. Mine, which had carried my light luggage like a feather all the way from La Unión, had gone on with admirable steadiness up hill and down dale, but when we stopped she trembled in every limb, and before the cargo was removed I expected to see her fall. Nicolás and the muleteer said she would certainly die, and the faithful brute seemed to look at me reproachfully for having suffered so heavy a load to be put upon her back. I tried to buy or hire another, but all were removed one or two days' journey out of the line of march of the soldiers.

It was agreed that I should go on to Ahuachapán and endeavor to have other mules ready early the next morning; but in the meantime the captain conceived some suspicions of the old man and woman and resolved not to remain that night in the village. Fortunately, my mule revived and began to eat. Don Saturnino repeated his *'stá bueno*, with which he had cheered us through all the perplexities of the day, and we determined to set out again. Neither of us had any luggage he was willing to leave, for in all probability we would never see it again. We loaded our saddle beasts

---

2. The editor was unable to identify Aguisalco. The only place name in this part of El Salvador that bears any similarity to it is Nahuizalco, which is undoubtedly the village meant.

and walked. Immediately upon leaving the village we commenced ascending the mountain of Ahuachapán, the longest and worst in the whole road, which in the wet season required two days to cross. A steep pitch at the beginning made me tremble for the result. The ascent was about three miles; on the very crest, imbowered among the trees, was a blacksmith's shop, which in one direction commanded a view of the whole country back to the village, and in another, the slope of the mountain to the plain of Ahuachapán. The clink of the hammer and the sight of a smith's grimed face seemed a profanation of the beauties of the scene. Here our difficulties were over; the rest of our road was downhill. The road lay along the ridge of the mountain. On our right we looked down the perpendicular side to a plain two thousand feet below us; and in front, on another part of the same plain, were the lake and town of Ahuachapán.

Instead of going direct to the town, we turned round the foot of the mountain and came into a field smoking with hot springs. The ground was incrusted with sulphur and dried and baked by subterranean fires. In some places were large orifices from which steam rushed out violently and with noise; in other places were large pools or lakes, one of which, a hundred and fifty feet in circumference, of dark brown water, was boiling with monstrous bubbles three or four feet high, which Homer might have made the headwaters of Acheron. All around, for a great extent, the earth was in a state of combustion, burning our boots and frightening the horses, and we were obliged to be careful to keep the horses from falling through. At some distance was a stream of sulphur water, which we followed up to a broad basin where we made a dam with stones and bushes and had a most refreshing warm bath.

It was nearly dark when we entered the town, the frontier of the state and the outpost of danger. All were on tiptoe of expectation for news from Guatemala. Riding through the plaza, we saw a new corps of about two hundred "patriot soldiers," uniformed and equipped, at evening drill, which was a guarantee against the turbulence we had seen in Izalco. It had been Colonel Angoula, the commandant, who had

broken up the band of Rascón. Everyone we met was astonished at our purpose of going on to Guatemala, and it was
vexatious and discouraging to have ominous cautions per-
petually dinned into our ears. We rode to the house of the
widow Padilla, a friend of Don Saturnino, whom we found
in great affliction. Her eldest son, on a visit to Guatemala
on business, with a regular passport, had been thrown into
prison by Carrera, and had then been a month in confinement; and she had just learned, what had been concealed
from her, that the other son, a young man just twenty-one,
had joined Morazán's expedition. Our purpose of going to
Guatemala opened the fountain of her sorrows. She mourned
for her sons, but the case of the younger seemed to give her
most distress. She mourned that he had become a soldier;
she had seen so much of the horrors of war. Speaking as if of
a truant boy, she begged us to urge General Morazán to
send him home. She was still in black for their father, who
was a personal friend of General Morazán, and she had,
besides, three daughters, all young women, the eldest of
which, not more than twenty-three, was married to Colonel
Molina, the second in command. All her daughters were
celebrated in that country for their beauty; and though the
circumstances of the night prevented my seeing much of
them, I looked upon them all as one of the most lady-like
and interesting family groups I had seen in the country.

Our first inquiry was for mules. Colonel Molina, the son-
in-law, after endeavoring to dissuade us from continuing,
sent out to make inquiries; it was found that, although there
were none to hire, there was a man who had two to sell, and
who promised to bring them early in the morning. We had
vexations enough without adding any between ourselves;
but, unfortunately, the captain and Don Saturnino had an
angry quarrel, growing out of the breaking down of the
mules. I was appealed to by both, and in trying to keep the
peace came near having both upon me. The dispute was so
violent that none of the female part of the family appeared
in the *sala*; while it was pending Colonel Molina was called
off by a message from the commandant. In half an hour he
returned and told us that two soldiers had just entered the

town, who reported that Morazán had been defeated in his attack on Guatemala and his whole army routed and cut to pieces; he said that Morazán himself with fifteen dragoons was making his escape by way of the coast with the whole of Carrera's army in full pursuit. The soldiers were at first supposed to be deserters, but they were recognized by some of the town's people; after a careful examination and calculation of the lapse of time since the last intelligence, the news was believed to be true. The consternation it created in our little household cannot be described. Morazán's defeat was the death knell of sons and brothers. It was not a moment for strangers to offer idle consolation, and we withdrew.

Our own plans were unsettled; the very dangers I had feared had happened; the soldiers, who had been kept together in masses, were disbanded to sweep every road in the country with the ferocity of partisan war. But for the night we could do nothing. Our men were already asleep and, not without apprehensions, the captain and I retired to a room opening upon the courtyard. Don Saturnino wrapped himself in his poncho and lay down under the corridor.

None of us had undressed, but the fatigue of the day had been so great that I soon fell into a profound sleep. At one o'clock we were roused by Colonel Molina shouting in the doorway *La gente viene!* (The people are coming!) His sword glittered, his spurs rattled, and by the moonlight I saw men saddling horses in the courtyard. We sprang up in a moment, and he told us to save ourselves; *la gente* were coming, and were within two hours' march of the town. My first question was, What had become of the soldiers? But they were already marching out; everybody was preparing to flee. The Colonel intended to escort the ladies to a hiding place in the mountains, and then to overtake the soldiers.

I must confess that my first thought was "devil take the hindmost," and I ordered Nicolás, who was fairly blubbering with fright, to saddle for a start. The captain, however, objected, insisting that to fly would be to identify ourselves with the fugitives; if we were overtaken with them, we should certainly be massacred. Don Saturnino proposed to set out on our journey and go straight on to a hacienda two leagues beyond; if we met the soldiers on the road, we would appear to be travelers and, in their hurry, they would let us pass; at all events, we would avoid the dangers of a general sacking and plunder of the town. I approved of this suggestion, for the fact was, I was for anything that put us on horseback, but the captain again opposed it violently. Unluckily, he had four large, heavy trunks containing jewelry and other valuables, and no mules to carry them. I made a hurried but feeling comment upon the comparative value of life and property. But the captain said that all he was worth in the world was in those trunks; that he would not leave them; that he would not risk them on the road; and that he would defend them as long as he had life. Taking them up one by one from the corridor, he piled them inside of our little sleeping room; then he shut the door and swore that nobody should get into them without passing over his dead body.

Now I, for my own part, would have taken a quiet stripping, and I by no means approved this desperate purpose of the captain's. The fact was, I was very differently situated from him. My property was chiefly in horseflesh and muleflesh, at the moment the most desirable thing in which money could be invested; with two hour's start, I would have defied all the *Cachurecos*[3] in Guatemala to catch me. But the captain's determination put an end to all thoughts of testing the soundness of my investment; and perhaps, at all events, it was best to remain.

I entered the house, where the old lady and her daughters were packing up their valuables, and passed through to the street. The church bells were tolling with a frightful sound, and a horseman, with a red banneret on the point of his lance, was riding through the streets warning the inhabitants to flee. Horses were standing before the doors saddled and bridled, and all along men were issuing from the doors with loads on their backs, and women, with packages and bundles in their hands, were hurrying children before them. The

---

3. Stephens explains who the *Cachurecos* were in chapter II of volume I.

moon was beaming with unrivaled splendor; the women did
not scream; the children did not cry; terror was in every
face and movement, but too deep for utterance. I walked
down to the church; the cura was at the altar, receiving hurried confessions and administering the sacrament to wretched
inhabitants who left the altar to flee from the town. I saw
a poor mother searching for a missing child; but her friends,
in hoarse whispers, said, *La gente viene!* and hurried her
away. A long line of fugitives, with loaded mules interspersed, was moving from the door of the church and disappearing beneath the brow of the hill. It was the first time
I ever saw terror operating upon masses, and I hope never
to see it again.

I went back to the house. The family of Padilla had not
left, and the poor widow was still packing up. We urged
Colonel Molina to hasten; as commandant, he would be the
first victim. He knew his danger, but in a tone of voice that
told the horrors of his partisan war, he said he could not
leave behind him the young women. In a few moments all
was ready; the old lady gave us the key to the house, we
exchanged the Spanish farewell with a mutual recommendation to God, and sadly and silently they left the town.
Colonel Molina remained a moment behind. Again he urged
us to flee, saying that the enemy were robbers, murderers, and
assassins, who would pay no respect to person or character,
and that disappointment at finding the town deserted would
make them outrageous with us. He drove his spurs into his
horse, and we never saw him again. On the steps of the
church were sick and infirm old men and children, and the
cura's house was thronged with the same helpless beings.
Except for these, we were left in sole possession of the town.

It was not yet an hour since we had been roused from
sleep. We had not been able to procure any definite information as to the character of the approaching force. The alarm
was *La gente viene!* No one knew or thought of more. No
one paid any attention to us, and we did not know whether
the whole army of Carrera was approaching, or merely a
roving detachment. If the former, my hope was that Carrera
was with them, and that he had not forgotten my diplomatic

coat; I felt rejoiced that the soldiers had marched out, and that the inhabitants had fled; there could be no resistance, no bloodshed, nothing to excite a lawless soldiery. Again we walked down to the church; old women and little boys gathered around us, and wondered that we did not flee. We went to the door of the cura's house; the room was small and full of old women. We tried to cheer them, but old age had lost its garrulity; they waited their fate in silence. We returned to the house, smoked, and waited in anxious expectation. The enemy did not come, the bell ceased its frightful tolling, and after a while we began to wish they would come and let us have the thing over. We went out, and looked, and listened; but there was neither sound nor motion. We became positively tired of waiting and, since there were still two hours to daylight, we lay down and strange to say again fell asleep.

Chapter V

~~~~~~

*Approach of Carrera's forces. Terror of the inhabitants.
The flight. Surrender of the town. Ferocity of the sol-
diery. A bulletin. Diplomacy. A passport. A breakfast.
An alarm. The widow Padilla. An attack. Defeat of
Carrera's forces. The town taken by General Morazán.
His entry. The widow's son. Visit to General Morazán.
His appearance, character, etc.
Plans deranged.*

IT was broad daylight when we woke without any machete cuts and still in undisturbed possession of the town.
My first thought was for the mules; they had eaten up their
zacate and had but a poor chance for more, but I sent them
immediately to the river for water. They had hardly gone
when a little boy ran in from the church and told us that *la
gente* were in sight. We hurried back with him, and the
miserable beings on the steps, with new terrors (supposing
that we were friends of the invaders) begged us to save
them. Followed by three or four trembling boys, we
ascended to the steeple and saw the *Cachurecos* at a distance
descending the brow of a hill in single file, their muskets
glittering in the sunbeams. We saw that it was not the whole
of Carrera's army but, apparently, only a pioneer company.
But they were too many for us, and the smallness of their
numbers gave them the appearance of a lawless predatory
band. They had still to cross a long plain and ascend the hill
on which the town was built. The bell rope was in reach of
my hand; I gave it one strong pull, and telling the boys to
sound loud the alarm, I hurried down from the steeple. As

we passed out of the church, we heard loud cries from the old women in the house of the cura; and the old men and children on the steps asked us whether they would be murdered.

The mules had not returned. Afraid of their being intercepted in the street, I ran down a steep hill toward the river, but, on meeting them, I hurried back to the house. While doing so I saw at the extreme end of the street a single soldier moving cautiously. Watching carefully every house, as if suspecting treachery, he advanced with a letter directed to Colonel Angula. The captain told him that he must seek Angula among the mountains. We inquired the name of his commanding officer and how many men he had. Then, telling him that there was no one to oppose him, we forthwith surrendered the town. The man could hardly believe that it was deserted. General Figoroa did not know it; he had halted a short distance away, afraid to make the attack at night, and was at the moment expecting immediate battle. The general himself could not have been much better pleased at avoiding it than we were. The envoy returned to him, and in a short time we saw at the extreme end of the street the neck of a horse protruding from the cross street on the left. A party of cavalry armed with lances followed; they formed at the head of the street, looking about them carefully as if still suspecting an ambush. In a few moments General Figoroa, mounted on a fierce little horse, came up, leading the van. He was without uniform but wore pistols and a basket-hilted sword, which gave him a warlike appearance. We took off our hats as he approached our door, and he returned the salute. About a hundred lancers followed him two abreast, with red flags on the ends of their lances and pistols in their holsters. In passing, one ferocious-looking fellow looked fiercely at us, and grasping his lance, cried *Viva Carrera!* We did not answer it immediately, and he repeated it in a tone that brought forth a response which was louder and more satisfactory from the spite with which it was given. The next man repeated the cry, and the next; before we were aware of our position, every lancer that passed, in a tone of voice regulated by the gentleness or the ferocity of his disposition, and sometimes with a most threatening scowl, put to us as a touchstone *Viva Carrera!* The infantry were worse than the lancers in appearance, being mostly ragged, half-naked Indians, with old straw hats; they were barefooted and armed with muskets and machetes, many with old-fashioned Spanish blunderbusses. They vied with each other in sharpness and ferocity; sometimes they actually leveled their pieces, crying at us *Viva Carrera!* We were taken completely unawares. There was no escape. I believe they would have shot us down on the spot if we had refused to echo the cry. I compromised with my dignity by answering no louder than the urgency of the case required, but I never passed through a more trying ordeal. Don Saturnino had had the prudence to keep out of sight; but the captain, who had intended to campaign against these fellows, never flinched, and when the last man passed he added an extra *Viva Carrera!* I again felt rejoiced that the soldiers had left the town and that there had been no fight. It would have been a fearful thing to fall into the hands of such men, with their passions roused by resistance and bloodshed.

When they reached the plaza, they gave a general shout of *Viva Carrera!* and stacked their arms. In a few minutes a party of them came down to our house and asked for breakfast and, when we could not give them that, they begged a *medio*, or sixpence. By degrees others came in until the room was full. They were really no great gainers by taking the town; they had had no breakfast, and the town was completely stripped of eatables. We inquired the news from Guatemala, and bought from them several copies of the *Parte Official* of the Supreme Government, headed *Viva la Patria! Viva el General Carrera!* We read that "The enemy has been completely exterminated in his attack upon this city, which he intended to devastate. The tyrant Morazán flies terrified, leaving the plaza and streets strewed with corpses sacrificed to his criminal ambition. The principal officers associated in his staff have perished. . . . *Eternal glory to the Invincible Chief, General Carrera,* and the valiant troops under his command."

The soldiers told us that Carrera, with three thousand men, was in full pursuit. In a little while the demand for sixpences became so frequent that, afraid of being supposed to have *mucha plata,* we walked to the plaza to present ourselves to General Figoroa and settle the terms of our surrender, or, at all events, to "define our position." We found him at the cabildo, quite at home with a parcel of officers, white men, mestizos, and mulattoes; they were smoking and interrogating some old men from the church as to the movements of Colonel Angula and the soldiers, the time of their setting out, and the direction they had taken. He was a young man—all the men in that country were young—about thirty-two or three, dressed in a snuff-colored cloth roundabout jacket with pantaloons of the same color; off his warhorse and away from his assassin-like band, he had very much the air of an honest man.

It was one of the worst evils of this civil war that no respect was paid to the passports of opposite parties. The captain had only his El Salvador passport, which was here worse than worthless. Don Saturnino had a variety from partisan commandants, and upon this occasion made use of one from a colonel under Ferrera. The captain introduced me by the title of *Señor Ministro de Norte America,* and I made myself acceptable by saying that I had been to El Salvador in search of a government, but had not been able to find any. The fact is, although I was not able to get into regular business, I was practising diplomacy on my own account all the time; and in order to define at once and clearly our relative positions, I undertook to do the honors of the town and invited General Figoroa and all his officers to breakfast. This was a bold stroke, but Talleyrand could not have touched a nicer chord. They had not eaten anything since noon the day before, and I believe they would have evacuated their empty conquest for a good breakfast all round. They accepted my invitation with a promptness that put an end to my small stock of provisions for the road. General Figoroa confirmed the intelligence of Morazán's defeat and flight, and Carrera's pursuit, and the "invincible chief" would perhaps have been somewhat surprised at the pleasure I promised myself in meeting him.

With a very few moments' interchange of opinion, we made up our minds to get out of this frontier town as soon as possible, and again to go forward. I had almost abandoned ulterior projects, and looked only to personal safety. To go back, we reasoned, would carry us into the very focus of war and danger. The El Salvador people were furious against strangers, and the Honduras troops were invading them on one side and Carrera's hordes on the other. To remain where we were meant certain exposure to attacks from both parties. By going on we would meet Carrera's troops, and if we passed them we left war behind us. We had but one risk, and that would be tested in a day. Under this belief, I told the general that we designed proceeding to Guatemala, and that it would add to our security to have his passport. It was the general's first campaign. He was then only a few days in service, having set off in a hurry to get possession of this town and cut off Morazán's retreat. He was flattered by the request and said that his passport would be indispensable. His aide and secretary, who had been clerk in an apothecary's shop in Guatemala and therefore understood the respect due to a *ministro*, said that he would make it out himself. I was all eagerness to get possession of this passport. The captain, in courtesy, said we were in no hurry; but I dismissed courtesy and said that we were in a hurry, that we must set out immediately after breakfast. I was afraid of postponements, delays, and accidents, and in spite of impediments and inconveniences, I persisted till I got the secretary down at the table, where, without any trouble and by a mere flourish of the pen, he made me *ministro plenipotenciario*. The captain's name was inserted in the passport, General Figoroa signed it, and I put it in my pocket, after which I breathed more freely.

We returned to the house, and in a few minutes the general, his secretary, and two mulatto officers came over to breakfast. It was very considerate of them that they did not bring more. Our guests cared more for quantity than quality, and this was the particular in which we were most deficient. We had plenty of chocolate, a stock of bread for the road, and some eggs that were found in the house. We put on the table all that we had, and gave the general the seat of honor at the head. One of the officers preferred sitting away on a bench and eating his eggs with his fingers. It is unpleasant for a host to be obliged to mark the quantity that his guests eat, but I must say I was agreeably disappointed. If I had been breakfasting with them instead of vice versa, I could have astonished them as much as their voracious ancestors did the Indians. The breakfast was a neat fit; there was none over and, I believe, nothing short.

There was but one unpleasant circumstance attendant upon it, and that was when General Figoroa requested us to wait an hour until he could prepare despatches to Carrera advising him of his occupation of Ahuachapán. I was extremely anxious to get away while the game was good. Of General Figoroa and his secretary we thought favorably, but we saw that he had no control over his men, and that as long as we were in the town, we should be subject to their visits, inquiries, and importunities, from which some difficulties might arise. At the same time, despatches to Carrera would be a great security on the road. Don Saturnino undertook to set off with the luggage, and we, glad of the opportunity of traveling without any encumbrance, charged him to push on as fast as he could and not stop for us because we would overtake him.

In about an hour we walked over to the plaza for the despatches, but unluckily found ourselves in a new scene of confusion. Figoroa was already in the saddle, the lancers were mounting in haste, and all were running to arms. A scout had brought in word that Colonel Angoula with soldiers of the town was hovering on the skirt of the mountain, and our friends were hurrying to attack him. In a moment the lancers were off on a gallop, and the ragged infantry snatched up their guns and ran after them, keeping up with the horses. The letter to Carrera was partly written, and the aide-de-camp asked us to wait, telling us that the affair would soon be over. He was left in command of about seventy or eighty men, and we sat down with him under the corridor of the cuartel. He was several years younger than Figoroa and more intelligent; he seemed very amiable except on political matters, in which case he was savage against the Morazán party. He was gentlemanly in his manners, but his coat was out at the elbows and his pantaloons were torn. He said he had a new frock coat, for which he had paid sixteen dollars, but which he wished to sell since it did not fit him. I afterward spoke of him to one of Morazán's officers, whom I would believe implicitly except in regard to political opponents, and he told me that this same secretary stole a pair of pantaloons from him, and he had no doubt the coat was stolen from somebody else.

There was no order or discipline among the men, the soldiers lay about the cuartel, joined in the conversation, or strolled through the town as they pleased. The inhabitants had fortunately carried away everything portable; two or three times a foraging party returned with a horse or mule, and once they were all roused by an alarm that Angoula was returning upon the town from another direction. Immediately all snatched up their arms, and at least one half, without a moment's warning, took to their heels. We had a fair chance of having the town again upon our hands, but the alarm proved groundless. We could not, however, but feel uncomfortable at the facility with which our friends abandoned us, and at the risk we ran of being identified with them. Three brothers, the only lancers who did not go out with Figoroa, were disposed to cultivate an acquaintance with us; they were young and athletic white men, the best dressed and best armed in the company and swaggering in their manner. They told us that they purposed going to Guatemala, but I shrank from them instinctively and eluded their questions as to when we intended to set out. I heard later that they were natives of the town who had been compelled to leave it on account of their notorious character as assassins. One of them, as we thought in a mere spirit of bravado, provoked a quarrel with the aide-de-camp; he strutted before the cuartel and in the hearing of all said that they were under no man's orders, that they had only joined

General Figoroa to please themselves, and that they would do as they thought proper.

In the meantime, a few of the townsmen who had nothing to lose, among them an alguacil, finding there was no massacring, had returned or emerged from their hiding places. We procured a guide to be ready the moment General Figoroa should return, went back to the house, and to our surprise found the widow Padilla there. She had been secreted somewhere in the neighborhood, and had heard, by means of an old woman servant, of the general's breakfasting with us and of our intimacy with him. We inquired for her daughters' safety, but not where they were, for we had already found that we could answer inquiries better when we knew nothing.

We waited till four o'clock and, hearing nothing of General Figoroa, made up our minds that we should not get off till evening. We therefore strolled up to the extreme end of the street, where Figoroa had entered and where stood the ruins of an old church. We sat on the foundation walls and looked through the long and desolate street to the plaza, where there were a few stacks of muskets and some soldiers. All around were mountains, and among them rose the beautiful and verdant volcano of Chingo. While we were sitting there, two women ran past and, telling us that the soldiers were returning in that direction, hid themselves among the ruins. We turned down a road and were intercepted on a little eminence, where we were obliged to stop and look down upon them as they passed. We saw that they were irritated by an unsuccessful day's work, and that they had found *aguardiente,* for many of them were drunk. A drummer on horseback, and so tipsy that he could hardly sit, stopped the line to glorify General Carrera. Very soon they commenced the old touchstone, *Viva Carrera!* and one fellow, with the strap of his knapsack across his naked shoulders, again stopped the whole line and, turning round with a ferocious expression, said, "You are counting us, are you?"

We disappeared, and by another street got back to the house. We waited a moment and then, determined to get out of the town and sleep at the first hacienda on the road,

we left the house to go again to General Figoroa for his
despatches; but before reaching it we saw new confusion in
the plaza, a general remounting and rushing to arms. As
soon as General Figoroa saw us, he spurred his horse down
the street to meet us and told us, in great haste, that General
Morazán was approaching and almost upon the town. He
had that moment received the news, and was going out to
attack him. He had no time to sign the dispatches, and while
he was speaking the lancers galloped past. He shook hands,
bade us good-by, *hasta luego* (until presently), asked us to
call upon Carrera in case we did not see him again, and
dashing down the line, put himself at the head of the lancers.
The foot soldiers followed in single file on a run, carrying
their arms as was most convenient. In the hurry and excitement we forgot ourselves till we heard some flattering
epithets and saw two fellows shaking their muskets at us
with the expression of fiends. Although hurried on by those
behind, they cried out ferociously, *Estos pícaros otra vez!*
(These rascals again!)

The last of the line had hardly disappeared before we
heard a volley of musketry, and in a moment the fifty or
sixty men left in the plaza snatched up their arms and ran
down a street opening from the plaza. Very soon a horse
without a rider came clattering down the street at full speed;
three others followed, and in five minutes we saw thirty or
forty horsemen with our friend Figoroa at their head dash
across the street, all running for their lives; but in a few
moments they rallied and returned. We were walking toward the church to ascend the steeple when a sharp volley
of musketry rolled up the street on that side; and before we
got back into the house there was firing along the whole
length of the street. Knowing that a chance shot might kill
a non-combatant, we secured the doors and windows. Finally,
however, as the firing was sharp and the balls went beyond
us and struck the houses on the opposite side, with an old
servant woman (what had become of the widow I do not
know) we retired into a small room on the courtyard, with
delightful walls and a bullet-proof door three inches thick.
Shutting the door, we listened valiantly in utter darkness.

Here we considered ourselves out of harm's way, but we had
serious apprehensions for the result. The spirit on both sides
was to kill; giving quarter was not thought of. Morazán's
party was probably small, but they would not be taken without a desperate fight, and from the sharpness of the firing
and the time occupied, there was probably a sanguinary affair
going on. Our quondam friends, roused by bloodshed,
wounds, and loss of companions, without anyone to control
them, would be very likely to connect "those rascals" with
the arrival of Morazán. I will not say that we wished they
might all be killed, but we did wish that their bad blood
might be let out, and that was almost the same thing. In
fact, I did most earnestly hope never to see their faces again.
I preferred being taken by any roving band in the country
than by them, and I never felt more relieved than when we
heard the sound of a bugle. It was the Morazán blast of
victory; and, though sounding fiercely the well-known notes
of *degollar, degollar* (cutthroat, cutthroat), it was music to
our ears.

Very soon we heard the tramp of cavalry, and leaving our
hiding place, we returned to the *sala* and heard a cry of
Viva la Federación! This was a cheering sound. It was now
dark. We opened the door an inch or two, but a lancer riding
by struck it wide open with his lance and asked for water.
We gave him a large calabash, which another took from his
hands. We threw open the door and kept two large calabashes on the sill, and the soldiers, as they passed, took a
hasty draught. Asking a question of each, we learned that
it was General Morazán himself with the survivors of his
expedition against Guatemala. Our house was well known;
many of the officers inquired for the family, and an aide-de-
camp gave notice to the servant woman that Morazán himself intended stopping there. The soldiers marched into the
plaza, stacked their arms, and shouted *Viva Morazán!* In
the morning the shout had been *Viva Carrera!* None cried
Viva la Patria!

There was no end to our troubles. In the morning we surrendered to one party, and in the evening we were captured
out of their hands by another; probably before daylight

Carrera would be upon us. There was only one comfort: the fellows who had broken our rest the night before and scared the inhabitants from their homes, were now looking out for lodgings in the mountains themselves. I felt sorry for Figoroa and his aide, and, on abstract principles, for those killed. As for the rest, I cared but little what became of them.

In a few moments a party of officers came down to our house. For six days they had been in constant flight through an enemy's country, changing their direction to avoid pursuit and only stopping to rest their horses. Entering under the excitement of a successful skirmish, they struck me as the finest set of men I had seen in the country. Figoroa had come upon them so suddenly that General Morazán, who rode at the head of his men, had two bullets pass by his head before he could draw his pistol, and he had a narrower escape than in the whole of his bloody battle in Guatemala. Colonel Cabañas, a small, quiet, gentlemanly man, the commander of the troops massacred in Honduras, struck the first blow; he broke his sword over a lancer, and, wresting the lance out of the owner's hands, ran it through his body, but he was himself wounded in the hand. A tall, gay, rattling young man, who was wiping warm blood from off his sword and drying it on his pocket handkerchief, mourned that he had failed to cut off their retreat; and a quiet middle-aged man, wiping his forehead, drawled out that if their horses had not been so tired they would have killed every man. Even they talked only of killing; taking prisoners was never thought of. The verb *matar* (to kill) with its inflections was so continually ringing in my ears that it made me nervous.

In a few minutes the widow Padilla, who I am inclined to believe was secreted somewhere in the neighborhood, knowing of General Morazán's approach, rushed in crying wildly for her sons. All answered that the eldest was with them; all knew her, and one after another put his right arm respectfully over her shoulder and embraced her. But the young man who was wiping his sword drove it into its scabbard and, catching her up in his arms, lifted her off the floor and whirled her about the room. The poor old lady, half laughing and half crying, told him he was as bad as ever, and continued asking for her sons. At this moment a man about forty, whom I had noticed before as the only one without arms, with a long beard, pale and haggard, entered from the courtyard. The old lady screamed, rushed toward him, and fell upon his neck, and for some moments rested her head upon his shoulder. This was the one who had been imprisoned by Carrera. General Morazán had forced his way into the plaza, broken open the prisons, and liberated the inmates; and when he was driven out this son made his escape. But where was her younger and dearer son? The young man answered that he had escaped and was safe. The old lady looked at him with distrust and, calling him by his Christian name, told him he was deceiving her; but he persisted and swore that her son had escaped, that he himself had given him a fresh horse; that he had been seen outside the barrier, and that he was probably concealed somewhere and would soon make his appearance. The other officers had no positive knowledge. One had seen him at such a time, and another at such a time during the battle; but all agreed that the young man ought to know best, for their posts had been near each other. But this ardent, reckless young man, the dearest friend of her son, and loving her as a mother, told me afterward that she deserved to have one night's comfort, and that she would know the truth soon enough. And the older brother, having narrowly escaped from death himself and looking as if smiles had been forever driven from his face, told me he had no doubt his mother's darling was killed. Long after I learned that he did manage to escape and to return to his mother's home.

During these scenes the captain and I were not unnoticed. The captain found among the officers several with whom he had become acquainted at the port, and he learned that others had made their last campaign. In the first excitement of meeting them, he determined to turn back and follow their broken fortunes; but, luckily for me, those trunks had gone on. He felt that he had had a narrow escape. Among those who had accompanied General Morazán were the former secretary of state and war, and all the principal officers, civil and military, of the shattered general government. They had heard of my arrival in the country, and I had been expected at San Salvador. I was known to them all by reputation, and very soon personally, particularly to Colonel Saravia with whom I became acquainted. He was a young man about twenty-eight, handsome, brave, and accomplished in mind and manners, with an enthusiastic attachment for General Morazán, from whom, he said, Providence seemed to turn the bullets away.

I had often heard of Colonel Saravia in Guatemala, and his case shows the unhappy rending of private and social ties produced by these civil wars. His father had been banished by the Liberal Party eight years before, and was at this time a general in the Carlist [1] service in Spain. His mother and three sisters lived in Guatemala, and I had visited at their house perhaps oftener than at any other in that city. They lived near the plaza, and while Morazán had possession of it, the Colonel had run home to see them; and, in the midst of a distracted meeting rendered more poignant by the circumstance of his being joined in an attack upon his native city, he had been called away to go into action. His horse had been shot from under him, and he himself had been wounded; he escaped with the wreck of the army. His mother and sisters knew nothing of his fate, and he said, what I was sure was but too true, that they would have dreadful apprehensions about him. He begged me, immediately on my arrival in Guatemala, to visit them and inform them of his safety.

In the meantime, General Morazán, apprehensive of a surprise from Carrera during the night, sent word that he would sleep in the plaza. Escorted by Colonel Saravia, I went to pay my respects to him. From the time of his entry I felt perfectly secure, and I never had a moment of apprehension from unruly soldiers. For the first time I saw something like discipline. A sentinel was pacing the street leading from the plaza to prevent the soldiers straggling into the town; but the poor fellows seemed to have no disposition

---

1. The Carlists were supporters of Don Carlos de Bourbon (1788–1855), pretender to the Spanish throne.

for straggling. The town was stripped of everything; even the poor horses had no food. Some of the soldiers were gathered at the window of the cabildo, each in his turn holding up his hat for a portion of hard corn bread; some were sitting around fires eating this miserable fare; but most were stretched on the ground already asleep. It was the first night they had lain down except in an enemy's country.

General Morazán, with several officers, was standing in the corridor of the cabildo; a large fire was burning before the door, and a table stood against the wall with a candle and chocolate cups upon it. He was about forty-five years old, five feet ten inches high, thin, with a black mustache and a week's beard. He wore a military frock coat buttoned up to the throat, and carried a sword. His hat was off, and the expression of his face was mild and intelligent. Though still young, for ten years he had been the first man in the country and the eighth president of the Republic. He had risen and had sustained himself by military skill and personal bravery; he always led his forces himself; and though he had been in innumerable battles and often wounded, he had never been beaten. A year before, the people of Guatemala of both parties had implored him to come to their relief as the only man who could save them from Carrera and destruction. At that moment he added another to the countless instances of the fickleness of popular favor. After the expiration of his term he had been elected chief of the State of El Salvador, which office he had resigned. He was now acting as commander-in-chief under the Federal government. Denounced personally, and the Federation under which he served disavowed, he had marched against Guatemala with fourteen hundred men. He had forced his way into the plaza of the capital, where forty of his oldest officers and his eldest son were shot down by his side. Cutting his way through masses of human flesh, with about four hundred and fifty men then in the plaza, he had made his escape.

I was presented to him by Colonel Saravia. From the best information I could acquire, and from the enthusiasm with which I had heard him spoken of by his officers, and, in fact, by everyone else in his own state, I had conceived al-

most a feeling of admiration for General Morazán, and
my interest in him was increased by his misfortunes. I was
really at a loss how to address him, but, while my mind
was full of his ill-fated expedition, his first question was
whether his family had arrived in Costa Rica and whether I
had heard anything of them. I did not tell him what I then
thought, that his calamities would follow all who were connected with him, and that probably his wife and daughters
would not be permitted an asylum in that state. But it spoke
volumes that, at such a moment, with the wreck of his followers before him and the memory of his murdered companions fresh in his mind, in the overthrow of all his hopes
and fortunes, his heart had turned to his domestic relations.
He expressed his sorrow for the condition in which I saw
his unhappy country and regretted that my visit was at such
a most unfortunate moment. He spoke of Mr. DeWitt [2]
and the relations of his country with ours, and of his regret
that our treaty had not been renewed, and that it could not
be done now; but these things were not in my mind. Feeling
that he must have more important business, I remained but
a short time and then returned to the house.

The moon had risen, and I was now extremely anxious to
set out, but our plans were entirely deranged. The guide
whom we had engaged to conduct us to the Río Paz was
missing, and no other could be found; in fact, not a man
could be induced, either by promises or threats, to leave the
town that night for fear of falling in with the routed troops.
Several of the officers took chocolate with us, and at the head
of the table sat a priest with a sword by his side. I had breakfasted men who would have been happy to cut their throats,
and they were now hiding among the mountains or riding
for life. If Carrera came, my new friends would be scattered. They all withdrew early to sleep under arms in the
plaza, and we were left with the widow and her son. There
followed a distressing scene of inquiries and forebodings by
the widow for her younger son, which the elder could only

2. Charles G. DeWitt was the American chargé d'affaires in Guatemala just prior to Stephens visit.

get rid of by pleading excessive fatigue and begging to be permitted to go to sleep. It was rather singular, but it had not occurred to us before to inquire about the dead and wounded in the skirmish. There were none of the latter; all who fell were lanced, and the dead were left on the ground. The elder son had been in the rear of the Morazán party; the fire had been scattering, but on the line by which he entered the town he had counted eighteen bodies.

Chapter VI

〰〰〰〰〰〰〰〰〰〰〰〰〰〰〰〰〰〰〰〰〰〰〰〰〰〰〰〰〰

*Visit from General Morazán. End of his career. Procuring
a guide. Departure for Guatemala. Fright of the people.
The Río Paz. Hacienda of Palmita. A fortunate escape.
Hacienda of San José. An awkward predicament. A kind
host. Rancho of Jocotilla. Oratorio and León. Río de los
Esclavos. The village. Approach to Guatemala. Arrival
at Guatemala. A sketch of the wars. Defeat of
Morazán. Scene of massacre.*

IN the morning, to our surprise, we found several shops
open and people in the street; many persons had been
concealed somewhere in the neighborhood and had returned
as soon as they knew of Morazán's entry. The alcalde reappeared and our guide was found, but he would not go
with us; he told the alcalde that he could kill him on the
spot, that he would rather die where he was than later by
the hands of the *Cachurecos.*

While I was taking chocolate, General Morazán called
upon me. Our conversation was longer and more general
than before. I did not ask him his plans or purposes, but
neither he nor his officers exhibited despondency. Once a
reference was made to the occupation of Santa Ana[1] by
General Cascara and, with a spirit that reminded me of
Claverhouse in *Old Mortality,*[2] he said, "We shall visit that
gentleman soon." He spoke without malice or bitterness
of the leaders of the Central Party, and of Carrera as an
ignorant and lawless Indian from whom the party that was
now using him would one day be glad to be protected. He

1. A city in El Salvador not far from the Guatemalan border.
2. The novel by Sir Walter Scott.

referred with a smile to a charge current among the *Cachurecos* that an effort had been made by him to have Carrera assassinated; he said that a great parade had been made of this charge, with details of time and place, and that it was generally believed. He had supposed the whole story a fabrication, but in retreating from Guatemala he had accidentally found himself in the very house where the attempt was said to have been made. The man of the house told him that Carrera had offered outrage to a member of his family, and that he himself had stabbed him, as was supposed, mortally. Carrera, in order to account for his wounds and turn away inquiries from the cause, had fastened the blame upon Morazán, and so the story flew all through the country. One of Morazán's officers accompanied the story with details of the outrage, and I felt very sure that, if Carrera ever fell into his hands, Morazán would shoot him on the spot.

With the opinion that he entertained of Carrera and his soldiers, he of course considered it unsafe for us to go on to Guatemala. But I was exceedingly anxious to set out and, as the captain's trunks had gone on, he was equally anxious. Carrera might arrive at any moment, in which case we might again change owners, or, at all events, be the witnesses of a sanguinary battle, for Morazán would defend the frontier town of his own state to the death.

I told General Morazán my wish and purpose, and of my difficulty in procuring a guide. He said that an escort of soldiers would expose us to certain danger, that even a single soldier without his musket and cartridge box (these being the only distinguishing marks of a soldier) might be recognized, but that he would send for the alcalde and procure us some trusty person from the town. I bade him farewell with an interest greater than I had felt for any man in the country. Little did we then know the calamities that were still in store for him; that very night most of his soldiers deserted, having been kept together only by the danger to which they were exposed while in an enemy's country. With the rest he marched to Sonsonate, seized a vessel at the port, manned her with his own men, and sent her to La Libertad, the port of San Salvador. He then marched to the capital, where the people who had for years idolized him in power turned their backs upon him in misfortune and received him with open insults in the streets. With many of his officers, who were too deeply compromised to remain, he embarked for Chile. Suffering from confinement on board a small vessel, he stopped in Costa Rica and asked permission for some of them to land. He did not ask it for himself, for he knew it would be refused. Leaving some of them behind, he went on to join his family in Chile.

Amid the fierceness of party spirit it was impossible for a stranger to form a true estimate of the character of a public man. The great outcry against General Morazán was due to his hostility to the church and his forced loans. For his hostility to the church there is the justification that it is at this day a pall upon the spirit of free institutions, degrading and debasing instead of elevating the Christian character; and for forced loans constant wars may plead. His worst enemies admit that he was exemplary in his private relations, and, what they consider no small praise, that he was sanguinary. He is now fallen and in exile, probably forever, and under sentence of death if he returns. All the truckling worshippers of a rising sun are blasting his name and memory, but I verily believe, and I know I shall bring down upon me the indignation of the whole Central Party by the assertion, I verily believe they have driven from their shores the best man in Central America.

The population of the town was devoted to General Morazán. An old man brought to us his son, a young man about twenty-two, as a guide, but when he learned that we wanted him to go with us all the way to Río Paz, he left us, as he said, to procure a horse. We waited nearly an hour, and then the old man reappeared with a little boy about ten years old, dressed in a straw hat and shirt, and mounted on a bare-backed horse. The young man had disappeared and could not be found; in fact, he was afraid to go, and it was thought this little boy would run less risk. I was never much disturbed by general reports of robbers or assassins, but there was palpable danger in meeting any of the routed troops. These men were desperate by defeat and assassin-like in disposition; they had not been very amiable to us before, and now, from having seen us lounging about the town at that inauspicious moment and likely to connect us with the movements of Morazán, I believed that they would murder us if we fell into their hands. But, on the other hand, they had surely not let the grass grow under their feet; they had probably been flying all night in apprehension of pursuit, and, shunning the main road, had perhaps already crossed the Río Paz. Once in Guatemala, they would disperse to their own villages. Besides, the rout had been so total that they were probably escaping three or four together, and would be as likely to run from us as we from them. At all events, it was better to go than wait till Carrera came upon the town.

With these calculations and really uncomfortable feelings, we bade farewell to some of the officers who were waiting to see us off, and at nine o'clock set out. Descending from the tableland on which the town is built, we entered an open plain over which we could see to a great distance, and which would furnish, if necessary, a good field for the evolutions of our cavalry. We passed a lake near Ahuachapán,[3] the beauty of which under other circumstances would have attracted our admiration. As our little guide seemed at fault, we stopped at a hut to inquire the road. The people were afraid to answer any questions. Figoroa's soldiers and Morazán's had passed by, but they did not know it; they could not tell whether any fugitive soldiers had passed, and they only knew the road to the Río Paz. It was easy to see that they thought of nothing else; but they said they were poor people and at work all the time, and did not know what was going on.

In half an hour we met three Indians with loads of pottery on their backs. The poor fellows pulled off their hats, and trembled when we inquired if there were any routed soldiers on the road before us. It occurred to us that such an inquiry would expose us to the suspicion of being officers of Morazán

---

3. The lake is called La Laguna del Llano.

in pursuit, and that, if we met anyone, we had better ask no questions.

Beyond this there were many roads, all of which, the boy said, led to the Río Paz; but he had never been there before and did not know the right one. We followed one which took us into the woods, and soon commenced descending. The road was broken, stony, and very steep; we descended rapidly, and soon it was manifest that no horses had passed on this road for a long time before. Trees lay across it so low that we dismounted and were obliged to slip our high-peaked saddles to pass under them. It was evidently an old cattle path, now disused even by cattle. After descending for some distance, I proposed to return. My only argument was that it was safer; we knew we were wrong and might get down so low that our physical strength would not carry us back. The captain said that I had chosen this path, and if we had followed his advice we should have been safe, but now it was impossible to return. We had an angry quarrel, and fortunately, in consideration of my having led us into the difficulty, I gave way, and very soon we were cheered by hearing below us the rushing of the river. After a most difficult descent we reached the bank but at a point where there was no fording place and no path on the opposite side.

The river itself was beautiful. The side which we had descended was a high and almost perpendicular mountain, and on both sides trees spread their branches over the water. It was called the River of Peace but was now the dividing line of deadly war, the boundary between Guatemala and El Salvador. The inhabitants of the opposite side were in enemy country, and the routed troops, both of Morazán and Figoroa, had fled to it for refuge. Riding some distance up the stream, we worked our way across, and on the opposite side found a *guacal*, or drinking shell, which had probably been left there by some fleeing soldier. We drank from it as if it had been intended for our use, and left it on the bank for the benefit of the next comer.

We were now in the State of Guatemala, on the banks of a wild river, without any visible path; and our situation was rather more precarious than before, for here the routed soldiers would· consider themselves safe, and probably many, after a day and night of toil and fighting, would lie down to rest. We were fortunate in regard to a path, for, riding a short distance through the woods along the bank of the river, we struck one which turned off to the left and terminated in the *camino real* leading from the regular fording place. Here we dismissed our little guide, and set out on the main road. The face of the country was entirely changed; it was broken and stony, and we saw no one till we reached the hacienda of Palmita.

This too seemed desolate. We entered the yard and did not see a single person till we pushed open the door of the house. The proprietor was an old gentleman, opposed to Morazán; he sat in the *sala* with his wife's saddle and his own and two bundles of bed and bedding packed upon the floor, ready for a start. He seemed to feel that it was too late, and with an air of submission answered our questions, and then asked us how many men we had with us. It was amusing that, while half frightened to death ourselves, we carried terror wherever we went. We relieved him by inquiring about Don Saturnino and our luggage, then remounted and rode on.

In an hour we reached the hacienda del Cacao, where Don Saturnino was to sleep. Owing to the position of the ground, we came suddenly upon the front of the house, and saw under the piazza three *Cachureco* soldiers eating tortillas. They saw us at the same moment, snatched up their muskets, and ran; but suddenly one stopped and leveled at us a blunderbuss. The barrel looked as big as a church door, and seemed to cover both the captain and me. We were in awful danger of being shot by mistake when one of them rushed back, knocked up the blunderbuss, and cried out, *"Amigos, los ingleses!"* This amiable and sensible young *Cachureco* vagabond was one of those who had paid us a visit to beg a breakfast and a *medio*. Probably there never was a sixpence put out at better interest. He had seen us intimate with Figoroa, and taught by his betters to believe that General Morazán was a cutthroat and murderer, and not conceiving that we could be safe with him, he considered us sharers of the same danger, and inquired how we had escaped. As it turned out, we were extremely happy to meet with these particular soldiers; another party might have received us very differently. They also relieved us in an important point, for they told us that most of the routed soldiers had fled on the Santa Ana road. Don Saturnino, who had passed the night at this hacienda, had set out very early in the morning.

The soldiers returned to finish their meal, after which, giving their thanks in payment, they set out again with us. They had a good horse, which they had stolen on the road and which they said paid them very well for the expedition, and they rode him bareback by turns. Passing El Cacao their appearance created a sensation, for they brought the first intelligence of the rout of Figoroa. This was ominous news, for all had considered Morazán completely crushed by his defeat at Guatemala. In his retreat he had avoided the villages, and they did not know that he had escaped with so strong a force. We endeavored to procure a guide, but not a man could be induced to leave the village, so we rode on. In a short time it began to rain; the road was very stony, and we crossed a high, bleak volcanic mountain. Late in the afternoon the captain conceived suspicions of the soldiers, and we rode on very unceremoniously, leaving them behind. About five o'clock we avoided the road that led to a village and, taking el Camino de los Partidos, which was very rough and stony, we soon came to a place where there were branches from the road, and we were at a loss which to take. Our course lay through a broad valley bounded by two ranges of mountains; we felt sure that our road did not cross either of these ranges, and they were our only guides. A little before dark we passed beyond the range of mountains and on our right saw a road leading into the woods. Presently we heard the sound of a bell and saw through the trees a hacienda, to arrive at which we had to go on for some distance and then turn back by a private road.

The hacienda was situated in a large clearing, with *cocina* and sheds and a large sugar mill. Twenty or thirty workmen, principally Indians, were assembled to give an account of their day's work and receive orders for the next. Our appearance created a great sensation. The proprietors of the hacienda, two brothers, were standing in the door while we were talking with the men, and we rode up and asked permission to stop there for the night. The elder assented, but with an embarrassment that showed the state of alarm and suspicion existing in the country. The gentlemen wore the common hacienda dress; the interior was miserably poor, but it had a hammock and two rude frames with matting over them for beds. There was a small room adjoining, in which was the wife of one of them with a child. The proprietors were men of education and intelligence and thoroughly acquainted with the condition of the country; we told them what had happened at Ahuachapán, and that we were hurrying on to Guatemala. We had supper at a small table placed between the hammock and one of the beds; the meal consisted of fried eggs, *frijoles,* and tortillas, as usual without knife, fork, or spoon.

After supper our elder host was called out, but in a few minutes he returned; closing the door, he told us that there was great excitement among the workmen on our account. They did not believe our story of going to Guatemala, for a woman had seen us come in from the Guatemala road; they believed that we were officers of Morazán retreating from the attack on Guatemala and endeavoring to escape into El Salvador. Here was a ground of suspicion we had not anticipated. The gentleman was much agitated; he regretted that he was obliged to violate the laws of hospitality, but said we knew the distracted state of the country and the frenzy of party spirit. He himself was against Morazán but his men were violent *Cachurecos* who at this moment were capable of committing any outrage. He said that he had incurred great peril by receiving us for a moment under his roof, and begged us, both for our own sake and his, to leave his house, adding that, even if we were of those unfortunate men, our horses would be brought up and we should go away unharmed, but more he could not promise. Now if we had really been the fugitives he supposed us, we should have been no doubt very thankful for his kindness; but to be turned out by mistake on a dark night in unknown country, and without any guide, was almost as bad as coming at us with a blunderbuss. Fortunately, he was not a suspicious man; if he had been another Don Gregorio we should have "walked Spanish." [4] More fortunately still, my pertinacity had secured Figoroa's passport; it was the only thing that could have cleared our character. I showed it to him, pointing to the extra flourish which the secretary had made of *plenipotenciario*, and I believe he was not more astonished at finding who had honored him by taking possession of his house than he was pleased that we were not Morazán's officers. Though an intelligent man, he had passed a retired life on his hacienda. He had heard of such a thing as a *ministro plenipotenciario*, but had never seen one. My accouterments and the eagle on my hat sustained the character, and he called in the major-domo and two leading men on the hacienda, read to them the passport, and explained to them the character of a *ministro plenipotenciario*. Meanwhile I sat up on the bed with my coat off and hat on to show the eagle, and the captain suppressed all partialities for Morazán and talked of my intimacy with Carrera. The people are so suspicious that, having once formed an idea, they do not willingly abandon it, and it was uncertain whether all this would satisfy them; but our host was warm in his efforts, the major-domo was flattered by being made the medium of communicating with the men, and his influence was at stake in satisfying them. It was one of Talleyrand's maxims never to do today what you can put off till tomorrow. On this occasion at least of my diplomatic career I felt the benefit of the old opposite rule. From the moment I saw Figoroa I had an eye only to getting a passport from him, and I did not rest until I had it in my pocket. If we had waited to receive this with his letters, we should now have been in a bad position. If we had escaped immediate violence, we should have been taken to the village, shut up in the cabildo, and exposed to all the dangers of an ignorant populace at that moment excited by learning the success of Morazán and the defeat of Figoroa.

---

4. That is, they would have been hustled off the premises by force.

In setting out, our idea had been that, if taken by the *Cachurecos*, we should be carried up to Guatemala; but we found that there was no accountability to Guatemala. The people were in a state to act entirely from impulses; and nothing could induce any party of men to set out for Guatemala, or under any circumstances to go farther than from village to village.

Having satisfied the men, the major-domo promised us a guide before daylight for the next village. At three o'clock we were wakened by the creaking of the sugar mill. We waited till daylight for a guide, but as none came we bade farewell to our kind host and set out alone. The name of the hacienda is San José, but in the hurry of my movements I never learned the name of the proprietor. In the constant revolutions of Central America, it may happen that he will one day be fleeing for his life; in his hour of need, may he meet a heart as noble as his own.

At a distance of five leagues we reached the rancho of Jocotilla, where Don Saturnino and our men had slept. The road lay in a magnificent ravine, with a fine bottom land and noble mountain sides. We passed through the straggling settlements of Oratorio and León,[5] mostly single huts, where several times we saw women snatch up their children and run into the woods at sight of us. Bury the war knife and this valley would be equal to the most beautiful in Switzerland. At twelve o'clock we came upon four posts with a thatched roof occupied by a scouting party of *Cachureco* soldiers. We would have been glad to avoid them, but they could not have judged so from the way in which we shouted *Amigos!* We inquired for Carrera and said that we expected to meet him on the road, that Figoroa had told us he was coming, and that Figoroa had entered Ahuachapán; taking special good care not to tell them that Figoroa had been driven out, we bade them good-by and hurried on.

At twelve o'clock we reached the Río de los Esclavos, a wild and noble river, the bridge across which is the greatest

---

5. At present, there is no such town in Guatemala.

structure in Central America, a memorial of the Spanish dominion. We crossed it and entered the village, a mere collection of huts standing in a magnificent situation on the bank of the river looking up to a range of giant mountains on the other side which were covered to the top with noble pines. The miserable inhabitants were insensible to its beauties, but there were reasons to make them so. Every hostile expedition between Guatemala and El Salvador passed through their village. Twice within one week Morazán's party had done so; the inhabitants carried off what they could and, locking their doors, fled to the mountains. The last time, Morazán's army was so straitened for provisions and pressed by fear of pursuit that huts had been torn down for firewood, and bullocks slain and eaten half raw in the street without bread or tortillas.

At two we set off again, and from the village entered a country covered with lava. At four we reached the hacienda of Coral de Piedra, situated on the crest of a stony country, looking like a castle, very large with a church and village; although it was raining, we did not stop, for the whole village seemed to be intoxicated. Opposite one house we were hailed by a *Cachureco* officer, so tipsy that he could hardly sit on his horse, who came at us and told us how many of Morazán's men he had killed. A little before dark, riding through a forest in the apprehension that we were lost, we emerged suddenly from the woods, and saw towering before us the great volcanoes of Agua and Fuego; at the same moment we were hailed by the joyful shouts of Don Saturnino and our men. They had encamped in a small hut on the borders of a large plain, and the mules had been turned out to pasture. Don Saturnino had been alarmed about us, but he had followed our parting injunction to go on, because, if any accident had happened, he could be of more service in Guatemala. They had not met Morazán's army, having been at a hacienda off the road when it passed, and in their hurried progress, they had not heard of the rout of Figoroa.

The rancho contained a single small room barely large enough for the man and woman who occupied it, but there was plenty of room out of doors. After a rough ride of more than fifty miles, with the most comfortable reflection of being but one day from Guatemala City, I soon fell asleep.

The next morning one of the mules was missing, and we did not get off till eight o'clock. Toward evening we descended a long hill and entered the plain of Guatemala City. It looked beautiful; I never thought I should be so happy to see it again. I had finished a journey of twelve hundred miles, and the gold of Peru could not have tempted me to undertake it again. At the gate the first man I saw was my friend Don Manuel Pavón. I could but think: if Morazán had taken the city, where would he be now? Carrera was not in the city; he had set out in pursuit of Morazán, but on the road he had received intelligence which induced him to turn off for Quezaltenango. I learned with deep satisfaction that not one of my acquaintances was killed, and, as I afterward found, not one of them had been in the battle.

I gave Don Manuel the first intelligence he had received of General Morazán. Not a word had been heard of him since he left Antigua. Nobody had come up from that direction; the people were still too frightened to travel, and the city had not recovered from its spasm of terror. As we advanced I met acquaintances who welcomed me back to Guatemala. I was considered as having run the gauntlet for life, and escape from dangers created a bond between us. I could hardly persuade myself that the people who received me so cordially, and whom I was really glad to meet again, were the same whose expulsion by Morazán I had considered probable. If he had succeeded, not one of them would have been there to welcome me. Repeatedly I was obliged to stop and tell again of the affair of Ahuachapán: how many men Morazán had; what officers; whether I spoke to him; how he looked and what he said. I introduced the captain and each of us had his circle of listeners. The captain, as a slight indemnification for his forced *Viva Carrera's* on the road, and feeling a comparative security for liberty of speech now that he was once more among civilized and well-dressed people, said that if Morazán's horses had not been so tired, every man of Figoroa's would have been killed. Unhappily, I could not but see that our news would have been more acceptable if we could have reported Morazán completely prostrated, or wounded, or even dead.

As we advanced I could perceive that the sides of the houses were marked by musket balls, and the fronts on the plaza were fearfully scarified. My house was near the plaza, and three musket balls picked out of the woodwork as a sample of the battle had been saved for my inspection. In an hour after my arrival I had seen nearly all my old friends. Engrossed by my own troubles, I had not imagined the full extent of theirs. I cannot describe the satisfaction with which I found myself once more among them, and for a little while, at least, at rest. I still had anxieties: I had no letters from home and Mr. Catherwood had not arrived; but I had no uneasiness about him, for he was not in the line of danger and, when I lay down, I had the comfortable sensation that there was nothing to drive me forward the next day. The captain took up his abode with me. It was an odd finale to his expedition against Guatemala, but, after all, it was better than remaining at the port.

Great changes had taken place in Guatemala since I had left, and it may not be amiss here to give a brief account of what had occurred in my absence. The reader will remember the treaty between Carrera and Guzmán, the general of the State of Los Altos,[6] by which the former surrendered to the latter four hundred old muskets. Since that time Guatemala had adopted Carrera (or had been adopted by him, I hardly know which) and, on the ground that the distrust formerly entertained of him no longer existed, Carrera demanded a restitution of the muskets to him. The State of Los Altos refused. This state was at that time the focus of Liberal principles, and Quezaltenango, the capital, was the asylum of Liberals banished from Guatemala. Apprehending, or pretending to apprehend, an invasion from that state, and using the restitution of the four hundred worthless muskets

---

6. The western highlands of Guatemala.

as a pretext, Carrera marched against Quezaltenango with one thousand men. The Indians, believing that he came to destroy the whites, assisted him. Guzmán's troops deserted him, and Carrera with his own hands took him prisoner. Sick and encumbered with a greatcoat, Guzmán had been in the act of dashing his horse down a deep ravine to escape. Carrera sent to Guatemala Guzmán's military coat, which had the names of Omoa, Trujillo, and other places where Guzmán had distinguished himself in the service of the Republic labeled on it, with a letter to the government, stating that he was sending the coat as a proof that he had taken Guzmán. A gentleman told me that he saw this coat on its way; he saw it stuck on a pole and paraded by an insulting rabble around the plaza of Antigua. After the battle, Carrera marched to the capital, deposed the chief of the state and other officers, garrisoned it with his own soldiers, and, not understanding the technical distinctions of state lines, destroyed its existence as a separate state, annexing it to Guatemala, or, rather, to his own command.

In honor of his distinguished services, public notice was given that on Monday the seventeenth he would make his triumphal entry into Guatemala. And on that day he did enter, under arches erected across the streets, amid the firing of cannon, waving of flags, and music. General Guzmán, who was personally known to all the principal inhabitants, and who but a year before had hastened at their piteous call to save them from the hands of this same Carrera, was placed sidewise on a mule, with his feet tied under him; his face was so bruised, swollen, and disfigured by stones and blows of machetes that he could not be recognized. Prisoners were tied together with ropes; and the chief of the state, secretary of state, and secretary of the constituent assembly rode by Carrera's side in this disgraceful triumph.

General Guzmán was one of those who had later been liberated from prison by General Morazán. He had escaped from the plaza with the remnant of his forces, but, unable to endure the fatigues of the journey, he had been left behind, secreted on the road. General Morazán told me that, in consequence of the cruelty exercised upon Guzmán and the horrible state of anxiety in which he was kept, reason had deserted its throne, and his once strong mind was gone.

From this time the city settled into a volcanic calm, quivering with apprehensions of an attack by General Morazán, a rising of the Indians, and a war of castes, and startled by occasional rumors that Carrera intended to bring Guzmán and the prisoners out into the plaza and shoot them. On the fourteenth of March intelligence was received from Figoroa that General Morazán had crossed the Río Paz and was marching against Guatemala. This swallowed up all other apprehensions. Carrera was the only man who could protect the city. On the fifteenth he marched out with nine hundred men toward Arazola, leaving the plaza occupied by five hundred men. Great gloom hung over the city. The same day Morazán arrived at the Coral de Piedra, eleven leagues from Guatemala. On the sixteenth, the soldiers commenced erecting parapets at the corners of the plaza; many Indians came in from the villages to assist and Carrera took up his position at the Aceytuna,[7] a league and a half from the city. On the seventeenth, Carrera rode into the city, and with the chief of the state and others, went around to visit the fortifications and rouse the people to arms. At noon he returned to the Aceytuna, and at four o'clock intelligence was received that Morazán's army was descending the Cuesta de Pinula, the last range before reaching the plain of Guatemala. The bells tolled the alarm, and great consternation prevailed in the city.

Morazán's army slept that night on the plain. Before daylight he marched upon the city and entered the gate of Buena Vista. He had left all his cavalry and part of his infantry at the Plaza de Toros and on the heights of Calvario under Colonel Cabanes to watch the movements of Carrera. With seven hundred men he occupied the Plaza of Guadaloupe, depositing his park, equipage, a hundred women (more or less of whom always accompany an expedition in that coun-

---

7. The editor was unable to identify a place by this name. The historian Bancroft calls this place *Aceituno*, which also eludes further identification.

try), and all his train in the Hospital of San Juan de Dios. From here he sent Pérez and Rivas, with four or five hundred men, to attack the central plaza. Passing up a street which descended from the center of the city, while covered by the brow of the hill they climbed over the yard wall of the Church of Escuela de Cristo and passed through the church into the street opposite the mint in the rear of one side of the plaza. Twenty-seven Indians had been engaged at the moment in making a redoubt at the door, and twenty-six bodies were found on the ground, nine killed and seventeen wounded. Entering the mint, the invaders were received with a murderous fire along the corridor; but, forcing their way through, they broke open the front portal and rushed into the plaza. The plaza was occupied by the five hundred men left by Carrera and two or three hundred Indians, who fell back and closed up near the porch of the cathedral; but in a few moments they all fled, leaving the plaza with all their ammunition in the possession of the assailants. Rivera Paz and Don Luis Batres, the chief and secretary of the state, were in the plaza at the time, and but few other white citizens. Carrera did not want white soldiers, and would not permit white men to be officers; many of them had presented themselves in the plaza, but they were told that there were no arms.

In the meantime, Carrera, strengthened by masses of Indians from the villages around, attacked the division on the heights of Calvario. Morazán, with the small force left at San Juan de Dios, went to the assistance of Cabanes. The battle lasted an hour and a half, fierce and bloody, and fought hand to hand. Morazán lost some of his best officers. Sánchez was killed by Sotero Carrera, a brother of the general. Carrera and Morazán met, and Carrera says that he cut Morazán's saddle nearly in two. Morazán was routed; he was pursued so closely that he could not take up his equipage and, having lost three hundred muskets, four hundred men killed, wounded, and prisoners, and all his baggage, he hurried on to the plaza. At ten o'clock his whole force was penned up in the plaza, surrounded by an immense mass of Indian soldiers, and fired upon from all the corners.

Manning the parapets and stationing pickets on the roofs of the houses, he kept up a galling fire in return.

Pent up in this fearful position, Morazán had time to reflect. But a year before he had been received with ringing of bells, firing of cannon, joyful acclamations, and deputations of grateful citizens, as the only man who could save them from Carrera and destruction. Among the few white citizens in the plaza at the time of the entry of the soldiers was a young man who was taken prisoner and brought before General Morazán. The latter knew him personally, and inquired for several of his old partisans by name, asking whether they were not coming to join him. The young man answered that they were not, and Morazán and his officers seemed disappointed. No doubt he had expected a rising of citizens in his favor, and again to be hailed as a deliverer from Carrera. In San Salvador I had heard that he had received urgent solicitations to come up to Guatemala City; but, whatever had been contemplated, there was no manifestation of any such intention; on the contrary, the hoarse cry was ringing in his ears, *Muera el tirano! Muera el General Morazán!* Popular feeling had undergone an entire revolution, or else it was kept down by the masses of Indians who came in from the villages around to defend the city against him.

In the meantime the fire slackened, and at twelve o'clock it died away entirely; but the plaza was strewed with dead, dense masses choked the streets, and at the corners of the plaza the soldiers, with gross ribaldry and jests, insulted and jeered at Morazán and his men. The firing ceased only from want of ammunition, Carrera's stock having been left in Morazán's possession. Carrera, in his eagerness to renew the attack, sat down to make cartridges with his own hands.

The house of Mr. Hall, the British vice-consul, was on one of the sides of the plaza. Mr. Chatfield, the consul-general, was at Escuintla, about twelve leagues distant, when intelligence was received of Morazán's invasion. He mounted his horse, rode up to the city, and hoisted the English flag on Mr. Hall's house, which was to Morazán's soldiers the most conspicuous object on the plaza. Carrera himself was hardly more obnoxious to them than Mr. Chatfield. A picket of soldiers was stationed on the roof of the house commanding the plaza on the one side and the courtyard on the other. Orellana, the former minister of war, who was on the roof, cut into the staff with his sword, but desisted on a remonstrance from the courtyard that it was the house of the vice-consul.

At sundown the immense mass of Indians who now crowded the city fell on their knees and set up the Salve, or Hymn to the Virgin. Orellana and others of Morazán's officers had let themselves down into the courtyard, and were at the moment taking chocolate in Mr. Hall's house. Mrs. Hall, a Spanish lady of the city, asked Orellana why he did not fall on his knees; and he answered, in jest, that he was afraid his own soldiers on the roof would take him for a *Cachureco* and shoot him. But, it is said, to Morazán the noise of this immense chorus of voices was appalling, bringing home to him a consciousness of the immense force assembled to crush him, and for the first time he expressed his sense of the danger they were in. The prayer was followed by a tremendous burst of *Viva la Religión! Viva Carrera! y Muera el General Morazán!* and the firing commenced more sharply than before. It was returned from the plaza, and for several hours it continued without intermission.

At two o'clock in the morning Morazán made a desperate effort to cut his way out of the plaza, but was driven back behind the parapets. The plaza was strewed with dead. Forty of his oldest officers and his eldest son had been killed. At three o'clock he stationed three hundred men at three corners of the plaza, directed them to open a brisk fire, threw all the powder into the fountain, and while attention was directed to these points, sallied by the other corner and left them to their fate. I state this on the authority of the Guatemala official account of the battle—of course I heard nothing of it at Ahuachapán—and if true, it is a blot on Morazán's character as a soldier and as a man. He escaped from the city with five hundred men, and strewing the road with wounded and dead, at twelve o'clock arrived at Antigua. Here he was urged to proclaim martial law and to make another attack on the city; but he answered No, that blood enough had been shed. He entered the cabildo, and, it is said, wrote a letter to

Carrera recommending the prisoners to mercy. Baron Ma-
helin, the French consul-general, related to me an anecdote
which does not, however, seem probable. He said that Morazán had laid his glove on the table and requested the alcalde to give it to Carrera as a challenge and to explain its
meaning to him. From Antigua he continued his retreat by
the coast until I met him at Ahuachapán.

In the meantime Carrera's soldiers poured into the plaza
with a tremendous *feu de joie*, and kept up a terrible firing
in the air till daylight. Then they commenced searching for
fugitives, and a general massacre took place. Colonel Arias,
lying on the ground with one of his eyes out, was bayoneted
to death. Pérez was shot. Marescal, concealed under the cathedral, was dragged out and shot. Padilla, the son of the
widow at Ahuachapán was found on the ground; while begging a Centralist whom he knew to save him, he had been
killed with bayonets. The unhappy fugitives were brought
into the plaza two, three, five, and ten at a time. Carrera
stood pointing with his finger to this man and that, and
everyone that he indicated was removed a few paces from
him and shot. Major José Viera and several of the soldiers
on the roof of Mr. Hall's house let themselves down into
the courtyard, but Carrera sent for all who had taken refuge
there. Viera was taking chocolate with the family, and he
gave Mrs. Hall a purse of doubloons and a pistol to take
care of for him. They were delivered up with a recommendation to mercy particularly in behalf of Viera; but a few moments later Mr. Skinner entered the house and said that he
saw Viera's body in the plaza. Mr. Hall could not believe
it; he walked round the corner, and, but a few paces from
his own door, saw Viera lying on his back, dead. In this
scene of massacre the Padre Zezena, a poor and humble
priest, exposed his own life to save his fellow beings. Throwing himself on his knees before Carrera, he implored him to
spare the unhappy prisoners, exclaiming that they were
Christians like themselves; by his importunities and prayers he induced Carrera to desist from murder and to send the
wretched captives to prison.

Carrera and his Indians had the whole danger and the
whole glory of defending the city. The citizens, who had

most at stake, took no part in it. The members of the government who were most deeply compromised fled or remained shut up in their houses. It would be hard to analyze the feelings with which they straggled out to gaze upon the scene of horror in the streets and in the plaza, and as they saw on the ground the well-known faces and mangled bodies of the leaders of the Liberal Party. There was one overpowering sense of escape from immense danger, and the feeling of the Central government burst out in its official bulletin: "Eternal glory to the invincible chief General Carrera and the valiant troops under his command!"

In the morning, as at the moment of our arrival, this subject was uppermost in every one's mind; no one could talk of anything else, and each one had something new to communicate. In our first walk through the streets our attention was directed to the localities, and everywhere we saw marks of the battle. Vagabond soldiers accosted us, begging *medios,* pointing their muskets at our heads to show how they shot the enemy, and boasting how many they had killed. These fellows made me feel uncomfortable, and I was not singular; but if there was a man who had a mixture of uncomfortable and comfortable feelings, it was my friend the captain. He was for Morazán; he had left La Unión to join his expedition, left San Salvador to pay him a visit at Guatemala and partake of the festivities of his triumph, and left Ahuachapán because his trunks had gone on before. Ever since his arrival in the country he had been accustomed to hear Carrera spoken of as a robber and assassin and the *noblesse* of Guatemala ridiculed, and all at once he found himself in a hornet's nest. He now heard Morazán denounced as a tyrant, his officers as a set of cutthroats banded together to assassinate personal enemies, rob churches, and kill priests; they had met the fate they deserved, and the universal sentiment was, "so perish the enemies of Guatemala." The captain had received a timely caution. His story, that Morazán would have killed every man of Figoroa's if the horses had not been so tired, had circulated; it was considered very partial, and special inquiries were made as to who that captain was. He was compelled to listen and assent, or say nothing. On the road he was an excessively loud talker; he spoke the language perfectly and, with his admirable arms and horse equipments, he always made a dashing entree into a village. He was called *muy valinte* (very brave). But here he was a subdued man, attracting a great deal of attention, but without any of the éclat which had attended him on the road, and with a feeling that he was an object of suspicion and distrust. But he had one consolation that nothing could take away: he had not been in the battle, or, to use his own expression, he might now be lying on the ground with his face upward.

In the afternoon, unexpectedly, Mr. Catherwood arrived. He had passed a month at Antigua, and had just returned from a second visit to Copán; he had also explored other ruins, of which mention will be made hereafter. In our joy at meeting we tumbled into each other's arms, and in the very first moment resolved not to separate again while in that distracted country.

Chapter VII

~~~~~~

Ruins of Quiriguá. Visit to them. Los Amates. Pyramidal structure. A colossal head. An altar. A collection of monuments. Statues. Character of the ruins. A lost city. Purchasing a ruined city.

TO recur for a moment to Mr. Catherwood, who during my absence had not been idle. When I reached Guatemala the first time from Copán, I had made it my business to inquire particularly for ruins. I did not meet a single person who had ever visited those of Copán, and but few who took any interest whatever in the antiquities of the country. Fortunately, a few days after my arrival, Don Carlos Meany, a Trinidad Englishman long resident in the country, who was proprietor of a large hacienda and extensively engaged in mining operations, made one of his regular business visits to the capital. Besides a thorough acquaintance with all that concerned his own immediate pursuits, this gentleman possessed much general information respecting the country, and a curiosity which circumstances had never permitted him to gratify in regard to antiquities. He told me of the ruins of Quiriguá on the Motagua River near Encuentros, the place at which we slept the second night after crossing Mico Mountain. He had never seen them, and I hardly believed it possible they could exist, for at that place we had made special inquiries for the ruins of Copán, and had not been informed of any others. I became satisfied, however, that Don Carlos was a man who did not speak at random. He told us that the ruins were on the estate of

Señor Payes,[1] a gentleman of Guatemala lately deceased, from whom he had learned of their existence. He had taken such interest in the subject as to inquire for and obtain the details of particular monuments.

Three sons of Señor Payes had succeeded to his estate, and at my request Don Carlos called with me upon them. Neither of the sons had ever seen the ruins or even visited the estate, an immense tract of wild land which had come into their father's hands many years before for a mere trifle. They said their father had visited it once and they, too, had heard him speak of these ruins. Lately the spirit of speculation had reached that country; and because of its fertility and position on the bank of a navigable river contiguous to the ocean, the tract had been made the subject of a prospectus, to be sold on shares in England. The prospectus set forth the great natural advantages of the location, and the inducements held out to emigrants were stated in terms and phrases that might have issued from a laboratory in New York before the crash.[2] The Señores Payes were in the first stage of anticipated wealth, and talked in the familiar strains of city builders at home. They were roused by the prospect of any indirect addition to the value of their real estate and, since two of them were then making arrangements to visit the tract, they immediately proposed that I should accompany them.

Mr. Catherwood, on his road from Copán, had fallen in with a person at Chiquimula who told him also of such ruins, with the addition that Colonel Galindo was then at work among them. Being in the neighborhood, he had had some idea of going to visit them; but, being much worn with his labors at Copán and knowing that the story was untrue as regarded Colonel Galindo, whom he knew to be in a different section of the country, he was incredulous as to the whole. We had some doubt whether the ruins themselves would repay the labor of searching for them, but as there

---

1. This unusual proper name may be Stephens' version of Páez, which is fairly common in Guatemala.
2. The panic of 1837.

was no occasion for him to accompany me to El Salvador,
it was agreed that during my absence he should, with the
Señores Payes, go to Quiriguá, which he accordingly did.

The reader must now go back to Encuentros, the place at
which we slept the second night of our arrival in the country.
From this place Mr. Catherwood and the Señores Payes embarked in a canoe about twenty-five feet long and four broad,
dug out of the trunk of a mahogany tree. After descending
for two hours, they disembarked at Los Amates, near El
Pozo, on the main road from Izabal to Guatemala. This was
the place at which we had breakfasted on the second morning of our arrival in the country, and where now the Señores
Payes were obliged to wait two or three days. The place was
a miserable collection of huts and scant of provisions; the
people drank a muddy water at their doors rather than take
the trouble of going to the river.

It was a fine morning after a heavy rain when they set
off again for the ruins. After a ride of about half an hour,
and over an execrable road, they again reached Los Amates.
The village was pleasantly situated on the bank of a river
and elevated about thirty feet. The river was here about two
hundred feet wide, and fordable in every part except for a
few deep holes. Generally it did not exceed three feet in
depth, and in many places was not so deep; but below it was
said to be navigable to the sea for boats not drawing more
than three feet of water. They embarked in two canoes dug
out of cedar trees, and proceeded down the river for a couple
of miles, where they took on board a negro man named Juan
Lima and his two wives. This black scoundrel, as Mr. Catherwood marks him down in his notebook, was to be their
guide. After proceeding two or three miles farther, they
stopped at a rancho on the left side of the river and, passing
through two cornfields, entered a forest of large cedar and
mahogany trees. The path was exceedingly soft and wet and
covered with decayed leaves, and the heat very great. Continuing through the forest toward the northeast, in three-
quarters of an hour they reached the foot of a pyramidal
structure like those at Copán, with the steps in some places
perfect. They ascended to the top, a distance of about twenty-

five feet; descending by steps on the other side, they came at
a short distance beyond to a colossal head two yards in diameter which was almost buried by an enormous tree and
covered with moss. Near it was a large altar, so covered with
moss that it was impossible to make anything out of it. The
two were within an enclosure.

Retracing their steps across the pyramidal structure, and
proceeding to the north about three or four hundred yards,
they reached a collection of monuments of the same general
character as those at Copán, but twice or three times as high.

The first was about twenty feet high, five feet six inches
on two sides, and two feet eight on the other two. The front,
which was well preserved, represented the figure of a man;
the back, which was much defaced, that of a woman. The
sides were covered with hieroglyphics in good preservation,
but in low relief, and of exactly the same style as those at
Copán.

Another monument near by (figure 1 facing page 146) was
twenty-three feet out of the ground, with figures of men on
the front and back, and hieroglyphics in low relief on the
sides; it was surrounded by a base projecting fifteen or sixteen feet from it.

At a short distance, standing in the same position as regards the points of the compass, was an obelisk or carved
stone, twenty-six feet out of the ground, and probably six or
eight feet under.[3] It was leaning twelve feet two inches out
of the perpendicular, and seemed ready to fall; it was probably prevented from doing so only by a tree that had grown
up against it and the large stones around the base. The side
toward the ground represented the figure of a man, very
perfect and finely sculptured. The upper side seemed to be
the same, but it was so hidden by vegetation as to make
identification somewhat uncertain. The other two sides contained hieroglyphics in low relief. In size and sculpture this
was the finest monument there.

A statue ten feet high was lying on the ground, covered
with moss and herbage, and another about the same size lay

---

3. A reproduction of the engraving of this obelisk is included in
the earlier editions of *Incidents of Travel*. . . .

with its face upward. Four others stood erect, about twelve feet high, but not in a very good state of preservation; several altars were so covered with herbage that it was difficult to ascertain their exact form. One of them was round and situated on a small elevation within a circle formed by a wall of stones. In the center of the circle, reached by descending very narrow steps, was a large round stone, with the sides sculptured in hieroglyphics; it was covered with vegetation and supported on what seemed to be two colossal heads. All these monuments were at the foot of a pyramidal wall, near each other, and in the vicinity of a creek which empties into the Motagua. Besides these, they counted thirteen fragments, and doubtless many others may yet be discovered.

At some distance from them is another monument, nine feet out of the ground, and probably two or three under, with the figure of a woman on the front and back; the two sides were richly ornamented but without hieroglyphics.

The next day the negro promised to show Mr. Catherwood eleven square columns which were higher than any he had seen and which stood in a row at the foot of a mountain. For three hours the negro dragged him through the mud, but when Mr. Catherwood found by the compass that he was constantly changing his direction, and knowing that the man, notoriously a bad fellow, was armed with pistols and indignant at the owners of the land for coming down to look after their squatters, he became suspicious of him and insisted upon returning. The Payes were engaged with their own affairs and, having no one to assist him, Mr. Catherwood was unable to make any thorough exploration or any complete drawings.

The general character of these ruins is the same as those at Copán. The monuments are much larger, but they are sculptured in lower relief, less rich in design, and more faded and worn; they were probably of a much older date.[4]

Of one thing there is no doubt: a large city once stood there; its name is lost, its history unknown. Except for a

4. On the contrary, the monuments are of more recent date. Quiriguá was founded later than Copán.

notice which was taken from Mr. Catherwood's notes and inserted by the Señores Payes in a Guatemala paper which found its way also to this country and Europe, no account of its existence has ever before been published. For centuries it has lain as completely buried as if covered with the lava of Vesuvius. Every traveler from Izabal to Guatemala has passed within three hours of it; we ourselves had done the same; and yet, there it lay, like the rock-built city of Edom, unvisited, unsought, and utterly unknown.

The morning after Mr. Catherwood returned, I called upon the only one of the Payes brothers then in Guatemala, and opened a negotiation for the purchase of these ruins. Besides their entire newness and immense interest as an unexplored field of antiquarian research, the monuments were but about a mile from the river, the ground was level to the bank, and the river from that place was navigable; the city might be transported bodily and set up in New York. I expressly stated (and my reason for doing so will be obvious) that I was acting in this matter on my own account, that it was entirely a personal affair. But Señor Payes considered me as acting for my government, and he said, what I am sure he meant, that if his family was as it had been once, they would be proud to present the whole to the United States. In his country, he said, the ruins were not appreciated, and he would be happy to contribute to the cause of science in ours had they not been impoverished by the convulsions of the country; at all events, he could give me no answer till his brothers returned in two or three days. Unfortunately, as I believe, for both of us, Señor Payes consulted with the French consul-general, who put an exaggerated value upon the ruins, referring him to the expenditure of several hundred thousand dollars by the French government in transporting one of the obelisks of Luxor from Thebes to Paris. Probably, before the speculating scheme referred to, the owners would have been glad to sell the whole tract, consisting of more than fifty thousand acres, with everything on it, known and unknown, for a few thousand dollars. I was anxious to visit the ruins myself, and learn with more certainty the possibility of their removal, but I was afraid of increasing the extravagance of his notions. His brothers did not arrive, and one of them unfortunately died on the road. I had not the government for paymaster, and it might be necessary to throw up the purchase on account of the cost of removal. But I left an offer with Mr. Savage, the result of which is still uncertain; I trust, however, that by the time these pages reach the hands of the reader, two of the largest monuments will be on their way to this city.[5]

5. Mr. Stephens, unfortunately, was doomed to disappointment. For details of his negotiations, *see* Appendix.

Chapter VIII

~~~~~~

Reception at the Government House. The captain in trou-
ble. A change of character. Arrangements for journey to
Palenque. Arrest of the captain. His release. Visit from
a countryman. Dangers in prospect. Last stroll through
the suburbs. Hospital and cemetery of San Juan de Dios.
Fearful state of the country. Last interview with Carrera.
Departure from Guatemala. A Don Quixote. Ciudad
Vieja. Plain of Ciudad Vieja. Volcanoes, plains, and
villages. San Andrés Itzapa. Dangerous
road. A molino.

THE next day I called upon the chief of the state. At
this time there was no question of presenting credentials; I was received by him and all gentlemen connected
with him without any distrust or suspicion, and more as one
identified with them in feelings and interests than as a foreign agent. I had seen more of their country than anyone
present, and spoke of its extraordinary beauty and fertility,
its volcanoes and mountains, its immense resources and the
great canal which might make it known to all the civilized
world, if they would let the sword rest and be at peace
among themselves. Some of the remarks in these pages will
perhaps be considered harsh, and a poor return for the kindness shown to me. My predilections were in favor of the
Liberal Party, not only because they sustained the Federation, but because they gave me a chance for a government;
but I have a warm feeling toward many of the leading members of the Central Party. If I speak harshly, it is of their
public and political character only; and if I have given offence, I regret it.

As I was leaving the Government House a gentleman
followed me and asked me who that captain was that had

accompanied me, adding, what surprised me not a little, that
the government had advices of his traveling up with me from
La Unión, of his intention to join Morazán's expedition, and
of his change of purpose in consequence of meeting Morazán
defeated on the road. He told me that as yet the captain had
not been molested only because he was staying at my house.
I was disturbed by this communication; I was open to the
imputation of taking advantage of my official character to
harbor a partisan. I was the only friend the captain had, and
of course determined to stand by him. He was, however, not
only an object of suspicion, he was actually known; for much
less cause men were imprisoned and shot. In case of any out-
break, my house would not be a protection; consequently it
was best to avoid any excitement and to have an understanding at once. With this view I returned to the chief of the
state and mentioned the circumstances under which we had
traveled together. As to myself, I informed him that I
would have taken a much more questionable companion
rather than travel alone; and as to the captain, I assured
him that if the captain had happened to be thrown ashore
on the coast, he would very likely have taken a campaign on
their side. Besides, I added, he had not been on his way to
join the expedition when we met Morazán. Finally I assured
him most earnestly that the captain now understood better
the other side of the question, and that I would answer for
his keeping quiet. Don Mariano Rivera Paz, who, I felt, was
desirous to allay rather than create excitement in the city,
received my communication in the best spirit possible, and
said the captain had better present himself to the government. I returned to my house and found the captain alone,
already by no means pleased with the turn of his fortunes.
My communication did not relieve him, but he accompanied
me to the Government House. I could hardly persuade myself that he was the same man whose dashing appearance on
the road had often made the women whisper *muy valiente*,
and whose answer to all intimations of danger was that a
man can only die once. To be sure, the soldiers in the corridor seemed to intimate that they had found him out; the
gentlemen in the room surveyed him from head to foot, as

if taking notes for an advertisement of his person, and their looks appeared to say they would know him when they met him again. On horseback and with a fair field, the captain would have defied the whole noblesse of Guatemala, but now he was completely cowed; he spoke only when he was spoken to, and walked out with less effrontery than I supposed possible.

And now I would fain let the reader sit down and enjoy himself quietly in Guatemala, but I cannot. The place did not admit of it. I could not conceal from myself that the Federal government was broken up; there was not the least prospect of its ever being restored, nor, for a long time to come, of any other being organized in its stead. Under these circumstances I did not consider myself justified in remaining any longer in the country. I was perfectly useless for all the purposes of my mission, and I made a formal return to the authorities of Washington, in effect, "after diligent search, no government found."

I was once more my own master, at liberty to go where I pleased, at my own expense, and immediately we commenced making arrangements for our journey to Palenque.[1] We had no time to lose; it was a thousand miles distant, and the rainy season was approaching, during which part of the road was impassable. There was no one in the city who had ever made the journey. The archbishop, on his exit from Guatemala eight years before, had fled by that road, and since his time it had not been traveled by any resident of Guatemala; but we learned enough to satisfy us that it would be less difficult to reach Palenque from New York than from where we were. We had many preparations to make, and, from the impossibility of getting servants upon whom we could rely, we were obliged to attend to all the details ourselves. The captain was uncertain what to do with himself, and talked of going with us.

The next afternoon, as we were returning to the house, we noticed a line of soldiers at the corner of the street. As usual, we gave them the sidewalk, and in crossing I remarked to

---

1. In the State of Chiapas in southeast Mexico.

the captain that they eyed us sharply as they spoke to each other. The line extended past my door and up to the corner of the next street. Supposing that they were searching for General Guzmán or other officers of General Morazán who were thought to be secreted in the city, and that they would not spare my house, I determined to make no difficulty and to let them search. We went in, and the porter, with great agitation, told us that the soldiers were in pursuit of the captain. He had hardly finished speaking when an officer entered to summon the captain before the corregidor. The captain turned pale as death. I do not mean it as an imputation upon his courage; any other man would have done the same. I was as much alarmed as he, and told him that if he said so I would fasten the doors; but he answered that it was of no use, that they would break them down, and it was better for him to go with the officers. I followed him to the door, telling him not to make any confessions, not to commit himself, and that I would be with him in a few minutes. I saw at once that the affair was out of the hands of the chief of the state, and had gotten before an inferior tribunal.

Mr. Catherwood and Mr. Savage entered in time to see the captain moving down the street with his escort. Mr. Savage, who had had charge of my house during my absence and had hoisted the American flag during the attack upon the city, had lived so long in that country and had beheld so many scenes of horror that he was not easily disturbed; he knew exactly what to do. He accompanied me to the cabildo, where we found the captain sitting bolt upright within the railing, and the corregidor and his clerk, with pen, ink, and paper, and ominous formality, examining him. The captain's face brightened at sight of the only man in Guatemala who took the least interest in his fate. Fortunately, the corregidor was an acquaintance of mine. He had been pleased with the interest I took in the sword of Alvarado, an interesting relic in his custody, and was one of the many whom I found in that country who were proud of showing attentions to a foreign agent. Claiming the captain as my traveling companion, I said that we had a rough journey together and I did not like to lose sight of him. The corregidor welcomed me back to Guatemala, and appreciated the peril I must have encountered in meeting on the road the tyrant Morazán. I told him that the captain had taken advantage of the opportunity to detach himself, without any compunctions, from such dangerous fellowship. We conversed till it was too dark to write, and then I suggested that, as it was dangerous to be out at night, I wished to take the captain home with me, and would be responsible for his forthcoming. He assented with great courtesy, and told the captain to return at nine o'clock the next morning. The captain was immensely relieved; but he had already made up his mind that he had come to Guatemala on a trading expedition, and would make great use of his gold chains.

The next day the examination was resumed. The captain certainly did not commit himself by any confessions; indeed, the revolution in his sentiments was most extraordinary—the Guatemala air was fatal to partialities for Morazán. The examination, by favor of the corregidor, was satisfactory, but the captain was advised to leave the city. In case of any excitement he would be in danger. Carrera was expected from Quezaltenango in a few days, and if he took up the captain's case, which he was not unlikely to do, it might be a bad business. The captain did not need any urging. A council was held to determine which way he should go, and it was decided that the road to the port was the only one open. He had a horse and one cargo mule, and he wanted another for those trunks. I had seven in my yard, and I told him to take one. On a bright morning he pulled off his frockcoat, put on his traveling dress, and set off for Belize. I watched him as he rode down the street till he was out of sight. Poor captain, where is he now? The next time I saw him was at my own house in New York. He was taken sick at Belize, and had boarded a brig bound for Boston; he was there at the time of my arrival and came to New York to see me. The last I saw of him, afraid to return across the country to get the account sales of his ship, he was about to embark for the Isthmus of Panama, where he would cross over and go up the Pacific. I was knocked about myself in that country, but I think the captain will not soon forget his campaign with Morazán.

At this time I received a visit from a countryman whom I regretted not to have seen before. It was Dr. Weems, of Maryland, who had resided several years at Antigua, and had lately returned from a visit to the United States with an appointment as consul. He came to consult me in regard to the result of my search for a government, as he was on the track with his own credentials.

The doctor advised me not to undertake the journey to Palenque. In my race from Nicaragua I had cheered myself with the idea that, on reaching Guatemala, all difficulty would be over, and that our journey to Palenque would be attended only by the hardships of traveling in a country destitute of accommodations. But, unfortunately, the horizon in that direction was lowering. The whole mass of the Indian population of Los Altos was in a state of excitement, and there were whispers of a general rising and massacre of the whites. General Prem, to whom I have before referred, and his wife, while traveling toward Mexico, had been attacked by a band of assassins; he himself was left on the ground for dead, and his wife was murdered, her fingers cut off, and the rings torn from them. Lieutenant Nichols, the aide-de-camp of Colonel MacDonald, arrived from Belize with a report that Captain Caddy and Mr. Walker, who had set out for Palenque by the Belize River, had been speared by the Indians. There was a rumor of some dreadful atrocity committed by Carrera in Quezaltenango, and that he was hurrying back from that place infuriate, with the intention of bringing all the prisoners out into the plaza and shooting them. Every friend in Guatemala, and Mr. Chatfield particularly, urged us not to undertake the journey. We felt that it was a most inauspicious moment, and we almost shrunk from our purpose. I have no hesitation in saying that it was a matter of most serious consideration whether we should not abandon it altogether and go home; but we had set out to go to Palenque, and we could not return without seeing it.

Among the petty difficulties of fitting ourselves, I may mention that we wanted four iron chains for trunks, but could only get two, for every blacksmith in the place was making chains for prisoners. In a week from the time of my arrival everything was ready for our departure. We provided ourselves with all the facilities and safeguards that could be procured. Besides passports, the government furnished us special letters of recommendation to all the corregidores; a flattering notice appeared in the government paper, *El Tiempo,* mentioning my travels through the provinces and my intended route, and recommending me to hospitality; and, upon the strength of the letter of the Archbishop of Baltimore, the venerable provisor gave me a letter of recommendation to all the curas under his charge. But these were not enough; Carrera's name was worth more than them all, and we waited two days for his return from Quezaltenango. On the sixth of April, early in the morning, he entered the city. At about nine o'clock I called at his house and was informed that he was in bed, that he had ridden all night and would not rise till the afternoon. The rumor of the atrocity committed at Quezaltenango was confirmed.

After dinner, in company with Mr. Savage, I made my last stroll in the suburbs of the city. I never felt so strongly as at that moment, its exceeding beauty of position, and for the third time I visited the hospital and cemetery of San Juan de Dios. In front was the hospital, a noble structure, which was formerly a convent supported principally by the active charity of Don Mariano Aycinena. In the center of the courtyard was a fine fountain, and beyond it the cemetery, which was established at the time of the cholera. The entrance was by a broad passage with a high wall on each side, intended for the burial of "heretics." There was but one grave, and the stone bore the inscription

Teodoro Ashadl,
de la Religione Reformada.
July 19 de 1837.

At the end of this passage was a deadhouse, in which lay, on separate beds, the bodies of two men, both poor; one was entirely naked, with his legs drawn up, as though no friend had been by to straighten them, and the other was wrapped in matting. On the right of the passage a door opened into a square enclosure, in which were vaults built above the ground, bearing the names of the wealthy inhabitants of the city. On the left a door opened into an enclosure running in the rear of the deadhouse, about seven hundred and fifty feet long and three hundred wide. The walls were high and thick, and the graves were square recesses lengthwise in the wall, three tiers deep, each closed up with a flat stone on which the name of the occupant was inscribed. These, too, were for the rich. The area was filled with the graves of the common people, and in one place was a square of new-made earth, under which lay the bodies of about four hundred men killed in the attack upon the city. The table of land commanded a view of the green plain of Guatemala and the volcanoes of Antigua. Beautiful flowers were blooming over the graves, and a voice seemed to say

Oh do not pluck these flowers,
They're sacred to the dead.

A bier approached with the body of a woman, which was buried without any coffin. Nearby was a line of new-made graves waiting for tenants. They were dug through skeletons, and skulls and bones lay in heaps beside them. I rolled three skulls together with my foot. It was a gloomy leave-taking of Guatemala. The earth slipped under my feet and I fell backward, but saved myself by stepping across a new-made grave. I verily believe that if I had fallen into it, I should have been superstitious and afraid to set out on my journey.

I have mentioned that there were rumors in the city of some horrible outrage committed by Carrera at Quezaltenango. He had set out from Guatemala in pursuit of Morazán. Near Antigua he met one of his own soldiers from Quezaltenango, who reported that there had been a rising in that town, and that the garrison had been compelled to lay down their arms. Enraged at this intelligence, Carrera abandoned his pursuit of Morazán; without even advising the government of his change of plan, he marched to Quezaltenango and, among other minor outrages, seized eighteen of the municipality, the first men of the state; without the slightest form of trial he shot them in the plaza. To heighten the gloom which this news cast over the city, a rumor had preceded him that, immediately on his arrival, he intended to order out all the prisoners and shoot them also. At this time the repressed excitement in the city was fearful. An immense relief was experienced on the repulse of Morazán, but there had been no rejoicing; again the sword seemed suspended by a single hair.

And here I would remark, as at a place where it has no immediate connection with what precedes or what follows, and, consequently, where no application of it can be made, that some matters of deep personal interest which illustrate more than volumes the dreadful state of the country, I am obliged to withhold altogether, lest, perchance, these pages should find their way to Guatemala and compromise individuals. In my long journey I had had intercourse with men of all parties, and was spoken to freely, and sometimes confidentially. Heretofore, in all the wars and revolutions the whites had had the controlling influence, but at this time the Indians were the dominant power. Roused from the sloth of ages, and with muskets in their hands, their gentleness was changed into ferocity; and, even among the adherents of the Carrera party, there was a fearful apprehension of a war of castes, and a strong desire on the part of those who could get away, to leave the country. I was consulted by men having houses and large landed estates, but who could only command two or three thousand dollars in money, as to their ability to live on that sum in the United States; and individuals holding high offices under the Central Party told me that they had their passports from Mexico, and were ready at any moment to flee.

There seemed ground for the apprehension that the hour of retributive justice was nigh, and that a spirit had been awakened among the Indians to make a bloody offering to the spirits of their fathers, and to recover their inheritance. Carrera was the pivot on which this turned. He was talked of as *El Rey de los Indios*, The King of the Indians. He had relieved them from all taxes, and, as they said, supported his army by levying contributions upon the whites. His power by a word to cause the massacre of every white inhabitant, no one doubted. Their security was, as I conceived, that, in the constant action of his short career, he had not had time to form any plans for extended dominion, and that he knew nothing of the immense country from Texas to Cape Horn occupied by a race sympathizing in hostility to the whites. He was a fanatic, and, to a certain extent, under the dominion of the priests; and his own acuteness told him that he was more powerful with the Indians themselves while supported by the priests and the aristocracy than at the head of the Indians only. But all knew that, in a moment of passion, he forgot entirely the little of plan or policy that ever governed him.

When he returned from Quezaltenango, his hands red with blood and preceded by the fearful rumor that he intended to bring out two or three hundred prisoners and shoot them, the citizens of Guatemala felt that they stood on the brink of a fearful gulf. A leading member of the government, whom I wished to call on him with me to ask for a passport, declined doing so, lest, as he said, Carrera should think the government was trying to lead him. Others paid him formal visits of ceremony and congratulation upon his return and compared notes with each other as to the manner in which they were received. Carrera made no report, official or verbal, of what he had done; and though all were full of it, no one of them dared ask him any questions, or refer to it. They will perhaps pronounce me a calumniator, but even at the hazard of wounding their feelings, I cannot withhold what I believe to be a true picture of the state of the country as it was at that time.

I was unable to induce any of the persons I wished to call with me upon Carrera; and I was afraid, after such a long interval and such exciting scenes as he had been engaged in, that he might not recognize me. Feeling, however, that it was all important not to fail in my application to him, I recalled that in my first interview he had spoken warmly of a doctor who had extracted a ball from his side. This doctor I did not know, but I called upon him and asked him to accompany me, to which, with great civility, he immediately assented.

It was under these circumstances that I made my last visit to Carrera. He had moved into a much larger house, and his guard was more regular and formal. When I entered, he was standing behind a table on one side of the room with his wife and Rivera Paz and one or two others examining some large Costa Rica chains; at the moment he had in his hands one which had formed part of the contents of those trunks of my friend, the captain, and which had often adorned his neck. I think it would have given the captain a spasm if he had known that anything once around his neck was between Carrera's fingers. His wife was a pretty, delicate-looking mestiza not more than twenty, and seemed to have a woman's fondness for chains and gold. Carrera himself looked at them with indifference. My idea at the time was that these jewels had been sent in by the government as a present to his wife, hoping through her to propitiate him, but perhaps I was wrong. The face of Rivera Paz seemed anxious.

Carrera had passed through so many terrible scenes since I saw him that I feared he had forgotten me; but he recognized me in a moment and made room for me behind the table next to himself. His military coat lay on the table, and he wore the same roundabout jacket; his face had the same youthfulness, quickness, and intelligence, his voice and manners the same gentleness and seriousness, and he had again been wounded. I regretted to meet Rivera Paz there, for I thought it must be mortifying to him, as the head of the government, to see that his passport was not considered a protection without Carrera's endorsement; but I could not stand upon ceremony, and I took advantage of Carrera's leaving the table to say to Rivera Paz that I was setting out on a dangerous road and considered it indispensable to fortify myself with all the security I could get. When Carrera returned I told him my purpose, showed him the passport of the government, and asked him to put his stamp upon it. Carrera had no delicacy in the matter. Taking the passport out of my hand, he threw it on the table, saying he would make me out a new one and sign it himself. This was more than I had expected. In a quiet way telling me to "be seated," he sent his wife into another room for the secretary, and told him to make out a passport for the "Consul of the North." He had an indefinite idea that I was a great man in my own country, but he had a very indefinite idea as to where my country was. I was not particular about my title so long as it was big enough, but "the North" was rather a broad range, and to prevent mistakes I gave the secretary the other passport. He took it into another room, and Carrera sat down at the table beside me.

Carrera had heard of my having met Morazán on his retreat, and inquired about him, though less anxiously and more to the purpose than the others. He said that he was making preparations, and that in a week he intended to march upon El Salvador with three thousand men, adding that if he had had cannon he would have driven Morazán from the plaza very soon. I asked him whether it was true that he and Morazán had met personally on the heights of Calvary, and he said that they had, that it was toward the last of the battle, when the latter was retreating. One of Morazán's dismounted troopers had torn off his holsters; Morazán had fired a pistol at him and he had struck at Morazán with his sword and cut his saddle. Morazán, he said, had very handsome pistols; and it struck me that he was thinking if he had killed Morazán he would have the pistols. I could not but think of the strange positions into which I was thrown: shaking hands and sitting side by side with men who were thirsting for each other's blood, well received by all, hearing what they said of each other, and in many cases their plans and purposes, as unreservedly as if I were a traveling member of both cabinets. In a few minutes the secretary called him, and he went out and brought back the passport himself, signed with his own hand, the ink still wet. It had taken him longer than it would have done to cut off a head, and he seemed more proud of it. Indeed, it was the only occasion in which I saw in him the slightest elevation of feeling. I made a comment upon the excellence of the handwriting, and with his good wishes for my safe arrival in the North and speedy return to Guatemala, I took my leave. Now, I do not believe if he knew what I say of him, that he would give me a very cordial welcome; but I do believe him honest, and if he knew how and could curb his passions, he would do more good for Central America than any other man in it.

I was now fortified with the best security we could have for our journey. We passed the evening writing letters and packing up things to be sent home (among which was my diplomatic coat), and on the seventeenth of April we rose to set out. The first movement was to take down our beds. Every man in that country has a small cot called a *catre*, made to double with a hinge, which may be taken down and with pillows and bedclothes wrapped up in an oxhide to carry on a journey. Our great object was to travel lightly. Every additional mule and servant gave additional trouble, but we could not do with less than a cargo mule apiece. Each of us had two *petacas*, or trunks made of oxhide lined with thin straw matting with a top like that of a box secured by a clumsy iron chain with large padlocks. They contained besides other things, a hammock, a blanket, one pair of sheets, and a pillow, all of which, with alforjas of provisions, made one load apiece. We carried one *catre* in case of sickness. We had one spare cargo mule, the gray mule with which I had ascended the volcano of Cartago, and my macho for Mr. Catherwood and myself, and a horse for relief, in all six animals; we had two untried *mozos*, or men of all work. While we were in the act of mounting, Don Saturnino Tinoca, my companion from Sonsonate, rode into the yard to accompany us two days on our journey. We bade farewell to Mr. Savage, my first, last, and best friend, and in a few minutes, with a mingled feeling of regret and satisfaction, we left for the last time the barrier of Guatemala.

Don Saturnino was most welcome to our party. His purpose was to visit two brothers of his wife, curas whom he had never seen, and who lived at Santiago Atitlán, two or three days' journey distant. His father had been the last governor of Nicaragua under the royal rule, with a large estate which had been confiscated at the time of the revolution. Don Saturnino was about forty, tall, and as thin as a man could be to have activity and vigor; he wore a roundabout jacket and trousers of dark olive cloth, and carried large pistols in his holsters, and a long sword with a leather scabbard, which was worn at the point, leaving about an inch of steel naked. He sat his mule as stiff as if he had swallowed his own sword; he held the reins in his right hand, and his left arm, crooked from the elbow, stood out like a pump handle, the hand dropping from the wrist and shaking with the movement of the mule. He rode on a Mexican saddle plated with silver, and carried behind a pair of alforjas with bread and cheese, and *atole*, a composition of pounded parched corn, cocoa, and sugar, which, mixed with water, was almost his living. His *mozo* was as fat as he was lean, and wore a bell-crowned straw hat, cotton shirt, and drawers reaching down to his knees. Instead of Rocinante and the ass, the master rode a mule and the servant went afoot, but in other respects, they were a genuine Don Quixote and Sancho Panza, the former of which appellations we gave to Don Saturnino very early in our acquaintance.

Although we had set out for Quezaltenango, we intended to turn aside and visit ruins. That day we went three leagues out of our road to say farewell to our friend Padre Alcántara at Ciudad Vieja. At five o'clock in the afternoon we reached the convent, where I had the pleasure of meeting again not only him but also Señor Vidaurre, and Don Pepe, the same party with whom I had passed the day with so much satisfaction before. Mr. Catherwood had in the meantime passed a month at the convent. Padre Alcántara had fled at the approach of the *tyrant* Morazán; Don Pepe had had a shot at Morazán as he was retreating from Antigua, and the padre had a musket which a fleeing soldier had left at night against the wall of the convent.

The morning opened with troubles. The gray mule was sick. Don Saturnino bled her on both sides of her neck, but the poor animal was not in a condition to be ridden. Then, shortly afterward, Mr. Catherwood had one of the *mozos* by the throat, but Padre Alcántara patched up a peace. Don

Saturnino said that the gray mule would be better for exercise, so we set out, bidding farewell for the last time to our kind host.

Don Pepe escorted us and, crossing the plain of Ciudad Vieja in the direction in which Alvarado had entered it, we ascended a high hill. Turning the summit, through a narrow opening we looked down upon a beautiful plain, cultivated like a garden, which opened to the left as we advanced, and ran off to the Lake of Duenos [2] between the two great volcanoes of Fire and Water. Descending to the plain, we entered the village of San Antonio, occupied entirely by Indians. The cura's house stood on an open plaza, with a fine fountain in front, and the huts of the Indians were built with stalks of sugar cane. Early in the occupation of Guatemala, the lands around the capital were partitioned out among certain *canónigos*, or canons, and Indians were allotted to cultivate them. Each village was called by the *canónigo's* own name. A church was built, and a fine house for the *canónigo*, and by judicious management the Indians became settled and the artisans for the capital. In the stillness and quiet of the village, it seemed as if the mountains and volcanoes around had shielded it from the devastation and alarm of war.

Passing through it, on the other side of the plain we commenced ascending a mountain. About halfway up, looking back over the village and plain, we saw a single white line over the mountain we had crossed to Ciudad Vieja; the range of the eye embraced the plain and lake at our feet, the two volcanoes of Agua and Fuego, and the great plain of Escuintla extending to the Pacific Ocean. The road was very steep, and our mules labored. On the other side of the mountain the road lay for some distance between shrubs and small trees, emerging from which we saw an immense plain broken by the track of the direct road from Guatemala, and afar off the spires of the town of Chimaltenango. At the foot of the mountain we reached the village of Parramos. We

---

2. The editor was unable to identify a lake by this name. There is in this vicinity a village called Las Dueñas.

had been three hours and a half making six miles. Don Pepe
summoned the alcalde, showed him Carrera's passport, and
demanded a guide to the next village. The alcalde called his
alguaciles, and in a very few minutes a guide was ready. Don
Pepe told us that he was leaving us here in "Europa," and
with many thanks we bade him farewell.

We were now entering upon a region of country which at
the time of the conquest was the most populous, the most
civilized, and the best cultivated in Guatemala. The people
who occupied it were the descendants of those found tnere
by Alvarado, and perhaps four-fifths of them were Indians
of untainted blood. For three centuries they had submitted
quietly to the dominion of the whites, but the rising of Carrera had wakened them to a recollection of their fathers, and
it was rumored that their eyes rolled strangely upon the
white men as the enemies of their race. For the first time we
saw fields of wheat and peach trees. The country was poetically called Europa; and though the Volcán de Agua still
reared in full sight its stupendous head, it resembled the
finest part of England on a magnificent scale.

But it was not like traveling in England. The young man,
with whose throat Mr. Catherwood had been so familiar,
loitered behind with the sick mule and a gun. He had started
from Ciudad Vieja with a drawn knife in his hand, the blade
about a foot and a half long, and we made up our minds to
get rid of him. We feared that he might have anticipated us
and gone off with the mule and gun, but he caught up to us,
and we relieved him of the gun and made him go on ahead
while we drove the mule. At the distance of two leagues we
reached the Indian village of San Andrés Itzapa. Don
Saturnino flourished Carrera's passport, introduced me as
El Ministro de Nueva York, demanded a guide, and in a
few minutes an alguacil was trotting before us for the next
village.

At this village, on the same requisition, the alcalde ran
out to look for an alguacil, but could not find one immediately, and ventured to beg Don Saturnino to wait a moment.
Don Saturnino told him he must go himself; that Carrera
would cut off his head if he did not; "the minister of New

York" could not be kept waiting. Don Saturnino, like many others of my friends in that country, had no very definite notions in regard to titles or places. A man happened to be passing whom the alcalde pressed into service, and he trotted on before with the halter of the led horse, and Don Saturnino hurried him along. As we approached the next village Carrera's soldiers were in sight, returning on the direct road to Guatemala, fresh from the slaughter at Quezaltenango. Don Saturnino told the guide that he must avoid the plaza and go on to the next village. When the guide begged, Don Saturnino rode up, drew his sword, and threatened to cut his head off. The poor fellow trotted on with his eye fixed on the uplifted sword; but when Don Saturnino turned to me with an Uncle Toby expression of face, the guide threw down the halter, leaped over a hedge fence, and ran toward the town. Don Saturnino, not disconcerted, caught up the halter and, spurring his mule, pushed on.

The road lay on a magnificent tableland, which in some places had trees on each side for a great distance. Beyond this we had a heavy rainstorm, and late in the afternoon reached the brink of an immense precipice, on which, at a great distance, we saw a *molino,* or wheat mill, looking like a New England factory. The descent was very steep and muddy, winding in places close along the precipitous side of the ravine. Great care was necessary with the mules, for their tendency was to descend sidewise, which was very dangerous; in the steepest places, if we kept their heads straight, they would slip in the mud several paces, but, bracing their feet, they would not fall.

At dark, wet and muddy, and in the midst of a heavy rain, we reached the *molino.* The major-domo was a Costa Rican, a countryman of Don Saturnino; fortunately, he gave us a room to ourselves, though it was damp and chilly. Here we learned that Tecpán Guatemala, one of the ruined cities we wished to visit, was but three leagues distant, and the major-domo offered to go there with us in the morning.

Chapter IX

IN the morning the major-domo furnished us with fine
horses, and we started early. Almost immediately we
commenced ascending the other side of the ravine which
we had descended the night before, and on the top we entered on a continuation of the same beautiful and extensive
tableland. On one side, for some distance, were high hedge
fences, in which aloes were growing, and in one place were
four in full bloom. In an hour we arrived at Patzún, a large
Indian village. Here we turned off to the right from the
highroad to Mexico by a sort of bypath. The country was
beautiful, and in parts well cultivated; and the morning was
bracing, the climate like our own in October. The immense
tableland was elevated some five or six thousand feet, but
none of these heights have ever been taken. We passed on
the right two mounds, such as are seen all over our own
country, and on the left an immense barranca. The table was
level to the very edge, where the earth seemed to have
broken off and sunk, and we looked down into a frightful
abyss two or three thousand feet deep. Gigantic trees at the
bottom of the immense cavity looked like shrubs. At some
distance beyond we passed a second of these immense barrancas, and in an hour and a half reached the Indian village
of Tecpán Guatemala.

For some distance before we reached the village, the road
was shaded by trees and shrubs, among which were aloes

thirty feet high. The long street by which we entered was paved with stones from the ruins of the old city; it was filled with drunken Indians and, rushing across it, was one with his arms around a woman's neck. At the head of this street was a fine plaza, with a large cabildo and twenty or thirty silent Indian alguaciles under the arcade with wands of office in their hands; they were dressed in full suits of blue cloth, the trousers open at the knees, and cloaks with a hood like the Arab burnoose. Adjoining this plaza was the large court-yard of the church, paved with stone. The church itself, the second built after the conquest, was one of the most magnificent in the country. The façade was two hundred feet long, very lofty, with turrets and spires gorgeously ornamented with stuccoed figures, and on its high platform were Indians, the first we had seen in picturesque costume. With the widely extended view of the country around, the scene was one of wild magnificence in nature and in art. We stopped involuntarily, lost in surprise and admiration, and the Indians, in mute astonishment, gazed at us.

As usual, Don Saturnino was the pioneer; we rode up to the house of the padre, where we were shown into a small room in which the padre was dozing in a large chair. The window was closed and a ray of light was admitted from the door. Before he had fairly opened his eyes, Don Saturnino told him that we had come to visit the ruins of the old city and wanted a guide; he thrust into his hands Carrera's passport and the letter of the provisor. The padre was old, fat, rich, and infirm; he had been thirty-five years cura of Tecpán Guatemala and was not used to doing things in a hurry. But our friend, knowing the particular objects of our visit, with great earnestness and haste told the padre that the minister of New York had heard in his country of a remarkable stone here, and that the provisor and Carrera were anxious for him to see it. The padre said that it was in the church on the top of the grand altar; that the cup of the sacrament stood upon it; that it was covered up and very sacred; and that he himself had never seen it. He was evidently unwilling to let us see it, but said he would endeavor to do so when we returned from the ruins. He sent for a guide, and we went out to the courtyard of the church.

While Mr. Catherwood was attempting a sketch, I walked up the steps. The interior was lofty, spacious, richly ornamented with stuccoed figures and paintings, and dark and solemn. In the distance was the grand altar, with long wax candles burning upon it and Indians kneeling before it. At the door a man stopped me and said that I must not enter with sword and spurs, and that I must even take off my boots. I would have done this, but I saw that the Indians did not like a stranger going into *their* church. They were evidently entirely unaccustomed to the sight of strangers; Mr. Catherwood was so annoyed by their gathering round him that he gave up his drawing. However, fearing it would be worse on our return, I told Don Saturnino that we must make an effort to see the stone now. Don Saturnino had a great respect for the priests and the Church. He was not a fanatic, but he thought that a powerful religious influence was good for the Indians. Nevertheless, he said we ought to see it, and we went back in a body to the padre; Don Saturnino told him that we were anxious to see the stone now in order to prevent delay on our return. The good padre's heavy body was troubled. He asked for the provisor's letter again, read it over, went out on the corridor and consulted with a brother about as old and round as himself, and at length told us to wait in that room and he would bring the stone. As he went out he ordered all the Indians in the courtyard, about forty or fifty, to go to the cabildo and tell the alcalde to send the guide. In a few minutes he returned, and opening with some trepidation the folds of his large gown, he produced the stone.

Fuentes,[1] in speaking of the old city, says, "To the westward of the city there is a little mount that commands it, on which stands a small round building about six feet in height, in the middle of which there is a pedestal formed of a shining substance resembling glass, but the precise quality of which has not been ascertained. Seated around this building, the judges heard and decided the causes brought before

1. Although Fuentes is undoubtedly the original source, Stephens is actually quoting Juarros here. (Domingo Juarros, *A History of the Kingdom of Guatemala*, translated by John Baily, London, 1823, p. 384.)

them, and their sentences were executed on the spot. Previous to executing them, however, it was necessary to have them confirmed by the oracle, for which purpose three of the judges left their seats and proceeded to a deep ravine, where there was a place of worship containing a black transparent stone, on the surface of which the Deity was supposed to indicate the fate of the criminal. If the decision was approved, the sentence was executed immediately; if nothing appeared on the stone, the accused was set at liberty. This oracle was also consulted in the affairs of war. The Bishop Francisco Marroquín [2] having obtained intelligence of this slab, ordered it to be cut square, and consecrated it for the top of the grand altar in the Church of Tecpán Guatemala. It is a stone of singular beauty, about a yard and a half each way." *The Modern Traveller* [3] refers to it as an "interesting specimen of ancient art;" and in 1825 concludes, "we may hope, before long, to receive some more distinct account of this oracular stone."

The world—meaning thereby the two classes into which an author once divided it, that is, of subscribers and non-subscribers to his work—the world that reads these pages is indebted to Don Saturnino for some additional information. When we saw it, the stone was sewed up in a piece of cotton cloth drawn tight, which looked certainly as old as the thirty-five years it had been under the cura's charge; it was probably the same covering in which it was enveloped when first laid on the top of the altar. One or two stitches were cut in the middle, and this was perhaps all we would have seen, if Don Saturnino, with a hurried jargon of "strange, curious, sacred, incomprehensible, the provisor's letter, minister of New York, etc." had not whipped out his penknife. The good old padre, heavy with agitation and his own weight, sank into his chair, still holding on with both hands. Don Saturnino ripped till he almost cut the good old man's fingers and slipped out the sacred tablet, leaving the sack in the padre's hands. The padre was a picture of self-abandon-

2. Francisco Marroquín became the first Bishop of Guatemala when, in 1534, it was advanced to the rank of Bishopric.
3. A series of travel books. Stephens refers to *Mexico and Guatemala*, by Josiah Conder, London: James Duncan, 1825, 2 vols.

ment, helplessness, distress, and self-reproach. We moved toward the light, and Don Saturnino, with a twinkle of his eyes and a ludicrous earnestness, consummated the padre's fear and horror by scratching the sacred stone with his knife. This oracular slab was only a piece of common slate, fourteen inches by ten, and about as thick as those used by boys at school; it was without characters of any kind. With a strong predilection for the marvelous, and scratching it most irreverently, we could make nothing more out of it. Don Saturnino handed it back to the padre and told him that he had better sew it up and put it back; and probably it is now in its place on the top of the grand altar, with the sacramental cup upon it, an object of veneration to the fanatic Indians.

But the agitation of the padre destroyed whatever there was of comic in the scene. Recovering from the shock, he told us not to go back through the town, that there was a road direct to the old city. Concealing the tablet under his gown, he walked out with a firm step, and in a strong, unbroken voice, rapidly, in their own unintelligible dialect, he called to the Indians to bring up our horses and directed the guide to put us on the road which led direct to the *molino*. He feared that the Indians might discover our sacrilegious act; and as we looked in their stupid faces, we were well satisfied to get away before any such discovery was made, rejoicing more than the padre that we could get back to the *molino* without returning through the town.

We had but to mount and ride. At the distance of a mile and a half we reached the bank of an immense ravine. We descended it, Don Saturnino leading the way, and at the foot, on the other side, he stopped at a narrow passage, barely wide enough for the mule to pass. This was the entrance to the old city. It was a winding passage cut in the side of the ravine; it was twenty or thirty feet deep and not wide enough for two horsemen to ride abreast, and it continued to the high table of land on which stood the ancient city of Patinamit.

This city flourished with the once powerful kingdom of the Cakchiquel Indians. Its name, in their language, means "*the* city." It was also called Tecpán Guatemala, which, according to Vázquez,[4] means "the Royal House of Guatemala," and he infers that it was the capital of the Cakchiquel kings. But Fuentes supposes that Tecpán Guatemala was the arsenal of the kingdom, and not the royal residence, which honor belonged to Guatemala; and that the former was so called from its situation on an eminence with respect to the latter, the word Tecpán meaning "above."[5]

According to Fuentes, Patinamit was seated on an eminence and surrounded by a deep defile, or natural fosse, the perpendicular height of which, from the level of the city, was more than one hundred fathoms. The only entrance was by a narrow causeway terminated by two gates constructed of *chaya* stone, or obsidian, one on the exterior and the other on the interior wall of the city. The plane of this eminence extends about three miles in length from north to south, and about two in breadth from east to west. The soil is covered with a stiff clay about three-quarters of a yard deep. On one side of the area are the remains of a magnificent building, perfectly square, each side measuring one hundred paces, constructed of hewn stones extremely well put together. In front of the building is a large square, on one side of which stand the ruins of a sumptuous palace, and near to it are the foundations of several houses. A trench three yards deep runs from north to south through the city, having a breastwork of masonry rising about a yard high. On the eastern side of this trench stood the houses of the nobles, and on the opposite side the houses of the *macehuales,* or commoners. The streets were, as may still be seen, straight and spacious, crossing each other at right angles.

When we went up on the table, for some distance it bore no marks of ever having been a city. Very soon we came upon

4. Father Francisco Vázquez, seventeenth-century Guatemalan historian and author of the *Crónica de la Provincia del Santísimo Nombre de Jesús de Guatemala,* first published in 1714.

5. Tecpán means "royal residence" as Vázquez supposed. Tecpán Guatemala is the name which Alvarado's Mexican allies gave to the Cakchiquel city. The Cakchiquel name was Iximché but the city was often referred to as Patinamit (meaning "principal city").

an Indian burning down trees and preparing a piece of ground for planting corn. Don Saturnino asked him to go with us and show us the ruins, but he refused. Soon after we reached a hut, outside of which a woman was washing. We asked her to accompany us, but she ran into the hut. Beyond this we reached a wall of stones, but broken and confused. We tied our horses in the shade of trees, and commenced exploring on foot. The ground was covered with mounds of ruins. In one place we saw the foundations of two houses, one of them about a hundred feet long by fifty feet broad. It had been one hundred and forty years since Fuentes published the account of his visit; during that time the Indians had carried away on their backs stones to build up the modern village of Tecpán Guatemala, and the hand of ruin had been busily at work. We inquired particularly for sculptured figures; our guide knew of two, and after considerable search brought us to them. They were lying on the ground, about three feet long, so worn that we could not make them out, though on one the eyes and nose of an animal were distinguishable. The position commanded an almost boundless view, and it was surrounded by an immense ravine, which warrants the description given of it by Fuentes. In some places it was frightful to look down into its depths. On every side it was inaccessible, and the only way of reaching it was by the narrow passage through which we entered. Its desolation and ruin added another page to the burdened record of human contentions, and proved that, as in the world whose history we know, so in this of whose history we are ignorant, man's hand has been against his fellow. The solitary Indian hut is all that now occupies the site of the ancient city; but on Good Friday of every year a solemn procession of the whole Indian population is made to it from the village of Tecpán Guatemala, and, as our guide told us, on that day bells are heard sounding under the earth.

Descending by the same narrow passage, we traversed the ravine and ascended on the other side. Our guide put us into the road that avoided the town, and we set off on a gallop.

Don Saturnino possessed the extremes of good temper, simplicity, uprightness, intelligence, and perseverance. Ever

since I fell in with him he had been most useful, but this day
he surpassed himself; and he was so well satisfied with us as
to declare that if it were not for his wife in Costa Rica, he
would bear us company to Palenque. He had an engagement in Guatemala on a particular day, and every day that
he lost with us was so much deducted from his visit to his
relatives. At his earnest request we had consented to pass a
day with them, though it was a little out of our road.

We reached the *molino* in time to walk around the mill.
On the side of the hill above was a large building to receive
grain; below it there was an immense reservoir for water in
the dry season, which did not answer the purpose for which
it was intended. The mill had seven sets of grindstones and,
working night and day, it ground from seventy to ninety
fanegas of wheat in the twenty-four hours, each fanega being
equal to six arrobas, or twenty-five pounds. The Indians
bring the wheat, and each one takes a stone and does his own
grinding, paying a *real*, or twelve and a half cents, per fanega
for the use of the mill. Flour is worth from about three dollars and a half to four dollars the barrel.

Don Saturnino was one of the best men that ever lived,
but in undress there was a lankness about him that was
ludicrous. In the evening, as he sat on the bed with his thin
arms wound around his thin legs and we reproved him for
his sacrilegious act in cutting open the cotton cloth, his little
eyes twinkled, and Mr. Catherwood and I laughed as we had
not before laughed in Central America.

But in that country one extreme followed close upon another. At midnight we were roused from sleep by that movement which, once felt, can never be mistaken. The building
rocked, our men in the corridor cried out *Temblor!* and Mr.
Catherwood and I at the same moment exclaimed "An earthquake!" Our *catres* stood transversely, and by the undulating movement of the earth he was rolled from side to
side, and I from head to foot. The sinking of my head induced an awful faintness of heart. I sprang upon my feet
and rushed to the door. In a moment the earth was still. We
sat on the sides of the bed and compared movements and
sensations; then we lay down again and slept till morning.

Early in the morning we resumed our journey. Unfortunately, the gray mule was no better. Perhaps she would recover in a few days, but we had no time to wait. And my first mule, purchased as the price of seeing Don Clementino's sister and a most faithful animal, was drooping. Don Saturnino offered me his own, a strong, hardy animal, in exchange for this mule, and the gray I left behind to be sent back and turned out on the pasture grounds of Padre Alcántara. There were few trials greater in that country than that of being obliged to leave on the road these tried and faithful companions.

To Patzún our road was the same as the day before. Before reaching it we had difficulty with the luggage, and left our only *catre* at a hut on the road. Leaving Patzún on the left, our road lay on the high, level table of land, and at ten o'clock we came to the brink of a ravine three thousand feet deep; at our feet we saw an immense abyss, and opposite, the high precipitous wall of the ravine. Our road lay across it. At the very commencement the descent was steep, and as we advanced, the path wound fearfully along the edge of the precipice. We met a caravan of mules at a narrow place where there was no room to turn out, and we were obliged to go back, taking care to give them the outside. All the way down we were meeting these caravans; perhaps more than five hundred passed us, loaded with wheat for the mills and cloths for Guatemala. In meeting so many mules loaded with merchandise, we lost the vague and indefinite apprehensions with which we had set out on this road. Altogether we were delayed by them more than half an hour, and with great labor reached the bottom of the ravine. A stream ran through it and for some distance our road lay in the stream; we crossed it thirty or forty times. The sides of the ravine were of an immense height. In one place we rode along a perpendicular wall of limestone rock smoking with spontaneous combustion.

At twelve o'clock we commenced ascending the opposite side. About halfway up we met another caravan of mules, with heavy boxes on their sides, tumbling down the steep descent. They came upon us so suddenly that our cargo mules got entangled among them, and got turned around and hurried down the mountain. Our men got them dis-engaged, and we drew up against the side. As we ascended, we saw far above us toward the summit rude fortifications, commanding the road up which we were toiling. This was the frontier post of Los Altos, and the position taken by General Guzmán to repel the invasion of Carrera. It seemed that it would be certain death for any body of men to ad-vance against it; but Carrera had sent a detachment of In-dians who clambered up the ravine at another place and attacked it in the rear. The fortifications had been pulled down and burned, the boundary lines demolished, and Los Altos annexed to Guatemala. Here we met an Indian, who confirmed what the muleteers had told us, that the road to Santiago Atitlán, the place of residence of Don Saturnino's relatives, was five leagues from here, and exceedingly bad; in order to save our luggage mules, we resolved to leave them at the village of Godínez, about a mile farther on.

The village consisted of but three or four huts, entirely desolate; there was not a person in sight. We were afraid to trust our *mozos* alone; they might be robbed, or they might rob us themselves; besides, they had nothing to eat. We were about at the head of the Lake of Atitlán. It was impossible, with the cargo mules, to reach Santiago Atitlán that day; it lay on the left border of the lake and our road was on the right. It was agreed for Don Saturnino to go on alone, and for us to continue on our direct road to Panajachel, a village on the right border opposite Atitlán, where we would cross the lake and pay our visit to him. We were advised that there were canoes there for this purpose, and we bade fare-well to Don Saturnino with the confident expectation of seeing him again the next day at the house of his relatives; but we never met again.

At two o'clock we came out upon the lofty table of land bordering the Lake of Atitlán. In general I have forborne attempting to give any idea of the magnificent scenery amid which we were traveling, but here forbearance would be a sin. From a height of three or four thousand feet [6] we looked

6. Actually Stephens was about eight or nine thousand feet above sea level, for the lake itself is situated at an altitude of approximately five thousand feet.

down upon a surface shining like a sheet of molten silver; it was enclosed by rocks and mountains of every form, some barren and some covered with verdure, rising from five hundred to five thousand feet in height. Opposite, down on the borders of the lake, and apparently inaccessible by land, was the town of Santiago Atitlán, to which our friend was wending his way. It was situated between two immense volcanoes eight or ten thousand feet high, and farther on was another volcano, and farther still, another more lofty than all, with its summit buried in clouds. There were no associations connected with this lake; until lately we did not know it even by name; but we both agreed that it was the most magnificent spectacle we ever saw. We stopped and watched the fleecy clouds of vapor rising from the bottom, moving up the mountains and the sides of the volcanoes.

We descended at first by a steep pitch, and then gently for about three miles along the precipitous border of the lake, leaving on our right the *camino real* and the village of San Andrés, and suddenly we reached the brink of the table-land, two thousand feet high. At the foot was a rich plain running down to the water; and on the opposite side another immense perpendicular mountainside, rising to the same height as that on which we stood. In the middle of the plain, buried in foliage, with the spire of the church barely visible, was the town of Panajachel. Although our first view of the lake had been the most beautiful we had ever seen, this surpassed it. All the requisites of the grand and beautiful were there: gigantic mountains, a valley of poetic softness, lake and volcanoes; and from the eminence on which we stood a waterfall marked a silver line down its side. A party of Indian men and women were moving in single file from the foot of the mountain toward the village, and they looked like children. The descent was steep and perpendicular, and, reaching the plain, the view of the mountain walls was sublime. As we advanced, the plain formed a triangle with its base on the lake, and the two mountain ranges converged to a point, communicating, by a narrow defile beyond, with the village of San Andrés.

Riding through a thick forest of fruit and flower trees, we entered the village, and at three o'clock rode up to the convent. The padre was a young man, cura of four or five villages; he was rich, formal, and polite, but all over the world women are better than men; his mother and sister received us cordially. They were in great distress on account of the outrage at Quezaltenango. Carrera's troops had passed through on their return to Guatemala, and they feared that the same bloody scenes were to be enacted all through the country. Part of Carrera's outrages were against the person of a cura, and this seemed to break the only chain that was supposed to keep him in subjection. Unfortunately, we learned that there was little or no communication with Santiago Atitlán, and no canoe on this side of the lake. Our only chance of seeing Don Saturnino again was that he might learn this fact at Atitlán, and if there was a canoe there, send it for us. After dinner, with a servant of the house as guide, we walked down to the lake. The path lay through a tropical garden. The climate was entirely different from the table-land above, and productions which would not grow there flourished here. Sapotas, *jocotes*, avocados, apples, pine-apples, oranges, and lemons, the best fruits of Central America, grew in profusion here. Aloes, cultivated in rows, grew thirty or thirty-five feet high and twelve or fourteen inches thick; they were used for thatching miserable Indian huts. We came down to the lake at some hot springs, so near the edge that the waves ran over the spring, the springs being very hot, and the waves very cold.

According to Juarros, the Lake of Atitlán is one of the most remarkable in the kingdom. It is about twenty-four miles from east to west, and ten from north to south,[7] entirely surrounded by rocks and mountains. There is no gradation of depth[8] from its shores, and the bottom has not been found with a line of three hundred fathoms. It receives several rivers and all the waters that descend from the mountains, but there is no known channel by which this great body of water is carried off. The only fish caught in it are crabs and a species of small fish about the size of the little

7. More recent measurements record a length of eighteen miles and a width of eleven miles.

8. From the editor's own experience in swimming in this lake, it appears that on one side, at least, there are gradations of depth.

finger. These are in such countless myriads that the inhabitants of the surrounding ten villages carry on a considerable fishing for them.

At that hour of the day, as we understood to be the case always at that season of the year, heavy clouds were hanging over the mountains and volcanoes, and the lake was violently agitated by a strong southwest wind; as our guide said, "*La laguna está muy brava.*" Santiago Atitlán was nearly opposite, at a distance of seven or eight leagues, and in following the irregular and mountainous border of the lake from the point where Don Saturnino left us, we doubted whether he could reach it that night. It was much farther off than we had supposed, and with the lake in such a state of agitation and subject, as our guide told us, at all times to violent gusts of wind, we had but little inclination to cross it in a canoe. It would have been magnificent to see there a tropical storm, to hear the thunder roll among the mountains and see the lightning flash down into the lake. We sat on the shore till the sun disappeared behind the mountains at the head of the lake. Mingled with our contemplations of it were thoughts of other and far distant scenes, and at dark we returned to the convent.

Chapter X

~~~~~~

Lake of Atitlán. Conjectures as to its origin, etc. A sail on the lake. A dangerous situation. A lofty mountain range. Ascent of the mountains. Commanding view. Beautiful plain. An elevated village. Ride along the lake. Sololá. Visit to Santa Cruz del Quiché. Scenery on the road. Barrancas. Santo Tomás. Whipping-posts. Plain of Quiché. The village. Ruins of Quiché. Its history. Desolate scene. A facetious cura. Description of the ruins. Plan of the ruins. The royal palace. The Place of Sacrifice. An image. Two heads, etc. Destruction of the palace recent. An arch.

EARLY in the morning we again went down to the lake. Not a vapor was on the water, and the top of every volcano was cleár of clouds. We looked over to Santiago Atitlán, but there was no indication of a canoe coming for us. We whiled away the time in shooting wild ducks, but could get only two ashore, which we afterward found of excellent flavor. According to the account given by Juarros, the water of this lake is so cold that in a few minutes it benumbs and swells the limbs of all who bathe in it. But it looked so inviting that we determined to risk it, and were not benumbed, nor were our limbs swollen. The inhabitants, we were told, bathed in it constantly; and Mr. Catherwood, who remained a long time in the water supported by his life preserver without taking any exercise, was not conscious of extreme coldness. In the utter ignorance that exists in regard to the geography and geology of that country, it may be that the account of its fathomless depth and the absence of any visible outlet, is as unfounded as that of the coldness of its waters.

The Modern Traveller, in referring to the want of specific information with regard to its elevation, and to other circumstances from which to frame a conjecture as to its origin and the probable communication of its waters with some other reservoir, states that the "fish which it contains are the same as are found in the Lake of Amatitlán," and asks, "May there not be some connection between these lakes, at least the fathomless one, and the Volcán de Agua?" We were told that the *mojarra*, the fish for which the Lake of Amatitlán is celebrated in that country, was not found in the Lake of Atitlán at all, so on this ground at least there is no reason to suppose a connection between the two lakes. In regard to any connection with the Volcán de Agua, if the account of Torquemada [1] be true, the deluge of water from that volcano was not caused by an eruption, but by an accumulation of water in a cavity on the top; consequently, the volcano has no subterraneous water power. The elevation of this lake has never been taken, and the whole of this region of country invites the attention of the scientific traveler.

While we were dressing, Juan, one of our *mozos*, found a canoe along the shore. It was an oblong dugout, awkward and rickety, and intended for only one person; but the lake was so smooth that a plank seemed sufficient. We got in, and Juan pushed off and paddled out; as we moved away the mountainous borders of the lake rose grandly before us. I had just called Mr. Catherwood's attention to a cascade opening upon us from the great height of perhaps three or four thousand feet when we were struck by a flaw which turned the canoe and drove us out into the lake. The canoe was overloaded, and Juan was an unskillful paddler. For several minutes he pulled, with every sinew stretched, but could barely keep her straight. Mr. Catherwood was in the stern, and I, on my knees in the bottom of the canoe. The loss of a stroke, or a tottering movement in changing places, might swamp her; and if we let her go she would be driven out into the lake and cast ashore, if at all, twenty or thirty miles distant,

---

1. Stephens reports this account by the Spanish historian, Torquemada, in chapter XIII of volume I.

whence we should have to scramble back over mountains. And there was a worse danger than this, for in the afternoon the wind always came from the other side, and might drive us back again into the middle of the lake. We saw the people on the shore looking at us and growing smaller every moment, but they could not help us. In all our difficulties we had none that came upon us so suddenly and unexpectedly, or that seemed more threatening. It had hardly been ten minutes since we were standing quietly on the beach, and if the wind had continued five minutes longer I do not know what would have become of us. But, most fortunately, it lulled; Juan's strength revived, and with a great effort he brought us under cover of the high headland beyond which the wind first struck us, and in a few minutes we reached the shore.

We had had enough of the lake; time was precious, and we determined to set out after dinner and ride four leagues to Sololá.[2] We took another *mozo*, whom the padre recommended as a *bobón*, or great fool. The first two were at swords' points, and with such a trio there was not much danger of combination. In loading the mules they fell to quarreling, Bobón taking his share. Ever since we left, Don Saturnino had superintended this operation, and without him everything went wrong. One mule slipped part of its load in the courtyard, and we made but a sorry party for the long journey we had before us.

From the village our road lay along the lake, to a point opposite the mountain which shut in the plain of Panajachel. Here we began to ascend. For a while the path commanded a view of the village and plain, but by degrees we diverged from it. After an hour's ascent we came out upon an eminence commanding a view of the lake and rode a short distance upon the brink; another immense mountain range lay before us, and breaking over the top was the cataract which I had seen from the canoe. Very soon we commenced ascending; the path ran zigzag, commanding alternately a view of the

---

2. A magnificently situated Indian town about two thousand feet above Lake Atitlán.

plain and of the lake. The ascent was terrible for loaded
mules, being in some places steps cut in the stone like a regular staircase. Every time we came upon the lake there was a
different view. At four o'clock, looking back over the high
ranges of mountains we had crossed, we saw the great volcanoes of Agua and Fuego. Six volcanoes were in sight at
one time, four of them above ten thousand, and two nearly
fifteen thousand feet high.

Looking down upon the lake we saw a canoe, so small as
to present a mere speck on the water; as we supposed, it had
been sent for us by our friend Don Saturnino. Four days
later, after diverging and returning to the main road, I
found a letter from him, directed to *El Ministro de Nueva
York,* stating that he had found the road so terrible that
night overtook him, and he had been obliged to stop three
leagues short of Atitlán. On arriving at that place he learned
that *the* canoe was on his side of the lake, but the boatmen
would not cross till the afternoon wind sprang up. The letter
was written after the return of the canoe, and sent by courier
two days' journey; it begged us to return and offered as a
bribe a noble mule, which, in our bantering on the road, he
affirmed was better than my macho.

Twice the mule track led us almost within the fall of
cataracts, and the last time we came upon the lake we looked
down upon a plain even more beautiful than that of Panajachel. Directly under us, at an immense distance below,
but itself elevated fifteen hundred or two thousand feet,
was a village, with its church conspicuous; it seemed as if we
could throw a stone down upon its roof. From the moment
this lake first opened upon us until we left it, our ride along
it presented a greater combination of beauties than any lo-
cality I ever saw. The last ascent occupied an hour and three
quarters. As old travelers, we would have avoided it if there
had been any other road, but, once over, we would not have
missed it for the world. Very soon we saw Sololá. In the
suburbs drunken Indians stood in a line, and took off their
old *petates*[3] (straw hats) with both hands. It was Sunday,

3. Literally a straw matting out of which hats and many other
things are made.

and the bells of the church were ringing for vespers, rockets were firing, and a procession, headed by violins, was parading round the plaza the figure of a saint on horseback, dressed like a harlequin. Opposite the cabildo, the alcalde with a crowd of mestizos was fighting cocks.

The town stands on the lofty borders of the Lake of Atitlán, and a hundred yards from it the whole water was visible. I tied my horse to the whipping post, and, thanks to Carrera's passport, the alcalde sent off for *zacate*, had a room swept out in the cabildo, and offered to send us supper from his own house. He was about ten days in office, having been appointed since Carrera's last invasion. Formerly this place was the residence of the youngest branch of the house of the Cakchiquel Indians.

It was our purpose at this place to send our luggage on by the main road to Totonicapán, one day's journey beyond, while we struck off at an angle and visited the ruins of Santa Cruz del Quiché. The Indians of that place, even in the most quiet times, bore a very bad name, and we were afraid of hearing such an account of them as would make it impossible to go there. Carrera had left a garrison of soldiers in Sololá, and we called upon the commandant, a gentlemanly man, who, suspected of disaffection to Carrera's government, was therefore particularly desirous to pay respect to his passport. He told me that there had been less excitement at that place than in some of the other villages, and promised to send the luggage on under safe escort to the corregidor of Totonicapán, and to give us a letter to his *comisionado* in Santa Cruz del Quiché.

On our return we learned that a lady had sent for us. Her house was on the corner of the plaza. She was a *chapetona* from Old Spain, which she had left with her husband thirty years before on account of wars. At the time of Carrera's last invasion her son, who was alcalde mayor, had fled toward Mexico; if he had been taken he would have been shot. The wife of her son was with her. They had not heard from him, but supposed him to be in the frontier town; they wished us to carry letters to him and inform him of their condition. Their house had been plundered, and they were in great distress. It was another of the instances we were constantly meeting of the effects of civil war. They insisted on our remaining at the house all night, which, besides the fact that they were interesting ladies, we were not loth to do on our own account. The place was several thousand feet higher than where we had slept the night before, and the temperature was cold and wintry by comparison. Hammocks, our only beds, were not used at all. There were not even supporters in the cabildo to hang them on. The next morning we found the mules all drawn up by the cold; their coats were rough and my poor horse was so chilled that he could hardly move. In coming in he had attracted the alcalde's attention, and he wanted to buy him. In the morning the alcalde told me that, being used to a hot climate, the horse could not bear the journey across the Cordilleras, which was confirmed by several disinterested persons to whom he appealed. I almost suspected him of having done the horse some injury so as to make me leave him behind. However, by moving him in the sun his limbs relaxed, and we sent him off with the men, the luggage, and the promised escort, recommended to the corregidor at Totonicapán.

At a quarter before nine we bade farewell to the ladies who had entertained us so kindly, and, charged with letters and messages for their son and husband, set out with Bobón for Santa Cruz del Quiché. At a short distance from the town we again rose upon a ridge which commanded a view of the lake and town; it was the last, and, as we thought, the loveliest of all. At a league's distance we turned off from the *camino real* into a narrow bridle path, and very soon entered a well-cultivated plain, passed a forest clear of brush and underwood, like a forest at home, and followed the course of a beautiful stream. Again we came out upon a rich plain, and in several places saw clusters of aloes in full bloom. The atmosphere was transparent, and, as in an autumn day at home, the sun was cheering and invigorating.

At twelve o'clock we met some Indians who told us that Santo Tomás⁴ was three leagues distant, and five minutes

---

4. The famous Quiché Indian village, Santo Tomás Chichicaste-nango, in the western highlands.

afterward we saw the town apparently not more than a mile
off; but we were arrested by another immense ravine. The
descent was by a winding zigzag path, part of the way with
high walls on either side, and so steep that we were obliged
to dismount and walk all the way, hurried on by our own
impetus and the mules crowding upon us from behind. At
the foot of the ravine was a beautiful stream, at which,
choked with dust and perspiration, we stopped to drink. We
mounted to ford the stream, and almost immediately dismounted again to ascend the opposite side of the ravine.
This was even more difficult than the descent, and when we
reached the top it seemed a good three leagues. We passed
on the right another awful barranca broken off from the
table of land, and riding close along its edge, we looked
down into an abyss of two or three thousand feet. Very soon
afterwards we reached Santo Tomás. A crowd of Indians was
gathered in the plaza; they were well dressed in brown cloth,
and wore no hats over their long black hair. The entire population was Indian. There was not a single white man in the
place, and the only one who could speak Spanish was an old
mestizo, the secretary of the alcalde. We rode up to the
cabildo, and tied our mules before the prison door. Groups
of villainous faces were fixed in the bars of the windows. We
called for the alcalde, presented Carrera's passport, and demanded *zacate*, eggs, and *frijoles* for ourselves, and a guide
to Quiché.

While these requests were being attended to, the alcalde
and as many alguaciles as could find a place, seated themselves silently on a bench occupied by us. In front was a new
whipping post. There was not a word spoken; but a man was
brought up before it, his feet and wrists tied together, and
he was drawn up by a rope which passed through a groove
at the top of the post. His back was naked, and on his left
stood an alguacil with a heavy cowhide whip. Every stroke
made a blue streak which rose into a ridge from which the
blood started and trickled down his back. The poor fellow
screamed in agony. After him, a boy was stretched up in the
same way. At the first lash, with a dreadful scream he jerked
his feet out of the ropes and seemed to fly up to the top of

the post. He was brought back and secured, and then whipped till the alcalde was satisfied.

This practice was one of the reforms instituted by the Central government of Guatemala. The Liberal Party had abolished this remnant of barbarity, but within the last month, at the wish of the Indians themselves and in pursuance of the general plan to restore old usages and customs, new whipping posts had been erected in all the villages. Not one of the brutal beings around seemed to have the least feeling for the victims. Among the amateurs were several criminals, whom we had noticed walking in chains about the plaza; and among them were a man and woman in rags, bareheaded, with long hair streaming over their eyes, chained together by the hand and foot, with strong bars between them to keep them out of each other's reach. They were a husband and wife, who had shocked the moral sense of the community by not living together. The punishment seemed the very refinement of cruelty, but while it lasted it was an effectual way of preventing a repetition of the offence.

At half past three, with an alguacil running before us and Bobón trotting behind, we set out again. Crossing a gently rolling plain, with a distant hillside on the left, handsomely wooded, we were reminded of scenes at home, except that on the near left was another immense *barranca*, with large trees, their tops two thousand feet below us. Leaving the village on the right, we passed a small lake, crossed a ravine, and rose to the plain of Quiché. At a distance on the left were the ruins of the old city, the once large and opulent capital of Utatlán, the court of the native kings of Quiché and the most sumptuous discovered by the Spaniards in this section of America. It was a site worthy to be the abode of a race of kings. We passed between two small lakes, rode into the village, and passed on, as usual, to the convent, which stood beside the church. As we stopped at the foot of a high flight of stone steps, an old Indian on the platform told us to walk in; we spurred our mules up the steps, rode through the corridor into a large apartment, and sent the mules down another flight of steps into a yard enclosed by a high stone fence.

The convent was the first erected in the country by the Dominican friars, and dated from the time of Alvarado. It was built entirely of stone, with massive walls, and corridors, pavements, and courtyard strong enough for a fortress; but most of the apartments were desolate or filled with rubbish; one was used for *zacate*, another for corn, and one was fitted up as a roosting place for fowls. The padre had gone to another village and his own apartments were locked. We were shown into an adjoining room, which was about thirty feet square and nearly as high, with stone floor and walls; it was absolutely empty except for a shattered and weather-beaten soldier in one corner, returned from campaigns in Mexico. As we had brought with us nothing but our ponchos, and the nights in that region were very cold, we were unwilling to risk sleeping on the stone floor. With the padre's Indian servant we went to the alcalde, who, on the strength of Carrera's passport, gave us the audience room of the cabildo, which had at one end a raised platform with a railing, a table, and two long benches with high backs. Adjoining was the prison, which was merely an enclosure of four high stone walls without any roof; it was filled with more than the usual number of criminals, some of whom, as we looked through the gratings, we saw lying on the ground with only a few rags of covering, shivering in the cold. The alcalde provided us with supper and promised to procure us a guide to the ruins.

Early in the morning, with a mestizo armed with a long basket-hilted sword, who advised us to carry our weapons as the people were not to be trusted, we set out for the ruins. At a short distance we passed another immense barranca, down which, but a few nights before, an Indian, chased by alguaciles, either fell or threw himself off into the abyss fifteen hundred feet deep, where he was dashed to pieces. At about a mile from the village we came to a range of elevations connected by a ditch and extending to a great distance, which had evidently formed the line of fortifications for the ruined city. They consisted of the remains of stone buildings, probably towers, the stones well cut and laid together; the mass of rubbish around abounded in flint arrowheads. Within this line, one elevation grew more imposing as we approached; one hundred and twenty feet hign, it was square in shape with terraces, and in the center was a tower. We ascended by steps to three ranges of terraces and, on the top, entered an area enclosed by stone walls and covered with hard cement, in many places still perfect. Thence we ascended by stone steps to the top of the tower; formerly covered with stucco, it had stood as a fortress at the entrance of the great city of Utatlán,[5] the capital of the kingdom of the Quiché Indians.

According to Fuentes, the chronicler of the kingdom of Guatemala, the kings of the Quiché and Cakchiquel Indians were descended from the Toltecan Indians, who, when they came into this country, found it already inhabited by people of different nations. According to the manuscript of Don Juan Torres, the grandson of the last king of the Quichés, which was in the possession of the lieutenant-general appointed by Pedro de Alvarado, and which Fuentes says he obtained by means of Father Francisco Vázquez, the historian of the order of Saint Francis, the *Toltecas* themselves descended from the house of Israel.[6] These Israelites, Torres goes on to explain, were released by Moses from the tyranny of Pharaoh and, after crossing the Red Sea, fell into idolatry; to avoid the reproofs of Moses, or from fear of his inflicting upon them some chastisement, they separated from him and his brethren. Under the guidance of Tanub, their chief, they passed from one continent to the other, until finally, in a place which they called the seven caverns, a part of the kingdom of Mexico, they founded the celebrated city of Tula. From Tanub sprang the families of the kings of Tula and Quiché, and the first monarch of the *Toltecas*.

---

5. Alvarado's Mexican allies are responsible for this name too. The Quiché Indians called their capital city Gumarkaaj.

6. Needless to say, no one now seriously believes that the Toltecs or the Quichés are the lost tribes of Israel, although in Stephens' day the belief was held.

Nimaquiché, the fifth king of that line and more beloved than any of his predecessors, was directed by an oracle to leave Tula with his people, who had by this time multiplied greatly, and conduct them from the kingdom of Mexico to that of Guatemala. In performing this journey they consumed many years, suffered extraordinary hardships, and wandered over an immense tract of country, until, discovering the Lake of Atitlán, they resolved to settle near it in a country which they called Quiché.

Nimaquiché was accompanied by his three brothers, and it was agreed to divide the new country between them. Nimaquiché died; his son Axcopil became chief of the Quichés, Cakchiquels, and Tzutuhiles, and was at the head of his nation when they settled in Quiché. He was also the first monarch to reign in Utatlán, and under him the monarchy rose to a high degree of splendor. To relieve himself from some of the fatigues of administration, he appointed thirteen captains or governors, and at a very advanced age divided his empire into three kingdoms: Quiché, Cakchiquel, and Tzutuhil, retaining the first for himself, and giving the second to his eldest son Jintemal and the third to his youngest son Acxigual. This division was made on a day when three suns were visible at the same time, which extraordinary circumstance, says the manuscript, has induced some persons to believe that it was made on the day of our Saviour's birth. There were seventeen Toltecan kings who reigned in Utatlán, the capital of Quiché; their names have come down to posterity, but they are so hard to write out that I will take for granted the reader is familiar with them.[7]

Their history, like that of man in other parts of the world, is one of war and bloodshed. Before the death of Axcopil his sons were at war, which, however, was settled by his mediation, and for two reigns peace existed. Although Balam-Acab, the next king of Quiché, lived on terms of

---

7. Evidently the authors of early writings found, like Stephens, that these names are "hard to write out," for they occur with a great variety of spellings. There appears to be no reliable recent summary in English of pre-Columbian Guatemalan history. (*See* Hubert H. Bancroft, *The Works*, San Francisco; 1886, vol. 5, pp. 540–602.)

great intimacy and friendship with his cousin Zutuhileb-Pop, king of the Tzutuhiles, the latter abused his generosity and ran away with his daughter Ixcunsocil; and at the same time Iloacab, his relative and favorite, ran away with Exelispua, his niece. The rape of Helen did not produce more wars and bloodshed than the carrying off of these two young ladies with unpronounceable names. Balam-Acab was naturally a mild man, but the abduction of his daughter was an affront not to be pardoned. With eighty thousand veterans he marched against Zutuhileb-Pop. He, himself, was in the center squadron, adorned with three diadems and other regal ornaments; in a rich chair of state splendidly ornamented with gold, emeralds, and other precious stones, he was carried upon the shoulders of the nobles of his court. Zutuhileb-Pop met him with sixty thousand men, commanded by Iloacab, his chief general and accomplice. The most bloody battle ever fought in the country took place; the field was so deeply inundated with blood that not a blade of grass could be seen. Victory long remained undecided, but at length Iloacab was killed, and Balam-Acab remained master of the field.

But the campaign did not terminate here. Balam-Acab, with thirty thousand veterans under his personal command and two other bodies of thirty thousand each, again met Zutuhileb Pop with forty thousand of his own warriors and forty thousand auxiliaries. The latter was defeated, and escaped at night. Balam-Acab pursued and overtook him, but while his bearers were hastening with him to the thickest of the fight, they lost their footing, and precipitated him to the earth. At this moment Zutuhileb-Pop was advancing with a chosen body of ten thousand lancers. Balam-Acab was slain, and fourteen thousand Indians were left dead on the field.

The war was prosecuted by the successor of Balam, and Zutuhileb-Pop sustained such severe reverses that he fell into a despondency and died. The war continued down to the time of Kicab Tanub, who, after a sanguinary struggle, reduced the Tzutuhiles and Cakchiquels to subjection to the kings of Quiché. At this time the kingdom of the Quichés had attained its greatest splendor, and this was contempora-

neous with that eventful era in American history, the reign
of Montezuma and the invasion of the Spaniards. The kings
of Mexico and Quiché acknowledged the ties of relationship,
and in a manuscript of sixteen quarto leaves, preserved by
the Indians of San Andrés Xecul, it is related that when
Montezuma was made prisoner, he sent a private ambassador
to Kicab Tanub to inform Kicab that some white men had
arrived in his state and had made war upon him with such
impetuosity that the whole strength of his people was unable
to resist them; that he was himself a prisoner, surrounded
by guards; and that, hearing it was the intention of his invaders to pass on to the kingdom of Quiché, he was sending
this notice of their design in order that Kicab Tanub might
be prepared to oppose them.

On receiving this intelligence, the King of Quiché sent
for four young diviners, whom he ordered to tell what the
result of this invasion would be. They requested time to
give their answers. Taking their bows, they discharged some
arrows against a rock but, seeing that no impression was
made upon it, they returned very sorrowfully and told the
king there was no way of avoiding the disaster, the white
men would certainly conquer them. Kicab, dissatisfied, then
sent for the priests, desiring to have their opinions on this
important subject. But they, too, because of the ominous circumstance of a certain stone brought by their forefathers
from Egypt having suddenly split into two, predicted the
inevitable ruin of the kingdom. At this time Kicab received
intelligence of the arrival of the Spaniards on the borders
of Soconusco to invade his territory and, undismayed by
the auguries of diviners or priests, he prepared for war.
Messages were sent by him to the conquered kings and chiefs
under his command, urging them to co-operate for the common defense. But, glad of an opportunity to rebel, Sinacam,
the king of Guatemala, declared openly that he was a friend
to the *Teules* or Gods, as the Spaniards were called by the
Indians; and the King of the Tzutuhiles answered haughtily
that he was able to defend his kingdom alone against a more
numerous and less famished army than that which was approaching Quiché. Irritation, wounded pride, anxiety, and

fatigue brought on a sickness which carried Tanub off in a
few days, and his son Tecún Umán succeeded to his honors
and troubles.

In a short time intelligence was received that the captain
(Alvarado) and his *Teules* had marched to besiege Xelahuh
(now Quezaltenango), which, next to the capital, was the
largest city of Quiché. At that time it had within its walls
eighty thousand men; but such was the fame of the Spaniards
that Tecún Umán determined to go to its assistance. He left
the capital, at the threshold of which we stood, borne in his
litter on the shoulders of the principal men of his kingdom,
and preceded by the music of flutes, cornets, and drums,
with seventy thousand men, commanded by his general
Ahzol, his lieutenant Ahzumanche, the grand shield-bearer
Ahpocob, other officers of dignity with still harder names,
and numerous attendants bearing parasols and fans of
feathers for the comfort of the royal person. An immense
number of Indian carriers followed with baggage and provisions. At the populous city of Totonicapán the army was
increased to ninety thousand fighting men. At Quezaltenango he was joined by ten more chiefs, who, well-armed
and supplied with provisions and displaying all the gorgeous
insignia of their rank, were attended by twenty-four thousand soldiers. At the same place he was re-enforced by
forty-six thousand more, adorned with plumes of different
colors, and with arms of every description, the chiefs decorated with the skins of lions, tigers, and bears, as distinguishing marks of their bravery and warlike prowess.

Tecún Umán marshaled under his banners on the plain
of Tzakahá two hundred and thirty thousand warriors and
fortified his camp with a wall of loose stones, enclosing
within its circuit several mountains. In the camp were several
military machines, formed of beams on rollers, to be moved
from place to place. But after a series of desperate and bloody
battles, the Spaniards routed this immense army, and entered the city of Xelahuh. The fugitives rallied outside, and
made a last effort to surround and crush the Spaniards.
Tecún Umán commanded in person; he singled out Alvarado, attacked him three times hand to hand, and wounded
his horse; but the last time Alvarado pierced him with a

FIG. 1 *Stone Idol at Quiriguá*

View of the Place of Sacrifice in Ruins.
AT SANTA CRUZ DEL QUICHE.

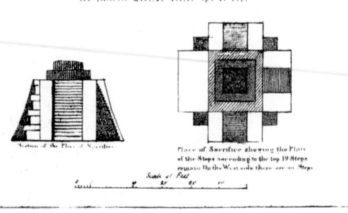

Section of the Place of Sacrifice

Place of Sacrifice showing the Place
of the Steps ascending to the top 19 Steps
remain On the West side there are no Steps

Scale of Feet

FIG. 2 *Ruins of the Place of Sacrifice, Santa Cruz
del Quiché, with sectional drawings of its
original form*

lance and killed him on the spot. The fury of the Indians increased to madness; in immense masses they rushed upon the Spaniards and, seizing the tails of their horses, endeavored by main force to bring horse and rider to the ground. But, at a critical moment, the Spaniards attacked in close column, broke the solid masses of the Quichés, routed the whole army and, slaying an immense number, became complete masters of the field. But few of the seventy thousand who had marched out from the capital with Tecún Umán ever returned; hopeless of being able to resist any longer by force, those still alive had recourse to treachery. At a council of war called at Utatlán by the king, Chinanivalut, son and successor of Tecún Umán, it was determined to send an embassy to Alvarado, with a valuable present of gold, suing for pardon, promising submission, and inviting the Spaniards to the capital. In a few days Alvarado with his army, in high spirits at the prospect of a termination of this bloody war, encamped upon the plain.

This was the first appearance of strangers at Utatlán, the capital of the great Indian kingdom, the ruins of which were now under our eyes; it had once been the most populous and opulent city, not only of Quiché, but of the whole kingdom of Guatemala. According to Fuentes, who visited it for the purpose of collecting information and who gathered his facts partly from the remains and partly from manuscripts, the city was surrounded by a deep ravine that formed a natural fosse, leaving only two very narrow roads as entrances, both of which were so well defended by the castle of Resguardo,[8] as to render the city impregnable. The center of the city was occupied by the royal palace, which was surrounded by the houses of the nobility; the extremities were inhabited by the plebeians. Some idea may be formed of its vast population from the fact, before mentioned, that the king drew from it no less than seventy-two thousand fighting men to oppose the Spaniards.

It contained many very sumptuous edifices, the most superb of which was a seminary, where between five and

---

8. *Resguardo* and *Atalaya* (see p. 148), Spanish common nouns meaning *defense* and *watchtower* are the names which the Spaniards gave to these buildings undoubtedly because of their appearance and use.

six thousand children were educated at the charge of the royal treasury. The castle of the Atalaya was a remarkable structure, four stories high, and capable of furnishing quarters for a very strong garrison. The castle of Resguardo was five stories high, extending one hundred and eighty paces in front, and two hundred and thirty in depth. The grand *alcázar*, or palace of the kings of Quiché, surpassed every other edifice; in the opinion of Torquemada, it could compete in opulence with that of Montezuma in Mexico or that of the Incas in Cuzco. The front extended three hundred and seventy-six geometrical paces from east to west, and it was seven hundred and twenty-eight paces in depth. It was constructed of hewn stones of various colors. There were six principal divisions. The first contained lodgings for numerous troop of lancers, archers, and other troops, which constituted the royal bodyguard; the second was assigned to the princes and relations of the king. The third division was for the use of the monarch himself, containing distinct suites of apartments for the mornings, evenings, and nights; in one of the salons stood the throne, under four canopies of feathers. In this portion of the palace were also the treasury, tribunals of the judges, armory, aviaries, and menageries. The fourth and fifth divisions were occupied by the queen and royal concubines, with gardens, baths, and places for breeding geese, which were kept to supply feathers for ornaments. The sixth and last division was the residence of the daughters and other females of the blood royal.

Such is the account as derived by the Spanish historians from manuscripts composed by some of the caciques who first acquired the art of writing; and it is related that from Tanub, who conducted them from the old to the new continent, down to Tecún Umán, was a line of twenty monarchs.[9]

Alvarado, on the invitation of the king, entered this city with his army. Observing the strength of the place—that it

---

9. In this and other accounts of the early history of Guatemala, allowances should be made for the intrusion of legend and exaggerations. If, for example, the Indian armies were as large as reported here, Guatemala would have had a population of perhaps fifteen million people. Modern historians believe the population to have been less

was well walled and surrounded by a deep ravine with but two approaches to it, the one by an ascent of twenty-five steps, and the other by a causeway, and both extremely narrow; that the streets were but of trifling breadth, and the houses very lofty; that there were neither women nor children to be seen; and that the Indians seemed agitated— observing these things the soldiers began to suspect some deceit. Their apprehensions were soon confirmed by Indian allies of Quezaltenango, who discovered that the people intended that night to fire their capital and, while the flames were rising, to burst upon the Spaniards with large bodies of men concealed in the neighborhood and put everyone to death. These tidings were found to be in accordance with the movements of the Indians; and on examining the houses, the Spaniards discovered that there were no preparations of provisions to regale them, as had been promised, but everywhere was a quantity of light dry fuel and other combustibles. Alvarado called his officers together and laid before them their perilous situation and the immediate necessity of withdrawing from the place; and, pretending to the king and his caciques that their horses were better in the open fields, the troops were collected and without any appearance of alarm marched in good order to the plain. The king, with pretended courtesy, accompanied them, and Alvarado, taking advantage of the opportunity, made him prisoner and, after trial and proof of his treachery, hung him on the spot.

But neither the death of Tecún nor the ignominious execution of his son could quell the fierce spirit of the Quichés. A new ebullition of animosity and rage broke forth. A general attack was made upon the Spaniards, but Spanish bravery and discipline increased with danger. After a dreadful havoc by the artillery and horses, the Indians abandoned a field covered with their dead, and Utatlán, the capital, with the whole kingdom of Quiché, fell into the hands of Alvarado and the Spaniards.

---

than three million. Furthermore, the site of Utatlán is not large enough to accommodate the enormous buildings described by Stephens as having existed when the Spaniards arrived.

As we stood now on the ruined fortress of Resguardo, the great plain, consecrated by the last struggle of a brave people, lay before us grand and beautiful, its bloodstains all washed out, and smiling with fertility, but perfectly desolate. Our guide leaning on his sword in the area beneath was the only person in sight. But very soon Bobón introduced a stranger, who came stumbling along under a red silk umbrella, talking to Bobón and looking up at us. We recognized him as the cura, and descended to meet him. He laughed to see us grope our way down; by degrees his laugh became infectious, and when we met we all laughed together. All at once he stopped, looked very solemn, pulled off his neckcloth, and wiped the perspiration from his face; he took out a paper of cigars but, laughing, thrust it back and pulled out another, as he said, of *habanos*, and asked what was the news from Spain.

Our friend's dress was as unclerical as his manner. He wore a broad-brimmed black glazed hat, an old black coat reaching to his heels, glossy from long use, with pantaloons to match, and a striped roundabout, a waistcoat, flannel shirt, and under it a cotton one, perhaps washed when he shaved last, some weeks before. He laughed at our coming to see the ruins, and said that he laughed prodigiously himself when he first saw them. He was from Old Spain. He had seen the battle of Trafalgar, looking on from the heights on shore, and he said he laughed whenever he thought of it: the French fleet blown sky high and the Spanish with it, Lord Nelson killed—all for glory—he could not help laughing. He had left Spain to get rid of wars and revolutions (here we all laughed); sailing with twenty Dominican friars, he had been fired upon and chased into Jamaica by a French cruiser (here we laughed again); from there he got an English convoy to Omoa, where he arrived at the breaking out of a revolution. All his life he had been in the midst of revolutions, and it was now better than ever! Here we all laughed incontinently. His own laugh was so rich and expressive that it was perfectly irresistible. In fact, we were not disposed to resist, and in half an hour we were as intimate as if acquainted for years. The world was our butt, and we laughed at it outrageously. Except for the Church, there were few things which the cura did not laugh at; but politics was his favorite subject. He was in favor of Morazán, or Carrera, or *el Demonio; vamos adelante* (go ahead) was his motto, he laughed at them all. If we had parted with him then, we should always have remembered him as the laughing cura; but, on further acquaintance, we found in him such a vein of strong sense and knowledge, and, retired as he lived, he was so intimately acquainted with the country and all the public men, and as a mere looker-on his views were so correct and his satire so keen yet without malice, that we improved his title by calling him the laughing philosopher.

Having finished our observations at this place, stopping to laugh as some new greatness or folly of the world, past, present, or to come occurred to us, we descended by a narrow path and, after crossing a ravine, entered upon the table of land on which stood the palace and principal part of the city. Mr. Catherwood and I began examining and measuring the ruins, and the padre followed us, talking and laughing all the time. When we were on some high place out of his reach, he seated Bobón at the foot, discoursing to him of Alvarado and Montezuma and the daughter of the king of Tecpán of Guatemala, and of books and manuscripts in the convent, to all of which Bobón listened without comprehending a word or moving a muscle, looking him directly in the face and answering his long low laugh with a respectful *Sí, señor.*

The ground in the heart of the city, which was occupied by the palace and other buildings of the royal house of Quiché, was surrounded by an immense barranca, or ravine,[10] and the only entrance to it was through that part of the ravine by which we reached it, which is defended by the fortress before referred to. The cura pointed out to us one part of the ravine which, he said, according to old manuscripts formerly existing in the convent but now carried

---

10. A distant view of Santa Cruz del Quiché and surrounding topography is reproduced from an engraving in earlier editions of *Incidents of Travel. . . .*

away, was artificial, on the work of which forty thousand men had been employed at one time.

The whole area was once occupied by the palace, seminary, and other buildings of the royal house of Quiché, which now lie for the most part in confused and shapeless masses of ruins. The palace with its courts and corridors, the cura told us, once covered the whole diameter; now completely destroyed, the materials have been carried away to build the present village. In part, however, the floor remains entire, with fragments of the partition walls, so that the plan of the apartments can be distinctly made out. This floor is of a hard cement, which, though washed year after year by the floods of the rainy season, is hard and durable as stone. The inner walls were covered with plaster of a finer description, and in corners where there had been less exposure were the remains of colors; no doubt the whole interior had been ornamented with paintings. It gave a strange sensation to walk the floor of that roofless palace and think of that king who left it at the head of seventy thousand men to repel the invaders of his empire. Corn was now growing among the ruins, the ground being used by an Indian family which claimed to be descended from the royal house. In one place was a desolate hut, occupied by them at the time of planting and gathering the corn. Adjoining the palace was a large plaza or courtyard, also covered with hard cement, in the center of which were the relics of a fountain.

The most important part remaining of these ruins, which appears in the engraving (figure 2 facing page 147), is called *El Sacrificadero,* or The Place of Sacrifice. It is a quadrangular stone structure, sixty-six feet on each side at the base, and rising in a pyramidal form to the height, in its present condition, of thirty-three feet. On each of three sides there is a range of steps in the middle, each step seventeen inches high and but eight inches on the upper surface, which makes the range so steep that in descending some caution is necessary. At the corners are four buttresses of cut stone, diminishing in size from the line of the square, and apparently intended to support the structure. On the side facing the west there are no steps, but the surface is smooth and covered with stucco, gray from long exposure. By breaking a little at the corners we saw that there were different layers of stucco, doubtless put on at different times, and all had been ornamented with painted figures. In one place we made out part of the body of a leopard, well drawn and colored.

The top of the *Sacrificadero* is broken and ruined, but there is no doubt that it once supported an altar for those sacrifices of human victims which struck even the Spaniards with horror. It was barely large enough for the altar and officiating priests, and the idol to whom the sacrifice was offered. The whole was in full view of the people at the foot.

The barbarous ministers carried up the victim entirely naked; they pointed out the idol to which the sacrifice was to be made, that the people might pay their adorations, and then extended him upon the altar. This had a convex surface, and the body of the victim lay arched, with the trunk elevated and the head and feet depressed. Four priests held the legs and arms, and another kept his head firm with a wooden instrument made in the form of a coiled serpent, so that he was prevented from making the least movement. The head priest then approached, and with a knife made of flint cut an aperture in the breast, and tore out the heart, which, yet palpitating, he offered to the sun and then threw at the feet of the idol. If the idol was gigantic and hollow, it was usual to introduce the heart of the victim into its mouth with a golden spoon. If the victim was a prisoner of war, as soon as he was sacrificed they cut off the head to preserve the skull, and threw the body down the steps to be taken by the officer or soldier to whom the prisoner belonged and carried to his house to be dressed and served up as an entertainment for his friends. If he was not a prisoner of war, but a slave purchased for the sacrifice, the proprietor carried off the body for the same purpose. In recurring to the barbarous scenes of which the spot had been the theater, it seemed a righteous award that the bloody altar was hurled down, and the race of its ministers destroyed.

It was fortunate for us, in the excited state of the country, that it was not necessary to devote much time to an examination of these ruins. In 1834 a thorough exploration had been made under a commission from the government of Guatemala. Don Miguel Rivera y Maestre, a gentleman distinguished for his scientific and antiquarian tastes, was the commissioner, and he kindly furnished me with a copy of his manuscript report to the government, written out by himself. This report is full and elaborate, and I have no doubt is the result of a thorough examination, but it does not refer to any objects of interest except those I have mentioned. He procured, however, the image of which a front and side view appear in figure 3 and which, without my venturing to express a wish for it, he kindly gave to me. It is made of baked clay, very hard, with a surface as smooth as if coated with enamel. It is twelve inches high, and the interior is hollow, including the arms and legs. In his report to the government, Don Miguel calls it Cabuahuil, or one of the deities of the ancient inhabitants of Quiché. I do not know upon what authority he has given it this name, but to me it does not seem improbable that his supposition is true, and that to this earthen vessel human victims have been offered in sacrifice.

The heads in the engraving (figure 3) were given me by the cura. They are of terra cotta; the lower one is hollow and the upper is solid with a polished surface. They are hard as stone, and in workmanship will compare with images in the same material by artists of the present day.

In our investigation of antiquities we considered this place important from the fact that its history is known and its date fixed. It was in its greatest splendor when Alvarado conquered it. It proves the character of the buildings which the Indians of that day constructed, and in its ruins confirms the glowing accounts given by Cortes and his companions of the splendor displayed in the edifices of Mexico. The point to which we directed our attention was to discover some resemblance to the ruins of Copán and Quiriguá; but we did not find statues, or carved figures, or hieroglyphics, nor could we learn that any had ever been found there. If there had been such evidences we should have considered these remains the works of the same race of people, but in the absence of

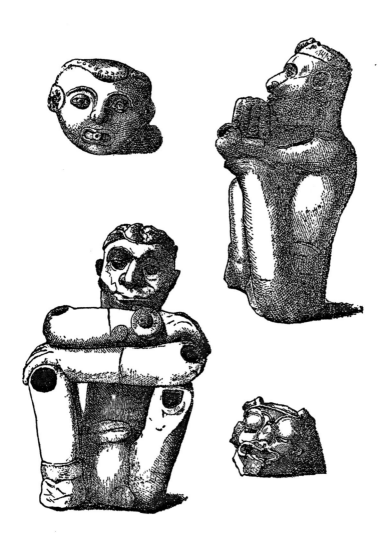

FIG. 3 *Terra Cotta Figures at Santa Cruz del Quiché*

such evidences we believed that Copán and Quiriguá were cities of another race and of a much older date.[11]

The padre told us that thirty years before, when he first saw it, the palace was entire to the garden. He was then fresh from the palaces of Spain, and it seemed as if he was again among them. Shortly after his arrival a small gold image was found and sent to Saravia, the president of Guatemala,[12] who ordered a commission from the capital to search for hidden treasure; in this search the palace was destroyed. The Indians, roused by the destruction of their ancient capital, rose and threatened to kill the workmen unless they left the country; and but for this, the cura said, every stone would have been razed to the ground. The Indians of Quiché have at all times a bad name; at Guatemala it was always spoken of as an unsafe place to visit, and the padre told us that they looked with distrust upon any stranger coming to the ruins. At that moment they were in a state of universal excitement. Coming close to us, the padre said that in the village they stood at swords' points with the mestizos, ready to cut their throats, and with all his exertions he could barely keep down a general rising and massacre. (Even this information he gave us with a laugh.) We asked him if he had no fears for himself. He said No, he was beloved by the Indians; he had passed the greater part of his life among them, and as yet the padres were safe: the Indians considered them almost as saints. Here he laughed again: Carrera was on their side; but if he turned against them it would be time to flee. All this was both communicated and received with peals of laughter; and the more serious the subject, the louder was our cachinnation. And all the time the padre made continual references to books and manuscripts, showing antiquarian studies and profound knowledge.

---

11. According to modern scholarship, Copán and Quiriguá are much older than Utatlán. The Quiché Indians are, however, one branch of the great Maya family.

12. Guatemala was not independent at that time. Saravia was captain-general and president of the *audiencia* of Guatemala from 1801–11.

Under one of the buildings was an opening which the Indians called a cave, and by which they said one could reach Mexico in an hour. I crawled under, and found a pointed-arch roof formed by stones lapping over each other, but was prevented from exploring it by want of light and the padre's crying to me that it was the season of earthquakes. He laughed more than usual at the hurry with which I came out, but all at once he stopped, and grasping his pantaloons, hopped about, crying, "a snake, a snake." The guide and Bobón hurried to his relief. By a simple process, but with great respect, one at work on each side, they were in a fair way of securing the intruder, but the padre could not stand still, and with his agitation and restlessness he tore loose from their hold and brought to light a large grasshopper. While Bobón and the guide, without a smile, restored him and put each button in its place, we finished with a laugh outrageous to the memory of the departed inhabitants, and to all sentiment connected with the ruins of a great city.

As we returned to the village the padre pointed out on the plain the direction of four roads, which led (according to him they were still open) to Mexico, Tecpán Guatemala, Los Altos, and Verapaz.

Chapter XI

~~~~~~

Interior of a convent. Royal bird of Quiché. Indian languages. The Lord's Prayer in the Quiché language. Numerals in the same. Church of Quiché. Indian superstitions. Another lost city. Tierra de Guerra. The aboriginals. Their conversion to Christianity. They were never conquered. A living city. Indian tradition respecting this city. Probably has never been visited by the whites. Presents a noble field for future enterprise. Departure. San Pedro. Virtue of a passport. A difficult ascent. Mountain scenery. Totonicapán. An excellent dinner. A country of aloes. "River of Blood." Arrival at Quezaltenango.

IT was late when we returned to the convent. The good padre, who regretted not being at home when we arrived, said that he always locked his room to prevent the women throwing things into confusion. When we entered, it was in what he called order, but this order was of a class that beggars description. The room contained a table, chairs, and two settees, but there was not a vacant place even on the table on which to sit or lay a hat. Every spot was encumbered with articles, of which four bottles, a cruet of mustard and another of oil, bones, cups, plates, sauceboat, a large lump of sugar, a paper of salt, minerals and large stones, shells, pieces of pottery, skulls, bones, cheese, books, and manuscripts formed part. On a shelf over his bed were two stuffed quetzales, the royal bird of Quiché, the most beautiful that flies, and so proud of its tail that it builds its nest with two openings, that it may pass in and out without turning. The plumes of these birds were not permitted to be used except by the royal family.

Amid this confusion a corner was cleared on the table for dinner. The conversation continued on his part in the same unbroken stream of knowledge, research, sagacity, and satire. Political matters were spoken of in whispers when any servants were in the rooms, and a laugh was the comment upon everything. By evening we were deep in the mysteries of Indian history.

Besides the Mexican or Aztec language spoken by the Pipil Indians along the coast of the Pacific, there are twenty-four dialects peculiar to Guatemala.[1] Though they sometimes bear such a strong resemblance in some of their idioms that the Indians of one tribe can understand those of another, in general the padres, after years of residence, can only speak the language of the tribe among which they live. This diversity of language had seemed to me an insuperable impediment in the way of any thorough investigation and study of Indian history and traditions; but the cura, profound in everything that related to the Indians, told us that the Quiché was the parent tongue, and that, if one were familiar with it, the others could be easily acquired. If this be true, a new and most interesting field of research is opened. During my whole journey, even at Guatemala City, I was unable to procure any grammar of an Indian language, nor any manuscripts. I made several vocabularies, which I have not thought it worth while to publish; but the padre had a book prepared by some of the early fathers for the church service, which he promised to have copied for me later and sent to a friend at Guatemala, and from which I copied the Lord's prayer in the Quiché language. It is as follows:

Cacahan chicah lae coni Vtzah. Vcahaxtizaxie mayih Bila Chipa ta pa Cani Ahauremla Chibantah. Ahuamla Uaxale Chiyala Chiqueeh hauta Vleus quehexi Caban Chicah. Uacamic Chiyala. Chiqueeh hauta. Eihil Caua. Zachala Camac quehexi Cacazachbep qui. Mac Xemocum Chiqueeh: moho Estachcula maxa Copahic Chupamtah Chibal mac xanare Cohcolta la ha Vonohel itgel quehe Chucoe. Amen.[2]

---

1. Most linguists would call them languages rather than dialects. At present only about fifteen are spoken in Guatemala. Except for Pipil, they all belong to the Mayan family.

2. It is difficult to say how inaccurate this version is.

I will add the following numerals,[3] as taken from the same book:

Hun, *one*	Uaelahuh, *sixteen*
Quieb, *two*	Velahuh, *seventeen*
Dxib, *three*	Uapxaelahuh, *eighteen*
Quieheb, *four*	Belehalahuh, *nineteen*
Hoob, *five*	Huuinac, *twenty*
Uacacguil, *six*	Huuinachun, *twenty-one*
Veuib, *seven*	Huuinachlahuh, *thirty*
Uahxalquib, *eight*	Cauinae, *forty*
Beleheb, *nine*	Lahuh Raxcal, *fifty*
Lahuh, *ten*	Oxcal, *sixty*
Hulahuh, *eleven*	Lahuh Vhumuch, *seventy*
Cablahuh, *twelve*	Humuch, *eighty*
Dxlahuh, *thirteen*	Lahuh Rocal, *ninety*
Cahlahuh, *fourteen*	Ocal, *a hundred*
Hoolahuh, *fifteen*	Otuc Rox Ocob, *a thousand*

Whether there is any analogy between this language and that of any of our Indian tribes, I am not able to say.[4]

For a man who has not reached that period when a few years tell upon his teeth and hair, I know of no place where, if the country becomes quiet, he might pass them with greater interest than at Santa Cruz del Quiché, in studying, by means of their language, the character and traditionary history of the Indians; for here they still exist, in many respects, an unchanged people, cherishing the usages and customs of their ancestors. Though the grandeur and magnificence of the churches and the pomp and show of religious ceremonies affect their rude imaginations, the padre told us that in their hearts they were full of superstitions and still idolaters; in the mountains and ravines they had their idols, and in silence and secrecy they practised the rites received from their fathers. He was compelled to wink at these things, but there was one proof which he saw every day: The church of Quiché stands east and west; on entering it for vespers the

3. For a more accurate spelling of these numerals, *see* Otto Stoll, *Etnografía de la República de Guatemala*, translated by Antonio Goubaud Carrera, Guatemala, 1938, p. 80 ff.

4. The Quiché language is not known to be related to any of the Indian languages of the United States.

Indians always bowed to the west in reverence to the setting sun. He told us, too, what requires confirmation, and what we were very curious to judge of for ourselves, that in a cave near a neighboring village were skulls much larger than the natural size which were regarded with superstitious reverence by the Indians. He had seen them, and vouched for their gigantic dimensions. Once he had placed a piece of money in the mouth of the cave and, a year afterward, found the money still lying in the same place, while, he said, if it had been left on his table, it would have disappeared with the first Indian who entered.

The padre's whole manner was now changed; his keen satire and his laugh were gone. There was interest enough about the Indians to occupy the mind and excite the imagination of one who laughed at everything else in the world; and his enthusiasm, like his laugh, was infectious. Notwithstanding our haste to reach Palenque, we felt a strong desire to track the Indians in the solitude of their mountains and deep ravines, and to watch them in the observance of their idolatrous rites; but the padre did not give us any encouragement. In fact, he opposed our remaining another day, even to visit the cave of skulls. He made no apology for hurrying us away. He lived in unbroken solitude, in a monotonous routine of occupations, and the visit of a stranger was to him an event most welcome. But there was danger in our remaining. The Indians were in an inflammable state; they were already inquiring what we came there for, and he could not answer for our safety. In a few months, perhaps, the excitement might pass away, and then we could return. He loved the subjects we took interest in, and would join us in all our expeditions, and aid us with all his influence.

The padre's knowledge was not confined to his own immediate neighborhood. His first curacy had been at Cobán,[5] in the province of Verapaz; and he told us that four leagues from that place was another ancient city, as large as Santa Cruz del Quiché, deserted and desolate, and almost as per-

---

5. In the department of Alta Verapaz in north central Guatemala; not to be confused with the Old Empire Mayan city of Copán in Honduras.

fect as when evacuated by its inhabitants. He had wandered through its silent streets and over its gigantic buildings, and its palace was as entire as that of Quiché when he first saw it. This ancient city is within two hundred miles of Guatemala, and in a district of country not disturbed by war; yet, with all our inquiries, we had heard nothing of it. And now the information really grieved us, for going to the place would add eight hundred miles to our journey. Our plans were fixed, our time already limited; and in that wild country and its unsettled state, we had superstitious apprehensions that it was ominous to return. My impression, however, of the existence of such a city is most strong. I do most earnestly hope that some future traveler will visit it.[6] He will not hear of it even at Guatemala, and perhaps will be told that it does not exist. Nevertheless, let him seek for it and, if he does find it, experience sensations which seldom fall to the lot of man.

But the padre told us more—something that increased our excitement to the highest pitch. On the other side of the great traversing range of Cordilleras lies the district of Verapaz, once called *Tierra de Guerra*, or Land of War, from the warlike character of its aboriginal inhabitants. Three times the Spaniards were driven back in their attempts to conquer it. Las Casas,[7] vicar of the convent of the Dominican order in the city of Guatemala, mourning over the bloodshed caused by what was called converting the Indians to Christianity, wrote a treatise to prove that Divine Providence had instituted the preaching of the Gospel as the only means of conversion to the Christian faith; that war could not with justice be made upon those who had never committed any aggressions against Christians; and that to harass and destroy the Indians was to prevent the accomplishing of this desired

6. The only Mayan ruins anywhere near Cobán are those of Chamá which has been classed by S. G. Morley, the archeologist, as a fourth-class center.

7. Bartolomé de las Casas (1474–1566), Spanish missionary and historian whose zeal in defending the Indians won for him the title "Apostle of the Indians."

object. This doctrine he preached from the pulpit and enforced in private assemblies. He was laughed at, ridiculed, and sneeringly advised to put his theory in practice.

Undisturbed by this mockery, Las Casas accepted the proposal; he chose as the field of his operations the unconquerable district called *Tierra de Guerra,* and made an arrangement that no Spaniards should be permitted to reside in that country for five years. This agreed upon, the Dominicans composed some hymns in the Quiché language describing the creation of the world, the fall of Adam, the redemption of mankind, and the principal mysteries of the life, passion, and death of our Saviour. These were learned by some Indians who traded with the Quichés; and a principal cacique of the country, afterward called Don Juan, having heard them sung, asked those who had repeated them to explain in detail the meanings of things so new to him. The Indians excused themselves, saying that they could only be explained by the fathers who had taught them. The cacique sent one of his brothers with many presents to entreat that they would come and make him acquainted with what was contained in the songs of the Indian merchants. A single Dominican friar returned with the ambassador, and the cacique, having been made to comprehend the mysteries of the new faith, burned his idols and preached Christianity to his own subjects. Las Casas and another associate followed, and, like the apostles of old, without scrip or staff, effected what Spanish arms could not, bringing a portion of the Land of War to the Christian faith. The rest of the *Tierra de Guerra* never was conquered. Even at this day the northeastern section, bounded by the range of the Cordilleras and the State of Chiapas, is occupied by Candones [8] or unbaptized Indians, who live as their fathers did, acknowledging no submission to the Spaniards; and the government of Central America does not pretend to exercise any control over them.

But the thing that roused us was the assertion by the padre, that, four days on the road to Mexico, on the other side of

8. Stephens must mean the Lacandones, who are the least civilized of all the Indians now living in Guatemala.

the great sierra,[9] was a living city, which was large and populous, and occupied by Indians in precisely the same state
as before the discovery of America. He had heard of it many
years before at the village of Chajul, and he had been told
by the villagers that from the topmost ridge of the sierra
this city was distinctly visible. He was then young, and with
much labor climbed to the naked summit of the sierra, from
which, at a height of ten or twelve thousand feet, looking
over an immense plain extending to Yucatán and the Gulf
of Mexico, he saw at a great distance a large city spread over
a great space, a city with turrets white and glittering in the
sun. The traditional account of the Indians of Chajul is: that
no white man has ever reached this city; that the inhabitants
speak the Maya language; and that, aware that a race of
strangers has conquered the whole country around, they will
murder any white man who attempts to enter their territory.
They have no coin or other circulating medium; no horses,
cattle, mules, or other domestic animals except fowls, and
they keep the cocks under ground to prevent their crowing
being heard.

There was a wild novelty—something that touched the
imagination—in every step of our journey in that country.
The old padre, in the deep stillness of the dimly lighted
convent, with his long black coat like a robe, and his flashing
eye, called up an image of the bold and resolute priests who
accompanied the armies of the conquerors; as he drew a map
on the table and pointed out the sierra to the top of which
he had climbed, and the position of the mysterious city, the
interest awakened in us was the most thrilling I ever experienced. One look at that city would be worth ten years of an
everyday life. If he is right, a place is left where Indians
and an Indian city exist as Cortes and Alvarado found them;
a place where there are living men who can solve the mystery that hangs over the ruined cities of America, who can,
perhaps, go to Copán and read the inscriptions on its monuments. No subject more exciting and attractive presents itself

9. Probably the Cuchumatanes, the highest mountains in Central
America.

to my mind, and the deep impression of that night will never be effaced.

Can it be true? Being now in my sober senses, I do verily believe there is much ground to suppose that what the padre told us is authentic. That the region referred to does not acknowledge the government of Guatemala, that it has never been explored,[10] and that no white man ever pretends to enter it, I am satisfied of. From other sources we heard that from this sierra a large *ruined* city was visible; we were also told of still another person who had climbed to the top of the sierra but, who, on account of the dense cloud resting upon it, had been unable to see anything. At all events, the belief at the village of Chajul is general, and it rouses a curiosity that burns to be satisfied. We had a craving desire to reach the mysterious city. No man, even if willing to peril his life, could undertake the enterprise with any hope of success without hovering for one or two years on the borders of the country, studying the language and character of the adjoining Indians and making acquaintance with some of the natives. Five hundred men could probably march directly to the city, and the invasion would be more justifiable than any ever made by the Spaniards; but the government is too much occupied with its own wars, and the knowledge could not be procured except at the price of blood. Two young men of good constitution, and who could afford to spare five years, might succeed. If the object of search prove a phantom, in the wild scenes of a new and unexplored country there are other objects of interest; but if real, besides the glorious excitement of such a novelty, they will have something to look back upon through life. As to the dangers, these are always magnified, and, in general, peril is discovered soon enough for escape. But in all probability, if any discovery is ever made it will be by the padres. As for ourselves, to attempt it alone, ignorant of the language, and with *mozos* who were a constant annoyance to us, was out of the question. The most

---

10. The region to which Stephens refers here has been explored and the ruins of ancient cities have been found there. But, unfortunately for both science and romance, the autonomous city Stephens pictures was not among them.

we thought of was a climb to the top of the sierra, thence to look down upon the mysterious city; but we had difficulties enough on the road before us; it would add ten days to a journey already almost appalling in propect; and for days the sierra might be covered with clouds. In attempting too much, we might lose all. Palenque was our great point, and we determined not to be diverted from the course we had marked out.

The next morning we had one painful moment with the cura, and that was the moment of parting. He was then calm and kind, his irresistible laugh and his enthusiasm all gone. He told us that we had one village to pass where the Indians were bad; for this reason he gave us a letter to the *justicia*. In the kindness of his heart before parting he insisted on my accepting one of his beautiful quetzales.

As this was Holy Week, we had great difficulty in procuring a guide. None of the Indians wished to leave the village, and the alcalde told an alguacil to take a man out of prison. After a parley with the inmates through the grating, one was selected but kept in confinement till the moment of starting when the alguacil opened the door and let him out; our roll of luggage was put on his back, and he set off. The battered soldier accompanied us a short distance, and Bobón went before, carrying on a stick the royal bird of Quiché. Crossing the plain and the ravine on which the city stood, we ascended a mountain in the rear which commanded a magnificent view of the plain of Quiché, and descending on the other side, at the distance of two leagues we reached the village of San Pedro. A thatched church, with a cross before it, stood near the road, and the huts of the village were a little in the rear.

The padre had told us that the Indians of this place were *muy malos* (very bad). As our guide, when he returned, would be locked up in prison, to avoid the necessity of stopping, we tried to induce him to continue; but he dropped his load at the foot of the cross, and ran back in such haste that he left behind his ragged *chamarra*, or poncho. The *justicia*, a mestizo, sent for the alcalde, and presently that worthy trotted down with six alguaciles, marching in single file, all

with wands in their hands and dressed in handsome cloth
cloaks, the holiday costume for the Holy Week. We told
them that we wanted a guide, and the whole six set off to
look for one. In about ten minutes they returned single file,
exactly on the same trot as before, and said they could not
find any; the whole week was holiday, and no one wanted
to leave home. I showed Carrera's passport, and told the
justicia he must go himself, or send one of his alguaciles, and
they set off again in pursuit. After waiting a little while, I
walked to the top of a hill near by, and saw them all seated
below, apparently waiting for me to go. As soon as they saw
me they ran back in a body to repeat that they could not find
a guide. I offered them double price, but they were immova-
ble; and feeling rather uncertain what turn things might
take, I talked largely of Carrera's vengeance; not contenting
myself with merely turning them out of office, I had their
heads taken off at once. After a few moments' consultation
they all rose quietly; one doffed his dignity and dress, and
the rest rolled up the cargo and, throwing it on his bare back,
placed the band across his forehead and set him off on a run.
We followed, the secretary begging me to write to Carrera
that it was not through his fault I was kept waiting, and that
he would have been my guide himself if I had not found another. At a short distance another alguacil, by a crosscut,
intercepted and relieved the first; and they ran so fast that
on the rough road we could not keep up with them.

The road was indeed rough and wild beyond all description; and very soon, after reaching and descending another
immense ravine, we commenced an ascent on the opposite
side, which occupied three hours. Through openings in the
woods we looked down precipices one or two thousand feet
deep, with the mountainside still higher above us. The whole
mountain was clothed with luxuriant vegetation, and though
wanting the rocky, savage grandeur of Alpine scenery, at
every turn the view was sublime. As we climbed up we met
a few Indians who could speak no language but their own,
and reaching the top, we saw a wretched spectacle of the
beings made in God's image. A drunken Indian was lying
on the ground, his face cut with a machete; he was weltering

in his blood and a drunken woman was crying over him. Our Indians stopped and spoke to them, but we could not understand what they said.

At about three o'clock we emerged from the woods and very soon saw Totonicapán, at a great distance and far below us, on a magnificent plain with a high table of land behind it; a range of mountains sprung from the table and rising above them was the volcano of Quezaltenango.[11] The town was spread over a large space, and the flat roofs of the houses seemed one huge covering, broken only by the steeple of the church. We descended the mountain to the banks of a beautiful stream along which Indian women were washing; following it, we entered the town and rode up to the house of the corregidor, Don José Azmitia. Our luggage had arrived safely, and in a few minutes our men presented themselves to receive us.

Much might be said of Totonicapán, surrounded as it was by mountains visible on all sides from the plaza; but I stop only to record an event. All along, with the letters to corregidores, the passport of Carrera, and the letter of the archbishop, our road had been a sort of triumphal march; but at this place we dined, that is, we had a dinner. The reader may remember that in Costa Rica I promised to offend but once more by referring to such a circumstance. That time has come, and I should consider myself an ingrate if I omitted to mention it. We were kept waiting perhaps two hours, and we had not eaten anything in more than twelve. We had clambered over terrible mountains; and at six o'clock, on invitation, with hands and faces washed, and in dress coats, we sat down with the corregidor. Courses came regularly and in right succession. Servants were well trained, and our host did the honors as if he was used to the same thing every day. But it was not so with us. Like Rittmaster Dugald Dalgetty,[12] we ate very fast and very long, on his principle deeming it the duty of every commander of a fortress, on all occasions

---

11. The volcano of Santa María near the city of Quezaltenango.
12. A character in Sir Walter Scott's *Legend of Montrose*.

which offer, to secure as much munition and vivers as his magazines could possibly hold.

We were again on the line of Carrera's operations; the place was alive with apprehensions; white men were trembling for their lives; and I advised our host to leave the country and come to the United States.

The next morning we breakfasted with him, and at eleven o'clock, while a procession was forming in the plaza, we started for Quezaltenango. We descended a ravine commanding at every point a beautiful view, ascended a mountain from which we looked back upon the plain and town of Totonicapán, and on the top entered a magnificent plain, cultivated with cornfields and dotted with numerous flocks of sheep, the first we had seen in the country; on both sides of the road were hedges of gigantic aloes (*Agave americana*). In one place we counted upward of two hundred in full bloom. In the middle of the plain at a distance of two and a half leagues, we crossed on a rude bridge of logs a broad river memorable for the killed and wounded thrown into it in Alvardo's battle with Quiché Indians, and called the "River of Blood." Two leagues beyond we came in sight of Quezaltenango, standing at the foot of a great range of mountains, surmounted by a rent volcano constantly emitting smoke; before it was a mountain ridge of lava, which, if it had taken its course toward the city, would have buried it like Herculaneum and Pompeii.

Chapter XII

∿∿∿∿∿∿∿∿∿∿∿∿∿∿∿∿∿∿∿∿∿∿∿∿∿∿∿∿∿∿∿∿∿∿∿

Quezaltenango. Account of it. Conversion of the inhabitants to Christianity. Appearance of the city. The convent. Insurrection. Carrera's march upon Quezaltenango. His treatment of the inhabitants. Preparations for Holy Week. The Church. A procession. Good Friday. Celebration of the Resurrection. Opening ceremony. The Crucifixion. A sermon. Descent from the Cross. Grand procession. Church of El Calvario. The case of the cura. Warm springs of Almolonga.

WE were again on classic soil. The reader perhaps requires to be reminded that the city stands on the site of the ancient Xelahuh, which next to Utatlán was the largest city in Quiché. The word *Xelahuh* means "under the government of ten"; the city was governed by ten principal captains, each captain presiding over eight thousand dwellings, in all eighty thousand, and it contained, according to Fuentes, more than three hundred thousand inhabitants.[1] On the defeat of Tecún Umán by Alvarado, the inhabitants had abandoned the city, and fled to their ancient fortresses: Excanul, the volcano, and Cekxak, another mountain adjoining. The Spaniards entered the deserted city and, according to a manuscript found in the village of San Andrés Xecul, their vedettes captured the four celebrated caciques, whose names, the reader doubtless remembers, were Calel Ralek, Ahpopqueham, Calelahau, and Calelaboy; the Spanish records say that they fell on their knees before Pedro

---

1. Fuentes says eight thousand subjects, not dwellings. Modern scholars do not believe the population of Xelahuh reached even a third of three hundred thousand.

Alvarado while a priest explained to them the nature of the
Christian faith and they declared themselves ready to embrace it. Two of them were retained as hostages, and the
others sent back to the fortresses to return with such multi-
tudes of Indians ready to be baptized that the priests from
sheer fatigue could no longer lift their arms to perform
the ceremony. As we approached, seven towering churches
showed that the religion so hastily adopted had not died
away.

In a few minutes we entered the city. The streets were
handsomely paved, and the houses picturesque in architecture; the cabildo had two stories and a corridor. The cathedral, with its façade richly decorated, was grand and imposing. The plaza [2] was paved with stone, having a fine
fountain in the center, and commanding a magnificent view
of the volcano and mountains around. It was the day before
Good Friday; the streets and plaza were crowded with people in their best attire. The Indians wore large black cloaks
with broad-brimmed felt sombreros, and the women a white
frock which covered the head except for an oblong opening
for the face; some wore a sort of turban of red cord plaited
with the hair. The bells were hushed and wooden clappers
sounded in their stead. As we rode through, armed to the
teeth, the crowd made way in silence. We passed the door of
the church, and entered the great gate of the convent. The
cura was absent at the moment, but a respectable-looking
servant woman received us in a manner that assured us of a
welcome from her master. There was, however, an air of excitement and trepidation in the whole household, and it was
not long before the good woman unburdened herself of matters fearfully impressed upon her mind.

After chocolate we went to the corregidor, to whom we
presented our letters from the government and Carrera's
passport. He was one of Morazán's *expulsados*, a fine, military-looking man, but, as he told us, not a soldier by profession; he was in office by accident, and exceedingly anxious to
lay down his command; indeed, his brief service had been no

---

2. See figure 4 facing page 178.

sinecure. He introduced us to Don Juan Lavanigno, an Italian from Genoa, banished on account of a revolution headed by the present king who was then heir apparent; the revolution had intended to put the king on the throne, but the king basely withdrew himself from it, leaving his followers to their fate. How the *signor* found his way to this place I did not learn, but he had not found peace; and, if I am not deceived, he was as anxious to get out of it as ever he was to leave Genoa.

On our return to the convent we found the cura, who gave us personally the welcome assured to us by his housekeeper. With him was a respectable-looking Indian, bearing the imposing title of *Gobernador*, being the Indian alcalde. It was rather singular that, in an hour after our arrival at Quezaltenango, we had become acquainted with the four surviving victims of Carrera's wrath, all of whom had narrowly escaped death at the time of the outrage, the rumor of which had reached us at Guatemala. The place was still quivering under the shock of that event. We had heard many of the particulars on the road and, in Quezaltenango, except for the parties concerned, no one could speak of anything else.

On the first entry of Morazán's soldiers into the plaza at Guatemala, in an unfortunate moment a courier was sent to Quezaltenango to announce the capture of the city. The effect there was immediate and decided; the people rose upon the garrison left by Carrera and required them to lay down their arms. The corregidor, not wishing to fire upon the townsmen, and finding it would be impossible with his small force to repress the insurrection, by the advice of the cura and Don Juan Lavanigno, to prevent bloodshed and a general massacre, induced the soldiers to lay down their arms and leave the town. The same night the municipality, without his knowledge, nominated Don Juan Lavanigno as commandant. He refused to serve; but the town was in a violent state of excitement, and they urged him to accept for that night only, representing that if he did not, the fury of the populace would be directed against him. The same night they made a *pronunciamiento* in favor of Morazán, and addressed a letter of congratulation to him, which they dispatched immediately by an Indian courier. It will be remembered, however, that in the meantime Morazán had been driven out of Guatemala, and that Carrera had pursued him in his flight. At Antigua the latter met a disarmed sergeant, who informed him of the proceedings at Quezaltenango, whereupon, abandoning his pursuit of Morazán, he marched directly thither.

Early intelligence was received of his approach, and the corregidor, the cura, and Don Juan Lavanigno were sent as a deputation to receive him. They met him at Totonicapán. Carrera had heard on the road of their agency in inducing the soldiers to surrender their arms, and his first greeting was a furious declaration that their heads should lie at that place; laying aside his fanaticism and respect for the priests, he broke out against the cura in particular, who, he said, was a relative of Morazán. The cura said he was not a relative, but only a fellow countryman (which in that region means a townsman), and that he could not help the place of his birth; but Carrera forthwith ordered four soldiers to remove him a few paces and shoot him on the spot. The *Gobernador,* the old Indian referred to, threw himself on his knees and begged the cura's life; but Carrera drew his sword and struck the Indian twice across the shoulder, and the wounds were still unhealed when we saw him; but he desisted from his immediate purpose of shooting the cura, and delivered him over to the soldiers. Don Juan Lavanigno was saved by Carrera's secretary, who exhibited in *El Tiempo,* the government paper of Guatemala, an extract from a letter written by Don Juan to a friend in Guatemala, praising Carrera's deportment on his previous entry into Quezaltenango, and the discipline and good behaviour of his troops.

Early the next morning Carrera marched into Quezaltenango, with the cura and Don Juan as prisoners. The municipality waited upon him in the plaza; but, unhappily, the Indian intrusted with the letter to Morazán had loitered in the town, and at this unfortunate moment presented it to Carrera. Before his secretary had finished reading it, Carrera, in a transport of fury, drew his sword to kill them on the spot with his own hand; he wounded Molina, the alcalde-mayor, and two other members of the municipality, but then checked himself and ordered the soldiers to seize them   He then rode to the corregidor, where he again broke out into fury and drew his sword upon him. A woman in the room threw herself before the corregidor, and Carrera struck around her several times, but finally checked himself again and ordered the corregidor to be shot unless he raised five thousand dollars by contributions upon the town.

Don Juan and the cura he had locked up in a room with the threat to shoot them at five o'clock that afternoon unless they paid him one thousand dollars each, and the former two hundred, and the latter one hundred to his secretary. Don Juan was the principal merchant in the town, but even for him it was difficult to raise that sum. The poor cura told Carrera that he was not worth a cent in the world except his furniture and books. No one was allowed to visit him except the old housekeeper who first told us the story. Many of his friends had fled or hidden themselves away, and the old housekeeper ran from place to place with notes written by him, begging five dollars, ten dollars, anything she could get. One old lady sent him a hundred dollars. At four o'clock, with all his efforts he had raised but seven hundred dollars; but, after undergoing all the mental agonies of death, when the cura had given up all hope, Don Juan, who had been two hours at liberty, made up the deficiency, and he was released.

The next morning Carrera sent to Don Juan to borrow his shaving apparatus, and Don Juan took them over himself. He had always been on good terms with Carrera, and the latter asked him if he had got over his fright, talking with him as familiarly as if nothing had happened. Shortly afterward he was seen at the window playing on a guitar; and in an hour thereafter, eighteen members of the municipality, without the slightest form of trial, not even a drum-head court martial, were taken out into the plaza and shot. They were all the very first men in Quezaltenango; Molina, the alcalde-mayor, in family, position, and character was second to no other in the republic. His wife was clinging to Carrera's knees, and begging for his life when he passed with a file of soldiers. She screamed "Robertito"; he looked at her, but did not speak. She shrieked and fainted, and before she recovered her husband was dead. He was taken around the corner of the house, seated on a stone, and dispatched at once. The others were seated in the same place, one at a time; the stone and wall of the house were still red with their blood. I was told that Carrera shed tears for the death of the first two, but for the rest he said he did not care. Heretofore, in all their revolutions, there had been some show of regard for the tribunals of justice, and the horror of the citizens at this lawless murder of their best men cannot be conceived. The facts were notorious to everybody in Quezaltenango. We heard them, with but little variation of detail, from more than a dozen different persons.

Having consummated this enormity, Carrera returned to Guatemala, and the place had not yet recovered from its consternation. It was considered a blow at the whites, and all feared the horrors of a war of castes. I have avoided speaking harshly of Carrera when I could. I consider myself under personal obligations to him, and without his protection I never could have traveled through the country; but it is difficult to suppress the feelings of indignation excited against the government, which, conscious of the enormity of his conduct and of his utter contempt for them, never dared call him to account, and which now cajoles and courts him, sustaining itself in power by his favor alone.

To return to the cura. He was about forty-five, tall, stout, and remarkably fine-looking; he had several curacies under his charge, and next to a canónigo's, his position was the highest in the country—but it had its labors. He was at that time engrossed with the ceremonies of the Holy Week, and in the evening we accompanied him to the church. At the door the *coup d'oeil* of the interior was most striking. The church was two hundred and fifty feet in length, spacious and lofty, richly decorated with pictures and sculptured ornaments, blazing with lights, and crowded with Indians. On each side of the door was a grating, behind which stood an Indian to receive offerings. The floor was strewed with pine leaves. On the left was the figure of a dead Christ on a bier, upon which every woman who entered threw a handful of roses, and near it stood an Indian to receive money. Opposite, behind an iron grating, was the figure of Christ bearing the cross; the eyes were bandaged and large silver chains, attached to the arms and other parts of the body, were fastened to the iron bars. Here, too, stood an Indian to receive contributions. The altar was beautiful in design and decorations, consisting of two rows of Ionic columns, one above another, gilded, surmounted by a golden glory, and lighted by candles ten feet high. Under the pulpit was a piano. After a stroll around the church, the cura led us to seats under the pulpit. He asked us to give them some of the airs of our country, and then himself sat down at the piano. On Mr. Catherwood's suggesting that the tune was from one of Rossini's operas, he said that this was hardly proper for the occasion and changed it.

At about ten o'clock the crowd in the church formed into a procession, and Mr. Catherwood and I went out and took a position at the corner of a street to see it pass. It was headed by Indians, two abreast, each carrying in his hand a long lighted wax candle. And then, borne aloft on the shoulders of four men, came the figure of Judith, with a bloody sword in one hand, and in the other the gory head of Holofernes. Next, also on the shoulders of four men, came the archangel Gabriel, dressed in red silk with large wings puffed out. The next were men in grotesque armor made of black and silver paper to resemble Moors, with shield and spear like ancient cavaliers. Four little girls followed, dressed in white silk and gauze and looking like little spiritualities, with men on each side bearing lighted candles. Then came a large figure of Christ bearing the cross, supported by four Indians; on each side were young Indian lads, carrying long poles horizontally to keep the crowd from pressing upon it, and followed by a procession of townsmen. In turning the corner of the street at which we stood, a dark mestizo, with a scowl of fanaticism on his face, said to Mr. Catherwood, "Take off your spectacles and follow the Cross." Next followed a procession of women fancifully dressed with silver caps and headdresses, with children in their arms, half of them asleep.

Finally came a large statue of the Virgin, in a sitting posture, magnificently attired, with Indian lads on each side, as before, supporting poles with candles. The whole was accompanied with the music of drums and violins; and, as the long train of light passed down the street, we returned to the convent.

The night was very cold, and the next morning was like one in December at home. It was the morning of Good Friday, and throughout Guatemala, in every village, preparations were being made to celebrate, with the most solemn ceremonies of the Church, the resurrection of the Saviour. In Quezaltenango, at that early hour, the plaza was thronged with Indians from the country around; but the whites, terrified and grieving at the murder of their best men, avoided, to a great extent, taking part in the celebration.

At nine o'clock the corregidor called for us, and we accompanied him to the opening ceremony. On one side of the nave of the church, near the grand altar and opposite the pulpit, were high cushioned chairs for the corregidor and members of the municipality, and we had seats with them. The church was thronged with Indians, estimated at more than three thousand. Formerly at this ceremony no women or children were admitted, but now the floor of the church was filled with Indian women on their knees; with red cords plaited in their hair, perhaps one third of them had children on their backs, only the heads and arms of whom were visible. Except for ourselves and the padre, there were no white people in the church; and, with all eyes turned upon us, and a lively recollection of the fate of those who but a few days before had occupied our seats, we felt that the post of honor was a private station.

At the steps of the grand altar stood a large cross, apparently of solid silver, which was richly carved and ornamented, and over it was a high arbor of pine and cypress branches. At the foot of the cross stood a figure of Mary Magdalene weeping, with her hair in a profusion of ringlets, her frock low in the neck, and altogether rather immodest. On the right was the figure of the Virgin gorgeously dressed, and in the nave of the church stood John the Baptist, placed there, as it seemed, only because they had the figure on hand. Very soon strains of wild Indian music rose from the other end of the church, and a procession advanced, headed by Indians with broad-brimmed felt hats, dark cloaks, and lighted wax candles, who preceded the body of the Saviour on a bier borne by the cura and attendant padres and followed by Indians with long wax candles. The bier advanced to the foot of the cross and ladders were placed behind against it. The *Gobernador*, with his long black cloak and broad-brimmed felt hat, mounted on the right and leaned over, holding in his hands a silver hammer and a long silver spike; another Indian dignitary mounted on the other side, while the priests raised the figure up in front. The face was ghastly, blood trickled down the cheeks, the arms and legs were moveable, and in the side was a gaping wound, with a stream of blood oozing from it. The back was affixed to the cross, the arms were extended and spikes driven through the hands and feet, and then the ladders were taken away. Thus the figure of Christ was nailed to the cross.

This over, we left the church, and passed two or three hours in visiting. The white population was small, but equal in character to any in the republic; there was hardly a respectable family that was not afflicted by the outrage of Carrera. We knew nothing of the effect of this enormity until we entered domestic circles. The distress of women whose nearest connections had been murdered or obliged to flee for their lives and to wander they knew not where, only those can realize who can appreciate woman's affection.

I was urged to visit the widow of Molina. Her husband was but thirty-five, and his death under any circumstances would have been lamented, even by political enemies. I felt a painful interest in one who had lived through such a scene, but at the door of her house I stopped. I felt that a visit from a stranger must be an intrusion upon her sorrows.

In the afternoon, we were again seated with the municipality in the church to behold the descent from the cross. The spacious building was thronged to suffocation. The floor was covered by a dense mass of kneeling women, with tur-

FIG. 4 *Plaza at Quezaltenango*

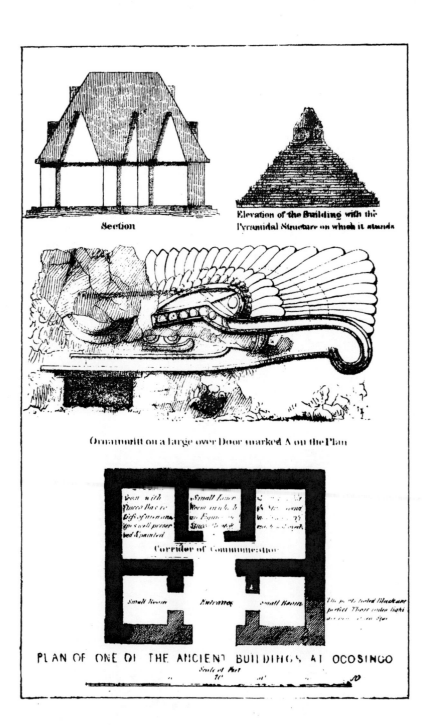

Section

Elevation of the Building with the Pyramidal Structure on which it stands

Ornament on a large over Door marked A on the Plan

PLAN OF ONE OF THE ANCIENT BUILDINGS AT OCOSINGO

Scale of Feet

FIG. 5 *Ancient Building at Ococingo
a section; elevation; detail over door; and
place of building*

baned headdresses and crying children on their backs, their imaginations excited by gazing at the bleeding figure on the cross; but among them all I did not see a single interesting face. A priest ascended the pulpit, thin and ghastly pale, who, in a voice that rang through every part of the building, preached emphatically a passion sermon. Few of the Indians understood even the language, and at times the cries of children made his words inaudible; but the thrilling tones of his voice played upon every chord in their hearts, and mothers, regardless of their infants' cries, sat motionless, their countenances fixed in high and stern enthusiasm. It was the same church, and we could imagine them to be the same women who, in a frenzy and fury of fanaticism, had dragged the unhappy vice-president by the hair and murdered him with their hands. Every moment the excitement grew stronger. The priest tore off his black cap, and leaning over the pulpit, stretched forward both his arms and poured out a frantic apostrophe to the bleeding figure on the cross. A dreadful groan, almost curdling the blood, ran through the church. At this moment, at a signal from the cura, the Indians sprang upon the arbor of pine branches, tore it asunder, and with a noise like the crackling of a great conflagration, struggling and scuffling around the altar, broke into bits the consecrated branches to save as holy relics. Two Indians in broad-brimmed hats mounted the ladders on each side of the cross and, with embroidered cloth over their hands and large silver pincers, drew out the spikes from the hands. The feelings of the women burst forth in tears, sobs, groans, and shrieks of lamentation, so loud and deep, that coming upon us unexpectedly, our feelings were disturbed, and even with sane men the empire of reason tottered. Such screams of anguish I never heard called out by mortal suffering. The body, smeared with blood, was held aloft under the pulpit, while the priest leaned down and apostrophized it with frantic fervor, and the mass of women wild with excitement heaved to and fro like the surges of a troubled sea. The whole scene was so thrilling, so dreadfully mournful, that, without knowing why, tears started from our eyes. Four years before, at Jerusalem, on Mount Calvary itself,

and in the presence of the scoffing Mussulman, I had beheld
the same representation of the descent from the cross; but
the enthusiasm of Greek pilgrims in the Church of the Holy
Sepulchre was nothing compared with this whirlwind of
fanaticism and frenzy. By degrees the excitement died away
and the cracking of the pine branches ceased, the whole
arbor being broken up and distributed; and very soon commenced preparations for the grand procession.

We went out with the corregidor and officers of the municipality, and took our place in the balcony of the cabildo.
The procession opened upon us in a manner so extraordinary,
that, screening myself from observation below, I endeavored to make a note of it on the spot. The leader was a man
on horseback, called the centurion. He wore a helmet and
cuirass of pasteboard covered with silver leaf, a black crape
mask, black velvet shorts and white stockings, a red sash, and
blue and red ribands on his arms; he carried a silver-hilted
sword and a lance, with which, from time to time turning
round, he beckoned and waved the procession on. Then
came a led horse, having on its back an old Mexican saddle
richly plated with silver. Then two men wearing long blue
gowns, with round hoods covering their heads and having
only holes for the eyes; they were leading two mules abreast
covered with black cloth dresses enveloping their whole
bodies to their feet, the long trains of which were supported
by men attired like the other two. There followed the large
silver cross of the crucifixion, with a richly ornamented
silver pedestal and with ornaments that looked like lanterns
dangling from each arm of the cross; it was supported by
four men in long black dresses. Next came a procession of
Indians, two abreast, who wore long black cloaks and black
felt hats, the brims six or eight inches wide, and who were
carrying lighted candles in their hands. Four more Indians
followed; they were in the same costume, but with crowns
of thorns on their heads; they were dragging a long low
carriage or bier filled with pine leaves, on the top of one end
of which had been laid a naked skull.

Next, and in striking contrast with this emblem of mortality, advanced an angel in the attitude of an opera dancer;

she was borne on the shoulders of six men, was dressed in flounced purple satin, with lace at the bottom, gauze wings, and a cloud of gauze over her head, and was holding in her right hand a pair of silver pincers, and in her left a small wooden cross. Her train of white muslin, ten yards long, was supported by a pretty little girl fancifully dressed. Then another procession of Indians with lighted candles; then a group of devils in horrible masquerade. Then another angel, still more like an opera dancer; she was dressed in azure blue satin, with rich lace wings, and clouds, and fluttering ribands, and she was holding in her right hand a ladder, and in her left a silver hammer. Her train was supported in the same fashion as the preceding angel, and we could not help seeing that she wore black velvet small-clothes. Still another angel followed, who was dressed in yellow; in her right hand she was holding a small wooden cross, and in the other, I could not tell what.

The next in order was a beautiful little girl about ten years old, armed cap-a-pie with breastplate and helmet of silver; she, too, was called the centurion. She moved along in a slow and graceful dance, keeping time to the music, turning round, stopping, resting on her sword, and waving on a party worthy of such a chief, being twelve beautiful children fancifully dressed who were intended to represent the twelve apostles; one of the children carried in his arms a silver cock to signify that he was the representative of St. Peter. After these came the great object of veneration, the figure of the Christ crucified, on a bier, in a full-length case of plate glass, strewed with roses inside and out, and protected by a mourning canopy of black cloth; it was supported by men in long black gowns, with hoods covering all but their eyes. This was followed by the cura and priests in their richest robes and bareheaded, the muffled drum, and soldiers with arms reversed.

The Virgin Mary, in a long black mourning dress, closed the procession, which passed on to make the tour of the city. Twice we intercepted it, and then went to the Church of El Calvario. It stands on an elevation at the extreme end of a long street, and the steps were already crowded with women dressed in white from the head to the feet, with barely an oval opening for the face. It was dark when the procession made its appearance at the foot of the street, but by the blaze of innumerable lighted candles every object was exhibited with more striking wildness, and fanaticism seemed written in letters of fire on the faces of the Indians. The centurion cleared a way up the steps, the procession with a loud chant entered the church, and we went away.

In the evening we made several visits, and late at night we were called to a conference by some friends of the cura, and on his behalf. His troubles were not yet over. On the day of our arrival he had received a peremptory order from the provisor to repair to Guatemala, with notice that "some proper person" would be appointed in his place. We knew that the terms of the order afflicted the cura, for they implied that he was not a proper person. All Quezaltenango, he said, could answer for his acts, and he could answer to God that his motives were only to prevent the effusion of blood. His house was all in confusion; he was packing up his books and furniture and preparing to obey the provisor's order. But his friends considered that it was dangerous for him to go to Guatemala. At that place, they said, he would be under the eyes of Carrera, who, meeting him in an angry moment, might cut him down in the street. If he did not go, the provisor would send soldiers after him, such was the rigor of church discipline. His friends wished him to flee from the country, to go with us into Mexico; but he could not leave without a passport from Guatemala, and this would be refused.

The reason for their unburdening themselves to us showed the helplessness of his condition. They supposed that I might have influence with the provisor, and begged me to write to Guatemala and state the facts as they were known to all Quezaltenango. I had determined to take no part in the public or personal affairs of this unhappy revolution, but here I would not have hesitated to incur any trouble or risk to serve the cura, could it have done him any good; but I knew the sensitiveness of the men in power, and I believed that the provisor and the government would resent

my interference. I proposed, however, to write to a friend
who I knew stood well with the provisor and request him
to call upon that dignitary and state the facts as from me;
and I suggested that he should send some friend to Guatemala expressly to see the provisor in person. Returned to a
land of government and laws, I can hardly realize that it is
so short a time since I was called into counsel for the safety
of a man of the cura's character and station. Relatively, the
most respectable clergyman in our country does not stand
higher than he did.

The next morning we were invited to breakfast with another friend and counsellor, and about as strange a one as
myself, being the old lady who sent the cura the one hundred dollars before mentioned. The plan was discussed and
settled, and in the course of the day two friends undertook
to visit Guatemala on the cura's behalf. We intended that
day to ascend the volcano of Quezaltenango, but were disappointed in our guide. In the morning we made purchases
and provisions for continuing our journey; as one of our
mules' backs was badly galled, we requested the *Gobernador*
to procure us Indian carriers.

In the afternoon, in company with the corregidor, we rode
to the warm springs of Almolonga. The road crosses a spur
of the volcano and descends precipitously into a deep valley,
in which, about a league distant, stand the village and hot
springs. There is a good bathing house, at which we were
not allowed to pay, being considered the guests of the city.
Outside, in a beautiful natural reservoir, Indian men,
women, and children were bathing together.

We returned by another road, passing up a valley of extraordinary beauty, and the theme of conversation was the
happiness the country might enjoy but for wars and revolutions. Beautiful as it was, all wished to leave it and seek a
land where life was safe—*México* or *El Norte*. Toward
evening, descending the spur of the volcano, we met several
hundred Indians returning from the ceremonies of the Holy
Week, who exceeded in drunkenness all the specimens we
had yet encountered. In one place, a man and woman, the
latter with a child on her back, were staggering so near the

brink of a precipice that the corregidor dismounted and took the child from them and made them go before us into the town.

There was no place we had visited, except ruined cities, which was so unique and interesting, and which deserved to be so thoroughly explored, as Quezaltenango. A month at least, might be satisfactorily and profitably employed in examining the many curious objects in the country around. For botanical researches it is the richest region in Central America. But we had no time even for rest.

I passed the evening in writing, packing things to be sent to Guatemala, among others my quetzal, which, however, never arrived, and in writing letters. One of these letters was on account of the cura. In it, intending even if it fell into wrong hands to be out of the country myself, I spoke in no measured terms of the atrocity committed by Carrera.

Chapter XIII

~~~~~~

Journey continued. A mountain plain. Lost guides. A trying moment. Agua Caliente. A magnificent view. Gold ore. San Sebastián. Huehuetenango. Sierra Madre. A huge skeleton. The ruins. Pyramidal structures. A vault. Mounds. A welcome addition. Interior of a mound. Vases. Ascent of the Sierra Madre. Buena Vista. The descent. Todos Santos. San Martín. Santiago Petatán. A forest on fire. Suffering of the mules from swarms of flies. San Antonio Huista.

EARLY in the morning our mules were saddled for the journey. The *Gobernador* and another friend of the cura came to receive parting instructions and set off for Guatemala. The Indians engaged for us did not make their appearance and, desirous to save the day, we loaded the mules and sent Juan and Bobón forward with the luggage. In a little while two women came and told us that our Indians were in prison. I accompanied the women to two or three officials and, with much difficulty and loss of time, found the man who had charge of them; he told us that, on finding that we had paid them part of their hire in advance, he had been afraid they would buy *aguardiente* and be missing, so he had shut them up the night before to have them ready for us in the morning, and that he had left word to that effect with one of the servants of the cura. I went with him to the prison and, after paying a shilling apiece for their lodging, took them over to the convent. The poor fellows had not eaten since they were shut up, and, as usual, wanted to go home for tortillas for the journey. We refused to let them go, but gave them money to buy some in the plaza, keeping the women and their *chamarras* with us as hostages for their return. But we became tired of waiting. Mr. Catherwood picked up their *chamarras* and threw them across his saddle as a guarantee for their following, and we set off.

We had added to our equipments *armas de agua*, being undressed goatskins embroidered with red leather, which hung down from the saddlebow to protect the legs against rain. Now we were fully accoutered in Central American style.

It was cold and wintry. We ascended and crossed a high plain, and at the distance of a league descended to a village, where we learned that Juan and Bobón had passed on some time before. Beyond this we ascended a high and rugged mountain, and on the top reached a magnificent plain. We rode at a brisk pace, and it was one o'clock before our jail-birds overtook us. By this time we were surprised at not overtaking our men with the luggage; we could not have passed them, for there was but one road. Since leaving the village we had not seen a single person, but at two o'clock we met a man with a loaded mule coming from Agua Caliente, the end of our day's journey, but he had not met them. Mr. Catherwood became alarmed, fearing that they had robbed us and run away. I was always careless with luggage but never lost any, and I was slow in coming to this belief. In half an hour we met another man who told us that he had not seen them and that there was no other road than the one by which he had come. Since our apprehensions began, we had not been able to discover any track of them, but we went on to within two leagues of our halting place before we stopped and held one of the most anxious consultations that occurred in our whole journey. We knew but little of the men. Juan cheated us every day in the little purchases for the road, and we had detected him in the atrocity of keeping back part of the money we gave him to buy corn and *zacate*, and of starving the mules. After a most unhappy deliberation, we concluded that they had broken open the trunks, taken out the money, thrown the rest of the contents down some ravine, mounted the mules, and made off. Besides money, beds, and bedding, these trunks contained all Mr. Catherwood's drawings, and the precious notebooks to which the reader is indebted for these pages. The fruits of all our labor were gone. In all our difficulties and perplexities we never had a more trying moment. We were two leagues from Agua Caliente. Our first idea was to go on, rouse the village, get fresh horses, and return in pursuit, but this would widen the distance between us, and we should probably not be able to get horses.

With hearts so heavy that nothing but the feeble hope of catching them in the act of dividing the money kept us from sinking, we turned back. It was four o'clock in the afternoon; neither our mules nor we had eaten anything since early in the morning. Night would be upon us, and it was doubtful whether our mules would hold out. Our prisoners told us we had been very imprudent to let the men set out alone, and took for granted that they had not let slip the opportunity of robbing us.

As we rode back, both Mr. Catherwood and I brooded over an apprehension which for some time neither mentioned to the other. It was the letter I had written on behalf of the cura. We should again be within reach of Carrera. If the letter by accident fell into his hands, he would be indignant at what he considered my ingratitude, and he could very easily take his revenge. Our plans, however, we made at once. We determined, at all events, not to go back to Guatemala, nor, broken as we were in fortune and spirit, to give up Palenque, but, if possible, to borrow money for the road, even if we set out on foot. But, O GLORIA ETER-NAL, as the official bulletin said of Carrera's victory, on reaching the top of a mountain we saw the men climbing up a deep ravine on the other side. We did not tell them of our agony, but we had not gone far before the Indians told all; and they were not surprised or hurt. How we passed them neither of us knew; but another such spasm would have put a period to our journey of life, and from that time, however tedious, or whatever might be the inducements, we resolved to keep by our luggage. At dusk we reached the top of a high mountain, and by one of those long, steep, and difficult descents of which it is impossible to give the reader any idea, we entered the village of Agua Caliente.

It was occupied entirely by Indians, who gathered round us in the plaza and, by the light of pine sticks, looked at Carrera's passport. Not one of them could read it, but it was enough to pronounce the name, and the whole village was put in requisition to provide us with something to eat. The alcalde distributed the money we gave him, and one brought sixpence worth of eggs, another of beans, another of tortillas, another of lard, another of candles, and a dozen or more received sixpence for *zacate;* not one of them would bring anything until he had the money in hand. A fire was kindled in the square, and in process of time we had supper. Our usual supper of fried eggs, beans, tortillas, and chocolate—any one of them enough to disturb digestion in a state of repose—with the excitement and vexation of our supposed loss, made me ill. The cabildo was a wretched shed, full of fleas, with a coat of dust an inch thick to soften the hard earthen floor. It was too cold to sleep out of doors, and there were no pins to hang hammocks on, for in this region hammocks were not used at all. We made inquiries with the view of hiring for the night the bedsteads of the principal inhabitants, but there was not one in the village; all slept on the bosom of mother earth, and we had part of the family bed. Fortunately, however, and most important for us, our mules fared well.

Early in the morning we resumed our journey. There are warm springs in this neighborhood, but we did not go out of our way to visit them. A short distance from the village we crossed a river and commenced ascending a mountain. On the top we came upon a narrow table of land with a magnificent forest on both sides far below us. The wind swept over the lofty height, so that with our ponchos, which were necessary on account of the cold, it was difficult to keep the saddle. The road was broken and stony, and the track scarcely perceptible. At about ten o'clock the whole surface of the mountain was a bare ridge of limestone, from which the sun was reflected with scorching heat; the whiteness was dazzling and painful to the eyes. Below us, on each side, continued an immense forest of gigantic pines. The road was perfectly desolate; we met no travelers. In four hours we saw on our left, at a great distance below, a single hacienda with a clearing around it, seemingly selected for magnificent seclusion from the convulsions of a distracted country. The ridge was broken by gullies and deep ravines; and we came to one across which, by way of a bridge, lay the trunks of two gigantic pines. My macho always pulled back when I attempted to lead him, and I remained on his back and was carried steadily over; but at the other end we started at a noise behind us. Our best cargo mule had fallen and rolled over; she hung on the brink of the precipice with her feet kicking in the air, and was kept from falling to the bottom only by being entangled among bushes. In a moment we scrambled down to get her, got her head turned up the bank, and by means of strong halters heaved her out; but she was bruised and crippled, and barely able to stagger under her load.

Continuing along the ridge, swept by fierce blasts of wind, we descended again to a river, rode some distance along its bank, and passed a track up the side of a mountain on the right; it was so steep that I had no idea it could be our road and passed it, but was called back. It was the steepest ascent we had yet had in the country. It was cruel to push my brave macho, but I had been tormented all day with a violent headache and could not walk; so I beat my way up, making the best tacks I could and stopping every time I put about. On the top there broke upon us one of those grand and magnificent views which, when we had wiped off perspiration and recovered breath, always indemnified us for our toil. It was the highest ground on which we had yet stood. Around us was a sea of mountains, and peeping above them, but so little as to give full effect to our own great height, were the conical tops of two new volcanoes. The surface was of limestone rock in immense strata with quartz, in one piece of which we discovered a speck of gold. Here again, in this vast wilderness of mountains, deep in the bowels of the earth, are those repositories of the precious ores for which millions upon millions all over the world are toiling, bargaining, craving, and cheating every day.

Continuing on this ridge, we came out upon a spur commanding a view, far below us, of a cultivated valley and the village of San Sebastián. We descended to the valley, left the village on our right, crossed the spur, and saw the end of our day's journey, the town of Huehuetenango, situated on an extensive plain, with a mild climate, luxuriant with tropical productions, and surrounded by immense mountains. Before us was the great Sierra Madre,[1] the natural bulwark of Central America; the grandeur and magnificence of the view was disturbed only by the distressing reflection that we had to cross it. My macho, brought up on the plains of Costa Rica, had long seemed puzzled to know what mountains were made for; if he could have spoken, he would have cried out in anguish:

Hills peep o'er hills, and Alps on Alps arise.

Our day's journey was but twenty-seven miles, but it was harder for man and beast than any sixty since we left Guatemala. We rode into the town, the chief place of the last district of Central America and of the ancient kingdom of Quiché. It was well built, with a large church and plaza, and again a crowd of mestizos were engaged in their favorite occupation of fighting cocks. As we rode through the plaza the bell sounded for the *oración,* or vesper prayers. The people fell on their knees and we took off our hats. We stopped at the house of Don Joaquín Monte, an old Spaniard of high consideration, by whom we were hospitably received, and who, though a Centralist, on account of some affair of his sons, had had his house at Chiantla plundered by Carrera's soldiers. His daughters had been compelled to take refuge in the church, and forty or fifty mules were driven from his hacienda. In a short time we had a visit from the corregidor; he had seen our proposed journey announced

---

1. The mountains which Stephens refers to here as the Sierra Madre are called in Guatemala the Cuchumatanes.

in the government paper, and he treated us with the consideration due to persons specially recommended by the government.

We reached Huehuetenango in a shattered condition. Our cargo mules had their backs so galled that it was distressing to use them, and the saddle horse was no better off. Bobón, in walking barefooted over the stony road, had bruised the ball of his foot so that he was disabled, and that night Juan's enormous supper gave him indigestion. He was a tremendous feeder; on the road nothing eatable was safe. We owed him a spite for pilfering our bread and bringing us down to tortillas, and were not sorry to see him on his back; but he rolled over the floor of the corridor, crying out uproariously, so as to disturb the whole household, *Voy a morir! voy a morir!* (I am going to die! I am going to die!) He was a hard subject to work upon, but we took him in hand strongly, and unloaded him.

Besides our immediate difficulties, we heard of others in prospect. In consequence of the throng of emigrants from Guatemala toward Mexico, no one was admitted into that territory without a passport from Ciudad Real, the capital of Chiapas, four or five days' journey from the frontier. The frontier was a long line of river in the midst of a wilderness, and there were two roads, the lower one but little traveled on account of the difficulty of crossing the rivers, but at that time passable. As we intended, however, at all events, to stop at this place for the purpose of visiting the ruins, we postponed our decision till the next day.

The next morning Don Joaquín told us of the skeleton of a colossal animal, supposed to be a mastodon, which had been found in the neighborhood. Some of the bones had been collected and were then in the town and, having seen them, we took a guide and walked to the place where they had been discovered, on the borders of the Río Chinaca, about half a mile distant. At this time the river was low, but the year before, swelled by the immense floods of the rainy season, it had burst its bounds, carried away its left bank, and laid bare one side of the skeleton of a huge animal. The bank was perpendicular, about thirty feet high, and the animal had been buried in an upright position. Besides the bones in the town, some had been carried away by the flood and others remained imbedded in the earth; but the impression of the whole animal, from twenty-five to thirty feet long, was distinctly visible. We were told that about eight leagues above, on the bank of the same river, the skeleton of a much larger animal had been discovered.

In the afternoon we rode to the ruins, which in the town were called *las cuevas* (the caves). They lie about half a league distant, on a magnificent plain, bounded in the distance by lofty mountains, among which is the great Sierra Madre.

The site of the ancient city, as at Patinamit and Santa Cruz del Quiché, was chosen for its security against enemies. It was surrounded by a ravine, and the general character of the ruins is the same as at Quiché, but the hand of destruction has fallen upon it more heavily. The whole is a confused heap of grass-grown fragments. The principal remains are two pyramidal structures of this form: ⌐▢ One of them measures at the base one hundred and two feet; the steps are four feet high and seven feet deep, making the whole height twenty-eight feet. They are not of cut stone as at Copán, but of rough pieces cemented with lime, and the whole exterior was formerly coated with stucco and painted. On the top is a small square platform, and at the base lies a long slab of rough stone, apparently hurled down from the top, perhaps the altar on which human victims were extended for sacrifice.

The owner of the ground, a mestizo, whose house was near by, and who accompanied us to the ruins, told us that he had bought the land from Indians, and that, for some time after his purchase, he had been annoyed by their periodical visits to celebrate some of their ancient rites on the top of this structure. This annoyance had continued until he whipped two or three of the principal men and drove them away.

At the foot of the structure was a vault faced with cut stone, in which were found a collection of bones and a terra cotta vase, then in the mestizo's possession. The vault was not long enough for the body of a man extended, and the bones must have been separated before they were placed there.

The owner believed that these structures contained interior apartments with hidden treasures; there were several mounds, supposed to be sepulchers of the ancient inhabitants, which also, he had no doubt, contained treasure. The situation of the place was magnificent. We had never before enjoyed so good an opportunity of working; we agreed with him to come the next day and make excavations, promising to give him all the treasure and to take for my share only the skulls, vases, and other curiosities.

The next morning before we were up, the door was thrown open, and to our surprise we received a salutation in English. The costume of the stranger was of the country; his beard was long, and he looked as if he had already made a hard morning's ride. To my great surprise and pleasure I recognized Pawling, whom the reader will perhaps remember I had seen as superintendent of a cochineal hacienda at Amatitlán. He had heard of our setting out for Mexico and, disgusted with his occupation and the country, had mounted his horse, and with all he was worth tied on behind his saddle, pushed on to overtake us. On the way he had bought a fine mule, and by hard riding, and changing from one animal to the other, he had reached us in four days. He was in difficulty about a passport, and was anxious to have the benefit of mine in order to get out of the country, offering to attach himself to me in any capacity necessary for that purpose. Fortunately, my passport was broad enough to cover him, and I immediately constituted him the general manager of the expedition, the material of which was now reduced to Juan sick and but one cargo mule sound.

At nine o'clock, attended by three men and a boy with machetes, being all we could procure at so short a notice, we were again among the ruins. We were not strong enough to pull down a pyramid, and we lost the morning in endeavoring to make a breach in one of the sides, but we did not accomplish anything.

In the afternoon we opened one of the mounds. The interior was a rough coat of stones and lime, and after an hour's digging we came to fragments of bones and two vases.[2] One of the vases was entire when we discovered it, but, unfortunately, was broken in getting it out, though we obtained all the pieces. It is graceful in design, the surface is polished, and the workmanship very good. The other was already broken, and though of more complicated design, the surface was not polished. We discovered no treasure, but our day's work was most interesting, and we only regretted that we had not time to explore more thoroughly.

In the meantime Don Joaquín had made arrangements for us, and the next morning we resumed our journey. We left behind a mule, a horse, and Bobón, and were re-enforced by Pawling, who was well mounted and armed with a pair of pistols, with a short double-barreled gun slung to his saddlebow. Santiago, a Mexican fugitive soldier, and Juan, an interesting invalid mounted on a mule, were also with us, and the whole was under escort of a respectable old muleteer, who was setting out with empty mules to bring back a load of sugar.

At a short distance from the village we commenced ascending the Sierra Madre. The first range was stony, and on the top of it we came upon a cultivated plain, beyond which rose a second range, covered with a thick forest of oak. On the top of this range stood a cross. The spot was called Buena Vista, or Fine View, and commanded a magnificent expanse of mountains and plains, five lakes, and two volcanoes, one of which, called Tajumulco, our guide said was a water volcano. Beyond this rose a third range. At some distance up was an Indian rancho, at which a fine little boy thrust his face through a bush fence, and said *adiós* to everyone that passed. Beyond was another boy, to whom we all in succession said *adiós*, but the surly little fellow would not answer one of us. On the summit of this range we were almost on a level with the tops of the volcanoes.

As we ascended the temperature grew colder, and we were compelled to put on our ponchos. At half past two we

2. An engraving of these vases is reproduced in earlier editions of *Incidents of Travel*. . . .

reached the top of the Sierra Madre, the dividing line of the waters, being twelve miles from Huehuetenango, and in our devious course this made the second time that we had crossed the sierra. The ridge of the mountain was a long level table about half a mile wide, with rugged sides rising on the right to a terrific peak. Riding about half an hour on this table by the side of a stream of clear and cold water, which passed on, carrying its tribute to the Pacific Ocean, we reached a miserable rancho, in front of which the *arriero*, or muleteer, proposed to encamp, as he said it would be impossible to reach the next village. At a distance it was a glorious idea, that of sleeping on the top of the Sierra Madre, and the scene was wild enough for the most romantic imagination; but, being poorly provided against cold, we would have gladly exchanged it for an Indian village.

The occupants of the hut were a man and woman, who lived there rent free. Like the eagle, they had fixed their habitation where they were not likely to be disturbed. While the men were unloading, Juan, as an invalid, asked permission to stretch his huge body before the fire, but the woman told him there was more room out of doors. I succeeded, however, in securing him a place inside. We had an hour to wander over the top of the sierra. It belonged to our friend Don Joaquín Monte, and was what would be called at home a pretty substantial piece of fast property. At every step there was some new opening, which presented a new view of the grand and magnificent in nature. In many places, between cliffs and under certain exposures, were fine pieces of ground, and about half a mile distant there was a *potrero*, or pastureground for brood mares, which we visited to buy some corn for our mules. A vicious jack reigned lord of the sierra!

Adjoining the occupied hut was another about ten feet square, made of small upright poles and thatched with branches of cypress, which was open on all sides to the wind. We collected a quantity of wood, made a fire in the center, had supper, and passed a social evening. The muleteers had a large fire outside, and with their packsaddles and cargoes built a breastwork to shelter themselves against the wind.

Fancy called up a picture of far-distant scenes: a small circle of friends, perhaps at that moment thinking of us, perhaps, to tell the truth, we wished to be with them; and, above all, as we looked to our sleeping places, we thought of the comforts of home. Nevertheless, we soon fell asleep.

Toward morning, however, we were reminded of our elevated region. The ground was covered with a hoarfrost, and water was frozen a quarter of an inch thick. Our guide said that this happened regularly every night in the year when the atmosphere was clear. It was the first ice we had seen in the country. The men were shivering around a large fire, and, as soon as they could see, went out to look for the mules. One of them had strayed, and while the men were looking for her, we had breakfast. We did not get off till a quarter before eight. Our road traversed the ridge of the sierra, which for two leagues was a level table, a great part composed of immense beds of red slate and blue limestone or chalk rock, lying in vertical strata.

At ten o'clock we began to descend, the cold being still severe. The descent surpassed in grandeur and magnificence all that we had yet encountered. It was by a broad passage with perpendicular mountain walls rising in rugged and terrific peaks higher and higher as we descended, out of which gigantic cypress trees were growing, their trunks and all their branches dead. Before us, between these immense walls, was a vista reaching beyond the village of San Andrés, twenty-four miles distant. A stream of water was dashing down over rocks and stones, hurrying on to the Atlantic; we crossed it perhaps fifty times on bridges wild and rude as the stream itself and the mountains between which it rolled. As we descended the temperature became milder. At twelve o'clock the immense ravine opened into a rich valley a mile in width, and in half an hour we reached the village of Todos Santos. On the right, far below us, was a magnificent table cultivated with corn and bounded by the side of the great sierra; and in the suburbs of the village were apple and peach trees covered with blossoms and young fruit. We had again reached the *tierras templadas*, and in

Europe or North America the beauty of this miserable unknown village would be a theme for poetry.

As we rode through it, at the head of the street we were
stopped by a drunken Indian supported by two men hardly
able to stand themselves, who, we thought, were taking
him to prison; but, staggering before us, they blocked up
the passage and shouted *pasaporte*. Not one of the three
could read the passport and they sent for the secretary, a
bare-headed Indian, habited in nothing but a ragged cotton
shirt, who examined it very carefully; he read aloud the
name of Rafael Carrera, which, I think, was all that he attempted to make out. We were neither sentimental, nor
philosophical, nor moralizing travelers, but it gave us pangs
to think that such a magnificent country was in the possession of such men.

Passing the church and convent, we ascended a ridge, then
descended an immense ravine, crossed another magnificent
valley, and at length reached the Indian village of San
Martín, which, with loveliness and grandeur all around us,
might have been selected for its surpassing beauty of position. We rode to the cabildo, and then to the hut of the
alcalde. The people were all Indians; the secretary was a
bare-legged boy, who spelled out every word in the passport
except our names, but his reading sufficed to procure supper
for us and provender for the mules, and early in the morning we pushed on again.

For some distance we rode on a lofty ridge, with a precipitous ravine on each side, in one place so narrow that, as
our *arriero* told us, when the wind is high there is danger of
being blown off. We continued descending, and at a quarter
past twelve reached Santiago Petatán, fifteen miles distant, blooming with oranges, sapotas, and other fruit trees.
Passing through the village, at a short distance beyond we
were stopped by a fire in the woods. We turned back and
attempted to pass by another road, but were unable. Before
we returned, the fire had reached the place we left, and it
increased so fast that we had apprehensions for the luggage
mules, and we hurried them back with the men toward the

village. The flames came creeping and crackling toward us, shooting up and whirled by currents of wind, and occasionally, when fed with dry and combustible materials, flashing and darting along like a train of gunpowder. We fell back, keeping as near as we could to the line of fire. The road lay along the side of a mountain; the fire came from the ravine below, crossing the road and moving upward. The clouds of smoke and ashes, the rushing of currents of wind and flames, the crackling of burning branches and trees wrapped in flames, and the rapid progress of the destroying element, made such a wild and fearful scene that we could not tear ourselves away. At length we saw the flames rush up the side of the ravine, intercepting the path before us. We spurred our horses, shot by, and in a moment the whole was a sheet of flame. The fire was now spreading so rapidly that we became alarmed. We hurried back to the church, which, on an elevation strongly defined against the immense mountain in the background, stood before us as a place of refuge.

By this time the villagers had become alarmed, and men and women were hurrying to the height to watch the progress of the flames. The village was in danger of conflagration; it would be impossible to urge the loaded mules up the hill we had descended, so we resolved to deposit the luggage in the church and save the mules by driving them up unburdened. It was another of those wild scenes to which no effect can be given in words. We stopped on the brow of the hill before the square of the church and, while we were watching the fire, the black clouds and sheets of flame rolled up the side of the mountain and spared the village. Relieved from apprehension, we sat down under a tree in front of the church to the calm enjoyment of the terrific spectacle and a cold fowl. The cinders and ashes fell around, and the destructive element rushed on, sparing the village before us, perhaps to lay some other to ruins.

We were obliged to wait two hours. From the foot of the hill on which the village stood the ground was hot and covered with a light coat of ashes; the brush and underwood were burned away; in some places were lying trees reduced to masses of live coal, and in other places they were standing with their trunks and branches all on fire. In one place we passed a square of white ashes, the remains of some miserable Indian hut. Our faces and hands were scorched and our whole bodies heated when we emerged from the fiery forest. For a few moments the open air was delightful; but we were hardly out of one trouble before we had another. Swarms of enormous flies, perhaps driven out by the fire, and hovering on the borders of the burned district, fell upon the mules. Every bite drew blood, and the tormentors clung to the suffering animals until brushed off by a stick. For an hour we labored hard, but could not keep their heads and necks free. The poor beasts were almost frantic, and, in spite of all we could do, their necks, the inside of their legs, mouths, ears, nostrils, and every tender part of their skin, were trickling with blood.

Hurrying on, in three hours we saw the Church of San Antonio Huista, and in a few minutes entered the village, beautifully situated on a tableland projecting from the slope of a mountain, looking upon an immense opening, and commanding on all sides a magnificent view. At this time we were beyond the reach of war, and free from all apprehensions. With the addition of Pawling's pistols and double-barreled gun, and our faithful muleteer Santiago, and with Juan on his legs again, we could have stormed an Indian village and locked up a refractory alcalde in his own cabildo. We took possession of San Antonio Huista, dividing ourselves between the cabildo and the convent, sent for the alcalde (even on the borders of Central America the name of Carrera was omnipotent), and told him to stay there and wait upon us, or send an alguacil. The convent stood adjoining the church, on an open table of land, commanding a view of a magnificent valley surrounded by immense mountains; and on the left was a vista between two mountain ranges, wild, rugged, and lofty, losing their tops in the clouds. Before the door of the convent was a large cross on a high pedestal of stone, with the coating decayed and covered with wild flowers. The convent was enclosed by a brush fence, without any opening until we made one. The padre was not at home, which was very fortunate for him, as there would not have been room enough for us all. In fact, everything seemed exactly intended for our party; there were three beds, just as many as we could conveniently occupy, and the style of them was new; they were made of long sticks about an inch thick, tied with bark strings at top and bottom, which rested on crotches about two feet high, driven into the dirt floor.

The alcalde and his major had roused the village. In a few moments, instead of the mortifying answer *no hay* (there is none), the provision made for us was almost equal to the offers of the Turkish paradise. Twenty or thirty women were in the convent at one time, with baskets of corn, tortillas, *dulces*, plantains, *jocotes*, sapotas, and a variety of other fruits, each one's stock in trade being the value of three cents; and among them was a species of tortillas, thin and baked hard, about twelve inches in diameter, one hundred and twenty for six cents, of which, as they were not expensive, we laid in a large supply.

At this place our muleteer was to leave us. We had but one cargo mule fit for service, and we applied to the alcalde for two carriers to go with us across the frontier to Comitán. He went out, as he said, to consult with the mozos, and told us that they asked six dollars apiece. We spoke to him of our friend Carrera, and on a second consultation the demand was reduced by two-thirds. We were obliged to make provision for three days, and even to carry corn for the mules; and Juan and Santiago had a busy night boiling fowls and eggs.

Chapter XIV

~~~~~~

Comfortable lodgings. Journey continued. Stony road. Beautiful river. Suspension bridge. The Dolores. Río Lagartero. Enthusiasm brought down. Another bridge. Entry into Mexico. A bath. A solitary church. A scene of barrenness. Zapaluta. Comitán. Another countryman. More perplexities. Official courtesy. Trade of Comitán. Smuggling. Scarcity of soap.

THE next morning we found the convent was so comfortable, we were so abundantly served—the alcalde or his major, staff in hand, being in constant attendance—and the situation so beautiful that we were in no hurry to go; but the alcalde told us that all was ready. We did not see our carriers, and found that the alcalde and his major were the mozos whom he had consulted. They could not let slip two dollars apiece and, laying down their staves and dignity, they bared their backs, placed the straps across their foreheads, took up the loads, and trotted off.

We started at five minutes before eight. The weather was fine but hazy. From the village we descended a hill to an extensive stony plain and, at about a league's distance, reached the brink of a precipice, from which we looked down into a rich oblong valley, two or three thousand feet deep, shut in all around by a mountain wall, and seeming an immense excavation; toward the other end of the valley was a village with a ruined church. The road led up a precipitous ascent to a plain on the same level with that on which we stood, undulating and boundless as the sea. Below us it seemed as if we could drop a stone to the bottom. We descended by one of the steepest and most stony paths we had yet encountered in the country, which crossed and recrossed in a zigzag course along the side of the height, perhaps making the descent a mile and a half long. Very soon we reached the bank of a beautiful river, running lengthwise through the valley, bordered on each side by immense trees, throwing their branches clear across, and having their roots washed by the stream; and while the plain beyond was dry and parched, they were green and luxuriant.

Riding along the bank of the river, we reached a suspension bridge of the most primitive appearance and construction, which had existed there from time immemorial; it was called by the natives La Hamaca. Made of osiers twisted into cords, about three feet apart, it stretched across the river with a hanging network of vines, the ends fastened to the trunks of two opposite trees. It hung about twenty-five feet above the river, which was here some eighty feet wide, and was supported in different places by vines tied to the branches. The access was by a rude ladder to a platform in the crotch of the tree. In the bottom of the Hamaca were two or three poles to walk on. The bridge waved with the wind, and was an unsteady and rather insecure means of transportation. From the center the vista of the river both ways under the arches of the trees was beautiful, and in every direction the Hamaca was a most picturesque-looking object. We continued on to the village and, after a short halt and a smoke with the alcalde, rode on to the extreme end of the valley, and by a steep and stony ascent, at twenty minutes past twelve, we reached the level ground above. Here we dismounted, slipped the bridles off our mules, and seated ourselves to wait for our Indians, looking down into the deep embosomed valley, and back at the great range of Cordilleras crowned by the Sierra Madre, seeming a barrier fit to separate worlds.

Free from all apprehensions, we were now in the full enjoyment of the wild country and wild mode of traveling. But our poor Indians, perhaps, did not enjoy it so much. The usual load was from three to four *arrobas*, or seventy-five to one hundred pounds; ours were not more than fifty; but the sweat rolled in streams down their naked bodies, and every limb trembled. After a short rest they started again. The day was hot and sultry, the ground dry, parched, and stony. After two sharp descents, we reached the River Dolores. On both sides were large trees, furnishing a beautiful shade, which, after our scorching ride, we found delightful. The river was about two hundred feet broad. In the rainy season it was impassable, but in the dry season it was not more than three or four feet deep, very clear and the color a grayish green, probably from the reflection of the trees. We had had no water since we left the suspension bridge, and both our mules and we were intemperate.

We remained here half an hour; and now apprehensions, which had been operating more or less all the time, made us feel very uncomfortable. We were approaching, and very near, the frontier of Mexico. This road was so little traveled, that, as we had been advised, there was no regular guard; but piquets of soldiers, who were scouring the whole line of frontier to prevent smuggling, might consider us contraband. Our passports were good for going out of Central America; but to go into Mexico, the passport of the Mexican authorities at Ciudad Real,[1] four days' journey, was necessary. Turning back was not in our vocabulary; perhaps we should be obliged to wait in the wilderness till we could send for one.

In half an hour we reached the Río Lagartero, the boundary line between Guatemala and Mexico, a scene of wild and surpassing beauty, with banks shaded by some of the noblest trees of the tropical forests, water as clear as crystal, and fish a foot long playing in it as gently as if there were no fishhooks. No soldiers were visible; all was as desolate as if no human being had ever crossed the boundary before. We had a moment's consultation on which side to encamp, and determined to make a lodgment in Mexico. I was riding Pawling's horse, and I spurred him into the water to be the first to touch the soil. With one plunge his forefeet

---

1. Ciudad Real was the first name of the city. Later it was called San Cristóbal de las Casas, and now it is known as Ciudad de las Casas.

were off the bottom and my legs under water. For an instant I hesitated; but as the water rose to my holsters my enthusiasm gave way, and I wheeled back into Central America. As we afterward found, the water was ten or twelve feet deep.

We waited for the Indians, in some doubt whether it would be possible to cross at all with the luggage. At a short distance above was a ledge of rocks, forming rapids, over which there had once been a bridge with a wooden arch and stone abutments, the latter of which were still standing, the bridge having been carried away by the rising of the waters seven years before. It was the last of the dry season; the rocks were in some places dry, with the body of the river running in channels on each side. A log was laid to the rocks from the abutments of the bridge and, taking off the saddles and bridles of the mules, cautiously, with the water breaking rapidly up to our knees, we carried everything across by hand, an operation in which an hour was consumed. One night's rain on the mountains would have made it impassable. The mules were then swum across, and we were all landed safely in Mexico.

On the bank opposite the place where I had attempted to cross was a semicircular clearing, from which the only opening was the path leading into the Mexican provinces. We closed this up and, turning the mules loose, hung our traps on the trees and bivouacked in the center. The men built a fire, and while they were preparing supper, we went down to the river to bathe. The rapids were breaking above us. The wildness of the scene, its seclusion and remoteness, the clearness of the water, the sense of having accomplished an important part of our journey, all revived our physical and moral being. Clean apparel consummated the glory of the bath. For several days our digestive organs had been out of order, but when we sat down to supper they could have undertaken the bridles of the mules; and my brave macho—it was a pleasure to hear him crunch his corn. We were out of Central America, safe from the dangers of revolution; we stood on the wild borders of Mexico, in good health, with good appetites, and something to eat. We had still a tremendous journey before us, but it seemed nothing. We strode the little clearing as proudly as the conquerors of Mexico, and in our extravagance resolved to have a fish for breakfast. We had no hooks, and there was not even a pin in our traveling equipage; but we had needles and thread. Pawling, with the experience of seven years' "roughing," had expedients, and he put a needle in the fire, which softened its temper so that he bent it into a hook. A pole was on every tree, and we could see the fish in the water; all that we wanted was for them to open their mouths and hook themselves to the needle; but this they would not do, and for this reason alone we did not catch any. Our men then cut some poles, and resting them in the crotch of a tree, covered them with branches, under which we spread our mats, and our roof and beds were ready. The men piled logs of wood on the fire, and our sleep was sound and glorious.

At daylight the next morning we were again in the water. Our bath was even better than that of the night before, and when I mounted I felt able to ride through Mexico and Texas to my own door at home. Returned once more to steamboats and railroads, how flat, tame, and insipid all their comforts seem.

We started at half past seven. At a very short distance three wild boars crossed our path, all within gunshot; but our men carried the guns, and in an instant it was too late. Very soon we emerged from the woods that bordered the river, and came out into an open plain. At half past eight we crossed a low stony hill and came to the dry bed of a river. The bottom was flat and baked hard, and the sides smooth and regular as those of a canal. At the distance of half a league water appeared, and at half past nine it became a considerable stream. We again entered a forest, and riding by a narrow path, saw directly before us, closing the passage, the side of a large church. We came out, and saw the whole gigantic building, without a single habitation, or the vestige of one, in sight. The path led across the broken wall of the courtyard. We dismounted in the deep shade of the front. The façade was rich and perfect. It was sixty feet front and two hundred and fifty feet deep, but roofless, with trees growing out of the area above the walls. Nothing could exceed the quiet and desolation of the scene; but there was something strangely interesting in these roofless churches, standing in places entirely unknown. Santiago told us that this was called Conata, and according to tradition, it was once so rich that the inhabitants carried their water jars by silken cords. Giving our mules to Santiago, we entered the open door of the church. The altar was thrown down, the roof lay in broken masses on the ground, and the whole area was a forest of trees. At the foot of the church, and connected with it, was a convent. There was no roof, but the apartments were as entire as when a good padre stood there to welcome a traveler. In front of the church, on each side, was a staircase leading up to a belfry in the center of the façade. We ascended to the top. The bells which had called to matin and vesper prayers were gone; the crosspiece was broken from the cross. The stone of the belfry was in solid masses of petrified shells, worms, leaves, and insects. On one side we looked down into the roofless area, and on the other over a region of waste. One man had written his name there:

Joaquim Rodrigues,
Conata, Mayo 1°, 1836

We wrote our names under his and descended. Mounting again, and riding over a stony and desolate country, we crossed a river and saw before us a range of hills, and beyond them a range of mountains. Then we came upon a bleak stony table and, after riding four hours and a half, saw the road leading across a barren mountain on our right; afraid of having missed our way, we halted under a low spreading tree to wait for our men. We turned the mules loose, and after waiting some time sent Santiago back to look for the men. The wind was sweeping over the plain, and while Mr. Catherwood was cutting wood, Pawling and I descended to a ravine to look for water. The bed was entirely dry, and one of us took his course up, and the other down. Pawling found a muddy hole in a rock, which, even to thirsty men, was not tempting.

Returning, we found Mr. Catherwood warming himself by the blaze of three or four young trees, which he had piled one upon another. The wind was at this time sweeping furiously over the plain, and night was approaching. We had not eaten anything since morning; our small stock of provisions was in unsafe hands, and we began to fear that none would be forthcoming. Our mules were as badly off. The pasture was so poor that they required a wide range, and we let all go loose except my poor macho, which, from certain roving propensities acquired before he came into my possession, we were obliged to fasten to a tree. It was some time after dark when Santiago appeared with the *alforjas* of provisions on his back. When he had gone back six miles he found the track of Juan's foot, one of the squarest ever planted, and followed it to a wretched hut in the woods, at which we had expected to stop. We had lost nothing by not stopping; all they could get to bring away was four eggs. We supped, piled up our trunks to windward, spread our mats, lay down, gazed for a few moments at the stars, and fell asleep. During the night the wind changed, and we were almost blown away.

The next morning, preparatory to entering once more upon habitable regions, we made our toilet: we hung a looking glass on the branch of a tree, and shaved the upper lip and a small part of the chin. At a quarter past seven we started, having eaten up our last fragment. Since we had left Huista, we had not seen a human being, and the country was still desolate and dreary; there was not a breath of air, and the hills, mountains, and plains were all barren and stony. But, as the sun peeped above the horizon, its beams gladdened this scene of barrenness. For two hours we ascended a barren stony mountain. Even before this the desolate frontier had seemed almost an impregnable barrier; but Alvarado had crossed it to penetrate an unknown country teeming with enemies, and twice a Mexican army had invaded Central America.

At half past ten we reached the top of the mountain, and on a line before us saw the Church of Zapaluta, the first village in Mexico. Here our apprehensions revived from want of a passport. Our great object was to reach Comitán, and there bide the brunt. Approaching the village, we avoided the road that led through the plaza; leaving the luggage to get along as it could, we hurried through the suburbs, startled some women and children, and before our entry was known at the cabildo, were beyond the village. We rode briskly for about a mile, and then stopped to breathe. An immense weight was removed from our minds, and we welcomed each other to Mexico. Coming in from the desolate frontier, it opened upon us like an old, long-settled, civilized, quiet, and well-governed country.

Four hours' ride over an arid and sandy plain brought us to Comitán. Santiago, being a deserter from the Mexican army and afraid of being caught, left us in the suburbs to return alone across the desert we had passed, and we rode on into the plaza. In one of the largest houses fronting it lived an American. Part of the front was occupied as a shop, and behind the counter was a man whose face called up the memory of home. I asked him in English if his name was MacKinney, and he answered *Sí, señor*. I put several other questions in English, which he answered in Spanish. The sounds were familiar to him, yet it was some time before he could fully comprehend that he was listening to his native tongue; but when he did, and understood that I was a countryman, it awakened feelings to which he had long been a stranger, and he received us as one in whom absence had only strengthened the links that bound him to his country.

Dr. James MacKinney, whose unpretending name is in Comitán transformed to the imposing one of Don Santiago Maquene, was a native of Westmoreland County, Virginia, who went out to Tobasco to pass a winter for the benefit of his health and the practice of his profession. Circumstances induced him to make a journey into the interior, and he had established himself at Ciudad Real. At the time of the cholera in Central America he had gone to Quezaltenango, where he was employed by the government and where he lived two years on intimate terms with the unfortunate General Guzmán, whom he described as one of the most gentlemanly, amiable, intelligent, and best men in the country. He afterward returned to Comitán and married a lady of a once rich and powerful family, which had been stripped of a portion of its wealth by a revolution only two years before.

In the division of what was left, the house on the plaza had fallen to his share; and disliking the practice of his profession, he abandoned it and took to selling goods. Like every other stranger in the country, by reason of constant wars and revolutions he had become nervous. He had none of this feeling when he first arrived, and at the time of the first revolution in Ciudad Real he stood in the plaza looking on, when two men were shot down by his side. Fortunately, he took them into a house to dress their wounds, and during this time the attacking party forced their way into the plaza and cut down every man in it.

Up to this place we had traveled on the road to Mexico City; here Pawling was to leave us and go on to the capital; Palenque lay on our right, toward the coast of the Atlantic. The road Dr. MacKinney described was more frightful than any we had yet traveled, and there were other difficulties. War was again in our way; and, while all the rest of Mexico was quiet, Tobasco and Yucatán, two points in our journey, were in a state of revolution. This might have disturbed us greatly but for another difficulty. It was necessary to present ourselves at Ciudad Real, three days' journey directly out of our road, to procure a passport, without which we could not travel in any part of the Mexican republic. And, serious as these things were, they merged in a third, for the government of Mexico had issued a peremptory order to prevent all strangers from visiting the ruins of Palenque. Dr. Mac-Kinney told us that of his own knowledge three Belgians, who had been sent out on a scientific expedition by the Belgian government, had gone to Ciudad Real expressly to ask permission to visit them and had been refused. These communications damped somewhat the satisfaction of our arrival in Comitán.

By Dr. MacKinney's advice we presented ourselves immediately to the commandant, who had a small garrison of about thirty men, well uniformed and equipped; compared with the soldiers of Central America, they gave me a high opinion of the Mexican army. I showed the commandant my passport, and a copy of the government paper of Guatemala, which fortunately stated that I intended going to Campeche to embark for the United States. With great courtesy he immediately undertook to relieve us from the necessity of presenting ourselves in person at Ciudad Real, offering to send a courier to the governor for a passport. This was a great point, but still this, too, would mean detention. Therefore, by his advice, we called upon the Prefecto, who received us with the same courtesy; regretting the necessity of embarrassing my movements, he showed us a copy of the order of the government, which was imperative and made no exceptions in favor of Special Confidential Agents. He was really anxious, however, to serve us; he said he was willing to incur some responsibility and would consult with the commandant. We left him with a warm appreciation of the civility and good feeling of the Mexican officials, satisfied that whatever might be the result they were disposed to pay great respect to their neighbors of the North. The next morning the Prefecto sent back the passport, with a courteous message that they considered me in the same light as if I had come accredited to their own government, that they would be happy to render me every facility in their power, and that Mexico was open to me to travel which way I pleased. Thus one great difficulty was removed. I recommend all who wish to travel to get an appointment from Washington.

As to the revolutions, after having gone through the crash of a Central American, we were not to be put back by a Mexican. But the preventive order against visiting the ruins of Palenque was not so easily disposed of. If we made an application for permission, we felt sure of the good disposition of the local authorities; but if they had no discretion, if they were bound by imperative orders and obliged to refuse, it would be uncourteous and improper to make the attempt. At the same time, it was discouraging, in the teeth of Dr. MacKinney's information, to undertake the journey without permission; yet to be obliged to retrace our steps and make the long journey to the capital to ask for it would be terrible. But we learned that the ruins were removed some distance from any habitation; we did not believe, in the midst of a formidable revolution, that the government had any spare soldiers to station there as guard. From what we knew of other ruins, we had reason to believe that the place was entirely desolate; we might be on the ground before anyone knew we were in the neighborhood, and then make terms either to remain or evacuate, as the case might require; it would be worth the risk if we got one day's quiet possession. With this uncertain prospect we immediately commenced repairing and making preparations for our journey.

The comfort of finding ourselves at this distant place in the house of a countryman can hardly be appreciated. In dress, manner, appearance, habits, and feelings, the doctor was as natural as if we had met him at home. The only difference was in his use of the English language, which he could not speak connectedly, interlarding it with Spanish expressions. He moved among the people but he was not of them; and the only tie that bound him was a dark-eyed Spanish beauty, one of the few that I saw in that country for whom a man might forget kindred and home. He was anxious to leave the country, but was trammeled by a promise made his mother-in-law not to do so during her life. He lived, however, in such constant anxiety that he hoped she would release him.

Comitán, the frontier town of Chiapas, contains a population of about ten thousand. It has a superb church and well-filled convent of Dominican friars. The better classes, as in Central America, have dwelling houses in the town, and derive their subsistence from the products of their haciendas, which they visit from time to time. It was a place of considerable trade, and has become so by the effect of bad laws, for, in consequence of the heavy duties on regular importations at the Mexican ports of entry, most of the European goods consumed in this region were smuggled in from Belize and Guatemala. The proceeds of confiscations and the perquisites of officers are such an important item of revenue that the officers are vigilant, and the day before we arrived twenty or thirty muleloads that had been seized were brought into Comitán; but the profits were so large that smuggling was a regular business, the risk of seizure being considered one of the expenses of carrying it on. The whole community, not excepting the revenue officers, were interested in it, and its effect upon public morals was deplorable. The markets, however, were but poorly supplied, as we found out. We sent for a washerwoman, but there was no soap in the town. We wanted our mules shod, but there was only iron enough to shoe one. Buttons for pantaloons made up in size for other deficiencies. The want of soap was a deplorable circumstance. For several days we had indulged in the pleasing expectation of having our sheets washed. The reader may perhaps consider us particular, as it had only been three weeks since we left Guatemala, but we had slept in wretched cabildos and on the ground, and they had become of a very doubtful color. In time of trouble, however, commend me to the sympathy of a countryman. Don Santiago, alias Doctor MacKinney, stood by us in our hour of need; he provided us with soap and our sheets were purified.

I have omitted a circumstance which from the time of our arrival in Central America we had noticed as extraordinary. The horses and mules were never shod, except for perhaps a few pleasure horses used for riding about the streets of Guatemala. On the road, however, we were advised, after we had set out, that it was proper to have ours shod; but there was no good blacksmith except at Quezaltenango, and as we were at that place during a fiesta, he would not work. In crossing long ranges of stony mountains, not one of the animals suffered except Mr. Catherwood's riding mule, and her hoofs were worn down even with the flesh.

Pawling's difficulties were now over. I procured for him a separate passport, and he had before him a clear road to Mexico City; but his interest had been awakened; he was loth to leave us, and after a long consultation and deliberation resolved that he would go along with us to Palenque.

Chapter XV

~~~~~~

Parting. Sotaná. A millionaire. Ococingo. Ruins. Begin-
ning of the rainy season. A female guide. Arrival at the
ruins. Stone figures. Pyramidal structures. An arch. A
stucco ornament. A wooden lintel. A curious cave. Build-
ings, etc. A causeway. More ruins. Journey to Palenque.
Río Grande. Cascades. Succession of villages. A maniac.
The Yajalón. Tumbalá. A wild place. A scene of grandeur
and sublimity. Indian carriers. A steep
mountain. San Pedro.

ON the first of May, with a bustle and confusion like
that of May Day at home, we moved out of Don
Santiago's house, mounted, and bade him farewell. Doubtless his daily routines have not since been broken by the visit
of a countryman, and communication is so difficult that he
never hears from home. He charged us with messages to
his friend Doctor Coleman, United States consul at Tabasco,
not knowing at the time that he was dead; and the reader
will perhaps feel for Don Santiago when I mention that
probably a copy of this work, which I intend to send him,
will never reach his hands.

I must pass over the next stage of our journey, which was
through a region less mountainous but not less solitary than
that we had already traversed. The first afternoon we
stopped in a soft and lovely valley at the hacienda of Sotaná,
belonging to a brother-in-law of Don Santiago; attached to
the hacienda was a chapel with a bell that at evening called
the Indian workmen, women, and children to vesper prayers.
The next day, we stopped at the abode of Padre Solís, a

rich old cura, short and broad of figure. He lived on a fine hacienda and we dined off solid silver dishes, drank out of silver cups, and washed in a silver basin. He had lived at Palenque, talked of Lacandones, or unbaptized Indians, and wanted to buy my macho, promising to keep him till he died; the only thing that relieves me from self reproach in not securing him such pasture grounds is the recollection of the padre's weight.

At four o'clock on the third day we reached Ococingo, likewise in a beautiful situation surrounded by mountains; in the center of the square was a large ceiba tree. It had a large church, and in the wall of the yard we noticed two sculptured figures from the ruins we proposed to visit, somewhat in the same style as those at Copán. We rode up to the house of Don Manuel Pasada, the prefect, and, except for an old woman servant, we had it entirely to ourselves, the family being at his hacienda. The house was a large enclosure with a shed in front, and was furnished with bedsteads made of reeds split in two and supported on sticks resting in the ground.

The alcalde was a mestizo, very civil and glad to see us; he spoke of the neighboring ruins in the most extravagant terms, but said they were so completely buried in *el monte* that it would require a party of men for two or three days to cut a way to them. He laid great stress upon a cave, the mouth of which was completely choked up with stones, which communicated by a subterraneous passage with the old city of Palenque, about one hundred and fifty miles distant. He added that if we would wait a few days to make preparations, he and all the village would go with us and make a thorough exploration. We told him that first we wished to make preliminary observations, and he promised us a guide for the next morning.

That night there broke upon us the opening storm of the rainy season. Peals of crashing thunder reverberated from the mountains, lightning illuminated with fearful flashes the darkness of night, rain poured like a deluge upon our thatched roof. The worst mountains in the whole road were

yet to be crossed; all our efforts to anticipate the rainy season
had been fruitless.

In the morning, dark clouds still obscured the sky, but
they fell back and hid themselves before the beams of the
rising sun. The grass and trees, parched by six months'
drought, started into a deeper green, and the hills and mountains seemed glad. The alcalde, I believe, being vexed at
our unwillingness to make an immediate affair of exploring
the ruins, had gone away for the day without sending us any
guide; he had left word that all the men were engaged in
repairing the church. We endeavored to entice one of them
away, but unsuccessfully. Returning to the house, we found
that our piazza was the schoolhouse of the village. Half a
dozen children were sitting on a bench, and the schoolmaster,
half tipsy, was educating them, that is, teaching them to
repeat by rote the formal parts of the church service. We
asked him to help us, but he advised us to wait a day or two:
in that country nothing could be done *violenter*.

We were excessively vexed at the prospect of losing the
day; but at the moment when we thought there was nothing
left to do but submit, a little girl came to tell us that a
woman, on whose hacienda the ruins were, was about to go
to visit it and had offered to escort us. Her horse was already
standing before the door, and before our mules were ready
she rode over for us. We paid our respects, gave her a good
cigar, and, lighting all around, set out. She was a pleasant
mestizo, and had a son with her, a fine lad about fifteen. We
started at half past nine, and, after a hot and sultry ride, at
twenty minutes past eleven reached her rancho. It was a
mere hut, made of poles and plastered with mud, but the
situation was one of those that warmed us to country life.
Our kind guide sent with us her son and an Indian with his
machete, and in half an hour we were at the ruins.

Soon after leaving the rancho and at nearly a mile distant,
on a high elevation we saw through openings in trees growing around it, one of the buildings of Tonila,[1] the Indian

---

1. The reference is probably to the ruins of Toniná, an Old Empire Mayan city near Ococingo.

name in this region for stone houses. Approaching it, we
passed on the plain in front of us two stone figures lying on
the ground with the faces upward; they were well carved,
but the characters, though still distinct, were somewhat faded
by long exposure to the elements. Leaving them, we rode
on to the foot of a high structure, probably a fortress, rising
in a pyramidal form, with five spacious terraces. These terraces had all been faced with stone and stuccoed, but in many
places they were broken and overgrown with grass and
shrubs. Taking advantage of one of the broken parts, we
rode up the first pitch, and, following the platform of the
terrace, ascended by another breach to the second, and in
the same way to the third. There we tied our horses and
climbed up on foot.

On the top was a pyramidal structure overgrown with
trees, supporting the building which we had seen from the
plain below. Among the trees were several wild lemons,
loaded with fruit of very fine flavor, which, if not brought
there by the Spaniards, must be indigenous. The building,
which was fifty feet front and thirty-five feet deep, was constructed of stone and lime; the whole front had once been
covered with stucco, of which part of the cornice and mouldings still remained. The entrance was by a doorway ten feet
wide, which led into a sort of antechamber, on each side of
which was a small doorway leading into an apartment ten
feet square. The walls of these apartments had once been
covered with stucco, which had fallen down; part of the
roof had given way, and the floor was covered with ruins.
In one of them was the same pitchy substance we had noticed
in the sepulcher at Copán. The roof was formed of stones,
lapping over in the usual style, and forming as near an approach to the arch as was made by the architects of the New
World.

In the back wall of the center chamber was a doorway,
of the same size as that in front, leading to an apartment
which did not have any partitions, but which did have in the
center an oblong enclosure eighteen feet by eleven, intended,
manifestly, as the most important part of the edifice. The
door was choked up with ruins to within a few feet of the

top, but over it, and extending along the whole front of the structure, was a large stucco ornament which at first impressed us most forcibly by its striking resemblance to the winged globe over the doors of Egyptian temples. Part of this ornament had fallen down and, striking the heap of rubbish underneath, had rolled beyond the door of entrance. We endeavored to roll it back and restore it to its place, but it proved too heavy for the strength of four men and a boy. The part which remains is represented in the engraving (figure 5 facing page 179) and differs in detail from the winged globe; the wings are reversed, and a fragment of a circular ornament which may have been intended for a globe, had no remains of serpents entwining it.

There was another surprising feature in this door. The lintel was *a beam of wood;* of what species we did not know, but our guide said it was of the sapota tree. It was so hard that on being struck it rang like metal; it was perfectly sound, without a wormhole or other symptom of decay. The surface was smooth and even, and from a very close examination we were of the opinion that it must have been trimmed with an instrument of metal.

The opening under this doorway was what the alcalde had mentioned as the mouth of the cave that led to Palenque, and which, by the way, he had told us was so completely buried in *el monte* that it would require two days digging and clearing to reach it. Our guide laughed at the ignorance prevailing in the village in regard to the difficulty of reaching it, but stoutly maintained the story that it led to Palenque; but we could not prevail on him to enter it. A short cut to Palenque was exactly what we wanted, so I took off my coat and, lying down on my breast, began to crawl under. When I had advanced about half the length of my body, I heard a hideous hissing noise and, starting back, saw a pair of small eyes, which in the darkness shone like balls of fire. The precise portion of time that I employed in backing out is not worth mentioning. My companions had heard the noise, and the guide said it was *un tigre.* I thought it was a wildcat; but, whatever it was, we determined to have a shot at it. We took it for granted that the animal would dash past us, and in a few moments our guns and pistols, swords and machetes were ready. When we had taken our positions, Pawling standing close against the wall thrust under a long pole, and with a horrible noise out fluttered a huge turkey buzzard, which flapped itself through the building and took refuge in another chamber.

This peril over, I renewed the attempt, and holding a candle before me, quickly discovered the whole extent of the cave that led to Palenque. It was a chamber corresponding with the dimensions given of the outer walls. The floor was encumbered with rubbish two or three feet deep, the walls were covered with stuccoed figures, among which that of a monkey was conspicuous, and against the back wall, among curious and interesting ornaments, were two figures of men in profile, with their faces toward each other, well drawn and as large as life, but with their feet concealed by the rubbish on the floor. Mr. Catherwood crawled in to make a drawing of them, but, on account of the smoke from the candles, the closeness, and the excessive heat, it was impossible to remain long enough. In general appearance and character they were the same as we afterward saw carved on stone at Palenque.

By means of a tree growing close against the wall of this building, I climbed to the top and saw another edifice very near and on top of a still higher structure. We climbed up to this and found it of the same general plan, but in a more dilapidated condition. Descending, we passed between two other buildings on pyramidal elevations and came out upon an open table which had probably once been the site of the city. It was protected on all sides by the same high terraces, which overlooked for a great distance the whole country round, rendering it impossible for an enemy to approach from any quarter without being discovered. Across the table was a high and narrow causeway extended till it joined a range of mountains. From the few Spanish books within my reach I have not been able to learn anything whatever of the history of this place, or whether or not it existed at the time of the conquest. I am inclined to think, however, that it did, and that mention is made of it in some Spanish authors.[2] At all events, there was no place we had seen which gave us such an idea of the vastness of the works erected by the aboriginal inhabitants. Pressed as we were, we determined to remain and make a thorough exploration.

It was nearly dark when we returned to the village. Immediately we called upon the alcalde, but found on the very threshold detention and delay. He repeated the schoolmaster's warning that nothing could be done *violenter*. It would take two days to get together men and implements, and these last, of the kind necessary, could not be had at all. There was not a crowbar in the place, but the alcalde said one could be made and, in the same breath, that there was no iron. There was half a blacksmith, but no iron nearer than Tabasco, about eight or ten days' journey. While we were with him another terrible storm came on. We hurried back in the midst of it, and determined forthwith to push on to Palenque. I am strongly of the opinion that there is at this place much to reward the future traveler; we were told also that there were other ruins about ten leagues distant, along the same range of mountains. This place has additional interest in our eyes, from the circumstance that it would be the best point from which to attempt the discovery of the mysterious city seen from the top of the Cordilleras.

At Ococingo we were on the line of travel of Captain Dupaix,[3] whose great work on Mexican antiquities, published in Paris in 1834–5, awakened the attention of the learned in Europe. His expedition to Palenque was made in 1807. He reached this place from the city of Mexico, under a commission from the government, attended by a draughtsman and secretary, and part of a regiment of dragoons. "Palenque," he says, "is eight days' march from Ococingo. The journey is very fatiguing. The roads, if they can be so called, are only narrow and difficult paths, which wind across mountains and precipices, and which it is necessary to follow

---

2. Toniná was no longer inhabited when the Spaniards arrived.
3. Guillelmo Dupaix. *Antiquités Mexicaines*, Paris, 1834, 2 vols.

sometimes on mules, sometimes on foot, sometimes on the shoulders of Indians, and sometimes in hammocks. In some places it is necessary to pass on bridges, or, rather, trunks of trees badly secured, and over lands covered with wood, desert and dispeopled, and to sleep in the open air, excepting a very few villages and huts.

"We had with us thirty or forty vigorous Indians to carry our luggage and hammocks. After having experienced in this long and painful journey every kind of fatigue and discomfort, we arrived, thank God, at the village of Palenque."

This was now the journey before us and, according to the stages we had arranged to avoid sleeping out at night, it was to be made in five instead of eight days. The terrible rains of the two preceding nights had infected us with a sort of terror, and Pawling was completely shaken in his purpose of continuing with us. The people of the village told him that after the rains had fairly set in it would be impossible to return, and in the morning, though reluctantly, he determined abruptly to leave us and go back. We were very unwilling to part with him, but, under the circumstances, could not urge him to continue. Our luggage and little traps, which we had used in common, were separated. Mr. Catherwood bade him good-bye and rode on; but while mounted and in the act of shaking hands to pursue our opposite roads, I made him a proposition which induced him again to change his determination at the risk of remaining on the other side of the mountains until the rainy season was over, and in a few minutes we overtook Mr. Catherwood.

The fact is, we had some apprehensions from the badness of the roads. Our route lay through an Indian country, in parts of which the Indians bore a notoriously bad character. We had no dragoons, our party of attendants was very small, and, in reality, we had not a single man upon whom we could rely. Under such a state of things, Pawling's pistols and double-barreled gun were a matter of some consequence.

We left Ococingo at a quarter past eight. So little impression did any of our attendants make upon me, that I have entirely forgotten every one of them. Indeed, this was the case throughout the journey. In other countries a Greek muleteer, an Arab boatman, or a Bedouin guide was a companion; but here the people had no character and nothing in which we took any interest except their backs. Each Indian carried besides his burden a net bag containing his provisions for the road: a few tortillas and large balls of mashed Indian corn wrapped in leaves. A drinking cup, being half a calabash, he carried sometimes on the crown of his head. At every stream he filled his cup with water, into which he stirred some of his corn, making a sort of cold porridge; throughout the country this is the staff of life for the Indian on a journey. In half an hour we passed at some distance on our right large mounds, formerly structures which formed part of the old city. At nine o'clock we crossed the Río Grande, or Huacachahoul, followed some distance on the bank, and passed three cascades spreading over the rocky bed of the river, unique and peculiar in beauty; probably there were many more of the same character breaking unnoticed and unknown in the wilderness through which the Río Grande rolled, but, turning up a rugged mountain, we lost sight of the river.

The road was broken and mountainous. We did not meet a single person, and at three o'clock, moving in a north-northwest direction, we entered the village of Huacachahoul,[4] standing in an open situation surrounded by mountains, and peopled entirely by Indians, wilder and more savage than any we had yet seen. The men were without hats, but wore their long black hair reaching to their shoulders; and the old men and women, with harsh and haggard features and dark rolling eyes, had a most unbaptized appearance. They gave us no greetings, and their wild but steady glare made us feel a little nervous. A collection of naked boys and girls called Mr. Catherwood *Tata*, mistaking him for a padre. We had some misgivings when we put the village behind us, and felt ourselves enclosed in the country of wild Indians. We stopped an hour near a stream, and at

---

4. The editor has been unable to identify a village by this name. Between Ococingo and Chilón there is, however, a village called Bachajón, which is probably that referred to.

half past six arrived at Chilón, where, to our surprise and pleasure, we found a sub-prefect, a white man, and intelligent, who had traveled to San Salvador and knew General Morazán. He was very anxious to know whether there was any revolution in Ciudad Real, as, with a pliancy becoming an officeholder, he wished to signify his adhesion to the new government.

The next morning, at a quarter before seven, we started with a new set of Indians. The road was good to Yajalón, which we reached at ten o'clock. Before entering it we met a young Indian girl with her father; she was of extraordinary beauty of face and was in the costume of the country, but she had a modest expression of countenance, which we all particularly remarked as evidence of her innocence and unconsciousness of anything wrong in her appearance. Every village we passed was most picturesque in position, and here the church was very effective; as in the preceding villages, it was undergoing repairs.

Here we were obliged to take another set of Indians, and perhaps we should have lost the day but for the padre, who called off some men working at the church. At a quarter past eleven we set off again; at a quarter before one we stopped at the side of a stream to lunch. At this place a young Indian with a very intelligent face overtook us and, seating himself beside me, said in remarkably good Spanish that we must beware of the Indians. I gave him some tortillas. He broke off a small piece, and holding it in his fingers, looked at me, and with great emphasis said he had eaten enough; it was of no use to eat; he ate all he could get and did not grow fat; and, thrusting his livid face into mine, he told me to see how thin he was. His face was calm, but one accidental expression betrayed him as a maniac. Then I noticed in his face and all over his body white spots of leprosy, and I started away from him. I endeavored to persuade him to go back to the village, but he said it made no difference whether he went to the village or not; he wanted a *remedio* for his thinness.

Soon after, we came upon the banks of the River of Yajalón. It was excessively hot, and with the river as pure as water could be, we stopped and had a delightful bath. After this we commenced ascending a steep mountain, and when high up we saw the poor crazed young Indian standing in the same place on the bank of the river. At half past five, after a toilsome ascent, we reached the top of the mountain and rode along the borders of a table of land several thousand feet high, which looked down into an immense valley; turning to the left, around the corner of the forest we entered the outskirts of Tumbalá. The huts were distributed among high, rugged, and picturesque rocks, which had the appearance of having once formed the crater of a volcano. Drunken Indians were lying in the path, so that we had to turn out to avoid treading on them. Riding through a narrow passage between these high rocks, we came out upon a corner of the lofty perpendicular table several thousand feet high, on which stood the village of Tumbalá. In front were the church and convent; the square was filled with wild-looking Indians preparing for a fiesta, and on the very corner of the immense table was a high conical peak, crowned with the ruins of a church. Altogether it was the wildest and most extraordinary place we had yet seen, and though not consecrated by associations, for unknown ages it had been the site of an Indian village.

It was one of the circumstances of our journey in this country that every hour and day produced something new. We never had any idea of the character of the place we were approaching until we entered it, and one surprise followed close upon another. On one corner of the table of land stood the cabildo. The *justicia* was the brother of our silver-dish friend Padre Solís, and as poor and energetic as the padre was rich and inert. At the last village we had been told that it would be impossible to procure Indians for the next day on account of the fiesta, and had made up our minds to remain. But my letters from the Mexican authorities were so effective that immediately the *justicia* held a parley with forty or fifty Indians, and, breaking off occasionally to cuff one of them, he arranged our journey through to Palenque in three days, and we paid and distributed the money. Although the wildness of the Indians made us feel a little uncomfortable, we almost regretted this unexpected promptness. But the *justicia* told us we had come at a fortunate moment, for many of the Indians of San Pedro, who were notoriously a bad set, were then in the village, but he could select those he knew, and would send an alguacil of his own with us all the way. As he did not give us any encouragement to remain and seemed anxious to hurry us on, we made no objections; in our anxiety to reach the end of our journey, we had a superstitious apprehension of the effect of any voluntary delay.

With the little of daylight that remained, he conducted us along the same path trodden by the Indians centuries before to the top of the cone rising at the corner of the table of land, from which we looked down on one side into an immense ravine several thousand feet in depth; and on the other, over the top of a great mountain range, we saw the village of San Pedro, the end of our next day's journey, and beyond, over the range of the mountains of Palenque, the Lake of Términos and the Gulf of Mexico. It was one of the grandest, wildest, and most sublime scenes I ever beheld. On the top were ruins of a church and tower, probably once used as a lookout, and near it were thirteen crosses erected over the bodies of Indians, who, a century before, had tied the hands and feet of the curate and thrown him down the precipice, and who had been killed and buried on the spot. Every year new crosses are set up over their bodies to keep alive in the minds of the Indians the fate of murderers. All around, on almost inaccessible mountain heights and in the deepest ravines, the Indians have their *milpas* or corn patches, living almost as when the Spaniards broke in upon them; the *justicia* pointed with his finger to a region still occupied by the "unbaptized": the same strange people whose mysterious origin no man knows and whose destiny no man can foretell. Among all the wild scenes of our hurried tour, none is more strongly impressed upon my mind than this; but with the untamed Indians around, Mr. Catherwood was too much excited and too nervous to attempt to make a sketch of it.

At dark we returned to the cabildo, which was decorated with evergreens for the fiesta. At one end was a table with a figure of the Virgin fantastically dressed and sitting under an arbor of pine leaves.

In the evening we visited the padre, the delegate of Padre Solís, a gentlemanly young man from Ciudad Real, who was growing as round, and bade fair to grow as rich out of this village, as Padre Solís himself. He and the *justicia* were the only white men in the place. We returned to the cabildo; the Indians came in to bid the *justicia* "*buenas noches*" and kiss the back of his hand, after which we were left to ourselves.

Before daylight we were roused by an irruption of Indian carriers with lighted torches, who, while we were still in bed, began tying on the covers of our trunks to carry them off. At this place the mechanic arts were lower than in any other we had visited. There was not a rope of any kind in the village; the fastenings of the trunks and the straps to go around the forehead were all of bark strings. Here it was customary for those who intended to cross the mountains to take *hamacas* or *sillas;* the former was a cushioned chair with a long pole at each end, to be borne by four Indians before and behind, the traveler sitting with his face to the side; it was only used, as the *justicia* told us, by very heavy men and padres. The *silla* was an armchair to be carried on the back of an Indian. We had a repugnance to this mode of conveyance, considering, though unwilling to run any risk, that where an Indian could climb with one of us on his back we could climb alone, and so we set out without either *silla* or *hamaca*.

Immediately from the village the road, which was a mere opening through the trees, commenced descending, and very soon we came to a road of *palos*, or sticks; it was like a staircase and so steep that it was dangerous to ride down them. But for these sticks, in the rainy season the road would be utterly impassable. Descending constantly, at a little after twelve we reached a small stream, where the Indians washed their sweating bodies.

From the banks of this river we commenced ascending the steepest mountain I ever knew. Riding was out of the question; encumbered with sword and spurs and leading our mules, which sometimes held back and sometimes sprang upon us, we had to toil excessively. Every few minutes we were obliged to stop and lean against a tree or sit down. The Indians did not speak a word of any language but their own. We could hold no communication whatever with them, and could not understand how far it was to the top. At length we saw up a steep pitch before us a rude cross, which we hailed as being the top of the mountain. We climbed up to it and, after resting a moment, mounted our mules, but before riding a hundred yards, the descent began, and immediately we were obliged to dismount.

The descent was steeper than the ascent. In a certain college in our country a chair was transmitted as an heirloom to the laziest man in the senior class. One held it by unanimous consent, but when he was seen running down hill, and was tried and found guilty, he avoided sentence by the frank avowal that a man pushed him and he was too lazy to stop himself. So it was with us. It was harder work to resist than to give way. Our mules came tumbling after us; and after a most rapid, hot, and fatiguing descent, we reached a stream covered with leaves and insects. Here two of our Indians left us to return that night to Tumbalá! Our labor was excessive; what must it have been to them! Though accustomed to carrying loads from their boyhood, they probably suffered less than we; and the freedom of their naked limbs relieved them from the heat and confinement which we suffered from clothes wet with perspiration. It was the hottest day we had experienced in the country. We had a further violent descent through woods of almost impenetrable thickness, and at a quarter before four reached San Pedro. Looking back over the range we had just crossed, we saw Tumbalá and the towering point on which we stood the evening before on a right line, only a few miles distant, but by the road twenty-seven.

If a bad name could kill a place, San Pedro was damned. From the hacienda of Padre Solís to Tumbalá, everyone we met cautioned us against the Indians of San Pedro. Fortunately, however, nearly the whole village had gone to the fête at Tumbalá. There was no alcalde, no alguaciles; a few Indians were lying about in a state of utter nudity and, when we looked into the huts, the women ran away, probably alarmed at seeing men with pantaloons. The cabildo was occupied by a traveling party with cargoes of sugar for Tabasco. The leaders of the party and owners of the cargoes were two mestizos, having servants well armed, with whom we formed an acquaintance and tacit alliance. One of the best houses was empty; the proprietor with his family and household furniture, except for reed bedsteads fixed in the ground, had gone to the fiesta. We took possession and piled our luggage inside.

Without giving us any notice, our men deserted us to return to Tumbalá, and we were left alone. We could not speak the language, and could get nothing for the mules or for ourselves to eat; but, through the leader of the sugar party, we learned that a new set of men would be forthcoming in the morning to take us on. With the heat and fatigue I had a violent headache. The mountain for the next day was going to be worse and, afraid of the effort and of the danger of breaking down on the road, Mr. Catherwood and Pawling endeavored to procure a *hamaca* or *silla*, which was promised for the morning.

Chapter XVI

~~~~~~

A wild country. Ascent of a mountain. Ride in a silla.
A precarious situation. The descent. Rancho of Nopa.
Attacks of mosquitoes. Approach to Palenque. Pasture
grounds. Village of Palenque. A crusty official. A courte-
ous reception. Scarcity of provisions. Sunday. Cholera.
Another countryman. The conversion, apostacy, and re-
covery of the Indians. River Chacamal.
The Caribs. Ruins of Palenque.

EARLY the next morning the sugar party started, and at five minutes before seven we followed with *silla* and men; altogether our party had swelled to twenty Indians.

The country through which we were now traveling was as wild as before the Spanish conquest, and without a habitation until we reached Palenque. The road was through a forest so overgrown with brush and underwood as to be impenetrable; the branches were trimmed barely high enough to admit a man's traveling under them on foot, so that on the backs of our mules we were constantly obliged to bend our bodies and even to dismount. In some places, for a great distance around, the woods seemed killed by the heat; the foliage was withered and the leaves dry and crisp, as if burned by the sun. In addition, a tornado had swept the country, of which no mention had been made in the San Pedro papers.

We met three Indians carrying clubs in their hands; they were naked except for a small piece of cotton cloth wound around the loins and passed between the legs. One of them, young, tall, and of admirable symmetry of form, looked the freeborn gentleman of the woods. Shortly afterward, we passed a stream where naked Indians were setting rude nets for fish—wild and primitive as in the first ages of savage life.

At twenty minutes past ten we commenced ascending the mountain. It was very hot, and I can give no idea of the toil of ascending these mountains. Our mules could barely clamber up with their saddles only. We disencumbered ourselves of sword, spurs, and all useless trappings; in fact, we came down to shirt and pantaloons, and as near the condition of the Indians as we could. Our procession would have been a spectacle on Broadway: first were four Indians, each with a rough oxhide box, secured by an iron chain and large padlock, on his back; then Juan, with only a hat and pair of thin cotton drawers, driving two spare mules and carrying a double-barreled gun over his naked shoulders; then ourselves, each one either driving before him or leading his own mule; then an Indian carrying the *silla*, with relief carriers and several boys bearing small bags of provisions, the Indians of the *silla* being much surprised at our not using their services, according to contract and the price paid. Though toiling excessively, we felt a sense of degradation at being carried on a man's shoulders. At that time I was in the worst condition of the three, and the night before had gone to bed at San Pedro without supper, which for any of us was a sure evidence of being in a bad way.

We had brought the *silla* with us merely as a measure of precaution, without much expectation of being obliged to use it; but at a steep pitch, which made my head almost burst to think of climbing, I resorted to it for the first time. It was a large, clumsy armchair, put together with wooden pins and bark strings. The Indian who was to carry me was, like all the others, small and not more than five feet seven; he was very thin but symmetrically formed. A bark strap was tied to the arms of the chair and, sitting down, he placed his back against the back of the chair, adjusting the length of the strings and smoothing the bark across his forehead with a little cushion to relieve the pressure. An Indian on each side lifted it up, and the carrier rose on his feet, stood still a moment, threw me up once or twice to adjust me on his shoulders, and set off with one man on each side. It was a great relief, but I could feel every movement, even to the heaving of his chest. The ascent was one of the steepest on the whole road. In a few minutes he stopped and sent forth a sound, usual with Indian carriers, between a whistle and a blow; it was a sound which was always painful to my ears, but which I had never before felt to be quite so disagreeable. My face was turned backward; I could not see where he was going but observed that the Indian on the left fell back.

Not to increase the labor of carrying me, I sat as still as possible; but in a few minutes, looking over my shoulder, I saw that we were approaching the edge of a precipice more than a thousand feet deep. Here I became very anxious to dismount; but I could not speak intelligibly, and the Indians could or would not understand my signs. My carrier moved along carefully: he put his left foot out to feel whether the stone on which he put it down was steady and secure before he brought up the other: by degrees and after a particularly careful movement, he brought both feet up to within half a step of the edge of the precipice where he stopped and gave a fearful whistle and blow. I rose and fell with every breath, feeling his body trembling under me and his knees seeming to give way. The precipice was awful, and the slightest irregular movement on my part might bring us both down together. I would have given him a release in full for the rest of the journey to be off his back; but he started again, and with the same care ascended several steps, so close to the edge that even on the back of a mule it would have been very uncomfortable. My fear lest he should break down or stumble was excessive.

To my extreme relief, the path finally turned away; but I had hardly congratulated myself upon my escape before he descended a few steps. This was much worse than ascending; if he fell, nothing could keep me from going over his head; but I remained till he put me down of his own accord. The poor fellow was wet with perspiration and trembled in every limb. Another stood ready to take me up, but I had had enough. Pawling tried it, but only for a short time. It was bad enough to see an Indian toiling with a dead weight on his back; but to feel him trembling under one's own body, hear his hard breathing, see the sweat rolling down him, and feel the insecurity of the position, made this a mode of traveling which nothing but constitutional laziness and insensibility could endure. Walking, or rather climbing, stopping very often to rest, and riding when it was at all practicable, we reached a thatched shed, where we wished to stop for the night, but there was no water.

We could not understand how far it was to Nopa, our intended stopping place, which we supposed to be on the top of the mountain. To every question the Indians answered *una legua*. Thinking it could not be much higher, we continued. For an hour more we had a very steep ascent, and then commenced a terrible descent. At this time the sun had disappeared; dark clouds overhung the woods and thunder rolled heavily on the top of the mountain. As we descended a heavy wind swept through the forest; the air was filled with dry leaves, branches were snapped and broken, trees bent, and there was every appearance of a violent tornado. To hurry down on foot was out of the question, we were so tired that it was impossible. But, afraid of being caught on the mountain by a hurricane and deluge of rain, we spurred down as fast as we could go. It was a continued descent, without any relief, stony, and very steep. Very often the mules stopped, afraid to go on; and in one place the two empty mules bolted into the thick woods rather than proceed. Fortunately for the reader, this is our last mountain, and I can end honestly with a climax: it was the worst mountain I ever encountered in that or any other country, and, under our apprehension of the storm, I will venture to say that no travelers ever descended in less time. At a quarter before five we reached the plain. The mountain was hidden by clouds, and the storm was now raging above us. We crossed a river, and continuing along it through a thick forest, reached the rancho of Nopa.

It was situated in a circular clearing about one hundred feet in diameter, near the river, with the forest around so thick with brush and underwood that the mules could not penetrate it, and with no opening but for the passage of the road through it. The rancho was merely a pitched roof covered with palm leaves and supported by four trunks of trees. All around were heaps of snail shells; the ground of the rancho was several inches deep with ashes, the remains of fires for cooking them. We had hardly congratulated ourselves upon our arrival at such a beautiful spot before we suffered such an onslaught of mosquitoes as we had not before experienced in the country. We made a fire and, with appetites sharpened by a hard day's work, sat down on the grass to dispose of a San Pedro fowl; but we were obliged to get up and, while one hand was occupied with eatables, use the other to brush off the venomous insects. We soon saw that we had bad prospects for the night; we lighted fires all around the rancho and smoked inordinately. We were in no hurry to lie down, and sat till a late hour, consoling ourselves with the reflection that, but for the mosquitoes, our satisfaction would be beyond all bounds. The dark border of the clearing was lighted up by fireflies of extraordinary size and brilliancy; they darted among the trees, not flashing and disappearing, but carrying a steady light; they seemed like shooting stars except that their course was serpentine. In different places there were two that remained stationary; emitting a pale but beautiful light, they seemed like rival belles holding levees. The fiery orbs darted from one to the other; and when one, more daring than the rest, approached too near, the coquette withdrew her light and the flutterer went off. One, however, carried all before her, and at one time we counted seven hovering around her.

At length we prepared for sleep. Hammocks would leave us exposed on every side to the merciless attacks of the mosquitoes, and we spread our mats on the ground. We did not undress. Pawling, with a great deal of trouble, rigged his sheets into a mosquito net, but it was so hot that he could not breathe under them, and he roamed about or was in the river nearly all night. The Indians, who had occupied themselves in catching snails and cooking them for supper, then lay down to sleep on the banks of the river. But at midnight, with sharp thunder and lightning, the rain broke in a deluge and they all came under the shed, lying there perfectly naked, and mechanically and without seeming to disturb themselves, slapping their bodies with their hands. The incessant hum and bite of the insects kept us in a constant state of wakefulness and irritation. Our bodies we could protect, but with a covering over the face the heat was insufferable. Before daylight I walked to the river, which was broad and shallow, and stretched myself out on the gravelly bottom, where the water was barely deep enough to run over my body. It was the first comfortable moment I had had. My heated body became cooled, and I lay till daylight. When I rose to dress they came upon me with appetites whetted by a spirit of vengeance. Our day's work had been tremendously hard, but the night's was worse.

The morning air, however, was refreshing, and as day dawned our tormentors disappeared. Mr. Catherwood had suffered least, but in his restlessness he had lost from his finger a precious emerald ring which he had worn for many years and prized for associations. We remained some time looking for it, but at length mounted and made our last start for Palenque. The road was level, but the woods were still as thick as on the mountain. At a quarter before eleven we reached a path which led to the ruins, or somewhere else. We had abandoned the intention of going directly to the ruins, for, besides being in a shattered condition, we could not communicate with our Indians, and probably they did not know where the ruins were. At length we came out upon an open plain and looked back at the range we had crossed, running off to Petén and the country of unbaptized Indians.

As we advanced we came into a region of fine pasture grounds, and saw herds of cattle. The grass showed the effect of early rains, and the picturesque appearance of the country reminded me of many a scene at home; but there was one tree of singular beauty that was a stranger: it had a high, naked trunk and spreading top, leaves of vivid green, and was covered with yellow flowers. Continuing carelessly and stopping from time to time to enjoy the smiling view around and to realize our escape from the dark mountains behind, we rose upon a slight table of land and saw the village before us; it consisted of one grass-grown street, unbroken even by a mule path, with a few straggling white

houses on each side and, at the further end, on a slight elevation, a thatched church with a rude cross and belfry before it.
A boy could roll on the grass from the church door out of
the village. In fact, it was the most dead-and-alive place I
ever saw; but, coming from villages thronged with wild Indians, its air of repose was most grateful to us. In the suburbs
were scattered Indian huts and, as we rode into the street,
eight or ten white people, men and women, came out, more
than we had seen since we left Comitán. The houses had a
comfortable and respectable appearance, and in one of them
lived the alcalde. He was a white man of about sixty, with
a stoop to his shoulders; dressed in white cotton drawers and
shirt outside, he was respectable in his appearance. But the
expression of his face was very doubtful. With what I intended as a most captivating manner, I offered him my passport. But we had disturbed him at his siesta and he had risen
wrong side first; looking me steadily in the face, he asked
me what he had to do with my passport. This I could not
answer, and he went on to say that he had nothing to do
with it and did not want to have, that we must go to the
prefect. Then he turned round two or three times in a circle
to show he did not care what we thought of him; and, as if
conscious of what was passing in our minds, he volunteered
to add that complaints had been made against him before,
but it was of no use; they couldn't remove him, and if they
did he didn't care.

   This greeting at the end of our severe journey was rather
discouraging, but it was important for us not to have any
difficulty with this crusty official; and, endeavoring to hit a
vulnerable point, we told him that we wished to stop a few
days to rest, and should be obliged to purchase many things.
We asked him if there was any bread in the village; he answered *no hay* (there is none); corn? *no hay;* coffee? *no
hay;* chocolate? *no hay.* His satisfaction seemed to increase
as he was still able to answer *no hay;* but our unfortunate
inquiries for bread roused his ire. Innocently, and without
intending any offence, we betrayed our disappointment; and
Juan, looking out for himself, said that we could not eat

tortillas. This he recurred to, repeating several times to himself and to every newcomer, saying with peculiar emphasis: "They can't eat tortillas." Following it up, he said there was an oven in the place, but no flour, and the baker went away seven years before, and the people there could do without bread. To change the subject, and determined not to complain, I threw out the conciliatory remark, that, at all events, we were glad to escape the rain on the mountains, which he answered by asking if we expected anything better at Palenque. He repeated with great satisfaction an expression common in the mouths of Palenquians: *tres meses de agua, tres meses de aguaceros y seis meses de nortes* (three months rains, three months heavy showers, and six months north wind), and the latter in that country brings cold and rain.

Finding it impossible to hit a weak point, while the men were piling up the luggage I rode to the prefect, and his reception at that critical moment was most cheering and reviving. With habitual courtesy he offered me a chair and a cigar, and as soon as he saw my passport said he had been expecting me for some time. This surprised me and, when he added that Don Patricio had told him I was coming, I was surprised still more, as I did not remember any friend of that name, but I soon learned that this imposing cognomen meant my friend, Mr. Patrick Walker, of Belize. This was the first notice of Mr. Walker and Captain Caddy I had received since Lieutenant Nicols brought to Guatemala the report that they had been speared by the Indians. They had reached Palenque by the Belize River and Lake of Petén without any difficulties other than the badness of the roads; they had remained two weeks at the ruins and then left for the Laguna and Yucatán. This was most gratifying intelligence, first, as it assured me of their safety, and second, as I gathered from it that there would be no impediment to our visiting the ruins. The apprehension of being met at the end of our toilsome journey with a peremptory exclusion had constantly disturbed us more or less, and sometimes it had weighed upon us like lead. We had determined to make no reference to the ruins until we had an opportunity of ascertaining our ground, and up to that moment I did not know but that all our labor was bootless. To heighten my satisfaction, the prefect said that the place was perfectly quiet, that it was in a retired nook which revolutions and political convulsions never reached. He had held his office twenty years, acknowledging as many different governments.

I returned to make my report, and in regard to the old alcalde, in the language of a ward-meeting manifesto, I determined to ask for nothing but what was right, and to submit to nothing that was wrong. In this spirit we made a bold stand for some corn. The alcalde's *no hay* was but too true; the corn crop had failed, and there was an actual famine in the place. The Indians, with accustomed improvidence, had planted barely enough for the season; when this turned out bad, they were reduced to fruits, plantains, and roots instead of tortillas. Each white family had about enough for its own use, but none to spare. The shortness of the corn crop made everything else scarce, as they were obliged to kill their fowls and pigs from want of anything to feed them with. The alcalde, who to his other offences added that of being rich, was the only man in the place who had any to spare, and he was holding on for a greater pressure. At Tumbalá we had bought good corn at thirty ears for sixpence; here, with great difficulty, we prevailed upon the alcalde to spare us a little at eight ears for a shilling, and these were so musty and worm-eaten that the mules would hardly touch them. At first it surprised us that some enterprising capitalist did not import several dollars' worth from Tumbalá; but on going deeper into the matter we found that the cost of transportation would not leave much profit, and, besides, the course of exchange was against Palenque. A few backloads would overstock the market; for as each white family was provided till the next crop came in, the Indians were the only persons who wished to purchase, and they had no money to buy with. The brunt of the famine fell upon us, and particularly upon our poor mules. Fortunately, however, there was good pasture, and not far off. We slipped the bridles at the door and turned them loose in the streets; but after making the circuit they came back in a body and poked their heads in at the door with an imploring look for corn.

Our prospects were not very brilliant; nevertheless, we had reached Palenque. Toward evening storms came on, with terrific thunder and lightning, which made us feel but too happy that our journey was over. The house assigned to us by the alcalde was next his own, and belonged to himself. It had a *cocina* adjoining and two Indian women, who did not dare look at us without permission from the alcalde. It had an earthen floor, three beds made of reeds, and a thatched roof which was very good, except that over two of the beds it leaked. Under the peaked roof and across the top of the mud walls there was a floor made of poles, which served as a granary for the alcalde's mouldy corn, and which was inhabited by industrious mice, which scratched, nibbled, squeaked, and sprinkled dust upon us all night. Nevertheless, we had reached Palenque, and we slept well.

The next day was Sunday, and we hailed it as a day of rest. The place was so tranquil, and seemed in such a state of repose, that as the old alcalde passed the door we ventured to wish him a good morning; but again he had gotten up wrong and, without answering our greeting, he stopped to tell us that our mules were missing, and, when this did not disturb us sufficiently, he added that they had probably been stolen. Then, when he had got us fairly roused and on the point of setting off to look for them, he said there was no danger, they had only gone for water and would return of themselves.

The village of Palenque, as we learned from the prefect, was once a place of considerable importance through which all the goods imported for Guatemala passed; but Belize had diverted that trade and destroyed its commerce. And but a few years before more than half the population had been swept off by the cholera; whole families had perished, and their houses were desolate and falling to ruins. The church stood at the head of the street in the center of a grassy square. On each side of the square were houses with the forest directly upon them; as we were a little elevated in the plaza, we were on a line with the tops of the trees. The largest house on the square was deserted and in ruins. There were a dozen other houses occupied by white families, with whom, in the course of an hour's stroll, I became acquainted. I had but to stop before the door to receive an invitation, *Pase adelante, Capitán* (Walk in, Captain), for which title I was indebted to the eagle on my hat. Each family had its hacienda in the neighborhood, and in the course of an hour I knew all that was going on in Palenque; that is, I knew that nothing *was* going on.

At the upper end of the square, commanding this scene of quiet, was the house of an American named William Brown. It was a strange place for the abode of an American, and Mr. Brown was a regular "go-ahead" American. In the great lottery he had drawn a Palenquian wife, which in that quiet place probably saved him from dying of ennui. What first took him to the country I do not know; but he had an exclusive privilege to navigate the Tabasco River by steam, and would have made a fortune had his steamboat not foundered on the second trip. He then took to cutting logwood on a new plan, and came very near making another fortune, but something went wrong. At the time of our visit he was engaged in making a short cut to the sea by connecting two rivers near his hacienda. To the astonishment of the Palenquians, he was always busy, when he might live quietly on his hacienda in the summer and pass his winters in the village. Very much to our regret, he was not then in the village. It would have been interesting to meet a countryman of his stamp in that quiet corner of the world.

The prefect was well versed in the history of Palenque. It is in the province of Tzentales,[1] and for a century after the conquest of Chiapas it remained in possession of the Indians. Two centuries ago, Lorenzo Mugil, an emissary direct from Rome, set up among them the standard of the cross. The Indians still preserve his dress as a sacred relic, but they are jealous of showing it to strangers and I could not obtain a sight of it. The bell of the church, too, was sent from the

---

1. Tzental is the name applied to the branch of the Maya family in the area around Palenque.

holy city. The Indians submitted to the dominion of the
Spaniards until the year 1700, when the whole province revolted, and in Chilón, Tumbalá, and Palenque they apos-
tatized from Christianity, murdered the priests, profaned
the churches, paid impious adoration to an Indian female,
massacred the white men, and took the women for their
wives. But, as soon as the intelligence reached Guatemala,
a strong force was sent against them, the revolted towns were
reduced and recovered to the Catholic faith, and tranquillity
was restored. The right of the Indians, however, to the
ownership of the soil was still recognized, and down to the
time of the Mexican Independence they received rent for
land in the villages and the *milpas* in the neighborhood.

A short distance from Palenque the River Chacamal separates it from the country of the unbaptized Indians, who are
here called Caribs.[2] Fifty years ago the Padre Calderón, an
uncle of the prefect's wife, attended by his sacristan, an Indian, was bathing in the river when the latter cried out in
alarm that some Caribs were looking at them; the sacristan
attempted to flee, but the padre took his cane and went toward them. The Caribs fell down before him and conducted
him to their huts, giving him an invitation to return and
make them a visit. On the day appointed the padre went
with his sacristan, and found a gathering of Caribs and a
great feast prepared for him. He remained with them some
time, and invited them in return to the village of Palenque
on the day of the fête of St. Dominic. A large party of these
wild Indians attended, bringing with them tiger's meat,
monkey's meat, and cocoa as presents. They listened to mass
and beheld all the ceremonies of the Church, whereupon
they invited the padre to come among them and teach them;
they erected a hut at the place where they had first met him
which he consecrated as a church, and he taught his sacristan
to say mass to them every Sunday. As the prefect said, if he

2. The reader might infer from this that all the "unbaptized" are
the same, merely being called Lacandones in one region and Caribs in
another. The Lacandones and Caribs are separate tribes, however,
speaking different languages. The latter are unrelated to the Maya.

had lived, many of them would probably have been Christianized, but, unfortunately, he died, whereupon the Caribs retired into the wilderness, and not one had appeared in the village since.

The ruins lie about eight miles from the village, perfectly desolate. The road was so bad that, in order to accomplish anything, it was necessary to remain there, and we had to make provision for that purpose. There were three small shops in the village, the stock of all together not worth seventy-five dollars, but in one of them we found a pound and a half of coffee, which we immediately secured. Juan communicated the gratifying intelligence that a hog was to be killed the next morning, and that he had engaged a portion of the lard; also, that there was a cow with a calf running loose, and an arrangement might be made for keeping her up and milking her. This was promptly attended to, and all necessary arrangements were made for visiting the ruins the next day. The Indians generally knew the road, but there was only one man in the place who was able to serve as a guide on the ground and he had on hand the business of killing and distributing the hog, by reason whereof he could not set out with us, although he promised to follow.

Toward evening the quiet of the village was disturbed by a crash, and on going out we found that a house had fallen down. A cloud of dust rose from it, and the ruins probably lie as they fell. The cholera had stripped it of tenants, and for several years it had been deserted.

Chapter XVII

~~~~~~

*Preparations for visiting the ruins. A turnout. Departure.
The road. Rivers Micol and Otula. Arrival at the ruins.
The palace. A feu-de-joie. Quarters in the palace. Inscriptions by former visitors. The fate of Beanham. Discovery
of the ruins of Palenque. Visit of del Río. Expedition of
Dupaix. Drawings of the present work. First dinner at the
ruins. Mammoth fireflies. Sleeping apartments. Extent of
the ruins. Obstacles to exploration.
Suffering from mosquitoes.*

EARLY the next morning we prepared for our move to
the ruins. We had to make provision for housekeeping
on a large scale; our culinary utensils were of rude pottery,
and our cups the hard shells of some round vegetables, the
whole cost, perhaps, amounting to one dollar. We could not
procure a water jar in the place, but the alcalde lent us one
free of charge unless it should be broken, and as it was
cracked at the time he probably considered it sold. By the
way, we forced ourselves upon the alcalde's affections by
leaving our money with him for safekeeping. We did this
with great publicity, in order that it might be known in the
village that there was no *plata* at the ruins, but the alcalde
regarded it as a mark of special confidence. Indeed, we could
not have shown him a greater. He was a suspicious old miser,
who kept his own money in a trunk in an inner room and
never left the house without locking the street door and
carrying the key with him. He made us pay beforehand for
everything we wanted, and he would not have trusted us for
half a dollar on any account.

It was necessary to take with us from the village all that
could contribute to our comfort, and we tried hard to get a

woman; but no one would trust herself alone with us. This was a great privation; a woman was desirable, not, as the reader may suppose, for embellishment, but to make tortillas. These, to be tolerable, must be eaten the moment they are baked; but we were obliged to make an arrangement with the alcalde to send them out daily with the product of our cow.

Our turnout was equal to anything we had had on the road. One Indian set off with a cowhide trunk supported on his back by a bark string as the groundwork of his load, while on each side a fowl wrapped in plantain leaves hung by a bark string, with only the head and tail visible. Another had on the top of his trunk a live turkey, with its legs tied and wings expanded like a spread eagle. Another had on each side of his load strings of eggs, each egg being wrapped carefully in a husk of corn, and all fastened like onions on a bark string. Cooking utensils and water jar were mounted on the backs of other Indians, and they contained rice, beans, sugar, chocolate, etc., while strings of pork and bunches of plantains were pendent. And Juan carried in his arms our traveling tin coffee canister filled with lard, which in that country was always in a liquid state.

At half past seven we left the village. For a short distance the road was open, but very soon we entered a forest which continued unbroken to the ruins, and probably for many miles beyond. The road was a mere Indian footpath; the branches of the trees, beaten down and heavy with the rain, hanging so low that we were obliged to stoop constantly; very soon our hats and coats were perfectly wet. From the thickness of the foliage the morning sun could not dry up the deluge of the night before. The ground was very muddy, broken by streams swollen by the early rains, with gullies, in some places very difficult to cross, in which the mules floundered and stuck fast. Amid all the wreck of empires, nothing ever spoke so forcibly the world's mutations as this immense forest shrouding what was once a great city. Once it had been a great highway, thronged with people who were stimulated by the same passions that give impulse to human action now, but they were all gone, their habitations buried, and no traces of them left.

In two hours we reached the River Micol, and in half an hour more that of Otula, darkened by the shade of the woods and breaking beautifully over a stony bed. Fording this, very soon we saw masses of stones, and then a round sculptured stone. We spurred up a sharp ascent of fragments, so steep the mules could barely climb it, to a terrace which, like the whole road, was so covered with trees it was impossible to make out the form. Continuing on this terrace, we stopped at the foot of a second when our Indians cried out *El palacio* (The palace), and through openings in the trees we saw the front of a large building richly ornamented with stuccoed figures on the pilasters, curious and elegant, with trees growing close against it, their branches entering the doors; in style and effect it was unique, extraordinary, and mournfully beautiful. We tied our mules to the trees, ascended a flight of stone steps forced apart and thrown down by trees, and entered the palace. For a few moments we ranged along the corridor and into the courtyard, and after the first gaze of eager curiosity was over, went back to the entrance. Standing in the doorway, we fired a *feu-de-joie* of four rounds each, using up the last charge of our firearms. But for this way of giving vent to our satisfaction we should have made the roof of the old palace ring with a hurrah. It was intended, too, for effect upon the Indians, who had probably never heard such a cannonade before, and who, almost like their ancestors in the time of Cortes, regarded our weapons as instruments which spit lightning. They would, we knew, make such a report in the village as would keep any of their respectable friends from paying us a visit at night.

We had reached the end of our long and toilsome journey, and the first glance indemnified us for our toil. For the first time we were in a building erected by the aboriginal inhabitants. It had been standing there before the Europeans knew of the existence of this continent, and we prepared to take up our abode under its roof. We selected the front corridor as our dwelling, turned turkey and fowls loose in the courtyard, which was so overgrown with trees that we could barely see across it. Since there was no pasture for the mules except the leaves of the trees, and since we could not turn them loose into the woods, we brought them up the steps through the palace, and turned them also into the courtyard. At one end of the corridor Juan built a kitchen, which operation consisted in laying three stones anglewise, so as to have room for a fire between them. Our luggage was stowed away or hung on poles reaching across the corridor. Pawling mounted a stone about four feet long on stone legs for a table and, with the Indians, cut a number of poles, which they fastened together with bark strings and laid on stones at the head and foot for beds. We cut down the branches that entered the palace, and some of the trees on the terrace, and from the floor of the palace we looked over the top of an immense forest stretching off to the Gulf of Mexico.

The Indians had superstitious fears about remaining at night among the ruins and left us alone, the sole tenants of the palace of unknown kings. Little did they who built it think that in a few years their royal line would perish and their race be extinct, that their city would be a ruin and Mr. Catherwood, Pawling, I, and Juan its sole tenants. Other strangers had been there, wondering like ourselves. Their names were written on the walls, with comments and figures; and even here were marks of those low, groveling spirits which delight in profaning holy places. Among the names, but not of the latter class, were those of acquaintances: Captain Caddy and Mr. Walker; and one was that of a countryman, Noah O. Platt, New York. He had gone out to Tabasco as supercargo of a vessel, ascended one of the rivers for logwood, and while his vessel was loading visited the ruins. His account of them had given me a strong desire to visit them long before the opportunity of doing so presented itself.

High up on one side of the corridor was the name of William Beanham, and under it was a stanza written in lead pencil. By means of a tree with notches cut in it, I climbed up and read the lines. The rhyme was faulty and the spelling bad, but they breathed a deep sense of the moral sublimity pervading these unknown ruins. The author, too, seemed an acquaintance. I had heard his story in the village. He was a young Irishman who had been sent by a merchant of Tabasco into the interior for purposes of small traffic. Having passed some time at Palenque and in the neighborhood, his thoughts and feelings turned strongly toward the Indians and, after dwelling upon the subject for some time, he resolved to penetrate into the country of the Caribs. His friends endeavored to dissuade him, and the prefect told him, "You have red hair, a florid complexion, and white skin, and they will either make a god of you and keep you among them, or else kill and eat you." But he set off alone and on foot, and crossed the River Chacamal; after an absence of nearly a year he returned safe, but naked and emaciated, with his hair and nails long, having been eight days with a single Carib on the banks of a wild river searching for a crossing place and living upon roots and herbs. He then built a hut on the borders of the Chacamal River and lived there with a Carib servant while he prepared for another and more protracted journey among them; at length some boatmen who came to trade with him found him lying in his hammock dead, with his skull split open. He had escaped the dangers of a journey which no man in that country dared encounter only to die by the hands of an assassin in a moment of fancied security. His arm was hanging outside, and a book was lying on the ground; probably he had been struck while reading. The murderers, one of whom was his servant, were caught and were at this time in prison in Tabasco. Unfortunately, the people of Palenque had taken but little interest in anything except the extraordinary fact of his visit among the Caribs and his safe return. All his papers and collection of curiosities were scattered and destroyed, and with him died all the fruits of his labors; but, were he still living, he would be the man, of all others, to accomplish the discovery of that mysterious city which had so much affected our imaginations.

As the ruins of Palenque are the first which awakened attention to the existence of ancient and unknown cities in America, and as, on that account, they are perhaps more interesting to the public, it may not be amiss to state the circumstances of their first discovery.

In the year 1750, a party of Spaniards traveling in the interior of Mexico penetrated to the lands north of the district of Carmen in the province of Chiapas, when all at once they found, in the midst of a vast solitude, ancient stone buildings, the remains of a city still embracing from eighteen to twenty-four miles in extent, which was known to the Indians by the name of Casas de Piedras. From my knowledge of the country I am at a loss to conjecture why a party of Spaniards were traveling in that forest, or how they could have done so. I am inclined to believe rather that the existence of the ruins was discovered by the Indians who had clearings in different parts of the forest for their cornfields, or perhaps they had been known to them from time immemorial, and on their report the Spaniards were induced to visit them.

The existence of such a city was entirely unknown; there is no mention of it in any book, and no tradition that it had ever been. To this day it is not known by what name it was called, and the only appellation given to it is that of Palenque, after the village near which the ruins stand.

The news of the discovery passed from mouth to mouth, reaching some cities of the province, and finally the seat of government. But little attention was paid to it, and the members of the government, through ignorance, apathy, or the actual impossibility of occupying themselves with anything except public affairs, took no measures to explore the ruins. It was not till 1786, thirty years subsequent to the discovery, that the King of Spain ordered an exploration. On the third of May, 1787, Captain Antonio del Río arrived at the village under a commission from the government of Guatemala, and on the fifth he proceeded to the site of the ruined city. In his official report, he says that, on making his first essay, owing to the thickness of the woods and a fog so dense that it was impossible for the men to distinguish each other at five paces' distance, the principal building was completely concealed from their view.

He returned to the village, and after concerting measures with the deputy of the district, an order was issued to the inhabitants of Tumbalá requiring two hundred Indians with axes and billhooks. On the seventeenth seventy-nine Indians arrived, furnished with twenty-eight axes, after which twenty more were obtained in the village. With these he again moved forward and immediately commenced felling trees, which was followed by a general conflagration.

The report of Captain del Río, with the commentary of Doctor Paul Felix Cabrera of New Guatemala, which deduced an Egyptian origin for the people, either through the supineness or the jealousy of the Spanish government, was locked up in the archives of Guatemala until the time of the revolution, when, by the operation of liberal principles, the original manuscripts came into the hands of an English gentleman long resident in Guatemala, and, as a result, an English translation was published in London in 1822.[1] This was the first notice in Europe of the discovery of these ruins and, instead of electrifying the public mind, either from want of interest in the subject, distrust, or some other cause, so little notice was taken of it, that in 1831 the *Literary Gazette*, a paper of great circulation in London, announced it as a new discovery made by Colonel Galindo, whose unfortunate fate has been before referred to. If a like discovery had been made in Italy, Greece, Egypt, or Asia, within the reach of European travel, it would have created an interest not inferior to the discovery of Herculaneum, or Pompeii, or the ruins of Paestum.

While the report and drawings of del Río slept in the archives of Guatemala, Charles the Fourth of Spain ordered another expedition, at the head of which was placed Captain Dupaix, with a secretary and draughtsman, and a detachment of dragoons. His expeditions were made in 1805, 1806, and 1807, the last of which was to Palenque.

The manuscripts of Dupaix, and the designs of his draughtsman Castañeda, were about to be sent to Madrid, which was then occupied by the French army, when the revolution broke out in Mexico; they then became an object of secondary importance, and remained during the wars of independence under the control of Castañeda, who deposited them in the Cabinet of Natural History in Mexico. In 1828

---

1. Félix de Cabrera. *Description of the Ruins of an Ancient City Discovered near Palenque*, London, 1822.

M. Baradère disentombed them from the cartons of the museum, where, but for this accident, they might still have remained, and the knowledge of the existence of this city again been lost. The Mexican Congress had passed a law forbidding any stranger not formally authorized to make researches or to remove objects of art from the country; but, in spite of this interdict, Mr. Baradère obtained authority to make researches in the interior of the republic, with the agreement that, after sending to Mexico all that he collected, half should be delivered to him, with permission to transport them to Europe. Afterward, he obtained by exchange the original designs of Castañeda, and an authentic copy of the itinerary and descriptions of Captain Dupaix was promised in three months. From divers circumstances, that copy did not reach M. Baradère till long after his return to France, and the work of Dupaix was not published until 1834–5, twenty-eight years after his expedition, when it was brought out in Paris, in four volumes folio,[2] at the price of eight hundred francs, with notes and commentaries by M. Alexandre Lenoir, M. Warden, M. Charles Farcy, M. Baradère, and M. de St. Priest.

Lord Kingsborough's ponderous tomes,[3] so far as regards Palenque, are a mere reprint of Dupaix, and the cost of his work is four hundred dollars per copy. Colonel Galindo's communications to the Geographical Society of Paris are published in the work of Dupaix; and later Mr. Waldeck, with funds provided by an association in Mexico, passed two years among the ruins. His drawings, as he states in a work on another place, were taken away by the Mexican government; but he had retained copies, and before we set out his work on Palenque was announced in Paris. It, however, has never appeared,[4] and in the meantime Dupaix's is the textbook.

2. The only edition the editor was able to locate was in two volumes (*see* note 3, p. 219).

3. Lord Kingsborough. *Antiquities of Mexico*, London, 1831–48, 9 vols.

4. Waldeck brought it out in collaboration with Brasseur de Bourbourg after Stephens' death. *Monuments Anciens du Mexique: Palenqué et Autres Ruines de l'Ancienne Civilisation du Mexique*, Paris, 1866.

I have two objections to make to this work, not affecting Captain Dupaix, who, since his expedition took place thirty-four years ago, is not likely to be affected even if he is still living, but his Paris editors. The first is the very depreciating tone in which mention is made of the work of his predecessor del Río, and, secondly, this paragraph in the introduction:

"It must be considered that a government only can execute such undertakings. A traveller relying upon his own resources cannot hope, whatever may be his intrepidity, to penetrate, and, above all, to live in those dangerous solitudes; and, supposing that he succeeds, it is beyond the power of the most learned and skilful man to explore alone the ruins of a vast city, of which he must not only measure and draw the edifices still existing, but also determine the circumference and examine the remains, dig the soil and explore the subterraneous constructions. Mr. Baradère arrived within fifty leagues of Palenque, burning with the desire of going there; but what could a single man do with domestics or other auxiliaries,? without moral force or intelligence, against a people still half savage, against serpents and other hurtful animals, which, according to Dupaix, infest these ruins, and also against the vegetative force of a nature fertile and powerful, which in a few years re-covers all the monuments and obstructs all the avenues?"

The effect of this is to crush all individual enterprise, and, moreover, it is untrue. All the accounts, founded upon this, represent a visit to these ruins as one attended with immense difficulty and danger to such an extent that we feared to encounter them; but there is no difficulty whatever in going from Europe or the United States to Palenque. Our greatest hardships, even in our long journey through the interior, were from the revolutionary state of the countries and want of time; and as to a residence there, with time to construct a hut or to fit up an apartment in the palace, and to procure stores from the seaboard, "those dangerous solitudes" might be anything but unpleasant.

And to show what individuals can accomplish, I state that Mr. Catherwood's drawings include all the objects represented in the work of Dupaix, and others besides which do not appear in that work at all and have never before been presented to the public, among which are a stone tablet (figure 20) and the large tablets of hieroglyphics (figures 17, 22, and 23) which are the most curious and interesting pieces of sculpture at Palenque. I add, with the full knowledge that I will be contradicted by future travelers if I am wrong, that all of Mr. Catherwood's drawings are more correct in proportions, outline, and filling up than those of Dupaix, and that they furnish more true material for speculation and study. I would not have said this much but from a wish to give confidence to the reader who may be disposed to investigate and study these interesting remains. As to most of the places visited by us, he will find no materials whatever except those furnished in these pages. In regard to Palenque he will find in Dupaix a splendid work, the materials of which were procured under the sanction of a commission from government, which was brought out with explanations and commentaries by the learned men of Paris, by the side of which my two octavos shrink into insignificance; but I uphold the drawings against these costly folios, and against every other book that has ever been published on the subject of these ruins. My object has been, not to produce an illustrated work, but to present the drawings in such an inexpensive form as to place them within reach of the great mass of our reading community.

But to return to ourselves in the palace. While we were making our observations, Juan was engaged in a business that his soul loved. As with all the *mozos* of that country, it was his pride and ambition to *servir a mano*. He scorned the manly occupation of a muleteer and aspired to that of a menial servant. He was anxious to be left at the village and did not like the idea of stopping at the ruins, but was reconciled to it by being allowed to devote himself exclusively to cookery. At four o'clock we sat down to our first dinner. The tablecloth was two broad leaves, each about two feet long, plucked from a tree on the terrace before the door. Our salt cellar stood like a pyramid, being a case made of husks of corn put together lengthwise, and holding four or five pounds in lumps from the size of a pea to that of a hen's egg. Juan was as happy as if he had prepared the dinner exclusively for his own eating; and all went merry as a marriage bell until the sky became overcast and a sharp thunderclap heralded the afternoon's storm. From the elevation of the terrace, the floor of the palace commanded a view of the top of the forest and we could see the trees bent down by the force of the wind; very soon a fierce blast swept through the open doors, followed instantaneously by heavy rain. The table was cleared by the wind, and, before we could make our escape, was drenched by the rain. We snatched away our plates and finished our meal as we could.

The rain continued, with heavy thunder and lightning, all the afternoon. In the absolute necessity of taking up our abode among the ruins, we had hardly thought of our exposure to the elements until it was forced upon us. At night we could not light a candle, but the darkness of the palace was lighted up by fireflies of extraordinary size and brilliancy, shooting through the corridors and stationary on the walls, forming a beautiful and striking spectacle. They were of the description of those we saw at Nopa, known by the name of shining beetles, and are mentioned by the early Spaniards, among the wonders of a world where all was new, "as showing the way to those who travel at night." The historian describes them as "somewhat smaller than sparrows, having two stars close by their eyes, and two more under their wings, which gave so great a light that by it they could spin, weave, write, and paint; and the Spaniards went by night to hunt the *utios*,[5] or little rabbits, of that country; and a-fishing, carrying these animals tied to their great toes or thumbs: and they called them *cocuyos*, being also of use to save them from the gnats, which are there very troublesome. They took them in the night with firebrands, because they made to the light, and came when called by their name; and they are so unwieldy that when they fall they cannot rise again; and the men stroaking their faces and hands with a sort of moisture that is in those stars, seemed to be afire as long as it lasted."

It always gave us high pleasure to realize the romantic and seemingly half-fabulous accounts of the chroniclers of

5. Probably *hutías*, an American rodent.

the conquest. Very often we found their quaint descriptions so vivid and faithful as to infuse the spirit that breathed through their pages. We caught several of these beetles, not, however, by calling them by their names, but with a hat, as schoolboys used to catch fireflies, or, less poetically, lightning bugs, at home. They are more than half an inch long, and have a sharp movable horn on the head; when laid on the back they cannot turn over except by pressing this horn against a membrane upon the front. Behind the eyes are two round transparent substances full of luminous matter, about as large as the head of a pin, and underneath is a larger membrane containing the same luminous substance. Four of them together threw a brilliant light for several yards around and, by the light of a single one, we read distinctly the finely printed pages of an American newspaper, one of a packet, full of debates in Congress, which I had as yet barely glanced over. It seemed stranger than any incident of my journey to be reading by the light of beetles in the ruined palace of Palenque the sayings and doings of great men at home. In the midst of it Mr. Catherwood, in emptying the capacious pocket of a shooting jacket, handed me a Broadway omnibus ticket:

> Good to the bearer for a ride,
> A. Brower.

These things brought up vivid recollections of home, and among the familiar images present were the good beds into which our friends must have been about that time turning.

Our beds were set up in the back corridor, fronting the courtyard. This corridor consisted of open doors and pilasters, alternately. The wind and rain were sweeping through and, unfortunately, our beds were not out of reach of the spray. They had been set up with some labor on four piles of stones each, and we could not then change their position; nor did we have any spare articles to put up as screens. But, happily, two umbrellas, tied up with measuring rods and wrapped in a piece of matting, had survived the wreck of the mountain roads, and these Mr. Catherwood and I secured at the head of our beds. Pawling swung a hammock across the corridor so high that the sweep of the rain only touched the foot of the beds. So passed our first night at Palenque. In the morning, umbrellas, bedclothes, wearing apparel, and hammocks were wet through, and there was not a dry place to stand on. Already we considered ourselves booked for rheumatism. We had looked to our residence at Palenque as the end of troubles, and for comfort and pleasure, but all we could do was to change the location of our beds to places which promised a better shelter for the next night.

A good breakfast would have done much to restore our equanimity; but, unhappily, we found that the tortillas which we had brought out the day before, probably made of half-mouldy corn, by the excessive dampness were matted together, sour, and spoiled. We went through our beans, eggs, and chocolate without any substitute for bread, and, as often before in time of trouble, composed ourselves with a cigar. Blessed be the man who invented smoking, the soother and composer of a troubled spirit, allayer of angry passions, a comfort under the loss of breakfast, and to the roamer in desolate places, the solitary wayfarer through life, serving for "wife, children, and friends."

At about ten o'clock the Indians arrived with fresh tortillas and milk. Our guide, too, having finished cutting up and distributing the hog, was with them. He was the same who had been employed by Mr. Waldeck, and also by Mr. Walker and Captain Caddy, and he had been recommended by the prefect as the only man acquainted with the ruins. Under his escort we set out for a preliminary survey. By ourselves, leaving the palace in any direction, we should not have known which way to direct our steps.

Even in this practical age the imagination of man delights in wonders. In regard to the extent of these ruins the Indians and the people of Palenque say that they cover a space of sixty miles; in a series of well-written articles in our own country they have been set down as ten times larger than New York; and lately I have seen an article in some of the newspapers, which, referring to our expedition, represents this city, *discovered* by us, as having been three times as large as London! It is not in my nature to discredit any marvelous story. I am slow to disbelieve, and would rather sustain all such inventions; but it has been my unhappy lot to find marvels fade away as I approached them: even the Dead Sea lost its mysterious charm; and besides, as a traveler and "writer of a book," I know that if I go wrong, those who come after me will not fail to set me right. Under these considerations, not from any wish of my own, and with many thanks to my friends of the press, I am obliged to say that the Indians and people of Palenque really know nothing of the ruins personally, and the other accounts do not rest upon any sufficient foundation. The whole country for miles around is covered by a dense forest of gigantic trees, with a growth of brush and underwood unknown in the wooded deserts of our own country, and impenetrable in any direction except by cutting a way with a machete. What lies buried in that forest it is impossible to say of my own knowledge; without a guide, we might have gone within a hundred feet of all the buildings without discovering one of them.

Captain del Río, the first explorer, with men and means at command, states in his report that in the execution of his commission he cut down and burned all the woods; he does not say how far, but, judging from the breaches and excavations made in the interior of the buildings, probably for miles around. Captain Dupaix, acting under a royal commission, and with all the resources such a commission would give, did not discover any more buildings than those mentioned by del Río. And we saw only the same, but, having the benefit of them as guides, at least of del Río (for at that time we had not seen Dupaix's work), we of course saw things which escaped their observation, just as those who come after us will see what escaped ours. This place, however, was the principal object of our expedition, and it was our wish and intention to make a thorough exploration. Respect for my official character, the special tenor of my passport, and letters from Mexican authorities gave me every facility. The prefect assumed that I was sent by my government expressly to explore the ruins; and every person in Palenque except our friend the alcalde, and even he as much as the perversity of his disposition would permit, was disposed to assist us.

But there were accidental difficulties which were insuperable. First, it was the rainy season. This, under any circumstances, would have made it difficult; but as the rains did not commence till three or four o'clock, and as the weather was always clear in the morning, it alone would not have been sufficient to prevent our attempting the exploration. There were other difficulties, which had embarrassed us from the beginning and continued to do so during our whole residence among the ruins. There was not an axe or spade in the place, and, as usual, the only instrument was the machete, which here was like a short and wide-bladed sword. And the difficulty of procuring Indians to work was greater than at any other place we had visited; it was the season of planting corn, and the Indians, under the immediate pressure of famine, were all busy with their *milpas*. The price of an Indian's labor was eighteen cents per day, and the alcalde, who had the direction of this branch of the business, would not let me advance to more than twenty-five cents, and the greatest number he would engage to send me was from four to six a day. They would not sleep at the ruins; they came late and went away early. Sometimes only two or three appeared, and the same men rarely came twice, so that during our stay we had all the Indians of the village in rotation. This increased very much our labor, as it made it necessary to stand over them constantly to direct their work, and just as one set began to understand precisely what we wanted, we were obliged to teach the same to others; and I may remark that their labor, though nominally cheap, was dear in reference to the work done.

At that time I expected to return to Palenque; whether I shall do so now or not is uncertain. But I am anxious that it should be understood that the accounts which have been published of the immense labor and expense of exploring these ruins, which, as I before remarked, made it almost seem presumptuous for me to undertake it with my own resources, are exaggerated and untrue. Being on the ground at the commencement of the dry season with eight or ten young "pioneers" with a spirit of enterprise equal to their bone and muscle, in less than six months the whole of these ruins could be laid bare. Any man who has ever cleared a hundred acres of land is competent to undertake it, and the time and money spent by one of our young men in a "winter in Paris" would determine beyond all peradventure whether the city ever did cover the immense extent which some have supposed.

But to return. Under the escort of our guide we had a fatiguing but most interesting day. What we saw does not need any exaggeration. It awakened admiration and astonishment. In the afternoon came on the regular storm. We had distributed our beds, however, along the corridors under cover of the outer wall, and were better protected, but we suffered terribly from mosquitoes, the noise and stings of which drove away sleep. In the middle of the night I took up my mat to escape from these murderers of rest. The rain had ceased, and the moon, breaking through the heavy clouds, with a misty face lighted up the ruined corridor. I climbed over a mound of stones at one end where the wall had fallen and, stumbling along outside the palace, entered a lateral building near the foot of the tower, groped in the dark along a low damp passage, and spread my mat before a low doorway at the extreme end. Bats were flying and whizzing through the passage, noisy and sinister; but these ugly creatures drove away mosquitoes. The dampness of the passage was cooling and refreshing; and, with some twinging apprehensions of the snakes and reptiles, lizards and scorpions, which infest the ruins, I fell asleep.

Chapter XVIII

AT daylight I returned and found Mr. Catherwood and Pawling sitting on the stones, half dressed, in rueful conclave. They had passed the night worse than I, and our condition and prospects were dismal. Rains, hard work, bad fare, seemed nothing; but we could no more exist without sleep than the "foolish fellow" of Æsop, who, at the mo-ment when he had learned to live without eating, died. In all his travels through the country Pawling had never en-countered such hard work as since he met us.

The next night the mosquitoes were beyond all endur-ance; the slightest part of the body, the tip end of a finger, exposed, was bitten. With the heads covered, the heat was suffocating, and in the morning our faces were all in blotches. Without some remedy we were undone. It is on occasions like this that the creative power of genius displays itself. Our beds, it will be remembered, were made of sticks lying side by side and set on four piles of stones for legs. Over these we laid our *pellones* and *armas de agua*, or leathern armor, against rain, and over these our straw matting. This prevented our enemies invading us from between the sticks. Our sheets were already sewed up into sacks. We ripped one side, cut sticks, and bent them in three bows about two feet high over the frame of the beds. Over these the sheets were stretched, and sewed down all around with a small space open at the head, they had much the appearance of biers. At night, after a hard day's work, we crawled in. Hosts were waiting for us inside. We secured the open places, then each, with the stump of a lighted candle, hunted and slew, and with a lordly feeling of defiance we lay down to sleep. We had but one pair of sheets apiece, and this was a new way of sleeping under them; but, besides the victory it afforded us over the mosquitoes, it had another advantage: the heat was so great that we could not sleep with our clothes on, and since it was impossible to place the beds entirely out of reach of the spray, the covering, held up a foot or two above us and kept damp, cooled the heated atmosphere within. The Indians came out in the morning with provisions, and as the tortillas were made in the alcalde's own kitchen, not to disturb his household arrangements, they seldom arrived till after breakfast. In this way we lived.

In the meantime work went on. As at Copán, it was my business to prepare the different objects for Mr. Catherwood to draw. Many of the stones had to be scrubbed and cleaned; and, as it was our object to have the utmost possible accuracy in our drawings, in many places scaffolds had to be erected on which to set up the camera lucida. Pawling relieved me from a great part of this labor. That the reader may know the character of the objects we had to interest us, I proceed to give a description of the building in which we lived, called the palace.

The front view of this building (figure 10) [1] does not purport to be given with the same accuracy as the other drawings, the front being in a more ruined condition. It stood on an artificial elevation of an oblong form, forty feet high, three hundred and ten feet in front and rear, and two hundred and sixty feet on each side. This elevation had formerly been faced with stone, which had been so thrown down by the growth of trees that its form was hardly distinguishable.

The building stood with its face to the east, and measured two hundred and twenty-eight feet front by one hundred

1. Figures 10 through 23 follow page 274.

and eighty feet deep. Its height was not more than twenty-five feet, and it had a broad projecting cornice of stone all around. The front contained fourteen doorways, about nine feet wide each, and the intervening piers were between six and seven feet wide. On the left (in approaching the palace) eight of the piers had fallen down, as had also the corner on the right, and the terrace underneath was cumbered with the ruins. But six piers remained entire, and the rest of the front was open.

The engraving (figure 11) represents the ground plan of the whole. The black lines represent walls which were still standing; the faint lines indicate remains only, which were, in general, so clearly marked that we had no difficulty in connecting them together.

The building was constructed of stone, with a mortar of lime and sand, and the whole front was covered with stucco and painted. The piers were ornamented with spirited figures in bas-relief, one of which is represented in figure 15. On the top were three hieroglyphics sunk in the stucco. They were enclosed by a richly ornamented border, about ten feet high and six wide, of which only a part then remained. The principal personage stood in an upright position and in profile, exhibiting an extraordinary facial angle of about forty-five degrees. The upper part of the head seemed to have been compressed and lengthened, perhaps by the same process employed upon the heads of the Choctaw and Flathead Indians of our own country. The head represented a different species from any now existing in that region of country; and supposing the statues to be images of living personages, or the creations of artists according to their ideas of perfect figures, they indicated a race of people now lost and unknown.[2] The headdress was evidently a plume of feathers. Over the shoulders was a short covering decorated with studs, and a breastplate; part of the ornament of the girdle was broken and the tunic was probably a leopard's

2. The descendants of the ancient Mayas still occupy much the same territory as in pre-Columbian times. It is known that the Mayas used to flatten their babies' heads, which could account for the cranial differences observed by Stephens.

skin. The whole dress no doubt exhibited the costume of this unknown people. He held in his hand a staff or scepter, and opposite his hands were the marks of three hieroglyphics, which have decayed or been broken off. At his feet were two naked figures seated cross-legged, and apparently suppliants. A fertile imagination might find many explanations for these strange figures, but no satisfactory interpretation presents itself to my mind. The hieroglyphics doubtless tell their history. The stucco was of admirable consistency, and hard as stone. It had been painted, and in different places about it we discovered the remains of red, blue, yellow, black, and white.

The piers which were still standing contained other figures of the same general character, but they, unfortunately, were more mutilated, and from the declivity of the terrace it was difficult to set up the camera lucida in such a position as to draw them. The piers which were fallen were no doubt enriched with the same ornaments. Each one had some specific meaning, and the whole probably presented some allegory or history; when entire and painted, the effect in ascending the terrace must have been imposing and beautiful.

The principal doorway was not distinguished by its size or by any superior ornament, but was only indicated by a range of broad stone steps leading up to it on the terrace. The doorways had no doors, nor were there the remains of any. Within, on each side, were three niches in the wall, about eight or ten inches square, with a cylindrical stone about two inches in diameter fixed upright, by which perhaps a door had been secured. Along the cornice outside, projecting about a foot beyond the front, holes had been drilled at intervals through the stone; and our impression was that an immense cotton cloth, running the whole length of the building, perhaps painted in a style corresponding with the ornaments, had been attached to this cornice and raised and lowered like a curtain, according to the exigencies of sun and rain. Such a curtain is used now in front of the piazzas of some haciendas in Yucatán.

The tops of the doorways were all broken. They had evidently been square, and over every one were large niches in the wall on each side, in which the lintels had been laid. These lintels had all fallen, and the stones above formed broken natural arches. Underneath were heaps of rubbish, but there were no remains of lintels. If they had been single slabs of stone, some of them must have been visible and prominent; and we made up our minds that these lintels were of *wood*. We had no authority for this. It is not suggested either by del Río or Captain Dupaix, and perhaps we should not have ventured the conclusion had it not been for the wooden lintel which we had seen over the doorway at Ococingo; by what we saw afterward in Yucatán, we were confirmed, beyond all doubt, in our opinion. I do not conceive, however, that this gives any conclusive data in regard to the age of the buildings. The wood, if such as we saw in the other places, would be very lasting; its decay must have been extremely slow, and centuries may have elapsed since it perished altogether.

The building had two parallel corridors running lengthwise on all four of its sides. In front these corridors were about nine feet wide, and extended the whole length of the building upward of two hundred feet. In the long wall that divided them there was but one door, which was opposite the principal door of entrance, with a corresponding one on the other side leading to a courtyard in the rear. The floors were of cement, as hard as the best seen in the remains of Roman baths and cisterns. The walls were about ten feet high, plastered, and on each side of the principal entrance ornamented with medallions, of which the borders only remained; these perhaps contained the busts of the royal family. The separating wall had apertures of about a foot, probably intended for purposes of ventilation. Some were of the form which has been called the Greek Cross and some of that called the Egyptian Tau, which has made them the subject of much learned speculation.

The Indian builders were evidently ignorant of the principles of the arch, and they supported their ceilings by lapping stones over as they rose, as at Ococingo and among the Cyclopean remains in Greece and Italy. Along the top was a layer of flat stone, and the sides, being plastered, presented a flat surface. The long, unbroken corridors in front of the palace were probably intended for lords and gentlemen in waiting; or perhaps, in that beautiful position, which, before the forest grew up, must have commanded an extended view of a cultivated and inhabited plain, the king himself sat in it to receive the reports of his officers and to administer justice. Under our dominion Juan occupied the front corridor as a kitchen, and the other was our sleeping apartment.

From the center door of this corridor a range of stone steps thirty feet long led to a rectangular courtyard, eighty feet long by seventy broad. On each side of the steps were grim and gigantic figures carved on stone in basso-relievo, nine or ten feet high, and in a position slightly inclined backward from the end of the steps to the floor of the corridor. The engraving (figure 12) represents this side of the courtyard, and in figure 6 are shown the figures alone, on a larger scale. They are adorned with rich headdresses and necklaces, but their attitude is that of pain and trouble. The design and anatomical proportions of the figures are faulty, but there is a force of expression about them which shows the skill and conceptive power of the artist. When we first took possession of the palace this courtyard was encumbered with trees, so that we could hardly see across it, and it was so filled up with rubbish that we were obliged to make excavations of several feet before these figures could be drawn.

On each side of the courtyard the palace was divided into apartments, probably for sleeping. On the right the piers had all fallen down. On the left they were still standing, and ornamented with stucco figures. In the center apartment, in one of the holes of the arch, were the remains of a wooden pole about a foot long, which once stretched across, but the rest had decayed. It was the only piece of wood we found at Palenque, and we did not discover this until some time after we had made up our minds in regard to the wooden lintels over the doors. It was much worm-eaten, and probably, in a few years, not a vestige of it will be left.

At the farther side of the courtyard was another flight of stone steps, corresponding with those in front, on each side

FIG. 6 *Colossal Bas Reliefs on West Side of*
Courtyard at Palace Palenque

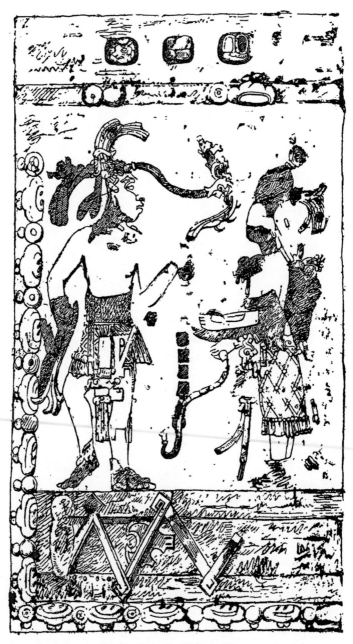

FIG. 7 *Stucco Bas Relief on West Side of Palace Palenque*

of which were carved figures, and on the flat surface beween were single cartouches of hieroglyphics (figure 14).

The whole courtyard was overgrown with trees, and it was encumbered with ruins several feet high, so that the exact architectural arrangements could not be seen. Having our beds in the corridor adjoining, when we woke in the morning, and when we had finished the work of the day, we had it under our eyes. Every time we descended the steps the grim and mysterious figures stared us in the face, and it became to us one of the most interesting parts of the ruins. We were exceedingly anxious to make excavations, clear out the mass of rubbish, and lay the whole platform bare; but this was impossible. It was probably paved with stone or cement; and from the profusion of ornament in other parts, there is reason to believe that many curious and interesting specimens may be brought to light. This agreeable work is left for the future traveler, who may go there better provided with men and materials, and with more knowledge of what he will encounter; in my opinion, if he finds nothing new, the mere spectacle of the courtyard entire will repay him for the labor and expense of clearing it.

The part of the building which formed the rear of the courtyard, communicating with it by the steps, consisted of two corridors, the same as the front, paved, plastered, and ornamented with stucco. The floor of the corridor fronting the courtyard sounded hollow, and a breach had been made in it which seemed to lead into a subterraneous chamber; but in descending by means of a tree with notches cut in it, and with a candle, we found merely a hollow in the earth, not bounded by any wall.

In the farther corridor the wall was in some places broken, and had several separate coats of plaster and paint. In one place we counted six layers, each of which had the remains of colors. In another place there seemed a line of written characters in black ink. We made an effort to get at them, but in endeavoring to remove a thin upper stratum, they came off with it, and we desisted.

This corridor opened upon a second courtyard, eighty feet long and but thirty across. The floor of the corridor was ten feet above that of the courtyard, and on the wall underneath were square stones with hieroglyphics sculptured upon them. On the piers were stuccoed figures, but in a ruined condition.

On the other side of the courtyard were two ranges of corridors, which terminated the building in this direction. The first of them was divided into three apartments, with doors opening from the extremities upon the western corridor. All the piers were standing except that on the northwest corner. All were covered with stucco ornaments, and one with hieroglyphics. The rest contained figures in bas-relief, two of which, being those least ruined, are represented in figures 7 and 8.

The first was enclosed by a border, very wide at the bottom, part of which was destroyed. The subject consisted of two figures with facial angles similar to those in figure 8, and plumes of feathers and other decorations for head-dresses, necklaces, girdles, and sandals; each had hold of the same curious baton, part of which was destroyed, and opposite their hands were hieroglyphics, which probably give the history of these incomprehensible personages. The others were more ruined, and no attempt has been made to restore them. One is kneeling as if to receive an honor,[3] and the other (figure 8) a blow.

So far the arrangements of the palace are simple and easily understood; but on the left were several distinct and independent buildings, as will be seen by the plan, the particulars of which, however, I do not consider it necessary to describe. The principal of these is the tower, on the south side of the second court. This tower was conspicuous by its height and proportions, but on examination in detail it was found unsatisfactory and uninteresting. The base was thirty feet square, and it had three stories. Entering over a heap of rubbish at the base, we found within another tower, distinct from the outer one, and a stone staircase, so narrow that a large man could not ascend it. The staircase terminated against a dead stone ceiling, closing all further passage, the

3. This engraving is reproduced in earlier editions of *Incidents of Travel.* . . .

FIG. 8 *Stucco Bas Relief on West Side of*
Palace Palenque

FIG. 9 *Stone Oval Bas Relief in Wall of Apartment
in Palace Palenque*

last step being only six or eight inches from it. For what purpose a staircase had been carried up to such a bootless termination we could not conjecture. The whole tower was a substantial stone structure, and in its arrangements and purposes about as incomprehensible as the sculptured tablets.

East of the tower was another building with two corridors, one richly decorated with pictures in stucco, and having in the center the elliptical tablet represented in the engraving (figure 9). It was four feet long and three wide, of hard stone set in the wall, and the sculpture was in bas-relief. Around it were the remains of a rich stucco border. The principal figure sat cross-legged on a border ornamented with two leopards' heads; the attitude was easy, the physiognomy the same as that of the other personages, and the expression calm and benevolent. The figure wore around its neck a necklace of pearls, to which was suspended a small medallion containing a face, perhaps intended as an image of the sun. Like every other subject of sculpture we had seen in the country, the personage had earrings, bracelets on the wrists, and a girdle round the loins. The headdress differs from most of the others at Palenque in that it wants the plumes of feathers. Near the head were three hieroglyphics.

The other figure, which seems that of a woman, was sitting cross-legged on the ground, richly dressed, and apparently in the act of making an offering. In this supposed offering was seen a plume of feathers, in which the headdress of the principal person was deficient. Over the head of the sitting personage were four hieroglyphics. This was the only piece of sculptured stone about the palace except those in the courtyard. Under it formerly stood a table—of which the impression against the wall was still visible, and which is given in the engraving in faint lines—after the model of other tables still existing in other places.

At the extremity of this corridor there was an aperture in the pavement leading by a flight of steps to a platform; from this a door, with an ornament in stucco over it, opened by another flight of steps upon a narrow, dark passage, terminating in other corridors, which ran transversely. These were called subterraneous apartments; but there were windows opening from them above the ground, and, in fact, they were merely a ground floor below the pavement of the corridors. In most parts, however, they were so dark that it was necessary to visit them with candles. There were no bas-reliefs or stucco ornaments; and the only objects which our guide pointed out or which attracted our attention were several stone tables, one crossing and blocking up the corridor, about eight feet long, four wide, and three high. One of these lower corridors had a door opening upon the back part of the terrace, and we generally passed through it with a candle to get to the other buildings. In two other places there were flights of steps leading to corridors above. Probably these were sleeping apartments.

In that part of the plan marked *Room No. 1*, the walls were more richly decorated with stucco ornaments than any other in the palace; but, unfortunately, they were much mutilated. On each side of the doorway was a stucco figure.[4] Near one of the figures was an apartment in which was marked *small altar*. It was richly ornamented, like those which will be hereafter referred to in other buildings; and from the appearance of the back wall we supposed there had been stone tablets. In our utter ignorance of the habits of the people who had formerly occupied this building, it was impossible to form any conjecture for what uses these different apartments were intended; but if we are right in calling it a palace, the name which the Indians give it, it seems probable that the part surrounding the courtyard was for public and state occasions, and that the rest was occupied as the place of residence of the royal family; this room with the small altar was, we may suppose, what would be called in our own times a royal chapel.

With these helps and the aid of the plan, the reader will be able to find his way through the ruined palace of Palenque; he will form some idea of the profusion of its ornaments, of their unique and striking character, and of their mournful effect, shrouded by trees; and perhaps with him, as with us, fancy will present it as it was before the hand of

---

4. The engraving for one of these figures is reproduced in earlier editions of *Incidents of Travel* . . .

ruin had swept over it, perfect in its amplitude and rich decorations, and occupied by the strange people whose portraits and figures now adorn its walls.

The reader will not be surprised that, with such objects to engage our attention, we disregarded some of the discomforts of our princely residence. We expected at this place to live upon game, but were disappointed. A wild turkey we could shoot at any time from the door of the palace; but, after trying one, we did not venture to trifle with our teeth upon another. And besides these, there was nothing but parrots, monkeys, and lizards, all very good eating, but we kept them in reserve for a time of pressing necessity. The density of the forest and the heavy rains would, however, have made sporting impracticable.

Once only did I attempt an exploration. From the door of the palace, almost on a line with the front, rose a high steep mountain, which we thought must command a view of the city in its whole extent, and perhaps itself contain ruins. I took the bearing and, with a compass in my hand and an Indian before me with his machete, from the rear of the last-mentioned building I cut a straight line up east-northeast to the top. The ascent was so steep that I was obliged to haul myself up by the branches. On the top was a high mound of stones, with a foundation wall still remaining. Probably a tower or temple had stood there, but the woods were as thick as below, and no part of the ruined city, not even the palace, could be seen. Trees were growing out of the top, up one of which I climbed, but could not see the palace or any one of the buildings. Back toward the mountain was nothing but forest; in front, through an opening in the trees, we saw a great wooded plain extending to Tabasco and the Gulf of Mexico; and the Indian at the foot of the tree, peering through the branches, turned his face up to me with a beaming expression, and pointing to a little spot on the plain, which was to him the world, cried out, *Allí está el pueblo* (There is the village). This was the only occasion on which I attempted to explore, for it was the only time I had any mark to aim at.

I must except, however, the exploration of an aqueduct which Pawling and I attempted together. It was supplied by a stream which ran at the base of the terrace on which the palace stands. At the time of our arrival the whole stream passed through this aqueduct. It was now swollen, and ran over the top and alongside. At the mouth we had great difficulty in stemming the torrent. Within it was perfectly dark, and we could not move without candles. The sides were of smooth stones about four feet high, and the roof was made by stones lapping over like the corridors of the buildings. At a short distance from the entrance the passage turned to the left and, at a distance of one hundred and sixty feet, it was completely blocked up by the ruins of the roof, which had fallen down. What was its direction beyond, it was impossible to determine, but certainly it did not pass under the palace as has been supposed.

Besides the claps of thunder and flashes of lightning, we had one alarm at night. It was from a noise that sounded like the cracking of a dry branch under a stealthy tread, which, as we all started up together, I thought was that of a wild beast, but which Mr. Catherwood, whose bed was nearer, imagined to be that of a man. We climbed up the mound of fallen stones at the end of this corridor, but beyond all was thick darkness. Pawling fired twice as an intimation that we were awake, and we arranged poles across the corridor as a trap, so that even an Indian could not enter from that quarter without being thrown down with some considerable noise and detriment to his person.

Besides mosquitoes and *garrapatas,* or ticks, we suffered from another worse insect, called by the natives *niguas,* which, we are told, pestered the Spaniards on their first entry into the country, and which, says the historian, "ate their way into the flesh, under the nails of the toes, then laid their nits there within, and multiplied in such manner that there was no ridding them but by cauteries, so that some lost their toes, and some their feet, whereas they should at first have been picked out; but being as yet unacquainted with the evil, they knew not how to apply the remedy."

This description is true even to the last clause. We had escaped them until our arrival at Palenque, and being unacquainted with the evil, did not know how to apply the remedy. I carried one in my foot for several days, conscious that something was wrong, but not knowing what, until the nits had been laid and multiplied. Pawling undertook to pick them out with a penknife, which left a large hole in the flesh; unluckily, from the bites of various insects my foot became so inflamed that I could not get on shoe or stocking. I was obliged to lie by, and, sitting an entire day with my foot in a horizontal position, uncovered, it was assaulted by small black flies, the bites of which I did not feel at the moment of infliction, but which left marks like the punctures of a hundred pins. The irritation was so great and the swelling increased so much that I became alarmed and determined to return to the village. It was no easy matter to get there. The foot was too big to put in a stirrup, and, indeed, to keep it but for a few moments in a hanging position made it feel as if the blood would burst through the skin, and the idea of striking it against a bush makes me shudder even now. It was indispensable, however, to leave the place. I sent in to the village for a mule, and on the tenth day after my arrival at the ruins, hopped down the terrace, mounted, and laid the unfortunate member on a pillow over the pommel of the saddle. This gave me, for that muddy road, a very uncertain seat. I had a man before me to cut the branches, yet my hat was knocked off three or four times, and twice I was obliged to dismount; but in due season, to my great relief, we cleared the woods. After the closeness and confinement of the forest, coming once more into an open country quickened every pulse.

As I ascended to the table on which the village stood, I observed an unusual degree of animation, and a crowd of people in the grass-grown street, probably some fifteen or twenty, who seemed roused at the sight of me; presently three or four men on horseback rode toward me. I had borne many different characters in that country, and this time I was mistaken for three padres who were expected to arrive that morning from Tumbalá. If the mistake had continued I should have had dinner enough for six at least; but unluckily, it was soon discovered, and I rode on to the door of our old house. Presently the alcalde appeared, with his keys in his hands and in full dress, that is, his shirt was inside of his pantaloons. I was happy to find that he was in a worse humor at the coming of the padres than at our arrival; indeed, he seemed now rather to have a leaning toward me, as one who could sympathize in his vexation at the absurdity of making such a fuss about them. When he saw my foot too, he really showed some commiseration, and endeavored to make me as comfortable as possible. The swelling had increased very much. I was soon on my back, and lying perfectly quiet, by the help of a medicine chest, starvation, and the absence of irritating causes, in two days and nights I reduced the inflammation very sensibly.

FIG. 10 *Palace at Palenque*

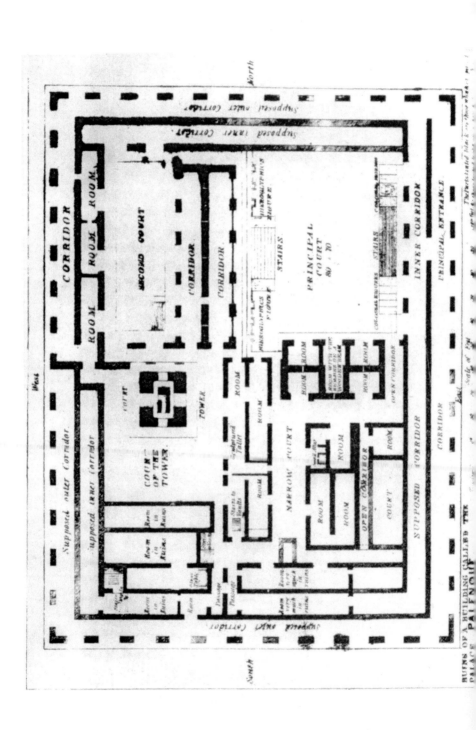

RUINS OF A BUILDING (CALLED THE PALACE).

FIG. 12 *West Courtyard at Palace Palenque*

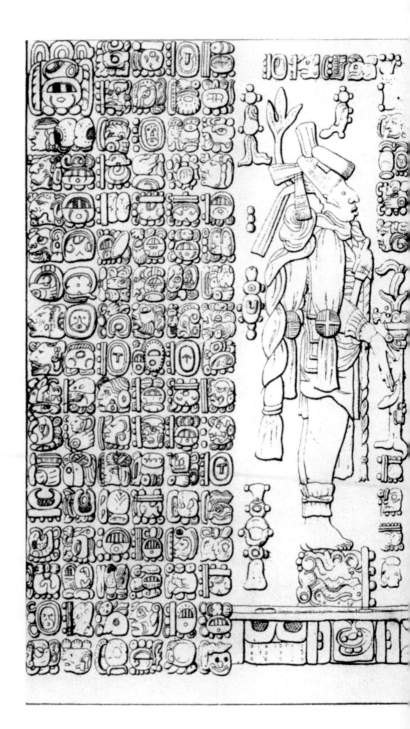

FIG. 13 *Tablet on Be*

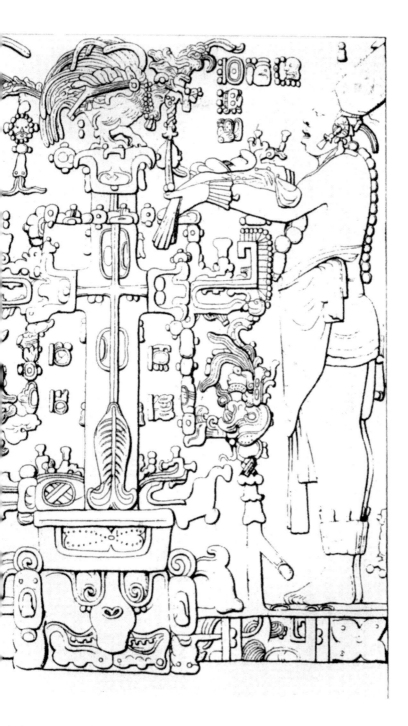

of Altar, Casa No. 2

FIG. 14 *East Courtyard at Palace Palenque*

FIG. 15 *Stucco Bas Relief at the Palace Palenque*

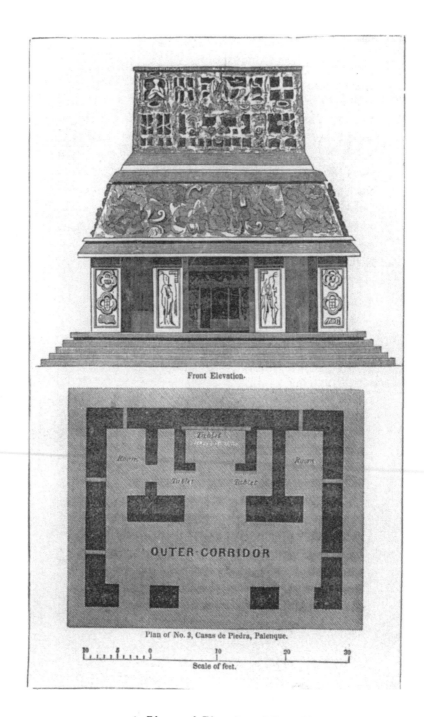

Front Elevation.

Tablet

Room

Tablet   Tablet

Room

OUTER-CORRIDOR

Plan of No. 3, Casas de Piedra, Palenque.

Scale of feet.

FIG. 16 *Plan and Elevation of Casa No. 3*

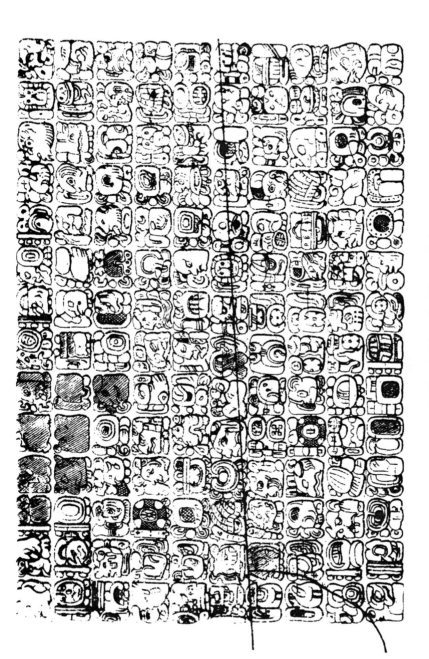

FIG. 17 *Tablet of Hieroglyphics at Palenque*

FIG. 18 *Altar, Casa No. 3*

FIG. 19 *Bas Relief on Side of Door of Altar, Casa No. 3*

FIG. 20 *Tablet on Ba...*

f Altar, Casa No. 3

FIG. 21 *Bas Relief on Side of Door of Altar, Casa No. 3*

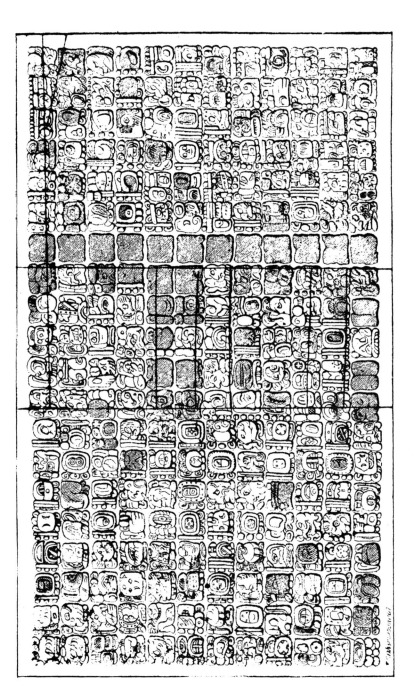

FIG. 22 *Tablet of Hieroglyphics at Palenque*

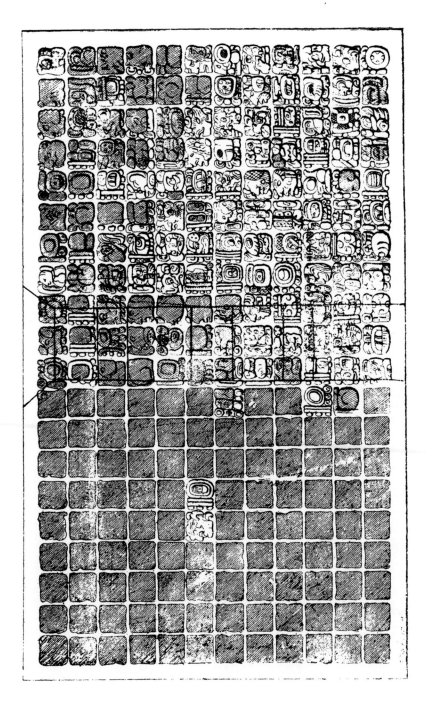

FIG. 23 *Tablet of Hieroglyphics at Palenque*

Chapter XIX

~~~~~~

A voice from the ruins. Buying bread. Arrival of padres.
Cura of Palenque. Card playing. Sunday. Mass. A dinner
party. Mementos of home. Dinner customs. Return to the
ruins. A marked change. Terrific thunder. A whirl-
wind. A scene of the sublime and terrible.

THE third day I heard from the ruins a voice of wail-
ing. Juan had upset the lard, and every drop was gone.
The imploring letter I received roused all my sensibilities
and, forgetting everything in the emergency, I hurried to
the alcalde's and told him a hog must die. The alcalde made
difficulties, and to this day I cannot account for his concealing from me a fact of which he must have been aware, to
wit, that on that very night a porker had been killed. Very
early the next morning I saw a boy passing with some strings
of fresh pork; I hailed him and he guided me to a hut in
the suburbs, which but yesterday had been the dwelling
of the unfortunate quadruped. I procured the portion destined for some honest Palenquian and returned, happy in
the consciousness of making others so.

That day was memorable, too, for another piece of good
fortune, for a courier arrived from Ciudad Real with despatches for Tabasco and a backload of bread on private
account. As soon as the intelligence reached me, I despatched
a messenger to negotiate for the whole stock. Unfortunately,
it was sweetened, made up into diamonds, circles, and other
fanciful forms about two inches long and an inch thick, to
be eaten with chocolate, and that detestable lard was oozing
out of the crust. Nevertheless, it was bread, and placing it
carefully on a table with a fresh cheese, the product of our

cow, I lay down at night full of the joy that morning would diffuse over the ruins of Palenque. But, alas! All human calculations are vain. In my first sleep, roused by a severe clap of thunder, I detected an enormous cat on the table. While my boot was sailing toward her, with one bound she reached the wall and disappeared under the eaves of the roof. I fell asleep again; she returned and the consequences were fatal.

The padres who had been expected when we first arrived in Palenque, were slow in movement. After keeping the village in a state of excitement for three days, this morning they made a triumphal entry, escorted by citizens and with a train of more than a hundred Indians, carrying hammocks, chairs, and luggage. The villages of Tumbalá and San Pedro had turned out two or three hundred strong, and had carried them on their backs and shoulders to Nopa, where they had been met by a deputation from Palenque and transferred to the village. It is a glorious thing in that country to be a padre, and next to being a padre is the position of being a padre's friend. In the afternoon I visited them, but after the fatigues of the journey they were all asleep, and the Indians around the door were talking in low tones so as not to disturb them. Inside were enormous piles of luggage, which showed the prudent care the good ecclesiastics took of themselves. The siesta over, very soon they appeared, one after the other, in dresses, or rather undresses, difficult to describe, but certainly by no means clerical; none of them had coat or jacket. Two of them were the curas of Tumbalá and Yajalón, whom we had seen on our journey. The third was a Franciscan friar from Ciudad Real, and they had come expressly to visit the ruins. All had suffered severely from the journey.

The cura of Yajalón was a deputy to Congress, and in Mexico many inquiries had been made of him about the ruins on the supposition that they were in his neighborhood, which erroneous supposition he mentioned with a feeling reference to the intervening mountains. The padre of Tumbalá was a promising young man of twenty-eight, and weighed at that time about twelve stone, or two hundred and forty pounds—a heavy load to carry about with him over such roads as they had traversed. But the Franciscan friar had suffered most, and he sat sideways in a hammock, with his vest open, wiping the perspiration from his breast. They were all intelligent men, and, in fact, the circumstance of their making the journey for no other purpose than to visit the ruins was alone an indication of their superior character. The Congressman we had seen on our way through his village, and we had been struck then with his general knowledge and particularly with his force of character. He had borne an active part in all the convulsions of the country from the time of the revolution against Spain, of which he had been an instigator, and ever since that time, to the scandal of the Church party, he had stood forth as a Liberal. He had played the soldier as well as priest, laying down his blood-stained sword after a battle to confess the wounded and dying; he had been twice wounded, once chronicled among the killed, and an exile in Guatemala. With the gradual recovery of the Liberal Party, he had been restored to his place and sent as a deputy to Congress, where very soon he was to take part in new convulsions. They were all startled by the stories of mosquitoes, insects, and reptiles at the ruins, and particularly by what they had heard of the condition of my foot.

While we were taking chocolate the cura of Palenque entered. At the time of our first arrival he had been absent at another village under his charge, and I had not seen him before. He was more original in his appearance than any of the others, being very tall, with long black hair, and an Indian face and complexion. He was certainly four-fifths Indian blood; indeed, if I had seen him in Indian costume (and what that is the reader by this time understands) I should have taken him for a *puro*, or Indian of unmixed descent. His dress was as unclerical as his appearance, consisting of an old straw hat, with the rim turned up before, behind, and at the sides, so as to make four regular corners, with a broad blue velvet riband for a hatband, both soiled by long exposure to wind and rain. Beneath this were a check shirt, an old blue silk neckcloth with yellow stripes, a striped

roundabout jacket, black waistcoat, and pantaloons made of
bedticking which did not meet the waistcoat by two inches,
the whole tall figure ending below in yellow buckskin shoes.
But under this *outré* appearance existed a charming simplicity and courtesy of manner, and when he spoke his face
beamed with kindness.

The reception given him showed the good feeling existing
among the padres; and after some general conversation, the
chocolate cups were removed and one of the padres went to
his chest, whence he produced a pack of cards which he
placed upon the table. The cards had evidently done much
service; he said that he always carried them with him, and
it was very pleasant to travel with companions, as, wherever
they stopped, they could have a game at night. There was
something orderly and systematic in the preliminary arrangements that showed the effect of regular habits and a
well-trained household. An old Indian servant laid on the
table a handful of grains of corn and a new bundle of paper
cigars. The grains of corn were valued at a *medio*. I declined
joining in the game, whereupon one of the reverend fathers
kept aloof to entertain me and the other three sat down to
monte, still taking part in the conversation. Very soon they
became abstracted, and I left them playing as earnestly as
if the souls of unconverted Indians were at stake. I had
often heard the ill-natured remark of foreigners, that two
padres cannot meet in that country without playing cards,
but it was the first time I had seen its verification; perhaps
(I feel guilty in saying so) because, except on public occasions, it was the first time I had ever seen two padres together. Before I left them the padres invited me to dine
with them the next day, and on returning to my own quarters I found that Don Santiago, the gentleman who was
giving them the dinner, and next to the prefect the principal inhabitant, had called upon me with a like invitation,
which I need not say I accepted.

The next day was Sunday; the storm of the night had
rolled away, the air was soft and balmy, the grass was green,
and, not being obliged to travel, I felt what the natives aver,
that the mornings of the rainy season were the finest in the

year. It was a great day for the little church at Palenque. The four padres were there, all in their gowns and surplices; all assisted in the ceremonies and the Indians from every hut in the village went to mass. This over, all retired, and in a few minutes the village was as quiet as ever.

At twelve o'clock I went to the house of Don Santiago to dine. The three stranger padres were there, and most of the guests were assembled. Don Santiago, the richest man in Palenque, and the most extensive merchant, received us in his *tienda*, or store, which was merely a few shelves with a counter before them in one corner; his whole stock of merchandise was worth perhaps twenty or thirty dollars. But Don Santiago was entirely a different style of man from one in such small business in this country or Europe; he was courteous in manners and intelligent for that country. He was dressed in white pantaloons and red slippers, a clean shirt with an embroidered bosom, and suspenders, which having probably cost more than all the rest of his habiliments, were not to be hidden under coat and waistcoat.

In this place, which had before seemed to me so much out of the world, I was brought more directly in contact with home than at any other I visited. The chair on which I sat came from New York, as well as a small looking-glass, two pieces of American "cottons," and the remnant of a box of vermicelli, of the existence of which in the place I was not before advised. The most intimate foreign relations of the inhabitants were with New York through the port of Tabasco. They knew a man related to a family in the village who had actually been to New York, and a barrel of New York flour, the bare mention of which created a yearning, had once reached the place. In fact, New York was more familiar to them than any other part of the world except the capital. Don Santiago had a copy of Zavala's [1] tour in the United States, which, with the exception of a few volumes of the lives of saints, was his library, and which he knew almost by heart. They had kept up with our political history

---

1. Lorenzo de Zavala who in 1833 wrote *Viaje a los Estados Unidos.*

so well as to know that General Washington was not president, but General Jackson.

The padre of Tumbalá, he of two hundred and forty pounds' weight, was somewhat of an exquisite in dress for that country, and had brought with him his violin. He was curious to know the state of musical science in my country, and whether the government supported good opera companies; he regretted that I could not play some national airs, and entertained himself and the company with several of their own.

In the meantime the padre of Palenque was still missing, but, after being sent for twice, he made his appearance. The dinner was in fact his, but, on account of the want of conveniences in the convent from his careless housekeeping, it was being given by his friend Don Santiago on his behalf; the answer he gave to the boy who had been sent to call him was that he had forgotten all about it. He was absent and eccentric enough for a genius, though he made no pretensions to that character. Don Santiago told us that he once went to the padre's house, where he found inside a cow and a calf; the cura, in great perplexity, apologized, saying that he could not help himself, they would come in, and when Don Santiago suggested to him the plan of driving them out, he considered it a good idea.

As soon as he appeared the other padres rallied him upon his forgetfulness, which they insisted was all feigned; they had won sixteen dollars from him the night before and said that he was afraid to come. He answered in the same strain that he was a ruined man. They offered him his revenge, and forthwith the table was brought out, cards and grains of corn were spread upon it as before, and while the padre of Tumbalá played the violin, the other three played monte. Being Sunday, in some places this would be considered rather irregular, at least; to do so with open doors would be considered setting a bad example to children and servants; and, in fact, considering myself on a pretty sociable footing, I could not help telling them that in my country they would all be read out of Church. The padre Congressman had met an Englishman in Mexico who told him the same thing, and also the manner of observing the Sunday in England, which they all thought must be very stupid.

Perhaps upon less ground than this the whole Spanish American priesthood has at times been denounced as a set of unprincipled gamblers, but I have too warm a recollection of their many kindnesses to hold them up in this light. They were all intelligent and good men, who would rather do benefits than an injury. In matters connected with religion they were most reverential; they labored diligently in their vocations and were without reproach among their people. By custom and education they did not consider that they were doing wrong. From my agreeable intercourse with them, and my regard for their many good qualities, I would fain save them from denunciations of utter unworthiness which might be cast upon them. Nevertheless, it is true that dinner was delayed, and all the company kept waiting until they had finished their game of cards.

The table was set in an unoccupied house adjoining. Every white man in the village, except the prefect and alcalde, was present; the former was away at his hacienda, and the latter, from the sneering references he made to it, I suspected was not invited. In all there were fifteen or sixteen, and I was led to the seat of honor at the head of the table. I objected, but the padres seated me perforce. After the gentlemen were seated, it was found that, by sitting close, there was room for some ladies, and after the arrangements for the table were completed, they were invited to take seats. Unluckily, there was only room for three, who sat all together on my left. In a few minutes I felt very much as if the dinner was got up expressly for me. It was long since I had seen such a table, and I mourned in spirit that I had not sent notice for Mr. Catherwood to come to the village accidentally in time to get an invitation. But it was too late now; there was no time for reflection; every moment the dinner was going. In some places my position would have required me to devote myself to those on each side of me, but at Palenque they devoted themselves to me. If I stopped a moment my plate was whipped away and another brought, loaded with something else. It may seem unmannerly, but I watched the fate of certain dishes, particularly some *dulces*, or sweetmeats, hoping they would not be entirely consumed, as I purposed to secure all that should be left to take with me to the ruins. Wine was on the table, which was recommended to me as coming from New York, but this was not enough to induce me to taste it. There was no water, and, by the way, water is never put on the table, and never drunk until after the *dulces*, which come on as the last course, when it is served in a large tumbler, which passes round for each one to sip from. It is entirely irregular and ill bred to ask for water during the meal. Each guest, as he rose from the table, bowed to Don Santiago, and said *muchas gracias*, which I considered in bad taste and not in keeping with the delicacy of Spanish courtesy, as the host ought rather to thank his guests for their society than they to thank him for his dinner. Nevertheless, as I had more reason to be thankful than any of them, I conformed to the example set me. After dinner my friends became drowsy and retired to siesta. I found my way back to Don Santiago's house, where, in a conversation with the ladies, I secured the remains of the *dulces* and bought out his stock of vermicelli.

In the morning, my foot being sufficiently recovered, I rode up to the house of the padres to escort them to the ruins. They had passed the evening sociably at cards, and again the padre of Palenque was wanting. We rode over to his house and waited while he secured carefully on the back of a tall horse a little boy, who looked so wonderfully like him that, out of respect to his obligation of celibacy, people felt delicate in asking whose son he was. This done, he tied an extra pair of shoes behind his own saddle, and we set off with the *adiós* of all the village. The padres intended to pass the night at the ruins, and had a train of fifty or sixty Indians loaded with beds, bedding, provision, *zacate* for mules, and multifarious articles, down to a white earthen washbowl; besides which, more favored than we, they had four or five women.

Entering the forest, we found the branches of the trees, which had been trimmed on my return to the village, again weighed down by the rains; and the streams were very bad. The padres were well mounted but no horsemen, and they had to dismount very often. Under my escort we got lost, but at eleven o'clock, very much to the satisfaction of all, our long, strange-looking, straggling party reached the ruins. The old palace was once more alive with inhabitants.

There was a marked change in it since I had left: the walls were damp, the corridors wet; the continued rains were working through cracks and crevices, and opening leaks in the roof; saddles, bridles, boots, shoes, etc., were green and mildewed, and the guns and pistols covered with a coat of rust. Mr. Catherwood's appearance startled me. He was wan and gaunt; he was lame, like me, from the bites of insects, his face was swollen, and his left arm hung with rheumatism as if paralyzed.

We sent the Indians across the courtyard to the opposite corridor, where the sight of our loose traps might not tempt them to their undoing, and selecting a place for that purpose, we set up the *catres* immediately, and, with all the comforts of home, the padres lay down for an hour's rest. I had no ill-will toward these worthy men; on the contrary, I had the most friendly feeling, and, to do the honors of the palace, I invited them to dine with us. Catherwood and Pawling objected, and the padres would have done better if left to themselves; but they appreciated the spirit of the invitation, and returned me *muchas gracias*. After their siesta I escorted them over the palace, and left them in their apartment. Singularly enough, that night there was no rain, so, with a hat before a candle, we crossed the courtyard and paid them a visit; we found the three reverend gentlemen sitting on a mat on the ground, winding up the day with a comfortable game at cards, with the Indians asleep around them.

The next morning, with the assistance of Pawling and the Indians to lift and haul them, I escorted them to the other buildings, heard some curious speculations, and at two o'clock, with many expressions of good will and pressing invitations to their different convents, they returned to the village.

Late in the afternoon the storm set in with terrific thunder, which at night rolled with fearful crashes against the walls, while the vivid lightning flashed along the corridors.

The padres had laughed at us for their superior discrimination in selecting a sleeping place, and this night their apartment was flooded. From this time my notebook contains memoranda only of the arrival of the Indians, with the time that the storm set in, its violence and duration, the deluges of rain, and the places to which we were obliged to move our beds. Every day our residence became more wet and uncomfortable. On Thursday, the thirtieth of May, the storm opened with a whirlwind. At night the crash of falling trees rang through the forest, rain fell in deluges, the roaring of thunder was terrific, and as we lay looking out, the aspect of the ruined palace, lighted by the glare of lightning such as I never saw in this country, was awfully grand; in fact, there was too much of the sublime and terrible. The storm threatened the very existence of the building; and, knowing the tottering state of the walls, for some moments we had apprehensions lest the whole should fall and crush us. In the morning the courtyard and the ground below the palace were flooded, and by this time the whole front was so wet that we were obliged to desert it and move to the other side of the corridor. Even here we were not much better off; but we remained until Mr. Catherwood had finished his last drawing; and on Saturday, the first of June, like rats leaving a sinking ship, we broke up and left the ruins. Before leaving, however, I will present a description of the remaining buildings.

Chapter XX

~~~~~~

Plan of the ruins. Pyramidal structure. A building. Stucco
ornaments. Human figures. Tablets. Remarkable hiero-
glyphics. Range of pillars. Stone terrace. Another building.
A large tablet. A cross. Conjectures in regard to this cross.
Beautiful sculpture. A platform. Curious devices. A statue.
Another pyramidal structure surmounted by a building.
Corridors. A curious bas-relief. Stone tablets with figures
in bas-relief. Tablets and figures. The oratorio. More py-
ramidal structures and buildings. Extent of the ruins.
These ruins the remains of a polished and peculiar
people. Antiquity of Palenque.

THE plan [1] indicates the position of all the buildings
which have been discovered at Palenque. There were
remains of others in the same vicinity, but they were so utterly dilapidated that we have not thought it worth while
to give any description of them, nor even to indicate their
places on the plan.

From the palace no other building is visible. Passing out
by what is called the subterraneous passage, you descend the
southwest corner of the terrace, and at the foot immediately
commence ascending a ruined pyramidal structure, which
appears once to have had steps on all its sides. These steps
have been thrown down by the trees, and it is necessary to
clamber over stones, aiding the feet by clinging to the
branches. The ascent is so steep that if the first man displaces
a stone it bounds down the side of the pyramid, and woe to
those behind. About halfway up, through openings in the

---

1. The drawing of the general plan of the ruins is reproduced in
earlier editions of *Incidents of Travel* . . . , although its usefulness
is very much reduced because of indistinct lettering.

trees, is seen the building represented in figure 24. The height of the structure on which it stands is one hundred and ten feet on the slope. The engraving represents the actual

FIG. 24 *Casa No. 1 at Palenque*

condition of the building, surrounded and overgrown by trees, but no description and no drawing can give effect to the moral sublimity of the spectacle. From the multiplicity of engravings required to illustrate the architecture and arts of this unknown people, I have omitted a series of views, exhibiting the most picturesque and striking subjects that ever presented themselves to the pencil of an artist. The ruins and the forest made a deep and abiding impression upon our minds; but our object was to present the building as restored, as subjects for speculation and comparison with the architecture of other lands and times. The supposed restorations were made after a careful examination, and in each case the reader will see precisely what we had to guide

us in making them. I must remark, however, that the buildings are the only parts which we attempted to restore; the
specimens of sculpture and stuccoed ornaments were drawn
as we found them.

The engraving (figure 25) represents the same building
(Casa No. 1) cleared from forest and restored. This engraving shows (beginning at the bottom), the ground-plan,
the front elevation, a section showing the position of tablets
within, and on a smaller scale, the front elevation with the
pyramidal structure on which it stands.

The building is seventy-six feet in front and twenty-five
feet deep. It has five doors and six piers, all standing. The
whole front is richly ornamented in stucco, and the corner
piers are covered with hieroglyphics, each of which contains
ninety-six squares. The four piers are ornamented with human figures, two piers on each side facing each other; the
figures are represented in the engravings (figures 26, 27, 28,
and 29).

The first (figure 26) is that of a woman with a child in her
arms; at least we supposed it to be intended for a woman
from the dress; the head is destroyed. It is enclosed by an
elaborate border and stands on a rich ornament. Over the
top are three hieroglyphics, and there are traces of hieroglyphics broken off in the corner. The other three (figures
27, 28, and 29) are of the same general character; each
probably had an infant in her arms, and over each are
hieroglyphics.

At the foot of the two center piers, resting on the steps,
are two stone tablets with what seemed interesting figures,
but they were so encumbered with ruins that it was impossible to draw them.

The interior of the building is divided into two corridors
running lengthwise, with a ceiling rising nearly to a point,
as in the palace, and paved with large square stones. The
front corridor is seven feet wide. The separating wall is very
massive, and has three doors, a large one in the center, and
a smaller one on each side. In this corridor, on each side of
the principal door, is a large tablet of hieroglyphics (figures
22 and 23 preceding page 275), each thirteen feet long and

eight feet high; each tablet is divided into two hundred and forty squares of characters or symbols. Both are set in the wall so as to project three or four inches. In one place a hole had been made in the wall close to the side of one of them, apparently for the purpose of attempting its removal; by means of this hole we discovered the stone to be about a foot thick. The tablets had been constructed by placing a large stone on each side, and smaller ones in the center, as indicated by the dark lines in the engravings. The sculpture is in bas-relief.

In the right-hand tablet (figure 22) one line is obliterated by water trickling down for an unknown length of time and forming a sort of stalactite, or hard substance, which has incorporated itself with the stone, and which we could not remove, though perhaps it might be detached by some chemical process. In the other tablet (figure 23), nearly one half of the hieroglyphics are obliterated by the action of water and the decomposition of the stone. When we first saw them, both tablets were covered with a thick coat of green moss, and it was necessary to wash and scrape them, clear the lines with a stick, and scrub them thoroughly, for which last operation a pair of blacking brushes that Juan had picked up in my house at Guatemala and disobeyed my order to throw away upon the road, proved exactly what we wanted and could not have been otherwise procured. On account of the darkness of the corridor from the thick shade of the trees growing before it, it was necessary to burn candles or torches, and to throw a strong light upon the stones while Mr. Catherwood was drawing.

The corridor in the rear is dark and gloomy, and divided into three apartments. Each of the side apartments has two narrow openings about three inches wide and a foot high. They have no remains of sculpture, or painting, or stuccoed ornaments. In the center apartment, set in the back wall and fronting the principal door of entrance, is another tablet of hieroglyphics (figure 17), four feet six inches wide and three feet six inches high. The roof above it is tight, consequently it has not suffered from exposure, and the hieroglyphics are

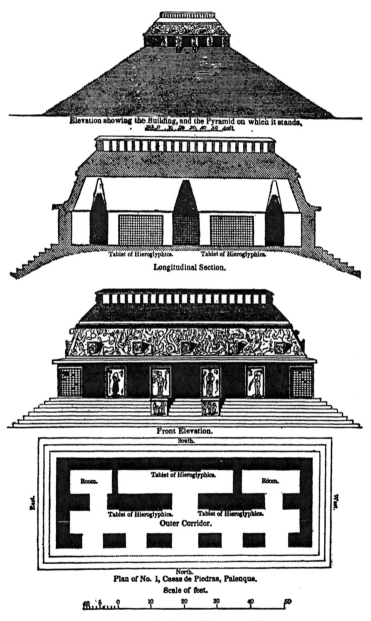

Elevation showing the Building, and the Pyramid on which it stands.

Longitudinal Section.

Tablet of Hieroglyphics.   Tablet of Hieroglyphics.

Front Elevation.

South.

Room.   Tablet of Hieroglyphics.   Room.

East.   West.

Tablet of Hieroglyphics.   Tablet of Hieroglyphics.

Outer Corridor.

North.

Plan of No. 1, Casas de Piedras, Palenque.

Scale of feet.

10 5 0   10   20   30   40   50

FIG. 25 *Plan of Casa No. 1 at Palenque*

perfect, though the stone is cracked lengthwise through the middle, as indicated in the engraving.

The impression made upon our minds by these speaking but unintelligible tablets I shall not attempt to describe. From some unaccountable cause they have never before been presented to the public. Captains del Río and Dupaix both refer to them, but in very few words, and neither of them has given a single drawing. Acting under a royal commission, and selected, doubtless, as fit men for the duties intrusted to them, they cannot have been ignorant or insensible of their value. It is my belief they did not give them because in both cases the artists attached to their expedition were incapable of the labor and the steady, determined perseverance required for drawing such complicated, unintelligible, and anomalous characters. As at Copán, Mr. Catherwood divided his paper into squares; the original drawings were reduced, and the engravings corrected by himself, and I believe they are as true copies as the pencil can make: the real written records of a lost people. The Indians call this building an *escuela*, or school, but our friends, the padres, called it a tribunal of justice, and these stones, they said, contained the tables of the law.

There is one important fact to be noticed. The hieroglyphics are the same as those found at Copán and Quiriguá. The intermediate country is now occupied by races of Indians speaking many different languages, entirely unintelligible to each other; but there is room for the belief that the whole of this country was once occupied by the same race, speaking the same language, or at least, having the same written characters.

There is no staircase or other visible communication between the lower and upper parts of this building, and the only way of reaching the latter was by climbing a tree which grows close against the wall, the branches of which spread over the roof. The roof is inclined, and the sides are covered with stucco ornaments, which, from exposure to the elements and the assaults of trees and bushes, are faded and ruined, so that it was impossible to draw them; but enough remained to give the impression that, when perfect and painted, they

FIG. 26 *Bas Relief in Stucco on Casa No. 1*

FIG. 27 *Bas Relief in Stucco on Casa No. 1*

FIG. 28 *Bas Relief in Stucco on Casa No. 1*

FIG. 29 *Bas Relief in Stucco on Casa No. 1*

must have been rich and imposing. Along the top was a range
of pillars eighteen inches high and twelve apart, made of
small pieces of stone laid in mortar and covered with stucco,
crowning which is a layer of flat projecting stones, having
somewhat the appearance of a low open balustrade.

In front of this building, at the foot of the pyramidal
structure, is a small stream, part of which supplies the
aqueduct before referred to. Crossing this, we come upon a
broken stone terrace about sixty feet on the slope with a level
esplanade at the top one hundred and ten feet in breadth,
from which rises another pyramidal structure, now ruined
and overgrown with trees; it is one hundred and thirty-four
feet high on the slope, and on its summit is a building (Casa
No. 2) which like the first is shrouded among trees, but
which is presented in the engraving as restored (figure 30).
The engraving contains, as before, the ground plan, front
elevation, section, and front elevation on a smaller scale,
with the pyramidal structure on which it stands.

This building is fifty feet front, thirty-one feet deep, and
has three doorways. The whole front was covered with
stuccoed ornaments. The two outer piers contain hieroglyphics; one of the inner piers is fallen, and the other is ornamented with a figure in bas-relief, but it is faded and ruined.

The interior, again, is divided into two corridors running
lengthwise, with ceilings as before, and pavements of large
square stones, in which forcible breaches have been made
(doubtless by Captain del Río) and excavations underneath.
The back corridor is divided into three apartments, and
opposite the principal door of entrance is an oblong enclosure, with a heavy cornice or moulding of stucco and a
doorway richly ornamented over the top, but now much
defaced; on each side of the doorway was a tablet of sculptured stone, which, however, has been removed. Within, the
chamber is thirteen feet wide and seven deep. There was
no admission of light except from the door; the sides were
without ornament, but in the back wall, covering the whole
width, was another tablet (figure 13 following page 274).
It was ten feet eight inches wide, six feet four inches in
height, and consisted of three separate stones. That on the

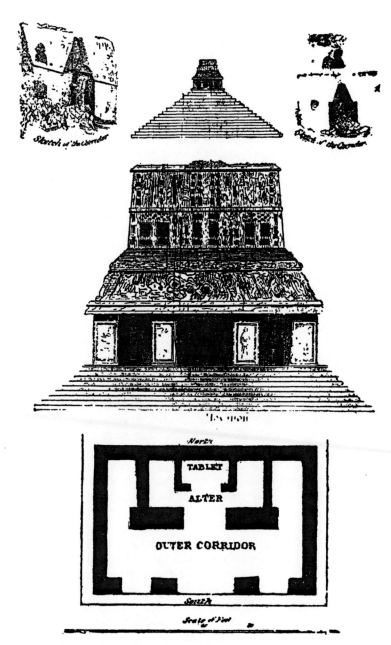

FIG. 30 *Plan and Elevation of Casa No. 2*

left, facing the spectator, is still in place. The middle one has been removed and carried down the side of the structure, and now lies near the bank of the stream. It was removed many years ago by one of the inhabitants of the village with the intention of carrying it to his house; but, after great labor, with no other instruments than the arms and hands of Indians, and poles cut from trees, it had only advanced so far when its removal was arrested by an order from the government forbidding any farther abstraction from the ruins. We found it lying on its back near the banks of the stream, washed by many floods of the rainy season and covered with a thick coat of dirt and moss. We had it scrubbed and propped up, and probably the next traveler will find it with the same props under it which we placed there. In the engraving it is given in its original position on the wall. The stone on the right is broken, and unfortunately altogether destroyed; most of the fragments have disappeared, but, from the few we found among the ruins in the front of the building, there is no doubt that it contained ranges of hieroglyphics corresponding in general appearance with those of the stone on the left.

The tablet, as given in the engraving, contains only two-thirds of the original. In del Río's work it is not represented at all. In Dupaix it is given, not, however, as it exists, but as made up by the artist in Paris, so as to present a perfect picture. The subject is reversed, with the cross in the center, and on each side a single row of hieroglyphics, only eight in number. Probably, when Dupaix saw it (thirty-four years before), it was entire, but the important features of six rows of hieroglyphics on each side of the principal figures, each row containing seventeen in a line, do not appear. This is the more inexcusable in his publishers, as in his report Dupaix expressly refers to these numerous hieroglyphics; but it is probable that his report was not accompanied by any drawings of them.

The principal subject of this tablet is the cross. It is surmounted by a strange bird, and loaded with indescribable ornaments. The two figures are evidently those of important personages. They are well drawn, and in symmetry of proportion are perhaps equal to many that are carved on the walls of the ruined temples in Egypt. Their costume is in a style different from any heretofore given, and the folds would seem to indicate that they were of a soft and pliable texture like cotton. Both are looking toward the cross, and one seems in the act of making an offering, perhaps of a child; all speculations on the subject are of course entitled to little regard, but perhaps it would not be wrong to ascribe to these personages a sacerdotal character. The hieroglyphics doubtless explain all. Near them are other hieroglyphics, which reminded us of the Egyptian mode for recording the name, history, office, or character of the persons represented.

This tablet of the cross has given rise to more learned speculations than perhaps any others found at Palenque. Dupaix and his commentators, assuming for the building a very remote antiquity, or, at least, a period long antecedent to the Christian era, account for the appearance of the cross by the argument that it was known and had a symbolical meaning among ancient nations long before it was established as the emblem of the Christian faith. Our friends the padres, at the sight of it, immediately decided that the old inhabitants of Palenque were Christians, and by conclusions which are sometimes called jumping, they fixed the age of the buildings in the third century.

There is reason to believe that this particular building was intended as a temple, and that the enclosed inner chamber was an *adoratorio*, or oratory, or altar. What the rites and ceremonies of worship may have been, no one can undertake to say.

The upper part of this building differs from the first. As before, there was no staircase or other communication inside or out, nor were there the remains of any. The only mode of access was, in like manner, by climbing a tree, the branches of which spread across the roof. The roof was inclined, and the sides were richly ornamented with stucco figures, plants, and flowers, but mostly ruined. Among them were the fragments of a beautiful head and of two bodies, in justness of proportion and symmetry approaching the Greek models. On the top of this roof is a narrow platform, supporting what, for the sake of description, I shall call two stories. The platform is but two feet ten inches wide, and the super-structure of the first story is seven feet five inches in height, that of the second eight feet five inches, the width of the two being the same. The ascent from one to the other is by square projecting stones; the covering of the upper story is of flat stones laid across and projecting over. The long sides of this narrow structure are of open stucco work formed into curious and indescribable devices, human figures with legs and arms spreading and apertures between; and the whole was once loaded with rich and elegant ornaments in stucco relief. Its appearance at a distance must have been that of a high, fanciful lattice. Altogether, like the rest of the architecture and ornaments, it was perfectly unique, dif-ferent from the works of any other people with which we were familiar, and its uses and purposes entirely incompre-hensible. Perhaps it was intended as an observatory. From the upper gallery, through openings in the trees growing around, we looked out over an immense forest, and saw the Lake of Términos and the Gulf of Mexico.

Near this building was another interesting monument, which had been entirely overlooked by those who preceded us in a visit to Palenque, and I mention this fact in the hope that the next visitor may discover many things omitted by us. It lies in front of the building, about forty or fifty feet down the side of the pyramidal structure. When we first passed it with our guide it lay on its face with its head down-ward, and it was half buried by an accumulation of earth and stones. The outer side was rough and unhewn, and our at-tention was attracted by its size; our guide said it was not sculptured, but, after he had shown us everything that he had knowledge of and we had discharged him, in passing it again we stopped and dug around it and discovered that the under surface was carved. The Indians cut down some saplings for levers, and rolled it over. It is the only statue (figure 31) that has ever been found at Palenque. We were at once struck with its expression of serene repose and its strong resemblance to Egyptian statues, though in size it does not compare with the gigantic remains of Egypt. In

Stone Statue in front of Casa No. 2.

Scale of feet.

Scale for the small Figure.

FIG. 31 *Stone Statue in Front of Casa No. 2*

height it is ten feet six inches, of which two feet six inches were under ground. The headdress is lofty and spreading; there are holes in the place of ears, which were perhaps adorned with earrings of gold and pearls. Round the neck is a necklace, and pressed against the breast by the right hand is an instrument apparently with teeth. The left hand rests on a hieroglyphic, from which descends some symbolical ornament. The lower part of the dress bears an unfortunate resemblance to the modern pantaloons, but the figure stands on what we have always considered a hieroglyphic, analogous again to the custom in Egypt of recording the name and office of the hero or other person represented. The sides are rounded, and the back is of rough stone. Probably it stood imbedded in a wall.

From the foot of the elevation on which the last-mentioned building stands, their bases almost touching, rises another pyramidal structure of about the same height, on the top of which is another building (Casa No. 3). Such is the density of the forest, that even on the sides of the pyramidal structure, though in a right line but a short distance apart, one of these buildings cannot be seen from the other.

Figure 16 (following page 274) shows this building as restored, not from any fancied idea of what it might have been, but from such remains and indications that it was impossible to make anything else of it. It is thirty-eight feet front and twenty-eight feet deep, and has three doors. The end piers are ornamented with hieroglyphics in stucco, two large medallions in handsome compartments, and the intermediate ones with bas-reliefs, also in stucco; they were in general character similar to those before given, and for that reason, not to multiply engravings, I omit them.

The interior, again, is divided into two corridors, about nine feet wide each, and paved with stone. The engraving (figure 32) represents the front corridor, with the ceiling rising nearly to a point and covered at the top with a layer of flat stones. In several places on each side are holes, which are found also in all the other corridors; they were probably used to support poles for scaffolding while the building was in process of erection and had never been filled up. At the

FIG. 32 *Front Corridor, Casa No. 3*

extreme end, cut through the wall, is one of the windows before referred to, which have been the subject of speculation from analogy to the letter Tau.

The back corridor is divided into three apartments. In the center, facing the principal door of entrance, is an enclosed chamber similar to that which in the last building we called an oratory, or altar. Its shadow is seen in the engraving. The top of the doorway was gorgeous with stuccoed ornaments, and on the piers at each side were stone tablets in bas-relief. Within, the chamber was four feet seven inches deep and nine feet wide. There were no stuccoed ornaments or paintings, but set in the back wall was a stone tablet (figure 20 following page 274) covering the whole width of the chamber, nine feet wide and eight feet high.

I beg to call this tablet to the particular attention of the reader as the most perfect and the most interesting monument in Palenque. Neither Captain del Río nor Captain Dupaix has given any drawing of it, and it is now for the first time presented to the public. It is composed of three separate stones, the joints of which are shown by the blurred lines in the engraving. The sculpture is perfect, and the characters and figures stand clear and distinct on the stone. On each side are rows of hieroglyphics. The principal personages will be recognized at once as the same who are represented in the tablet of the cross. They wear the same dress, but here both seem to be making offerings. Both personages stand on the backs of human beings; one supports himself by his hands and knees, and the other seems crushed to the ground by the weight. Between them, at the foot of the tablet, are two figures, sitting cross-legged, one bracing himself with his right hand on the ground, and with the left supporting a square table; the attitude and action of the other are the same, except that they are in reverse order. The table also rests upon their bended necks, and their distorted countenances may perhaps be considered expressions of pain and suffering. They are both clothed in leopard skins. Upon this table rest two batons crossed, their upper extremities richly ornamented, supporting what seems to be a hideous mask, the eyes widely expanded and the tongue hanging out. This seems to be the object to which principal personages are making offerings.

The piers on each side of the doorway each contained a stone tablet, with figures carved in bas-relief (figures 19 and 21 following page 274). These tablets, however, have been removed from their place to the village, and set up in the wall of a house as ornaments. They were the first objects which we saw, and the last which Mr. Catherwood drew. The house belonged to two sisters, who had an exaggerated idea of the value of these tablets; though always pleased with our coming to see them, they made objections to having them copied. We obtained permission only by promising a copy for them also, which, however, Mr. Catherwood, worn out with constant labor, was entirely unable to make. I cut out of del Río's book the drawings of the same subjects, which I thought, being printed, would please them better; but they had examined Mr. Catherwood's drawing in its progress and were not at all satisfied with the substitute. The moment I saw these tablets I formed the idea of purchasing them and carrying them home as a sample of Palenque, but it was some time before I ventured to broach the subject. They could not be purchased without the house, but that was no impediment, for I liked the house also. It was afterward included among the subjects of other negotiations which were undetermined when I left Palenque.

The two figures stand facing each other, the first on the right hand, fronting the spectator. The nose and eyes are strongly marked, but altogether the development is not so strange as to indicate a race entirely different from those which are known. The headdress is curious and complicated, consisting principally of leaves of plants with a large flower hanging down; and among the ornaments are distinguished the beak and eyes of a bird, and a tortoise. The cloak is a leopard's skin, and the figure has ruffles around the wrists and ankles.

The second figure, standing on the left of the spectator, has the same profile which characterizes all the others at Palenque. Its headdress is composed of a plume of feathers, in which is a bird holding a fish in its mouth; and in different parts of the headdress there are three other fishes. The figure wears a richly embroidered tippet and a broad girdle with the head of some animal in front, sandals, and leggings: the right hand is extended in a prayerful or deprecating position, with the palm outward. Over the heads of these mysterious personages are three cabalistic hieroglyphics.

We considered the *oratorio*, or altar, the most interesting portion of the ruins of Palenque; in order that the reader may understand it in all its details, figure 18 (following page 274) is presented, showing distinctly all the combinations of the doorway, with its broken ornaments and the tablets on each side; within the doorway is seen a large tablet on the back of the inner wall. The reader will form from this drawing some idea of the whole and of its effect upon the stranger, when, as he climbs up the ruined pyramidal structure, on the threshold of the door this scene presents itself. We could not but regard it as a holy place, dedicated to the gods and consecrated by the religious observances of a lost and unknown people. Comparatively, the hand of ruin has spared it, and the great tablet, surviving the wreck of elements, stands perfect and entire. Lonely, deserted, and without any worshippers at its shrine, the figures and characters are as distinct as when the people who reared it went up to pay their adorations before it. To us it was all a mystery, silent and defying the most scrutinizing gaze and reach of intellect. Even our friends the padres could make nothing of it.

Near this, on the top of another pyramidal structure, was another building entirely in ruins, which apparently had been shattered and hurled down by an earthquake. The stones were strewed on the side of the pyramid, and it was impossible even to make out the ground plan.

Returning to Casa No. 1 and proceeding south, at a distance of fifteen hundred feet, and on a pyramidal structure one hundred feet high from the bank of the river, is another building (Casa No. 4), twenty feet front and eighteen feet deep, but in an unfortunately ruined condition. The whole of the front wall has fallen, leaving the outer corridor entirely exposed. Fronting the door, and against the back wall of the inner corridor, was a large stucco ornament representing a figure sitting on a couch; but a great part had fallen or been taken off and carried away. The body of the couch, with tiger's feet, is all that now remains. The outline of two tiger's heads and of the sitting personage is seen on the wall. The loss or destruction of this ornament is more to be regretted, as from what remains it appears to have been superior in execution to any other stucco relief in Palenque. The body of the couch is entire, and the leg and foot hanging down the side are elegant specimens of art and models for study. Figure 33 (following page 354) represents this relief, and also a plan, section, and general view of the building.

I have now given, without speculation or comment, a full description of the ruins of Palenque. I repeat what I stated in the beginning, there may be more buildings, but after a close examination of the vague reports current in the village, we are satisfied that no more have ever been discovered; and from repeated inquiries of Indians who have traversed the forest in every direction in the dry season, we are induced to believe that no more exist. The whole extent of ground covered by those as yet known is not larger than our Park or Battery. In stating this fact I am very far from wishing to detract from the importance or interest of the subject. I give our opinion, with the grounds for it, and the reader will judge for himself how far these are entitled to consideration. It is proper to add, however, that, considering the space now occupied by the ruins as the site of palaces, temples, and public buildings, and supposing the houses of the inhabitants to have been, like those of the Egyptians and the present race of Indians, of frail and perishable materials and, as at Memphis and Thebes, to have disappeared altogether, the city may have covered an immense extent.

The reader is perhaps disappointed, but we were not. There was no necessity for assigning to the ruined city an immense extent, or an antiquity coeval with that of the Egyptians or of any other ancient and known people. What we had before our eyes was grand, curious, and remarkable enough. Here were the remains of a cultivated, polished, and peculiar people, who had passed through all the stages incident to the rise and fall of nations, had reached their golden age, and had perished, entirely unknown. The links connecting them with the human family were severed and lost; these were the only memorials of their footsteps upon earth. We lived in the ruined palace of their kings; we went up to their desolate temples and fallen altars; and wherever we moved we saw evidences of their taste, their skill in arts, their wealth and power. In the midst of desolation and ruin we looked back to the past, cleared away the gloomy forest, and fancied every building perfect, with its terraces and pyramids, its sculptured and painted ornaments, grand, lofty, and imposing, and overlooking an immense inhabited plain. We called back into life the strange people who gazed at us in sadness from the walls; pictured them, in fanciful costumes and adorned with plumes of feathers, ascending the terraces of the palace and the steps leading to the temples. Often we imagined a scene of unique and gorgeous beauty and magnificence, realizing the creations of oriental poets, the very spot which fancy would have selected for the "Happy Valley" [2] of Rasselas. In the romance of the world's history nothing ever impressed me more forcibly than the spectacle of this once great and lovely city, overturned, desolate, and lost; discovered by accident, overgrown with trees for miles around, it did not have even a name to distinguish it. Apart from everything else, it was a mourning witness to the world's mutations.

Nations melt
From Power's high pinnacle, when they have felt
The sunshine for a while, and downward go.

As at Copán, I shall not at present offer any conjecture in regard to the antiquity of these buildings, merely remarking that at ten leagues' distance is a village called Las Tres Cruces, or the Three Crosses, from three crosses which, according to tradition, Cortes erected at that place when on his conquering march from Mexico to Honduras by the Lake of Petén. Cortes, then, must have passed within twenty

2. The "Happy Valley" was a natural paradise described in Dr. Samuel Johnson's oriental romance *Rasselas.*

or thirty miles of the place now called Palenque. If it had been a living city, its fame must have reached his ears, and he would probably have turned aside from his road to subdue and plunder it. It seems, therefore, but reasonable to suppose that it was at that time desolate and in ruins, and even the memory of it lost.

Chapter XXI

~~~~~~

*Departure from the ruins. Bad road. An accident. Arrival
at the village. A funeral procession. Negotiations for pur-
chasing Palenque. Making casts. Final departure from
Palenque. Beautiful plain. Hanging birds' nests. A sitio.
Adventure with a monstrous ape. Hospitality of padres.
Las Playas. A tempest. Mosquitoes. A youthful merchant.
Alligators. Another funeral.
Disgusting ceremonials.*

AMONG the Indians who came out to escort us to the
village was one whom we had not seen before, and
whose face bore a striking resemblance to those delineated
on the walls of the buildings. In general, the faces of the Indians were of an entirely different character, but this one
might have been taken for a lineal descendant of the perished race. The resemblance was perhaps purely accidental,
but we were anxious to procure his portrait. He was, however, very shy, and unwilling to be drawn. Mr. Catherwood,
too, was worn out, and in the confusion of removing we
postponed it upon his promising to come to us at the village,
but we could not get hold of him again.

We left behind our kitchen furniture, consisting of the
three stones which Juan put together the first day of our
residence, vessels of pottery and calabashes, and also our
beds, for the benefit of the next comer. Everything susceptible of injury from damp was rusty or mouldy and in a
ruinous condition; we ourselves were not much better. With
the clothes on our backs far from dry, we bade farewell to
the ruins. We had been happy when we reached them, but
our joy at leaving them burst the bounds of discretion and

broke out into extravagances poetical, which, however, fortunately for the reader, did not advance much beyond the first line:

Adiós, Las Casas de Piedra.

The road was worse than at any time before; the streams were swollen into rivers, and along the banks were steep, narrow gullies, very difficult to pass. At one of these, after attempting to ascend with my macho, I dismounted. Mr. Catherwood was so weak that he remained on the back of his mule; and after he had crossed, just as he reached the top, the mule's strength gave way and she fell backward, rolling over in the stream with Mr. Catherwood entirely under. Pawling was behind and at that time in the stream. He sprang off and extricated Mr. Catherwood, unhurt, but very faint; as he was obliged to ride in his wet clothes, we had great apprehensions for him. At length we reached the village, when, exhausted by hard and unintermitted labor, he gave up completely and took to bed and the medicine chest. In the evening nearly all my friends of the dinner party came to see us. That one day had established an intimacy. All regretted that we had had such an unfortunate time at the ruins, wondered how we had lived through it, and were most kind in offers of services. The padre remained after the rest, and went home with a lantern in the midst of one of those dreadful storms which had almost terrified us at the ruins.

The next day again was Sunday. It was my third Sunday in the village, and again it was emphatically a day of rest. In the afternoon a mournful interruption was given to the stillness of the place by the funeral of a young Indian girl, once the pride and beauty of the village, whose portrait Mr. Waldeck had taken to embellish his intended work on Palenque. Her career, as often happens with beauty in higher life, was short, brilliant, and unhappy. She married a young Indian who abandoned her and went to another village. Ignorant, innocent, and unconscious of wrong, she was persuaded to marry another, and soon after she drooped and died. The funeral procession passed our door. The corpse was borne on a rude bier, without coffin, in a white cotton dress with a shawl over the head, and was followed by a slender procession of women and children only. I walked beside it, and heard one of them say, *"buen cristiano,* to attend the funeral of a poor woman." The bier was set down beside the grave, and in lifting the body from it the head turned on one side and the hands dropped: the grave was too short, and as the dead was laid within, the legs were drawn up. Her face was thin and wasted, but the mouth had a sweetness of expression which seemed to express that she had died with a smile of forgiveness for him who had injured her.

I could not turn my eyes from her placid but grief-worn countenance, and so touching was its expression that I could almost have shed tears. Young, beautiful, simple, and innocent, abandoned and dead, with not a mourner at her grave. All seemed to think that she was better dead: she was poor and could not maintain herself. The men went away, and the women and children with their hands scraped the earth upon the body. It was covered up gradually and slowly; the feet stuck out, and then all was buried but the face. A small piece of muddy earth fell upon one of the eyes, and another on her sweetly smiling mouth, changing the whole expression in a moment; death was now robed with terror. The women stopped to comment upon the change; then the dirt fell so as to cover the whole face except the nose, and for two or three moments this alone was visible. Another brush covered this, and the girl was buried. The reader will excuse me. I am sorry to say that if she had been ugly, I should, perhaps, have regarded it as an everyday case of a wife neglected by her husband; but her sweet face speaking from the grave created an impression which even yet is hardly effaced.

But to return to things more in my line. We had another long journey before us; our next move was for Yucatán. From Mr. Catherwood's condition I had great fear that we would not be able to accomplish what we purposed; but, at all events, it was necessary to go down to the seacoast. There were two routes, either by Tabasco or the Laguna, to Campeche, and war again confronted us. Both Tabasco and Campeche were besieged by the Liberals, or, as they were called, the Revolutionists. The former route required three days' journey by land, the latter one short day; as Mr. Catherwood was not able to ride, we determined to take the latter. In the meantime, while waiting for his recovery, and so as not to rust and be utterly useless when I returned home, I started another operation, that is, the purchase of the city of Palenque. I am bound to say, however, that I was not bold enough to originate this, I fell into it accidentally in a long conversation with the prefect about the richness of the soil, the cheapness of land, its vicinity to the seaboard and the United States, and the easy communication with New York. He told me that a merchant of Tabasco, who had visited the place, had proposed to purchase a tract of land and establish a colony of emigrants, but that he had gone away and never returned. He added, that for two years a government order from the State of Chiapas, to which the region belonged, had been lying in his hands for the sale of all land in the vicinity lying within certain limits; but there had been no purchasers and no sales had ever been made. Upon inquiry I learned that this order, in its terms, embraced the ground occupied by the ruined city. No exception whatever was made in favor of it. He showed me the order, which was imperative; and he said that if any exception was intended, it would have been so expressed; wherefore he considered himself bound to receive an offer for any portion of the land. The sale was directed to be by appraisement, the applicant to name one man, the prefect another, and, if necessary, they two to name a third; and the application, with the price fixed and the boundaries, was to be sent to Ciudad Real for the approval of the governor and for a deed.

The tract containing the ruins consisted of about six thousand acres of good land, which, according to the usual appraisement, would cost about fifteen hundred dollars; and the prefect said that it would not be valued a cent higher because of the ruins. I resolved immediately to buy it. I would fit up the palace and repeople the old city of Palenque. But there was one difficulty: by the laws of Mexico no stranger can purchase lands unless married to a *hija del país,* or daughter of the country. This, by the way, is a grand stroke of policy, holding up the most powerful attraction of the country to seduce men from their natural allegiance and radicate them in the soil. And it is taking them where weak and vulnerable, for, when wandering in strange countries, alone and friendless, buffeted and battered, with no one to care for him, there are moments when a lovely woman might root the stranger to any spot on earth. On principal I always resisted such tendencies, but I never before found it to my interest to give way. The ruined city of Palenque was a most desirable piece of property.

The case was embarrassing and complicated. Society in Palenque was small; the oldest young lady was not more than fourteen, and the prettiest woman, who already had contributed most to our happiness (she made our cigars), was already married. The house containing the two tablets belonged to a widow lady and a single sister, good-looking, amiable, and both about forty. The house was one of the neatest in the place. I always liked to visit it, and had before thought that, if passing a year at the ruins, it would be delightful to have this house in the village for recreation and occasional visits. With either of these ladies would come possession of the house and the stone tablets; but the difficulty was that there were two of them, both equally interesting and equally interested. I am particular in mentioning these little circumstances, to show the difficulties that attended every step of our enterprise in that country. There was an alternative, and that was to purchase in the name of some other person, but I did not know of anyone I could trust.

At length, however, I hit upon Mr. Russell, the American consul at Laguna,[1] who was married to a Spanish lady, and already had large possessions in the country; and I arranged with the prefect to make the purchase in his name. Pawling

---

1. Ciudad del Carmen, situated on the island of Carmen in the Lake of Términos. In several instances in the following pages, Stephens speaks of this town by the name Laguna.

was to accompany me to the Laguna, for the purpose of procuring and carrying back evidence of Mr. Russell's cooperation and the necessary funds, and he was to act as my agent in completing the purchase. The prefect was personally anxious to complete it. The buildings, he said, were fast going to decay and, in a few years, more of them would be mounds of ruins. In that country they were not appreciated or understood, and he had the liberal wish that the tablets of hieroglyphics particularly might find their way to other countries, to be inspected and studied by scientific men, and their origin and history ascertained. Besides, he had an idea that immense discoveries were still to be made and that treasures were still to be found, and he was anxious for a thorough exploration in which he would himself co-operate. The two tablets which I had attempted to purchase were highly prized by the owners, but he thought they could be secured by purchasing the house, so I authorized him to buy it at a fixed price.

In my many conversations with the prefect I had broached the subject of making casts from the tablets. Like every other official whom I met, he supposed that I was acting under a commission from my government, which idea was sustained by having in my employ a man of such character and appearance as Pawling, though every time I put my hand in my pocket I had a feeling sense that the case was far otherwise. In the matter of casts he offered every assistance, but there was no plaster of Paris nearer than Laguna or Campeche, and perhaps not there. We had made an experiment at the ruins by catching in the river a large quantity of snails and burning the shells, but it did not answer. He referred us to some limestone in the neighborhood, but this also would not do. Pawling knew nothing of casting. The idea had never entered his mind before, but he was willing to undertake the task. Mr. Catherwood, who had been shut up in Athens during the Greek Revolution when it was besieged by the Turks, and who in pursuing his artistical studies had perforce made castings with his own hands, gave him written instructions, and it was agreed that when he returned with the credentials from Mr. Russell he would bring back plaster of Paris, and, while the proceedings for completing the purchase were pending, he would occupy himself in this new branch of business.

On the fourth of June we took our final departure from Palenque. Don Santiago sent me a farewell letter, enclosing, according to the custom of the country, a piece of silk, the meaning of which I did not understand at first, but learned it was meant as a pledge of friendship, and I reciprocated with a penknife. The prefect was kind and courteous to the last; even the old alcalde, drawing a little daily revenue from us, was touched. Every male inhabitant came to the house to bid us farewell and wish us to return; and before starting we rode around and exchanged *adiós* with all their wives: good, kind, and quiet people, free from all agitating cares, and aiming only at an undisturbed existence in a place which I had been induced to believe the abode of savages and full of danger.

In order to accompany us, the cura had postponed for two days a visit to his hacienda, which lay on our road. Pawling continued with us for the purpose before mentioned, and Juan according to contract: I had agreed to return him to Guatemala. Completely among strangers, he was absolutely in our power, and following blindly, but with great misgivings he asked the padre where we were taking him. His impression was that he was setting out for my country, and he had but little hope of ever seeing Guatemala again.

From the village we entered immediately upon a beautiful plain, picturesque, ornamented with trees, and extending five or six days' journey to the Gulf of Mexico. The road was very muddy, but, being open to the sun in the morning, was not so bad as we feared. On the borders of a piece of woodland were singular trees, with a tall trunk, the bark very smooth and the branches festooned with hanging birds' nests. The bird was called the *jagua*,[2] and had built his nest in this tree, as the padre told us, to prevent serpents from

---

2. In the state of Oaxaca, at least, *jagua* is the local name of the royal palm. Stephens must have mistaken the name of a tree for that of a bird.

getting at the young. The cura, notwithstanding his strange figure and a life of incident and danger, was almost a woman in voice, manner, tastes, and feelings. He had been educated at the capital, and been sent as a penance to this retired curacy. The visit of the padres had for the first time broken the monotony of his life. In the political convulsions of the capital he had made himself obnoxious to the church government by his liberal opinions. Unable, as he said, to find in him any tangible offence, his superiors had called him up on a charge of polluting the surplice, founded on the circumstance that, in the time of the cholera, when his fellow creatures were lying all around him in the agonies of death, in leaning over their bodies to administer the sacrament, his surplice had been soiled by saliva from the mouth of a dying man. For this he was condemned to penance and prayers from midnight till daybreak for two years in the cathedral, and was deprived of a good curacy and sent to Palenque.

At half past two we reached his *sitio*, or small hacienda. In the apprehension of the afternoon's rain we would have continued to the end of our afternoon's journey; but the padre watched carefully the appearance of the sky, and, after satisfying himself that the rain would not come on till late, positively forbade our passing on. His *sitio* was what would be called at home a "new" place, being a tract of wild land of I do not know what extent, but some large quantity, which had cost him twenty-five dollars; it had cost about as much more to make the improvements, which consisted of a hut made of poles and thatched with corn-husks, and a *cocina*, or kitchen, at a little distance. The stables and outhouses were in a clearing bounded by a forest so thick that cattle could not penetrate it, and on the roadside by a rude fence. Altogether, in that mild climate the effect was good; and it was one of those occasions which make a man feel, away from the region of fictitious wants, how little is necessary for the comforts of life. The furniture of the hut consisted of two reed bedsteads, a table, and a bench, and in one corner was a pile of corn.

The cura sent out for half a dozen fresh pineapples; while we were refreshing ourselves with them we heard an extraordinary noise in the woods, which an Indian boy told us was made by *un animal*. Pawling and I took our guns and entered a path in the woods; as we advanced the noise sounded fearful, but all at once it stopped. The boy opened a way through thickets of brush and underwood, and through an opening in the branches I saw on the limbs of a high tree a large black animal with fiery eyes. The boy said it was not a *mico*, or monkey, but I supposed it to be a catamount. Having barely an opening through which to take aim, I fired, and the animal dropped below the range of view; but, not hearing him strike the ground, I looked again and saw him hanging by his tail, dead, with the blood streaming from his mouth. Pawling attempted to climb the tree; but it was fifty feet to the first branch, and the blood trickled down the trunk. Wishing to examine the creature more closely, we sent the boy to the house for a couple of Indians. They cut down the tree, which fell with a terrible crash, and still the animal hung by its tail. The ball had hit him in the mouth and knocked out the fore teeth, and then passed out at the top of his back between his shoulders; it must have killed him instantly. The tenacity of his tail seemed marvelous, but was easily explained. It had no grip, and had lost all muscular power, but was wound round the branch with the end under, so that the weight of the body tightened the coil, and the harder the strain, the more secure was the hold. It was not a monkey, but so near a connection that I would not have shot him if I had known it. In face, he was even more nearly related to the human family. He was a *mono*, or ape, and measured six feet including the tail; very muscular, in a struggle he would have been more than a match for a man; and the padre said they were known to have attacked women. The Indians carried him up to the house, and skinned him; and when he was lying on his back, with his skin off and his eyes staring, the padre cried out, *es hombre* (it is a man) and I almost felt liable to an indictment for homicide. The Indians cooked the body, and I contrived to preserve the skin as a curiosity, for its extraordinary size; but, unluckily, I left it on board a Spanish vessel at sea.

In the meantime the padre had a fowl boiled for dinner. Three guests at a time were not too much for his open hospitality, but they went beyond his dinner service, which consisted of three bowls. There was no plate, knife, fork, or spoon, and for the cura himself not even a bowl. The fowl was served in an ocean of broth, which had to be disposed of first. Tortillas and a small cake of fresh cheese composed the rest of the meal. The reader will perhaps connect such an entertainment with vulgarity of manners; but the curate was a gentleman and made no apologies, for he gave us the best he had. We had sent our carriers on before, the padre gave us a servant as a guide, and at three o'clock we bade him farewell. He was the last padre whom we met, and put a seal upon the kindness we had received from all the padres of that country.

At five o'clock, by a muddy road through a picturesque country remarkable only for swarms of butterflies with large yellow wings which filled the air, we reached Las Playas.[3] This village is the head of navigation of the waters that empty in this direction into the Gulf of Mexico. The whole of the great plain to the sea is intersected by creeks and rivers, some of which, although dry in summer, on the rising of the waters overflow their banks. At this season the plain on one side of the village was inundated, and seemed a large lake. The village was a small collection of huts upon what might be called its banks. It consisted of one street or road, grass-grown and still as at Palenque, at the extreme end of which was the church, under the pastoral care of our friend the padre. Our guide, according to the directions of the padre, conducted us to the convent and engaged the sexton to provide us with supper. The convent was built of upright sticks, with a thatched roof and mud floor, and was furnished with three reed bedsteads and a table.

At this place we were to embark in a canoe, and we had sent a courier the day before with a letter from the prefect to the *justicia*, to have one ready for us. The *justicia* was a portly mulatto, well dressed and very civil, who had a canoe of his own for which he promised to procure us two *bogadores*, or rowers, in the morning. Very soon the mosquitoes made alarming demonstrations, and gave us apprehensions of a fearful night. To make a show of resistance, we built a

3. The editor was unable to identify this village. Probably it has disappeared or changed its name.

large fire in the middle of the convent. At night the storm
came on with a high wind, which made it necessary to close
the doors. For two hours we had a tempest of wind and rain,
with terrific thunder and lightning. One blast burst open the
door and scattered the fire, so that it came very near burning
down the convent. Between the smoke and mosquitoes, it was
a matter of debate which to choose: suffocation or torture.
We preferred the former, but we had the latter also, and
passed a miserable night.

The next morning the *justicia* came to say that the *bogadores* were not ready and could not go that day. The price
which he named was about twice as much as the cura told us
we ought to pay, and it was in addition to the cost of *pozol*
(balls of mashed Indian corn), tortillas, honey, and meat.
I remonstrated, and he went off to consult the *mozos*, but
returned to say that they would not take less, and after treat-
ing him with but little of the respect due to office, I was
obliged to accede; but I ought to add that throughout that
country prices in general were fixed, and that there was less
advantage taken of the necessity of travelers than in most
others. We were loth to remain, for, besides the loss of time
and the mosquitoes, the scarcity of provisions was greater
than at Palenque.

The sexton bought us some corn and his wife made us
tortillas. The principal merchant in the place, or, at least, the
one who traded most largely with us, was a little boy about
twelve years old, who was dressed in a *petate*,[4] or straw hat.
He had brought us some fruit, and we saw him coming again
with a string over his naked shoulder, dragging on the
ground what proved to be a large fish. The principal food
of the place was young alligators. They were about a foot
and a half long, and at that youthful time of life they were
considered very tender. At their first appearance on the table
they had not an inviting aspect, but *ce n'est que le premier
pas qui coûte*, they tasted better than the fish, and they were
the best food possible for our canoe voyage, being dried and
capable of preservation.

Go where we will, to the uttermost parts of the earth, we
are sure to meet one acquaintance: death is always with us.

4. See note 3, p. 136.

In the afternoon was the funeral of a child. The procession consisted of eight or ten grown persons, and as many boys and girls. The sexton carried the child in his arms; it was dressed in white with a wreath of flowers around its head. All were huddled around the sexton, walking together, the father and mother with him; and even more than in Costa Rica I remarked, not only an absence of solemnity, but cheerfulness and actual gaiety, from the same happy conviction that the child had gone to a better world. I happened to be in the church as they approached; it was more like a wedding than a burial party. The floor of the church was earthen and the grave was dug inside, because, as the sexton told me, the father was rich and could afford to pay for it; the father seemed pleased and proud that he could give his child such a burial place. The sexton laid the child in the grave and folded its little hands across its breast, placing there a small rude cross; he covered it over with eight or ten inches of earth and then got into the grave and stamped it down with his feet. After throwing in more earth, he went outside of the church, and brought back a pounder, being a log of wood about four feet long and ten inches in diameter, like the rammer used among us by paviors. Again taking his place in the grave, he threw up the pounder to the full swing of his arm and brought it down with all his strength over the head of the child. My blood ran cold. As he threw it up a second time I caught his arm and remonstrated with him, but he said that they always did so with those buried inside the church; that the earth must be all put back, and the floor of the church made even. My remonstrances seemed only to give him more strength and spirit. The sweat rolled down his body, and when perfectly tired with pounding he stepped out of the grave. But this was nothing. More earth was thrown in, and the father laid down his hat, stepped into the grave, and the pounder was handed to him. I saw him throw it up twice and bring it down with a dead, heavy noise. I never beheld a more brutal and disgusting scene. The child's body must have been crushed to atoms.

Toward evening the mosquitoes began their operations. Pawling and Juan planted sticks in the ground outside the convent and spread sheets over them for nets; but the rain came on and drove them within, and we passed another wretched night. It may be asked how the inhabitants live. I cannot answer. They seemed to suffer as much as we, but at home they could have conveniences which we could not carry in traveling. Pawling suffered so much, and heard such dreadful accounts of what we would meet with below, that in a spirit of impetuosity and irritation he resolved not to continue any further. From the difficulty and uncertainty of communications, however, I strongly apprehended that in such case all the schemes in which he was concerned must fall through and be abandoned, as I was not willing to incur the expense of sending materials, subject to delays and uncertainties, unless in special charge, and once more he changed his purpose.

I had but one leave-taking, and that was a trying one. I was to bid farewell to my noble macho. He had carried me more than two thousand miles over the worst roads that mule ever traveled. He stood tied to the door of the convent and saw the luggage, even his own saddle, carried away by hand; he seemed to have a presentiment that something unusual was going on. I had often been solicited to sell him, but no money could have tempted me. He was in poorer condition than when we reached Palenque. Deprived of corn and exposed to the dreadful rains, he was worse than when worked hard and fed well every day; in his drooping state he seemed to reproach me for going away and leaving him forlorn. I threw my arms around his neck; his eyes had a mournful expression, and at that moment he forgot the angry prick of the spur. I laid aside the memory of a toss from his back and ineffectual attempts to repeat it, and we remembered only mutual kind offices and good-fellowship. Tried and faithful companion, where are you now? I left him, with two others, tied at the door of the convent, to be taken by the sexton to the prefect at Palenque, there to recover from the debilitating influence of the early rains, and to roam on rich pasture grounds, untouched by bridle or spur, until I should return to mount him again.

Chapter XXII

~~~~~~

Embarkation. An inundated plain. Río Chico. The Usu-
macinta. Río Palizada. Yucatán. More revolutions. Ves-
pers. Embarkation for the Laguna. Shooting alligators.
Tremendous storm. Boca Chica. Lake of Términos. A
calm succeeded by a tempest.
Arrival at Laguna.

AT seven o'clock we went down to the shore to embark.
The boatmen whom the justice had consulted, and
for whom he had been so tenacious, were His Honor himself
and another man, who, we thought, was hired as the cheap-
est help he could find in the village. The canoe was about
forty feet long, with a *toldo,* or awning, of about twelve
feet at the stern covered with matting. All the space before
this was required by the boatmen to work the canoe; with all
our luggage under the awning, we had but narrow quarters.
The seeming lake on which we started was merely a large
inundated plain covered with water to the depth of three
or four feet; and with the justice in the stern and his assistant up front, by walking in the bottom of the canoe with
poles against their shoulders, they set her across. At eight
o'clock we entered a narrow, muddy creek, not wider than a
canal, but very deep and with the current against us. The
setting pole could not touch bottom, but it was forked at one
end, and, keeping close to the bank, the *bogador,* or rower,
fixed it against the branches of overhanging trees and pushed,
while the justice, whose pole had a rude hook, fastened his to
other branches forward and pulled. In this way, with no view
but that of the wooded banks, we worked slowly along the
muddy stream.

In turning a short bend, suddenly we saw on the banks
eight or ten alligators, some of them twenty feet long, huge,

hideous monsters, appropriate inhabitants of such a stream, and, considering the frailty of our little vessel, not very attractive neighbors. As we approached they plunged heavily into the water; sometimes they rose in the middle of the stream and swam across or disappeared. At half past twelve we entered the Río Chico, or Little River, varying from two to five hundred feet in width, deep, muddy, and very sluggish, with wooded banks of impenetrable thickness. At six o'clock we entered the great Usumacinta, five or six hundred yards across, one of the noblest rivers in Central America, which rose among the mountains of Petén and emptied into the Lake of Términos.

At this point the three provinces of Chiapas, Tabasco, and Yucatán meet, and the junction of the waters of the Usumacinta and the Río Chico presents a singular spectacle. Since leaving the sheet of water before Las Playas we had been ascending the stream, but now, continuing in the same direction and crossing the line of junction, we came from the ascending current of the Río Chico into the descending flow of the Usumacinta. Working out into the middle and looking back, we saw the Usumacinta and Río Chico coming together to form an angle of not more than forty degrees, one running up and the other down. Amid the wildness and stillness of the majestic river, and floating in a little canoe, the effect was very extraordinary; but the cause was obvious. The Usumacinta, descending swiftly and with immense force, broke against a projecting headland on the left of its course and, while the main body forced its way past and hurried on to the ocean, part was turned back at this sharp angle with such power as to form the creeks which we had ascended and to flood the plain of Las Playas.

At this time, away from the wooded banks, with the setting poles at rest, and floating quietly on the bosom of the noble Usumacinta, our situation was pleasant and exciting. A strong wind sweeping down the river drove away the mosquitoes, and there were no gathering clouds to indicate rain. We had expected to come to for the night, but the evening was so clear that we determined to continue. Unfortunately, we were obliged to leave the Usumacinta, and,

about an hour after dark, turned to the north into the Río
Palizada. The whole great plain from Palenque to the Gulf
of Mexico is broken by creeks and streams. The Usumacinta
in its stately course receives many, and sends off others to
find their way by other channels to the sea.

Leaving the broad expanse of the Usumacinta with its
comparative light, the Río Palizada, narrow, and with a dark
line of forest on each side, had an aspect fearfully ominous
of mosquitoes. Unfortunately, at the very beginning we
brushed against the bank and took on board enough to show
us the bloodthirsty character of the natives. Of course that
night afforded us little sleep.

At daylight we were still dropping down the river. This
was the region of the great logwood country. We met a large
bungo with two masts moving against the stream; she was
set up by hauling and pushing on the branches of trees and
was on her way for a cargo. As we advanced, the banks of
the river in some places were cleared and cultivated; there
were white-washed houses, small sugar mills turned by oxen,
and canoes lying on the water. Altogether the scene was
pretty, but the richness of the soil suggested the idea of how
beautiful this country might be made.

At two o'clock we reached Palizada, which was situated
on the left bank of the river on a luxuriant plain elevated
some fifteen or twenty feet. Several bungos lay along the
bank, and in front was a long street, with large and well-
built houses. This, our first point, was in the State of Yucatán, then in revolution against the government of Mexico.
Our descent of the river had been watched from the bank,
and before we landed we were hailed for our passports and
directed to present ourselves immediately to the alcalde. The
intimation was peremptory, and we proceeded forthwith to
the alcalde. Don Francisco Hebreo was superior to any man
I had yet found at the head of a municipality; in fact, he was
chief of the Liberal Party in that section of the state and, like
all the other officials in the Mexican provinces, received us
with the respect due an official passport of a friendly nation.
We were again in the midst of a revolution, but we had not
the remotest idea what it was about. We were most inti-

mately acquainted with Central American politics, but this
was of no more use to us than a knowledge of Texan politics
would be to a stranger in the United States. For several
months the names of Morazán and Carrera had rung in our
ears like those of our own candidates for the presidency at a
contested election; but we had passed the limits of their
world, and were obliged to begin anew.

For eight years the Central Party had maintained the
ascendancy in Mexico, during which time, as a mark of the
sympathy between neighboring people, the Liberal or Democratic Party had been ascendant in Central America. Within
the last six months the Centralists had overturned the Liberals in Central America; during the same time in Mexico
the Liberalists had almost driven out the Centralists. Along
the whole coast of the Pacific the Liberals were in arms,
waging a strong revolutionary war and threatening the capital, which they afterward entered, but whence, after great
massacre and bloodshed, they were expelled. On the Atlantic
side, the states of Tabasco and Yucatán had declared their
independence of the general government, and in the interior
of both states the officials of the Central government had
been driven out. The seaports of Tabasco and Campeche,
garrisoned by Central troops, still held out, but they were
at that time blockaded and beseiged on land by the Federal
forces. All communications by sea and land were cut off, their
supplies were short, and Don Francisco thought they would
soon be obliged by starvation to surrender.

The revolution seemed to be of a higher tone and to be
conducted for greater cause and with more moderation than
in Central America. The grounds of revolt here were the
despotism of the Central government, which, far removed
by position and ignorant of the condition and resources of
the country, used its distant provinces as a quartering place
for rapacious officers, and as a source of revenue for money
to be squandered in the capital. One little circumstance
showed the impolicy and inefficiency of the laws. On account of high duties, smuggling was carried to such an extent on the coast that many articles were regularly sold at
Palizada for much less than the duties.

The revolution, like all others in that country, began with *pronunciamientos*, that is, declarations of the municipality, or what we would call the corporation of a town, in favor of any particular party. Palizada had made its *pronunciamiento* but two weeks before, the Central officers had been turned out, and the present alcalde was hardly warm in his place. The change, however, had been effected with a spirit of moderation and forbearance, and without bloodshed. Don Francisco, with a liberality unusual, spoke of his immediate predecessor as an upright but misguided man who had not been persecuted and was then living in the place unmolested. The Liberals, however, did not expect the same treatment at the hands of the Centralists. An invasion had been apprehended from Tabasco. Don Francisco had his silver and valuables packed up and kept his bungo before the door to save his effects and family; the place was alive with patriots brushing up arms and preparing for war.

Don Francisco was a rich man: he had an hacienda of thirty thousand head of cattle, logwood plantations and bungos, and was rated at two hundred thousand dollars. The house in which he lived was on the bank of the river; it was newly built with one hundred and fifty feet front, and had cost him twenty thousand dollars. While we were with him, dinner was about to be served in a liberal style of housekeeping unusual in that country, and, with the freedom of a man who felt sure that he could not be taken unaware, he asked us to join him at table. In all his domestic relations he was like the respectable head of a family at home. He had two sons, whom he intended to send to the United States to be educated; minor things, too, called up home feelings. For the first time in a long while we had bread, and it was made of flour from New York, judging from the Rochester label on the barrel-head. Don Francisco had never traveled farther than Tabasco and Campeche, but he was well acquainted with Europe and the United States, geographically and politically; indeed, he was one of the most agreeable companions and best-informed men we met in that country. We remained with him all the afternoon, and toward evening moved our chairs outside in front of the house, which at evening was the regular gathering-place of the family. The bank of the river was a promenade for the people of the town, who stopped to exchange greetings with Don Francisco and his wife; a vacant chair was always at hand, and from time to time one of them took a seat with us. When the vesper bell struck, conversation ceased, and all rose from their seats and made a short prayer; when it was over, they turned to each other with a *buenas noches*, reseated themselves, and renewed the conversation. There was always something imposing in the sound of the vesper bell, presenting the idea of an immense multitude of people at the same moment offering up a prayer.

During the evening a courier arrived with dispatches for Don Francisco, advising him that a town which had "pronounced" in favor of the Liberals had pronounced back again, which seemed to give both him and his wife much uneasiness. At ten o'clock an armed patrol came for orders, and we retired to what we much needed, a good night's rest.

In the morning Don Francisco, half in jest and half in earnest, told us of the uneasiness we had given his wife. Pawling's Spanish and his constant use of idioms well known as belonging to the city of Mexico had excited her suspicions; she said he was not an American, but a Mexican from the capital, and she believed him to be a spy of the Centralists. Pawling did not like the imputation; he was a little mortified at this visible mark of long absence from his country, and not at all flattered at being taken for a Mexican. Don Francisco laughed at it, but his wife was so pertinacious that, if it had not been for the apparent propriety of my being attended by one perfectly familiar with the language of the country, I believe, in the state of apprehension and distrust, Pawling would have lost the benefit of his birthright and been arrested as a spy.

We passed the next day in a quiet lounge and in making arrangements for continuing our journey, and the next day after, furnished with a luxurious supply of provisions by the señora, and accompanied to the place by Don Francisco, we embarked on board a bungo for the Laguna. The bungo was about fifteen tons, flat-bottomed, with two masts and sails,

and loaded with logwood. The deck was covered with man-
goes, plantains, and other fruits and vegetables, and so encumbered that it was impossible to move about on it. The
stern had movable hatches. A few tiers of logwood had been
taken out, and the hatches put over so as to give us a shelter
against rain; a sail was rigged into an awning to protect us
from the sun, and in a few minutes we pushed off from the
bank.

We had as passengers two young Central Americans from
Petén, both under twenty, who were fleeing on account of
the dominion of the Carrera party. Coming, as we did, direct from Central America, we called each other countrymen. We soon saw that the bungo had a miserable crew. On
our last trip, the men had been called *bogadores*, or rowers;
but here, as they were on board a bungo with sails and going
down to the seacoast, they called themselves *marineros*, or
sailors. The patron, or master, was a mild, inoffensive, and
inefficient man, who prefaced all his orders to his breechless
marineros with the conciliatory words, *Señores, hágame el
favor* (Gentlemen, do me the favor).

Below the town commenced an island about four leagues
in length, at the end of which, on the mainland, was a large
clearing and farming establishment, with canoes lying on the
water. All traveling here is along the river and in canoes.
From this place on there were no habitations; the river was
very deep and the banks densely wooded, with branches
spreading far over.

Very soon we came to a part of the river where the alligators seemed to enjoy undisturbed possession. Some lay
basking in the sun on mudbanks like logs of driftwood, and
in many places the river was dotted with their heads. The
Spanish historian says that "They swim with their head
above the water, gaping at whatsoever they see, and swallow
it, whether stick, stone, or living creature, which is the true
reason of their swallowing stones; and not to sink to the
bottom, as some say, for they have no need to do so, nor
do they like it, being extraordinary swimmers; for the tail
serves instead of a rudder, the head is the prow, and the
paws the oars, being so swift as to catch any other fish as it

swims. An hundred weight and an half of fresh fish has been found in the maw of an alligator, besides what was digested; in another was an Indian woman whole, with her cloathes, whom he had swallowed the day before, and another with a pair of gold bracelets, with pearls, the enamel gone off, and part of the pearls dissolved, but the gold entire."

Here they still maintained their dominion. Accidents frequently happen; at Palizada Don Francisco told us that a year before a man had had his leg bitten off and was drowned. Three were lying together at the mouth of a small stream which emptied into the river. The patron told us that at the end of the last dry season upward of two hundred had been counted in the bed of a pond emptied by this stream. The boatmen of several bungos went in among them with clubs, sharp stakes, and machetes, and killed upward of sixty. The river itself, discolored, with muddy banks and a fiery sun beating upon it, was ugly enough; but these huge and ugly monsters, neither fish nor flesh, made it absolutely hideous. The boatmen called them *enemigos de los cristianos,* by which they mean "enemies of mankind." In a canoe it would have been unpleasant to disturb them, but in the bungo we brought out our guns and made indiscriminate war. One monster, twenty-five or thirty feet long, lay on the arm of a gigantic tree which projected forty or fifty feet; the lower part was covered with water but the whole of the alligator was visible. I hit him just under the white line; he fell off with a tremendous convulsion, reddening the water with a circle of blood, and turned over on his back, dead. A boatman and one of the Petén lads got into a canoe to bring him alongside. The canoe was small and tottering, and had not proceeded fifty yards before it dipped, filled, upset, and threw them both into the water. At that moment there were perhaps twenty alligators in sight on the banks and swimming in different parts of the river. We could do nothing for the man and boy, and the old bungo, which before hardly moved, seemed to start forward purposely to leave them to their fate. Every moment the distance between us and them increased, and on board all was confusion; the *patrón* cried out in agony to the señores, and the señores, straining every nerve, turned the old bungo in toward the bank but got the masts foul of the branches of the trees, which held her fast. In the meantime our friends in the water were not idle. The Petén lad struck out vigorously toward the shore, and we saw him seize the branch of a tree which projected fifty feet over the water, so low as to be within reach, and haul himself up like a monkey and run along it to the shore. The *marinero,* having the canoe to himself, turned her bottom upward, got astride, and paddled down with his hands. Both got safely on board, and, apprehension over, the affair was considered a good joke.

In the meantime our masts had become so locked in the branches of the trees that we carried away some of our miserable tackle in extracting them; but at length we were once more in the middle of the river, and renewed our war upon *los enemigos de los cristianos.* The sun was so hot that we could not stand outside the awning, but the boatmen gave us notice when we could have a shot. Our track down the river will be remembered as a desolation and scourge. Old alligators, by dying injunction, will teach the rising generation to keep the head under water when the bungos are coming. We killed perhaps twenty, and others are probably at this moment sitting on the banks with our bullets in their bodies, wondering how they came there. With rifles we could have killed at least a hundred.

At three o'clock the regular afternoon storm came on, beginning with a tremendous sweep of wind up the river, which turned the bungo round and drove her broadside up the stream; before we could come to the bank, we had a deluge of rain. At length we made fast, secured the hatch over the place prepared for us, and crawled under. It was so low that we could not sit up, and, lying down, there was about a foot of room above us. On our arrival at Palizada we had considered ourselves fortunate in finding a bungo ready, although she had already on board a full load of logwood from stem to stern. Don Francisco said it would be too uncomfortable, and wished us to wait for a bungo of his own; but delay was to us a worse evil, and I made a bargain to have a portion of the logwood taken out behind the main-

mast, so as to admit of a hatch on deck and give room below.
But we had not given any personal superintendence and
when we came on board, though the logwood seemed of a
rather hard species for sleeping on, we did not discover the
extreme discomfort of the place until forced below by the
rain. Even this small place which we had engaged and paid
for, we did not have to ourselves. The Petén lads crawled
under with us, and the patron and señores followed. We
could not drive them out into a merciless rain, and all lay
like one mass of human flesh, animated by the same spirit of
suffering, irritation, and helplessness. During this time the
rain was descending in a deluge, the thunder rolled fearfully
over our heads, and lightning flashed in through the crevices of our dark burrowing place, dazzling and blinding our
eyes; and we heard near us the terrific crash of a falling tree,
snapped by the wind, or, as we then supposed, shivered by
lightning.

Such was our position. Sometimes the knots in the logwood fitted well into the curves and hollows of the body,
but in general they were just where they should not be. We
thought we could not be worse off, but very soon we found
out our mistake and looked back upon ourselves as ungrate-
ful murmurers without cause. The mosquitoes claimed us as
waifs, and in murderous swarms found their way under the
hatches, humming and buzzing

Fee, faw, fum,
I smell the blood of an English-mun,
Dead or alive I will have some.

I now look back upon our troubles at that place with perfect
equanimity; but at the moment, with the heat and confinement, we were in anything but an amiable humor, and at ten
o'clock we broke out furiously, upbraiding the patron and his
lazy señores for not reaching the mouth of the river before
night, as is usually done and as he had been charged by the
alcalde to do; we insisted upon his hauling out into the
stream.

The rain had ceased, but the wind was still furious, and
dead ahead. By the misty light we saw a large bungo, with

one sail set, seemingly flying up the river like a phantom. We made the patron haul out from the bank, but we could not keep with the river, and, after a few zigzag movements, were shot across to the opposite side, where we brought upon us new and more hungry swarms of mosquitoes. Here we remained an hour longer, when the wind died away and we pushed out into the stream. This was a great relief. The señores, though more used to the scourge of mosquitoes than we, suffered quite as much. The clouds rolled away, the moon broke out, and, but for the abominable insects, our float down the wild and desolate river would have been an event to live in memory. As it was, not one of us attempted to sleep, and I verily believe a man could not have passed an entire night on the banks and lived.

At daylight we were still in the river. Very soon we reached a small lake, and, making a few tacks, entered a narrow passage called the Boca Chica, or Little Mouth. The water was almost even with the banks, and on each side were the most gigantic trees of the tropical forests, their roots naked three or four feet above the ground, gnarled, twisted, and interlacing each other, gray and dead-looking, and so held up as to afford an extended view under the first branches of a forest of vivid green. At ten o'clock we passed the Boca Chica and entered the Lake of Términos. Once more in salt water and stretching out under full sail, on the right we saw only an expanse of water; on the left was a border of trees with naked roots, which seemed to grow out of the water; and in front, but a little to the left, and barely visible, a long line of trees marked the island of Carmen, on which stood the town of Laguna, our port of destination. The passage into the lake was shoal and narrow, with reefs and sand bars, and our boatmen did not let slip the chance of running her ashore. Their efforts to get her off capped the climax of their stupidity and laziness; one or two of them at a time would push on poles as if they were shoving off a rowboat, and then after a few minutes they would stop to rest and give up to others; of what could be done by united force they seemed to have no idea. After a few in-effectual efforts, the patron said we must remain till the tide

rose. But we had no idea of another night on board the bungo
and took entire command of the vessel ourselves. This we
were entitled to do from the physical force we brought into
action. Even Mr. Catherwood assisted; and, besides him, we
were three able-bodied and desperate men. Juan's efforts
were gigantic. From the great surface exposed, the mosquitoes had tormented him dreadfully, and he was even more
disgusted with the bungo than we. We put two of the men
into the water to heave against the bottom with their shoulders, and ourselves bearing on poles all together, we shoved
her off into deep water. With a gentle breeze we sailed
smoothly along until we could distinguish the masts of vessels at Laguna rising above the island, when the wind died
away entirely and left us under a broiling sun in a dead calm.

At two o'clock we saw clouds gathering, and immediately
the sky became very black, the harbinger of one of those
dreadful storms which even on dry land were terrible. The
hatches were put down, and a tarpaulin spread over for us
to take refuge under. The squall came on so suddenly that
the men were taken unaware, and the confusion on board was
alarming. The patron, with both hands extended and a most
beseeching look, begged the señores to take in sail; and the
señores, all shouting together, ran and tumbled over the logwood, hauling upon every rope but the right one. The mainsail stuck halfway up, and would not come down; and while
the patron and all the men were shouting and looking up at
it, the *marinero* who had been upset in the canoe, with tears
of terror actually streaming from his eyes, in a start of desperation ran up the mast by the rings, and springing violently upon the top one and holding fast by a rope, brought
the sail down with a run. A hurricane blew through the
naked masts, a deluge of rain followed, and the lake was
lashed into fury. We lost sight of everything.

At the very beginning, on account of the confusion on
board, we had determined not to go under the hatch; if the
bungo swamped, the logwood cargo would carry her to the
bottom like lead. We disencumbered ourselves of boots and
coats, and brought out life preservers ready for use. The
deck of the bungo was about three feet from the water and

perfectly smooth, without anything to hold on to, and, to keep from being blown or washed away, we lay down and took the whole brunt of the storm. The atmosphere was black; but by the flashes we saw the bare poles of another bungo, tossed like ourselves at the mercy of the storm. This continued more than an hour, when it cleared off as suddenly as it had come up, and we saw Laguna crowded with more shipping than we had seen since we left New York.

In our long inland journey we had almost forgotten the use of ships, and the very sight of them seemed to bring us into close relations with home. The squall having spent its fury, there was now a dead calm. The men took to their sweeps, but made very little headway and, with the port in full sight, we had great apprehensions of another night on board; just then another squall came on, not so violent, but blowing directly from the harbor and accompanied by tremendous rain. We made two or three tacks under a close-reefed foresail—the old bungo seemed to fly through the water—and, when under full way, the anchor, or, to speak more correctly, the stone, was thrown out at some distance below the shipping and brought us up all standing. There were breakers between us and the shore, and we hallooed to some men to come and take us off, but they answered that the breakers were too rough. The rain came on again, and for half an hour we stowed ourselves away under hatches.

As soon as it cleared off we were on deck, and in a little time we saw a fine jolly boat, with a cockswain and four men, coasting along the shore against a rapid current, the men at times jumping into the water and hauling the boat by ropes fixed for the purpose. We hailed them in English, and the cockswain answered in the same language that it was too rough, but after a consultation with the sailors they pulled toward us and took Mr. Catherwood and me on board. The cockswain was the mate of a French ship, and he spoke English. His ship was to sail the next day, and he was going to take in some large turtles which lay on the beach waiting for him. As soon as we struck we mounted the shoulders of two square-built French sailors and were set down on shore, and perhaps in our whole tour we were never so happy as at that moment in being rid of the bungo.

The town extended along the bank of the lake. We walked the whole length of it, saw numerous and well-filled stores, cafés, and even barbers' shops, and at the extreme end reached the American consul's. Two men were sitting on the portico, of a most homelike appearance. One was Don Carlos Russell, the consul. The face of the other was familiar to me; learning that we had come from Guatemala, he asked news of me, which I was most happy to give him in person. It was Captain Fensley, whose acquaintance I had made in New York when seeking information about that country, and with whom I had spoken of sailing to Campeche; but at the moment I did not recognize him, and in my costume from the interior it was impossible for him to recognize me. He was direct from New York and gave us the first information we had received in a long time from that place, with budgets of newspapers burdened with suspension of specie payments and universal ruin. Some of my friends had been playing strange antics; but in the important matters of marriages and deaths I did not find anything to give me either joy or sorrow.

Don Carlos Russell, or Mr. Charles Russell, was a native of Philadelphia, married to a Spanish lady of large fortune, and though long absent from home, he received us as one who had not forgotten it. His house, his table, all that he had, even his purse, were at our service. Our first congratulations over, we sat down to a dinner which rivaled that of our friend of Totonicapán. We could hardly believe ourselves the same miserable beings who had been a few hours before tossing on the lake, in dread alike of the bottom and of another night on board the bungo. The reader would have to go through what we went through to form any idea of our enjoyment. The negro who served us at table had been waiter at the house of an acquaintance on Broadway; we seemed but a step from home, and at night we had clean sheets furnished us by our host.

Chapter XXIII

THE town of Laguna stands on the island of Carmen, which is about seven leagues long; with another island about four leagues in length, it separates the Lake of Términos from the Gulf of Mexico. It is the depot of the great logwood country in the interior, and a dozen vessels were then in port awaiting cargoes for Europe and the United States. The town was well built and thriving; its trade had been trammeled by the oppressive regulations of the Central government, but it had made its *pronunciamiento*, disarmed and driven out the garrison, and considered itself independent, subject only to the state government of Yucatán. The anchorage is shoal but safe and easy of access for vessels not drawing over twelve or thirteen feet of water.

We could have passed some time with satisfaction in resting and strolling over the island, but our journey was not yet ended. Our next move was for Mérida, the capital of Yucatán. The nearest port was Campeche, a hundred and twenty miles distant, and the voyage was usually made by bungo, coasting along the shore of the open sea. With our experience of bungos this was most disheartening. Nevertheless, this would have been our unhappy lot but for the kindness of Mr. Russell and Captain Fensley. The latter

was bound directly to New York, and his course lay along
the coast of Yucatán. Personally he was disposed to do all in
his power to serve us, but there might be some risk in putting
into port to land us; knowing his favorable disposition, we
could not urge him. But Mr. Russell was his consignee, and
by charter party had a right to detain him ten days, and intended to do so; but he offered to load him in two days upon
condition of his taking us on board and, as Campeche was
blockaded, of landing us at Sisal, the seaport of Mérida
sixty miles beyond Campeche. Captain Fensley assented,
and we were relieved from what at the time we should have
considered a great calamity.

In regard to the project for the purchase of the ruins of
Palenque, which I have before referred to, Mr. Russell entered into it warmly; with a generosity I cannot help mentioning, hardly to be expected from one so long from home,
he requested to be held liable for two thousand dollars as
part of the cost of introducing the ruins into the United
States. In pursuance of my previous arrangement, I wrote
to the prefect advising him of Mr. Russell's co-operation
and referring him to Pawling as my agent in settling the
details of the purchase. This was enclosed in a letter from
Mr. Russell to the same effect, which stated besides that the
money would be paid the moment it was required; both letters with full instructions were given to Pawling. The interest which Mr. Russell took in this matter gave me a
flattering hope of success, and but for him, the scheme for
making castings would have failed entirely. He was engaged
in building an unusually fine house and, in order to finish
it, had sent to Campeche for plaster of Paris, but not finding
any there, he had imported some from New York. Fortunately, he had a few barrels left; and but for this accident—
there was none other nearer than Vera Cruz or New Orleans
—Pawling's journey, so far as related to this object, would
have been fruitless. We settled the details of sending the
plaster with Pawling to Palenque, and of receiving and shipping the castings to me at New York. On Saturday morning
at seven o'clock we bade farewell to Mr. Russell and embarked on board the *Gabrielacho*. Pawling accompanied us
outside the bar, and we took leave of him as he got on board

the pilot boat to return. We had gone through such rough scenes together since he overtook us at the foot of the Sierra Madre that it may be supposed we did not separate with indifference. Juan was still with us, for the first time at sea, and wondering where we would take him next.

The *Gabrielacho* was a beautiful brig of about one hundred and sixty tons, built under Captain Fensley's own direction, one half belonging to himself, and fitted up neatly and tastefully as a home. He had no house on shore; one daughter was at boarding school in the United States, and the rest of his family, consisting of his wife and a little daughter about three years old, were with him on board. Since his marriage seven years before, his wife had remained but one year on shore, and she determined not to leave him again as long as he followed the seas, while he resolved that every voyage should be the last, and looked forward to the consummation of every sailor's hopes, a good farm. His daughter Vicentia, or Poor Centy, as she called herself, was the pet of all on board. We had twelve passengers which would be interesting to the Common Council of New York, for they were enormous turtles, one of which the captain hoped would gladden the hearts of the fathers of the city at their Fourth of July dinner.

The reader cannot realize the satisfaction with which we found ourselves in such comfortable quarters on board this brig. We had an afternoon squall, but we considered ourselves merely passengers and, with a good vessel, master, and crew, laughed at a distant bungo crawling close along the shore. For the first time we feared that a voyage would end too soon. Perhaps no captain ever had passengers so perfectly contented under storm or calm. Oh you who cross the Atlantic in packet ships, complaining of discomforts and threatening to publish the captain because the porter does not hold out, may you one day be caught on board a bungo loaded with logwood!

The wear and tear of our wardrobe was manifest to the most indifferent observer; and Mrs. Fensley, pitying our ragged condition, sewed on our buttons, darned, patched, and mended us, and put us in order for another expedition. On the third morning Captain Fensley told us we had passed

Campeche during the night and, if the wind held, would reach Sisal that day. At eight o'clock we came in sight of the long low coast, and moving steadily toward it, at a little before dark anchored off the port, about two miles from the shore. One brig was lying there, a Spanish trader bound for Havana; it was the only vessel in port. The anchorage is an open roadstead outside of the breakers which is considered perfectly safe except during a northeast storm, when Spanish vessels always slip their cables and stand out to sea.

In the uncertainty whether what we were going to see was worth the trouble, and the greater uncertainty of a conveyance when we wanted it, it was trying to leave a good vessel which in twenty days might carry us home. Nevertheless, we made the exertion. It was dusk when we left the vessel. We landed at the end of a long wooden dock, built out on the open shore of the sea, where we were challenged by a soldier. At the head of the pier was a guard and customhouse, where an officer presented himself to escort us to the commandant. On the right, near the shore, was an old Spanish fortress with turrets. A soldier, barely distinguishable on the battlements, challenged us; and, passing the cuartel, we were challenged again. The answer, as in Central America, was *Patria Libre*. The tone of the place was warlike, the Liberal Party dominant. The revolution, as in all the other places, had been conducted in a spirit of moderation; but when the garrison was driven out, the commandant, who had been very tyrannical and oppressive, was taken, and the character of the revolution would have been stained by his murder had he not escaped on board a bungo.

We were well received by the commandant; and Captain Fensley took us to the house of an acquaintance, where we saw the captain of the brig in the offing which was to sail in eight days for Havana; no other vessel was expected for a long time. We made arrangements for setting out the next day for Mérida, and early in the morning we accompanied the captain to the pier and saw him embark in a bungo; we waited till he got on board, and saw the brig, with a fine breeze and every sail set, stand out into the ocean for home. We turned our backs upon it with regret. There was nothing to detain us at Sisal. Though prettily situated on the seashore and a thriving place, it was merely the depot of the exports and imports of Mérida. So at two o'clock we set out for the capital.

We were now in a country as different from Central America as if separated by the Atlantic, and we began our journey with an entirely new mode of conveyance. It was in a vehicle called a calèche, built somewhat like the old-fashioned cab, but very large and cumbersome; it was made for rough roads but was without springs, and was painted red, green, and yellow. One cowhide trunk for each was strapped on behind, and above them, reaching to the top of the calèche, was secured a pile of *zacate* for the horses. The whole of this load, with Mr. Catherwood and me, was drawn by a single horse with a rider on his back. Two other horses followed for change; they were harnessed and each had a boy riding him. The road was perfectly level and on a causeway a little elevated above the plain, which was stony and covered with scrub trees. At first it seemed a great luxury to roll along in a wheel carriage; but, with the roughness of the road, and without springs, in a little while this luxury began to be questionable.

After the magnificent scenery of Central America the country was barren and uninteresting, but we perceived the tokens of a rich interior in large cars with high wheels ten or twelve feet apart drawn by mules five abreast and loaded with hemp, bagging, wax, honey, and ox and deer skins. The first incident of the road was changing horses, which consisted in taking out the horse in the shafts and putting in one of the others, already in a sweat. This occurred twice before entering the village of Hunucmá at one o'clock. The village was pleasantly situated, embowered among trees, with a large plaza which at that time was decorated with an arbor of evergreens all around, preparatory to the great fête of Corpus Christi, which was to be celebrated the next day. Here we took three fresh horses, changing them as before, and passing two villages, through a vista two miles long we saw the steeples of Mérida, and at six o'clock rode into the city. The houses were well built, with balconied windows; many had two stories. The streets were clean, and many people in them well dressed, animated, and cheerful in appearance. There were calèches fancifully painted and curtained, within which were ladies handsomely dressed without hats and with their hair ornamented with flowers; they gave to the city an air of gaiety and beauty that, after the somber towns through which we had passed, was fascinating and almost poetic. No place had yet made so agreeable a first impression. There was a hotel in a large building kept by Doña Micaela, driving up to which we felt as if by some accident we had fallen upon a European city.

The reader will perhaps be surprised, but I had a friend in Mérida who expected me. Before embarking from New York, I had been in the habit of dining at a Spanish hotel in Fulton Street, frequented principally by Spanish Americans, and it was there that I had met a gentleman of Mérida and learned that he was the proprietor of the ruins of Uxmal. As yet I knew nothing of the position or character of my friend, but I soon found that everybody in Mérida knew Don Simón Peón. In the evening we called at his house. It was a large, aristocratic-looking mansion of dark gray stone with balconied windows and it occupied nearly the half of one side of the plaza. Unfortunately, he was then at Uxmal; but we saw his wife, father, mother, and sisters, the house being a family residence, with the different members of it having separate haciendas. They had heard from him of my intended visit, and received me as an acquaintance. Don Simón was expected back in a few days, but, in the hope of finding him at Uxmal, we determined to go on immediately. Doña Joaquina, his mother, promised to make all necessary arrangements for the journey and to send a servant with us. It was long since we passed so pleasant an evening; we saw many persons who in appearance and manner would do credit to any society, and we left with a strong disposition to make some stay in Mérida.

The plaza presented a gay scene. It was the eve of the fête of El Corpus. Two sides of the plaza were occupied by corridors, and the others were adorned with arbors of evergreens, among which lights were interspersed. Gay parties were promenading under them, and along the corridors and in front of the houses were placed chairs and benches for the use of the promenaders and all who chose to take them.

The city of Mérida contains about twenty thousand inhabitants. It is founded on the site of an old Indian village, and dates from a few years after the conquest. In different parts of the city are the remains of Indian buildings. As the capital of the powerful state of Yucatán, it had always enjoyed a high degree of consideration in the Mexican Confederacy, and throughout the republic it was famed for its *sabios*, or learned men. The state of Yucatán had declared its independence of Mexico; indeed, its independence was considered achieved. News had been received of the capitulation of Campeche and the surrender of the Central garrison. The last remnant of despotism was rooted out, and the capital was in the first flush of successful revolution: the pride of independence. Removed by position, it was manifest that it would be no easy matter for Mexico to reconquer it; and probably, like Texas, it is a limb forever lopped from that great but feeble and distracted republic. It was pleasant to find that political animosities were not cherished with the same ferocity we had observed elsewhere; Centralists and Liberals met like men of opposite parties at home.

The next day was the fête of Corpus Domini, throughout all Spanish America the greatest in the Catholic Church. Early in the morning, at the tolling of the bell, we went to the cathedral, which, with the palace of the bishop, occupied one entire side of the plaza. The interior was grand and imposing, having a vaulted roof of stone and two rows of lofty stone pillars; the choir was in the center, the altar richly adorned with silver. But the great attraction was the sight of the ladies kneeling before the altars with white or black veils laid over the top of the head, some of them of saintlike purity and beauty, in dress, manners, and appearance realizing the pictures of Spanish romance. Indeed, the Spanish ladies appear nowhere so lovely as in church.

The associations of one of my acquaintances having turned out so well, I determined to present a letter of introduction from friends in New York to Don Joaquín Gutiérrez, whose family name stood high in Mérida, and who, to my surprise, spoke English quite as well as we did. He had gone the rounds of society in Europe and the United States, and, like a good citizen, had returned to marry one of the belles and beauties of his own country. His family was from Mérida, but he himself was resident at Campeche; being a prominent Centralist, he had left that city on account of its blockade by the Federalists, and in apprehensions of excesses that might be committed against obnoxious individuals should the place fall into their hands. From his house we went to the plaza to see the procession.

After those we had seen in Guatemala this was inferior, and there were no devils. But the gathering of people under the arbor and in corridors presented a beautiful spectacle. There was a large collection of Indians, both men and women, the best-looking race we had seen, and all were neatly dressed. In the whole crowd there was not a single garment that was not clean that day, and we were told that any Indian too poor to appear in a fitting dress that morning would be too proud to appear at all. The Indian women were really handsome; all were dressed in white, with a red border around the neck, sleeves, and hem of their garments, and their faces had a mild, contented, and amiable expression. The higher class were seated under the arbors before the doors of the houses and along the corridors, elegantly attired, without hats, and with veils or flowers in their hair, combining an elegance of appearance with a simplicity of manners that made almost a scene of poetic beauty. They had an air of gaiety and freedom from disquietude so different from the careworn faces of Guatemala that they seemed as God intended them to be, happy. In fact, at this place it would have been no hardship to comply with the condition of purchasing Palenque; and yet perhaps some of the effect of this strong impression was only the result of comparison.

After the procession Don Joaquín proposed to call either upon the bishop or a lady who had a beautiful daughter. The bishop was the greatest man in Mérida and lived in the greatest style; but, determined to make the best of our day in Mérida, we chose the other branch of the alternative. In the evening, however, we did call upon him. His palace was adjoining the cathedral and before the door was a large cross; the entrance was through a courtyard with two rows of corridors. We ascended to a second flight, and entered an anteroom where we were received by a well-dressed official who notified the bishop of our coming; shortly afterward he conducted us through three stately salons with high ceilings and lighted lamps, in one of which was a chair of state covered with red damask which was carried up on the wall behind to the ceiling over it. From the last salon, a door opened into a large room elegantly fitted up as a sleeping apartment, in one corner of which was a large silver wash basin with a silver pitcher. In the center, not a movable nor very easily moved, sat the bishop, a man several feet round, handsomely dressed, and in a chair stuffed and covered with red morocco made to fit, neither pinching him nor permitting him to roll. It had a large, firmly secured projecting earpiece on each side to catch his head during the siesta and arms broad enough to support books and papers; it seemed the work of a man of genius.

The lines of the bishop's face indicated a man of high tone and character, and his conversation sustained the impression. He was a Centralist, and a great politician; he spoke of letters from generals, sieges, blockades, and battles, in tones which brought up a vivid picture of some priestly warrior or grand master of the Temple. In conclusion, he said that his influence, his house, and his *table* were at our service, and asked us to name a day for dining with him, adding that he would invite some friends to meet us. We had had many trials in our journey, and it was not the least to decline this invitation; but we had some hope that we might be able to share his hospitality on our return from Uxmal.

From the bishop's palace we went to the theatre, a large building built expressly for the purpose, with two rows of boxes and a pit. The upper tier of boxes was private. The prima donna was the lady who sat next me at dinner at the hotel; but I had better employment than attending to the performance, in conversation with ladies who would have graced any circle. One of them told me that there was to be a *tertulia* and a *baile* at a country house near the town in a few days, and to forego this was a harder trial than the loss of the bishop's dinner. Altogether, the evening at the theatre consummated the satisfaction of the only day we passed in Mérida, so that it remains impressed on my mind in bright relief to months of dullness.

The next morning at half past six we set out for Uxmal on horseback, escorted by a servant of Señor Peón, with Indians before us, one of whom carried a load not provided by us and in which a box of claret was conspicuous. Leaving the city, we entered upon a level stony road, which seemed one bed of limestone cut through a forest of scrub trees. At the distance of a league we saw through a vista in the trees a large hacienda belonging to the Peón family, the entrance to which was by a large gate into a cattle yard. The house was built of stone and had a front of about one hundred and fifty feet, with an arcade running the whole length. It was raised about twenty feet, and at the foot was a large water trough extending the whole length, about ten feet wide and of the same depth, filled with water for cattle. On the left was a flight of stone steps leading to a stone platform on which the hacienda stood. At the end of this structure was an artificial reservoir or tank, also built of stone and cemented, about one hundred and fifty feet square and perhaps twenty feet deep. At the foot of the wall of the tank was a plantation of henequen, a species of aloe,[1] from the fibers of which hemp is made. The style of the house, the strong and substantial character of the reservoir, and its apparent costliness gave an imposing character to the hacienda.

At this place our Indian carriers left us, and we took others from the hacienda with whom we continued three leagues further to another hacienda of the family of much the same character, where we stopped to breakfast. This over, we set out again, and by this time it had become desperately hot.

The road was very rough and over a bed of stone thinly covered with barely soil enough for the growth of scrub trees. Our saddles were of a new fashion and most painfully trying to those unused to them. We found the heat very oppressive and the leagues very long till we reached another hacienda, a vast, irregular pile of buildings of dark gray

---

1. Henequen is of the genus *Agave*.

stone that might have been the castle of a German baron in feudal times. Each of these haciendas had an Indian name; this was called the hacienda of Vayalquex, and it was the only one of which Doña Joaquina, in speaking of our route, had made any particular mention. The entrance was by a large stone gateway with a pyramidal top into a long lane, on the right of which was a shed, built by Don Simón since his return from the United States as a ropewalk for manufacturing hemp raised on the hacienda. One arrangement, which added very much to the effect, I did not observe anywhere else: the cattle yard and water tanks were on one side and out of sight. We dismounted under the shade of noble trees in front of the house and ascended by a flight of broad stone steps to a corridor thirty feet wide with large mattings which could be rolled up or dropped as an awning for protection against the sun and rain. On one side the corridor was continued around the building, and on the other it conducted to a door of a church having a large cross over it and an interior ornamented with figures like the churches in towns. The whole establishment was lordly in its appearance. It had fifteen hundred Indian tenants bound to the master by a sort of feudal tenure. As the friends of the master, we were made to feel the whole was ours.

We had fallen unexpectedly upon a state of things new and peculiar. The peninsula of Yucatán, lying between the bays of Campeche and Honduras, is a vast plain. Cape Catoche, the northeastern point of the peninsula, is but fifty-one leagues from San Antonio, the western extremity of the Island of Cuba, which is supposed at a remote period to have formed part of the American Continent. The soil and atmosphere are extremely dry; along the whole coast, from Campeche to Cape Catoche, there is not a single stream or spring of fresh water. The interior is equally destitute; and water is the most valuable possession in the country. During the season of rains, from April to the end of October, there is a superabundant supply; but the scorching sun of the next six months dries up the earth, and unless water were preserved man and beast would perish and the country be depopulated. All the enterprise and wealth of the landed proprietors, therefore, are exerted in procuring supplies of water, as without it the lands are worth nothing. For this purpose each hacienda has large tanks and reservoirs, constructed and kept up at great expense, to supply water for six months to all dependent upon it, and this creates a relation with the Indian population which places the proprietor somewhat in the position of a lord under the old feudal system.

By the Act of Independence, the Indians of Mexico, as well as the white population, became free. No man can buy and sell another, whatever may be the color of his skin; but as the Indians are poor, thriftless, and improvident, and never look beyond the immediate hour, they are obliged to attach themselves to some hacienda which can supply their wants; and, in return for the privilege of using the water, they come under certain obligations of service to the master, which place him in a lordly position. This state of things, growing out of the natural condition of the country, exists, I believe, nowhere in Spanish America except in Yucatán. Each hacienda has its major-domo, who attends to all the details of the management of the estate, and who in the absence of the master is his viceroy with the same powers over the tenants. At this hacienda the major-domo was a young mestizo who had fallen into his place in an easy and natural way by marrying his predecessor's daughter; he had just enough white blood to elevate the dullness of the Indian face into one of softness and sweetness; and it struck me that he thought quite as much of the place he got with her, as of herself.

It would have been a great satisfaction to pass several days at this lordly hacienda; but, not expecting anything to interest us on the road, we had requested Doña Joaquina to hurry us through, and the servant told us that the señora's orders were to conduct us to another hacienda of the family, about two leagues beyond, to sleep. At the moment we were particularly loth to leave on account of the fatigue of the previous ride. The servant suggested to the major-domo *llamar un coche* (to call a coach) which the latter proposed to do if we wished it. We made a few inquiries and said, unhesitatingly and peremptorily, in effect, "Go call a coach, and let a coach be called." The major-domo ascended by a flight of stone steps outside to the belfry of the church, whither we followed him; and, turning around with a movement and tone of voice that reminded us of a Mussulman in a minaret calling the faithful to prayers, he called for a coach. For several minutes, all was still as the sun beat upon the roof of the church, which with the whole pile of buildings connected, was made of stone, cemented firm and strong as a pavement.

At length we saw a single Indian trotting through the woods toward the hacienda, then two together, and in a quarter of an hour there were twenty or thirty. These were the horses; the coaches were yet growing on the trees. Selected for each coach were six Indians, who with a few minutes' use of the machete cut a bundle of poles which they brought up to the corridor to manufacture into coaches. This was done, first, by laying on the ground two poles about as thick as a man's wrist, ten feet long and three feet apart. These were fastened by cross sticks tied with strings of unspun hemp about two feet from each end. Grass hammocks were then secured between the poles, bows bent over them and covered with light matting, and the coaches were made. Placing our ponchos at the head for pillows, we crawled inside and lay down. The Indians took off little cotton shirts covering the breast and tied them around their hats as hatbands. Four of them raised up each coach and placed the end of the poles on little cushions on their shoulders. We bade farewell to the major-domo and his wife, and, feet first, descended the steps and set off on a trot, while an Indian followed leading the horses. In the great relief we experienced we forgot our former scruples against making beasts of burden of men. They were not troubled with any sense of indignity or abasement, and the weight was not much. There were no mountains; only some little inequalities which brought the head lower than the heels, and they seldom stumbled. In this way they carried us about three miles, and then laid us down gently on the ground. Like the Indians in Mérida, they were a fine-looking race, with a good expression of countenance, cheerful, and even merry in their toil. They were amused at us because we could not talk with them. There is no diversity of Indian languages in Yucatán; the Maya is universal, even all the Spaniards speak it.

Having wiped off the perspiration and rested, they took us up again; and, lulled by the quiet movement and the regular fall of the Indian's feet upon the ear, I fell into a doze from which I was roused by stopping at a gate. On entering, I found we were advancing to a range of white stone buildings, standing on an elevation about twenty feet high, which by measurement afterward I found to be three hundred and sixty feet long, with an imposing corridor running the whole length. On the extreme right of the building the platform was continued one or two hundred feet, forming the top of a reservoir, on which there was a windlass with long arms; and Indian women, dressed in white, were moving round in a circle, drawing water and filling their water jars. This was called the hacienda of Mucuyche. We entered, as usual, through a large cattle yard. At the foot of the structure on which the building stood, and running nearly the whole length, was a gigantic stone tank, about eight or ten feet wide and of the same depth, filled with water. We were carried up an inclined stone platform at about the center of the range of buildings, which consisted of three distinct sets, each one hundred and twenty feet front. Among the buildings on the left was the church, and through the door which was open, we saw an old Indian lighting candles at the altar for vesper prayers. In front, setting a little back, were the apartments of the major-domo and, at the other end of the range, the mansion of the master, in the corridor of which we were set down and crawled out of our coaches.

There was something monstrously aristocratic in being borne on the shoulders of tenants from such a hacienda as the one we had left to this stately pile. The whole appearance of things gave an idea of country residence upon a scale of grand hospitality, and yet we learned to our astonishment that most of the family had never seen it. The only one by whom it was ever visited was the son who had it in charge, and he came only for a few days at a time to see how things were being conducted and to examine the accounts of the major-domo. The range consisted of a single suite of rooms, one in the center about eighty feet long, and one on each side about forty feet long and communicating with the center room; a noble corridor extended along the whole front and rear.

We had an hour of daylight, which I could have employed very satisfactorily on the spot, but the servant urged us to go immediately and see a *cenote*. What a *cenote* might be, we had no idea. Mr. Catherwood, being much fatigued, turned into a hammock; but, unwilling to lose anything where all was strange and unexpected, I followed the servant. We crossed the roof of the reservoir, which was cemented as hard as stone, and passed on to an open tank built of stone and covered with cement inside and out, about one hundred and fifty feet square and twenty feet deep. It was filled with water in which twenty or thirty Indians were swimming. Descending to the foot of the tank, at the distance of about a hundred yards we came to a large opening in the ground with a broad flight of more than fifty steps. As we descended the steps, I saw unexpectedly a spectacle of such extraordinary beauty that I sent the servant back to tell Mr. Catherwood to come to me forthwith, even if he had to be carried in his hammock. It was a large cavern or grotto, with a roof of broken, overhanging rock; it was high enough to give an air of wildness and grandeur and, at mid-day, was impenetrable to the sun's rays. At the bottom, water pure as crystal, still and deep, rested upon a bed of white limestone rock. It was the very creation of romance; a bathing place for Diana and her nymphs. Grecian poet never imagined so beautiful a scene. It was almost a profanation, but in a few minutes we were swimming around the rocky basin with feelings of boyish exultation, only regretting that such a freak of nature was played where so few could enjoy its beauties. On a nobleman's estate in England it would be above price. The bath reinvigorated our frames, and it was after dark when we returned. Hammocks were waiting for us, and very soon we were in a profound sleep.

Chapter XXIV

~~~~~~

*Journey resumed. Arrival at Uxmal. Hacienda of Uxmal.
Major-domos. Adventures of a young Spaniard. Visit to
the ruins of Uxmal. First sign of the ruins. Character of the
Indians. Details of hacienda life. A delicate case.
Illness of Mr. Catherwood. Breaking up.*

AT daybreak the next morning, with new Indians and
a guide on horseback from the hacienda, we resumed
our journey. The surface of the country was the same, limestone with scrub trees. There was not soil enough to absorb
the water, which rested in puddles in the hollows of the
stones. At nine o'clock we reached another hacienda, smaller
than the last, but still with a lordly appearance; here, as
before, the women were drawing water by a wheel. The
major-domo, who expressed his sense of the honor conferred
upon him by our visit and of his anxiety to serve us, gave us
a breakfast of milk, tortillas, and wild honey, and furnished
us with other Indians and a guide. We mounted again and
very soon the sun became intensely hot; there were no trees
to shade us and we suffered excessively. At half past twelve
we passed some mounds of ruins a little off the road, but the
sun was so scorching that we could not stop to examine them,
and at two o'clock we reached Uxmal. Little did I think,
when I made the acquaintance of my unpretending friend at
the Spanish hotel in Fulton Street, that I should ride upward
of fifty miles on his family estate, be carried by his Indians,
and breakfast, dine, and sleep at his lordly haciendas. The
route marked out for our return would bring us to others,
one of which was larger than any we had seen. The family
of Peón under the Spanish dominion had given governors
to the province of Yucatán. On the establishment of inde-

pendence, its present head, a stanch Royalist, retired in disgust from all kinds of employment, and all the large family estates were managed by the Señora Doña Joaquina. Unfortunately, Don Simón had left for Mérida, and we had missed him on the way. Moreover, owing to the heat of the sun and our awkward saddles, we arrived at the end of this triumphal march in a dreadfully jaded and forlorn condition; perhaps we never dismounted more utterly worn out and uncomfortable.

The hacienda of Uxmal was built of dark gray stone; it was ruder in appearance and finish than any of the others and had a greater appearance of antiquity. At a distance it looked like an old baronial castle. A year before it had been given to Don Simón by his father, and he was making large repairs and additions to the building, though, as his family never visited it and he only for a few days at a time, for what purpose I could not conceive. It had its cattle yard in front, with tanks of water around, some with green vegetation on the top; all around there was an unwholesome sensation of dampness. It had, too, its church, which contained a figure of *Nuestro Señor* (Our Lord); revered by the Indians of all the haciendas around, its fame had reached the household servants at Mérida, and it was the first object that attracted the attention of our guide. The whole hacienda was immediately at our disposal; but, worn down with heat and fatigue, we took at once to our hammocks.

The hacienda had two major-domos, one a mestizo, who understood the language and business; in the other we found an acquaintance, or, at least what seemed to be one, for, at about the time that we left New York, he was a waiter at Delmonico's. It was a strange encounter at this out-of-the-way place to be brought into close connection with this well-known restaurant, which to us in that country seemed the seat of art and the fountain of happiness. He was a young Spaniard from Catalonia; having taken part in some defeated insurrection, he had fled with a friend to Cuba, whence, on the point of being discovered, they escaped, penniless, to New York. Ignorant of the language, with no means of getting a livelihood, both were received by Del-

monico as waiters at his restaurant, where the friend rose to
be head chocolate maker; but he was languishing as a simple
waiter when Don Simón proposed to him to go to Uxmal.
Without knowing where he was going, except that it was to
some part of Spanish America, or what was to be his business, he found himself in a retired place, surrounded by
Indians whose language he could not understand, and having no one near him with whom he could exchange a word
except the major-domo.

These major-domos form a class in Yucatán who need
sharp looking after. Like the Scotch servant applying for a
place, they are not particular about wages, and are satisfied
with what little they can pick up about the house. This is the
character of most of the major-domos; the position of the
young man, being white, intelligent, and honest, had advantages in that country, as Don Simón intended to give him,
as soon as he understood the business, a superintendence over
the major-domos of three or four haciendas. Unfortunately
he wanted energy, and he felt the want of society and the
loneliness of his situation; he remembered scenes of enjoyment with his friend and other waiters, and talked of the
opera, and at dinner time he drew such a feeling picture of
Delmonico's saloon, that we sympathized with him cordially.

In the afternoon, rested and refreshed, we set out for a
walk to the ruins. The path led through a noble piece of
woods in which there were many tracks, and our Indian
guide lost his way. Mr. Catherwood, being unwell, returned
to the hacienda. We took another road and, emerging suddenly from the woods, to my astonishment we came at once
upon a large open field strewed with mounds of ruins, and
vast buildings on terraces, and pyramidal structures, grand
and in good preservation, richly ornamented, without a bush
to obstruct the view, in picturesque effect almost equal to
the ruins of Thebes, for these, standing on the flat of the
river, nowhere burst in one view upon the sight. Such was
the report I made on my return to Mr. Catherwood, who,
lying in his hammock unwell and out of spirits, told me I
was romancing; but early the next morning when we were

on the ground, he commented that the reality exceeded my description.

The place of which I am now speaking was beyond all doubt once a large, populous, and highly civilized city, and the reader can nowhere find one word of it on any page of history. Who built it, why it was located on that spot away from water or any of those natural advantages which have determined the sites of cities whose histories are known, what led to its abandonment and destruction, no man can tell. The only name by which it is known is that of the hacienda on which it stands. In the oldest deed belonging to the Peón family, which goes back a hundred and forty years, the buildings are referred to in the boundaries of the estate as *Las Casas de Piedra*. This is the only ancient document or record in existence in which the place is mentioned at all, and there are no traditions except the wild superstitions of Indians in regard to particular buildings. Within the last year the trees had been cut down and burned, and the whole field of ruins, all exhumed, was in view, enclosed by the woods and planted with corn.

We passed a most interesting and laborious day, and at evening returned to the hacienda to mature our plans for a thorough exploration. Unfortunately, during the night Mr. Catherwood, affected, I believe, by the immensity of the work, had a violent attack of fever, which continued upon him in the morning with a prospect of serious illness.

It was Monday, and very early all the Indians of the hacienda, according to their obligation to the master, presented themselves to receive directions from the major-domo for the day's work. In remaining about the house I had an opportunity of learning something of hacienda discipline and the character of the Indians.

The hacienda of Uxmal is ten leagues, or thirty miles, square, but only a small portion is cultivated, and the rest is a mere roaming-ground for cattle. The Indians are of two classes: *vaqueros*, or tenders of cattle and horses, who receive twelve dollars per year, with five *almudes* [1] of maize per

---

1. A dry measure equivalent to about 0.8 of a liter.

week; and *labradores,* or laborers, who are also called *luneros,* from their obligation, in consideration of their drinking the water of the hacienda, to work for the master without pay on *lunes,* or Monday. These last constitute the great body of the Indians. When they marry and have families, and of course need more water, in addition to their work on Mondays they are obliged to clear, sow, and gather twenty *mecates* of maize for the master, each *mecate* being twenty-four square yards. When the bell of the church is struck five times, every Indian is obliged to go forthwith to the hacienda, and, for a *real* a day and a ration of three cents' worth of maize, do whatever work the master or his delegate, the major-domo, may direct. The authority of the master or his delegate over them is absolute. He settles all disputes between the Indians themselves, and punishes for offences, acting both as judge and executioner. If the major-domo should punish an Indian unreasonably, the latter may complain to his master; and if the master should refuse to give him redress, or, should he, himself, punish an Indian unreasonably, the latter may apply for his discharge. There is no obligation upon him to remain at the hacienda unless he is in debt to the master, but practically this binds him hand and foot.

The Indians are all improvident; they anticipate their earnings, never have two days' provisions in store, and never keep any accounts. A dishonest master may always bring them in debt, and generally they are really so. If able to pay off the debt, the Indian is entitled to his immediate discharge; but if not, the master is obliged to give him a writing to the effect following: "Whatever señor wishes to receive the Indian named — —, can take him, provided he pays me the debt he owes me." If the master refuses him this paper, the Indian may complain to the *justicia.* When he has obtained it, he goes round to the different haciendas until he finds a proprietor who is willing to purchase the debt, with a mortgage upon him until it is paid. The account is settled, and the master gives the Indian a writing of this purport: "The account of my former servant — — being adjusted, which is twenty dollars, and having paid me the said debt, I, his present master, give him this receipt"; and with this he enters into the service of a new master. There is but little chance of his ever paying off the smallest debt. He will never work merely to clear off the encumbrance; he considers all he can get on his body clear gain, and virtually, from the time he receives his first dollar, he goes through life on bondage, varied only by an occasional change of masters.

In general these Indians are mild, amiable, and very docile. They bear no malice; and when one of them is whipped and smarting under stripes, with tears in his eyes he makes a bow to the major-domo and says *Buenas tardes, señor* (Good evening, sir). But they require to be dealt with sternly and kept at a distance; they are uncertain and completely the creatures of impulse. One bad Indian or a bad mestizo may ruin a whole hacienda. They inherit all the indolence of their ancestors, are wedded to old usages, and unwilling to be taught anything new. Don Simón has attempted to introduce improvements in agriculture, but in vain; they cannot work except in their own old way. Don Simón brought out the common churn from the United States, and attempted to introduce the making of cheese and butter, but the Indians could not be taught the use of them; the churns were thrown aside and hundreds of cows wander in the woods unmilked. The master is not obliged to maintain the Indian when sick, though, as he derives a profit from his labor, it is his interest to do so; and, on broad grounds, as it is an object always to increase his *labradores,* it is his interest to treat them in such a manner as to acquire among the Indians a reputation as a good master.

In the course of the morning I visited many of the huts of the Indians. They were built in an oblong form, of round poles set upright in the ground and thatched, and some appeared clean and comfortable. The men were all away at work, and all day there was a procession of women in white cotton dresses moving from the gate to the well, drawing water. It was pleasant to find that marriage was considered proper and expedient; it was certainly conducive to good order and thrift, and probably to individual happiness. Don Simón encouraged it; he did not like to have any single men

on the estate, and he made every young Indian of the right
age take unto himself a wife. When, as often happened, the
Indian, in a deprecating tone, said, *No tengo mujer* (I have
no woman), Don Simón looked through the hacienda and
found one for him. On his last visit he made four matches,
and the day before our arrival the Delmonico major-domo
had been to the nearest village to escort the couples and pay
the padre for marrying them, the price being thirteen
shillings each. He was afraid to trust them with the money
for fear they would spend it and not get married.

The old major-domo was energetic in carrying out the
views of his master on this important subject, and that day
a delicate case was brought before him. A young Indian
girl brought a complaint against a married woman for
slander. She said that she was engaged to be married to a
young man whom she loved and who loved her, and that
the married woman had injured her fair fame by reporting
that she was already in "an interesting situation." The
woman had told the young man of it, saying that all the
women in the hacienda saw it, and she had taunted him with
marrying such a girl. Now, the girl said, the young man
would not have her. The married woman was supported by
a crowd of witnesses, and it must be admitted that appearances were very much against the plaintiff; but the old
major-domo, without going into the merits at all, decided in
her favor on broad grounds. Indignant at a marriage being
prevented, he turned to the married woman and asked what
was it to her, what right had she to meddle, and what if it
were true—it was none of her business. Perhaps the young
man knew it and was party to it, and still intended to marry
the girl, and they might have lived happily but for her busy
tongue; and, without more ado, he brought out a leather
whip cut into long lashes, and with great vigor began applying it to the back of the indiscreet communicator of unwel-
come tidings. He wound up with an angry homily upon
busybodies, and then upon women generally, who, he said,
made all the difficulties on the hacienda, and but for them
the men would be quiet enough. The matrons of the hacienda
stood aghast at this unexpected turn of things; and, when

the case was dismissed, all crowded around the victim and went away with her, giving such comfort as they could. The young girl went away alone; the hearts of her sex were steeled against her: in savage as in civilized life

> *Every woe a tear may claim,*
> *Except an erring sister's shame.*

In the afternoon Mr. Catherwood's fever left him, but he was in a very low state. The hacienda was unhealthy at this season; the great troughs and tanks of water around the house were green and, with the regular afternoon rains, they induced fatal fevers. Mr. Catherwood's constitution was already severely shattered. Indeed, I became alarmed and considered it indispensable for him to leave the hacienda and, if possible, the country altogether. To carry out my other plans, we intended at all events to return. We made a calculation that, by setting out the next morning, we could reach the Spanish brig in time to embark for Havana, and in ten minutes' consultation we determined to break up and go home. Immediately we communicated our purpose to the major-domo, who ascended the belfry of the church and called a coach to be ready at two o'clock the next morning.

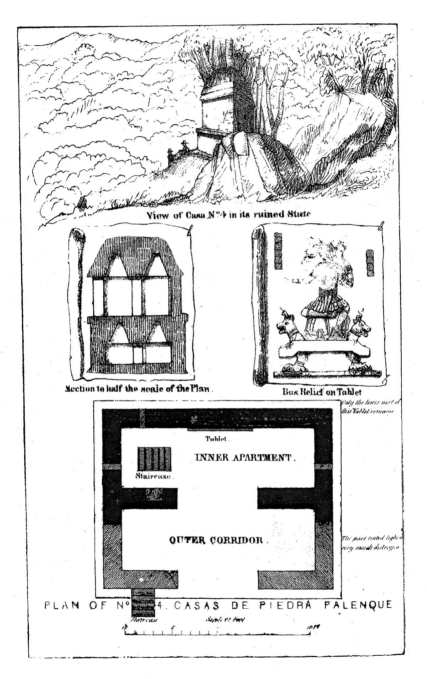

View of Casa N.º 4 in its ruined State

Section to half the scale of the Plan.

Bas Relief on Tablet

Only the lower part of this Tablet remains

Tablet.

INNER APARTMENT.

Staircase.

OUTER CORRIDOR.

The part tinted light is very much destroyed

PLAN OF Nº 4. CASAS DE PIEDRA PALENQUE

Staircase.   Scale 12 feet

FIG. 33 *Plan of Casa No. 4*

FIG. 34 *Front of Casa del Gobernador*

Chapter XXV

~~~~~~

Ruins of Uxmal. A lofty building. Magnificent view from its doorway. Peculiar sculptured ornaments. Another building, called by the Indians the "House of the Dwarf." An Indian legend. The House of the Nuns. The House of Turtles. The House of Pigeons. The Guardhouse. Absence of water. The House of the Governor. Terraces. Wooden lintels. Details of the House of the Governor. Doorways. Corridors. A beam of wood inscribed with hieroglyphics. Sculptured stones.

IN the meantime I returned for one more view of the ruins. Mr. Waldeck's work[1] on these ruins had appeared before we left the United States. It was brought out in Paris in a large folio edition with illustrations fancifully and beautifully colored, and it contains the result of a year's residence at Mérida and eight days at Uxmal. At the time of his visit the ruins were overgrown with trees, which within the last year have been cleared away and the whole laid bare and exposed to view. In attempting a description of these ruins, so vast a work rises up before me that I am at a loss where to begin. Arrested on the very threshold of our labors, I am unable to give any general plan; but fortunately the whole field was level, clear of trees, and in full sight at once. The first view stamped it indelibly upon my mind, and Mr. Catherwood's single day was well employed.

The first object that arrests the eye on emerging from the forest is the building represented on the right-hand side of the engraving (figure 35). Drawn off by mounds of ruins

---

1. Jean Frédéric Waldeck, *Voyage Pittoresque et Archéologique dans la Province de Yucatán*, Paris, 1838.

and piles of gigantic buildings, the eye returns and again
fastens upon this lofty structure. It was the first building I
entered. From its front doorway I counted sixteen elevations, with broken walls and mounds of stones, and vast,
magnificent edifices, which at that distance seemed untouched
by time and defying ruin. I stood in the doorway when the
sun went down, throwing from the buildings a prodigious
breadth of shadow, darkening the terraces on which they
stood, and presenting a scene strange enough for a work of
enchantment.

This building is sixty-eight feet long. The elevation on
which it stands is built up solid from the plain, entirely
artificial. Its form is not pyramidal, but oblong and round-
ing, being two hundred and forty feet long at the base, and
one hundred and twenty broad; it is protected all around,
to the very top, by a wall of square stones. Perhaps the high
ruined structures at Palenque, which we have called pyramidal, and which were so ruined that we could not make
them out exactly, were originally of the same shape. On the
east side of the structure is a broad range of stone steps
between eight and nine inches high and so steep that great
care is necessary in ascending and descending; of these we
counted a hundred and one in their places. Nine were wanting at the top, and perhaps twenty were covered with rubbish
at the bottom. At the summit of the steps is a stone platform
four feet and a half wide, running along the rear of the
building. There is no door in the center, but at each end a
door opens into an apartment eighteen feet long and nine
wide, and between the two is a third apartment of the same
width and thirty-four feet long. The whole building is of
stone; inside, the walls are of polished smoothness; outside,
up to the height of the door, the stones are plain and square.

Above this line there is a rich cornice or moulding, and
from this to the top of the building all the sides are covered
with rich and elaborate sculptured ornaments forming a
sort of arabesque. The style and character of these ornaments
were entirely different from those of any we had ever seen
before, either in that country or any other; they bore no
resemblance whatever to those of Copán or Palenque and

were quite as unique and peculiar. The designs were strange and incomprehensible, very elaborate, sometimes grotesque, but often simple, tasteful, and beautiful. Among the intelligible subjects are squares and diamonds, with busts of human beings, heads of leopards, and compositions of leaves and flowers, and the ornaments known everywhere as *grecques*.[2] The ornaments, which succeed each other, are all different, and the whole forms an extraordinary mass of richness and complexity; the effect is both grand and curious. And the construction of these ornaments is no less peculiar and striking than the general effect. There were no tablets or single stones, each representing separately and by itself an entire subject; but every ornament or combination is made up of separate stones, on each of which part of the subject was carved and then set in its place in the wall. Each stone by itself was an unmeaning fractional part; but, placed by the side of others, it helped to make a whole, which, without it, would be incomplete. Perhaps it may, with propriety, be called a species of sculptured mosaic.

From the front door of this extraordinary building a pavement of hard cement, twenty-two feet long by fifteen broad, leads to the roof of another building, seated lower down on the artificial structure, as shown in the engraving. There is no staircase or other visible communication between the two; but, descending by a pile of rubbish along the side of the lower one and groping around the corner, we entered a doorway in front four feet wide, and found inside a chamber twelve feet high, with corridors running the whole breadth, of which the front one was seven feet three inches deep, and the other three feet nine inches. The inner walls were of smooth and polished square stones, and there was no inner door or means of communication with any other place. Outside, the doorway was loaded with ornaments, and the whole exterior was the same as that of the building described above. The steps leading from the doorway to the foot of the structure were entirely destroyed.

The Indians regard these ruins with superstitious reverence. They will not go near them at night, and they have

2. Greek frets.

the old story that immense treasure is hidden among them. Each of the buildings has its name given to it by the Indians. This is called the *Casa del Enano*, or House of the Dwarf, and it is consecrated by a wild legend, which, as I sat in the doorway, I received from the lips of an Indian, as follows:

There was an old woman who lived in a hut on the very spot now occupied by the structure on which this building is perched, and opposite the *Casa del Gobernador* (which will be mentioned hereafter), who went mourning that she had no children. In her distress she one day took an egg, covered it with a cloth, and laid it away carefully in one corner of the hut. Every day she went to look at it, until one morning she found the egg hatched, and a *criatura*, or creature, or baby, born. The old woman was delighted; she called it her son, provided it with a nurse, and took good care of it, so that in one year it walked and talked like a man; and then it stopped growing. The old woman was more delighted than ever, and said he would be a great lord or king.

One day she told him to go to the house of the Gobernador and challenge him to a trial of strength. The dwarf tried to beg off, but the old woman insisted, and he went. The guard admitted him, and he flung his challenge at the Gobernador. The latter smiled, and told him to lift a stone of three *arrobas*, or seventy-five pounds, at which the little fellow cried and returned to his mother, who sent him back to say that if the Gobernador lifted it first, he would afterward. The Gobernador lifted it, and the dwarf immediately did the same. The Gobernador then tried him with other feats of strength, and the dwarf regularly did whatever was done by the Gobernador. At length, indignant at being matched by a dwarf, the Gobernador told him that, unless he made a house in one night higher than any in the place, he would kill him. The poor dwarf again returned crying to his mother, who bade him not to be disheartened, and the next morning he awoke and found himself in this lofty building. The Gobernador, seeing it from the door of his palace, was astonished, and sent for the dwarf, and told him to collect two bundles of *cocoyol*, a wood of a very hard species, with one of which he, the Gobernador, would beat the dwarf over the head, and *afterward* the dwarf should beat him with the other. The dwarf again returned crying to his mother; but the latter told him not to be afraid, and put on the crown of his head a *tortillita de trigo*, a small thin cake of wheat flour.

The trial was made in the presence of all the great men in the city. The Gobernador broke the whole of his bundle over the dwarf's head without hurting the little fellow in the least. He then tried to avoid the trial on his own head, but he had given his word in the presence of his officers and was obliged to submit. The second blow of the dwarf broke his skull in pieces, and all the spectators hailed the victor as their new Gobernador. The old woman then died; but at the Indian village of Mani, seventeen leagues distant, there is a deep well, from which opens a cave that leads underground an immense distance to Mérida. In this cave, on the bank of a stream, under the shade of a large tree, sits an old woman with a serpent by her side, who sells water in small quantities, not for money, but only for a *criatura*, or baby, to give the serpent to eat; and this old woman is the mother of the dwarf. Such is the fanciful legend connected with this edifice; but it hardly seemed more strange than the structure to which it referred.

The other building indicated in the plate (figure 35) is called by a name which may originally have had some reference to the vestals who in Mexico were employed to keep burning the sacred fire; but I believe in the mouths of the Indians of Uxmal it has no reference whatever to history, tradition, or legend, but is derived entirely from Spanish associations. It is called *Casa de las Monjas*, or House of the Nuns, or the Convent. It is situated on an artificial elevation about fifteen feet high. Its form is quadrangular, and one side, according to my measurement is ninety-five paces in length. It was not possible to pace all around it, from the masses of fallen stones which encumber it in some places, but it may be safely stated at two hundred and fifty feet square. Like the House of the Dwarf, it is built entirely of cut stone, and the whole exterior is filled with the same rich, elaborate, and incomprehensible sculptured ornaments.

The principal entrance is by a large doorway into a beautiful patio or courtyard, grass-grown but clear of trees, and the whole of the inner façade is ornamented more richly and elaborately than the outside, and is in a more perfect state of preservation. On one side the combination was in the form of diamonds, simple, chaste, and tasteful; and at the head of the courtyard two gigantic serpents, with their heads broken and fallen, were winding from opposite directions along the whole façade.

In front, and on a line with the door of the convent, is another building, on a lower foundation, of the same general character, called *Casa de Tortugas,* from sculptured turtles over the doorway. This building had in several places huge cracks, as if it had been shaken by an earthquake. It stands nearly in the center of the ruins, and the top commands a view all round of singular but wrecked magnificence.

Beyond this, a little to the right, approached by passing over mounds of ruins, was another building, which at a great distance attracted our attention by its conspicuous ornaments. We reached it by ascending two high terraces. The main building was similar to the others, and along the top ran a high ornamented wall in this form ⌐⌐⌐ , from which it was called *Casa de Palomas,* or House of Pigeons, and at a distance it looked more like a row of pigeon houses than anything else.

In front was a broad avenue with a line of ruins on each side leading beyond the wall of the convent to a great mound of ruins, which probably had once been a building with which it was connected; and beyond this is a lofty building in the rear, to which this seemed but a vestibule or porter's lodge. Between the two was a large patio or courtyard with corridors on each side; the ground of the courtyard sounded hollow. In one place the surface was broken, and I descended into a large excavation, cemented, which had probably been intended as a granary. At the back of the courtyard on a high, broken terrace, which it was difficult to climb, was another edifice more ruined than the others, but which, from the style of its remains and its commanding position overlooking

every other building except the House of the Dwarf, and
apparently having been connected with the distant mass of
ruins in front, must have been one of the most important in
the city, perhaps the principal temple. The Indians called
it the cuartel, or guardhouse. It commanded a view of other
ruins not contained in the enumeration of those seen from
the House of the Dwarf; and the whole presented a scene
of barbaric magnificence, utterly confounding all previous
notions in regard to the aboriginal inhabitants of this country, and calling up emotions which had not been wakened
to the same extent by anything we had yet seen.

There was one strange circumstance connected with these
ruins: no water had ever been discovered; and the Indians
did not know a single stream, fountain, or well nearer than
the hacienda, a mile and a half distant. The sources which
supplied this element of life had disappeared; the cisterns
were broken or the streams dried up. This, as we afterward
learned from Don Simón, was an object of great interest to
him and made him particularly anxious for a thorough exploration of the ruins. He supposed that the face of the
country had not changed, and that somewhere under ground
must exist great wells, cisterns, or reservoirs, which supplied
the former inhabitants of the city with water. The discovery
of these wells or reservoirs would, in that region, be like
finding a fountain in the desert, or, more poetically, like
finding money. The supply of water would be boundless.
Luneros without number might draw from it, and the old
city be repeopled without any new expense for wells or tanks.

While I was making the circuit of these ruins, Mr. Catherwood proceeded to the *Casa del Gobernador*,[3] which title,
according to the naming of the Indians, indicates the principal building of the old city, the residence of the governor,
or royal house. It is the grandest in position, the most stately
in architecture and proportions, and the most perfect in
preservation of all the structures remaining at Uxmal.

It stands on three ranges of terraces. The first terrace is

3. The drawing of the plan of this building is reproduced in earlier
editions of *Incidents of Travel* . . .

six hundred feet long and five feet high. It is walled with cut stone, and on the top is a platform twenty feet broad, from which rises another terrace fifteen feet high. At the corners this terrace is supported by cut stones, with the faces rounded so as to give a better finish than with sharp angles. The great platform above is flat and clear of trees, but abounding in green stumps of the forest but lately cleared away, and now planted, or, rather, from its irregularity, sown with corn, which as yet rose barely a foot from the ground. At the southeast corner of this platform is a row of round pillars eighteen inches in diameter and three or four feet high, which extend about one hundred feet along the platform; and these were the nearest approach to pillars or columns that we saw in all our exploration of the ruins of that country. In the middle of the terrace, along an avenue leading to a range of steps, was a broken, round pillar, inclined and falling, with trees growing around it. It was part of our purpose to make an excavation in this platform, from the impression that underneath would be found a vault forming part of the immense reservoirs for supplying the city with water.

In the center of the platform, at a distance of two hundred and five feet from the border in front, is a range of stone steps more than a hundred feet broad, and thirty-five in number, ascending to a third terrace, fifteen feet above the last, and thirty-five feet from the ground, about equal to the height of the City Hall; being elevated on a naked plain, it formed a most commanding position. The erection of these terraces alone was an immense work. On this third terrace, with its principal doorway facing the range of steps, stands the noble structure of the *Casa del Gobernador*. The façade measures three hundred and twenty feet. Away from the region of dreadful rains, and the rank growth of forest which smothered the ruins of Palenque, it stands with all walls erect and almost as perfect as when deserted by its inhabitants. The whole building is of stone; it is plain up to the moulding that runs along the tops of the doorway, and above it is filled with the same rich, strange, and elaborate sculpture, among which is particularly conspicuous the ornaments

before referred to as *grecques*. There is no rudeness or barbarity in the design or proportions; on the contrary, the
whole wears an air of architectural symmetry and grandeur;
and as the stranger ascends the steps and casts a bewildered
eye along its open and desolate doors, it is hard to believe
that he sees before him the work of a race in whose epitaph,
as written by historians, they are said to be ignorant of art
and to have perished in the rudeness of savage life. If it
stood at this day on its grand artificial terrace in Hyde Park
or the Garden of the Tuileries, it would form a new order,
I do not say equaling, but not unworthy to stand side by side
with the remains of Egyptian, Grecian, and Roman art.

But there was one thing which seemed in strange want of
conformity with all the rest. It was the first object that had
arrested my attention in the House of the Dwarf, and which
I had marked in every other building. I have mentioned
that at Ococingo we saw a wooden beam, and at Palenque a
fragment of a wooden pole; at this place *all the lintels had
been of wood, and throughout the ruins most of them were
still in their places over the doors.* These lintels were heavy
beams, eight or nine feet long, eighteen or twenty inches
wide, and twelve or fourteen thick. The wood, like that at
Ococingo, was very hard and rang under the blow of the
machete. As our guide told us, it was of a species not found
in the neighborhood, but came from the distant forests near
the Lake of Petén.[4] Why wood was used in the construction
of buildings otherwise of solid stone seemed unaccountable;
but if our guide was correct in regard to the place of its
growth, each beam must have been carried on the shoulders
of eight Indians, with the necessary relief carriers, a distance
of three hundred miles; consequently, it was rare, costly, and
curious, and for that reason may have been considered orna-
mental. The position of these lintels was most trying, as they
were obliged to support a solid mass of stone wall fourteen
or sixteen feet high, and three or four in thickness. Once,
perhaps, they were strong as stone, but they showed that

---

4. It is interesting to remember that the Old Empire of Mayan
civilization first flourished in El Petén.

they were not as durable, and they contained within them the seeds of destruction. Most, it is true, were in their places, sound, and harder than lignum vitæ, but others were perforated by wormholes. Some were cracked in the middle, and the walls, settling upon them, were fast overcoming their remaining strength; still others had fallen down altogether. In fact, except in the House of the Nuns the greatest destruction was from the decay and breaking of these wooden beams. If the lintels had been of stone, the principal buildings of this desolate city would at this day be almost entire; or, if the edifices had been still occupied under a master's eye, a decaying beam would have been replaced, and the buildings saved from ruin. At the moment of greatness and power, the builders never contemplated that the time would come when their city would be a desolation.

The *Casa del Gobernador* stands with its front to the east. In the center and opposite the range of steps leading up the terrace, are three principal doorways. The middle one is eight feet six inches wide, and eight feet ten inches high; the others are of the same height, but two feet less in width. The center door opens into an apartment sixty feet long and twenty-seven feet deep, which is divided into two corridors by a wall three and a half feet thick, with a door of communication between of the same size with the door of entrance. The plan is the same as that of the corridor in front of the palace at Palenque, except that here the corridor does not run the whole length of the building, and the back corridor has no door of egress. The floors are of smooth square stone, the walls of square blocks nicely laid and smoothly polished. The ceiling forms a triangular arch without the keystone, as at Palenque; but, instead of the rough stones overlapping or being covered with stucco, the layers of stone are beveled as they rise, and present an even and polished surface. Throughout, the laying and polishing of the stones are as perfect as under the rules of the best modern masonry.

In this apartment we determined to take up our abode, once more in the palace of an unknown king and under a roof tight as when sheltering the heads of its former occupants. Different from ruins in the Old World, where every fragment is exaggerated by some prating cicerone, in general, in this country, the reality exceeded our expectations. When we left Captain Fensley's brig we did not expect to find occupation for more than two or three days. But a vast field of interesting labor was before us, and we entered upon it with advantages of experience, the protection and kind assistance of the proprietor, and within the reach of comforts not procurable at any other place. We were not buried in the forest as at Palenque. In front of our door rose the lofty House of the Dwarf, seeming almost to realize the Indian legend, and from every part of the terrace we looked over a field of ruins.

From the center apartment the divisions on each wing correspond exactly in size and finish, and the same uniformity was preserved in the ornaments. Throughout the roof was tight, the apartments were dry, and, to speak understandingly, a few thousand dollars expended in repairs would have restored it and made it fit for the reoccupation of its royal owners. In one apartment the walls were coated with a very fine plaster of Paris, equal to the best seen on walls in our country. The rest were all of smooth polished stone. There were no paintings, stucco ornaments, sculptured tablets, or other decorations whatever.

In another apartment we found what we regarded as a most interesting object. It was a beam of wood, about ten feet long and very heavy, which had fallen from its place over the doorway and for some purpose or other been hauled inside the chamber into a dark corner. On the face was a line of characters carved or stamped, almost obliterated, but which we made out to be hieroglyphics, and, so far as we could understand them, similar to those at Copán and Palenque. Several Indians were around us watching our movements with an idle curiosity; and, not wishing to call their attention to it, we left it with an Indian who was at the moment sitting upon it. Before we were out of the doorway we heard the ring of his machete from a blow which, on rising, he had struck at random, and which chipped off a long shaving within a few inches of the characters. It almost gave us a shivering fit, and we did not dare tell him to spare it, lest from ignorance, jealousy, or suspicion, it should be the means of insuring its destruction. I immediately determined to secure this mystical beam. Compelled to leave in haste, on my arrival at Mérida, Don Simón kindly promised to send it to me, together with a sculptured stone which formed one of the principal ornaments in all the buildings. The latter is now in my possession, but the former has never arrived. In the multitude of regrets connected with our abrupt departure from these ruins, I cannot help deploring the misfortune of not being assured of the safety of this beam. By what feeble light the pages of American history are written! There are at Uxmal no "idols," as at Copán; not a single stuccoed figure or carved tablet, as at Palenque. Except for this beam of hieroglyphics, though searching earnestly, we did not discover any one absolute point of resemblance; and the wanton machete of an Indian may destroy the only link that can connect them together.

The ornament above referred to is the face of a death's head, with wings expanded and rows of teeth projecting, in effect somewhat like the figure of a death's head on tombstones with us. It is two feet wide across the wings, and has a stone staple behind, about two feet long, by which it is fastened in the wall. It had been removed by Don Simón entire, with the intention of setting it up as an ornament on the front of his hacienda.

It was our purpose to present full drawings of the exterior of this building, and, in fact, of all the others. Figure 34 represents one division with its sculptured ornaments, or what I have called mosaic. As at Copán, Mr. Catherwood was obliged to make several attempts before he could comprehend the subject so as to copy the characters. The drawing was begun late in the afternoon, was unfinished when we left to return to the hacienda, and, unfortunately, Mr. Catherwood was never able to resume it. It is presented in the state given by the last touches of the pencil on the spot, wanting many of the minute characters with which the subject was charged, and without any attempt to fill them in. The reader will see how utterly insufficient any verbal description must be, and he will be able to form from it some idea of the imposing exterior of the building. The exterior of every building in Uxmal was ornamented in the same elaborate manner. The part represented in the engraving embraces about twenty feet of the *Casa del Gobernador*. The whole exterior of this building presents a surface of seven hundred feet; the *Casa de las Monjas* is two thousand feet, and the extent of sculptured surface exhibited by the other buildings I am not able to give. Complete drawings of the whole would form one of the most magnificent series ever offered to the public, and such it is yet our hope one day to be able to present. The reader will be able to form some idea of the time, skill, and labor required for making them; and, more than this, to conceive the immense time, skill, and labor required for carving such a surface of stone, and the wealth, power, and cultivation of the people who could command such skill and labor for the mere decoration of their edifices. Probably all these ornaments have a symbolical meaning; each stone is part of an allegory or fable, hidden from us, inscrutable under the light of the feeble torch we may burn before it, but which, if ever revealed, will show that the history of the world yet remains to be written.

Chapter XXVI

~~~~~~

Exploration finished. Who built these ruined cities? Opinion of Dupaix. These ruins bear no resemblance to the architecture of Greece and Rome. Nothing like them in Europe. Do not resemble the known works of Japan and China, nor those of the Hindus. No excavations found. The pyramids of Egypt, in their original state, do not resemble what are called the pyramids of America. The temples of Egypt not like those of America. Sculpture not the same as that of Egypt. Probable antiquity of these ruins. Accounts of the Spanish historians. These cities probably built by the races inhabiting the country at the time of the Spanish Conquest. These races not yet extinct.

I HAVE now finished the exploration of ruins. The reader is perhaps pleased that our labors were brought to an abrupt close (my publishers certainly are); but I assure him that I could have found it in my heart to be prolix beyond all bounds, and that in mercy I have been very brief; in fact, I have let slip the best chance that author ever had to make his reader remember him. I will make no mention of other ruins of which we heard at more remote places. I have no doubt a year may be passed with great interest in Yucatán. The field of American antiquities is barely opened; but for the present I have done.

And here I would be willing to part, and leave the reader to wander alone and at will through the labyrinth of mystery which hangs over these ruined cities; but it would be craven to do so without turning for a moment to the important question: Who were the people that built these cities?

Since their discovery, a dark cloud has been thrown over the ruins in two particulars. The first is in regard to the immense difficulty and danger, labor and expense, of visiting and exploring them. It has been my object to clear away this cloud. It will appear from these pages that the accounts have been exaggerated; and, as regards Palenque and Uxmal at least, the only places which have been brought before the public at all, there is neither difficulty in reaching nor danger in exploring them.

The second is in regard to the age of the buildings; but here the cloud is darker and not so easily dispelled.

I will not recapitulate the many speculations that have already been presented. The most irrational, perhaps, is that of Captain Dupaix, who gives to the ruins of Palenque an antediluvian origin; and, unfortunately for him, he gives his reason, which is the accumulation of earth over the figures in the courtyard of the palace. His visit was thirty years before ours; and, though he cleared away the earth, the accumulation was again probably quite as great when we were there. At all events, by his own showing, the figures were not entirely buried. I have a distinct recollection of the condition of those monuments, and have no scruple in saying that, if entirely buried, one Irishman with the national weapon that has done such service on our canals would in three hours remove the whole of this antediluvian deposit. I shall not follow the learned commentaries upon this suggestion of Captain Dupaix, except to remark that much learning and research have been expended upon insufficient or incorrect data, or when a bias has been given by a statement of facts; and, putting ourselves in the same category with those who have furnished these data, for the benefit of explorers and writers who may succeed us I shall narrow down this question to a ground even yet sufficiently broad, that is, a comparison of these remains with those of the architecture and sculpture of other ages and people.

I set out with the proposition that they are not Cyclopean, and do not resemble the works of Greek or Roman; there is nothing in Europe like them. We must look, then, to Asia and Africa.

It has been supposed that at different periods of time vessels from Japan and China had been thrown upon the western coast of America. The civilization, cultivation, and science of those countries are known to date back from a very early antiquity. Of Japan I believe some accounts and drawings have been published, but they are not within my reach; of China, during the whole of her long history, the interior has been so completely shut against strangers that we know nothing of her ancient architecture. Perhaps, however, that time is close at hand. At present we know only that they have been a people not given to change; and if their ancient architecture is the same as their modern, it bears no resemblance whatever to these unknown ruins.

The monuments of India have been made familiar to us. The remains of Hindu architecture exhibit immense excavations in the rock, either entirely artificial or made by enlarging natural caverns, supported in front by large columns cut out of the rock, with a dark and gloomy interior.

Among all these American ruins there is not a single excavation. The surface of country, abounding in mountainsides, seems to invite it; but, instead of being underground, the striking feature of these ruins is, that the buildings stand on lofty artificial elevations; and it can hardly be supposed that a people emigrating to a new country, with that strong natural impulse to perpetuate and retain under their eyes memorials of home, would have gone so directly counter to national and religious associations.

In sculpture, too, the Hindus differ entirely. Their subjects are far more hideous, being, in general, representations of human beings distorted, deformed, and unnatural, very often many-headed, or with three or four arms or legs thrown out from the same body.

Lastly we come to the Egyptians. The point of resemblance upon which the great stress has been laid is the pyramid. The pyramidal form is one which suggests itself to human intelligence in every country as the simplest and surest mode of erecting a high structure upon a solid foundation. It cannot be regarded as a ground for assigning a

FIG. 35 *Nunnery and House of the Dwarf at Uxmal*

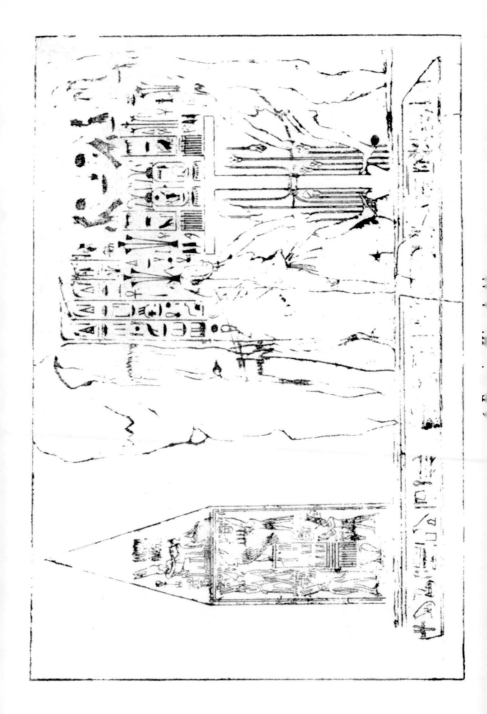

common origin to all people among whom structures of that character are found unless the similarity is preserved in its most striking features. The pyramids of Egypt are peculiar and uniform, and were invariably erected for the same uses and purposes, so far as those uses and purposes are known. They are all square at the base, with steps rising and diminishing until they come to a point. The nearest approach to this is at Copán; but even at that place there is no entire pyramid standing alone and disconnected, nor one with four sides complete, but only two, or, at most, three sides, and intended to form part of other structures. All the rest, without a single exception, were high elevations, with sides so broken that we could not make out their form; perhaps they were merely walled around with ranges of steps in front and rear, as at Uxmal, or terraces or raised platforms of earth, at most of three or four ranges, not of any precise form but never square, and with small ranges of steps in the center. Besides, the pyramids of Egypt are known to have interior chambers, and, whatever their other uses, to have been intended and used as sepulchers. These, on the contrary, are of solid earth and stone. No interior chambers have ever been discovered; probably none exist. And the most radical difference of all is that the pyramids of Egypt are complete in themselves, whereas the structures of this country were erected only to serve as foundations of buildings. There is no pyramid in Egypt with a palace or temple upon it; there is no pyramidal structure in this country without, at least none from whose condition any judgment can be formed.

But there is one further consideration, which must be conclusive. The pyramids of Egypt, as I have considered them and as they stand now, differ most materially from the original structures. Herodotus says that in his time the great pyramid was coated with stone, so as to present a smooth surface on all its sides from the base to the top. The second pyramid of Ghizeh, called the Pyramid of Cephrenes,[1] in its present condition, presents on the lower part ranges of steps, with an accumulation of angular stones at the base which originally filled up the interstices between the steps

---

1. This pyramid is usually called the Pyramid of Khafra.

which have now fallen down. In the upper part the intermediate layers are still in their places, and the sides present
a smooth surface to the top. There is no doubt that originally
every pyramid in Egypt was built with its sides perfectly
smooth. The steps formed no part of the plan. It is in this
state only that they ought to be considered, and in this
state any possible resemblance between them and what are
called the pyramids of America ceases.

Next to the pyramids, the oldest remains of Egyptian
architecture are temples, such as the temple of Absamboul in
Nubia. These temples, like those of the Hindus, are excavations in the rock, from which it has been supposed that the
Egyptians derived their style from that people. In later
times they commenced erecting temples above ground, retaining the same features of gloomy grandeur and remarkable for their vastness and the massiveness of the stone used
in their construction. This does not seem to have been aimed
at by the American builders. Among all these ruins we did
not see a stone worthy of being laid on the walls of an Egyptian temple. The largest single blocks were the "idols" or
"obelisks," as they have been called, of Copán and Quiriguá;
but in Egypt stones large as these are raised to the height
of twenty or thirty feet and laid in the walls, while the
obelisks which stand as ornaments at the doors, towering, a
single stone, to the height of ninety feet, so overpower them
by their grandeur that, if imitations, they are the feeblest
ever attempted by aspiring men.

Again: columns are a distinguishing feature of Egyptian
architecture, grand and massive, which at this day tower
above the sands, startling the wondering traveler in that
mysterious country. There is not a temple on the Nile without them; and the reader will bear in mind that among the
whole of these ruins not one column has been found. If this
architecture had been derived from the Egyptian, so striking
and important a feature would never have been thrown
aside. The dromos,[2] pronaos,[3] and adytum,[4] all equally

2. Avenue of approach to ancient temples.
3. Porch or vestibule of ancient temples.
4. Inner sanctum of ancient temples.

characteristic of Egyptian temples, are also here entirely wanting.

Next, as to sculpture. The idea of resemblance in this particular has been so often and so confidently expressed, and the drawings in these pages have so often given the same impression, that I almost hesitate to declare the total want of similarity. What the differences are I will not attempt to point out; that the reader may have the whole subject before him, I have introduced a plate of Egyptian sculpture (figure 36 facing page 371) from Mr. Catherwood's portfolio. The subject on the right is from the side of the great monument at Thebes known as the vocal Memnon, and has never before been engraved. The other is the top of the fallen obelisk of Karnak; and I think, by comparison with the engravings before presented, it will be found that there is no resemblance whatever. If there be any at all striking, it is only that the figures are in profile, and this is equally true of all good sculpture in bas-relief.

There is, then, no resemblance in these remains to those of the Egyptians; and, failing here, we look elsewhere in vain. The works of these people, as revealed by the ruins, are different from the works of any other known people; they are of a new order, and entirely and absolutely anomalous: they stand alone.

I invite to this subject the special attention of those familiar with the arts of other countries, for, unless I am wrong, we have a conclusion far more interesting and wonderful than that of connecting the builders of these cities with the Egyptians or any other people. It is the spectacle of a people skilled in architecture, sculpture, and drawing, and, beyond doubt, in other more perishable arts; and it possesses the cultivation and refinement attendant upon these, not derived from the Old World, but originating and growing up here, without models or masters, having a distinct, separate, independent existence: like the plants and fruits of the soil, indigenous.[5]

5. The independent creation of the brilliant Maya civilization is accepted by modern scholars.

I shall not attempt to inquire into the origin of this people, from what country they came, or when, or how; I shall confine myself to their works and to the ruins.

I am inclined to think that there are not sufficient grounds for the belief in the great antiquity that has been ascribed to these ruins; that they are not the works of people who have passed away and whose history has become unknown. Opposed as is my idea to all previous speculations, I am inclined to think that they were constructed by the races who occupied the country at the time of the invasion by the Spaniards, or of some not very distant progenitors.

And this opinion is founded, first, upon the appearance and condition of the remains themselves. The climate and rank luxuriance of soil are most destructive to all perishable materials. For six months every year exposed to the deluge of tropical rains, and with trees growing through the doorways of buildings and on the tops, it seems impossible that, after a lapse of two or three thousand years, a single edifice could now be standing.

The existence of wooden beams, and at Uxmal in a perfect state of preservation, confirms this opinion. The durability of wood depends upon its quality and exposure. In Egypt, it is true, wood has been discovered sound and perfect, and certainly three thousand years old; but even in that dry climate none has ever been found in a situation at all exposed. It occurs only in coffins in the tombs and mummy pits of Thebes, and in wooden cramps connecting two stones together, completely shut in and excluded from the air.

Secondly, my opinion is founded upon historical accounts. Herrera,[6] perhaps the most reliable of the Spanish historians, says of Yucatán: "The whole country is divided into eighteen districts, and in all of them were so many and such stately stone buildings that it was amazing, and the greatest wonder is, that having no use of any metal, they were able to raise such structures, which seem to have been temples, for their houses were always of timber and thatched. In those edifices

---

6. Antonio de Herrera. *Historia general de los hechos de los castellanos en las Indias*, Madrid, 1615.

were carved the figures of naked men, with earrings after the Indian manner, idols of all sorts, lions, pots or jarrs . . ." And again, ". . . after the parting of these lords, for the space of twenty years there was such plenty through the country, and the people multiplied so much, that old men said the whole province looked like one town, and then they applied themselves to build more temples, which produced so great a number of them."

Of the natives he says, "They *flattened their heads and foreheads, their ears bor'd with rings in them.* Their faces were generally good, and not very brown, but *without beards,* for they scorched them when young, that they might not grow. Their *hair was long like women,* and in tresses, with which they made a garland about the head, and a *little tail hung behind.* . . . The prime men wore a *rowler eight fingers broad round about them* instead of breeches, and going *several times round the waist, so that one end of it hung before and the other behind,* with fine feather-work, and had large *square mantles knotted on their shoulders,* and *sandals* or *buskins* made of deer's skins." The reader almost sees here, in the flattened heads and costumes of the natives, a picture of the sculptured and stuccoed figures at Palenque, which, though a little beyond the present territorial borders of Yucatán, was perhaps once a part of that province.

Besides the glowing and familiar descriptions given by Cortes of the splendor exhibited in the buildings of Mexico, I have within my reach the authority of but one eyewitness. It is that of Bernal Díaz del Castillo,[7] a follower and sharer in all the expeditions attending the conquest of Mexico. Beginning with the first expedition, he says, "On approaching Yucatán, we perceived a large town at the distance of two leagues from the coast, which, from its size, it exceeding any town in Cuba, we named Grand Cairo." Upon the invitation of a chief, who came off in a canoe, they went ashore and set out to march to the town, but on their way

---

7. *Historia verdadera de la conquista de la Nueva España,* Madrid, 1632.

were surprised by the natives, whom, however, they repulsed, killing fifteen. "Near the place of this ambuscade," he says, "were three buildings of *lime and stone*, wherein were idols of clay with *diabolical countenances* . . . The buildings of *lime and stone*, and the gold, gave us a high idea of the country we had discovered."

In fifteen days' further sailing, they discovered from the ships a large town, with an inlet, and went ashore for water. While filling their casks they were accosted by fifty Indians "dressed in cotton mantles," who "by signs invited us to their town." Proceeding thither, they "arrived at some large and very well-constructed buildings of *lime and stone*, with figures of *serpents* and of *idols* painted upon the walls."

In the second expedition, sailing along the coast, they passed a low island, about three leagues from the main, where, on going ashore, they found "two buildings of *lime and stone*, well constructed, each with steps, and an altar placed before certain hideous figures, the representations of the gods of these Indians."

His third expedition was under Cortes, and in this his regard for truth and the reliance that may be placed upon him are happily shown in the struggle between deep religious feeling and belief in the evidence of his senses, which appears in his comment upon Gómara's [8] account of their first battle:

"In his account of this action, Gómara says that, previous to the arrival of the main body under Cortes, Francisco de Morla appeared in the field upon a gray dappled horse, and that it was one of the holy apostles, St. Peter or St. James, disguised under his person. I say that all our works and victories are guided by the hand of our Lord Jesus Christ, and that in this battle there were so many enemies to every one of us, that they could have buried us under the dust they could have held in their hands, but that the great mercy of God aided us throughout. What Gómara asserts may be the case, and I, sinner as I am, was not permitted to see it. What I did see was Francisco de Morla riding in company with Cortes and the

8. Francisco López de Gómara. *Historia de las Indias* (Part I), *Crónica de la conquista de Nueva España* (Part II), Madrid, 1552.

rest upon a chestnut horse. But although I, unworthy sinner that I am, was unfit to behold either of these apostles, upward of four hundred of us were present. Let their testimony be taken. Let inquiry also be made how it happened that, when the town was founded on that spot, it was not named after one or other of these holy apostles, and called Santiago de la Vitoria or San Pedro de la Vitoria, as it was Santa María, and a church erected and dedicated to one of these holy saints. Very bad Christians were we, indeed, according to the account of Gómara, who, when God sent us his apostles to fight at our head, did not every day after acknowledge and return thanks for so great a mercy!"

Setting out on their march to Mexico, they arrived at Cempoala, entering which, he says, "We were surprised with the beauty of the buildings. . . . Our advanced guard having gone to the great square, the buildings of which had been lately whitewashed and *plastered, in which art these people are very expert,* one of our horsemen was so struck with the splendour of their appearance in the sun, that he came back in full speed to Cortes to tell him that the walls of the houses were of silver."

Offended by the abominable custom of human sacrifices, Cortes determined to suppress by force their idolatrous worship, and destroy their false gods. The chief ordered the people to arm in defence of their temple; "but when they saw that we were preparing to ascend *the great flight of steps,*" they said "they could not help themselves; and they had hardly said this, when fifty of us, *going up* for the purpose, threw down and broke in pieces the enormous idols which we found within the temple." Cortes then caused a number of *"Indian masons* to be collected, *with lime, which abounded* in that place, and had the walls cleared of blood and *new plastered."*

As they approached the territory of Mexico, he continues:

"Appearances demonstrated that we had entered a new country, for the *temples were very lofty,* and, together with the *terraced dwellings* and the houses of the cacique, being *plastered* and whitewashed, appeared very well, and resembled some of our towns in Spain."

Further on he says:

"We arrived at a kind of fortification, built of *lime and stone*, of so strong a nature that nothing but tools of iron could have any effect upon it. The people informed us that it was built by the Tlascalans, on whose territory it stood, as a defence against the incursions of the Mexicans."

At Tehuacingo,[9] after a sanguinary battle in which the Indians "drew off and left the field to them, who were too much fatigued to follow," he adds, "As soon as we found ourselves clear of them, we returned thanks to God for his mercy, and, entering a *strong and spacious temple*, we dressed our wounds with the fat of Indians."

Arrived at Cholula, Cortez immediately "sent some soldiers to a *great temple* hard by our quarters, with orders to bring, as quietly as they could, two priests." In this they succeeded. One of them was a person of rank and authority over *all the temples* of the city. Again: "*within the high walls of the courts* where we were quartered." And again: the city of Cholula, he says, "much resembled Valladolid." It "had at that time above a hundred *lofty white towers*, which were the temples of their idols. The principal temple was higher than that of Mexico, and each of these buildings was placed *in a spacious court*."

Approaching the city of Mexico, he gives way to a burst of enthusiasm:

"We could compare it to nothing but the enchanted scenes we had read of in *Amadis de Gaula*,[10] from the *great towers*, and *temples*, and other *edifices of lime and stone* which seemed to rise up out of the water. . . . We were received by great lords of that country, relations of Montezuma, who conducted us to our lodgings there in *palaces* magnificently built *of stone*, the timber of which was cedar, with *spacious courts* and apartments furnished with canopies of the *finest cotton*. The whole

---

9. Bernal Diaz speaks of Teoacingo near Tlaxcala, but modern maps do not reveal the existence of such a place.
10. A novel of chivalry which was very popular in sixteenth-century Spain.

was ornamented with *works of art painted*, and *admirably plastered* and whitened, and it was rendered more delightful by numbers of beautiful birds. . . . The palace in which we were lodged was very light, airy, clean, and pleasant, the entry being through a great court."

Montezuma, in his first interview with Cortes, says:

"The Tlascalans have, I know, told you that I am like a god, and that all about me is gold, and silver, and precious stones; but you now see that I am mere flesh and blood, and that my *houses are built like other houses, of lime, and stone, and timber*. . . .

"At the great square we were astonished at the crowds of people and the regularity which prevailed, and the vast quanities of merchandise. . . . The entire square was enclosed in piazzas."

"From the square we proceeded to the great temple, but before we entered it we made a circuit through a number of *large courts*, the smallest of which appeared to me to contain more ground than the great square of Salamanca, with double enclosures, *built of lime and stone*, and the *courts* paved with large white *cut* stones, or, where not paved, they were plastered and polished. . . . The ascent to the great temple was by *a hundred and fourteen steps*. . . . From the platform on the summit of the temple, Montezuma, taking Cortes by the hand, pointed out to him the different parts of the city and its vicinity, all of which were commanded from that place . . . We observed also the temples and oratories of the adjacent cities, built in the form of *towers* and *fortresses*, and others on the causeway, all whitewashed and wonderfully brilliant. . . . The noise and bustle of the market-place could be heard almost a league off, and *those who had been at Rome and Constantinople* said that for convenience, regularity, and population they had never seen the like."

During the seige he speaks of being "quartered in a *lofty temple*"; "marching *up the steps of the temple*"; "some *lofty temples* which we now battered with our artillery"; "the *lofty temples* where Diego Velázquez and Salvatierra were posted"; "the *breaches* which they had made in the *walls*"; "*cut stone* taken from the buildings from the terraces."

Arrived at the great temple, instantly more than four thousand Mexicans rushed up into it, who for some time prevented them from ascending:

"Although the cavalry several times attempted to charge, the stone pavements of the courts of the temple were so smooth that the horses could not keep their feet, and fell. . . . Their numbers were such that we could not make any effectual impression or *ascend the steps*. At length we *forced our way up*. Here Cortes showed himself the man that he really was. What a desperate engagement we then had! Every man of us was covered with blood. . . . They drove us *down six, and even ten of the steps*, while others who were in the corridors, or within-inside of the railings and concavities of the great temple, shot such clouds of arrows at us that we could not maintain our ground [and we] began our retreat, every man of us being wounded, and forty-six of us left dead on the spot. I have often seen this engagement represented in the *paintings* of the natives both of Mexico and Tlascala, and *our ascent into the great temple*."

Again, he speaks of arriving at a village and taking up their "quarters in *a strong temple*"; "assaulting them at their posts in *the temples and large walled enclosures*."
At Texcoco:

". . . we took up our quarters in some buildings which consisted of *large halls and enclosed courts*. . . . Alvarado, De Olid, and some soldiers, whereof I was one, then ascended to the top of *the great temple*, which was *very lofty*, in order to notice what was going on in the neighborhood. . . .
"We proceeded to another town called Terrayuco,[11] but which we named the town of the *serpents*, on account of the *enormous figures of those animals* which we found in their temples, and which they worshipped as gods."

Again:

"In this garden our whole force lodged for the night. I certainly never had seen one of such magnificence; and Cortes and the treasurer Alderete, after they had walked through and examined it, declared that it was admirable, and equal to

---

11. The editor was unable to identify a place by this name. The town referred to may, perhaps, be Tenayuca in the State of Zacatecas.

any they had ever seen in Castile. . . . I and ten more soldiers were posted as a guard upon a *wall of lime and stone*. . . .

"When we arrived at our quarters at Tacuba it rained heavily, and we remained under it for two hours in some *large enclosed courts*. The general, with his captains, the treasurer, our reverend father, and many others of us, mounted to the *top of the temple*, which commanded all the lake. . . .

"We crossed the water up to our necks at the pass they had left open, and followed them until we came to a place where were *large temples and towers of idols*. . . .

"As Cortes now lodged at Cuejoacan,[12] in large buildings with white walls, very well adapted for scribbling on, there appeared every morning libels against him in prose and verse. I recollect the words of one only:

Que triste está el alma mea
Hasta que la parte vea.
(How anxious I am for a share of the plunder. . . .)

"When our party (for I went with Sandoval) arrived at Tustepeque, I took up my lodgings in the summit of a *tower in a very high temple*, partly for the fresh air and to avoid the mosquitoes, which were very troublesome below, and partly to be near Sandoval's quarters. . . . We pursued our route to the city of Chiapas, in the same province with Palenque, and a city it might be called, from the regularity of its streets and houses. It contained not less than four thousand families, not reckoning the population of the many dependant towns in its neighborhood . . . We found the whole force of Chiapas drawn up to receive us. Their troops were adorned with plumage. . . .

"On our arrival we found it too closely built to be safely occupied by us, and we therefore pitched our camp in the open field. In their *temples* we found idols of a horrid figure."

Now it will be recollected that Bernal Díaz wrote to do justice to himself and others of the "true conquerors," his companions in arms, whose fame had been obscured by other historians not actors and eyewitnesses; all his references to buildings are incidental; he never expected to be cited as authority upon the antiquities of the country. The pettiest skirmish with the natives was nearer his heart than all the edifices of lime and stone which he saw, and it is precisely

---

12. The editor was unable to identify a place by this name.

on that account that his testimony is more valuable. It was written at a time when there were many living who could contradict him if incorrect or false. His "true history" never was impeached; on the contrary, while its style was considered rude and inelegant, its fidelity and truth have been acknowledged by all contemporaneous and subsequent historians. In my opinion, it is as true and reliable as any work of travels on the countries through which he fought his way. It gives the hurried and imperfect observations of an unlettered soldier, whose sword was seldom in its scabbard, surrounded by dangers, attacking, retreating, wounded, and fleeing, with his mind constantly occupied by matters of more pressing moment.

The reader cannot fail to be struck with the general resemblance between the objects described by him and the scenes referred to in these pages. His account presents to my mind a vivid picture of the ruined cities which we visited, as they once stood, with buildings of lime and stone, painted and sculptured ornaments, and plastered; idols, courts, strong walls, and lofty temples with high ranges of steps.

But if this is not sufficient, I have further and stronger support. After the siege of Mexico, on the re-entry of the Spaniards, a ruthless and indiscriminate destruction fell upon every building and monument in the city. No memorials of the arts of the Mexicans were left; but in the year 1790, two statues and a flat stone, with sculptured characters relative to the Mexican calendar, were discovered and dug up from among the remains of the great Teocalli in the plaza of the city of Mexico. The statues excited great interest among the Mexican Indians, and the priests, afraid of their relapsing into idolatry, and to destroy all memorials of their ancient rites, buried them in the court of the Franciscan convent. The calendar was fixed in a conspicuous place in the wall of the cathedral, where it now stands. In the center, and forming the principal subject of this calendar, is a face, published in Humboldt's work,[13] which in one particular bears

13. Alexander von Humboldt. *Vues des Cordillères, et Monuments des Peuples Indigènes de l'Amérique*, Paris, 1809.

FIG. 37 *Mayan Hieroglyphics*

FIG. 38 *Aztec Hieroglyphics*

so strong a resemblance to that called the mask, in figure 20, as to suggest the idea that they were intended for the same. There are palpable differences, but perhaps the expression of the eyes is changed and improved in the engraving published, and, at all events, the peculiar and striking feature in both is that of the tongue hanging out of the mouth. The calendar is in bas-relief, and, as I understand from a gentleman who has seen it, the sculpture is good.

And, lastly, among the hieroglyphical paintings which escaped destruction from monkish fanaticism are certain Mexican manuscripts now in the libraries of Dresden and Vienna. These have been published in Humboldt's work and in that of Lord Kingsborough, and, on a careful examination, we are strongly of the opinion that the characters are the same as those found on the monuments and tablets at Copán and Palenque. For the sake of comparison I have introduced again the engraving of the top of the altar at Copán, and another from a hieroglyphical manuscript published in Humboldt's work (figures 37 and 38). Differences, it is true, are manifest, but it must be borne in mind that in the former the characters are carved on stone, and in the latter written on paper (made of the *Agave mexicana*). Probably, for this reason, they want the same regularity and finish; but, altogether, the reader cannot fail to mark the strong similarity, and this similarity cannot be accidental. The inference is, that the Aztecs, or Mexicans, at the time of the conquest had the same written language as the people of Copán and Palenque.[14]

I have thus very briefly, and without attempting to controvert the opinions and speculations of others, presented our own views upon the subject of these ruins. As yet we perhaps stand alone in these views, but I repeat my opinion that we are not warranted in going back to any ancient nation of the Old World for the builders of these cities: that they are not the work of people who have passed away and whose history

---

14. Although the language of the Aztecs was different from that of the Mayas, the former did pattern their writing on that of the latter according to S. G. Morley.

is lost, but that there are strong reasons to believe them the creations of the same races who inhabited the country at the time of the Spanish conquest, or of some not very distant progenitors. And I would remark that we began our exploration without any theory to support; our feelings were in favor of going back to a high and venerable antiquity. During the greater part of our journey we were groping in the dark, in doubt and uncertainty, and it was not until our arrival at the ruins of Uxmal that we formed our opinion of their comparatively modern date. Some are beyond doubt older than others, some are known to have been inhabited at the time of the Spanish conquest, and others, perhaps, were really in ruins before; and there are points of difference which as yet cannot very readily be explained. But in regard to Uxmal, at least, we believe that it was an existing and inhabited city at the time of the arrival of the Spaniards. Its desolation and ruin since are easily accounted for. With the arrival of the Spaniards the scepter of the Indians departed. In the city of Mexico every house was razed to the ground, and, beyond doubt, throughout the country every gathering place or stronghold was broken up, the communities scattered, their lofty temples thrown down and their idols burned, the palaces of the caciques ruined, the caciques themselves made bondmen, and, by the same ruthless policy which from time immemorial has been pursued in a conquered country, all the mementos of their ancestors and lost independence were destroyed or made odious in their eyes. And, without this, we have authentic accounts of great scourges which swept over, and for a time depopulated and desolated, the whole of Yucatán.

It perhaps destroys much of the interest that hangs over these ruins to assign to them a modern date; but we live in an age whose spirit is to discard phantasms and arrive at truth, and the interest lost in one particular is supplied in another scarcely inferior; for, the nearer we can bring the builders of these cities to our own times, the greater is our chance of knowing all. Throughout the country the convents are rich in manuscripts and documents written by the early fathers, caciques, and Indians, who very soon acquired the

knowledge of Spanish and the art of writing. These have
never been examined with the slightest reference to this
subject; and I cannot help thinking that some precious memorial is now mouldering in the library of a neighboring
convent, which would determine the history of some one of
these ruined cities; moreover, I cannot help believing that
the tablets of hieroglyphics will yet be read. No strong curiosity has hitherto been directed to them; vigor and acuteness
of intellect, knowledge, and learning have never been expended upon them. For centuries the hieroglyphics of Egypt
were inscrutable, and, though not perhaps in our day, I feel
persuaded that a key surer than that of the Rosetta stone
will be discovered.[15] And if only three centuries have elapsed
since any one of these unknown cities was inhabited, the race
of the inhabitants is not extinct. Their descendants are still
in the land, scattered, perhaps, and retired, like our own
Indians, into wildernesses which have never yet been penetrated by a white man, but not lost; living as their fathers
did, erecting the same buildings of "lime and stone," "with
ornaments of sculpture and plastered," "large courts," and
"lofty towers with high ranges of steps," and still carving on
tablets of stone the same mysterious hieroglyphics; and if,
in consideration that I have not often indulged in specula-
tive conjecture, the reader will allow one flight, I turn to
that vast and unknown region, untraversed by a single road,
wherein fancy pictures that mysterious city seen from the
topmost range of the Cordilleras, of unconquered, unvisited,
and unsought aboriginal inhabitants.

In conclusion, I am at a loss to determine which would be
the greatest enterprise, an attempt to reach this mysterious
city, to decipher the tablets of hieroglyphics, or to wade
through the accumulated manuscripts of three centuries in
the libraries of the convents.

15. Stephens was again correct when he supposed that some manuscript to help interpret the hieroglyphics would be found. The Maya
"Rosetta Stone" is Bishop Diego de Landa's *Relación de las cosas de
Yucatán*, written in the second half of the sixteenth century. There is
an English translation edited with notes by Alfred M. Tozzer, Cam-
bridge, Mass., The Museum, 1941.

Chapter XXVII

BUT to return to ourselves. At three, by the light of the moon, we left Uxmal by the most direct road for Mérida, Mr. Catherwood in a coach and I on horseback, charged with a letter from the junior major-domo to his compatriot and friend, Delmonico's head chocolate maker. As I followed Mr. Catherwood through the woods, borne on the shoulders of Indians, the stillness broken only by the shuffle of their feet, and under my great apprehensions for his health, it almost seemed as if I were following his bier. At the distance of three leagues we entered the village of Muna; though a fine village having both white people and mestizos among its inhabitants, travelers were more rare than in the interior of Central America. We were detained two hours at the *casa real* waiting for a relief coach. At a short distance beyond, my guide led me out of the road to show me a pond of water, which in that country was a curiosity. It was surrounded by woods; wild cattle were drinking on the borders and started like deer at our approach.

At the distance of four leagues we reached the village of Abala, with a plaza enclosed by a rough picket fence, a good *casa real* and fine old alcalde, who knew our servant as belonging to the Peón family. There was no intermediate village, and he undertook to provide us with relief Indians to carry the coach through to Mérida, twenty-seven miles. It was growing late, and I went on before with a horse for change, in order to reach Mérida in time to make arrangements for a calèche the next day.

Toward evening it rained hard. At dark I began to have apprehension of leaving Mr. Catherwood behind, sent the servant on to secure the calèche, and dismounted to wait. Being too dreadfully fatigued to ride back, I sat down in the road; by degrees I stretched myself on a smooth stone, with the bridle around my wrist, and after a dreamy debate whether my horse would tread on me or not, fell asleep. I was roused by a jerk which nearly tore my arm off, and saw coming through the woods Indian runners with blazing pine torches, lighting the way for the coach, which had an aspect so funereal that it almost made me shudder. Mr. Catherwood had had his difficulties. After carrying him about a league, the Indians had stopped and laid him down; after an animated conversation, they took him up and went on, but in a little while laid him down again and, thrusting their heads under the cover of the coach, made him an eager and clamorous address, of which he did not understand one word. At length he picked up *dos pesos*, or two dollars, and gathered that they wanted two dollars more. As the alcalde had adjusted the account, he refused to pay and, after a noisy wrangle, they quietly took him up on their shoulders and began trotting back with him to the village. This made him tractable, and he paid the money, threatening them as well as he could with vengeance; but the amusing part was that they were right. The alcalde had made a mistake in the calculation; and, on a division and distribution on the road, by hard pounding and calculating, each one knowing what he ought to receive himself, they had discovered that they had been paid two dollars short. The price was twenty-five cents per man for the first, and eighteen cents for every subsequent league, besides fifty cents for making the coach; so that, with four men for relief, it was two dollars for the first league, and a dollar and a half for every subsequent one; and a calculation of the whole amount for nine leagues was rather complicated.

It was half past one when we reached Mérida, and we had been up and on the road since two in the morning. Fortunately, with the easy movement of the coach, Mr. Catherwood had suffered but little. I was tired beyond all measure; but I had what enabled me to endure any degree of fatigue, a good cot, and was soon asleep.

The next morning we saw my friend Don Simón, who was preparing to go back and join us. I cannot sufficiently express my sense of the kindness we received from him and from his family, and I only hope that I may have an opportunity at some future time of returning it in my own country. He promised, when we returned, to go down with us and assist in a thorough exploration of the ruins. The Spanish vessel was to sail the next day. Toward evening, after a heavy rain, as the dark clouds were rolling away and the setting sun was tinging them with a rich golden border, we left Mérida. At eleven o'clock we reached Hunucmá and stopped in the plaza two hours to feed the horses. While there, a party of soldiers arrived from the port, waving pine torches, having just returned victorious from the siege of Campeche. They were all young, ardent, well dressed, and in fine spirits, and full of praises of their general, who, they said, had remained at Sisal to attend a ball and was coming on as soon as it was over. Resuming our journey, in an hour more we met a train of calèches, with officers in uniform. We stopped, congratulated the general upon his victory at Campeche, inquired for a United States' sloop-of-war which we had heard was there during the blockade, and, with many interchanges of courtesy but without seeing a feature of each other's faces, we resumed our separate roads. An hour before daylight we reached Sisal, at six o'clock we embarked on board the Spanish brig *Alexandre* for Havana, and at eight we were under way.

It was the twenty-fourth of June; and now, as we thought, all our troubles were ended. The morning was fine. We had eight passengers, all Spanish; when one, who was from the interior, came down to the shore and saw the brig in the offing, he asked what animal it was. From my great regard for the captain, I will not speak of the brig or of its condition, particularly the cabin, except to say that it was Spanish. The wind was light; we breakfasted on deck, making the top of the companionway serve as a table under an awning. The captain told us we would be in Havana in a week.

Our course lay along the coast of Yucatán toward Cape Catoche. On Sunday, the twenty-eighth, we had made, according to the brig's reckoning, about one hundred and fifty miles, and were then becalmed. The sun was intensely hot, the sea of glassy stillness, and all day a school of sharks were swimming around the brig. From this time we had continued calms, and the sea was like a mirror, heated and reflecting its heat. On the Fourth of July there was the same glassy stillness, with light clouds, but fixed and stationary. The captain said we were *encantado*, or enchanted, and really it almost seemed so. We had expected to celebrate this day by dining with the American consul in Havana, but our vessel lay like a log, and we were scorching and already pinched for water; the bare thought of a Fourth of July dinner meanwhile made Spanish ship cookery intolerable. We had read through all the books in the mate's library, consisting of some French novels translated into Spanish, and a history of awful shipwrecks. To break the monotony of the calm, we had hooks and lines out constantly for sharks; the sailors called them, like the alligators, *enemigos de los cristianos*, hoisted them on deck, cut out their hearts and entrails, and then threw them overboard. We were already out ten days, and growing short of provisions; we had two young sharks for dinner. Apart from the associations, they were not bad—quite equal to young alligators; and the captain told us that in Campeche they were regularly in the markets and eaten by all classes.

In the afternoon they gathered around us fearfully. Everything that fell overboard was immediately snapped up; and the hat of a passenger which fell from his head had hardly touched the water before a huge fellow turned over on his side, opened his ugly mouth above the water, and swallowed it: luckily, the man was not under it. Toward evening we caught a leviathan, raised him four or five feet out of the water with a hook, and the sailors, leaning over, beat his brains with the capstan bars till he was motionless; then fastening a rope with a slipnoose under his fins, with the ship's tackle they hoisted him on deck. He seemed to fill half the side of the vessel. The sailors opened his mouth and fastened the jaws apart with a marlinspike, turned him over on his back, ripped him open, and tore out his heart and entrails. They then chopped off about a foot of his tail and threw him overboard; what he did I will not mention, lest it should bring discredit upon other parts of these pages which the reader is disposed to think may be true; but the last we saw of him he seemed to be feeling for his tail.

In the afternoon of the next day we crossed a strong current setting to northwest which roared like breakers; soundings before one hundred and twenty fathoms; during the evening there was no bottom, and we supposed we must have passed Cape Catoche.

On the sixth, seventh, eighth, ninth, tenth, eleventh, and twelfth, there was the same dead calm, with a sea like glass and intense heat. We were scant of provisions, and alarmed for entire failure of water. The captain was a noble Spaniard, who comforted the passengers by repeating every morning that we were enchanted, but for several days he had been uneasy and alarmed. He had no chronometer on board. He had been thirty years trading from Havana to different ports in the Gulf of Mexico, and had never used one; but out of soundings, among currents, with nothing but the log, he could not determine his longitude, and was afraid of getting into the Gulf Stream and being carried past Havana. Our chronometer had been nine months in hard use, jolted over severe mountain roads, and, as we supposed, could not be relied upon. Mr. Catherwood made a calculation with an old French table of logarithms which happened to be on board, but with results so different from the captain's reckoning that we supposed it could not be correct. At this time our best prospect was that of reaching Havana in the midst of the yellow fever season, sailing from there in the worst hurricane month, and a quarantine at Staten Island.

On the thirteenth of July everything on board was getting scarce, and with crew and passengers twenty in number, we broached our last cask of water. The heat was scorching, and the calm and stillness of the sea were fearful. All said we were enchanted; and the sailors added, half in earnest, that it was on account of the heretics. Sharks were more numerous than ever; we could not look over the side of the vessel without seeing three or four, as if waiting for prey.

On the fourteenth the captain was alarmed. The log was thrown regularly, but could not give his position. Toward evening we saw an enormous monster, with a straight black head ten feet out of water, moving directly toward us. The captain, looking at it from the rigging with a glass, said it was not a whale. Another of the same kind appeared at the stern, and we were really nervous; but we were relieved by hearing them spout and seeing a column of water thrown into the air. At dark they were lying huge and motionless on the surface of the water.

On the fifteenth, to our great joy, a slight breeze sprang up in the morning, and the log gave three miles an hour. At twelve o'clock we took the latitude, which was 25° 10', and found that in steering *southward* at the rate of three miles an hour by the log, we were fifty-five miles to the northward of the reckoning of the day before. The captain now believed that we were in the midst of the Gulf Stream, had been so perhaps for two or three days, and that we were then two or three hundred miles past Havana. Mr. Catherwood's chronometer gave 88° longitude, but this was so far out of the way by our dead reckoning, that, with our distrust of the chronometer, we all disregarded it, the captain especially. We were then in a very bad position, short of provisions and water, and drifted past our port. The captain called aft the passengers, sailors, cook, and cabin boy; he spread the chart on the companionway and pointed out our supposed position, saying that he wished to take the advice of all on board as to what was best to be done. The mate sat by with the logbook to take notes. All remained silent until the cook spoke and said that the captain knew best; the sailors and passengers assented; for, although we considered it all un-

certain, and that we were completely lost, we believed that
he knew better than anybody else. The captain pointed out
the course of the Gulf Stream, said it would be impossible
to turn back against it, and, having a light, favorable breeze,
recommended that we should follow the stream and bear up
for New Providence for a supply of provisions and water.
All assented, and so we put about from the south and squared
the yards for the northeast. At that moment we considered
ourselves farther from Havana than when we started.

   With most uncomfortable feelings we sat down to a scanty
meal. Supposing that we were in the Gulf Stream and in the
track of vessels, the captain sent a man aloft to look out for
a sail; very soon, to our great joy, he reported a brig to lee-
ward. We hoisted our flag and bore down upon her. As we
approached she answered our signal, and with a glass we
recognized the American ensign. In an hour we were nearly
within hailing distance. The captain could not speak English,
and gave me the speaking trumpet; but fancying, from his
movements, that our countryman did not like the Spanish
colors, and afraid of some technical irregularity in my hail
which would make us an object of suspicion, we begged our
captain to lower the jolly boat. This was lying on the deck,
with her bottom upward and her seams opened by the sun.
The water poured into her and before we were fifty yards
from the brig she was half full. We sat up on the gunwale,
and two of the men had as much as they could do to keep
her afloat, while we urged the others to pull. Sharks were
playing around us, and for a few moments we wished to be
back on board the old brig. A breeze seemed to strike the
vessel, which for two or three minutes kept steadily on; but,
to our great relief, she hove to and took us on board. Our
Spanish colors, and our irregular movement in attempting
to board without hailing, had excited suspicion, and the sailors said we were pirates; but the captain, a long, cool-headed
down-easter, standing on the quarter with both his hands in
his pockets, and seeing the sinking condition of our boat, said,
"Them's no pirates."

   The brig was the *Helen Maria* of North Yarmouth, and
its master, Sweetzer, was from Tabasco, and she was bound

for New York. My first question was whether he could take us on board, next for provisions and water for our friends, and then where we were. He showed us his observation for the day. We were about four hundred miles from the spot we supposed. The current which sets up between Cape Catoche and Cape Antonio the captain had taken for the Gulf Stream. If we had attended to Mr. Catherwood's chronometer we should not have been far out of the way. As it was, we were perfectly lost; and if we had not met this vessel, I do not know what would have become of us. The captain was but seven days from Tabasco, with a wind that had carried away one of his sails, and had lost one of his men. He had no surplus of provisions, particularly with two additional passengers; but he sent on board what he could, and a supply of water. We returned, told the captain, much to his surprise and astonishment, of his position, not more than two hundred miles from Sisal, and bade all hands farewell. They were not sorry to get rid of us, for the absence of two mouths was an object; and though, perhaps, in their hearts they thought their bad luck was on account of the heretics, it was pleasant, that with all our vexations, parting thus on the wide ocean, we shook hands with captain, passengers, sailors, cook, and cabin boy, having no unkind feeling with anyone on board. How long they were out I do not know, but I heard that they arrived at Havana in wretched condition, having eaten up the last morsel on board.

Our new vessel had a full cargo of logwood, the deck being loaded even with the quarter, and stowed so close that the cabin door was taken off and descent made over a water cask; but the change from the Spanish to the American vessel was a strange transition. The former had a captain, two mates, and eight sailors; the latter one mate and three sailors, with plank over the deckload for sailors to run on, an enormous boom mainsail, and a tiller instead of a wheel sweeping the whole quarter-deck and at times requiring two men to hold it. In the evening we had two or three hours of calm; we were used to it, but the captain was annoyed; he detested a calm; he had not had one since he left Tabasco; he could bear anything but a calm. In the evening the charm was broken by a squall. The captain hated to take in sail, held on till the last moment, and then, springing from the tiller, hauled on the ropes himself, and was back again at the rudder, all in a flash. Mr. Catherwood and I were so well pleased with the change that we were in no hurry; and, noticing the shortness of hands and the stumbling over logwood, we suggested to the captain that if he lost another man he would have difficulty in carrying his vessel into port; but he put this down at once by swearing that, if he lost every hand on board, the mate and he could carry her in themselves, deckload and all.

On the thirty-first of July we arrived at New York ten months less three days since we sailed, and nine without having received any intelligence whatever from our friends at home. Deducting the time passed at sea, we had spent but seven months and twenty-four days in the prosecution of our work. This, I am sure, must recommend us to every true American; and here, on the same spot from which we set out together, and with but little hope of ever journeying with him again, I bid the reader farewell.

Appendix

Having mentioned in the preceding pages efforts to introduce into this country some of the antiquities therein described, the author considers it proper to say that, immediately on his return home, a few friends, whose names he would have great pleasure in making known if he were at liberty to do so, undertook to provide the sum of twenty thousand dollars for the purpose of carrying that object into effect. Under their direction, the author wrote to his agent at Guatemala to purchase the ruins of Quiriguá, or such monuments as it might be considered advisable to remove, at a price beyond what would have been accepted for them when he left Guatemala. But, unfortunately, in the meantime, a notice taken from Mr. Catherwood's memoranda and inserted by the proprietors in a Guatemala paper, had reached this country, been translated, and copied into some of our own journals. One eulogistic paragraph, probably forgotten as soon as written, was sent back to Guatemala, which gave the proprietor such an exaggerated notion of their value that he refused our offer. From vague conversations with foreigners who had never seen and knew nothing of them, he conceived the idea that all the governments of Europe would vie with each other for their possession; and still entertaining the foolish belief that the author was acting on behalf of his government, the owner said that, if the President of the United States wanted them, he must pay twenty thousand dollars for them; in the meantime, he resolved to wait for offers from England and France. By the last advices he was still under the same hallucination.

In regard to Palenque, the author has just received a letter from Mr. Russell, enclosing four documents brought to him by Mr. Pawling, which, translated so far as the manuscripts can be made out, are as follows:

From Enrique Ruiz, dated San Cristóbal,[1] October 1, 1840.
"The governor has been informed that the vice-governor of Belize [meaning no doubt, Mr. Secretary Walker and Cap-

---

1. Or, Stephens notes, Ciudad Real, the capital of the State of Chiapas.

tain Caddy] came to explore the ruins a few days since, with fourteen armed men, and you have neither prevented him nor given any information to this government.

"Now he is again informed that some citizens of the United States of the North are doing the same; in virtue of which, his excellency orders me to tell you to inform him immediately upon the truth of these facts, that he may take the necessary measures.

"God and liberty.

"ENRIQUE RUIZ"

From Santiago Froncoso, Bartolo Bravo, and Miguel Castillo, dated Palenque, October 15, 1840.

"The subscribers, inhabitants of this town, as true patriots, and lovers of the prosperity and advancement of their country, before you, with due respect, and with the legal right that we may have, appear, saying that it is something like more than three months since a citizen of North America, named Henry Paulin, has fixed his residence on the ruins of this district, with the view of making moulds of every monument and precious thing that there is on them; as, in fact, he is making them, since, up to this date; he has already made something like thirty moulds of plaster of Paris, including two which he took to the town of Carmen, without giving notice to anybody, and with the object of shipping them for the North [these two have been received by the author]. The said moulds are so much like the originals, that at the first sight it may be observed that they may be taken, surely, for second originals, and no doubt they may serve to mould after them as many copies as might be wished, and in this manner they may supply the world with these precious things without a six cents' piece expense. Mr. William Brown, married to Doña Trinidad Garrido, offered from eight to ten thousand dollars only for the leave to extract four or six principal stones from these ruins, in quality of a loan . . . or to . . . [the precise nature of Mr. William Brown's offer cannot be made out, from the illegible character of the handwriting], promising all these things with the most satisfactory guarantees. Saving you, sir, from any responsibility, we take it upon ourselves, since we are aware of your bad state of health, and we suppose that you do not know of this fact . . . [manuscript illegible], on account of this master operation, or whosoever is concerned in it, make this gentleman pay four or five thousand dollars, to apply them to benevolent works, and to the embellishment of this town, or else let him in no manner take away with him any of the moulds of plaster of Paris he has made and continues making. Indeed, if this treasure is ours, and by right belongs to our town, why should it not be benefited by it?

"It is an honour to us, sir, to make a demand of this nature, since we have not heard that any offer whatever has been made at all about this undertaking up to this date. Let the visitors of these ruins make moulds, drawings, &c., but let them also contribute with sums proportionate to their operations. This is, sir, if we are not mistaken, a business of a great speculation. The persons concerned in this affair are men of importance. Therefore we beg of you most earnestly, and in virtue of our legal right, not to permit the removal of any of the said moulds of plaster of Paris from this town without the said sums being paid, grounded on the great utility that the extractors may derive from it, as well as on the aforesaid offer made by Mr. Brown.

"SANTIAGO FRONCOSO"
"BARTOLO BRAVO"
"MIGUEL CASTILLO"

From Domingo González, dated San Cristóbal, December 1, 1840.

"Don Santiago Froncoso having informed the governor that he and two other inhabitants of that town have presented a memorial before you in regard to the removal of the antiquities of the ruins at Palenque, his excellency consulted the departmental junta on the subject, which junta answered by approving the petition, which copy I send you enclosed, with the decree of his excellency written under it, that you may cause it to be fulfilled. I send you, likewise, two copies of the regulations for passports for the archives of that subprefecture, with the object that the subprefect should act according to it, in the introduction of foreigners in your district, and also a copy of the order of the 17th of June, 1835, and his excellency orders me to tell you to inform him immediately with regard to the issue of the fulfilment of his said decree.

"It is a copy.   God and liberty.

"DOMINGO GONZALEZ"

From Domingo González, dated San Cristóbal, November 30, 1840.

"His excellency the governor, having read your information of the 15th inst., orders me to tell you to keep a watchful eye upon the strangers who visit the ruins; and when any of them arrive, to give notice of it to this government without delay, expressing their numbers, whence they come, and what is their object, without allowing them to make any operation or excavation, and much less to remove anything whatever, however insignificant it may appear.

"Consequently, if they arrive with the only object of visiting, let them do it in company with one, two, or more officers of that subprefecture, that the above dispositions may be fulfilled.

"It is a copy from the original.

"God and liberty.

"DOMINGO GONZALEZ"

Under these orders Mr. Pawling has been compelled to leave the ruins; and the casts belonging to the author, for the making of which he had subjected himself to considerable expense, have been seized and detained by the prefect. Perhaps, instead of unavailing regrets, the author ought rather to congratulate himself that he had left the ruins, and that Mr. Catherwood's drawings were safe, before the news of their visit reached the capital. He can imagine the excitement in the village, and the annoyance and vexation to which future travelers will be subjected; but he cannot understand exactly the cause. His purpose of leaving Pawling to make casts was known in the village, and no objections whatever were made. Don Santiago Froncoso, the first of the "true patroits" whose names are signed to the complaint, was his particular friend, from whom, late in the evening before he left Palenque, he received the following note (translation):

"Mr. _____ (I do not know your surname), at his house June 3, 1840.

"My most respected sir,

"I have just arrived, because my wife sent me notice yesterday that *you* (permit me to address you on the footing of a friend [2]) and your estimable companion depart to-morrow without fail. If it is really true, continue your journey with all the felicity which my great affection desires. I send you, together with my gratitude and affection, this raw silk from the ruins to keep for my sake.

"Farewell, my friend and dearest sir. Command whatever you wish, and from whatever distance.

"Your most affectionate friend,

"SANTIAGO FRONCOSO"

"Senor ex-plenipotentiary envoy near the government of Central America from the government of North America."

---

2. Don Santiago apologizes, Stephens tells us, for not using the title *Your Excellency.*

The author feels assured that, if he had been on the spot himself, Don Santiago would have been the last man in the place to embarrass his operations. He is now violent against foreigners. The author has received no letter from Mr. Pawling, and fears that he has in some way got into difficulty with the people of the village, or else the author's plans have been defeated, and his casts are detained and kept from being introduced into the United States by the agency and offers of Mr. William Brown. In the absence of any farther information than what appears in these documents, the author makes no comments; but he mentions that this Mr. William Brown is an American, known in this city as Captain William Brown, having been for several years master of a vessel trading between this port and Tabasco.

It was the hope of the gentlemen before referred to, with the monuments of Quiriguá, casts from Copán and Palenque, or the tablets themselves, and other objects from other places within their reach, to lay the foundation of a Museum of American Antiquities which might deserve the countenance of the General Government, and draw to it Catlin's Indian Gallery, and every other memorial of the aboriginal races, whose history within our own borders has already become almost a romance and fable. The author does not despair of this yet. The difficulty will perhaps be increased (the author trusts he will not be considered presumptuous) by the attention that will be directed to the remains of Palenque and the other ruined cities by the publication of these pages, and the consequently exaggerated notions that the inhabitants will form of their value. But then he is persuaded that the Government of Mexico will, on proper representations, order a restitution of the casts now detained at Palenque, and that the republic, without impoverishing herself, will enrich her neighbors of the North with the knowledge of the many other curious remains scattered through her country. And he entertains the belief also that England and France, whose formidable competition has already been set up, as it were *in terrorem*, by one proprietor, having their capitals enriched by the remains of art collected throughout the Old World, will respect the rights of nations and discovery, and leave the field of American antiquities to us; that they will not deprive a destitute country of its only chance of contributing to the cause of science, but rather encourage it in the work of bringing together, from remote and almost inaccessible places, and retaining on its own soil, the architectural remains of its aboriginal inhabitants.

CPSIA information can be obtained at www.ICGtesting.com
Printed in the USA
LVOW061520220312

274341LV00003B/133/P

9 781605 204468